Nicholas Byfield

An Exposition Upon the Epistle to the Colossians

Nicholas Byfield

An Exposition Upon the Epistle to the Colossians

ISBN/EAN: 9783337384722

Printed in Europe, USA, Canada, Australia, Japan

Cover: Foto ©Lupo / pixelio.de

More available books at **www.hansebooks.com**

AN EXPOSITION

UPON THE

EPISTLE TO THE COLOSSIANS:

BEING THE SUBSTANCE OF

NEAR SEVEN YEARS' WEEK-DAY SERMONS.

BY

NICHOLAS BYFIELD,

LATE ONE OF THE PREACHERS FOR THE CITY OF CHESTER.

EDINBURGH: JAMES NICHOL.
LONDON: JAMES NISBET & CO.   DUBLIN: G. HERBERT.

M.DCCC.LXIX.

EDINBURGH:
BALLANTYNE AND COMPANY, PRINTERS,
PAUL'S WORK.

NICHOLAS BYFIELD.

THE author of this volume was a man of note, and a member of a notable family. His father was minister of Stratford-on-Avon; but it appears that his incumbency there began several years after Shakespeare had left the town. As, however, Nicholas is said to have been born in Warwickshire seventeen years before his father's settlement in Stratford, it is not improbable that the father may have been curate there, or in some neighbouring village, in which case the poet may have been one of his hearers. The life of our author was comparatively short, so that even Anthony à Wood acknowledges with astonishment the amount of work that he did in so short a time. The facts of his life are given with sufficient detail in this author's account of him. We, therefore, content ourselves with merely subjoining it:—

"N. Byfield, son of Richard Byfield (who became minister of Stratford-upon-Avon in January 1596), was born in Warwickshire, became a batler or a servitor of Exeter College in Lent Term, anno 1596, aged seventeen at least; continued under a severe discipline more than four years, but never took a degree. Afterwards, entering into the sacred function, he left the University, and had intentions to go into Ireland to obtain preferment in the Church, but at Chester, in his way thither, he was, upon the delivery of a noted sermon at that place, invited to be pastor of St Peter's Church there; which invitation being esteemed by him as a great providence, he willingly accepted; so that, continuing there several years a constant preacher, was much followed and admired by the precise party, who esteemed his preaching profitable and his life pious. He was a strict observer of the Lord's-day at that place, and preached and wrote for the sincere observance of it, which caused some pens to be active against him, particularly that of Edward Breerwood, who, being a native of that city, was sometimes his auditor. At length, being called thence, he had the benefice of Isleworth, in Middlesex, conferred on him, where he remained to his dying day. He was a person, in the opinion of the zealots, of profound judgment, strong memory, sharp wit, quick invention, and of unwearied industry; also, that in his ministry he was powerful, and that unto all turns and upon all occasions, not only at Chester, but at Isleworth, where his preaching and expounding were very frequent. The books that he hath written are these :—

 Assurance of God's Love and Man's Salvation.
 Exposition of Colossians : Substance of near Seven Years' Week-day Sermons at Chester.
 Directions for Private Reading of Scripture.
 How a Godly Christian may Support his Heart with Comfort.

Beginning of Doctrine of Christ.
Marrow of the Oracles of God.
Sermons on 1 Peter ii.
Principal Grounds of Christian Religion.
Sermons on 1 Peter iii. 1–10.
Afterwards on whole of 1 Peter.
Answer to Mr Brecrwood's Treatise of Liberty.
Exposition of Apostles' Creed.
Light of Faith and Way of Holiness.
Signs of God's Love to us.
Practice of Christianity; or, An Epitome of Mr R. Roger's Seven Treatises.
Several Sermons.

"It is commonly reported that this person died at Isleworth, before mentioned, in 1622, which, if true, his writings and works shew him (being not then above 44 years of age) to have been a person of great parts, industry, and readiness. He left behind him a son, named Adoniram Byfield, a most zealous and forward brother for the cause, of whom I shall make mention in R. Byfield in another part of this work.

"In an Epistle to the Christian Reader, by William Gouge, prefixed to Commentary on 1 Peter, we have the following character of the author's account of his acute sufferings:—'He was a man of profound judgment, strong memory, sharp wit, and true piety. Preached twice on the Lord's-day, and in summer on Wednesday and Friday. This course he kept on till about five weeks before his death, when the pain came so violently upon him as it wasted his vital vigour, yet did it in no way weaken his faith, but, as the outward perished, then was the inward man renewed in him. He earnestly prayed that the extremity of the pain might not make him utter or do anything unbecoming his vocation and profession, but withal he advised his friends to consider that he was but as other men, and thereupon to judge charitably of his carriage in that case.'"

From this Epistle of Gouge we learn that for fifteen years or more he suffered intense pain from stone in the bladder, which makes it all the more remarkable that he should have accomplished so much.

The present Commentary is a fine specimen of Puritan exposition, indicating an extensive and intensive knowledge of the Word of God, and great soundness of judgment, and great faithfulness in dealing with the hearts and consciences of men. There is no eloquence in it, but a serious, earnest desire is manifest to keep back nothing of the counsel of God; and we are much mistaken if ministers do not find it profitable, as suggestive of many hints which may enrich their own expositions of this Epistle.

T. S.

TO THE RIGHT HONOURABLE

EDWARD LORD RUSSELL, EARL OF BEDFORD,

AND

THE LADY LUCY, COUNTESS OF BEDFORD,

GRACE AND PEACE BE MULTIPLIED, WITH INCREASE OF ALL HONOUR AND HAPPINESS FOR EVER.

MOST NOBLE LORD, AND MY VERY HONOURABLE GOOD LADY,—

THIS Epistle to the Colossians contains an excellent epitome of the doctrine expressed in the rest of the books of the Old and New Testament, as will appear by a brief delineation or adumbration of the proportion and parts of that sacred body of truth, paralleled with the several parts of this epistle, using the benefit of this commentary upon it.

The whole word of God may be divided into two parts: the first concerns faith, or what we must believe; the second, love, or what we must do. So the apostles divided it, as may appear by the pattern used in their times, which stood of two parts, faith and love, 2 Tim. i. 13. And so is this epistle divided; for in the two first chapters he tells them what they must believe, and in the two last what they must do.

Now faith looks either upon God or upon the world. In God two things are to be believed: first, The attributes of the essence; secondly, The trinity of the persons. The attributes unfold the nature and proprieties of God, such as are his power, glory, knowledge, and the like. Of the power of God ye may read, chap. i. 11, and ii. 12; of the glory of God, chap. i. 11, and iii. 17; of the knowledge of God, chap. iii. 10.

The persons are three, the Father, the Son, and Holy Ghost. Of the Father, chap. i. 2, 12, and iii. 17; of the Son, chap. i. 2, 13, 15, &c.; of the Holy Ghost, chap. ii. 19. Thus of God.

In the consideration of the world, faith is taken up especially about the creation of it, and the government of it. In the creation it views the mighty workmanship of God, making all things of nothing, even the very angels, as well as men and other creatures. Of the creation, chap. i. 16; of angels, also chap. i. 16; both good, chap. ii. 9; and evil, chap. ii. 15.

The government of the world is two ways to be considered: first, In the general disposing and preservation of all things; secondly, and principally, Faith is taken up about the consideration of the government of men in the world; of the general providence, chap. i. 16, 17.

The providence of God over man may be considered according to his fourfold estate: first, Of innocency; secondly, Of corruption; thirdly, Of grace; fourthly, Of glory.

In the estate of innocency faith chiefly beholds and wonders at the glorious image of God, in which man was created. Of this image you may read, chap. iii. 10, by analogy.

In the state of corruption, two things do offer

themselves to our doleful contemplation: first, Sin; secondly, The punishment of sin. Sin is both original and actual; of original sin, chap. ii. 13; of actual sins, chap. ii. 11, 13, iii. 5, 6; of the punishment of sin, chap. iii. 25, and ii. 13, and iii. 6.

In the state of grace, faith views three things: first, The means of grace; secondly, The subject; thirdly, The degrees. The means is either before time, or in time; before time, it is the election of God, of which chap. iii. 12; in time, the means chiefly is Christ, and the covenant in him. In Christ two things are to be considered—his person, and his office. The theory concerning Christ's person is twofold: first, Concerning his two natures; secondly, Concerning his twofold estate in those natures. The natures of Christ are two, human and divine, joined in the bond of personal union; of the human nature, chap. i. 22; of his divine, chap. i. 15, 16, &c.; of the union of both, chap. ii. 9. The state of the person of Christ is twofold: first, Of humiliation; secondly, Of exaltation. His humiliation comprehends: first, His incarnation, as the antecedent; secondly, His obedience to the law of Moses; thirdly, His passion; of his incarnation and obedience, impliedly in divers places; of his passion, chap. i. 14, 20, 22; xiv. 15. His exaltation comprehends his resurrection, ascension, and session at the right hand of God; of his resurrection, chap. ii. 12; of his sitting at God's right hand, chap. iii. 1.

Thus of the person of Christ.

The office of Christ is to mediate between God and man. The parts are three: first, His prophetical office; secondly, His priestly office; thirdly, His regal office. His prophetical office stands in propounding of doctrine, and in making it effectual by his Spirit. His priestly office standeth in two things: first, Expiation of sin; secondly, Intercession for us to God. His regal office is partly in the government of the church, as the head thereof, and partly in the subduing of the enemies of God and the church; of the treasures of wisdom in Christ as a prophet, chap. ii. 3; of the sacrifice of Christ as a priest, chap. ii. 14; of the headship of Christ over the church, chap. i. 18, and ii. 19.

Thus of Christ.

The covenant followeth, which is considered both in itself and in the seals of it. Though the covenant of works be accidentally a means to drive us to Christ, yet the proper effectual means is the covenant of grace, which God hath made with the elect in Christ; this being recorded in the word of the gospel, both in the Old and New Testament is the ordinary means, by the power of Christ, to convert souls to God by the preaching of it in the ministry of his servants; of this, chap. i. 6.

The seals of this covenant are the sacraments, both of the Old and New Testament: of the Old Testament was circumcision and the rest, of which chap. ii. 11; of the New Testament are baptism and the Lord's supper; of baptism, chap. ii. 12.

Thus of the means of grace.

The subject of true grace is the church, the body of Christ united to him by mystical union. The church consists of two sorts of men, ministers and people; of the church in general, with her union with Christ, chap. i. 18–20, and ii. 19; of ministers and people, with their duties, chap. i. 25, 28, and ii. 1, and in divers other places.

Thus of the subject also.

The degrees of grace in the third estate are: first, Vocation; secondly, Faith; thirdly, Remission of sins; fourthly, Sanctification; of vocation, chap. iii. 15; of faith, chap. i. 4, 23, and ii. 12; of remission of sins, chap. i. 14, and ii. 13; of sanctification, in both parts, both mortification, chap. iii. 5, 8; and vivification, chap. ii. 13, and iii. 10.

Thus of the estate of grace.

The fourth and last estate of man is the estate of glory, which stands of three degrees: first, Resurrection; secondly, The last judgment; and thirdly, Life eternal; of resurrection, chap. i. 18; of the last judgment and eternal glory, chap. iii. 4. And thus of the first part of the pattern of wholesome words, and that is faith; now followeth the second, and that is love.

Love comprehends all the duties we owe to God or men, as being 'the bond of perfection' which ties together all holy services. Love must be considered both in the adjuncts and in the sorts of it.

The adjuncts are constancy, wisdom, zeal, care to avoid offences, and the like. Of love in general, chap. i. 4, ii. 2, and iii. 14; of constancy, chap. ii.

6; of zeal, chap. iv. 13; of wisdom, and care to avoid offences, chap. iv. 5. Thus of the adjuncts.

The sorts of works comprehended under love are two chiefly: first, Works of worship; secondly, Works of virtue. The works of worship are either internal only, or external and internal also. The internal are, the acknowledging of God, the love of God, the fear of God, the trust or hope in God, and which floweth from thence, patience; of the acknowledgment of God, chap. i. 9, 10; of the love of God, chap. i. 8; of the fear of God, chap. iii. 22; of the hope in God, chap i. 5; of patience, chap. i. 11. The works of worship that are both external and internal are prayer and thanksgiving; of prayer, chap. iv. 2, 3; of thanksgiving, chap. iii. 17.

Thus of works of worship.

Works of virtue either concern ourselves or others; the works that concern ourselves are chiefly two—the study of heavenly things, and temperance. Temperance contains chastity and sobriety in the use of all sorts of earthly things; of the study of heavenly things, chap. iii. 1, 2; of chastity, chap. iii. 5; of sobriety, chap. iii. 2.

Thus of virtue that concerns ourselves.

Works of virtue towards others are chiefly nine: mercy, courtesy, humility, meekness, long-suffering, clemency, peaceableness, thankfulness, and justice; of the first eight of these, chap. iii. 12–16. Now justice is either public or private; public justice is in magistrates, of which, chap. ii. 5; private justice is either commutative, in bargaining, or distributive, in giving that which is right to every one according to his degree, and so distributive justice is either civil or economical. Private justice in civil conversation with men abroad, is either to magistrates, of which, chap. i. 5, or to all men, and so consists of truth and faithfulness, with sincerity and observance. Economical justice is that which concerns the household, and so contains the duties of husbands and wives, children and parents, servants and masters; of which, chap. iii. 18, to the end, with the first verse of chap. iv.

Thus also of love.

Thus I have shewed the excellent completeness of this worthy scripture. It remains that I declare some of the reasons that have emboldened me to make choice of your Honours' names for the dedication of my exposition upon this scripture. Three things, swaying godly men in like case, have compelled me—protection, observance, and thankfulness. The preaching of this doctrine, as by the mercy of God it wrought abundant consolation and comfort able reformation in many hearers, so did it seldom rest from the assaults and calumnies which one while profaneness, another while envy, poured out upon it. Great cause there is, therefore, that it coming out now to a more public view, should seek shelter; and of whom should I seek it or hope for it sooner than of your Honours, who are pleased, by your daily countenance, to assure me a just patronage? For the second,—to omit the high reputation which the religious eminency of both your ancestors hath set your Honours in, and the praises of many singular endowments and gifts, in which you do worthily excel;—there are two things wherein your Honours daily win a great increase of observance—the one is piety towards God, the other is mercy towards the poor. The loins of the poor daily bless your Honours, and their mouths daily pray for you. Your piety is many ways expressed; to omit many undoubted proofs of it, your Lordship hath much confirmed the persuasion of your religious disposition by your daily and affectionate respect of the word of God and prayer in private, since the Lord hath made you less able to resort more frequently to the public assemblies. And, Madam, what thanks can we ever sufficiently give unto God for that rare and worthy example with which your Ladyship doth comfort and encourage the hearts of many in your care of God's Sabbaths, and in your never-failing attendance upon the ordinances of God with the congregation, morning and evening, not only in your own person, but with your whole family. For the third, I do ingenuously profess before God and men that I hold my obligation unto your Honours in the just debt of service and gratitude to be so great, as the labour here employed is no way answerable to a meet discharge, no, though it had been taken only for your Honour's use; for to omit the debt which I am in for a great part of my maintenance, and that singular encouragement I reap daily in your Honours' respect of my ministry, what thanks can ever be sufficient, or what service can ever be enough for that incomparable benefit which I have and shall ever esteem the greatest outward blessing did ever befall me; and which, Madam, by your Honour's singular care and furtherance, after an admirable manner I obtained; I mean the clearing of my reputation from the unjust aspersions of my adversaries, and that by the mouth and pen of the Lord's anointed, my most dread sovereign, whom the God of heaven, with all abundance of royal and divine blessings, recompense in all earthly felicity and eternal glory. And the same God of peace, and Father of mercies, 'sanctify your Honours wholly, that your whole spirits and souls and bodies may be preserved blameless unto the coming of our Lord Jesus Christ.' 'Faithful is he that hath called you, who also will do it.' And I doubt not but God that hath enriched your Honours with the true grace that is in Jesus Christ, will daily win unto you increase of honour from your perseverance in welldoing; so as thanksgiving for your sakes shall be abundantly given unto God by many. Thus, in most humble manner, craving your Honours' acceptance and patronage of this work, I end, and shall rejoice to remain,

Your Honours' Chaplain,

To be commanded in all service,

NI. BYFIELD.

THE ARGUMENT

OF THIS

EPISTLE TO THE COLOSSIANS.

THERE are four principal parts of this epistle: first, The proëm; secondly, Doctrine of faith; thirdly, Precepts of life; fourthly, The epilogue, or conclusion. The proëm is expressed in the first eleven verses of the first chapter; the doctrine of faith is expressed in the rest of the verses of the first chapter and the whole second chapter. The precepts of life are set down in the third chapter, and in the beginning of the fourth. And the epilogue is in the rest of the verses of the fourth chapter.

1. The proëm contains two things: first, The salutation, ver. 1, 2; and secondly, A preface, affectionately framed to win attention and respect, wherein he assures them of his singular constancy in remembering them to God, both in thanksgiving for their worthy graces and the means thereof, ver. 3–8; and in earnest prayer for their increase and comfortable perseverance in knowledge and the eminency of sincerity in holy life, ver. 9–11.

2. The doctrine of faith he expresseth two ways: first, By proposition; secondly, By exhortation. In the proposition of doctrine, he doth with singular force of words, and weight of matter, set out both the work of our redemption, ver. 12–14, and the person of our Redeemer; and that first in his relation to God, ver. 15; then in relation to the world, ver. 15–17; and thirdly, in relation to the church; both the whole in general, ver. 18–20; and the church of the Colossians in particular, ver. 21, 22. And thus of the proposition. Now his exhortation follows, from 23 of chap. i. to the end of chap. ii., and therein he both persuades and dissuades; he persuades by many strong and moving reasons, to a holy endeavour to continue and persevere with all Christian firmness of resolution, in the faith and hope, [which] was already begotten in them by the gospel; and this is contained in the seven last verses of the first chapter, and the seven first verses of the second chapter. He dissuades them from receiving the corrupt doctrine of the false apostles, whether it were drawn from philosophical speculations, or from the traditions of men, or from the ceremonial law of Moses; and he proceeds in this order: first, He lays down the matter of his dehortation, chap. ii. 8; then secondly, He confirms it by divers reasons, from ver. 9 to 16; and lastly, He concludes, and that severally, as against Mosaical rites, ver. 16, 17; against philosophy, ver. 18, 19; and against traditions, ver. 20, and so to the end of that chapter.

Thus of the second part.

3. Thirdly, In giving precepts of life, the apostle holds this order: first, He gives general rules that concern all, as they are Christians; then, he gives

special rules, as they are men of this or that estate of life. The general rules are contained in the first seventeen verses of the third chapter, and the special rules from the eighteenth verse of the third chapter, to the second verse of the fourth. The general rules he reduceth into three heads, viz.: first, The meditation of heavenly things, ver. 1-4; secondly, The mortification of vices and injuries, ver. 5-12; thirdly, The exercise of holy graces, a number of which he reckoneth, both in the kinds, means, and ends of them, from ver. 12-18. The particular rules concern principally household government; for he sets down the duty of wives, ver. 18; of husbands, ver. 19; of children, ver. 20; of parents, ver. 21; of servants, ver. 22-25; and of masters, chap. iv. 1.

4. The epilogue, or conclusion, contains in it both matter of general exhortation, as also matters of salutation. The general exhortation concerns prayer, ver. 2-4; wise conversation, ver. 5; and godly communication, ver. 6. Now, after the apostle hath disburdened himself of those general cares, then he taketh liberty to refresh himself and them. And first, he makes entrance by a narration of his care to know their estate, and to inform them of his. To which purpose he sendeth and prayeth Tychicus and Onesimus, ver. 7-9. The salutations then follow; and they are of two sorts; for some are signified to them, some are required of them. Of the first sort, he signifies the salutations of six men, three of them Jews, and three Gentiles, ver. 10-14. The salutations required, concern either the Laodiceans, ver. 15, 16, or one of the Colossian preachers, who is not only saluted, but exhorted, ver. 17. And then follows the apostle's general salutations to all in the last verse.

THE PLAIN LOGICAL ANALYSIS OF THE FIRST CHAPTER.

THIS chapter stands of three parts—a proëm, a proposition of doctrine, an exhortation to constancy and perseverance. The proëm is continued from ver. 1-12, the proposition from ver. 12-23, the exhortation from ver. 23 to the end.

The proëm is intended to win attention and affection, and stands of two parts—the salutation and the preface. The salutation is contained in the two first verses, and the preface in the third verse and those that follow to the twelfth.

In the salutation three things are to be observed: first, The persons saluting; secondly, The persons saluted; thirdly, The form of the salutation itself.

The persons saluting are two, ver. 1, 2; the author of the epistle and an evangelist, famous in the churches, who is named as one that did approve the doctrine of the epistle, and commend it to the use of the churches. The author is described: first, By his name, 'Paul;' secondly, By his office, 'an apostle,' which is amplified by the principal efficient, 'Jesus Christ,' and by the impulsive cause, 'the will of God.' The evangelist is described: first, By his name, 'Timotheus;' secondly, By his adjunct estate, 'a brother.' Thus of the persons saluting.

The persons saluted are described: first, By the place of their abode, and so they are citizens and inhabitants of 'Colosse;' secondly, By their spiritual estate, which is set out in four things: 1. They are 'saints;' 2. They are 'faithful;' 3. They are 'brethren;' 4. They are 'in Christ.'

The form of the salutation expresseth what he accounteth to be the chief good on earth, and that is, 'grace and peace,' which are amplified by the causes or fountains of them, 'from God our Father, and from our Lord Jesus Christ.' Thus of the salutation.

In the preface the apostle, ver. 3, demonstrateth his love to them by two things, which he constantly did for them; he 'prayed' for them, and he 'gave thanks' for them; and this he both propounds generally, ver. 3, and expounds particularly in the verses following.

In the general propounding three things are evidently expressed: first, What he did for them—he 'gave thanks,' 'he prayed;' secondly, To whom—even to 'God the Father of our Lord Jesus;' thirdly, How long—'always,' that is, constantly from day to day.

Now, in the verses that follow he expounds and opens this: first, His thanksgiving, ver. 4-8; secondly, His prayer, ver. 9-11. In the thanksgiving he shews for what he gave thanks; which he refers to two heads: 1. Their graces; 2. The means by which those graces were wrought and nourished.

The graces are three, faith, love, hope, ver. 4, 5. Their faith is amplified by the object, 'your faith in Jesus Christ:' and their love by the extent of it, 'your love to all the saints;' and their hope by the place, 'which is laid up for you in heaven.'

The means of grace was either principal, ver. 5, 6, or instrumental, ver. 7, 8. The principal ordinary outward means was the word, which is described and set out six ways: 1. By the ordinance in which it was most effectual, viz., hearing, 'whereof ye have heard;' 2. By the property that was most eminent in the working of it, viz., truth, 'by the word of truth;' 3. By the kind of word, viz., the gospel, 'which is the gospel;' 4. By the providence of God in bringing the means, 'which is come unto you;' 5. By the subject persons upon whom it wrought, viz., 'you and all the world;' 6. By the efficacy of it, 'it is fruitful and increaseth;' which is amplified by the repetition of the persons in whom, and the consideration both of the time, in those words, 'from the day that you heard,' &c., and also, of the adjunct cause, viz., the hearing and the true knowledge of the grace of God, from the day that you heard of it, and 'knew the grace of God in truth.'

Thus of the principal means, the ministry of the word.

The instrumental, or the minister followeth, ver. 7, 8, and he is described: 1. By his name, 'Epaphras;' 2. By the adjunct love of others to him, 'beloved;' 3. By his office, 'a servant;' 4. By his willingness to join with others, 'a fellow-servant;' 5. By his faithfulness in the execution of his office, 'which is for you a faithful minister of Christ;' and lastly, By his delight in his people, which he shews by the good report he cheerfully gives of them, viz., 'who also declared unto us your love in the spirit.' Thus of the thanksgiving.

Now in the opening or unfolding of his practice in praying for them: first, He affirms that he did pray for them; and then, Declares it by shewing what he prayed for. The affirmation is in the beginning of the ninth verse, and the declaration in the rest of the words to the end of the eleventh verse.

In the affirmation there are three things: first, An intimation of a reason, in those words, 'for this cause;' secondly, A consideration of the time, 'since the day we heard of it;' thirdly, The matter affirmed, 'we cease not to pray for you.'

In the declaration he instanceth in one thing he principally prayed about, and that was their 'knowledge;' which he sets out: first, By the object of it, 'the will of God;' secondly, By the parts of it, 'wisdom and understanding;' thirdly, By the end, viz., 'that they might walk worthy,' &c.; fourthly, By the cause, 'his glorious power;' and fifthly, By the effects, 'patience, long-suffering, and joyfulness.'

In setting down the object, he expresseth also the measure he desired; he would have them filled with the knowledge of God's will, and that he addeth in the second part, when he saith, 'all wisdom and understanding.' The end of all their knowledge he expresseth more largely, ver. 10, which in general is the eminence of holy life, which he expresseth in three several forms of speech, viz.: 1. To walk 'worthy of the Lord;' 2. To walk 'in all pleasing;' and 3. To be 'fruitful in all good works;' unto the fuller attainment of which he notes the means to be, an 'increase in the knowledge of God.'

Hitherto of the proëm.

The proposition of doctrine containeth excellent matter concerning our redemption; where he proceeds in this order: first, He considers the work of our redemption; and secondly, The person of our Redeemer. The work of our redemption, ver. 12-14; the person of our Redeemer, ver. 15 and those that follow to the 23; and all this he expresseth in form of thanksgiving.

The work of our redemption he describes two ways, after he hath touched the first efficient cause of it, viz., God the Father; for in the twelfth verse he seems to shew, that in respect of inchoation, it is a 'making of us fit;' and in respect of consummation, it is a causing of us to enjoy an immortal happiness in heaven, better than that Adam had in paradise, or the Jews in Canaan. And therein he expresseth: first, The manner of tenure or title, in the word 'inheritance;' secondly, The adjunct praise of the company, viz., the saints; and thirdly, The perfection of it, it is 'in light.'

Now, in the end of the 13th ver. he seems to shew that our redemption stands of two parts: first, 'Deliverance from the power of darkness;' secondly, 'Translating into the kingdom of the Son of his love,' one of the many excellent privileges of which estate is noted in the 14th ver., to be 'remission of sins, through the blood of Christ.' And thus of the work of our redemption.

The person of our Redeemer is described three ways, ver. 15-17: first, In relation to God; secondly, In relation to the whole world; thirdly, In relation to the church.

First, In relation to God, he is described in the beginning of the 15th ver.; and so he is said to be 'the image of the invisible God.'

Secondly, In relation to the whole world, five things are to be said of Christ: first, He is 'the first begotten of every creature,' in the end of the 15th ver.; secondly, He is the creator of all things, ver. 16. Where note the distinctions of creatures: 1. They are distinguished by their place, some 'in heaven,' some 'in earth;' 2. They are distinguished by their quality, some are 'visible,' some 'invisible;' 3. The invisible are again distinguished by either titles or offices, some are 'thrones,' some are 'principalities,' &c.; thirdly, 'All things are for him,' this is in the end of the 16th ver.; fourthly, 'He is before all things,' in the beginning of ver. 17; lastly, 'All things in him consist,' ver. 17, the end of it. Thus the Redeemer is described in relation to the whole world.

Thirdly, He is described as he stands in relation to the church; and so either to the whole church, ver. 18–20, or to the church of the Colossians, ver. 21, 22.

As he stands in relation to the whole church, he is said to be 'the head of the church,' in the beginning of the 18th ver., and this he proves, by shewing that he is a head in three respects.

First, In respect of the dignity of order towards his members, and so, in the state of grace, he is their beginning; and in the state of glory he is 'the first begotten of the dead;' that both among the living and the dead 'he might have the pre-eminence.'

Secondly, In respect of perfection in himself, in that 'all fulness dwelleth in him;' which is amplified by the cause, viz., 'the good pleasure of the Father,' who made him head of the church, ver. 19.

Thirdly, In respect of efficacy or influence through the whole body; for from him flows 'peace' and 'reconciliation,' ver. 20, concerning which reconciliation there are eight things to be noted: 1. The moving cause, which is to be supplied out of the former verse, as the conjunction 'and' importeth, viz., 'it pleased the Father;' 2. The instrument, 'by him,' viz., Christ, the head; 3. The benefit itself, viz., 'to reconcile;' 4. The subject, persons in general, 'all things;' 5. The end, 'to himself;' 6. The effect, 'making peace;' 7. The means,

'through the blood of his cross;' 8. The distribution of the persons, who, in those words, 'things in earth and things in heaven.' Thus of his relation to the whole church.

In the description of his relation to the church of the Colossians, he urgeth them with two things, ver. 21, 22: 1. Their misery without Christ; 2. The remedy of their misery by Christ.

Their misery stands in two things: first, They are 'strangers;' secondly, They are 'enemies,' and both are amplified: 1. By the subject wherein, viz., not outwardly only, but in 'their minds;' 2. By the cause, viz., 'wicked works,' ver. 22.

In setting down their remedy he notes: 1. The means; 2. The end. The means is, the 'death of the body of Christ's flesh.' The end is, that 'he might present them holy and unblamable, and without fault in God's sight,' ver. 22.

Thus of his relation to the church of the Colossians; and thus, also, of the second part of this chapter, viz., The proposition of doctrine.

The exhortation follows, ver. 23, where is to be considered: first, The exhortation itself, and then, The reasons. The exhortation is to perseverance, both in faith and hope.

In the exhortation to perseverance in faith, there is worthy to be noted: first, The manner of propounding it, which is with an 'if;' secondly, The duty required, 'continue;' thirdly, The manner of the duty, 'grounded and stablished;' fourthly, The object grace, 'in faith.'

In the exhortation to perseverance in hope, two things are to be observed: first, He sets down the evil to be avoided, viz., unsettledness or revolting, in the words, 'be not moved away;' secondly, He quickens them by remembering the cause and fountain of their hope, viz., 'the hearing of the gospel preached.'

Thus of the exhortation; the reasons follow.

There are seven reasons to enforce this exhortation to perseverance. The first is taken from the consent of God's elect, 'which are through the world,' who have, in the preaching of the gospel, received faith and hope as their common portion.

The second reason is taken from the testimony of Paul himself, and that is twofold: the first is, The testimony of his 'ministry;' this is that he preacheth, and therefore it should be that they should keep fast; the second is, The testimony of his 'sufferings;' he hath endured much for the doctrine of faith and hope, and therefore they should continue in it; and to stir them the more concerning his sufferings, he sheweth that he suffered with great joy, which he confirmeth by expressing the reasons of his joy: first, Because they were 'the afflictions of Christ;' secondly, Because he had his part allotted him by the decree of God; and it was his joy that he had almost finished what was left for him to suffer; there was but a little remaining; thirdly, Because they were but 'in his flesh;' fourthly, Because they were 'for them,' and the good of 'the church,' ver. 24.

The third reason is taken from the testimony of God, who enjoined unto Paul, and other ministers, this dispensation of the doctrine of faith and hope, with a charge that they should see his word fulfilled herein, ver. 25.

The fourth reason is taken from the excellency of the gospel, which is set out: first, By the nature of it, it is 'a mystery;' secondly, By the antiquity of it, it was, and was 'hid since the world began, from ages and generations;' thirdly, By the time of the revelation of it, 'now,' in the new world; fourthly, By the persons to whom it is revealed, viz., only 'the saints,' all which should move to care and constancy in keeping of it, ver. 26.

The fifth reason is taken from the excellency of the subject of the gospel, which is no less nor worse than Christ revealed by the preaching of the gospel. In this revelation of Christ in the gospel, consider: first, Who reveals him, God; secondly, The cause of his revelation, the will of God, 'he would;' thirdly, The manner, viz., 'in a rich and glorious mystery;' fourthly, The persons to whom, viz., the miserable 'Gentiles;' fifthly, The effects or fruits of it, which are: 1. The 'inhabitation of Christ;' 2. The 'hope of glory,' ver. 27.

The sixth reason is taken from the end, ver. 28, which is the 'presenting of them perfect in Jesus Christ;' which is amplified by the means to bring to this end, which is preaching; and that is amplified: first, By the parts of it, which are 'teaching' and 'admonishing;' and secondly, By the manner, 'in all wisdom,' ver. 28.

The seventh reason is taken from the holy strife of the apostle, to bring men to this; which is amplified by the great success which the Lord had given, ver. 28.

A METAPHRASE

UPON THE

FIRST CHAPTER OF THE EPISTLE TO THE COLOSSIANS.

VER. 1. Paul, the messenger or ambassador-general for all the churches of the Gentiles, by commission from the promised Messiah, now come in the flesh, the Lord anointed; separated hereunto, not for his own worthiness, or by any private motion of his own, or by commandment of any man, but by the express will of God, according to his everlasting counsel; as also Timotheus, a reverend brother, an evangelist of Christ, with full and free testimony approveth this epistle written.

Ver. 2. To the citizens and inhabitants of the city of Colosse, that are separate from the world, and sanctified with true grace, and faithfully walk in that holy calling in brotherly communion one with another, and indissoluble union with Christ your Saviour, grace be with you, and peace, even the free favour of God, with all internal, eternal, and needful external blessings, from him that both will and can, even God our Father, through the merits of the Lord our anointed Saviour.

Ver. 3, 4. We give thanks unto God, even that God that by an eternal and unexpressible generation is the Father of our Lord Jesus Christ, remembering you earnestly and constantly in our daily prayers, being exceedingly fired and inflamed since we heard by continual and true report of your precious faith, by which you have with firmness and steadfastness of assurance laid hold upon Jesus Christ, for life and righteousness; and the rather, because we likewise heard of your holy affection to such as have separated themselves from the profaneness of the world to the service of God, especially considering that you have not the glorious faith of Christ in respect of persons, but love all the saints as well as any.

Ver. 5. And as a people not destitute of any saving grace, we rejoice to hear of that lively hope by which you have laid hold on the promise of eternal glory, which God the Father hath prepared and laid up in heaven; and the more are we confirmed in this resolution constantly to praise God for these excellent graces, because they are not sudden fancies or presumptuous conceits, raised out of the forge of your own brain, or conceived for some corrupt or carnal ends, but were indeed begotten in you by the mighty working of the most sweet doctrine of reconciliation, proved in itself, and by effect, to be a word of truth; even that word of the Lord, long foretold, now truly revealed and accomplished also, begetting the true form of piety in you, with constancy and true uprightness, both of heart and life.

Ver. 6. This is the word of reconciliation which is come unto you, as by incredible power and swiftness it is now to the greatest part of the world, even to people of all sorts and nations, causing them to shew the soundness of their conversion by the daily fruits of amendment of life; and this increaseth continually in all places, as it doth and hath done with you since the very first day that you truly heard and effectually believed this rich doctrine of the grace of God.

Ver. 7. And this very doctrine, which you have heard of Epaphras, is the self-same divine truth that is gone all abroad the world; of Epaphras, I say, whom we all reverence as our dear fellow-servant, being assured that he is for your best good, a faithful and most humble minister of Jesus Christ.

Ver. 8, 9. He hath with great contentment boasted of you in reporting to us your spiritual and heavenly affection to God and godliness, and one towards another; and for the same cause since the first time we heard of your praises in the gospel, we have been importunate without ceasing, praying for you, and beseeching God to increase in you, and make complete your knowledge of His revealed will, not only for contemplation, but for practice also, with a gracious experience of the working of the Spirit.

Ver. 10. That ye might carry yourselves in a holy eminency of godly conversation, striving to proportion your obedience in a greater degree than ordinary, as might become the great measure of God's mercies of all sorts towards you, expressing a lively kind of pleasingness, both in carriage towards God and man, being refreshed with the sweetness of acceptation in your services; and that you might extend your carefulness to bear fruit, not in one kind, or some few, but in all kinds and sorts of good works, daily increasing in a holy acquaintance with the sacred nature of God, which is both the effect and cause of all comfortable progress in holy life.

Ver. 11. That so growing up to a ripe age in Christ, in the sanctification both of soul and body and spirit, in all the graces and duties of Christ and Christian life, through the assistance of the glorious power of God, in the use of all means and helps appointed by God, ye might accomplish your most holy profession, with singular comfort and contentment, being able cheerfully and with all patience and long-suffering to bear the crosses, temptations, infirmities, persecutions, and whatsoever wrongs or indignities might befall you, waiting for the promise of God, being never weary of well-doing.

Ver. 12. And as we have thought good thus to let you understand our love towards you, and our rejoicing for the prosperity of your souls, so we thought good to write unto you, both to put you in mind of the most holy doctrine of Christ, as also to exhort and beseech you to be constant in the faith and hope you have received, without listening to the enticing speeches of false teachers, which, as wicked seducers, would beguile your souls of that high prize of your most holy calling.

What thanks can we ever sufficiently give unto God, the Father of Christ and Christians, that of his mere grace and free love hath, by a holy calling, made us, in his account, meet to have a lot in that heavenly Canaan; in that sweet and eternal fellowship with the spirits of the just, not only revealed unto us in this light of the gospel, but to be enjoyed by us in the light of heaven;—

Ver. 13. And hath also already delivered us from that woeful estate in which the darkness of Gentilism and sin, and ignorance and adversity, and death and damnation had power over us, and hath translated us into the kingdom of Jesus Christ, the Son of his love, enrolling our names among the living, and accounting us as subjects of this kingdom of grace, and heirs, even co-heirs with Christ, of the glory to be revealed?

Ver. 14. And howsoever our sanctification be as yet unperfect, yet are we not only bought with a price, but effectually and truly redeemed, and in some sort fully too; for in our justification we are perfectly reconciled, and all our sins absolutely forgiven us, as if they had never been committed, through his merits that shed his blood for us.

Ver. 15. Who is a most lively and perfect image of the invisible God, not only as he works God's image in man, or because he appeared for God the Father, to the fathers in the old law; or because as man, he had in him the likeness of God in perfect holiness and righteousness; or because he did by his miracles, as it were, make God visible in his flesh; but as he was from everlasting the very essential natural image of God, most absolutely in his divine person, resembling infinitely the whole nature of his Father, and therefore is to be acknowledged as the begotten of God by an eternal generation; so the first begotten of every creature, as he was before them, so is he therefore the principal heir of all things, by whom, and in whose right, all the saints do inherit what they have or look for.

Ver. 16. For by him all things in heaven or earth, whether visible or invisible, were created; yea, the very angels themselves, of what order or office soever, whether thrones or dominions, principalities or powers, were all made by him of nothing; and therefore he, and not they, are to be worshipped; in short, all things were created by him, yea, and for him too.

Ver. 17. And he was from everlasting with God the Father, before all angels or other creature was made, and still all things are preserved and continued as consisting in him; yea, the very angels have their confirmation from him.

Ver. 18. And he is that glorious and alone mystical head of the church, which, in a holy order and relation, by the admirable work of the Spirit, as a bond uniting together, is a true body unto Christ; and worthily is he to be acknowledged a head unto the church, for three great reasons: first, In respect of dignity; for he alone hath the primacy, and ought to be acknowledged to have pre-eminence in all things; for if we respect the estate of grace, he is the beginning of all goodness, and if we respect the estate of glory, he is the firstborn of the dead; not only because he is risen himself in his body from the grave, but also because by his only power all his members shall rise at the last day; and also, because that in the death of all the righteous, he doth still continue to and in the very last gasp his assistance and holy presence.

Ver. 19. Secondly, He is fittest, yea, only fit, to be the head of the church, because it hath pleased the Father, that in him should all fulness only dwell, so that he is a head in respect of plenitude, for the behoof of the members.

Ver. 20–22. And thirdly, He is a head in respect of influence; for from him only comes down to the members all peace with God, and all the fruits of that reconciliation; for it is he that made peace, by the blood of his cross, and that hath estated happiness upon all the saints, reconciling them to God; I say, all the saints, both those that are in heaven already, and those that being yet on earth, hope for that glory in heaven hereafter. And that this is so, you are able out of your own experience to avouch; for whereas by nature you were strangers from God and the life of God, you were very enemies to God and all his goodness; and this alienation and enmity was apparently seated in your very minds, through the evil works of all sorts which abounded in your lives; yet you know that Christ taking our nature upon him, and in that nature suffering death for you, hath reconciled you to God, and by the gospel anew created you, that he might present you to God, as holy and unblamable, and without fault in his sight, covering your wants and hiding the evil of your works, through his own intercession, and allowing you the benefit of the covenant of grace, through which uprightness will be in him accepted instead of perfection.

Ver. 23. Now what remains, but that seeing we have such precious doctrine, you should be exhorted to hold out with all Christian perseverance, settling and establishing your hearts in the belief of the truth, suffering yourselves not to be carried away with any contrary wind of doctrine, from the confidence of that hope of your reconciliation with God, which hath been propounded and wrought in you, by the preaching of the gospel; and the rather, because unless you do so persevere, you cannot have sound comfort in your right to the benefits before named. Besides, there are many reasons may induce you to the resoluteness of perseverance in the doctrine you have already believed and hoped in: first, It is the doctrine which all God's elect, with one consent, have received throughout the world, and upon it have founded their faith and hope; secondly, The consideration of what ye see in me may somewhat move you, and that if you either consider my ministry or sufferings; for my ministry, I have so thoroughly informed myself concerning the doctrine which Epaphras hath taught you, that I see it in all things, for the substance of it, to be the same which I myself have taught in every place.

Ver. 24. Now for my sufferings, it is apparent to all sorts of men that I have endured my part of all kinds of troubles for the gospel, which I would not have done if I had not had full assurance of the truth of it, neither do I repent me of my afflictions, but rejoice in them rather, and that for divers reasons: first, Because they are the afflictions of Christ, that is, such as he accounts to be his; secondly, Because I know that in God's decree I have my part of troubles assigned me; and it is my joy to think, that in so good a cause I have almost fulfilled them; thirdly, Because these afflictions extend but to my flesh and outward man; and lastly, Because it is for your good I suffer, even for the confirmation of your faith, and for the good of the whole body of Christ, which is the church.

Ver. 25. Thirdly, I have received this commission concerning the gospel immediately from God himself, with strict charge that for your good I should pursue the execution of it, till not only faith and hope were wrought, but till we saw the work and word of God even accomplished and fulfilled.

Ver. 26. Fourthly, What can there be more excellent and worthy to be believed and trusted in, than this gospel of Jesus Christ, and our reconciliation in him, seeing it is that dreadful mystery which worlds of men have wanted, as being hid from whole ages and generations hitherto, and now by the unspeakable mercy of God is revealed by preaching unto the saints, as a peculiar treasure intrusted to them?

Ver. 27. And fifthly, The rather should you hereupon settle, considering the admirable subject of the gospel; for it is the good pleasure of God in this rich and glorious mystery of the gospel to make known to the poor Gentiles Christ Jesus himself, and that by giving him therein to dwell in your hearts by faith, and as your assured and only hope of immortal glory.

Ver. 28. Sixthly, Neither should you ever cast away the confidence of your assurance and hope, or grow weary herein, seeing it is the drift and end of all our preaching, wherein we either admonish or instruct you, leading you through all sorts of wisdom in the word of God. I say, the end of all is, to present you at the length, perfect and complete every one of you, in Christ Jesus, in some acceptable measure of sincerity and knowledge in him.

Ver. 29. And seventhly, Being encouraged with that success which the Lord hath given to my ministry, I will labour as I have laboured, and still strive with all possible diligence and endeavour in this glorious work; hoping that this also may prove a motive among the rest to persuade with you to keep faith and hope to the end, with all constancy and holy perseverance.

AN EXPOSITION

UPON THE

WHOLE EPISTLE TO THE COLOSSIANS.

VER. 1. *Paul, an apostle of Jesus Christ by the will of God, and Timotheus, a brother.*

Ver. 2. *To them which are at Colosse, saints and faithful brethren in Christ, grace be with you, and peace from God our Father, and the Lord Jesus Christ.*

Two things are worthy our consideration in this epistle, the author and the matter. The author was Paul, concerning whom memorable things are recorded. He was an Hebrew of the Hebrews; of the tribe of Benjamin, Phil. iii. 5; a pharisee, the son of a pharisee; born in Tarsus of Cilicia, circumcised the eighth day, brought up in the knowledge of the law and pharisaical institutions by Gamaliel, a great doctor among the Jews, Acts xxiii. 6; acquainted also with the language of foreign nations, as his quoting of the authorities of Greek poets shews, Acts xxii. 3; Titus i. 12. And in his youth, for the righteousness external, which was after the law, he was unrebukable and full of zeal, but withal a violent and blasphemous persecutor, Phil. iii. 6; Gal. i. 13, 14. His calling was exceeding glorious, his office unto which he was called was great and honourable, viz., to be legate of Christ, 1 Tim. i., the doctor of the Gentiles, the minister of God, of Christ, of the Spirit, of the New Testament, of the gospel of reconciliation and of righteousness, Acts ix. 15, xxvi. 16. He was famous for his labour in the word, by which he caused the gospel to run from Jerusalem to Illyricum with admirable swiftness, as also for his faithfulness of mind, for his pure conscience, for his affection to the faithful, for his humanity and courtesy, for his continency, for his humility, for his care for the churches, for his honest conversation, innocency, and constancy, he was of nature earnest, acute, and heroical, 1 Tim. ii.; 2 Cor. vi., xi., and iii.; Eph. iii.; 2 Cor. v., iii.; 1 Cor. xv.; Rom. xv. 19; 2 Cor. i. 12.

Add unto these the praises of his sufferings, what reproach, what stripes, what imprisonments, what beating with rods, and such like wrongs did he endure! Five times of the Jews received he forty stripes save one, once was he stoned, thrice he suffered shipwreck, night and day was he in the deep sea; in journeying often, in perils of waters, of robbers, of his own nation, of the Gentiles; in the city, in the wilderness, in the sea, and among false brethren. How he was daily pressed with weariness, painfulness, watchings, hunger, thirst, fastings, cold, and nakedness, besides the incumbrances and cares for the business of the churches, 2 Cor. xi. 22-30.

Finally, we may consider the testimony given to his doctrine to prove it to be without all mixture of error. And this testimony standeth of four branches: 1. His immediate calling; 2. His immediate instruction and information; 3. The visible donation of the Holy Ghost, which was not only given to himself, but he also conferred it by imposition of hands to others; 4. His working of miracles; for so he saith of himself, 'The signs of an apostle were wrought among you, with all patience, with wonders, and great works.' He raised a man from the dead, Acts ix., xix. 6; 2 Cor. xii. 12; Acts xx. Neither could the miracles wrought by him be small, when handkerchiefs were brought from his body to the sick, and their diseases departed from them; yea, devils went out of them, Acts xix. 12.

Lastly, this noble Jew, more famous among the apostles than ever the great Saul was among the prophets, was beheaded by the emperor Nero, the 29th of June, in the 70th year of the Lord.. And all this should cause us, with all reverence, both to teach and learn the celestial doctrine delivered in writing to the churches by him.

Thus of the author; the matter followeth. I mean not to search after the descants and conceits that some observe concerning the works of this worthy, as that he should write ten epistles to the churches, to answer the number of ten commandments; and four epistles to particular persons, to express his agreement with the four evangelists. Only this in general; for his hearers or auditory, he had the Romans, the greatest in the earth for power; the Grecians, the most famous for wit and learning; and the Jews or Hebrews, of greatest note for divine understanding of the law of God. But to leave this, I come to the matter of the epistle, and observe three things :

1. To whom he writeth.
2. Upon what occasion.
3. The treatise itself.

For the first, Colosse was a city in Phrygia, in Asia the less, near to Laodicea and Hierapolis. The church in this city was not first gathered by Paul, but, as some think, by Epaphras, whom they take to have been one of the seventy disciples, and an evangelist. Some say they were first converted by Archippus, who is mentioned, chap. iv. 17, and that Epaphras, one that was born amongst them, being instructed by Paul, was sent thither to build them up further.

For the second, the occasion of this epistle was this: After that there was a church here gathered by the power of the gospel, Satan, after his wonted manner, stirred up corrupt teachers, who by cross and contrary teaching did mightily labour to disgrace the ministry, and hinder the efficacy of the doctrine of their faithful minister. These men taught philosophical positions and vain speculations, urged the ceremonies of the Jews, and brought in praying to angels and such like infectious stuff. Epaphras hereupon being oppressed with the madness and fury of those imps of Satan, resorts to Paul, who lay in prison at Rome, and acquainting him with the state of the church, procures him to write this epistle.

Thirdly, The treatise itself stands of five parts: first, An exordium, chap. i. 1-12 ; secondly, A proposition, lively expressing the doctrine of Christ and his kingdom, from ver. 12-23; thirdly, An exhortation, containing a persuasion, from ver. 23 of chap. i. to ver. 8 of chap. ii., and a dissuasion, from ver. 8 of chap. ii. to the end of chap. ii. ; fourthly, An institution of manners, giving rules : first, In general, chap. iii. 1-18; secondly, In special, from ver. 18 of chap. iii. to ver. 2 of chap. iv. And lastly, A conclusion, from ver. 2 of chap. iv. to the end. Or briefly thus, setting aside the entrance and the conclusion, the apostle treats of matters of faith in the first two chapters, and of matters of life in the two last.

And thus in general of the whole epistle, with the persons to whom, and the occasion thereof. The first part of the epistle is the exordium ; and it stands of two members, a salutation and a preface. The salutation, ver. 1, 2, and the preface from ver. 3-12.

In the salutation I consider three things : first, The persons saluting; secondly, The persons saluted ; thirdly, The form of the salutation. The persons saluting are an apostle and an evangelist ; the apostle is described by his name, 'Paul;' by his office, 'an apostle;' by the principal efficient that preferred him to that office, and both appointed him his service, and protected him in it, viz., 'Jesus Christ;' and lastly, by the impulsive cause, viz., 'the will of God.' The evangelist is described: first, By his name, 'Timothy;' secondly, By his adjunct estate, 'a brother.'

First, Of the words that describe the apostle ; and here first the meaning of them, and then the doctrines to be observed of them.

Paul. The apostle at his circumcision was called Saul. For, being of the tribe of Benjamin, it seems the men of that tribe did, in honour of their king Saul, who was the first of all the kings of Israel; and by a kind of emulation to retain the first glory of their tribe (more respecting the outward honour of Saul, in that he was a king, than the curse of God in his rejection) did use to give the name of Saul to their children very often as a name of great honour.

And not unfitly did this name light upon this Benjamite, both if we regard him as he was before his calling or after: before his calling, as the old Saul persecuted David, so did this youngling Saul (coming freshly out of the mint of a pharisee) persecute Christ, who came of David. And after his calling, as it was said of old Saul, by way of proverb, 'Is Saul also among the prophets?' so may it be said of this Saul, by way of honour, 'Saul is among the apostles;' and that not the least of the apostles, for he 'laboured more abundantly than they all.'

Concerning this other name Paul, writers are diversely minded. Some think that thirteen years after Christ, by the conduct of the apostles, he received both his apostleship over the Gentiles, and this name. Others think that he took unto himself this name of 'Paulus,' to profess himself the least of all apostles. Others think the name was given him for some eminent praise of some quality or action, as Peter was called Cephas, and James and John called Boanerges, and Jacob called Israel. Some think he had two names, as Solomon was called also Jedidiah, and Matthew called Levi, and these should seem to be given by his parents, to profess his interest amongst both Jews and Romans; among Jews by the Hebrew name 'Saul,' and among the Romans by the Latin name 'Paulus.' Some think it is but the varying of the language, as John, Jochanan, Jehan, and Johannes, all are but differing in several languages. Lastly, it is most likely he was called Paul for memory of the first spoils he brought into the church of Christ, not the head but the heart of 'Sergius Paulus,' that noble Roman, Acts xiii. 9; and this is more probable, because in all the chapters before he is never called Paul.

Apostle. This word in the general signification importeth one that is sent, and so Epaphroditus is called an apostle, Phil. ii. 19; but the etymology of the word is larger than the usual application of it, for it is usually given to the twelve principal disciples, and to Paul and Barnabas; and so it is used as a term of distinction from other church officers; for, for the body, they had widows for the sick, and deacons for the poor; and for the soul, they had pastors and doctors for exhortation and instruction. And these were standing and ordinary officers. Now there were extraordinary, viz., apostles and evangelists. The apostles were men immediately called by Christ, and had general charge over all churches for planting and governing them; the evangelists were called most by the apostles, and sent with spiritual charge whither the apostles saw most convenient.

Jesus Christ. These titles given to the Messiah are not in vain used, or joined together; for by these names both his office and his work are described. In the one name 'Christ,' shewing what he undertook to be; in the other, shewing what he was, viz., 'Jesus,' a 'saviour.' The one name, viz., 'Jesus,' a Hebrew word, is for the Jews; and the other name, 'Christ,' a Greek word, is for the Gentiles,—the one shewing that he was God, for, 'besides me there is no Saviour,' Isa. xlv. 21; the others shewing that he was man, viz., Christ, the anointed. For in respect of his human nature chiefly is this anointing with graces or gifts attributed to Christ.

Again, Christs were of two sorts, viz., false Christs, Mat. xxiv., and true Christs. The true were either typical—and so the prophets, priests, and kings were anointed; hence in the Psalm, 'Touch not my Christs,' &c.—or essential, and so only the son of Mary.

By the will of God. These words are expounded, Gal. i. 1, where he is said to be an apostle; 'not of men,' as princes send civil ambassadors, or as the Jews sent false apostles; 'nor by men,' as Timothy, Titus, Luke, &c., who were ordained by man, and as Titus did ordain elders, Titus i. 4. Or else not by the commendation, pains, or instruction of any man.

Doct. 1. Paul an apostle. Here three doctrines may be observed: first, Great sinners may prove great saints; a great enemy of sincere religion may prove a great founder of churches; a great oppressor of God's servants may prove a great feeder of God's flock,—in a word, a persecutor, as we see here, may be an apostle.

Use 1. This doctrine, as it doth excellently sample out God's unsearchable mercy, so it teacheth us not to despair of any, but to continue to pray for even the vilest and most spiteful adversaries, and the most open oppugners and usual traducers of God's cause and people; and to wait upon God to see if at any time he will give them repentance to build that they have destroyed, and to gather that they have so much striven to scatter.

Use 2. Secondly, This doctrine is of singular use in the cure of the hardest of diseases, viz., affliction of conscience; for in some of the dear servants of God, that have appearing upon them some signs of effectual calling, a right evidence of hope from God's promises, sweet pledges, and signifying seals of God's favour, by the witness of the spirit of adoption, yet there ariseth some scruples about either the multitude or greatness of their sins. Now the healing of their errors and uncomfortable mistakings doth most an end arise from the right application of such examples as this. I say a right application, for the most men do dangerously and damnably mistake in alleging the instances of the great sins of God's servants. But if thou observe these four rules thou canst not mistake or misapply: first, If thou bring not in the examples of David, Peter, Paul, or any other, to patronise thy sin, or to defend or nourish thyself in a sinful course; secondly, If thou allege them not to wrest God's promises, as to make the promises of mercy general when they are restrained with their several limitations; thirdly, When they are not brought out to fortify a profane heart against the ordinances of God, as reproofs, either public or private; fourthly, When thou dost as well urge upon thyself the necessity of the repentance was in them, as seek the comfort of the remission of so great sins committed by them. These rules being observed, the example of Paul's sins may, with comfort, be applied, as he himself testifieth, 1 Tim. i. 16.

Doct. 2. Secondly, The apostle, to bring his doctrine into greater request, doth in the entrance of the epistle insinuate himself into their respects, by setting down the authority and praises of his office and person; which sheweth unto us that usually where the persons of the ministers are not regarded, their doctrine worketh little. The doctrine is not long in credit where the person and function itself is contemned.

And this yields us one reason why a number of profane men get so little by the doctrine they so ordinarily hear: and the cause is, they are contemners, and scoffers, and reproachers of God's ministers, and therefore God will give them no blessing by their ministry. Again, It shews how heavy and hurtful a sin it is to detract from the name and good esteem of ministers, by tales, lies, and slanders; for, though men believe thee not in thy slanders, yet it is the property of most defamations, that they leave a kind of lower estimation many times where they are not believed. Thirdly, It serves to teach all ministers, and others that are in government, to preserve by all lawful and holy endeavours the authority and credit both of their persons and callings. There is no doubt but the base carriage and indiscreet and sinful courses of many ministers have brought a contempt and barrenness upon the very ordinances of God; they can do no good with their doctrine, they are so wanting to that gravity and innocency that should shine in the lights and lamps of Christ.

Doct. 3. Lastly, Here may be observed, that he that will bear rule over other men's consciences, must be an apostle; less than an apostolical man cannot prescribe unto other men's consciences; and therefore it is a profane insolency in any whatsoever to urge their fancies and devices, and to press them, master-like, upon the judgments or practices of their brethren, when they are not warranted in the writings of the prophets and apostles.

Doctrine of Jesus Christ. No knowledge can be available to salvation without the knowledge of Christ, and therefore the apostle in the very forefront of the epistle professeth to teach the doctrine of Christ, and to aim at such a course of framing of doctrine, as above all things Christ Jesus may sound in his instructions, and be received into honour, application, and practice. And he doth in the very entrance intimate what the corrupt teachers must look for from him, viz., that he will batter the whole frame of their building, that have led men from Christ crucified, to vain traditions, philosophical speculations, Jewish observations, and given his glory to angels.

By the will of God. That is, by his approbation,

direction, protection, but especially by his singular vocation. The apostle then holds his calling from God, and therefore believes God's protection and blessing, because God had called him to his function. And as the apostle, so every member of the church, holds his particular standing and function from God; he is ranked into order by the special providence and calling of God.

And it is to great purpose that men should know it in their own particular. For, first, It enforceth diligence. If God have set thee in thy calling, then it stands thee upon to discharge the duties of thy calling with all heedfulness and painfulness. Secondly, It may teach men not to pass the bounds of their calling; for seeing they are in their places by God's will, they must take heed of going beyond their limits, either by using of unlawful ways and courses, or by intruding into other men's functions. Thirdly, It doth plainly appoint the particular calling to serve the general. Every Christian hath two callings: the one is the external designment of him to some outward service in the church or commmonwealth, and this is his particular calling; the other is the singling of him out by special sanctification to glorify God, and seek his own salvation in the things of the kingdom of Christ, and this is a calling general to him, with all believers. Now it is manifest, that God's commandment is, that men first seek the kingdom of God, and the righteousness thereof. And therefore he never meant that men should so follow their outward business and employments, as to omit the means of knowledge and grace, prayer, reading, hearing, conference, and such like. Lastly, the consideration of this, that we hold our particular callings from God, should teach us contentation in the willing undergoing of the daily molestations or troubles and crosses that do befall us, and to be content with our kind of life, seeing we are thus set and placed by God's will.

Thus far of the apostle. The evangelist is described: first, By his name, 'Timothy;' secondly, By his adjunct estate, 'a brother.'

Doct. 1. Three things briefly may be observed here: first, That consent in doctrine is a great means and effectual to persuade both to incorruption in faith, and integrity in living. This made Paul to join Timothy with him; and the consideration of this, as it should teach all faithful ministers to make themselves glorious by a brotherly harmony in matters of opinion, so it doth give occasion to bewail that great sin of wilful opposition and cross-teaching, which doth in many places too much abound, a course that is taken up by some of purpose to hinder the growth of knowledge and sincerity; some of these instruments of the devil, having for the most part, no life or heart either, in study or preaching, but when envy and malice and a desire to be contrary doth instigate and prick them forward. These are like them of whom the apostle complained, that were 'contrary to all men, and forbid us to preach to the churches that they might be saved, and fulfil the measure of their sins always: 'God they please not, and the wrath of God is come on them to the uttermost,' 1 Thes. ii. 15, 16.

Doct. 2. Secondly, Here we may learn that spiritual alliance is the best alliance, for it is a greater honour to Timothy to be a brother, than to be an evangelist; for he might have been an evangelist, and yet have gone to hell when he had done, as Judas, an apostle, did. And this cannot but be exceeding comfortable, seeing there is not the meanest child of God but he may attain to that which was Timothy's greatest title.

Doct. 3. Thirdly, The apostle doth intimate by the taking in of Timothy's assent, that the most glorious doctrine of God doth need the witness of men, such a vanity and secret sinfulness doth lodge in men's hearts. Which should teach ministers, with all good conscience and heedfulness, to weigh well and consider thoroughly of their doctrine before they deliver it, because there is a weakness too commonly found in the very dear children of God, namely, to receive doctrine upon the trust and credit of the messenger, without searching the scriptures as they ought to do.

Thus far of the persons saluting: the persons saluted are described, both by the place of their habitation, 'at Colosse,' and by their spiritual estate; in which he describes them by four things: they are 'saints,' they are 'faithful,' they are 'brethren,' and they are 'in Christ.'

Before I come to the particular handling of each of these, I consider four things in the general: first, Here we see the power of the gospel. But a little before, if Colosse had been searched with lights, as Jerusalem was, there would not have been found one saint nor one faithful man or woman in the whole city; and now behold by the preaching of the word, here are many saints and faithful brethren to be found in her. Secondly, We see here who be the true members of the church; the apostle acknowledgeth none but such as are saints, faithful, and in Christ. Thirdly, We see here that a church may remain a true church, notwithstanding gross corruptions remain in it unreformed, as here these titles are given to a church much poisoned with human traditions and vile corruptions in worship. Lastly, It is to be observed that the apostle joins all these together, to note that one cannot be without the other, one cannot be a saint unless he be faithful, and in Christ, and so of the rest. The last clause cuts off the Jews apparently from being saints or true believers, seeing they receive not Christ; and the first clause cuts off the carnal protestant, so as he cannot be a believer or in Christ, seeing he cares no more for sanctity; and the two middlemost cut off the papists and all heretics and schismatics, seeing they have with insolent pride made a rent and apostasy from the true apostolical churches, by advancing themselves with their 'man of sin' above their brethren, nay, above all that is called God, 2 Thess. ii. 4, &c.

Thus far in general, the first thing particularly given them, is, that they are saints.

Saints. This word is diversely accepted in scripture. Sometimes it is given to the angels, and so they are called saints, Deut. xxxiii. 2; Job xv. 15. Secondly, Men are said to be holy by a certain legal or ceremonial sanctity, Lev. xi. 44. And in this sense the superstitious are holy. This is the holiness and sanctity of papists and popish persons, which place all their holiness in the observation of rites and traditions, and superstitious customs. Thirdly, All that stand members of the church, by the rule of charity, or in respect of outward visibility and profession, are called saints, and so all that covenant with God by offering sacrifice are called saints, Ps. l. 5. Lastly, and properly, It is a term given to men effectually called: the children of God truly converted are called saints, not because they are perfectly holy without all sin, but in four respects:

first, In respect of separation, because they are elected and gathered out of the world, and joined unto God's people, and dedicated to holy services and uses, and thus the word is often taken; secondly, In respect of vocation, and therefore the apostle, 1 Cor. i. 2, when he had said they were sanctified, he said by way of explication, they were saints by calling; thirdly, In respect of regeneration, because they are now new creatures; and lastly, In respect of justification or imputation, because the holiness and sanctity of Christ is imputed to them.

Doct. The sense being thus given, the doctrine is plain, that men may be saints in this life; there are saints in earth as well as in heaven. This is apparent also in other scriptures, as Ps. xvi. 3; 'To the saints that are in earth.' And Ps. xxxvii. 28, 'He forsaketh not his saints.' And Ps. cxxxii. 9, 16, 'Let thy saints rejoice.' So in the Epistle to the Ephesians, chap. ii. 20, 'Citizens with the saints,' and, chap. iii. 8, Paul calleth himself 'the least of all saints,' and, chap. iv. 12, 'For the gathering together of the saints,' with many other places. The use of this serves: first, To confute the gross folly of the papists, that acknowledge no saints till three things come to them: first, They must be canonised by the pope; secondly, They must be dead first; thirdly, It must be an hundred years after their death. This last proviso was well added, lest their treasons and most vile practices should be remembered. Secondly, This serves for the severe reproof of numbers in our own church, that live as if there were no sanctity to be looked after, till they come to heaven. Thirdly, The scripture is not without singular comfort to the poor despised saints. I will take them in order as they lie, Deut. vii. 6, 7. If we be sure we be a holy people to the Lord, then this is our comfort, that God accounts of us above all the people upon the earth, and no man loves his pearls or precious jewels, so much as God loves the meanest saint. David saith, Ps. xvi. 3, these are the nobles of the earth; and Ps. xxx. 4, 5, these are willed with all cheerful thankfulness to laud and praise God, and that before the remembrance of his holiness—as they before the ark, so we before all the tokens and pledges of God's love, both the word and sacraments, and sweet witnesses of the spirit of adoption, and all other blessings as testimonies of God's favour.

Object. Oh, but it seems the saints have little cause of joy or praise, for they are much afflicted, and that by the judgments of God too, either in their consciences within, or in their bodies, or estates, or names without.

Sol. The prophet answers, that 'the Lord endureth but a while in his anger, but in his favour is life, though weeping may abide at evening, yet joy cometh in the morning.' And in the 37th Ps. 28th ver., a charge is given to 'fly from evil and do good,' in which words a saint is described by his practice.

Object. Oh, but what shall they get by this preciseness?

Sol. They shall dwell for ever; no men have so certain, sure, and durable estates as those that make conscience of their ways, hating the infection of all sin, and delighting themselves in well-doing.

Object. Oh, but we see they are much maliced and hated, disgraced and wronged in the world.

Sol. 'The Lord loveth judgment;' if men right not their wrongs, God will; nay, it is a delight unto the Lord to judge the righteous, and him that contemneth God every day, Ps. vii., those spiteful adversaries of sincerity shall never escape God's hands.

Object. Oh, but we see not only wicked men, but God himself, smiteth and afflicteth those that be holy.

Sol. Though God afflict and chastise his people as a father his beloved son, yet 'he forsaketh not his saints.'

Object. Oh, but the saints themselves are full of great doubts, whether they shall persevere, or God will change.

Sol. It is God's unchangeable promise, 'they shall be preserved for evermore.' Again, in the 85th Ps., though the church be in great perplexities in respect of outward afflictions, yet this comfort the saints have: first, That though God's strokes seem to be the strokes of war, yet God's words are the words of peace; the word and Spirit of God are sure fountains of rest and peace to the heart and conscience of God's afflicted people; secondly, When God smites his people, he ever hath a regard to this, not to smite them so long as they should be driven to 'turn again to folly;' by folly he meaneth sin, for all sinful courses are foolish courses. The Lord by crosses intends to bring them out of sin, not to drive them in; and if men find not these privileges true, it is because either they do not hearken, that is, observe and mark the word, Spirit, and works of God, or else because they are not his saints. In the 149th Psalm, there is an 'honour given to all the saints,' viz., that they should with a two-edged sword, 'execute vengeance upon the heathen, and corrections upon the people;' they should 'bind kings with chains, and nobles with fetters of iron;' thus should they, 'execute upon them the judgment that is written.' So forcible and powerful are the public threatenings and censures of the saints assembled in their holy ranks, as also their private prayers, that all the swords of great princes cannot so plague the enemies of the church, as do the saints by these weapons. So fearful are the corrections and judgments which the saints by prayers and censures may bring upon whole troops of wicked men, as no swords or fetters in nature can be comparable to them.

When Daniel had described the greatness and glory of the princes, potentates, and mighty states in the four monarchies, at last he comes to speak of a kingdom which is the greatest under the whole heaven; and that is 'the kingdom of the saints of the most high.' So glorious is the state of the poor despised servants of God, even here in this world, in the kingdom of grace, Daniel vii. 27. And if there be such suing on earth, to become freemen of great cities, especially to live in the courts of great princes, how great is the felicity of every child of God, who is no more now a 'foreigner or stranger,' but a 'citizen with the saints, and of the household of God,' Eph. ii. 19.

To conclude, This may be a great refreshing to every child of God against all the discomforts of this present transitory life, that in that great and last and terrible day Christ will be 'glorified in them, and made marvellous in the saints,' 2 Thes. i. 10. And last of all, though the saints be here despised and trodden under foot, judged and contemned by men, yet the time will come when 'the saints shall judge the world,' 1 Cor. vi. 2.

Oh, but some will say, all the difficulty lieth in this, to know who are saints.

Ans. To this end, besides the four things generally laid down before, I will for trial allege two or three places of scripture. First, In Deut. xxxiii. 3, when Moses had praised the love of God to the Jewish nation, he specially commendeth God's special care towards the saints of that nation, whom, as most dear to him, he had always in his hands, and giveth this sign to know them by, viz., they are 'humbled at his feet, to receive his words.'

Secondly, David having spoken of the excellency of the saints on earth, Ps. xvi. 3, 5, 6, to prove himself to be one of the number he yieldeth his reasons from four experimental signs. First, The Lord was his portion. Though he had hopes or possession of great things in the earth, yet God's favour was that he did most prize, and spiritual things were unto him the fairest part of his inheritance; and though he had many crosses, yet 'the line was fallen unto him in a fair place,' Ps. xvi. 5, 6, so long as he could see grace in his heart, and the God of grace to love him freely. Secondly, He could as heartily praise God for spiritual blessings, viz., counsel, knowledge, and direction out of the word of God, as wicked men could for temporal honours, riches, pleasures, and such things as they love best. Thirdly, His reins did teach him in the night, ver. 7. Something can wicked men learn by the word without, but God did never honour any with the feelings of the spirit of adoption, but only the saints.

Object. Oh, but might not David be deceived in that sign by illusions, &c. ?

Ans. David gives two reasons why he could not: first, His feelings did not make him more careless, presumptuous, and sinful, as illusions do wicked men; but they taught him, that is, he learned by them many worthy lessons, and directions, and encouragements to holy life, and never did he conceive a greater hatred against his sin than when his reins taught him; *secondly,* He shews that he had them in the night, —that is, when he was alone, and withdrawn from company, and the things of the world, and worldly occasions. Fourthly, His last sign is, that he did set the Lord always before him. He could be content to walk ever in God's presence, and to have him the witness of his actions. He was not careful only to approve himself to men, as wicked men may do, but his chief care was to walk in all good conscience before God.

Lastly, In the 4th of Isaiah the prophet foretells of men, that under the gospel they should be called 'holy' or 'saints;' and these he describes by their happiness, 'they shall be written among the living in Jerusalem;' and by their holiness, which will discover itself by these signs: first, They are not acquainted with the damnable and hateful extenuations and qualifications of sins; they are not heard to say it is a little sin, a small fault; no, their sins in their eyes are filthiness and blood; secondly, They are men that have felt the power of God in the practice of mortification; they are new creatures, they are washed and purged; thirdly, The Spirit of God in them hath been a 'spirit of judgment, and a spirit of burning:' a spirit of judgment, not only in respect of knowledge and illumination, but also because it hath kept an assize in the soul of the sinner—he hath been arraigned, indicted, and hath pleaded guilty, and been condemned; a spirit of burning, both in respect of the inward purifying of the heart from the dross that cleaves unto it, as also in respect of zeal and ardour for the glory of God. And thus far of the first thing given unto the people of God, they are saints. Now followeth the second—

Faithful. This word is diversely attributed in scripture. It is given to God, 2 Cor. i., and God is said to be faithful in the accomplishment of his promises. It is given to Christ, Rev. xix. 11, and he is called 'faithful and true.' It is given to the sun in the firmament, Ps. lxxxix. 37, because it keepeth its certain course. It is given to the word of God, Ps. xix. 7 and cxi. 7, so as whatsoever it promiseth or threateneth men may certainly bind upon it, for heaven and earth may fail, but one jot of it shall not fail. Lastly, It is given to men, especially and most ordinarily to such men as are true believers and walk in all good conscience both before God and men; and as it is thus taken, the words of the Holy Ghost, Prov. xx. 6, may be taken up, 'Many men will boast, every one of his own goodness, but who can find a faithful man?' These are they that David so earnestly searcheth for, and having found them, doth so steadfastly set his eyes upon them, and entertaineth them into his court, Ps. ci. 6. The names of these we do for the most part take upon ourselves, but the signs of these are but sparingly found amongst us. That we may examine ourselves, I will consider what is required of us that we may shew ourselves faithful.

The Christian man's faithfulness ought to shew itself: first, In spiritual things; secondly, In temporal things. Unto faithfulness in spiritual things five things are requisite: first, Faith in Christ, to get sound reasons from the word and Spirit of God, and a sure evidence for the particular persuasion of the heart, that God in Christ is graciously reconciled with the sinner. He cannot be a faithful man that hath not a justifying faith. All that time of a man's life only receiveth he this honour, to be accounted faithful, when above all things he travels after the sense of God's favour in the forgiveness of his sins; secondly, Faithfulness stands in the performance of all those promises, purposes, and vows, which men in their distress, inward or outward, do make unto God. And, therefore, the Israelites are charged, Ps. lxxviii. 31-38, not to be faithful, because, when 'the wrath of God turned upon them,' and the 'strongest of them were slain,' and 'their chosen men were smitten,' and that 'their days did consume in vanity, and their years hastily,' then 'they cry unto him, and seek him in their distress,' 'they return and seek him early; they acknowledge that God is their strength, and the Most High their Redeemer.' But when the Lord had been merciful unto them, forgiven their iniquities, so as 'he destroyed them not, and called back his anger,' then they 'returned and provoked the Lord' again, they 'flattered him with their tongue, they tempted God, and sinned still;' and therefore they are censured thus,—'Their heart was not upright, neither were they faithful in God's covenant,' ver. 37; thirdly, It shews itself in constant sincerity in God's worship, when men will worship God according to the rules of his revealed will, without mixture of men's inventions, or the customary sins of profaneness and hypocrisy. And thus, Hosea xi. 5, Judah is said to be faithful with God's saints, because as yet the worship of God was preserved amongst them in the ancient purity in which the old patriarchs and saints did sincerely worship the God of their fathers. He is a faithful man that will worship God no otherwise than the saints have done, —that is, precisely according to his will revealed in his word; fourthly, Faithfulness is exercised in the conscionable enjoyment of the gifts, graces, and talents received in our general calling to God's glory, the increase of our gifts, and the enriching of our souls with true spiritual gain. And thus he is said to be a good servant and faithful, that having received five talents, hath gained with them five more, or two talents, and doth gain two more, Mat. xxv. 21-23; and this we do when, having received knowledge, faith, love, hope, patience, spirit of prayer, &c., we do by a constant and daily practice bring them out into exercise for ourselves and for others. Thus doing, two commodities we shall reap: first, It is a sign of our faithfulness; secondly, The gifts will increase, and to him that hath such gifts to use them shall be more given. Lastly, Faithfulness shews itself in men's sincerity, diligence, constancy, and care to promote and further the causes of God and the church, with the conscionable discharge of all such duties as belong unto such service. Thus Timothy is praised to be 'faithful in the Lord,' 1 Cor. iv. 17. And thus the apostle and apostolical men were 'faithful' when they could 'do nothing against the truth, but for the truth,' 2 Cor. xiii. 8. And thus men are faithful that can patiently bear and willingly take up the cross of Christ, and that daily, Luke ix. 23, so as they may further the building up and edification of God's people. Those, then, are not faithful that 'do the works of the Lord negligently,' that 'set their hands to the plough and look back,' that 'mind their own things,' honours, pleasures, profits, and preferments, and those that 'in the time of temptation fall away.' These specialties of faithfulness receive a great increase of praise if two things come to them: first, That men's hearts be faithful,—that is, that though they have many wants and infirmities, and fail much and often in well-doing, yet the desire, delight, endeavour, resolution, and affection is 'in all pleasing,' and firmness to walk before God, without either hypocrisy or presumption. This was Abraham's praise, Neh. ix. 8; secondly, That men continue 'faithful unto the death,' with all constancy and holy perseverance, believing in Christ, and worshipping God, even to the end of their days; this is called for, and crowned, Rev. ii. 11. Thus of faithfulness in spiritual things.

Faithfulness in temporal things stands in three things. First, In the sincere, diligent, and careful discharge of the duties of our callings. It was a singular praise in Daniel, that when his enemies sought occasion against him, they could find none concerning the kingdom, he was so faithful and without blame, and therefore they must take him, if ever, 'concerning the law of his God,' Daniel vi. 5. Then doth the glory of God's people shine, when together with their constant zeal in matters of religion, they are found carefully diligent and faithful in their callings; then whatsoever befalls them for the law of their God, they may bear it with all comfort and constancy, as did Daniel. But how doth it blemish the glory of profession, when men can say and see that professors are idle, deceitful, busy-bodies, and careless in their places and callings! They cannot build so much by profession, as they destroy by their scandalous and careless courses.

Secondly, In the right use and profitable disposing of our riches, even the outward things God hath given us. This lieth upon us, as one of the tokens of our faithfulness; nay, this is necessary to the being of this praise. In the 16th of Luke, Christ exhorts to the wise and liberal bestowing of our riches unto the necessities of the poor, and for other holy and needful uses. And because there lie in the hearts of carnal men many objections against this exhortation, therefore he forceth it with reasons that meet with men's carnal conceits.

Object. 1. And first, Whereas men, out of an over-great estimation and liking of these earthly things, do easily object that they must be careful of the saving, and sparing in the use of their riches, for they are all the comfort they have in this world; he answereth that men should not so much love these earthly things: for they are 'riches of iniquity,'—that is, sin, that makes a man miserable and accursed, is most an end mixed with riches: either they are wrongfully gotten, and sinfully kept, or they are causes of much sinning against God, or men, or himself.

Object. 2. Oh, but what good shall a man get by parting with his goods?

Sol. 'They shall receive him into everlasting habitations,'—*they*, that is, either the angels, or the poor, or thy riches shall let thee into heaven; even to sure dwelling-places: and this should move the rich, because the time will come when thou shalt want, and all the riches in the world cannot help thee.

Object. 3. Oh, but a man may be saved and enjoy these everlasting habitations, though he do not part with his riches.

Sol. He cannot : for a man cannot be saved without grace, and God will never trust him with grace, 'the true treasure,' that is not faithful in bestowing riches, ver. 10, 11 : and good reason; for if God gave a wicked worldling grace, he would never be faithful in using it; for 'he that is unjust in the least,' that is, riches, would be 'unjust in much,' that is, grace.

Object. 4. Oh, but our goods are our own, and therefore why should we give them to others?

Sol. Ver. 12. That is false, for grace only is a man's own, but riches are another's; for God is the Lord of the whole, Ps. xxiv. 1 ; and the poor is the owner of a part, Prov. iii. 27.

Object. 5. Tush, but a man may have a good heart to God, and yet not deliver out his goods to other men's uses, nor leave his content that he hath in the fruition of them.

Sol. That is false too : for 'a man cannot serve two masters'—one man cannot serve God and riches, ver. 13. And thus our Saviour meeteth with the objections of worldly men. The words also contain notable reasons to persuade to faithfulness, which lieth in this good use of riches : first, They are riches of iniquity ; secondly, The right use of them makes way for heaven ; thirdly, He is like to be a godly man in the use of grace, that is a faithful man in the use of riches ; fourthly, God else will not trust us with grace ; fifthly, He will else be a very unjust man, and his riches wicked ; sixthly, Grace only is his own goods, and to be without grace is to live and die a beggar ; lastly, Thou canst never serve God and riches.

Thirdly, In temporal things faithfulness shews itself in the uprightness and harmlessness of our carriage towards others ; as in keeping of promises, Ps. xv., in the honest discharge of the trust laid upon men, either in church or commonwealth, Neh. xiii. 13 ; Prov. xiii. 17 ; in witness-bearing, Prov. xiv. 5, 25 ; in just gains and lawful means used for profit in our dealings with others, Prov. xxviii. 20 ; and such like duties of justice.

Thus then we see who is a faithful man, even he that knoweth his own reconciliation with God by faith; that performeth his vows to God; that sincerely worships God, and laboureth the increase of holy graces; that will do nothing against the truth, but for the truth; that is diligent in his calling; that is serviceable with his riches; and lastly, that is just in his dealing.

Now, if we be such, then is our estate most comfortable: for first, God will be faithful to us in the accomplishment of all his promises; secondly, The word will be faithful, even a sure fountain of comfort and help in all distress; thirdly, Christ will be a faithful, both high priest in heaven, Heb. ii. 17, by his intercession making request for us to God, and both in earth and heaven he will be a faithful witness, so as while we live, we shall find the testimony of Jesus in our hearts, and when we die he will not be ashamed of us before his Father and the holy angels; and lastly, We shall be sure to have a faithful reward, Prov. xi. 18. And this of the second title given to God's children.

Brethren. The children of God are said to be brethren in a fourfold relation: 1. To Christ; 2. To the apostle; 3. To the saints abroad; 4. To the saints at home. For the first, Are we brethren to Christ? Then it should teach us two things: first, To live comfortably, for a higher estate of excellence canst thou not have; secondly, To live nobly, like the sons of the Most High, not basely, like the sons of the earth. Why wallowest thou in base and filthy pleasures? Why dotest thou upon uncertain and sinful profits? Why doth thy heart degenerate to regard, and so aspire after, worldly preferment? Remember whence thou art descended, and with whom allied, and walk as becomes the 'co-heir of Christ,' Rom. viii. 17.

Secondly, Are they brethren to the apostles and other great governors of the church? It should then teach ministers, magistrates, and masters of families, so to rule as to remember that they rule their brethren: neither to neglect their good, (for 'why should thy brother perish?') nor with proud insolency or tyranny, either in correction, or severe carriage, to lord it over them.

Thirdly, Are they brethren to the saints abroad, and are they of the same family with them? Then it should teach them to pray for them, and to lay the distress of other saints and churches to their hearts; for though they be removed in place and carnal knowledge, yet are they near in the mystical union, if it be considered that the same mother bare them, and the same Father begat them.

Lastly, Are they brethren to the saints at home? Then they should learn to converse brotherly, to live and love together, as becometh saints and brethren. Oh that it could sink into men's minds, or that this were written in men's hearts! Then could there be nothing more glorious and comfortable in this earth than this communion of saints, especially in the fellowship of the gospel.

In Christ. Men are said to be in Christ three ways:—First, As the plant in the stock, John xv.; secondly, As the member in the body, 1 Cor. xii. 12; thirdly, As the wife is one with the husband, Eph. v. 25.

Dost thou ask, then, how thou mayest get into Christ?

Ans. Observe three things:

First, Before thou canst be ingrafted into Christ, thou must be cut off the old tree; either a new man or no man; either lose the world, or never find Christ; either disarm thyself of all vain confidence, love, delight, and support from the world and worldly men, or the arm of the Lord will never bear thee up and nourish thee.

Secondly, A true member is not but by generation in nature, nor canst thou be a true member of Christ but by regeneration. Great odds between a wooden leg, though never so exquisitely made, and a true leg. All members in creation be begotten, and in grace begotten again.

Thirdly, As they are not man and wife where there is no sure making by contract or marriage going before, so neither can any be in Christ unless he be received into the covenant of grace; and as it is a mad thing in nature for any woman to say, Such a man is my husband, for he is a kind man, and did cast his eye upon me, or did me a pleasure at such a time, &c., so it is as great spiritual madness for any soul to plead interest in Christ when they can allege no more but his general love to man, or that he offered grace to us in the word and sacraments, or that we together with the gospel received outward blessings, or such like, when men can show no contract, no mutual intercourse between Christ and the soul, no manner of evidence for their hopes, no witnesses from the word, Spirit, or children of God, for their spiritual marriage.

Again: Would a man know whether he be in Christ? These comparisons likewise resolve his doubt by a threefold answer: First, He is in Christ if he blossom, grow, and bear fruit, even such fruit as is to eternal life. If a man be abundant in the works of the Lord, and grow in such graces as are communicated only to the faithful, he is certainly a true plant in this stock; for, by growing and fruit is the plant that is ingrafted known from the sprig that is lopped off, and lieth by and is withered. A life barren and void of the works of piety and mercy is a manifest sign that the person is not in Christ.

Secondly, If there be in our souls the sense, and feeling, and motion of spiritual life, then are we members; for in a wooden leg is there no sense nor natural motion. When men have as much sense and feeling, savour and delight in the things of the Spirit, as the word, prayer, fellowship in the gospel, with the exercises of holy graces in the duties of God's worship, or things otherwise belonging to the kingdom of Christ, as the carnal man hath in the profits, pleasures, and fleshly things of this world, these certainly are men 'after the Spirit,' Rom. viii., and by the Spirit mystically united to Christ, the head. And, on the other side, a more plain and palpable sign cannot be given to prove demonstratively that a man is not in Christ, than when a man finds no taste, hath no feeling, can take no delight in spiritual meats, graces, or persons, and yet is easily affected with the least profits and delights of the world.

Thirdly, It will appear by the holy communion between Christ and the faithful soul; by his cohabitation and spiritual intercourse; when Christ meets a Christian with holy comforts, with heavenly refreshings, with sacred answers, with spiritual direction, and other sacred signs of the presence of Christ, in the use of the means, sporting himself with the Christian soul; this intercourse, I say, this secret and chamber-meeting, these inward and hearty feelings, wrought by the word and sacraments, by prayer and fasting, by reading and conference, are certain and sure signs and seals to prove a marriage going before. And thus far of the four titles given to the children of God, and also of the second thing, viz., the persons saluted. Now followeth the salutation itself.

Grace and peace be unto you, from God the Father, and from the Lord Jesus Christ.

It hath been an ancient custom, both in the Jewish, Christian, and Pagan world, to begin letters and epistles with salutations, and in these they were wont to wish to their friends that which was accounted the chiefest good. Hence the heathen, as they were opinionative about the chief good, they did differently wish good things to their friends in their salutations. Some wished health, τὸ ὑγιαινειν; some wished welfare or safety, τὸ χαιρειν; some to do well, τὸ εὐπραττειν; some joy and a merry life, as they were either stoics or epicures. But the apostle, finding that true felicity was in none of these, doth religiously wish that which in the kingdom of Christ was in greatest request, viz., 'Grace and peace.'

Grace. This word is diversely taken: For kindness, 2 Sam. xvi. 17; for ability to affect or persuade, Ps. xlv. 2; for the happiness that is had from Christ in this world, and so it is opposed to glory, Ps. lxxxiv. 11; for the preaching of the gospel, Rom. i, 4, Titus ii. 12; for approbation from God, Prov. xii. 2; for the spiritual liberty that we have from Christ, and so it is opposed to the law, Rom. vi. 14. Lastly, it is taken for the love and favour of God, receiving the sinner into covenant in Christ, as it is an ever-flowing spring of celestial grace to the soul justified; and so it is taken here.

Peace. This word also is diversely accepted, for rest and ease from pain, Ps. xxxviii. 3; for familiarity, so 'the man of my peace,' Ps. xli. 9; for concord, Eph. iv. 3; for prosperity in general, 1 Chron. xii. 18, Ps. cxxv. 5, Jer. xxix. 11; for all that felicity we have by Christ, Luke xix. 42; for glory in heaven, Isa. lvii. 2, Luke xix. 38, Rom. ii. 10, Luke i. 79; for reconciliation itself, Luke ii. 14, Isa. liii. 5; for the means of reconciliation, Eph. ii. 14; for the signs of reconciliation, Isa. lvii. 19, Ps. lxxxv. 8; for tranquillity of conscience, Rom. xiv. 17, and v. 2. Lastly, it is also taken for all that rest of conscience within, and synecdochically it signifieth all those blessings spiritual which, either in this world or that other better world, we receive from Christ, together with God's favour and grace; neither is temporal prosperity excluded, though not principally meant; and so I think it is taken here.

The meaning being thus found, I consider the observations first generally.

First, In that the apostle doth in the very salutation sow the seeds of the whole gospel, we might learn, even in our ordinary employments, to mind God's glory and the salvation of others.

Secondly, We may hence see that it is lawful to draw abridgments of holy things, and commend them to ordinary use, as here these graces to an ordinary salutation from man to man; and so I think of teaching the Lord's Prayer and Commandments, with other scripture, to children or servants, that yet understand not, and that for such reasons as these: first, That so they might have occasion much to think of the things [which] are so much and commonly urged; secondly, That if any time of extremity should come, they might have certain seeds of direction and comfort to guide and support them; thirdly, That their condemnation might be more just, if having grace and peace, and other principles of catechism so much in their mouths, they should not get them into their hearts.

Thirdly, A question may here be moved, how the apostle can here in these words wish unto them their chief good or felicity, seeing these are not all the graces or blessings needful to our happiness? I might answer this diversely: 1. Here is a synecdoche, all are understood, though not all named; or thus, these are the beginnings of all graces and blessings; or thus, one or two graces is worth a world besides; or thus, these are chiefly above others to be sought; but lastly, it is certain these cannot be had without the most of saving graces; as for example, true peace cannot be had without Christ, nor without godly sorrow, confession, knowledge, meekness, desires, faith, humility, love, and the like; as men may easily see, if they will be informed either by scripture or experience.

Doct. But the main doctrine which generally I observe out of these words is this, that spiritual things from God in Christ are the best things, and most to be sought, and desired, and wished, both for ourselves and others. The reasons are: 1. They serve for the excellentest part, (viz., the soul;) 2. They serve for eternity, and these outward things but for this life; 3. Spiritual things are given by God in Christ, the other by God without Christ; 4. They only are able to satisfy the soul; 5. In respect of continuance, for outward things can last but till death, but then their works will follow the faithful into the grave, yea, into heaven, and therefore much more these graces; 6. Spiritual things are only proper to the saints, temporal things are common both to good and bad; 7. These are to be had by virtue of an absolute promise, the other but conditionally assured; 8. These are more pleasing and acceptable to God—God's acceptation proves them best; lastly, 'What shall it profit a man to win the whole world, and lose his own soul?' Mat. xvi. 26.

Use 1. The use is first for the just reproof of the wonderful carelessness and strength of folly that hath possessed the most people, in the profane neglect, nay, contempt of spiritual things, with the means of them. Indeed, if men could be rid of death, the grave, hell, and God's curse, or if these things could be had without seeking, it were to some purpose for men to sleep still and never wake. Many are the sleights of Satan. Some are stubborn, and will not regard; some with very prejudice run wittingly to hell; some confess it to be meet that the best things should be chiefly sought, but forget; some purpose, but give over for difficulties in the beginning; some no sooner rid of terror, but as soon of care for the life to come.

Use 2. Secondly, This doctrine may be a singular comfort to us, if we can find grace and peace in our hearts, however it be with us in our bodies or estates otherwise.

Use 3. Thirdly, It should teach parents to be more careful to leave grace in their children's hearts, than treasures in their chests for them; and friends should more endeavour to help one another in the comforts of a holy fellowship in the gospel, than in the civil furtherances they do so much engage themselves to.

Use 4. Lastly, It should teach us to learn the lesson given by our Saviour Christ, Mat. vi., neither to enlarge our affections to the immoderate desires of superfluity in outward things, nor yet to rack our hearts with the faithless and fruitless care of things necessary. This latter branch is urged with eight or nine worthy reasons; but of these in another place afterwards. And this much generally.

Grace. If grace, that is, God's favour, and the graces spiritual that flow from thence, be of so great worth and excellence, divers things may be inferred by way of profitable instruction for our use, out of several scriptures: First, If it be so great a privilege to obtain grace from God, we should strive to be such as are within the compass of the promise of grace, especially we should get humble and lowly hearts; for God gives grace unto the humble, but resisteth the stubborn, wilful, and proud sinner, James iv. 6. Again, if God's love and Christ's grace be jewels of so great value, it should teach us, when grace is offered in the means, or any way bestowed by God's Spirit, never to 'receive it in vain,' 2 Cor. vi. 1, so as it should be tendered without effect, or kept without advantage; but especially, let it ever be far from us to 'turn the grace of God into wantonness,' Jude 4, to abuse either the promises of grace, or the pledges of God's love, to become either bawds for perseverance in sin, or props to secure and bold presumption. And above all things, we should with all watchfulness take heed of wronging the Spirit of grace, either by resisting, tempting, grieving, quenching, or despising it, Heb. x. And further, we should learn by all good means, as constant hearing, prayer, reading, conference, and meditation, to 'stir up the grace given us,' 2 Tim. i. 6, to labour for spiritual strength in grace, 2 Tim. ii. 1, and to search so carefully into the evidence of faith for what we have, and hope for what we want, as never to give over to examine ourselves by the signs and promises of God's love, till our hearts were settled and established in grace. Lastly, God's children should solace themselves in the feeling and experimental knowledge of God's grace, so as their hearts should never carry them away to make them account the consolations of God small, or to despise the grace given them, Job xv. 11, 12; but rather in the midst of all combats with temptations within, or afflictions without, to support their souls with that gracious promise, 'My grace shall be sufficient for you, and my power made known in your weakness,' 2 Cor. xii. 9.

Peace. The second thing here wished for, and to be desired of all that love their own good, is peace, that is tranquillity of heart, with other spiritual blessings accompanying it, with outward things also, so far as they may further our happiness; but the scripture lays a restraint upon the getting of this peace, and gives rules for the use of it. For if ever we would have peace, we must first be righteous persons, that is, men that are broken in heart for our sins, humbled at God's feet for forgiveness; and such as hang upon the word of God, to receive the certain means of our soul's reconciliation, and the righteousness of Christ imputed unto us; such as to whom 'there is a way, and their path is holy,' Isa. xxxv. 8. But, on the other side, 'unto the wicked is no peace,' Isa. lvii. 21; and they are taken by the prophet for wicked men that are never humbled in the duties of mortification for sin, that in the hardness of their hearts frustrate the power of God's ordinances, so as they cannot work upon them: these have no peace, neither with God, angels, men, the creatures, or their own consciences.

Again, hast thou gotten peace and tranquillity of heart, even rest and ease from Christ, then let this peace 'preserve thy heart and mind,' Phil. iv. 6, and let it 'rule,' Col. iii. 15. Be careful to reject all matters in thoughts or opinion, in affections or desires, in words or actions, that might any way interrupt thy peace; but by all means nourish it, delight in it, and let it guide to all holy meditations, and affections, and gainful practices and endeavours. Let the peace of thy heart and God's spiritual blessing be a rule for all thy actions. And lastly, with all good conscience and holy conversation hold out, that when Christ shall come, either by particular judgment to thee in death, or by general judgment to the whole world in the last day, thou mayest be 'found of him in peace,' 2 Pet. iii. 14, so shall Christ be unto thee a 'Prince of peace,' Isa. ix. 6, 7, and 'guide thy feet for ever into the way of peace,' Luke i. 79.

And thus far of the good things he wisheth unto them: now follow the efficient causes, viz., *From God the Father, and our Lord Jesus Christ.*

Divers things may be here observed.

First, A proof of the Trinity, or, at the least, a

plain proof of two persons, the Father and the Son, united in one essence.

Secondly, God is here plainly affirmed to be a Father, and that he is in divers respects: first, To all by creation; secondly, To all the faithful by adoption; thirdly, To Christ, by the grace of union as man, and a natural Father, as God.

Thirdly, Here we may observe that grace and blessings must not be looked upon without some honourable meditation of God and Christ, the givers.

Fourthly, Seeing believers have a God, a Father, a Christ, a Saviour, a Lord, they are sure to be in a happy case, and may have what is needful, if they will seek for it.

Fifthly, We may observe, we can have no comfort in the enjoying, or hope, or any favour, or blessing, spiritual or temporal, unless, first, God be our Father; secondly, We be in Christ.

Lastly, If God be a Father, and Christ a Lord, it stands us upon to look to it, that we perform both honour and service. And thus of the salutation. The preface followeth.

Ver. 3. *We give thanks to God, even the Father of our Lord Jesus Christ, always praying for you.*

The salutation hath been handled already, the preface followeth, and is contained in this verse and those that follow to the twelfth verse; in which the end and drift of the apostle is, to win affection to the doctrine afterwards to be propounded; and this he doth by showing his exceeding great love to them, which he demonstrates by two things which he did for them, viz., he both gives thanks unto God in their behalf, and also made many a prayer for them; which spiritual duties are better kindnesses and signs of true affection and respect than all civil courtesies or outward compliments are or can be.

These things in the preface are first generally set down in this verse, and then particularly enlarged in the verses afterwards: first, The thanksgiving, from ver. 4–9; secondly, Prayer, ver. 9–11. In this verse he doth two things: first, He gives thanks; secondly, He prays. In the thanksgiving, consider, first, what he doth in these words, 'We give thanks;' secondly, to whom he doth it, in these words, 'To God, even the Father of our Lord Jesus Christ.' Thus far of the order of the words.

The doctrines follow, which must be considered generally from the whole verse, and specially from the several words.

The first general doctrine is this, that it is not enough to salute others kindly, but we must do and perform the sound duties of love: this is from the coherence, and condemns the sinful barrenness of many that know a necessity of no duties of love unless it be to salute courteously.

Secondly, We see here that tyrants may take away the benefit of hearing, reading, conference, and such like, but they cannot hinder us of praying. Paul can pray and give thanks in prison, for himself and others, as well as ever before. Let wicked men do their worst, God's children will still pray unto God. And look how many promises are made in scripture to the prayers of the saints, so many consolations are inviolably preserved unto them, against the rage of whatsoever extremity wicked men can cast upon them: this is a singular comfort.

We. Doct. Misery breedeth unity. The apostle that in more prosperous times jarred with Peter and Barnabas, can now hold peace and firm unity with meaner men; and therefore he saith 'we,' not 'I.' And thus we see it was in the times of persecution in Queen Mary's days, the bishops and pastors that could not agree when they were in their seats and pulpits, willingly seek agreement when they are in prison, and must come to the stake. And so it many times falls out in common judgments, as the sword and pestilence; in such times the words of the prophet are fulfilled, 'Like people like priests, like servant like master, like buyer like seller, like borrower like lender, like giver like taker of usury,' Isa. xxiv. 2. Great and prevailing judgments take away all that vanity of conceit and swelling of pride which difference of gifts and places bred before.

The Lord for his mercy's sake grant, that at the length there may be found some remedy to cure the wound and heal the breach which proud contention hath made, and continued, with effects prodigious and unheard of, lest the Lord be at length provoked to plague with more fierce and cruel judgments, and work union, at least in one furnace of common calamity; the same God, for his Son's sake, work in all that anywise love the prosperity of Jerusalem, on all sides, that they more regard the glory of God and the good of the church than their own greatness, either of place or respects among men, and that they may more seek the truth than victory. And as for those that neither love the truth nor peace, the Lord open their eyes and convert them, or else give them to eat of the fruit of their own ways.

Doct. It is not safe to put over good motions. When Paul findeth fitness to pray and give thanks, he doth not omit the occasion. In spiritual things delay is always dangerous, but in sinful motions, the only way many times is to defer the execution. Many sins are prevented by the very benefit of taking time enough to execute them.

Give thanks. Paul gives them to understand, before he comes to dispraise their vices and the corruptions crept into the church, that he takes notice of their praiseworthy virtues. He reserves his taxation to the second chapter; and this course he holds with them for divers reasons: First, To assure them of his love, and that he did it not of malice, a thing especially to be looked to in all admonitions, in family, or elsewhere, as well to praise for virtue as dispraise for vice. Secondly, He holds this course to let them see that he did account them as Christians, though they had their infirmities. It is a secret corruption in the affection of the reproved to conceive that the reprover likes them not at all. They are not fit to reprove others that cannot love them for their virtues at the same time that they dispraise their faults; and therefore they are far short of holy affections that say, I never liked him since I saw that fault by him. Thirdly, He did thus that they might the more hate sin, seeing it did darken their graces, which else would more appear. Fourthly, That they might be made thankful themselves for their own graces; a shame that others should praise God for his mercies to us, and we never praise God ourselves. Lastly, It carrieth with it a secret taxation of unthankfulness, as the cause of their fall; for had they been more thankful for the sincerity of the preaching of the gospel, and for the riches of the grace of Christ offered, the honourable opinion of the excellency and sufficiency thereof to give all sound contentment, would have preserved them from mixing the worship of God with men's traditions, or admitting contrary doctrine, and from dishonouring the mediation of Christ with angel-worship. Then did popish traditions overflow, when the scriptures were contemned, and the light of them suppressed; and, in general, an unthankful man is ever a vicious man.

More especially in the duty here mentioned two things are to be considered:

1. What they do: 'We give thanks.'
2. To whom: viz., 'To God, even the Father,' &c.

We give thanks. Eucharist is sometimes appropriated only to the sacrament of the Lord's supper; but most commonly is general to all holy thankfulness, especially to God.

There is a flattering thankfulness to men, Acts xxiv. 3; and a pharisaical, proud, conceited thanksgiving to God, Luke xviii. 11.

Concerning the spiritual man's thankfulness to God, I propound three things only in the general briefly to be noted: first, Reasons to incite us to the practice of continual thankfulness to God; secondly, For what things we are to be thankful; thirdly, What rules to be observed for the manner of performance of it.

1. There are many reasons scattered in scripture to incite us to thankfulness: first, Because it is a special part of God's worship, or one way by which we yield worship to God. Hence that the apostle accounts it a great loss if the people cannot say Amen when the teacher blesseth in the spirit, or giveth thanks, 1 Cor. xiv. 16. Again, when he would exhort them to liberality, he urgeth them with this reason, that the supplying of the necessities of the saints would cause much thanksgiving to God, 2 Cor. ix. 12, 13. And in 2 Cor. iv. 16, he sheweth that the thanksgiving of many would breed both a plenty of grace and an abounding of much praise to God. Secondly, The apostle having dehorted the Ephesians from fornication and all uncleanness, and covetousness, filthiness, jesting, and foolish talking, he addeth, but 'rather use giving of thanks,' Eph. iv. 3, 4; as if he would note, that thankfulness for God's blessings and graces duly performed would preserve them from the filth and power of these base vices; besides, it is a thing that 'becometh the saints;' nothing better. Thirdly, It is a sign of three worthy things, wherein it behoveth every man to be well assured:

first, It is a sign of a heart that hath rightly received Christ, and is firmly 'rooted, built, and established in the faith,' Col. ii. 6, 7; secondly, If men 'in all things let their requests be showed unto God with givings of thanks,' it is a sign of the peace of God, even that 'the peace of God, that passeth all understanding, will preserve their hearts and minds in Christ Jesus,' Phil. iv. 6, 7; thirdly, It is a sign, nay, a very means, of a contented mind. He that can pray unto God for what he wants, and is able thankfully to acknowledge what he hath in possession or promise, he will in nothing be careful, as it appeareth in the same place to the Philippians. Lastly, It is one of the six principal means to make a man 'rejoice always,' as the apostle writeth, 1 Thes. v. 18. Thus of the reasons.

2. Secondly, We must consider for what we must give thanks: first, For spiritual things as well as temporal, as for the word, 2 Cor. iv. 16; for mercies in prayer, Col. iv. 2; for victory over a sin, Rom. vii. 25; for knowledge, Rom. i. 21; secondly, In adversity as well as in prosperity, and that in all sorts of afflictions; in danger, Acts xxvii. 35; in wrongs; thirdly, In outward things we must be thankful, Col. iii. 17, 1 Cor. x. 3, not only for great things done, for our states or names, but even for the lesser and more daily favours, as for our food, and the creatures for our nourishment. And in special manner have the saints in all ages bound themselves to a set course of prayer and praise over and for their food; and therefore their gross swinish profaneness is so much the greater that sit down and rise from their meat like brute beasts, without any prayer or thanksgiving. If any ask whether there be any express scripture for grace before and after meat, I answer, there is, and allege these three undeniable and plain places of Scripture: 1 Tim. iv. 3, 4, John vi. 23, Rom. xiv. 6.

3. Thirdly, For the manner of thanksgiving, it may be found in that phrase used by the prophets in the Old Testament, of sacrificing the calves of their lips, Ps. v. *ult*., Hosea xiv. 1, 2. For here four things may be observed: first, It must be a dead calf, to note that all thanksgiving must proceed from humble and mortified minds; and therefore the pharisee thanks did not a whit justify them, Luke xviii. 11, 14; secondly, It must be a sacrificed calf. Now in the sacrifice three things were required: an altar, fire, and to lay the hand upon the head of the beast. An altar; for not only our prayers must be made in the name of Christ, but our praises also must be tendered to God in his mediation, or they will never be accepted, no more than a calf not laid on the altar. Neither is it enough to lay the calf on the altar, but fire must be put to it, to note that the bare throwing out of words of thankfulness, though in the name of Christ, will not serve, unless we do also get some feeling, ardency, and zeal to burn the sacrifice; thirdly, We must lay our hands on the head of the calf, that is, in all humility we must confess our unworthiness of all the blessings or graces we give thanks for. Again, in that they offer a calf, it signifieth that we should not offer our thankfulness to God of that that costs us nothing. We should desire to express our praise by doing something to further God's worship, or relieve the necessities of others. If God bless us at home, we should carry a calf to the temple; lastly, We must not sacrifice to a strange god when we give thanks, and that men do when they sacrifice to their nets, as the prophet speaketh, Hab. i. 16; that is, when men attribute the glory and praise of God to the means or second causes.

Thus of thankfulness in the general.

But that which is here intended is, that we should give thanks for others as well as for ourselves, which is not a courtesy but a duty. This duty of praising God for others grows exceeding commendable, if we can exercise it in these particulars: first, If we can give thanks for those blessings upon others which the world accounts shameful to enjoy, as zeal for God's glory, religious sincerity, and uprightness of heart, the cross for Christ his sake, and such like; secondly, If we can first give thanks, that is, be more apt to praise God for the virtues of others, than be forward to tax their faults and frailties; thirdly, If we can do it for all sorts of men, 1 Tim. ii. 1, even our enemies; fourthly, If we can be thankful for the true joy we have had in other men's prosperities, 1 Thes. iii. 9.

To conclude this point, if we would have others to give thanks for us, we should labour to be such as for whom thanks may be given. And thus of what they do: now, to whom?

To God. These words having been used in the very verse before, teach us two things: first, That it is no cloying to a sanctified mind to be much and often, yea, upon every occasion, in the honourable mention and lauding of God, ascribing in everything glory to God: so in heaven they shall never be weary of God's praises, no, not unto all eternity. And certain it is, that the more men grow in sanctification, the more easy and apt are their hearts to entertain all occasions of communion with God, without weariness or deadness.

Secondly, 'To God' shuts out the praises of themselves or of men. It is fit our rejoicing and praise should be directed thither from whence the blessing came.

The Father. These words are considered in the former verse. Thus much of his thanksgiving.

Praying for you. First, in general, from the joining together of these two duties, two things may be observed: first, That a child of God never gives thanks but he hath cause to pray; for if it be for temporal things, he must pray both for their sanctified use, that they become not occasions of sin, and for their preservation according to God's will; if it be for spiritual things, he hath reason to pray for increase, strength, and preservation against falling, and such like; secondly, On the other side, I say also, that a child of God doth never pray but he may find reasons to give thanks; we may find mercies in any misery; yea, it is a singular mercy to have a heart to pray, and to have so many large promises made to them that call upon God in their distress. But the main particular doctrine is, that we ought not only to pray for ourselves but for others. And the apostle, 1 Tim. ii. 1, seems to make four sorts of prayers for others, viz., deprecations, requests, intercessions, and giving of thanks. Deprecations are prayers for help against hurtful things; requests are prayers for profitable things; the word rendered intercessions, is by some taken to signify complaints unto God against such as wrong them for whom we pray, or else it is a more set or serious imploring of God's aid with the united forces of the godly; and lastly, Giving of thanks stands in the lauding of God for blessings or graces; and in the 6th of the Ephesians, and in the 1st of Tim. ii. the apostle sets down rules to be observed in prayer for others: in the Ephesians, chap. vi. 18, he requires that they pray: 1. At all times; 2. With all manner of prayers; 3. In the spirit; 4. With watching; 5. With perseverance; 6. With spiritual importunity; and lastly, For all saints. And in 1 Tim. ii. 8, he requires that they pray: 1. Everywhere; 2. With pure hands; 3. Without wrath; 4. Without doubting.

Always. To pray always is to consecrate every day and night to God by prayer, and besides, to pray upon all occasions, with lifting up our hearts unto God, or by using short prayers, which they have been wont to call ejaculations. Neither was it the duty of Paul only to pray always, that is, to keep a set order of prayers, but it is our duty also to set apart time every day, evening and morning, to pray unto God ourselves, and our households. And because these exercises of religion are by the most wholly neglected, and in room of it, vile profaneness stains men's houses, I will here set down, by the way, some few reasons to warrant a daily set course of praying: first, Our Saviour Christ, Mat. vi. 11, teacheth us to pray for the bread of the day, every day; as God will not promise us bread for a week, a month, a year, so neither will God accept of a prayer for the necessities of a week, month, or year beforehand, but will have us to make as much conscience to pray daily, as we have sense of daily wants; secondly, We are commanded to 'pray continually,' 1 Thes. v. 17; now what sense can be probably given of these words, if that a daily set course of prayer be not included? thirdly, The saints prayed every day, an ancient practice some thousand of years ago; David prayed seven times a day, and Daniel three times a day. Let wicked and profane people say, What needs all this prayer? But let us be assured that as holiness and grace grows in any, so are they more abundant in this worship of prayer. The holiest men have ever prayed most, for though they have not most need, yet they have always most sense of their own needs and others' too. Fourthly, If our food must be every day sanctified by the exercise of the word and prayer, 1 Tim. iv. 2, then much more have we need to sanctify ourselves, our households, our callings, and our labours by daily prayer.

Lastly, Prayer is called incense and sacrifice, Ps.

cxli. 2, and li. 17. Now the Jews held it an abomination of desolation if the morning and evening sacrifice were wanting: neither do we less need to seek daily the benefits of the atonement made by the sacrifice of Christ and his intercession, than did the Jews; and we are every way as much bound as often to profess our faith in Christ slain as they did in Christ to be slain.

And thus of the demonstrative and undeniable signs of the apostle's love to the Colossians, as they are generally set down in this verse.

Ver. 4. *Since we heard of your faith in Christ Jesus, and your love towards all saints.*

Ver. 5. *For the hope's sake which is laid up for you in heaven.*

In these words, and the rest that follow to the 12th verse, he doth particularly explicate the two signs of affection: first, He sets down his thanksgiving to ver. 9; secondly, He prays, ver. 9–12. In the thanksgiving he gives thanks for their graces in these words; secondly, For the means of grace in the rest of the words to the 9th verse.

Their graces are three: faith, love, and hope.

Of faith. In the handling of the doctrine of faith, I consider it: first, In the coherence, as it stands in the text; secondly, As it is in itself, apart from that which went before or comes after. From the general consideration of the coherence I observe: first, That we can never be reconciled to God, or attain the chief good, without faith. 'Without faith it is impossible to please God,' Heb. xi. 6; therefore it is good for us to 'prove ourselves, whether we be in the faith,' and to know whether 'Christ be in us, except we be reprobates,' 2 Cor. xiii. 5.

Secondly. This faith is not natural; we are not born believers, we are all 'concluded under sin,' and 'kept under the law, and shut up to faith afterwards to be revealed,' Gal. iii. 22, 23. It is 'the work of God;' yea, of 'the power of God,' 2 Thes. i. 11; it is 'the gift of God,' Eph. ii. 8; all men have not faith,' 2 Thes. iii. 2; it must be gotten with much striving, 1 Tim. vi. 12; as not by nature, so not by natural means, and therefore we must seek for better grounds than I have been always thus: neither will it avail thee to show thy education, civility, moral virtues, outward holiness, &c.

Thirdly, Whatsoever we gain by the word of God, if we gain not faith and love, all is vain—knowledge is vain, zeal is vain, &c. Therefore it behoveth us to gather in our thoughts, and to mind that one thing that is necessary.

Lastly, Though nature deny strength to bear, or power to give this grace, yet there is power in the word of God preached to beget even faith, as well as other graces: 'Faith cometh by hearing,' &c., Rom. x. 17; and Gal. iii. 2–5, he saith, 'They received the Spirit by the hearing of faith preached,' &c. ; 'Hear and your soul shall live,' Isa. lv. 4.

Thus much of the doctrines from the coherence.

That the nature of this grace may appear, the several acceptations of the word, the sorts, objects, parts, and degrees of it must be considered. Faith is in scripture diversely taken; sometimes it is given to God, and signifieth his faithfulness in his promises, as Rom. iii. 3, 'shall their unbelief make the faith of God of none effect.' And when it is given to man, it is taken: first, For fidelity, as it is a virtue in the second table, Mat. xxiii. 23; secondly, Sometimes it is taken for the doctrine of faith, Rom. xii. 6, 'according to the analogy of faith;' thirdly, Sometimes for profession of religion; thus Elymas is charged to have 'laboured to turn the deputy from the faith,' Acts xiii. 8; fourthly, Sometimes for Christ himself, by a metonymy, who is both the object and cause of faith, Gal. iii. 25; fifthly, For knowledge; only thus the devils are said to believe, James ii.; sixthly, For the gift of working miracles; 'If I had all faith, so as I could remove mountains,' &c., 1 Cor. xiii. 2; lastly, For that grace by which felicity and the chief good is applied; and thus it is called 'the faith of God's elect,' Titus i. 1, and by divines, justifying faith.

Secondly, There are divers sorts of faith. I will not speak of faith general or special, infused or acquired, formed and unformed, but leave them to the troublesome schoolmen; only I rest in the usual distribution, which hath ground in scripture; thus faith is historical; temporary; of miracles; and justifying.

First, Historical faith is to believe the doctrine of the word of God to be true, and therein is supernatural, and differeth from all human knowledge whatsoever; neither is it in the power of nature

E

alone to persuade men that the scriptures are God's word, further than the remnants of God's former image do give a glimpse of it, and is cleared by the spirit of general illumination.

This historical faith doth both understand the doctrine, and give assent that it is true, yet doth not justify; and therefore their case is so much the more fearful, that have not so much as their ignorance any way redressed, nor gotten so much as any knowledge by the word of God.

Secondly, Temporary faith goeth yet further, for such as have that faith do not only get knowledge, and yield assent to the truth, but also profess the truth with some earnestness, not sticking at it, to give their names in some more special manner than others to a respect of religion; yea, they rejoice inwardly in the doctrine of the word; and lastly, bring forth some kind of fruit, and amend some faults, only because the word of God would have them so to do, Luke viii. 13, Heb. vi. 4, 5. Therefore is this faith unprofitable, because they never had the particular assurance of God's favour in forgiveness of sins, nor will be brought to dislike, much less to humble their souls for, those special sins wherein they have transgressed, but nourish some one particular presumptuous sin or sins, which reigning in them, doth wholly engross and take up that inward worship which is due to God only. And this is the faith of our better sort of people.

Thirdly, Faith of miracles was that faith by which many in the primitive Church were able to work miracles, and was of two sorts, either faith to heal, or faith to be healed. This faith may be in such as are reprobates, as Mat. vii., 'some shall say, Have we not cast out devils by thy name?' to whom Christ shall answer, 'Depart, I know you not.'

Fourthly, But that faith in the enjoying of which is comfort for evermore, is justifying faith. The nature of this faith will appear if we consider:

1. The objects; 2. The parts of it; 3. The degrees.

1. First, of the objects. This faith may be perceived by that which it carrieth the mind unto, and from which it seeketh the comfort of the chief good; and thus the object is threefold.

(1.) The merits of Christ; (2.) The promises of God; (3.) The providence of God.

So that, wouldst thou try thy faith? Consider then what it is that thou makest thy refuge, and the foundation of thy comfort. What is it that thou most labourest after? Is it the assurance of God's favour, by the application of Christ? Is it the distinct applying of such and such promises of life in scripture? Dost thou live by thy faith in the course of life? If so, thou hast met with the right faith. Without Christ it is not possible to attain the chief good, neither is it enough to believe that Christ died for sinners, &c., unless we labour in the day of our visitation, for the certain and particular apprehension of the efficacy and merit of Christ's righteousness, for the particular assurance of God's favour in remitting such and such our transgressions. And because it is not easy at all times to discern by the working of the Spirit of adoption, the imputation of righteousness from Christ, therefore hath the Lord discussed the cases of conscience so comfortably in scripture, that if men examine themselves before the conditions of God's promises, they may find in divers of them, the clear determining of their estate. Here may be justly taxed the gross oversight and security of many, (otherwise the dear servants of God,) that are no better acquainted with the promises of life, upon the truth of which depends their happiness, and both present and future comfort. And lastly, by the same faith whereby the just are saved, by the self-same they live in the course of life in this world; the ground of his faith for his preservation, is the providence of his God, while the men of this world wonderfully please themselves in sacrificing to their nets, ascribing, in their affections, the stay of their maintenance unto their labour, friends, inheritance, &c.

2. Secondly, That the nature of this faith may yet be further opened, the parts of it must be considered. Faith is either in the mind, or in the heart; and by the change of both, it may be discerned.

In the mind, it shows itself in two things: knowledge, judgment.

There is something in the very illumination of the understanding of the saints which is of the nature of faith. Hence it is that the prophet Isaiah saith of Christ, Isa. liii. 11, 'By his knowledge he shall justify many,' that is, make just.

Judgment is either of truth or of goodness.

Judgment of truth is when we give glory so far forth to the way of life, and the means of reconciliation, that our hearts being convinced, our understandings do clearly resolve that this is the way to be happy, and no other.

Judgment of goodness is when we do not only believe the doctrine of happiness to be true, as before, but to be the only good tidings our hearts can rest upon.

Faith, as it shows itself in the heart, stands in three things :—desires; fiduce, or confidence; persuasion, or apprehension and application.

It may not be dissembled that there are in the world many definitions or descriptions of faith, such as do not comprehend in them that only thing which is the chief stay of thousands of the dear servants of God, and that is, desires, which may not be denied to be of the nature of faith. I express my meaning thus:—that when a man or woman is so far exercised in the spiritual seeking of the Lord his God, that he would be willing to part with the world, and all the things thereof, if he had them in his own possession, so that by the Spirit and promises of God he might be assured that the sins of his former life, or such as presently do burthen his soul, were forgiven him, and that he might believe that God were now become his God in Christ, I would not doubt to pronounce that this person (thus prizing remission of sins at this rate, that he would sell all to buy this pearl) did undoubtedly believe, not only because it is a truth (though a paradox) that the desire to believe is faith, but also because our Saviour, Christ, doth not doubt to affirm, Mat. v. 6, that 'they are blessed that hunger and thirst after righteousness, because they shall be satisfied,' and, Rev. xxi. 6, 'to him that is athirst I will give to drink of the water of life freely;' and David doubteth not to say, Ps. lxix. 33, 'The Lord heareth the desires of his poor.'

Fiduce, or confidence in the heart, is a part of faith, and shows itself in this: when the soul resteth upon Christ and the promises of God as the only ground of all that happiness which he must ever get unto himself.

Persuasion, or an apprehending application, is the last thing in faith, and that, in the beginnings of faith, is more in the power of the Spirit than in the sense and feeling of the conscience; yet herein it appears, that though the soul be tossed with many temptations, and fears, and terrors, yet more or less, one time or other, they are much refreshed with a sweet joy, arising they know not how, from the very persuasion that they belong to God, in and for Christ.

So that, if we would try our faith, we must examine what knowledge we have gotten, what judgment of the way of life, what desires we have of remission of sins, how our hearts are settled, and what it is that supports us.

3. There are two degrees of faith: a weak faith, ὀλιγοπιστία, and a strong faith, πληροφορία. A weak faith is described before, for all the former parts of faith are found in the weakest faith that is: a strong faith hath in it a certain and full assurance of God's favour, in remission of sins, so as doubts and fears are stilled and overcome; and such was the faith of Abraham, commended Rom. iv. 18-21; and this faith may be attained unto by all sorts of the servants of God, if they live and may use the benefit of the ordinances of God. Yet a gross fault in the definition of faith, as it is made by many, must be carefully shunned, and that is, that they make the *genus* to be a full assurance, which is only proper to a strong faith, and is not usually found in the weak faith; and yet that faith is such as doth justify for the present, and will save for ever.

And that we may be affected with a holy desire after this necessary grace, two things are further to be considered:

1. The benefits men might have by faith.
2. The woeful estate of those that want it.

1. The benefits may be ordered into five ranks:
(1.) What faith delivereth us from.
(2.) What it preserves us against.
(3.) What the weakest faith getteth.
(4.) What we might get if we laboured for a greater growth in faith.
(5.) How it fits us for heaven.

(1.) For the first: Faith doth deliver us—

First, From the darkness and blindness we lived in before. 'Whosoever believeth in me shall not abide in darkness,' John xii. 46. We no sooner, by faith, taste of the bread of life, but the veil of ignorance, which naturally covereth all flesh, is torn and rent, as the prophet Isaiah sheweth notably, Isa. xxv. 7.

Secondly, It delivers us from those woeful evils, which, as so many abominations, do defile both the understanding and affections. Faith purifieth the heart, Acts xv. 9. No wonder though men be continually surcharged with evil thoughts, and most vile affections, and strange evils within, seeing we are so hardly gotten to set about the earnest labour after spiritual application of the merits and righteousness of Christ; which righteousness never can be imputed by faith, but grace is infused by the Spirit of sanctification at the same time. Neither is there any more clearer testimony of the want of justifying faith than the continual prevailing of evil thoughts and affections.

Thirdly, It delivers us from the law, not only from the ceremonial law, and other 'beggarly rudiments,' but also from the moral law in two things only: first, From the curse of it, which is wholly taken away by the imputation of Christ's passion; secondly, From the rigour of it; so that, as it is commanded in the gospel, it may not exact of believers an impossible perfection, but only an evangelical and accepted uprightness. We are not now under the law, but under grace, Rom. vi., as the apostle shews in the Epistles to the Romans and Galatians at large. And hence it is that the same apostle saith, 1 Tim. i. 9, that 'the law is not given unto a righteous man, but unto the lawless and disobedient,' meaning that so long as we continue in our natural estate, so long we have this, as one part of our miseries, that we are liable to the curses and impossible exactions of the most righteous law; but from the time that we are effectually called, and gathered unto Christ, we are not under this law in these two respects, which is an admirable mercy.

Fourthly, Faith delivers us from the power of the first death, John v. 29, being by nature 'dead in sins and trespasses,' Eph. ii. 2, having no more sense of the things that belong unto the kingdom of Christ, than a dead man in nature hath of the benefits of life. By the power of faith, eternal life is begun here, which is called, while we live here, the 'life of grace,' and after death is styled by the name of the 'life of glory.'

Lastly, It delivers men from eternal destruction, for 'whosoever believeth in him shall not perish,' John iii. 16.

Thus of the first sort of benefits.'

(2.) Secondly, Faith hath a power to preserve us, and that in three things:

First, It preserves us from many fearful spiritual diseases in the soul; hence cometh that metaphorical speech of being sound, or whole, or healthful in the faith, Tit. i. 13. Hence, that he saith, 'we follow faith unto the conservation of the soul,' Heb. x. 39.

Secondly, It preserves us against the use of ill means; for 'he that believeth maketh not haste,' Isa. xxviii. 16. Herein is a special trial of faith, and is a worthy testimony of uprightness, when men can so rest upon God, that they will not be entangled with those profits that either the time makes unseasonable, as the Sabbath, or the means make sinful, as deceit, lying, &c., but can cheerfully believe that the same God that now tries him with the occasions of profit in such time and manner, can give him as much profit at a lawful time, and by lawful means. It is most difficult for an unsanctified mind to forbear either time or means when profit and pleasure entice.

Lastly, How miserable is our life here many times in respect of the temptations with which Satan doth fire us! Now if there were in us conscionable respect of certain application of God's favour, there is a secret power in faith, as a shield, not only to keep off, but extinguish 'the fiery darts of the devil,' Eph. vi. 16. And the true reason why our life is continually assaulted, and why the world lieth vanquished under a thousand miseries, is only because men do not labour for a particular assurance of God's love in Christ, which being once had, we should soon see a happy victory over the world, hell, and death, in respect of the beginnings of many heavenly contentments.

(3.) In the third place, we are to consider the benefits which the weakest faith obtaineth; and they are especially six:

First, It justifies and gives us a portion in the most meritorious intercession of Christ at the right hand of God; it is not sooner had but it makes the sinner just before God. This is everywhere proved.

Secondly, It gathereth men into the family of Abraham, and that as sons: yea, the least faith makes a man 'blessed with faithful Abraham,' Gal. iii. 7–9 ; so that if Abraham's case were happy, then is every child of God so.

Thirdly, It makes men not only the sons of Abraham, but the sons of God also by adoption. 'As many as received him, to them he gave power to be the sons of God, even to them that believe in his name,' John i. 12.

Fourthly, By faith the Son of God, by an unutterable presence, doth dwell in the hearts of the sons of men, Eph. iii. 16.

Fifthly, The meanest faith, that is a true faith, doth ever come attended with many holy graces ; and therefore to dispute of faith, is to dispute of temperance, righteousness, &c., Acts xxiv. 25.

Lastly, Faith according to the measure of it, is the foundation of all the hope that makes men happy ; therefore it is called 'the ground of the things which are hoped for, and the evidence of things not seen,' Heb. xi. 1.

(4.) Fourthly, If men would labour for the increase of faith, and once get a certainty concerning God's favour, they might enjoy many blessings more than they do, even in this life.

First, It might be unto us according to our faith, Mat. ix. 29 : what greater indulgence can be desired from God ?

Secondly, Men might 'live by their faith,' Heb. ii. 5 ; that is, they might have from their faith continually arguments both of comfort and direction, even in their carriage about the things of this life.

Thirdly, We might have the sense of peace with God, access unto grace, wherein we might stand, and be filled with joy in the hope of the glory of God to be revealed, yea, to be made able to hold up their heads, and rejoice in afflictions, &c., Rom. v. 5.

Fourthly, There is a power in faith to put such life into the sacred scriptures, that they would be able to make us wise, even to salvation, 2 Tim. iii. 15.

Fifthly, How hard a thing it is for the creature to have access unto the Creator with any boldness or confidence, the lamentable experience of the world shews ; insomuch that the apostle saith, we are naturally 'without God in the world,' able to mind anything, and to affect anything but God. But now this which is impossible to nature, is become possible to faith, as the apostle shews, Eph. iii. 12. And how unspeakable a mercy it is to have a comfortable communion with God, and easy access for our prayers, the saints may conceive but not utter.

Sixthly, By faith we might be able to overcome the world, 1 John v. 4 ; so as we might easily contemn the glory of earthly things, the millions of evil examples and scandals, the thousands of temptations, allurements, dissuasives, lets, and impediments, which the world casteth in our way, and with which we are often entangled, ensnared, and many times most shamefully vanquished, to the dishonour of God and our religion, the wounding of our profession and our consciences, &c. If men had that power of faith which the ordinances of God were able to give, how might they astonish epicures, papists, and atheists, which now differ little from them !

Seventhly, Faith would even make our friendship and mutual society a thousand times more comfortable than now it is, as the apostle intimates, Rom. i. 12.

Eighthly, By faith we might 'work righteousness,' and attain to innocency of life ; we might 'receive the promises,' with all those sweet comforts contained in them, which are matters of as great wonder as to 'subdue kingdoms, to stop the mouths of lions,' &c., Heb. xi. 33, 34.

Ninthly, Faith would make us to contemn the pleasure of sin, and account affliction with God's people better than perfection of pleasure for a season, as it is observed in Moses, Heb. xi. 25 ; whereas now every base delight is able to captivate our affections, and we have scarce strength to stand against one temptation.

Tenthly, Faith, by continuance in the word of God, would 'make us free,' even God's spiritual freemen, John viii. 32 ; so as we should clearly see that no natural prentice or bond-slave could find so much ease and benefit by his release, as we might by faith.

Lastly, We might have the clear apprehension of

the remission of all our sins past, as is manifest, Rom. iii. 25, Acts x. 43; only for sins to come, God gives no acquittance before there be a debt, and the discharge sued out.

(5.) And as faith furnisheth, or would furnish, men with these wonderful benefits in this life, so it provideth an assurance of an immortal inheritance in heaven for all eternity, as these places shew: Acts xxvi. 18, John vi. 47, 1 Pet. i. 9, 1 Thes. i. 10, with many other.

Thus much of the benefits by faith.

Object. Oh, but what if men do not believe?

Ans. First, I might answer that it is yet a comfort, that though thousands neglect faith, yet 'their unbelief cannot make the faith of God of none effect,' Rom. iii. 3; though the whole world contemn the doctrine of faith, and please themselves in their spiritual security, yet God knows how to shew mercy to his servants that desire to believe in him and fear before him.

Secondly, I read in St Mark, chap. vi. 6, that Christ 'marvelled at their unbelief,' and justly. They were affected with his doctrine, it was confirmed by miracles, and yet they believed not: we miserable men are a wonderment to God, Christ, and angels, and an astonishment to heaven and earth for our incredible incredulity.

Thirdly, I read in St Matthew, chap. xiii. 58, that 'he did not great works there for their unbelief's sake.' Surely we are justly debarred the benefit and comfort of many of the works of God, which might discover the glory of his goodness to us, only because of our unbelief.

Fourthly, If the Jews were cut off for their unbelief, being natural branches, Rom. xi. 20, and such as God had reason to favour as much as any people under the sun, how fearful then is the case of many of us, that can have no other standing than by faith!

Fifthly, Nothing is pure to the unbelieving, Titus i. 15.

Sixthly, If we believe not we cannot be established, Isa. vii. 9.

Seventhly, If men refuse to believe when they have the means of faith, their sentence is already gone out: 'He that believeth not is condemned already,' John iii. 18.

Eighthly, It is a matter of ease and profit and pleasure to live in sin, especially some sins; but what is it to die in them? 'Except that ye believe that I am he, ye shall die in your sins,' John viii. 24.

Ninthly, Consider the contrary to the benefits before; if we get not faith we abide in darkness, we are under the rigour and curse the law, subject to the dominion of heart pollutions, dead in sin, full of spiritual diseases, hasting to evil means, pierced through with fierce temptations, wicked in God's account, not justified, neither the seed of Abraham nor of God, without Christ, without hope of immortal bliss, without peace with God, comfort in afflictions, without grace, without communion with God. The scriptures (while we are in this estate) are but as a dead letter; we are easily overcome of the world, unconstant in friendship, without the covenant of promise, entangled with every pleasure and bait, and as bond slaves abiding in the guilt and power of sins past.

Lastly, How fearful are those threatenings: Mark xvi. 16, Rev. xxi. 8, Heb. iii. 12.

There remain yet four things to be considered:

1. The encouragements to believe.
2. The lets of faith.
3. How faith may be known.
4. How far short the faith of the common protestant is.

1. For the first, we have many encouragements to believe.

First, Because we have a Saviour, in respect of merit, both in suffering and dying, able to deliver us, his redemption being both precious and plentiful.

Secondly, He is ready to make intercession for us, at the right hand of God, when we set ourselves in any measure to seek God's favour.

Thirdly, We have certain and sure ordinances, unto which if we seek we may find.

Fourthly, What greater joy to angels or saints than the coming home of the lost sheep? None greater in the house of the Father than the prodigal son returned.

Fifthly, There is no difficulty so great, either in respect of sin, or the means, &c., but it hath been overcome by every one of the saints, to shew that we may be cured and get faith.

Sixthly, God maketh a general proclamation, without exception of any in particular that will believe, but he may be saved: Isa. lv. 1, John iii. 16.

Seventhly, Christ himself most graciously invites men.

Object. Oh, but he doth not call me.

Ans. He calls all, therefore he excepteth not thee; but lest men should encourage themselves in sinfulness, he addeth a limitation, 'All that are weary and heavy laden,' Mat. xi. 28-30, Rev. iii. 18, John vii. 37. If we can once find that sin is the greatest burden that ever our souls bare, and that once we could come to be weary of them, we might have comfort in Christ.

Object. Oh, but if I should take that course, I should lead a dumpish and melancholy life.

Ans. It is a false imputation cast upon religion and Christ, for the promise is, 'I will ease you.'

Object. Oh, but to exercise such a communion with God and Christ, requires so many graces that I can never get them.

Ans. 'Learn of me, that I am lowly and meek;' as if he should say, Get this one grace which I myself have laboured in, and thou mayest continue in the case[1] and comfort once had from Christ without interruption. If men still think this improbable, he wills them to put it to trial, and they should certainly 'find rest to their souls.'

Object. Oh, but to be thus yoked is a most irksome and impossible servitude.

Ans. This he rejects as most false, and saith, 'My yoke is easy, and my burden light,' both in respect of the power of the means, and the secret comforts of God, able to support the soul.

Eighthly, We are commanded to believe, and therefore it is a heavy sin to disobey, 1 John iii. 23.

Ninthly, God doth 'beseech men to be reconciled,' 2 Cor. v. 20. Wonder at this admirable clemency in our God. Nay, then perish, and that justly, if so great and infinite goodness cannot persuade. These things should the rather affect, if we consider who it is that proclaimeth, inviteth, commandeth, beseecheth—namely, God, who is able to do it, and speaks out of his nature. If a covetous man should offer us any great kindness, we might doubt of performance, because it is contrary to his nature; but it

[1] Qu. 'case'?—Ed.

is not so with our God; his name is gracious, and his nature is to be faithful in performance where he hath been true in offer or promising.

Thus much of encouragements.

2. The hindrances of faith follow to be considered of. The lets of faith are sometimes in the minister, sometimes in the people.

Ministers are guilty of the want of faith in their hearers: first, When they teach not at all, because faith cannot be had without hearing, Rom. x.; secondly, If we teach not faith, and that plainly; if they intend not the chiefest part of their labours to inform men in the doctrine of faith, (under which is contained the whole doctrine of the sinner's conversion with his God,) though they inform manners both for piety and righteousness, and busy themselves in other contemplative divinity, yet have they not answered their calling, but are woeful hindrances of faith in the hearers.

Secondly, In the people faith is letted three ways.

(1.) By errors in their judgments.

(2.) By corrupt affection in the heart.

(3.) By certain things that befall their conversation.

There are five especial errors, with any of which whosoever is infected, faith is letted:

First, When men think they are bound to follow their callings, and to mind their worldly employments, and therefore cannot spend the time about thinking of sermons, &c. Our Saviour, Luke xiv. 16, in the parable, shews, that though men give heaven fair words, yet they take not a course to get it; but what lets them? Is it whoredom, drunkenness, idolatry, murder, breach of Sabbath, &c.? No such matter, but only the abuse of lawful profit and pleasures. What more lawful than a farm? what more honourable of all pleasures than marriage? Only observe that the voluptuous person saith flatly, he 'cannot come,' and the worldly man, 'I pray you have me excused.'

Object. Oh, but I confess it were a great fault to leave minding heavenly things to get superfluity, and more than needs, as farm upon farm. But I want necessaries; if I had but sufficient, my mind should not be so taken up, &c.

Ans. Our Saviour shews that this is no sufficient excuse, by bringing in the man that had bought his five yoke of oxen, than which what could be more needful, seeing he could not follow his husbandry without oxen?

Secondly, A second error letting faith, is a close opinion of merit, which sticks fast in our nature.

Thirdly, Faith is hindered when the mind is forestalled with an opinion that an outward serving of God will serve to bring them near enough to God. If they hear service and sermons, and receive the sacraments, &c., they have done so much as they think is enough, Ps. l., Isa. i.

Fourthly, Many therefore never labour to get faith, because they think it is impossible to take any such course, that they should get any assurance of the remission of their sins in this life, or if it be possible for others, yet it is not for them.

Lastly, Others think it possible to be had, and it is good to be humbled so far as to seek it with tears and prayers; and they think they do well that will not give over till they have comfort that way, but yet they think all this ado unnecessary, and that they may be saved without it.

(2.) In the heart faith is letted five ways:

First, When men nourish the secret evils of their hearts, both in thoughts and affections, and make not conscience to repent for them. An evil heart is always an unfaithful heart; therefore men are exhorted to 'take heed of being hardened through the deceitfulness of sin,' Heb. iii. 12, 13.

Secondly, Worldliness is a great let of faith, when men suffer their thoughts and affections to be continually taken up with minding of things here below, though they cannot be charged with any great covetousness.

Thirdly, There is in men's affections an unwillingness to part with worldly pleasure and delights, and they are loath to lose their credit with their carnal friends, which they say they must do if they take this course.

Fourthly, The world is full of common hope and presumption of God's mercy: men say, God is merciful, when they have neither comfort from the promises of God, nor ground of assurance, nor witness of the spirit of adoption.

Fifthly, Faith is letted, and men are kept from using the means to get faith, and to seek God while he may be found, only through a fear lest if they should examine themselves, and search whether they had a true faith or not, they should find they had none, and then they should be troubled, and driven into melancholy despair, &c.

(3.) *Lastly*, There are some things in men's carriage which greatly let and hinder faith.

First, A profane contempt of the word of God. Either men will not hear, or but by starts, or they attent not, or not apply it to themselves, or not meditate of the doctrine afterwards, or not labour for the power of it in practice, &c.

Secondly, The example of the multitude hinders much, Mat. vii. 13, 14, Luke xiii. 23, 24, especially the example of wise men and great men in the world, John vii. 45-50.

Thirdly, Some when they go about the duties of mortification and faith, they are turned off before they get faith, either because they find hardness of heart, or are overcharged with temptations or doubts of audience and acceptance, and that God will never look after such broken desires, &c., or else, because they have not comfort presently, they grow desperate, and say they shall have none at all, or else are vanquished with thoughts of atheism injected, which many times prevails so strongly, that they can hardly be recovered again to any care to labour for faith, till either bitter crosses, or fear of death, or hell awaken them.

Lastly, Closeness is a great cause of want of faith, when people will not discover their doubts and fears, especially to their pastors, being wise and merciful, and yet know not what to do, and cannot get information from public hearing. Here may be taken up a just complaint of the strangeness between the shepherds and the flocks: the one thinking he hath done enough if he preach to them, and the other if he hear him.

There remains two uses of this doctrine of faith.

3. *First*, Seeing there are divers sorts of faith, and that many benefits may be had by a true faith, and seeing that, on the other side, there are woeful effects of the want of faith, &c., it should teach us to try whether we have faith or no, and that this may be known, we must first understand:

First, That before faith can be wrought, the heart must be mollified by afflictions, by the continual dropping of the word of God, by the knowledge of our misery, by legal fear, or lastly, by terrors from God.

Secondly, Before faith can appear, repentance will show itself, and that especially in two things:

First, In godly sorrow for sin past.

Secondly, In the change of the thoughts, affections, and life.

As for godly sorrow, it may not be denied but that it may be without terrors in some, but never so easy in any but these three things are true: 1. That they grieve because they cannot grieve. 2. They hate their special sins. 3. They reform both inwardly and outwardly.

Thirdly, Faith, after the softening of the heart and repentance, shews itself in six things: first, In an honourable opinion, ready to believe all the word of God, though it make never so much against our pleasure or profit; secondly, By the combat between the flesh and spirit; thirdly, By the holy desires after remission of sins and holiness of life, witnessed by constant prayers and diligent use of the means; fourthly, By a fixed resolution reposed upon the way of God, though they find not comfort presently; fifthly, By the forsaking of the world and pleasures of sin, Heb. xi. 25; lastly, By the purging out of the evils of the thoughts and affections, Mat. v. 7, Acts xv. 9. As for joy, peace, thankfulness, admiration, love, and desire to convert others, &c., they belong to faith grown, not so apparently to faith begun.

4. Lastly, Here might justly be taxed the defects and wants that are found in the common protestant. The faith of the protestant at large is faulty: first, Because he knows no time of spiritual birth, and yet he can tell to a day when he was born in nature; secondly, They seek not unto the means spiritual to get faith; thirdly, They rest in other things instead of faith, as knowledge, hope, &c.; fourthly, Their faith is commonly either historical or temporary, for either it is enough to believe that Christ died for sinners; or else, if they believe the articles of the Creed to be true, and be no papists, but sound in the matter of justification, and receive the sacrament, especially when they are sick, all is well; or if they believe the word of God to be true, or especially if they can be willing to hear sermons, &c.; fifthly, They regard not God's promises to apply them, nor to live by faith—they hold both to be absurd; sixthly, They want the judgment that divines call the judgment of goodness; lastly, They do not believe that application is of the nature of faith.

Heard of. In that their graces are heard of, and by several relation the fame of them is spread, four things may be observed:

1. It is hard to have any saving grace, but it will be perceived and observed, and that for divers causes:

First, Grace cannot be without fruit external, and 'by their fruit ye shall know them.'

Secondly, God doth not ordinarily give saving grace, but it is gotten in or after some great affliction. A man may get much general knowledge, and go far in a temporary faith, without any great pain or perplexity, but the pains of travail do usually accompany the birth of any saving grace. Neither is there any such hearkening after a child born in nature as there is after an afflicted conscience now ready to be delivered of any eternal grace.

Thirdly, Grace cannot be received but it works a great change and alteration of disposition and practice of affection and carriage; it will work an alteration general, inward and outward. Now all this stir in reforming is liable to observation.

Fourthly, The devil usually lieth still while men please themselves with the effects of historical and temporary faith, because they feed presumption; but so soon as justifying faith is got in the least measure, and works by purifying both the heart and life from beloved sins, (though it work never so weakly,) he bestirs himself and his agents, by carnal counsel, temptations, reproaches, slanders, difficulties, and a thousand devices, to make this birth painful, and, if it were possible, abortive; the flesh boils, the devil darts fire by injection; the world hatefully pursues, and wonders at the sudden restraint and retiring, if 'men run not into the same excess of riot,' 1 Pet. iv. 4; 'He that restraineth himself from evil maketh himself a prey,' Isa. lix. 15.

Lastly, The graces of God are like lamps on a hill in a dark night, and like shining pearls, and therefore cannot be hid.

Use is, first, for confutation of their resolution that will serve God, but it must be secretly; they will be sincere, but they like not to do it so as every body may note them; they will go to heaven, but for ease, it must be in a feather-bed, and for closeness, it must be out of their closets. These men mean to steal their passages, and these kind of people commonly think, that the true cause why others are so talked of is their indiscretion, and rash and needless thrusting out of themselves into observation. But in the whole business they deceive themselves, for it is not possible to be friends with God and the world, to have God, his word, people, and Spirit to witness to us, and to have the world to praise and applaud us. And for indiscretion, it is a prejudice let fall by the devil, and taken up by carnal men, without considering that reproachful observation hath been the lot of the wisest and holiest saints that ever lived, yea, the portion of the Prince of the saints. Secondly, It may be an especial comfort to all the servants of God that find their names encountered with strange reports, and the world suddenly bent against them round about, (when yet many times they rather find purposes than practices of grace,) I say, they may gather comforts diversely: first, It is the portion of all God's people; secondly, It is a sign they are now no more carnal persons, for 'if they were of the world, the world would not thus hate his own,' John vii. 7; thirdly, Their praises are with the saints, and as now they taste of the cup of their affliction, so they shall reap the incomparable privileges of their communion.

Quest. A question, in the second place, may be propounded, and that is, How their faith can be heard of? seeing it is an inward grace, how it can so outwardly be known?

Ans. Faith, in itself hidden and secret, doth in people converted make itself known by certain demonstrative effects of it, as by confession in time of persecution, when the defence of the truth in any part of it is required; by constant profession, notwithstanding the scorns and disgraces of the world; by victory over the world, when men retire themselves, and will not live by example, contemn all earthly vanities, and use the world as if they used it not; by their love to the word of God more than their appointed food; by the reformation of their own lives; by the exercise of faith in their callings, not hasting to use ill and unlawful means, not sacrificing to their own nets; and lastly, by their love to God's people.

Seeing grace and fame are companions, we may learn that the surest way to get a good name is to get grace; for then their 'names are written in heaven,' Phil. iv. 3; they are known of angels, Mat. xviii. 10; they are imprinted in the hearts of God's people. A good man 'honoureth them that fear God,' Ps. xv. 4. And David saith, 'They are the only excellent ones, and all his delight is in them,' Ps. xvi. 3. And of the same mind is Solomon, even of the poor child of God, Prov. xix. 1. Yea, they have a name in the very conscience of wicked men, yea, their very enemies; which appears in this, that they spend more thoughts about them than the greatest potentate, and would gladly die their death, yea, a faithful man is honoured when he seems contemned. And on the other side, a wicked man is ever at the greatest in his own eyes, and is not able to conceive that they that so much depend upon him, and crouch to him, should contemn him, as certainly they do; for every sinful person is a shameful and vile person. Yea, so sovereign and sure a means is grace for the attaining of a good name, that it causeth the stains and blemishes of former infamous sins to be blotted out. When God takes away sin in the soul, he will take away rebuke from the name, Isa. xxv. 8. And this God (that hath the hearts of all men in his hands) works both wonderfully and secretly. Who doth not honour David, Peter, Magdalene, and Paul, notwithstanding their great sins and faults?

The last thing here to be inquired after is, whether it be not vainglory to seek fame and estimation, and to be heard of among men?

Ans. It is not simply a sin to seek an honest report amongst men; let them contemn their names that mean to be allowed to live in presumptuous sin. 'A good name is better than riches,' Eccles. vii. 1. And Christ commandeth that 'our light should shine that men might see our good works,' Mat. v. And the apostle wills them to 'hold forth the light of the word of truth in the midst of a crooked and froward generation,' Phil. ii. But glory is then vain: first, When it is sought in vain things; secondly, When men seek praise for the show of that that is not; thirdly, When they make it the chief end of their actions; fourthly, When it makes men proud and vicious—otherwise it is an honest joy that comes of a good name, and a reason to bear many crosses in other things patiently, where men may support themselves with this comfort of a good name.

And of your love to all saints. Hitherto of faith, by which we embrace Christ, the head. Now it remains that I entreat of love, by which we embrace the saints, the members. By the one we are joined to Christ, by the other to the members of Christ.

Love is either in God, John iii. 17, or in man. In God it is an attribute, in man an affection, or a quality in the affection.

Love in man is either a vice or a grace. It is a vice when it is set upon a wrong object, or is disordered, and that three ways: first, When we love things unlawful, as sin; secondly, When we love things lawful, but too much, as the world; thirdly, When love is turned unto lust, and so is the mother of fornication, adultery, incest, and such like.

As love is a grace, (for I omit bare natural affections,) it is only in the saints, and so they love, first, God and Christ, as the fountains of all natural and supernatural blessings; secondly, They love the means of communion with God and Christ, and thus they love the word of God, Ps. i. 2, and thus they love the second appearing of Christ, 2 Tim. iv. 8; thirdly, They love man, and so their love is either to all men, to their enemies, or to the saints. Of this last here.

Concerning this love to God's children, if the coherence and the general consideration of the words be observed, seven things may be noted:

First, That the love to God's children is a grace supernatural, as well as faith; 'Hereby we know that we are translated from death to life, because we love the brethren,' 1 John iii. 14. And again, 'Let us love one another, for love cometh of God, and every one that loveth is born of God,' 1 John iv. 7. Hence it is called 'The love that God hath in us,' 1 John iv. 16. Yea, it is derived from that precious love wherewith God loved Christ, John xvii. 26.

Secondly, We must first be joined to Christ by faith, before we can get any sanctified affection to man. All human affections in carnal men want their true comfort, profit, and constancy, because they are not seasoned by faith in God. Till a man do labour for his own reconciliation with God, he can never get a sound affection to God's children, nor reap the heavenly privileges of communion with saints.

Thirdly, To love God's children for any other respects than because they are saints is a mere natural affection, not a spiritual grace. A wicked man may love a child of God for his profit, pleasure, or credit's sake, for his company's sake, or for his amiable qualities, in conversing and such like; but the right love is to love them as they are sanctified, as they are begotten of God, 1 John v. 1, and for spiritual respects; and thus 'he that giveth a disciple a cup of cold water in the name of a disciple, shall not lose his reward,' Mat. x. 41, 42.

Fourthly, Nothing can make more to the praise and credit of men than faith and love. The highest praise of a man's good estate is to be able to shew that he believeth his own reconciliation with God, and that he loveth God's children. He doth not say he was glad at heart when he heard of their riches, honours, &c., but when 'he heard of their love to the saints,' and their faith in Christ. The good tidings of the faith and love in the Thessalonians was a great consolation to Paul in his affliction, and all his necessities, 1 Thes. iii. 6. No better news can be brought him, and therefore he prays the Lord to increase them, not in riches and the pleasures of this life, but to 'make them abound in love one to another.'

Fifthly, Whosoever doth actually believe, doth actually love, they are inseparable companions; 'faith worketh by love,' Gal. v. 6. Hence he wished the people not barely love, but 'love with faith,' Eph. vi. 23, 1 Tim. i. 14; so as commonly they are together in the same degrees also. If no faith, no love; if a show of faith, but a show of love; if but a purpose of faith, but a purpose of love; if a weak faith, a weak love; if an interrupted faith, an interrupted love; if often at odds with God, often at jars with men; they are begotten by the same seed, given by the same God; received by the same saints, and lodged in the same heart.

Sixthly, There is no hope of heaven if no love to the brethren. 'He that saith he is in the light, and hateth his brother, is in darkness until this time,' 1 John ii. 9, 10. And 'whosoever hateth his brother, is a man-slayer; and we know that no man-slayer hath eternal life,' 1 John iii. 15.

Seventhly and lastly, He that loves one saint truly, loves any saint; and therefore the apostle, in the praise of their love, commendeth it, for that it was towards 'all the saints.' To love God's children in respect of persons, is not to respect them at all aright; he that cannot love grace anywhere, loves not any for grace.

The uses of all these observations briefly follow: first, Here is reproof, and that first of such wicked wretches as can love any but the saints—these are in a woeful and damnable case, whatsoever their estate be in the world; secondly, Of such as allow themselves liberty to hold God's children in suspense; they do not hate them, but yet they will be better advised before they be too forward to join themselves with them; but let these be assured, that till they be loved, God will not be loved, 1 John v. 1.

Secondly, Here we may make trial by our love to God's children, both of our faith and hope; as also of our love to God; and lastly, the manner of our affection, viz., for what we love others. For natural affection hath his natural rewards. Lastly, The doctrine of love is a comfort two ways: first, If thou begin to love God's children, it is a comfortable sign thou art not without love to God and faith in Christ; secondly, It is a comfort against slanders, reproaches, and molestations from wicked men; thou hast as much credit with them as God; if they loved God, they would love thee. It is a great comfort when a man's enemies be enemies to religion, sincerity, and holiness of life.

Thus far of love in general. In particular I propound four things to be further considered: first, The nature of this grace; secondly, The reasons to persuade us to the conscionable exercise of it; thirdly, The helps to further us; and lastly, What defects are in the love the world commonly boasteth of.

1. For the first, That the nature of this sacred grace may be the better conceived, two things would be weighed: first, What things ought to be found in our love; secondly, In what manner love is to be expressed.

And for the former of these two, true Christian love hath in it these seven graces or duties: first, Uprightness in our own things, both in respect of right and truth; secondly, Peaceableness in the quiet order of our conversation; thirdly, Courtesy in needful and loving compliments; fourthly, Tenderness in the things that befall others, so as we can rejoice for them as for ourselves; fifthly, Liberality; sixthly, Society; seventhly, Clemency. Concerning these three last duties or branches of love, it will be expedient to add something for further explication of them.

Liberality is required, and it standeth of two main branches: first, Hospitality, and then the works of mercy. Hospitality is required in these places: Rom. xii. 13, 1 Tim. iii. 2, 1 Pet. iv. 9, Heb. xiii. 2. But this duty stands not in the entertainment of drunkards and vicious persons, or in keeping open house for gambling, and such lewd sports and disorders, or in feasting of carnal men; for this is so far from being the praise of great men, as it is a most shameful abuse, and one of the crying sins of a land, able to pull down the curse of God upon such houses, and such housekeeping; but hospitality stands in the kind entertainment of strangers that are in want, Heb. xiii. 2; and in welcoming of the poor that are in distresses; and lastly, in the friendly, and Christian, and mutual exercise of love, in inviting of God's children to our houses or tables.

Works of mercy are the second branch, and those are required of us as the needful duties of our love; and these works are either in temporal things, and so are alms-deeds, or in spiritual things. Love must shew itself in alms-deeds, that is, in 'distributing to the necessities of the saints,' Rom. xii. 13; in relieving those that are impoverished and fallen into decay, Lev. xxv. 26; by giving or lending, though they should not be paid again, upon the hope of a reward in heaven, Luke vi. 35; and this to be done both to our power and without compulsion, for that will shew the naturalness of our love, 2 Cor. viii. 3, 8. Thus being ready to distribute and communicate, men may 'lay up in store for themselves a good foundation against the time to come,' 1 Tim. vi. 18, 19; and that that is well given will be a greater help in time of need, than that that is spared and kept.

There are works of mercy also in spiritual compassion over the souls of men, and thus the poor may be merciful to the rich, viz., in labouring to win them to religion and sincerity, in praying, admonition, encouragements, and such like needful duties; and these are the best works of mercy that we can do for others whom we love or pity.

Thus of liberality. Another thing required unto the exercise of Christian love, is society. It is not enough to wish well to the saints, or salute them kindly, or relieve them according to their occasions, but we must converse lovingly and daily with them, make them our delight, company with them, and in all the mutual duties of fellowship in the gospel to solace them, and ourselves with them. This is that that Peter requires, when he chargeth that we should 'love brotherly fellowship,' ἀδελφότητα ἀγαπᾶτε, 1 Pet. ii. 17; we should not live like stoics, without all society, nor like profane men, in wicked society; but we should both entertain a brotherly fellowship, Rom. xii. 11, that is, society with the brethren, and love it too. This was their praise in the primitive times, that they 'continued in the apostles' doctrine, and in fellowship, and breaking of bread, and prayers,' Acts ii. 42; making conscience, as well of Christian society, as of hearing, praying, and receiving the sacraments.

The holy apostle, St Paul, blesseth God for the Philippians, chap. i. 5, ii. 1, that they did not only make conscience of receiving the gospel, but also of fellowship in the gospel, and that from the very first beginning of their entrance into religion. This was the comfort of their love and fellowship of the Spirit.

The last duty of love is clemency, and this stands in the right framing of ourselves in respect of others; and unto the practice of clemency divers things are required of us:

First, To cover the faults of others; 'Love covereth the multitude of sins,' 1 Pet. iv. 8. Secondly, To avoid the occasions of stirring the infirmities of others. And here we are bound to forbear our liberty in indifferent things, Gen. xiii. 8, rather than we should offend our brother: 'If thy brother be grieved for thy meat, now walkest thou not charitably,' Rom. xiv. 15. It is to be observed, that he saith, *thy brother*; for it matters not for the cavils and reproaches of idolatrous and superstitious persons that never regarded the sincerity of the gospel. Thirdly, To take things in the best part; 'Love believeth all things, it hopeth all things,' 1 Cor. xiii. 7. Fourthly, In our anger, both to be short, 'Let not the sun go down upon your wrath,' Eph. iv. 26; and also to be more grieved for their sin with whom we are angry than kindled against their persons; as it is said of our Saviour, Mark iii. 5, 'He looked round about upon them angrily, mourning for the hardness of their hearts.' Fifthly, To appease the anger of others, and that either by soft answers, Prov. xv. 1, or by parting with our own right, 1 Cor. vi. 7, or by overcoming evil with goodness, Rom. xii. 21.

Lastly, Clemency stands in the forgiving of trespasses done against us; 'Be tender-hearted, forgiving one another, even as God for Christ's sake forgave you,' Eph. iv. 31. So that unto Christian love is requisite a peaceable, courteous, and tender carriage, hospitality, and a liberal distributing to their wants, both in temporal and spiritual things, a covering of their faults, avoiding of occasions of scandal, a loving composing of ourselves in matters of wrong, and a daily and cheerful association with them.

Thus far of the gracious branches of Christian love. Now, the manner how we should love God's children is to be considered: first, in general, we should love them as ourselves, and therefore in all our dealings to do as we would be done by, Mat. xix. 19, and xxii. 39; we are to love man in measure, viz., as ourselves, but God above measure. But to consider of the manner of our love more specially, the particulars may be referred to the four heads mentioned, 1 Pet. i. 22. First, we must love brotherly, that is, not as we love our beasts, or as we love strangers, or as we love our enemies, but as we would love our dearest natural brother, with all tenderness and naturalness of our affection. Secondly, We must love without feigning, without hypocrisy, ἀνυποκρίτως, Rom. xii. 9; and this is explicated to be, 'not in word and tongue, but in deed, and in the truth,' 1 John ii. 18; not only truly, for it cannot be a true love unless it arise from a holy agreement in the truth. Thirdly, It must be with a pure heart, ἐκ καθαρᾶς καρδίας, and then we love with a pure heart: first, When our affection is grounded upon knowledge and judgment, Phil. i. 9; secondly, When it is expressed in a spirit of meekness, 1 Cor. iv. 21; thirdly, When it is free from wrath, or aptness to be offended, from envy, from pride, and swelling and boasting, from self-love, when men seek not their own things, and from evil suspicions, 1 Cor. xiii. 4, 5; fourthly, When it is exercised in holy things, so as no affection can make us rejoice in the wickedness of them we love, 1 Cor. xiii. 6; fifthly, When it is manifested in long-suffering, and all-suffering, when we 'believe all things, and hope all things,' 1 Cor. xiii. 7.

Lastly, We must love fervently, *ἐκτενῶς*, and this hath in it speediness, Prov. iii. 28, diligence, (called labour in love,) 1 Thes. i. 13, cheerfulness, Heb. vi. 10, earnestness, 2 Cor. ix. 17, and heat of affection, (and this is to follow after love,) Gal. v. 13, 1 Thes. iii. 12; and to the end it is without interruption, Eph. v. 2, 3.

2. Now, because these are the last days, wherein the most have no Christian love at all, and many have lost the affection they had, so as their love is grown cold, Mat. xxiv., and the most even of the children of God in all places are exceedingly wanting to their own comfort and spiritual content, in the neglect of the duties of love one to another, but especially in the duties of a holy fellowship, and mutual society in the gospel, and the rules of clemency; and that men might be kindled with some sparks of desire to redeem the time, and gain the comforts they have lost, and seek the blessings of God in a holy society, I have thought good, in the second place, to propound out of the scriptures motives, as they lie here and there scattered in the holy writings, to incite and persuade all sorts of men, especially professors, to a more conscionable respect of this mutual love.

The first motive may be taken from example, and that both of God and Christ. God made his infinite love apparent to us in 'that he sent his only-begotten Son into the world, that we might believe on him, and he might be a reconciliation for our sins, and therefore ought we to love one another, yea, so to love one another,' 1 John iv. 9–11. Shall the most high God fasten his love upon us, that are so many thousand degrees below him; and shall not we love them that are our equals, both in creation and regeneration? Shall the Lord be contented to respect with an appearing love; and shall we think it enough to carry good affections to our brethren, without manifestation of the outward signs and pledges of it? Was there nothing so dear unto God as his Son, and did he give us his Son also to assure us of his love; and shall the love of the saints be ever by us any more accounted a burthensome and costly love? Hath God sent his Son out of heaven into the world, and shall we stay ourselves up, and not daily run into the company of the members of Christ? Was Christ sent that we might have the life of grace in holy and heavenly and mystical union, and shall not we, as fellow-members in all the duties of a Christian society, stir up, nourish, and increase that life so given?

Note.—As sincerity is the life of religion, so society is the life of sincerity. Was Christ given a reconciliation for our sins; and shall not we strive to overcome one another in the religious temper of our affections, and the free and willing covering or forgiving of trespasses and wrongs? Our Head, our Saviour, our Lord, our Prophet, our Priest, our King, that we might perceive his love, 'laid down his life for us,' 1 John iii. 16; and should not we imitate so incomparable an example, though it were 'to lay down our lives one for another?'

The second motive is from commandment. It is not a thing arbitrary for us to love our brethren, as is before expressed. Courtesy, peaceableness, liberality, society, and clemency, are not things we may shew, or not shew, at our pleasures, but they are necessary; such as if they be wanting, a sin is committed, nay, grievous sins, even against the commandment of Christ, John xiii. 34: 'As I said to the Jews, whither I go can ye not come, so to you also I say now, a new commandment give I you, that ye love one another, even as I loved you.' He shews here that whereas they might be grieved that they should lose Christ's bodily presence, he had appointed them a course for their solace, and that was instead of Christ, as fellow-members in Christ's absence in the world, to strive by all means to delight themselves in loving society one with another. And this commandment he calls a new commandment, not in respect of the matter of the duty, for that was always required, but in respect of the form of observing it; for the old general rule was, that thou shouldst love thy neighbour as thyself; but now that form ('as I have loved you') hath in it something that is more expressly, and for the incomparable sufficiency of the precedent is matchless, and more full of incitations to fire affection. Again, the person that gives it, and the time, is to be considered : 'I now give this commandment.' Men are used, that have any sparks of good nature in them, to remember, and carefully to observe the last words of their dying friends, especially if they charge not many things. Why, these are the last words of Christ the night before his death ; even this one thing he doth especially charge upon us, namely, while we abide in this flesh, and are hated of this world, and want those glorious refreshings would come by the presence of Christ, to unite ourselves in a holy bond of peace and love, to be kept and strengthened by mutual endeavours in the performance of all the duties of holy affection, and that till Christ shall gather us unto the glory that he hath with the Father, John xvi. 12.

The third motive may be taken from the benefits that may be gotten by love ; and these are divers :

First, There is much 'comfort in love,' Phil. ii. 1. The Lord doth usually and graciously water the society, conferences, prayers, and other duties performed mutually by the saints, with the dews of many sweet and glorious refreshings, by which they are daily excited, inflamed, and encouraged to a holy contentation in godliness.

Secondly, 'Love is the fulfilling of the law,' Rom. xiii. 10. Not only all the duties belonging to human societies, of which he there entreats, are comprehended under love, as by that great band that tieth all estates and degrees, but also is the fulfilling of the law by effect, in that, first, It causeth abstinence from doing evil to our neighbour ; secondly, It causeth men to make conscience of fulfilling the law ; and that which is there generally spoken, if it be applied to the love of the saints, may have his special truth in this, that there is nothing in outward things doth more fire the heart of a man to the love of, and labour after a godly life, then a daily loving society with God's children, in whom we see godliness, even in an experimental knowledge, not laid before us in precept, but described unto us in practice, with the rewards and fruits of it. Yea, love may be said to be 'the filling up of the law,' πλή-ρωμα τοῦ νόμου, as the word seemeth to import in this, that it clotheth the duties of the law with the glory of a 'due manner,' and seateth them upon their due subjects, with the unwearied labours of constant well-doing.

Thirdly, The due performance and daily exercise of the mutual duties of love, would be a great testimony and witness unto us for the satisfying of our consciences in the knowledge of such great things as otherwise are exceeding hard to be known : as first, It is not everybody's case to have the Spirit of grace, or, when they have it, to discern it, yet, by this love, it may be discerned, for it is one of the inseparable fruits of the Spirit, Gal. v. 22 ; secondly, Many men follow not Christ at all, and among the followers of Christ a great number are not true disciples. Now, John xiii. 14, 'By love may all men know that we are Christ's disciples ; thirdly, 'The wind bloweth where it listeth,' and, 'that which is born of the flesh, is flesh,' John iii. ; and therefore great masters in Israel and teachers of other men may be ignorant of regeneration ; yet thereby 'may we know that we are born of God and do rightly know God, if we love one another,' 1 John iv. 7.

Fourthly, If we would seek God to find him, behold, 'If we go to the east, he is not there ; if to the west, yet we cannot perceive him ; if to the north, where he worketh, yet we cannot see him ; he will hide himself in the south, and we cannot behold him,' Job xxiii. 8, 9. How much more is the way of God in the heart of man unsearchable ? And yet, though 'no man hath seen God at any time,' 'if we love one another, God dwelleth in us,' 1 John iv. 12.

Fifthly, The election of man before time is like a boundless gulf, and the making of man blameless and holy in heaven is a dreadful mystery ; and yet those two glorious branches, whereof the one sprouts forth even beyond time, and the other reacheth up to heaven, nay, into heaven, are both fastened upon this stock of love in respect of one way and manner of coming to know them, Eph. iv. 1–4.

To conclude, salvation itself, even our own salvation, is known by the love to the brethren, as is clear, 1 John iii. 14, and in divers other places of that epistle.

Lastly, The day of the Lord is a terrible day, a day of trouble and heaviness: the strong-hearted man shall then cry bitterly, Zech. i. 14: then the heavens being on fire, shall be dissolved and pass away with a noise, and the elements shall melt with heat, 2 Pet. iii. 10, 11: the Lord himself shall descend from heaven with a shout, and with the voice of the archangels, and with the trumpet of God, 1 Thes. iv. 16: then shall all the kindreds of the earth mourn, and they shall see the Son of man come in the clouds of heaven with power and great glory, Mat. xxiv. 30. And who shall be able to stand in that great and fearful day? even all such as have finished their course in the love of God and his children; as certainly as we now find love in our hearts, so surely shall 'we have boldness in the day of judgment,' 1 John iv. 17.

The fourth motive may be taken from the miserable state of such as find not in themselves the love of God's children: first, It is a palpable sign they abide still in darkness, and under the bondage of the first death, and in danger of the second death.

Secondly, A man can never enter into the kingdom of heaven without it; for every man can say, a murderer shall not be saved, so continuing. Now it is certain God hates a man that loves not his children, as well as he doth murderers: 'He that loveth not his brother, is a man-slayer, and we know that no man-slayer can inherit eternal life,' 1 John iii. 15.

Thirdly, Till we love God's children we can never know what the length, breadth, and depth of the love of God and Christ is to us, Eph. iii. 17. God shews not his love to us till we shew our love to the saints. Lastly, for want of love in the heart, and the duties of love in conversation, the mystical body of Christ is exceedingly hindered from growing, both in the beauty and glory which otherwise would be found in the Church of Christ, Eph. iv. 16.

Lastly, To incite us yet more to the exercise of love, I propound three places of scripture more:

The first place is, Eph. iv. 12-17, where may be observed four things, gotten by a holy union with the members of Christ, and Christian society and affection. It furthers 'our gathering into the body.' It is an exceeding great help in the beginning of our effectual vocation; secondly, It furthers our edification in the building, and fits us for our room among the saints. Godly society doth frame us and square us, and many ways fit us for our place in this building; thirdly, Loving affection to the members of Christ and mutual society doth much profit us, in respect of our growth in the body, and that till we become perfect men, and attain to the age of the fulness of Christ; fourthly, This holy love is a great fence to the judgment against false and deceitful doctrine: he is not easily carried with every wind of doctrine, nor unsettled with the vain deceits of men, that can follow the truth, and the means thereof, in a settled and well grounded love to God's children. But, on the other side, how easily are such men deluded and thrown off from their purposes and comforts, that did never join themselves to God's children!

The second place is 1 Peter iv. 7, 8, where the apostle exhorteth to sobriety in the use of the profits and delights of the world in meats and drinks, riches, recreation, and apparel, and withal to spend their time here in spiritual duties, especially prayer, watching thereunto, both to observe all occasions and opportunities to pray, as also noting the mercies of God we find in prayer, with our own corruptions in the manner, and the glorious success of prayer in prevailing with God. But 'above all things,' he wills them to 'have fervent love;' and yieldeth two reasons or motives: first, 'The end of all things is at hand,' and therefore it is best loving and making much of those that after the dissolution shall be great heirs of heaven and earth; secondly, 'Love covereth the multitude of sins,' it hideth the blemishes of our natures, and fitteth us for the comforts of society. Notwithstanding the infirmities accompany even the saints while they are in this vale of misery.

The third place is 2 Peter i. 7, &c., where he largely persuadeth men to get holy graces into their hearts, and to express holy duties in their lives: among these, as chief, he instanceth in 'brotherly kindness and love;' to this end he bringeth divers reasons: first, It will set our knowledge a-work, which else would be idle and unfruitful; and where should we unload ourselves of the fruits of knowledge which men get in God's house better than in the houses of the people of God? Secondly, He that hath not these things 'is blind;' or if he have sight and wit enough for this world, yet he is purblind, μυωπαζων, so as 'he can see nothing that is far off,' as eternal things are, but only things near, such as are carnal things: the want of love to God's people is a palpable sign of a purblind carnal man; thirdly, The want of love, and the other graces there named, is a sign of a spiritual lethargy, even that a man is fallen into a 'forgetfulness of the purging of his old sins;' that is, it is a sign that a man lieth under the guilt and filth of all his former sins, and never feels the weight of them, or considers the danger of them; fourthly, Love, with the fruits of it, do 'make our calling and election sure;' fifthly, Loving society and brotherly kindness is a great means of perseverance—'if ye do these things ye shall never fall;' lastly, By this means 'an entrance shall be ministered unto us abundantly, into the everlasting kingdom of our Lord Jesus Christ,' both because it mightily furthereth faith and hope, as also, because by these means eternal life is begun on earth, in respect of communion both with God and the saints.

3. Thus far of the motives; helps follow. These helps are such as serve, both for the begetting and nourishing of a holy love, to and with God's people.

There are eight things that are great furtherances of holy life:

First, The conscionable hearing of the word of God; for in God's house doth the Lord fire the heart and holy affections, and teach the right ordering of them. How came those Colossians by their love to the saints? No otherwise but by 'hearing the word of truth,' which discovered unto them who were God's children, and did daily fence them against the scorns and reproaches which the world laded them withal.

Secondly, We must get faith and hope, as the coherence shows: for till we be soundly humbled to seek God's favour, and find our hearts possessed with the care for and hope of a better life, we cannot receive God's children aright into our hearts. But no man was ever truly touched in conscience, and had unfeigned desires of remission of his sins, neither did ever a man seriously seek after the things of a better life, but he did love God's children above all the people of the earth: and it is true of the measure, that as we grow in faith and hope, so we should grow in love and in the comforts of God's favour.

Thirdly, Would we love brotherly, without feigning, and fervently; then we must get our 'souls purified, through the Spirit, in obeying the truth;' we must make conscience of the duties of mortification, as of so many purges, to cleanse our thoughts and affections of dwelling and reigning lusts and evils; for secret sins entertained and delighted in within the affections and thoughts do exceedingly poison affection both to God and man: this is that the apostle meaneth where he saith, 'love must come out of a pure heart,' 1 Tim. i. 5.

Fourthly, We must stir up the spirit of love, 2 Tim. i. 6. The Spirit of God is a spirit of love, and we must stir it up by nourishing the motions of the same, putting courses or ways of expressing love into our minds, and by prayer, meditation, or any other means that may inflame our hearts to a holy affection.

Fifthly, It profiteth much hereunto to get and keep in our minds a pattern of faith and love, even a draught of the things that concern faith in God, and love to the saints, that we might always have a frame of all holy duties that concern this holy affection. This was their care in the primitive times, as appeareth, 2 Tim. i. 13.

Sixthly, To be found in these three things, faith, love, and patience, requires most an end experience, and a daily acquainting ourselves with the things of the kingdom of Christ. When we are driven by often crosses to seek comfort in God's children, and by much observation to find the worth of the comforts that arise from holy society with them, many are the incredible weaknesses that discover themselves in the hearts of younger and weaker Christians; but it is a shame for the elder men, if they be not 'found in love,' Titus ii. 2.

Seventhly, We must by all holy means strengthen, and encourage, and set ourselves upon perseverance in the profession of our hope, for if once we give over profession, it will be easy to see love vanish. A wavering profession is inconstant in love, Heb. x. 24.

Lastly, If we would never forsake the fellowship we have one with another, as the manner of some wicked hypocrites and damnable apostates is, then we must, with all Christian care, 'consider one another's' weaknesses and wants; and be continually ' provoking,' inciting, and encouraging 'one another to love, and to good works,' Heb. x. 25. Thus of the helps.

4. In the last place I propounded to be considered the defects that are found in the love that is abroad in the world, with which the common protestant pleaseth himself. I will not here complain that love is turned into lust, and that that damnable infection hath stained heaven and earth, and polluted our houses, brought a curse upon our assemblies, and debased our gentry, dishonoured our nobles, corrupted our youth, and made heavy our elder age, or shew how it hath brought upon us famine and pestilence; but, to let this pass, I will speak of the honester love. And wherein think you standeth it?

First, In the civiller sort—in compliments: never more compliments and less love. *Secondly,* In freedom from suits at law and quarrelling. They are in charity with all the world, if they can shew that they never were quarrelsome, or that they are friends again. *Thirdly,* In the baser sort it is mere ale-house friendship. Their love stands wholly in going to the ale-house together. These are the only fellows and good neighbours; and commonly here is set up the devil's bench, and proclamation made of free pardon for filthy ribaldry, for drunken spewings, and viper-like slanders belched out against good men. *Fourthly,* Many out of their ignorance know none other love than of themselves, or for themselves of others. But yet more plainly the defectiveness of the common protestant's love appears diversely:

First, By the usual sins which are rife amongst them, even such as batter the fortress of love. How can they please themselves in their charity, if we consider how malice, revenge, anger, slandering, backbiting, and all sorts of provocations to anger, are everywhere abounding? What more usual than self-love? What more common than envy? Shall I instance? The tradesman, while he is rising, is so flushed with success, and stuffed with the greedy desire of profit, that he cares not whom he wrongs, nor how much he becomes prejudicial to other men's trade. But this man is not so filled with self-love, but the declining tradesman that hath over-lived his prime, is every way as well filled with envy. And thus men are not in charity, neither full nor fasting.

Secondly, It appears to be defective in the objects of love, in a chief companion of love, in the parts of love, and in the manner of loving.

For the first, the only men that are chiefly to be loved, and our affections to be spent upon, are the saints, that is, such religious persons as make conscience of all their ways. But are these the men the common protestant loves? Oh times! oh manners! What men find worse entertainment in the world than these? Is not the least endeavour after holiness chased and pursued with open hates, dislikes, slanders? Can a man refrain himself from evil and not be made a prey? Doth there any live godly, and they persecute him not? Away, false wretch! sayest thou thou art in charity with all men, and yet canst not bear the image of God in a child of God?

For the second, all true love ought to be accompanied with faith, yea, it ought to be founded upon faith; and therefore herein is the common love of the world defective, that a communion with men is not first sanctified with a union with God. These men, that boast so much of their charity, never made conscience of seeking the assurance of God's favour in Christ, neither ever travailed under the burden of their sins, so as to seek forgiveness as the true blessedness.

Thirdly, The common protestant is exceedingly to blame in the very main duties of love. No tenderness of heart, no true hospitality; and for mercy to the poor, the old complaints may be taken up, ' There is no mercy in the land,' Hosea iv. 1; ' Merciful men are taken away,' Isa. lvii. 1. We may now-a-days wait for some Samaritan to come and prove himself a neighbour; and for society and fellowship in the gospel with God's people, it will never sink into the understanding of these carnal men, that that is any way expedient; and finally, in all the branches of clemency before expressed, where is the man that makes conscience of them?

And for the last, it is easily avouched that the love that is found in the most men is neither brotherly, nor without gross feigning and hypocrisy, nor proceedeth it from a heart in any measure purified; and lastly, it is so far from being fervent, that it is stone cold.

Thus of love.

Ver. 5. *For the hope's sake which is laid up for you in heaven.*

In these words is mentioned the third grace, for which the apostle gives thanks—and that is hope.

Hope is here taken both for the thing hoped for, viz., the glory of heaven, as also the grace by which it is apprehended, but especially the latter.

Heaven is diversely accepted in scripture. Sometimes it signifieth the air, Deut. xxviii. 12, Mat. xvi. 17; sometimes it signifieth the whole upper world that compasseth the earth, Gen. xlix. 25, Mat. iii. 16; sometimes for the kingdom of grace and the means thereof, Mat. iii. 2, and xi. 11; but most usually for the place of the blessed, and the glory thereof; and so it is taken here.

Hope, as it is here considered by the apostle, looks two ways: first, By relation to, and coherence with, faith and love, 'for the hope's sake ;' secondly, By a full aspect upon the object of it, which is intimated in the metaphor *laid up*, and expressed in the word *heavens*.

First, Of hope, as it is to be considered in the coherence :

Obser. 1. There is an admirable wisdom and mercy of God in the very manner of dispensing of his graces, for he makes one grace crown another, and become a recompense and reward to another, as here for hope's sake God's children break through the difficulties of faith, and the impediments and discouragements of love. When God sees how many ways the heart of man is beset in the spiritual combat, about the getting and exercise of those two graces, he is pleased, by his word and Spirit to trumpet out victory by shewing the glory of heaven, and to set on the crown of hope, as the assured pledge of full and final victory. It is hope that plucks up the heart of man to a constant desire of union with God by faith, and of communion with man by love. And the true reason why so many men utterly neglect the care to get a justifying faith and an inflamed affection to God's children, is because they have no taste of the comforts of the evidence of a better life by hope.

Obser. 2. Secondly, Faith and hope are two distinct things. Faith believes the promise to be true, with particular application of the promise to one's self; and hope waits for the accomplishment of it. Faith usually is employed about reconciliation and a godly life. Hope, for the most part, is taken up with the retired and affectionate contemplation of the glory of heaven, the coming of Christ, the resurrection of the body, and temporal blessings, and deliverance, as they are shadows and types of the last and great salvation..

Obser. 3. Thirdly, Hope is no more natural than faith and love. The carnal man is 'without hope in the world,' Eph. ii. 12. Not that wicked men are clean without all profession of hope, for few men are so vile but they possess and stoutly avouch their hope in God; but this hope is vain, empty, without evidence or promise, such as can never profit them; and therefore, in the 8th of Job he saith, that 'the hypocrite's hope shall perish, his confidence also shall be cut off, and his trust shall be as the house of a spider,' Job viii. 13, 14. It is to be observed, that he calls wicked men (even all carnal and unconverted people) hypocrites, and that fitly, for every sinner is a hypocrite in some degree; and if there were nothing else to prove it, their very hope and wilful confidence in the mercies of God, without all warrant from the word, or testimony of God's Spirit, or their own conscience, would undoubtedly prove it; and for the vanity of their hope, it is fitly expressed in the comparison of the spider's web. The silly spider, with many day's labour, weaves herself a web, in appearance able every way abundantly to cover her, and fit her turn; but at the end of the week, the maid with a besom sweeps all down. This poisonful spider is every unregenerate man or woman; this web is their hope, in the framing of which they daily busy themselves, and in the coverture of which they vainly repose themselves; but when any servant comes out of the Lord's army to sweep with the besom of judgment or death, the whole building of these imaginary hopes comes suddenly and totally down. In the 11th chapter of Job, and the 20th verse, it is said, 'The eyes of the wicked shall fail, and their refuge shall perish, and their hope shall be sorrow of mind.' In which words the Holy Ghost shews that the time shall come when those vain hopes shall be driven out of the souls of the wicked, and instead thereof, they shall be filled either with desperate sorrows on earth, or with eternal sorrows in hell. 'What hope hath the hypocrite, when he hath heaped up riches, if God take away his soul?' Job xxvii. 8. Noting that if carnal men (again called hypocrites) will not forego their fond presumptions while they live, yet by too late experience they shall find them vain when death comes.

Object. But then they mean to pray God to forgive them, and hope by their repentance then to find mercy for their souls.

Sol. In the ninth verse it is answered thus, 'Will God hear his cry when trouble comes upon him?'

Quest. But will not God hear men's prayers in the troublesome time of death?

Ans. Not the prayers at that time made by such men; for they are hypocrites, having upon them but the names of God and godliness, and will never in sincerity 'pray unto God at all times,' neither in their death do they pray unto God because they delight in the Almighty. And therefore he shews, ver. 10, that seeing they delight not in God and godliness, and will not pray at all times—that is, as well in health as sickness, in prosperity as in adversity, while they might yet sin as well as when they can sin no longer—therefore their hope of mercy in death shall fail them.

Quest. But if true hope be not natural, what is the difference between the hope of the faithful and this common hope that so ordinarily goeth up and down the world under the colours of it, or how may we try ourselves whether we have a right hope or no?

Ans. The true hope is described in several scriptures by divers properties, which are nowhere to be found in carnal men.

First, The true hope lays fast hold upon the merits of Jesus Christ only, and strives constantly to be established and assured, Titus i. 2; Ps. xxxi. 24. But the common hope is never emptied of carnal confidence and presumption that God loves them for some good things or parts that are in them; neither doth it brook assurance; for with one breath carnal people are assuredly confident of God's mercy, and encounter the doctrine of infallible assurance.

Secondly, True hope makes a man more humble, Lam. iii. 29; but the common hope makes men more wilful and obstinate against God and his ordinances.

Thirdly, True hope makes a man cheerful under all sorts of crosses, by virtue of the very reasons grounded upon hope, Rom. v. 2, 4; but the common hope of itself will not yield a man's heart support against any cross.

Fourthly, The faithful man can suffer for his hope, Acts xxviii. 20; Rom. viii. 24; but a wicked man can shew no chain, unless it be for his sin.

Fifthly, True hope rests upon God's promise, though never so unlikely to be performed by outward and ordinary means, Rom. iv. 18; but wicked men, with their common hope, are perhaps able to believe they shall live well so long as they see and feel means, but without means they are without hope.

Sixthly, True hope will acknowledge as well as know, Titus i. 2; but the common hope cannot abide profession of religion—it is enough there be a good heart to God.

Seventhly, True hope is industrious in the use of all means to come to the end hoped, Ps. xxxvii. 3; but the common hope is singularly slothful; it boasts of a sufficiency of knowledge, and yet neglects the sincere use of all God's ordinances; it affirms deeply of going to heaven, and yet cannot tell of one tear for sin, nor one hour truly spent in mortification—but 'trust thou in the Lord, and do good.'

Lastly, The true hope seeks God's presence, and strives in sense to draw near to God, Ps. lxxiii. 26; but the common hope is then at best rest when the heart is farthest off from the care, desire, or sense of God's presence, either in God's house or abroad.

Obser. 4. The fourth thing that I observe from the coherence concerning hope is the worth of the grace. It is one of the three golden habiliments to adorn a Christian soul. And this I note the rather, because it should move us to use carefully and constantly all the means that serve to breed or increase true hope in us, and to get, by prayers and practice, all those things that cause hope. And that we may get and increase our hope, we must labour for, first, True grace, 1 Thes. ii. 16; secondly, Saving knowledge, Ps. ix. 10, and lxxviii. 7; thirdly, Experience, Rom. v. 4; fourthly, Patience and comfort of the scriptures, Rom. xv. 4; fifthly, The joys of the Holy Ghost, and peace of conscience in believing, Rom. xv. 13; sixthly, Above all, and for all these, the Spirit of revelation, Eph. i. 18; seventhly, The often meditation of God's promises.

Thus of hope, as it is considered in relation to faith and love.

Which is laid up for you in heaven. In these words hope is described in the object of it.

Laid up. Viz., by God in his secret coffers, as a most worthy jewel. This metaphor gives occasion to observe three doctrines.

Doct. 1. First, That grace and glory are a man's best treasures, and therefore we should labour for them more than anything else; and if we have a comfortable evidence of them, to be contented though we want other things.

Doct. 2. Secondly, That hope is no common grace, in that, amongst many fair virtues which are common to wicked men, he locketh up this grace of hope as a special jewel he intends to keep only for his own children.

Doct. 3. Thirdly, That the evidence and grace of God's children be in God's keeping, and laid up safe in heaven, and therefore cannot be lost; and, besides, when they die, there is of theirs in heaven before they come.

Heaven. Here I observe two things:

1. First, That there is a heaven for the saints after this life. The doctrine of heaven is only proper to religion. Nature hath but a dark glimpse of immortality, or any being after this life, and is full of stronger objections than answers; and as any are more lewd in life, they are more senseless of immortality. But concerning the estate of the blessed in heaven, nature is wholly ignorant, yea, the doctrine hereof is so divine, that religion itself doth not fully portray it out in this world to any; yet as any are more holy, it is more discerned.

The consideration of heaven may urge us to many duties in general. If ever we would have heaven when we die, we must get holiness both imputed and infused while we live, Mat. v. 16; 2 Pet. i. 7; Mat. vii. 21; 1 Pet. ii. 11, 14; Ps. xv. We must be sure we be of God's family, Eph. iii. 16; and that we are born again, John iii. 5, Luke xiii. 5. In particular, we should therefore acquaint ourselves with the laws and mysteries of God's kingdom, Mat. xiii. 11, 52. And if we may come by the means to be effectually instructed in the way to heaven, we should account of this pearl, and rather than lose it, sell all we have to buy it, Mat. xiii. 44, 45. And we should above all things 'labour for the meat that perisheth not, but endures to everlasting life,' John vi. 27. Inasmuch as in the ministry of the word is many times found the keys that open unto us the kingdom of heaven, Mat. xvi. 19; Rom. x. 6. And inasmuch as riches may prove a singular hindrance, we should take warning, and see to it that they do not entangle us, Mat. xix. 23. And because in heaven are our treasures, we should set our affections there, Mat. vi. 20, Col. iii. 1; and prepare for our change and departure, 2 Cor. v. 1, 2, 1 Thes. i. 10. Giving allowance to no sin, no, not the least, Mat. v. 10-19; constantly professing and confessing Christ before men, that he may not deny us in that day, Mat. x. 32, 33, and v. 10. Yea, where God means to bestow heaven, he bestows heavenly qualities on men in this life. They are poor in spirit, Mat. v. 3; they are eager after heaven and the things thereof, Mat. xi. 12; they are like children, void of earthly carking and distressful cares, Mat. xviii. 2; they are merciful, Mat. xxv. 34-36; they love their enemies, Mat. v. 44.

Secondly, The meditation of heaven serves for reproof, not only of atheists, that would deny it, or papists, that claim so great glory for their base merits, but also of the most protestants; for are not the most such as 'can discern the face of the sky, and yet have no discerning of the season' to get grace and heaven? to say nothing of those that, by their gross and horrible sins, have forfeited over and over the claim of any interest in the kingdom of heaven, living in daily blasphemies, whoredoms, drunkenness, &c. Yea, do not the better sort give heaven fair words, and yet have their excuses why they will not come to God's feasts when he invites them? Luke xiv. 17. And thus, while men bless themselves, God's curses usually devour them.

Lastly, It is a doctrine of wonderful comfort to God's children, Heb. xii. 23; Luke xi. 20. Neither is this the peculiar advancement of some principal saints, as Abraham, David, &c., Mat. viii. 11, and xiii. 31. Neither should the miseries of this life before we come to heaven trouble us, seeing there is no comparison between the troubles of this life and the glory of the world to come, where there shall be no sin, sorrow, labour, weakness, disgrace, fear, death; where we shall enjoy the sweet presence of God, Christ, angels, and just men, with unspeakable joys, perfect holiness, exquisite knowledge, and a total righteousness; and all this for ever.

2. Secondly, From hence also doth plainly arise this second doctrine, viz., that the hope of Christians is in another world; there is their stay and comfort. When they seek by faith the comforts of God's favours, and by love separate themselves to the communion with God's children, they find presently such a rent from the world, and all sort of carnal men assaulting so their rest, that a little experience learns them the knowledge of this truth, that in this world, and from the men of this world, and the things thereof, they must look for no peace or contentment, Rom. viii. 24, 25.

Use. The use is first, for instruction, to teach us therefore to use the world as if we used it not, and so to care for earthly things and persons as to resolve that heaven is our portion, and there only must we provide to find some rest and contentment; yea, therefore, as 'strangers and pilgrims we should seek and provide for our abiding city,' Heb. xi. 13.

Secondly, This doctrine gives occasion to answer that imputation that is cast upon many professors, viz., that forwardness in religion makes them mindless of their business, and much hearing of sermons makes them careless of their callings. Men may here-hence inform themselves, that howsoever religion ties men to honest cares and daily diligence to provide for their families, else the very scripture brands such professors to be worse than infidels, that make religion as a mask for idleness, yet seeing our hope is not in the world, therefore God's children do well first and chiefly to seek the kingdom of God and the righteousness thereof, and so to mind an earthly calling as it hinder not a heavenly, and provide means for a temporal life as not to hinder the hope of an eternal life.

Thirdly, This doctrine may much settle and comfort God's children against the scorns and hates of the world and all sorts of carnal people—'the world will love his own.'

Object. Oh, but why should they hate us?

Ans. Because 'you are not of the world, and Christ hath chosen you out of the world, therefore the world hateth you,' John xv. 19. And therefore both provide for it, and bear it when you find it.

Object. But we will not be so rash and indiscreet to provoke men to hate and reproach.

Sol. Ver. 20. They have persecuted Christ, who was the fountain of all wisdom; and therefore it is a vain persuasion for any child of God to think, by any discretion, wholly to still the clamours and hates of wicked men; and those men are grossly deceived and prejudiced that think the true cause of the troubles of God's children is their own indiscretion.

Object. It is strange they should hate us so; we never did them wrong.

Sol. Ver. 21, 'All these things will they do unto you for my name's sake.' It is not your evil doing, but your holy profession of the name of Christ, which is named upon you, that they hate.

Quest. But how comes it they should dare to be so presumptuous and so palpably malicious?

Ans. It is because 'they have not known my Father,' ver. 21. Their ignorance of the majesty and justice of God is the cause of it.

Object. If it be of ignorance, it may be easily pardoned them.

Sol. Ver. 22, 'If I had not come and spoken unto them, they should have had no sin, but now there is no cloak for their sin;' that is, if Christ, by the preaching of the word, had not discovered their sins, and set before them the way of godliness, then it had been no such grievous and monstrous sin; but inasmuch as many men do lie in wilful ignorance, and will not be informed of the vileness of their course, therefore, before God, of all sinners, they are without colour or excuse.

Object. But may they not have good hearts to God, though they do thus intemperately and unjustly malign and abuse the preachers and children of God?

Sol. Ver. 23, He that hateth Christ in his ministers and members hateth the Father also, and cannot have a good heart to God.

Object. But it may be that Christ and Christians are hated the more securely by wicked worldlings, because they see nothing but their baseness and humiliation.

Sol. Ver. 24, 'If I had not done works among them which none other did,' &c. By which words our Saviour shews that no works of God for, by, or amongst God's servants can be so great testimonies of the undoubted certainty of the goodness and holiness of their cause, but wicked men will still, against all right, hate them. And, therefore, we should so inform ourselves by this and other scriptures, ver. 25, as to set down our rest, that in the world we must have troubles, and in Christ and heaven peace, and therefore lay up hope in our hearts, as God hath locked up our treasures in heaven.

Thus of hope. Thus also of the grace for which he gives thanks.

Whereof ye have heard before by the word of truth, which is the gospel.

Ver. 6. *Which is come unto you, even as it is unto all the world, and is fruitful as it is also among you, from the day that ye heard and truly knew the grace of God.*

In these words, with those that follow to the ninth verse, is contained the second part of the thanksgiving, viz., his praise to God for their means of grace.

The means is either principal, ver. 5, 6, or instrumental, ver. 7, 8.

The principal means is the word; and this is described by six things: first, By the ordinance in which it was most effectual, viz., *hearing*; secondly, By the property which was most eminent in the working of it, viz., *truth*; thirdly, By the kind of word, viz., *the gospel;* fourthly, By the providence of God in planting it amongst them—*is come unto you:* fifthly, By the subject persons upon whom it wrought—*you* (the Colossians) and *the whole world;* sixthly, By the efficacy—it is *fruitful from the day.* Thus for the order of the words.

From the general I observe, out of all the words, two things:

1. First, That nature directs not to the apprehension either of grace or glory: 'the natural man cannot perceive the things of God,' 1 Cor. ii. 14. These Colossians had never known the face of God, nor gained the grace of Christ, had not God sent them the means. Briefly, this may inform us of the lamentable condition of such as live in their natural estate, only pleased with the desire or possession of the riches or gifts of nature; and withal, shews us the fountain of the want of sense or care of grace, and holiness. In the most, sense comes not from nature, but from the word; and he is a natural man that is still lapped and covered with the veil of ignorance, whose wisdom is cross to God's wisdom, that lieth in gross sins, like a dead man without sense, that serves some particular gainful or pleasing sin, without using aright any ordinance of God against it, and is without the spirit of adoption, his heart never broken for sin, and without desire of righteousness—Isa. xxv. 8, Rom. viii. 6, Eph. ii. 1, Rom. vi.

2. Secondly, It is a worthy blessing of God to any people to have the word of God amongst them. This is that men should be exceeding thankful for to God—Ps. cxlvii. 19, 20, Isa. ii. 3. And by the contrary, the want of the word is a terrible famine.

Use 1. For reproof both of men's profaneness in neglecting and contemning of the word; as also of our great unthankfulness for such a mercy. 2. For comfort to God's children that enjoy the word and esteem it. The word should satisfy us whatsoever else we want, both because it doth abundantly make amends for all other wants; and besides, it fits us with strength, patience, and comfort, to make use of other wants. 3. For instruction, not only to such people as want the word to seek for it, and to plant themselves where they may have it, but also to such landlords and great men, and rulers of the people, as would be thought lovers of their country, to use all means to see the country and the parishes under their power provided of this holy treasure.

Thus of the general doctrines out of the whole verses.

The first thing in special, is the kind of ordinance in which the word was effectual, viz., hearing.

Whereof. That is, of which—heaven or hope. It is a great mercy of God to hear of heaven, before the time come it should be enjoyed or lost. If we heard not of heaven till death or judgment, we should continue still in our slumber, drowned in the lust after profit or pleasures; we should be so far from finishing our mortification, as we should hardly begin to set about the washing of our own uncleanness both of hands and life; we should look upon grace and holiness with a dull and feeble eye; yea, it is good even for God's children to hear of it before they have it, both to support them in their crosses and discouragements, as also to pluck up their minds to holy contemplation, and to wean them from the love of base things; yea, to inflame them to a greater desire to magnify and glorify the singular grace and mercy of God in these days of their pilgrimage.

Ye have heard. No man can get eternal graces or an enduring contentment, arising from the hope of a better life, without the hearing of the word of God—Mat. xvii. 50, Luke xvi. 29, 30, John viii. 47.

Quest. But tell us distinctly, what good shall men get by hearing of sermons?

Ans. Many are the singular benefits come to men thereby: *first*, The Holy Ghost is here given, Acts x. 44; *secondly*, Men's hearts are here opened, Acts xvi. 14; *thirdly*, The fear of God doth here fall upon men, Acts xiii. 16; *fourthly*, The proud and stony heart of man is here tamed, melted, and made to tremble, Isa. lxvi. 2; *fifthly*, The faith of God's elect is here begotten, Rom. x. 14; *sixthly*, Men are here sealed by the holy Spirit of promise, Eph. i. 13; *seventhly*, Here the Spirit speaketh to the churches, Rev. ii.; *eighthly*, Christ here comes to sup with men, Rev. iii. 20—let men tell of their experience, whether ever their hearts tasted of the refreshing of Christ, till they devoted themselves to the hearing of the word; *ninthly*, The painful distress of the afflicted conscience is here or nowhere cured—by hearing, the bones that God hath broken receive joy and gladness, Ps. li. 3; *tenthly*, What shall I say, but as the evangelical prophet saith, if you can do nothing else, yet 'hear, and your souls shall live,' Isa. lv. 3. Live, I say, the life of grace, yea, and the life of glory; for salvation is brought unto us by hearing.

Use 1. The use of this point is: *First*, For instruction—'let him that heareth hear,' Ezek. iii. 27; yea, let all rejoice in the mercies of their God, that have tasted of this bounty of the Lord— 'blessed are your ears, inasmuch as you have heard; many prophets and righteous men have desired to hear the things that you hear, and have not heard them,' Mat. xiii. 16, 17. *Secondly*, For humiliation, under the consideration of the lamentable estate of such people as have not the word preached unto them. How do the thousands even in Israel perish through the failing or wanting of vision? Is there not almost millions of men and women that have scarce heard, by preaching, whether there be any Holy Ghost? Oh the cruel torments that abide those soul-murderers! Shall I name them? I wish their repentance, that so they might have a new name; but because lamentable experience shews that the unsavoury salt seldom finds wherewith it may be salted, therefore it is the duty of all God's people to bow the knees of their hearts to God, beseeching him to inflame the hearts of those that are in authority with such bowels of compassion, that they would in due time purge the church of them, that so their names may no more be heard amongst us. While men lie sick of the spiritual lethargy in their own hearts, they are little troubled with the distress of others; but if men would even in God's sight duly weigh, without shifting and prejudice, these propositions, viz., that the hearing of the word is the ordinary means to convert men's souls to God, Rom. x. 14, 1 Pet. i. 23, &c.; and that 'except men be born again they cannot enter into the kingdom of God,' John iii. 3;—if, I say, these things be weighed, how should our bowels turn within us to consider the case of some hundreds of parishes in this famous kingdom, that in the midst of this great light, in this respect, yet sit in darkness? *Thirdly*, For the reproof of the disorders and vicious dispositions of men in the hearing of the word. Many are the sorts of evil hearers; exceeding many are the wicked humours of men, by which they sin against the word heard. The scripture hath noted and taxed divers corruptions in men in hearing, and fearfully threatened them. For the better explication of this use I consider two things: first, The sorts of evil hearers; secondly, Their state in respect of it.

1. The sorts of evil hearers may be distinguished into two kinds: some are openly impious and audacious, some more civil and restrained. Of the first kind: First, Some are so wayward nothing can please them; either the preacher is too terrible, or he is too comfortable. If John fast, he hath a devil; if Christ eats, he is a glutton, Mat. xi. 16, &c. Secondly, Some hear and are scandalised, Mat. xv. 12. Men are so wedded to their own conceits,

and stuffed with prejudice, that they many times wilfully study and strive to frame scandal and offence out of the words of the teacher. Thirdly, Some hear, and are filled with wrath and envy, and that sometimes so as they cannot restrain the signs of their rage and fretting, no, not in the sermon-time, Luke iv. 28. They gnash with their teeth, and their hearts are ready to burst for anger, Acts vii. 54. And this comes many times, because men cannot abide wholesome doctrine, but are given to fables, 2 Tim. iv. 3, 4. Fourthly, Some hear, and their mouths make jests, while their hearts go after their lusts, Ezek. xxxiii. 30; they hear and mock, Acts xvii. 32. Fifthly, Some make the auditory of Christians the study of all manner of base filthiness; thither comes the adulterer, the covetous, the deceiver, the accuser of the brethren, &c., and there they damnably frame their dogged and swinish imaginations. Sixthly, Some hear, and if they find any power in the doctrine of the preacher, they inquire whether he be not a Puritan; for they have heard so much evil of that sect everywhere, that that one colour may serve to make them cautelous, and better advised than to be much troubled with his doctrine, Acts xxviii. 22. Seventhly, Some will hear if he speak of this world, 1 John iv. 5. He is an excellent preacher that in their understanding gives them liberty, and sows pillows under their fleshly and worldly elbows. Eighthly, Some hear fearfully, as loath to be drawn to the sermon of any that rebukes sin, as the people of Israel were to come near the mount, Heb. xii. 19. Ninthly, Some, like the chief priests and pharisees, when they perceive that the preacher rebukes their sins, seek to lay hands upon him, Mat. xxi. 45, 46, and as far as the fear of the people restraineth them not, they practise to remove him.

The civiller sorts of hearers are diversely sinful in their several humours: first, Some hear, but it is to be rid of their diseases, that is, to see whether by hearing sermons, and coming to church, they can assuage the trouble of their minds, and dull the stinging cares of their hearts; secondly, Some are like the young man, for they go from the sermon sorry that the word requireth such things as they are not willing to do, Mat. xix.; thirdly, Some hear and say, God forbid, Luke xx. 16—it is pity it should be so as the preacher says; fourthly, Some hear because a great report goeth of the teacher, Mat. iii. 8; fifthly, But above all others, they are strange hearers that are mentioned, Mat. xxii. 22— they hear and admire, and yet leave and forsake, for any reformation or practice of what they hear.

Under this rank I may refer the three sorts of hearers, Mat. xiii. The first sort suffer the devil presently to take away the word. The second sort choke it with cares and lusts. The third forsakes the profession, and hearing, and liking of it, in the time of temptation or persecution. Thus of their sorts.

2. The state of men transgressing against the word, by refusing to hear it aright, is exceeding fearful; if they could see their misery they would do as the prophets require, they would cut their hair and cast it away, under the sense of the horror of God's indignation, Jer. vii. 22-29. The dust of the feet of God's messengers will rise in judgment against such hearers, Mat. x. 14. It shall be easier for Nineveh, and Tyrus, and Sidon, and Sodom, and Gomorrah, than for such hearers, Mat. xii. 41; yea, all their suits for mercy are abomination in God's sight, Prov. xxviii. 9. A heavy care is noted for a singular judgment, Mat. xiii. 13, 14, &c.; Isa. xxx. 8, 9. Yea, because men will not hear the word they must bear the rod, Mic. vi. 9; and their ears (if they belong to God) must be forced open by corrections, Job iii. 3. To conclude, if all this cannot affect men, then I say, as the Lord said to the prophet of such persons, 'He that leaveth off to hear, let him leave off,' Ezek. iii. *ult*. Thus of the first part of the description, viz., the ordinance in which it is most effectual, viz., hearing.

The second part is the property of the word, which is most eminent in the working of it, viz., truth.

Word of truth. He meaneth not the personal Word, which is Christ, but the enunciative word, made known either singularly by revelation, oracles, visions, dreams, or commonly by tradition of doctrine, from hand to hand for two thousand years; or by a more excellent manner, afterwards by scripture. The word of holy scripture is here meant.

There are many properties of the word of God wherein it doth excel: first, It is divine, the testimony of God's mouth, wonderful, 1 Thes. ii. 13, Ps. cxix. 18, 88, 129; secondly, It is eternal and incorruptible, a living word, or the word of life, Ps. cxix. 89, 144, 152, Philip. ii. 16, 1 Pet. i. 22; thirdly, It is swift, Ps. cxlvii. 15-18; fourthly, it is powerful and terrible, Heb. iv. 12; the sword of the Spirit, Hosea vi. 5, Isa. xi. 2, Heb. iv. 12, Eph. vi.; fifthly, It is nourishing and healing, it hath a property to nourish and heal, Ps. cvii. 20; sixthly, It sanctifieth both our persons and the use of the creature; seventhly, It is comfortable, joyful, sweet, Ps. cxix. 14, 52, 143, 162; eighthly, It is apt for generation, it hath a quickening power, Ps. cxix. 25-28, 1 Pet. i. 22; ninthly, It is preservative, both from sin, Ps. cxix. 11, and from shame, Ps. cxix. 22—so will not gold and silver; tenthly, It is wise and exceeding large, Ps. cxix. 96, 98, 99, 100, 104; eleventhly, It is light, and pure, and just, Ps. cxix. 105, 130, 140, 128, 138. But here the word is commended for the truth of it, and that a most eminent property in men's conversions.

Truth is taken diversely: for a virtue in speech, in the second table; for truth of doctrine, John v. 33; for the substance of a type, John i. 17; for uprightness and sincerity, John iii. 21; for the true form of a thing, Rom. i. 28.

Here the word of God is said to be ' the word of truth,' in regard of the use of the word in the conversion of a sinner; and that, first, as it is apprehended to be in itself; secondly, as it is by effect in the hearer. For the first, before a man can have experience of the power of the word in the gathering of his soul, he must know it to be a word of truth four ways:

First, That it is the very word of God, and therefore true: considering the admirable antiquity of the story before all other histories; the dreadful miracles by which it was confirmed; the certain event of the vaticinies or prophecies; the immutable and every way sufficient frame of piety, righteousness, and divine worship, contained in it; the durableness of the wisdom thereof, which no punishments could ever extort out the heart of the professor thereof; and lastly, the dreadful judgments upon the enemies of it.

Secondly, That it is true, whatsoever doctrine it revealeth, though it make never so much against our profits, or pleasures, or lusts. Till a man be brought to this, the word never worketh soundly.

Thirdly, That there is an especial glory of truth in the promises, both in the promise itself, and the condition.

Fourthly, That we acknowledge truth in the performance of what God hath promised, and so give glory to his faithfulness; and thus of the word as it is apprehended in itself.

In the second place, the word is the word of truth by effect, because it worketh truth in us, and imprinteth itself in us, and fits us for godliness, Titus i. 2; and thus it worketh truth in us six ways:

First, In that it worketh knowledge, and so truth in the understanding. *Secondly*, In that it worketh in us the truth of worship, John xiv. 23, 24. *Thirdly*, In that it worketh in us plainness and uprightness, in the exercise of grace and holiness, and so it is opposed to hypocrisy, Eph. iv. 24. *Fourthly*, In that it worketh truth of constancy, that is, an everlasting resolution to hear and keep the word of truth, John viii. 37, 1 John iv. 6. *Fifthly*, In that it begets in us the sincerity and truth that becomes our callings and behaviour in the world, as we are free from lying, calumnies, perfidiousness, slandering, boasting, flattery, &c., 1 Cor. v. 8. *Sixthly*, In that it makes all our conversation virtuous, and so guides us to do the truth, Job iii. 22, James iii. 17.

Use is both for instruction and for reproof.

For instruction: therefore we should labour that the word may be a word of truth to us; and to this end: first, We should pray God to give us 'the Spirit of truth,' John xvi. 13; secondly, We must repent, that we may ' come to the knowledge of the truth,' 2 Tim. ii. 25; thirdly, We may not rest in the form of truth, Rom. ii. 20, Job iii. 32.

For reproof of four sorts of men: first, Such as ' will not receive the love of the truth '—with these ' gain is godliness,' 1 Tim. vi. 5, 2 Thes. ii. 10, 12; secondly, Such as strangle the light of the truth, either of nature, conscience, or the word, and ' withhold it in unrighteousness '—that strive against the light of the truth in their hearts, that they might sin the more freely, Rom. i. 18; thirdly, Such as will not obey the truth which yet they admire, commend, affect, &c., Gal. iii. 1, and v. 7; fourthly, Such as by their wicked lives 'cause the way of truth to be blasphemed,' which truth they both hear, and profess to obey. Thus of the second part of the description.

Thirdly, The word of God is described by the kind of word, viz., the gospel.

Which is the gospel. By the gospel is meant the doctrine of the reconciliation of man with his God after the fall. Concerning the gospel, we may in the general here observe, that of all other doctrines, the doctrine of man's reconciliation with God is especially to be urged and explained by the preacher, and to be most minded and inquired into by the hearer. The knowledge and experience of this point acquaints a man with the saving power of God. Never do men indeed see the beauty of the feet of God's servants, Rom. x. 15, till they have travailed about the obtaining of their peace with God. If ministers would bend the very force of their ministries about the sound and daily enforcing of the doctrine of man's particular assurance of his peace and reconciliation, it would produce, by God's blessing, singular fruit. This doctrine would judge the very secrets of men, and give them a glimpse of their last doom. It is a most prevailing doctrine, and therefore extremely envied in the world. The high priests and scribes, with the elders of the people, many times shew they cannot abide it, Luke xx. 1. Hence it is that life is not dear unto God's faithful servants, so they may in the comfort thereof fulfil their course and ministration received of the Lord Jesus, in testifying the gospel of the grace of God, Acts xx. 24. Of all other doctrines, the devil labours to keep the world ignorant of the necessity and power of this, 2 Cor. iv. 3, 4. But woe is to those preachers that teach it not, 1 Cor. ix. 16; and horrible woeful shall the estate of those people appear to be at the last day that obey it not, 2 Thes. i. 8. And therefore we should strive to keep afoot the sparkles of light in this point; and whatsoever we lose in hearing, this doctrine should never run out.

In particular, concerning the gospel, I inquire into three things: first, Wherein this doctrine lieth; secondly, Who receive this doctrine of the gospel; thirdly, What are the effects of it.

1. For the first, the gospel, or the doctrine of it, lieth in two things:

First, In our true repentance for our sins; and, *secondly,* In the infallible assurance of faith in God's favour in Christ forgiving us our sins, Mat. iii. 2, Mark i. 15. And this duly weighed: first, Reproves those that dream of salvation and the benefits of the gospel, without mortification; and, secondly, It should teach us to nourish faith by all means, by nourishing of desires, by removing of lets, praying for it, waiting upon hearing, beholding the faith of God's children, and delivering up our souls to some able and wise pastor.

2. The second question is, Who receive the gospel?

Ans. We must consider: first, Who *may* receive it; and that is answered, Mark xvi. 15, 'every creature;' that is, any man or woman, of what nation, language, profession, calling, state, and condition soever; and, secondly, we must consider who *do* receive it; and this may be answered generally or more specially. Generally, none receive the gospel but they find in it the very power of God to salvation, Rom. i. 16. None but such as are begotten again by it to God, 1 Cor. i. 16. If there be no change in thy life, thou hast yet no part in the gospel; without conversion, no glad tidings. In special, the persons that receive this treasure are signed out by divers properties in scripture: they are poor in spirit, Mat. xi. 5, Luke iv. 18; they find such need of it, that heaven suffers violence, and they press to it, Luke xvi. 16, Mat. xi. 10; and they so highly esteem the comforts of it, that they can be content to lose liberty, friends, means, and life too, for Christ's sake and the gospel, Mark viii. 35, and x. 29. And it works so forcibly upon men's souls, that they consecrate themselves to God, to sincerity, and godliness, Rom. xv. 16; and learn conscionably to practise the service of God in their spirit, minding the reformation of their thoughts and affections within, as well as of their words and actions without, Rom. i. 9.

3. And, thirdly, For the effects of it. Great are the praises of the power of it: it begets men to God; it is the power of God to salvation; it judgeth the secrets of men. Of these before. It brings abundance of blessings, Rom. xv. 19; it makes men heirs and co-heirs with Christ; it is a witness to all

nations, Mat. xxiv. 14; and, lastly, life and immortality is brought to light by it, 2 Tim. i. 10.

The uses. The consideration hereof should much encourage ministers to press this doctrine, and never cease to preach it in the temple, and from house to house, and make use of all opportunities when a door is opened unto them, either in respect of power in their own hearts, or in respect of tenderness and affection, and desire in the people, Acts v. 42, 1 Cor. i. 12. God's people also should so labour for the assurance of God's favour, and peace in Christ by the word, as they should store their hearts with provision of that kind, not only for their death-bed when they die, but renew the persuasion of it in their hearts daily, the better to fit them even in their callings and special standings. This knowledge is not only a crown and shield for their heads, but shoes also for their feet, against the filth of the times, and thorny cares of the world, and all the difficulties of a daily diligence in their standings, Eph. vi. 15.

Thus of the third part of the description; the fourth followeth.

4. The manner of providence in planting it amongst them, in these words:

And is come unto you. Where we may observe, that if the means of happiness find us not out to work upon us, we would never look after it. If God were not more careful to send it than we to seek it, it would never be had. We see this by common experience, that whole multitudes of people live without any sense of the want of the word, and did not God by some great providence send it them, and persuade them to the use of it, it would never be had. And this comes to pass because men are dead in sin, and sick of a lethargy, in the very use of the light of nature in matters of godliness; and, besides, there is an incredible inclination in our natures to seek for contentment in things below, and to be pleased with any condition rather than soundly to digest a sense of the necessity of using the means for happiness in better things. And lastly, this neglect of seeking the word comes from errors about men's estate, while they think that they may be in God's favour, and like enough to be saved, without any such ado.

Thus of the fourth part.

5. The fifth thing in the description is the subject persons to whom the gospel came, viz., the Colossians, and all the world.

Unto you, as it is even unto all the world. Hence we may note: first, The truth of God in his promises; he promised flourishing churches of the Gentiles, and lo, it is effected; the word is gone out into all the world; secondly, That the true trial of all doctrine is by inquiring whether it be agreeable to that doctrine wherein the world was overcome to God. Though an angel from heaven should preach otherwise, yet his doctrine were to be detested as accursed, 1 Gal. i. 8. And therefore we may justly complain of the papists, and all popish men, that chain men down to a necessity of looking upon the hundreds of years near unto us, and will not bear it that men should seek ground for their conscience, by overlooking all the hundreds of years since Christ, and minding only conformity to the doctrine that first founded the churches of the Gentiles; all doctrines since then, though in the purest times, are to be received no further than they agree with the doctrine of Christ and his apostles.

Thirdly, That men are bound to seek the word wheresoever it may be heard; for if this had not been so, how could all the world receive the light of the gospel? And further, we may see that the want of teachers was no warrant to commit the churches to the care of such as could not teach; a necessity lieth in the people to seek the word where it may be had. And therefore those church governors sin grievously that in this light create so many insufficient men, and set them over the flocks of Christ. For if want of able men had been a reason, the apostles should have seen into this necessity, to ease the labour and care of the churches; but it is a more grievous sin to admit, ordain, and place them, and yet see many worthy and able men wholly want places.

Fourthly, We might here note the vanity of their argument that would prove universal grace, because Christ died for all men; for in this place here is not only *the world*, but *all the world*; and yet here cannot, in any reasonable sense, be meant all the singular men and women in the world; for there were many thousands of particular persons to whom the gospel came not, and therefore by all the world (as here, so in that question) may be understood all the elect world; or if the world universally, then it is true in respect of offer, or not excepting out of any of any nation; or by all the world is meant men of all sorts and conditions in the world.

Fifthly, We might here note the incredible power and swiftness of the gospel, that could overcome, and that in so short a time; and the rather if that we consider that the magistrates generally drew the sword against it, and there were not wanting ministers to oppugn it, even false teachers of all sorts; and besides, the people had been so long time settled in their false religion; and lastly, if we look upon the meanness or the fewness of those that were God's ambassadors to the Gentiles.

Thus of the fifth part of the description.

The last thing by which the word of God is described is the efficacy of it. And here the apostle sheweth: first, What it doth—'it bringeth fruit,' and 'it increaseth,' for so it is added in some copies; secondly, Upon whom—'as even in you;' thirdly, When it began to be so, viz., 'from the day that you heard,' &c.; fourthly, What made it work so, viz., ' the hearing and true knowledge of the grace of God.'

And is 'fruitful.' Concerning fruitfulness, required as an effect of the word, I consider four things: first, The reasons to move us to fruitfulness; secondly, The sort of fruits we should bear; thirdly, The means to make us fruitful; lastly, The uses.

1. For the first, there are many things might move us to make conscience of glorifying God in our places, by bearing the fruit of the gospel, even expressing the power of it in our lives.

First, It is a special glory to God, and to our adoption and calling, John xv. 8; secondly, It is a testimony that we are indeed Christ's disciples, *ibid.*; thirdly, The practising of those things which are within the compass of God's promises (such as are all the fruits of righteousness) is the very ground-work of true prosperity, Ps. i. 3; fourthly, To this end did God by election before time, and special vocation in the gospel, choose us, and call and single us out of the world, John xv. 16; fifthly, It procures unto us an unstained and inoffensive glory, even until the day of Christ, Phil. i. 21; sixthly, If a man endeavour to bring forth fruit, and to walk as becomes the gospel, he is sure to speed when he hath any suit to God, John xv. 16; seventhly, Against such there is no law, Gal. v. 23; eighthly, It shall be to us according to our fruit, Jer. xvii. 8; ninthly, The fruits of righteousness are better treasures for a Christian than all riches, Jer. xvii. 10; tenthly, If we be not fruitful we shall be cut off from Christ, and utterly for ever remain frustrate of all his merits and virtue, John xv. 2, 4, 6.

2. Now for the second, The fruits that we should bear are such as these:—the forsaking of our particular beloved reigning sins, (this is all fruit, Isa. xxvii. 9;) the exercise of the true love and fear of God in a conscionable both worship of God and practice of life; the fruits of zeal for God's glory, humility, patience, and the exercise of the duties of mortification—as prayer, sorrow, fasting, and the rest; fidelity in the diligent discharge of the duties required of us in our families and calling; sobriety in the use of God's creatures, contentation, just dealing, and to be rightly ordered in matters of report; finally, works of mercy, and all duties of love.

3. Thirdly, That we may be more fruitful: first, We must labour for greater tenderness in our hearts, and plough our ground deep with long furrows of mortification—the seed will not grow if it fall upon the trampled and smooth heart of man, Mat. xiii., the stones must be taken from the roots, Isa. lxii. 10; secondly, We must learn to make God our trust, and God's promise our treasure, else in many parts of Christian fruitfulness, worldliness will teach us to deny to obey, Jer. xvii. 8, 9; thirdly, We may not neglect to send forth the leaves of profession, for, as these leaves are of medicinal use, Ezek. xlvii. 12, so they are good inducements to force a necessity of more fruit—if no profession there will be little fruit; fourthly, We should labour to be abundant in storing up of saving knowledge, for the wisdom that is from above is full of good fruit, James iii. 17; fifthly, We should seek the prayers of God's ministers for us, and subject ourselves to be directed by their care and pains, Luke xiii. 6, 7—though the ungrateful world contemns God's messengers and vine-dressers, yet the truth is, that if many times they did not rise up in the gap, woe would be unto men for their barrenness; sixthly, We should make use of our crosses, and learn humility and acknowledgment of our sins by them, breaking our hearts in God's sight, and beseeching him for the compassions of a father to be

shewed to us, that so we might, after much exercise under our crosses, 'bring forth the quiet fruit of righteousness,' Heb. xii.; seventhly, We should importune the Lord, for our sakes, to visit the great leviathan, the devil, and to receive us under his protection, to watch us, and daily to water us, Isa. xxvii. 1-4, &c.

Lastly, In the first Psalm are divers rules: first, We must not sit with wicked men; secondly, We must privately and constantly exercise ourselves in the word of God; thirdly, We must seat ourselves under the powerful ministry of the word, near the rivers of these waters of life; and lastly, We must take heed of procrastination, delay no time, but with great heedfulness respect the season, or due time of fruit—all the year is not seed-time or harvest.

4. The use is for bitter reproof of the barrenness and perverseness of our hearts. Some men are so ignorant that they know not that they owe any things of necessity unto religion. Some bear fruit, and more than enough of it, but it is only to the flesh, Hosea x. 1, Rom. vi. Some hear the preacher, with Herod, gladly, but they mend but what they list. Some rest in the means of fruitfulness. It is enough with them, for their praise,[1] that they have the means and frequent it. Some will bear fruit, but they choose which fruit; for some will do somewhat in civil righteousness in their dealings with men, but are little or nothing in sincere piety to God. Others bear fair leaves of profession in the first table, but in the second table bear such wild fruit as it is a shame to behold it in this light, and a sorrow it ought to be to them to hear God, with disdain, expostulate about it. Some are good abroad, but naught at home; but at the hands of all these will the Lord of the vineyard require fruit, and judge them according to their works.

And increaseth. This also is added in some copies. Here I observe two things: first, In what it increaseth; secondly, By what means. For the first, the word increaseth five ways:

First, In the number of hearers, so Acts ix. 31. Secondly, In the power of working, the efficacy of it is, and is felt of godly minds, more and more. Thirdly, In the fairness of the leaves of profession. It is noted of a good tree that his leaves shall not fail; and it is certain that the word maketh the glory of profession both more and more inoffensive. Fourthly, In the goodness of fruit. It causeth men to bring forth more and better fruit at the last than at the first; yea, Christians refreshed with the daily comforts of God's word, bring forth new fruit every month, Ezek. xlvii. 12. Fifthly, In the height of growth. God's children are made every day more heavenly-minded than another.

Secondly, That the word of God may increase by making us to increase in fruitfulness, we must do five things: first, We must labour to continue near the waters of the sanctuary, Ezek. xlvii., Ps. i. We should never, but in case of necessity, withdraw our hearts from the directions and comforts of a daily and settled effectual ministry. Secondly, We must take root downward, and then the world will be filled with fruit, Isa. xxvii. 6. The tree groweth two ways, upward in branches, and downward by rooting itself more and more in the earth; so ought a Christian to grow upward in the external fruits of holy life, and downwards in the roots of faith, hope, and other holy graces; and it is certain if men be careful to fasten their roots more and more, there will be a happy increase in the outward life of man. Thirdly, We must arm ourselves against the heat of tribulations, or persecutions, as against the means of failing, Jer. xvii. 8. Fourthly, We must abide in Christ, John xv. 4, labouring to nourish the sense of his presence, and the contentment arising from the communion with his members, &c. Lastly, We must be much in the exercises of mortification. "Every branch that beareth fruit the husbandman purgeth, that it may bear more fruit,' John xv. 2, 3.

Before I pass from these words it is to be observed, that he saith not they were fruitful, or increased; but the word is fruitful, &c. To note that when men have given their names to the gospel, that which befalleth them is said to befall the gospel; partly because what good men do, they do it by direction from the word, and assistance of the Spirit of Christ, and partly because the world attributes what is done by professors of the word to the word they hear. If their lives be full of good fruits, the word of God is glorified; but if they be any way vicious, the word is blasphemed, Rom. ii. 24. Then they say, This is their preaching; this comes of

---

[1] Qu. 'part'?—Ed.

gadding to sermons, and tossing of their bibles! &c.

The use is both for instruction and comfort. For instruction: therefore, God's children should 'work out their salvation with fear and trembling,' and labour to be 'filled with the fruits of righteousness,' living inoffensively, and 'holding forth the word of life' in all holy conversation, 'shining as lights in the midst of a froward and crooked nation,' Phil. i. 11, and ii. 15, 16. For comfort also, because the Lord is pleased to communicate the honour of his word to his people, so as where the word is in credit they shall be in credit; and if they be despised they are not despised alone, but the word is despised with them.

Thus of the first thing in the efficacy of the word, viz., what it doth. The second thing is upon whom it worketh, or the subject persons.

As it is also in you. Doct. It helps not us that others, though many, be wrought upon by the word, gathered, made fruitful, and increased; unless we be sure of the efficacy of it in ourselves. It had been a small comfort to the Colossians to know that the word was fruitful all over the world, if it had no power amongst them. There is a windy vanity prevails in the heads of many hearers. They think they do worthily when they commend the sermon, praise the preacher, tell of the working of the word in such and such, though they perceive not that when it is but a dead letter. Many are full-mouthed, but have empty hearts and hands; but it should be our discretion to labour the cure of this looseness and wandering of heart, and not to suffer our souls to be led aside from considering our own way by any such smooth wiles of Satan. Thus of the persons; the time followeth.

From the day. Here I observe three things:

First, That there is a season for men to be fruitful in. We are naturally dry trees or no trees. We are but dead stocks; neither if we should stand in God's orchard to all eternity, would we of ourselves bear the fruits of the gospel, or exercise ourselves in those fair fruits that are unto eternal life. If before this day the city of Colosse had been searched with lights, there would had been found no true fruits of grace or righteousness amongst them. Our season to bear fruit is, then, when God calls for it. At some time of our life, God, giving us the means, doth set before us the way of life and death, affects us inwardly with sense of our misery, or the glory of conversion, or the necessity of our repentance. Now when the axe of God's word is laid thus near to the root of the tree, it is then time to bear fruit, or else we are in danger. The consideration hereof, as it shews that the works of civil honest men are but shadows or blasted fruit, so it should enforce upon us a fear of standing out the day of our visitation. Consider with thyself, God calls now for repentance and the duties of new obedience. If now thou answer God's call, and pray God to make thee such as he requires thee to be, thou mayest find favour in his eyes; for God is 'near them that call upon him,' if they seek him in due time, while he may be found; but if thou delay, consider, first, That thy heart of itself, without dressing, will never be fruitful; secondly, That thou art not sure of the means hereafter; thirdly, If thou wert sure, yet who can prescribe unto the Most High? 'He hath called, and thou hast not answered;' therefore fear his justice. Thou mayest call and he will not answer.

Secondly, That it is exceeding praiseworthy, and a singular mercy of God, if the word of God work speedily upon us, if we yield and stoop with the first, if it make us fruitful from the first day. This lively working of the word, first, Is a seal to the word itself, for hereby it is out of all doubt that it is the true word of God; and this effectual work of grace upon our consciences doth fence us against a thousand objections about the word; secondly, It is the minister's seal,—as soon as he seeth this power of doctrine, he hath his seal from God—the fruitfulness of the people is the preacher's testimonial, 2 Cor. iii. 2; thirdly, So soon as we find the word to be a savour of life unto us, it becomes a seal to our own adoption to life; and therefore we should again, every man, be admonished to take heed of delaying the time, for not only we want the testimony of our own happiness while we live without subjecting our souls to the power of the word, but exceedingly provoke God against us. We should consider that the Holy Ghost saith peremptorily, 'Now is the axe laid to the root of the tree, and every tree that bringeth not forth fruit is cut down and cast unto the fire.' Not that he requireth present fruit, or threateneth present execution, Mat. iii. 10, John xv. 2. Neither may we harden our own hearts with presumption, because we see not present execution upon this rebellion of man against God, and the offer of his grace; for we must know that men are cut off by more ways than one. Some are cut off by death, as an open revenge of the secret rebellion of the heart, not opening when the Spirit of grace knocketh. Some are cut off by spiritual famine, God removing the means from them, or suffering them to be their own executioners, by withdrawing themselves from the means. Some men are cut off by God's fearful judgment, being cast into a reprobate sense. Some are cut off by church censures, God ratifying in heaven what is done in earth by the church.

Thirdly, Hence we learn, that if we would be truly faithful, we must be constantly so; not lose a leaf, much less give over bearing fruit, Ps. i. 3, Ezek. xlvii. 12. Sudden flashes will not serve turn. The Lord knows not how to entreat them whose goodness is but like the morning dew, Hosea vi. 4. Either (from the day) constantly, or not (upon the day) truly. Thus of the time.

Fourthly, This efficacy is limited: first, By the kind of doctrine which especially makes men fruitful, viz., the doctrine of the grace of God; secondly, By the application of it, both by hearing and knowledge; and both are limited, in that they are required to be in the truth.

That ye heard and knew the grace of God in truth. In the opening of these words I consider: first, The words apart; secondly, The doctrines out of the whole. For the first, here are three things to be considered: 1. What grace of God the gospel propounds to men; 2. What we must do that we may have the comfort of this, that we do truly hear; 3. What it is to know truly.

1. For the first, the gospel requires of men a deep sense of the singular grace or free mercy of God towards men, and that principally in five things: first, In giving Christ to mankind fallen, and finding out so happy a means of our deliverance; secondly, In accepting of the mediation of Christ in particular for the believer, in the age that he liveth in; thirdly, In forgiving sins past, through his patience; fourthly, In blessing the means, for man's sanctification; and lastly, in allowing unto men their lot in the inheritance of the saints in heaven.

2. Secondly, That we may have the comfort of this, that we do truly hear the word, seven things are to be done: first, We must deny our own carnal reason, wit, parts, and outward praises, and 'become fools that we may be wise,' 1 Cor. iii. 18; secondly, We must fear God, and set our souls in God's presence, Ps. xxv. 14, Acts x. 33; thirdly, We must come with a purpose and willingness to be reformed by it, Ps. l. 16; fourthly, We must labour for a meek and humble spirit, mourning over pride, malice, and passion, James i. 22, Isa. lviii. 15, 1 Chron. xxxiv. 27; fifthly, We must hear all, Deut. v. 27, both at all times, that is, constantly, and all doctrines that concern the grace of God; sixthly, We must hear with faith and assurance, Heb. iv. 1, 1 Thes. i. 5; lastly, We should especially in hearing wait for a blessing from God, in the particular knowledge of God's grace to us, else all hearing is to little purpose.

3. Thirdly, Men may be said to know, and yet not truly: first, When they know false things, as, in the Church of Rome, to know the doctrine of purgatory, intercession of saints, image worship, the supremacy of the Pope, or, in Germany, to know the ubiquity of Christ's human nature, universal grace, falling from grace, or that the sacraments confer to all the graces they signify, and such like; secondly, When men have the form of words, and understand not the meaning; thirdly, when the notions of the truth are entertained in the mind, and not let down into the affections, when men have knowledge in their heads, and no affections in their hearts—the law should be 'written in their hearts;' fourthly, When men know things by opinion, not by faith, as the most men know the greatest part of religion; fifthly, When our knowledge is not experimental in practice; sixthly, When men know other things, but not the grace of God to themselves.

Thus of the words apart. The doctrines follow.

Doct. 1. First, Men may hear and yet not know. Knowledge is not attained by all that hear; and this comes to pass either as a curse for men's home-sins unrepented—where manners will not be informed, there faith cannot—or by reason of pride and conceit of our own wits, and that we need not be informed. Thus the pharisees are blind, though they hear Christ himself. Or it comes to pass by reason of men's faultiness in hearing; they hear carelessly, or without application, or with prejudice, or not all; or else it is because men smother their doubts, and seek not resolution in private by conference, or seeking the law at the priest's mouth; and in many fruitless hearing is caused by want of catechising, when people are not fitted for preaching by information in the principles before.

Doct. 2. Secondly, The hearing and true knowledge of God's grace to a man in particular doth make fruitful. The salutary appearance of God's grace in a man's heart works in a man a desire and endeavour to shew all good faithfulness that may adorn that doctrine by which he comes to know God to be his Saviour. 'It teacheth men to deny ungodliness and worldly lusts, and to live godly, righteously, and soberly;' it purgeth from iniquity, and inflames the zeal for good works, Titus ii. 10–14. When God's children have the tidings of grace given unto them, it kindles in them a singular encouragement to go about God's work, and to hold out to lay the very last stone with joy, Zech. iv. 7.

Doct. 3. Thirdly, As other doctrines, so especially the doctrine of our reconciliation with God, or of our particular assurance of God's grace to us, is exceeding hard, and men are strangely turned off from the right knowledge of it. This comes to pass (where it is effectually preached) because it is hindered by common hope, and by a resolution in many to part with no sin for the attaining of it, and by a natural darkness in the understanding of man in matters of the kingdom of Christ, and by the special malice of the devil, and by pride in other knowledges; and lastly, by an incredible averseness in our natures, that will not be brought to set time apart to mind this point seriously, and to apply ourselves unto the means that might further us thereunto. Whereas if men were assured of God's favour, and possessed of saving grace, the profit of the knowledge of it would appear to be exceeding great. Though the heart of man be exceeding dull, yet it could not but marvellously refresh us to think of the pardon of all our sins; yea, if we were sure of this point, and had travelled soundly about the experience of God's grace to us in particular, it would for ever settle us in the plerophory of our religion. A man needs never care for disputes and the thousands of volumes about which should be the true church or true religion; for if a man by sound reasons from the word and Spirit of God, had gotten the assurance of God's love, he would become as Mount Zion, that could not be moved. This also would make a man able to contemn all earthly mutations, and live in firmness of heart, in some measure, out of the fear of any afflictions, or of death itself; and besides, it would preserve us from the poison and infection of earthly pleasures, and vain delights and profits. And to conclude, it is to enjoy a kind of heaven upon earth, as being an entrance into the first degree of eternal life.

When men get from under the law to live under grace, it works not only a dissolution of the dominion of sin, but a consecration of the members for the service of righteousness, Rom. vi. 13, 14; of the fulness of Christ do all the faithful receive, even grace for grace, John i. 14–16; the truth of sanctification and new obedience, together with the perfection of redemption and justification. To conclude, every faithful man may say as the apostle said, ' By the grace of God I am what I am,' 1 Cor. xv. 10.

The use is, first, for instruction: even to labour so much the more earnestly for the certainty of assurance of God's grace and free favour to us in particular, because it will make us abundant in the work of the Lord, and enrich us with those things that may further our reckoning against the last day. But that we may speed in suing for God's grace, and waiting for the tidings of his special love, we must labour to be good men, and shew it by this, that we be men of holy imaginations, Prov. xii. 2. Our understanding will never be capable of this knowledge till the evils of the thoughts be in some measure purged out and subdued. Besides, we must take heed of scorning and contemning the means of grace, Prov. iii. 34, and labour for a hatred of every sin; for till then we never get any sound experience of God's favour. So long as a man makes a mock of any sin, and securely against the light will commit it. so long he remains under power of folly and unregeneration, Prov. xiv. 6. But especially we must labour to get and grow in humility; for God bestows his graces on the humble,

1 Pet. v. 4, James iv. 6. And if God ever comfort us with his graces, let us so learn to make it our portion, and to trust perfectly upon it, 1 Pet. i. 13, as not to receive it in vain, 2 Cor. vi. 1, but obey all the counsel of God, and his ministers, that beseech us to express the power of it in our lives.

Secondly, The doctrine of the power of God's grace doth bitterly reprove four sorts of men: first, Such as neglect God's grace, and seek not any particular evidence for it; secondly, Such as fall away from the grace of God, and give over the use of the means of grace, Gal. i. 6, which apostasy many times befalls such men as will not wash off the pollution, nor by mortification stay the springing up of some bitter root or other within their hearts,—such apostates, when they were at the best, had in their hearts some imperious lusts and passions or other, that they made not conscience of to subdue, Heb. xii. 15; thirdly, Such as turn the grace of God into wantonness; men that before they have any reason of comfort, upon the bare hearing of the promises of the gospel, take liberty to live licentiously, and follow their sins with presumptuous abuse of God's mercy,—these are ungodly men, ordained before to condemnation, Jude 4; lastly, Such as cannot abide the doctrine of God's grace, but despise and hate the very Spirit of grace, —how sore shall their punishment be! Heb. x. 29.

Thus far of the thanksgiving for the principal means of grace. The instrumental follows.

Ver. 7. *As ye also learned of Epaphras our fellow-servant, who is for you a faithful minister of God;*

Ver. 8. *Who hath also declared unto us your love, which you have in the Spirit.*

He hath given thanks for the ministry; now he gives thanks for the minister, who is here described by his name, 'Epaphras;' by the adjunct love of others to him, 'beloved;' and by his office, 'a servant;' by his willingness to join with others, ὁμόδουλος, a fellow-servant; by his faithfulness in the execution of his office, 'which is for you a faithful minister of Christ;' lastly, by his love to his people, which he shews by the good report he thankfully gives of them, ver. 8.

From the general consideration of all the words I observe:

Doct. 1. First, It much matters to the efficacy of the doctrine what the ministers be. He that would profit his hearers must be: first, Able to teach; secondly, He should be beloved, not a man against whom the hearts of the people had conceived incurable prejudice, or such a one as was scandalous; thirdly, He had need to be a fellow-servant, one that will draw with others; fourthly, He must consecrate his service to God and the church; fifthly, He must be faithful; and lastly, One that will love his people.

Doct. 2. Secondly, Ministers of greater gifts, or places, or learning, may here learn how to carry themselves towards their fellow-ministers. Paul commends Epaphras, confirms and countenances his doctrine, and gives him the right hand of fellowship; which example much condemns the haughty pride and arrogancy of many great clergymen, in whose eyes their brethren are despised; sometimes swelling against them with envy; sometimes openly pursuing them with censures, especially if God bless their labours with any good success; easily setting out with the foremost to detract from their just praises for gifts, sincerity, or pains. Woe and a fall will be to the great pride of clergymen.

Doct. 3. Thirdly, The apostle strives to win a greater estimation to the minister, that so he might the better fasten their respects to his ministry,—to note that where the messenger is not in credit, the message is easily neglected or contemned. And therefore, as men would desire good success in the ministry of the word, they should labour to get and retain an honourable opinion of the ministers. And to this end consider that they are called God's coadjutors, ministers of the Spirit, God's stewards, candlesticks, the mouth of Christ, stars, angels, and have many other titles of dignity.

From these words, *as ye also have learned of Epaphras*, I observe: First, That if men would be effectually wrought upon by the word, they must plant themselves under some settled ministry. They that hear now one and then another, at one end of the quarter hear a sermon of this man, and at the other end of that man, have their knowledge much like their pains.

Secondly, He is a true member of the church that can shew sound grace and knowledge, learned of the teachers of the church. It is neither the account of the world, nor profession of true religion, nor coming to church, demonstrates necessarily a true member of the church, but the effectual subjection of the soul to be formed and wrought upon by the ministry of the word.

Thirdly, It is an ordinary infirmity in the better sort of hearers that in many points they receive doctrine upon the credit of the teachers, yielding no other reason but Epaphras taught so; which should awaken affection and conscience in ministers, out of the fear of God, and sound and infallible knowledge and premeditation, to deliver what they do deliver, and to utter nothing for certain but the word of God.

From these words, *the beloved, our fellow-servant*, I observe: First, That common affliction for the cause of God works in men tenderness of love. The prison makes a great apostle embrace with singular love a poor and mean minister. The smell of the prison and sight of the stake (if such times should ever come again) would frame a better amity amongst our churchmen; ambitious men might then lay down their personal and guileful eagerness of haste and hate; and humorous men would then be ashamed to devise how to enlarge the dissension by coining new exceptions and urging of peremptory new scruples; modest and humble men on both sides, that have sought the peace of Zion, would then have double honour.

Secondly, That he that is faithful is beloved; beloved, I say, of God and God's household. It is an ill sign in a minister that he is not sound, when he finds no tokens of God's love in his heart, nor signs of respect with God's servants in his life.

Thirdly, That to be God's servant is a high dignity. It is here the special glory of an apostle, and was acknowledged and proclaimed to be the best part of a king's title, Ps. xxxvi., the title of it; which may serve for comfort to poor Christians. They can get no wealth, offices, nor honours in the world; but here is their joy—they may get to be God's servants, which is better and more worth than all honour. Besides, it condemns the aspiring of the clergy; yet, when they have done all they can to make themselves great men, he is a better man in God's books, that by faithful service can win souls to God, than he that by his money or pains can only purchase many livings and great dignities to himself.

Which is for you a faithful minister or deacon. Concerning the word Διάκονος, rendered *minister*, it is expressly a *deacon;* and it is a title of office, service, or administration, given sometimes to Christ. He is called the Deacon of circumcision, Rom. xv. 8; sometimes to magistrates, Rom. xiii. 4; yea, sometimes to women, Rom. xvi. 1; sometimes to a special calling or sort of church officers, Phil. i. 1, 1 Tim. iii. 8, 12; sometimes to the ministers of the gospel, both ordinary and extraordinary; so Timothy is a deacon, 1 Tim. iv. 6; so Judas, Acts i. 17, 15. But the doctrine I observe is:

That every faithful minister is Christ's deacon; and this may comfort painful ministers; for to be Christ's deacon is no base office, or to be called so a title of disgrace; for it is a title given to Christ and the greatest magistrates. And concerning them is that promise that he that receiveth one of them in Christ's name shall not be without his reward, Mark ix. 41. Besides, Christ saith of them, that where he is, there shall his deacon or servant be, and his Father will honour him, though the world do not, John xii. 26. Further, it may refresh them that they are said to be 'deacons, not of the letter, but of the Spirit,' 2 Cor. iii. 6-8. Lastly, We may see what power these deacons have, Mat. xxii. They call, they persuade; they are heard of the great king, if they complain and inform; and they bind men hand and foot and cast them into utter darkness. Only, if ministers would have the privileges of Christ's deacons, they must put on and practise their properties: first, They must become as little children, for humbleness of mind and confidence in God's fatherly care and providence, and for freedom from malice, Mark ix. 35, 36; secondly, They must follow their master Christ, in doctrine, in life, and in sufferings, John xii. 26; thirdly, 'Seeing they have this deaconship, as they have received mercy, they should not faint, but cast from them the cloaks of shame, and not walk in craftiness, nor handle the word of God deceitfully, but in declaration of the truth should approve themselves to every man's conscience in the sight of God,' 2 Cor. iv. 1, 2, so as for the daily expressing of their doctrine upon the hearts and lives of the people, their people might be their epistle, 2 Cor. iii. 2, 3.

Thus of the seventh verse. Out of the eighth verse I observe divers things.

First, From the word *declared*, as it is here used and applied to reports, I note that those things are to be reported and spoken that may give light to the hearers. A good man's report tends to clear things in the minds of them that hear him; there should be light and a lantern in our words, Prov. vi. 23. To this end we should use wisdom and truth and meekness when we speak; wisdom, by preparing ourselves to speak; truth, to report things as they are; and meekness, to avoid passion; for anger is a great darkener. We should also take heed of divers sins in both tables that greatly corrupt the hearers, not only in the general, but in this that they greatly darken and make muddy the understanding of man. As in the first table, discourses or disputes of atheism against the word, religion, or ordinances of God, apologies for idolaters or idolatrous religion in whole or in part, the very naming of vices or idols without disgracing or hating of them, impatience or murmuring against God, and such like, and, in the second table, flattery, tale-bearing, false accusing, rash judgment, answering of matters before they be heard, are great darkeners of the understanding.

Secondly, In that Epaphras, intending to complain of them for their corruptions in opinion and worship, doth here first declare their praises and graces of God's Spirit; it shews that it is a worthy grace to be apt to express others' just praises, especially when we are to speak of their faults; for that will shew that we are free from envy, ostentation, or disdain, and that we seek not our own things, that we are not suspicious, nor think evil, nor rejoice in evil.

Love in the Spirit. Love is either in God or in man; in God there is the personal love of Christ, the love of the creature, Φιλοκτισις, the love of man, Φιλανθρωπια, and the love of goodness or good men, Φιλαγαθια. In man there is both the love by which he loves God, and the love by which he loves man. I take it, here it is meant of whatsoever love the Spirit worketh in man. Of love I have spoken at large before; here only I note briefly two things in general: first, The necessity of love; secondly, The trial of it; both in the negative. For the first: If the true love of God and God's children be not in us, we have not faith, Gal. v. 6, nor the Spirit of God; for love is the fruit of the Spirit, Gal. v. 22, 2 Tim. i. 7; nor the seal of our election, Eph. i. 4; nor a pure heart or good conscience, 1 Tim. i. 5; nor strength to hold out against errors, 2 Thes. ii. 10. And for trial: first, of our love to God. We must know that he loves not God that will not come to Christ for life, John v. 42; that keeps not his commandments, John xv. 10; that is ashamed of the cross and profession of Christ, Rom. v. 5; that loves not the word, so as to hide, as precious treasure in his heart, the instructions and comforts of the word, 1 John ii. 6; that is not inflamed and inwardly constrained to an ardent desire of holy duties in that place God hath set him in, 2 Cor. v. 13, 14; that serves the lust or love of his profit, sports, and carnal delight, 1 John ii. 15. And for trial of our love to men, he loves not his neighbour: first, That cannot do it in the Spirit, that is, in spiritual things and from his heart, according to the directions and motions of God's Spirit; secondly, That doth or worketh evil to his neighbour, Rom. xiii. 10; thirdly, That wilfully will offend his brother in a thing indifferent, Rom. xiv. 15; fourthly, That will not pray for his neighbour, Rom. xv. 30; fifthly, That is not prone to shew mercy, 2 Cor. viii. 8.

Quest. But how must I love my neighbour?

Ans. As Christ loved us: and that hath four things in it; for Christ loved us first, and though we were his inferiors, and for our profit, and with an everlasting love; so should we: first, We must love with a preventing love; secondly, We must love, though they be meaner persons in place or gifts than we; thirdly, We must love them for their profit and good, not for our own; and lastly, We must love continually and fervently.

Ver. 9. *For this cause we also, since the day we heard of it, cease not to pray for you, and to desire that ye might be fulfilled with the knowledge of his will, in all wisdom and spiritual understanding.*

Ver. 10. *That ye might walk worthy of the Lord, in all pleasing, being fruitful in all good works, and increasing in the knowledge of God.*

Ver. 11. *Strengthened with all might, through his glorious power, unto all patience and long-suffering with joyfulness.*

These words are the second part of the preface, wherein he sheweth that he prayed for them, which he both generally affirms, and specially declares.

The general affirmation is in these words: 'For this cause we also, since the day we heard of it, cease not to pray for you.'

The special declaration is in the words that follow: 'And to desire that ye might be fulfilled with the knowledge of his will;' and so forward to the end of the 11th verse.

In the affirmation are three things: first, An intimation of a reason, 'for this cause;' secondly, The notation of time, 'since the day we heard of it;' thirdly, The matter affirmed, 'we cease not to pray for you.'

In general we may plainly observe that the desires of our hearts and endeavours of our lives ought not to be employed for our own good only, but for the good of others. We are neither born, nor born again, for ourselves. Sanctified and holy men have been full of constant and ardent affections and desires after the good of God's children: 'the manifestation of the Spirit is given to every member to profit withal,' 1 Cor. xii. 7. Religious love seeketh not her own things, 1 Cor. xiii. We should not seek our own things, as many do, but that which is Jesus Christ's, viz., that which tends to his glory, and the profit of his members, yea, Christians should 'serve one another by love.' He is not of God that hath not holy affections to promote, so far as in him lieth, the good of God's children, 1 John iii. 10. 'Herein are the children of God, and the children of the devil (usually) known:' certainly that which any man is in religion, he is relatively; if not fit to serve the body, then not fit to be of the body; he is not a saint, that seeks not communion of saints.

Uses. This may serve: First, To shew the misery of such as have no inflamed desires after the good of God's children. Secondly, It may give us occasion to examine ourselves what good the body of Christ reaps by us. If any Christian of less power, gifts and means in the world, ask, what good can I do to Christians? I answer, if thou canst do nothing else, thou canst pray to God for them, and desire their good, rejoice in their prosperity, and mourn for their miseries; neither let this be thought a mean and unprofitable service to the body, for we see here a great apostle employing himself about such works; yea, thou dost benefit the body by keeping a holy order in thine own work, walking inoffensively. If one stone fly out of the building it may breed great annoyance to the whole. Thirdly, This should teach us to avoid what lets our desires or abilities to serve the brethren by love, and what may wrong the body. Take heed of worldliness, even these carking cares or plodding thoughts about earthly things; use the world, but serve it not. Take heed of irreligiousness, or the common profaneness of the world. Take heed of rash censuring, and the customary liberty of speech to judge, and masterlike to tax the actions of others. Lastly, Take heed of presumptuous and scandalous courses of life. And here also may be gathered a comfort to afflicted consciences that are distressed because they find not what they would in themselves. They must know that one great way of trial of sincerity is by the constant uprightness of their heart in the desires of good to the church and people of God. And therefore, though they cannot speak so much good of themselves as were meet, yet it is a great grace of God, that they have inflamed affections to wish all spiritual prosperity to God's people, and to bless them in the name of the Lord.

For this cause. Doct. When we see the word of God beginning to work effectually in any people, and that they wax fruitful, it is the duty of all that love Sion, to bestir themselves, and cry mightily to God with incessant prayers for them. If it be asked, what we should pray for, or wish unto them? I answer, we should pray: first, That God would restrain the devil and all wicked men, that profession be not dishonoured in the birth of it by scandalous persons, for it is one of the first practices of the devil to thrust up wicked men into profession, that so the glory of sincerity might be darkened; secondly, That the word might have free passage without interruption or hurtful opposition. Seldom doth powerful preaching make a division in the heap, but the devil and devilish men strive to wring the fan out of Christ's hand, that the winnowing may cease. The doctrine that separates the precious from the vile, and without respect of persons yields comfort to the gracious, and terrors as the only present portion of the profane, is exceedingly opposed of the world; thirdly, That they may grow in grace. But, to omit other things, the apostle here shews, by his own example, that we should pray: first, That they may truly 'know the will of God' in Christ; secondly, That they be discreet and 'wise' in carriage, as well as in 'understanding;' thirdly, That they may 'walk worthy of the Lord,' &c.; fourthly, That they may 'increase in knowledge;' fifthly, That they might persevere, being strengthened with God's might; lastly, That they may lead a 'patient and joyful' life. And we should be thus careful of the good of others, both because God requires it, and the saints have practised it; and besides, if thou have any grace, thou standest or fallest with others, in respect of the credit of profession.

Since that day that we heard of it, we cease not to pray for you. First, from the coherence of these words with the words following, we may note the great efficacy of prayer, how mightily it prevails with God. It is a way by which a Christian may exceedingly help himself, and pleasure his friends: 'the prayer of the righteous availeth much,' both for helping of the body, and healing of the soul, James v. 16. If two sound-hearted men agree in earth in a suit to God the Father in heaven, they prevail with incredible success, they get what they would have, Mat. xviii. 19.

And that we may be encouraged to prayer, there are divers things that might undoubtedly persuade us to resolve of the efficacy of prayer. First, God's commandment; certainly God will not require prayer but that he means to hear it, Ps. l. 15. Secondly, The nature of God; he is a Father, and hath the compassions of a Father. 'Though Abraham would not know' his seed if they had suits to him, 'and Jacob be ignorant of his posterity, yet God will hear and redeem,' Isa. lxiii. 16. Though a mother should forget her motherly compassions, yet God will not forget his, Isa. xlix. 15; and therefore, if earthly fathers, that have a great deal of ill nature in them, can give good gifts to their children, and that because their children ask them, how much more shall God our Father, who is perfectly compassionate, give good things, yea, the best things, yea, the very fountain of all good, his Holy Spirit, if we ask him? Mat. vii. 9. Thirdly,

The manner of God's presence of grace. When we have any suits, he is not far off, or hard to come to, as earthly princes are, and great men in the world many times; but he is 'near to all that call upon him in truth,' Ps. cxlv. 18; yea, for more assurance of this, that he is ready to receive petitions, it is said, 'His ears are open to the cry of the righteous,' he is so far from being absent, that there is not so much as any little impediment in his ear. God is ever ready to hear, if our hearts were ready to pray. Fourthly, The property of God's liberality. He holds it a great blemish and dishonour to his bounty, either to deny when he is asked, or to reproach when he hath given; either to accept against the person, or to stick at the greatness of the gift, James i. 5. Fifthly, The assistance of the Spirit of adoption; 'The Spirit helps our infirmities, though we know not how to pray as we ought,' yet that shall not let audience; for 'The Spirit itself will make request for us, even in the sighs which cannot be expressed,' Rom. viii. 26. Sixthly, The merits of Christ and his intercession. He hath prayed for us, so as 'what we ask the Father in his name, he will grant it,' John xiv. 13, 14. Seventhly, The hate God bears to the enemies of his people. God's servants shall speed in their suits, even because of them that rise up against them. Lastly, Our prayers are furthered by the very faith and holiness of our godly and spiritual ancestors; the posterity speeds the better for their sakes; yea, without question we speed the better in England because we are the seed or successors of the martyrs.

Object. But I have prayed for myself and others, and yet find not success.

Sol. First, If thou speed not, it is either because thou art not a righteous person, Ps. xxxiv. 16, cix. 7, or thou art disordered in thy carriage in the family, 1 Pet. iii. 7, or thou didst not continue in prayer, Luke xviii. 1-8, or thou dost ask amiss.

Quest. But how may I know whether I did ask amiss?

Ans. Thou didst ask amiss: first, If thou didst pray and doubt, James i. 6, Job xxi. 15; secondly, If thou didst make prayers thy refuge, but not thy recompense,—when thou camest to pray, thou consideredst what thou didst want for thyself, not what thou shouldst render to God—thou usedst prayer to serve thy turn, but when thou hadst sped, thou didst not return by prayer to render unto God his honour, Ps. cxvi. 12; thirdly, If thou didst not make conscience of the use of other ordinances of God, for God will not give all to any one ordinance; fourthly, If thy prayers were ignorant, proud, hypocritical prayers, Mat. vi.; fifthly, If thou wast not in charity, but broughtest thy gift, and didst not forgive, or seek reconciliation with thy brother, Mat. v.; sixthly, If thou didst ask of God for wrong ends, or wrong things, as to spend on thy lusts, James iv. 3, or for temporal things only or chiefly, Hosea vii. 14; besides, many times it comes to pass that men speed not because they are not humble. We should so prize and esteem holy things, as we should exceedingly rejoice if we could get but the crumbs that fall from the Father's table. This humility is ever joined with great faith and wished success in all suits to God. Again, it is to be noted that men may be deceived about the success of prayer, for the decree for our succours may go forth at the very beginning of our supplications, though the knowledge of it be not revealed unto us till afterwards. Further, God heareth prayers diversely; sometimes he heareth to grant the very thing we desire; sometimes he heareth, and granteth, and giveth, not the very things we desire, but that which he holds to be best for us, and for the distress we are in; so he was said to hear Christ, Heb. v. Lastly, God doth hear and grant, and yet defer to give, and that for our great good many times. He defers that he may prove us, that our faith may be the more kindled, that his benefits may be more sweet when they do come, and that we may know by the want that it is his gift when they are bestowed, and that we may be more careful of the good use of his graces, gifts, and benefits, when we have them. Thus of the coherence.

For you. *Ibid.* We are bound to pray for others, as well as ourselves. In this place I consider in this point only two things: first, The kinds of prayers for others; secondly, The sorts of persons for whom we must pray.

For the first, I observe here in the original two words—προσευχαὶ and αἰτήματα, in the translation, *prayers* and *desires.* As I take it, all the sorts of prayers for others may be referred to these two heads, and these two differ not so much in the matter as in the motives to prayer: προσευχαὶ, *prayers*, are such suits unto God as we are vehemently moved to by the contemplation of God and his attributes. The difference between εὐχή and προσευχή is somewhat shadowed out by *oration* and *adoration.* Αἰτήματα, here rendered *desires*, are all suits unto God, arising from the deep sense of man's estate, either in dangers, wants, or blessings; and under this kind may be placed the three sorts of prayers in 1 Tim. ii. 1; for our desires for others are either deprecations, in which we desire God to turn away or keep from them some great evil; or intercessions, which are either complaints of wrongs, or most importunate supplications unto God for their conversion and the pardon of their sins; or, lastly, thanksgivings for God's mercies and blessings.

Secondly, To the question, for whom we must pray. It is shortly answered, 1 Tim ii. 1, 'for all men,' excepting dead men, or such as sin unto death, or such concerning whom the will of God is revealed for their perdition, as the Man of sin, 2 Thes. ii.; so as also by *all men* we understand all sorts of men, not all the particular men of every sort, for we may not desire salvation for all the men that God hath made, (universally considered,) seeing the counsel of God is unchangeably passed concerning reprobates. But that which in this text is principal is, that ministers and people must pray one for another. Ministers must pray for their people; thus do the apostles in every epistle; yea, Samuel saith, 'God forbid I should cease praying for you,' as if he knew it to be a detestable thing for a minister to be so reckless or careless, as either not to pray or not to continue to pray for his people. The people must also pray for their ministers, and that especially for these things: that God may deliver them from the rage of the disobedient and the practices of their enemies, Rom. xv. 30; that God would open their mouths and give them utterance, Eph. vi. 19, with a fitness to discover the secrets and mysteries of Christ, Col. iv. 3; and that their gospel may run and grow, both in efficacy and credit, 2 Thes. iii. 1, 2; yea, inasmuch as they labour about saving other men's souls, the people should by prayers labour to further the salvation of their ministers.

We cease not. Note, first, He that loves the people of God truly, loves them constantly.

Secondly, That a heart truly sanctified is much

in prayer, cannot give it over. It is a woeful thing to neglect prayer, but how cursedly miserable is their case whose hearts rise against prayer, and cannot abide it, but persecute it in others!

Thirdly, The not ceasing in prayer hath in it constancy and perseverance in prayer, and teacheth that as we are bound to pray, so are we bound to persevere in prayer; yea, if we must not cease to pray, it implies: first, That we must pray in all places; secondly, That we must watch to pray; thirdly, That we must believe and hope we shall obtain what we pray for; fourthly, We must not appoint God either time or means; fifthly, That we must pray with all manner of prayers; for all these five things are requisite, or, if any of them be wanting, there will not be constant and faithful prayer; yea, not ceasing, notes that there is singular comfort in prayer, else men would never hold out.

Object. But not ceasing implies multiloquy, vain babbling.

Sol. Not so; a man may pray earnestly and often, and yet not use many words.

Object. But to pray without ceasing is to be tied to use idle repetitions; for how can men be furnished and find matter to pray so often and so much?

Sol. A Christian is furnished many ways with needful occasions of continual prayer: first, He is tied to a daily sacrifice, both morning and evening, by prayer and praises; secondly, He finds continually new mercies, and those require new songs of praise and prayer, Ps. xl. 4; thirdly, As his knowledge increaseth by the use of the means, he finds an increase of matter to drive him to prayer, and make him pray better; fourthly, New infirmities breaking out in himself and others, and that daily, gives an occasion to renew his suits to God; fifthly, The creatures and his calling must be 'sanctified by the word and prayer;' sixthly, Variety of crosses breaking in upon him gives him cause to run to God for the sanctifying or removing of them.

Let such pray seldom as think they owe God no sacrifice, or receive no blessing from God, or care not for knowledge, or find no infirmities in themselves, or have no crosses, or need no blessing upon their callings and labours; but let all that fear God stir up themselves to pray without ceasing, because God requires it, and hath made gracious promises,—because they find daily necessities, and may hereby exercise their faith, and shew their love to God and to others, after the example of the saints, and by the motion of the Spirit of adoption, which will not be idle in them.

Thus of the affirmation, the declaration follows: *That ye might be fulfilled with the knowledge of his will in all wisdom and spiritual understanding, that ye might walk, &c.*

In this declaration he describeth the knowledge he prays for by five things:

1. By the object of it, 'The will of God.'
2. By the parts, 'Wisdom and understanding.'
3. By the end, 'That ye might walk,' &c., ver. 10.
4. By the cause, 'His glorious power,' ver. 11.
5. By the effects, 'Patience, long-suffering, joyfulness.'

The object is described in these words, *fulfilled with knowledge of his will.*

And here is, 1. The object itself, 'will of God;'
2. The means of apprehension, viz., 'knowledge;'
3. The measure, 'filled with it.'

Of his will. Will is a property in God. Properties in God are either personal or essential. The properties of the person are such as these: in the Father, to beget and send forth; of the Son, to be begotten and sent forth; and of the Holy Ghost, to proceed. The properties of the essence are of two sorts. Some note the essence, as they say, *à priori;* and these are such properties as are incommunicable, that is, are so in God as they are in no creature, as infiniteness and simplicity, free from all mixture, parts, or composition. Some note out the essence *à posteriori;* and these are such as are first and principally in God, but, in the second place, communicable to the creature; and of this sort are power, wisdom, and will in God.

The will of God is either the will of God's good pleasure, or the will of his pleasure.

The will of God's good pleasure is in things where the effect is good.

The will of his pleasure is in things where the effect is evil, and so he wills in respect of the end, but not in respect of the means to the end, as sin, and some miseries.

The will of God's good pleasure is here meant, and this is secret or revealed. The revealed will is here meant:

The revealed will of God is of four sorts. It is, first, His determining will concerning us, what shall become of us, Eph. i. 5 ; second, His prescribing will, where he requires either obedience—and this is revealed in the law—or faith and repentance, and so it is revealed in the gospel, Eph. i. 9, Acts xxii. 9 ; third, His approving will, and that is that will by which he graciously accepts, and tenderly regardeth, those that come to him in faith and repentance, Gal. i. 4, Mat. xviii. 14, John i. 23 ; fourth, His disposing will, and this is the will of his providence, 1 Cor. i. 1, Rom. i. 10. The prescribing will of God is wholly revealed ; the other three but in part, and by consequent.

Thus of the will of God.

Knowledge. This is the grace by which the will of God is apprehended. The original word, Ἐπίγνωσις, is three ways accepted. Sometimes for *knowledge*, so ordinarily ; sometimes for *acknowledgment*, as it is translated in these places, Luke i. 4, 1 Cor. xvi. 18, 2 Cor. vi. 9 ; sometimes for *knowing again*. All three senses may be here well considered of.

First, Of knowing God's will. Here I consider three things : first, What we must know ; secondly, Why, or the motives to persuade to seek for knowledge ; thirdly, The means to be used thereunto.

For the first, We must know that God doth approve of us in Christ—the approving will. And this is so necessary that our hearts can never be rid of the occasion of fear of our reprobation till we do know it, 2 Cor. xiii. 5. Secondly, We must know what God hath determined of us—his determining will. To this end hath God given us his word and Spirit, that we might know what he hath prepared for us if we love him, 1 Cor. ii. 9. Thirdly, We must labour to know what he requireth of us—his prescribing will. It is said of David, Acts xiii. 22, that he did all the wills of God ; and so should we also labour to know, and by practice express, the power of all God's wills ; and the rather seeing we have fulfilled not the will, but the wills of the flesh from time to time, Eph. ii. 3.

For the second, There are many things might inflame us to the desire of knowledge ; for this is the glory of God's elect, not riches, not strength, not carnal wit, Jer. ix. 24. It is the singular gift of God's grace, and special portion of his chosen, Mark iv. 11. It is a great sin and grievous curse to want it, Hosea iv. 11 ; but a damned plague to contemn it, Job xxi. 14. Knowledge! Why! It is more excellent than all things ; all but loss and dung in comparison of it, Phil. iii. 9. Without it zeal is little worth, Rom. x. 2, and sacrifice is in vain, Hosea vi. 6. What shall I say ? ' This is eternal life, to know God, and whom he hath sent, Jesus Christ,' John xvii. 3.

Thirdly, What must we do that we may attain to the knowledge of God's will ? I answer : first, We must get to be true members of Christ, for ' no man knoweth the Father but the Son, and they to whom the Son revealeth him,' Mat. xi. 27 ; secondly, We must conscionably practise what we do already know by the light of nature or general light of religion, and then Christ's gracious promise lieth for the further revelation, even of saving knowledge, John vii. 17 ; thirdly, Men never soundly prosper in the attainment of saving knowledge till they have been in the furnace of affliction of conscience,—after men have been wounded in spirit, and their hearts smitten within them, they will then know, and endeavour themselves to know, Hosea vi. 1-3.

But this question may be excellently answered out of two places of the apostle Paul :

First, in Rom. xii. 1-3, the apostle shews that a man must do five things if he would know what the good, and acceptable, and perfect will of God is : first, He must devote himself to a religious course of life—this he calls sacrificing of ourselves to God, ver. 1 ; secondly, He must no more follow the fashions of the world ; thirdly, He must by prayer and the use of all the means repent for the sins of his mind, and get a new mind to put his knowledge in, ver. 2 ; fourthly, He must be proving and trying, often examining himself, and trying his evidence concerning the faith of God's good will to him as the hope of his glory, ver. 2 ; fifthly, He must not be over-curious to pry into such knowledges as concern him not, but be wise to sobriety, labouring especially by hearing and practice to get within compass of the knowledge of his own justification, sanctification, and salvation, ver. 3.

Again, in the 5th of the Ephesians, ver. 14 to 22, to gain the true light of Christ, and understand God's will, the apostle shews that we must do nine things: first, We should awaken ourselves out of the spiritual slumber of our hearts, labouring, by prayer and meditation of our danger, to force open the eyes of our minds,—'awake thou that sleepest,' ver. 14; secondly, We must forsake the company of wicked and carnal men, that have no taste or feeling of things that belong to the kingdom of God,—'stand up from the dead,' ver. 14; thirdly, We must 'walk circumspectly,' (precisely, ἀκριβῶς, the original word is,) being resolved to make a conscience of all our ways, or else in vain to go about to dig for knowledge, ver. 15; fourthly, We must allow much time for hearing, and reading, and conference, even as men that mean to 'redeem' all the time past they have unprofitably spent, ver. 16; fifthly, We must bring a mind willing and desirous, in all humility, to understand God's will,—a froward spirit cannot prosper, or a man wise in his own conceit, ver. 17; sixthly, We should in special take heed of 'drunkenness,' or any kind of tippling, 'wherein is excess,' ver. 18; seventhly, We must labour for a cheerful spirit and a glad heart, and shew it by 'singing of psalms, making melody in our hearts to God,'—a heavy spirit is dull of apprehension, ver. 19; eighthly, We must 'give thanks' for all things, readily acknowledging every mercy, and rejoicing for any success in the means, ver. 20; lastly, We must 'submit ourselves one to another,' ever willing to learn in anything of anybody, Eph. v. 21,—he that scorneth information is a fool.

Thus of knowledge.

Secondly, It is not enough to know, but we must acknowledge, the will of God: that is, by a constant and open diligence in the use of the means, and conscionable heedfulness even in all things in practice, we must hold forth the light of the truth, in a religious profession of it, in communion with the saints, and separate from sinners; this is required in God's elect, as well as faith, Titus i. 1. Neither is it a precise humour in some few, but God 'would have all come to the acknowledgment of the truth,' 1 Tim. ii. 4; not to hear it or to know it only. Without this, I will not say absolutely a man cannot be in Christ, but this I say, with the apostle, 'a man cannot be perfect in Christ, and of ripe age,' Eph. iv. 13. By this acknowledgment we escape an exceeding great deal of filthiness that is in the world, 2 Pet. ii. 20; and because that many men will by no means be drawn to acknowledge the way of God, therefore, by a just judgment of God, they are delivered up to a reprobate sense, Rom. i. 28. Only two things are to be urged upon professors herein: first, That they do soundly repent of their sins before they make profession, and enter upon acknowledgment, 1 Tim. ii. 4, or else acknowledgment will be a veil for filthy hypocrisy; secondly, That they take heed of sinning presumptuously after acknowledgment,—fear the curse, Heb. x. 26.

Thirdly, We must know again. This hath three things in it: first, We must be often viewing and looking over our evidence, to be sure of the whole and every part of it, as we would do if we had assurances for matters of the world; secondly, Because sins after calling do greatly darken knowledge, therefore we must not only renew our repentance, but our knowledge also; thirdly, We must know the truth of God, not only in our minds, by understanding and thinking of it, but we must know it again in the affections of our hearts, in respect of sense and feeling; and again, after that, in the practice of our life; for that is experimental knowledge, and the very power of godliness.

Use. This doctrine of the knowledge of the will of God reproves many sorts of men: first, Such as desire not knowledge at all, Job xxi. 14, and so perish for want of it, Hosea iv. 6, 2 Thes. i. 8; secondly, Such as sometimes desire knowledge, but they will not use the means, or not constantly, or not all the means; thirdly, Such as will know something of the prescribing will of God, but never heed his approving or determining will; fourthly, Such as, though they use the means for knowledge, yet will at no hand abide acknowledgment; lastly, It reproves the carelessness even of God's people many times, neglecting to 'make their calling and election sure,' by looking often over their evidence, and renewing their knowledge, and labouring the cure of their natures from slumber and relapses. Thus of knowledge.

Filled, or fulfilled. From the observation of the measure I note four things: First, That we must not rest in beginnings,—we must be 'filled with all knowledge,' Rom. xv. 14; not only get grace and truth, but be filled with it, John i. 14; so full of wisdom, Acts vi. 3, 5, of faith and power, Acts vi. 8, of good works, Acts ix. 36, of joy in God's favour, Acts ii. 28, of all hope, Rom. xv. 13, full, even with the fulness of him that filleth all things, Eph. i. 23. But it is contrary with the most men, for we may complain out of divers scriptures, even of them that they are filled, not with grace, knowledge, faith, works, &c., but with the leprosy of all spiritual infections, Luke v. 12, with all deceit, Acts xiii. 10, with wrath, even when they hear God's word, Acts xix. 28, with worldly grief and passions, John xvi. 16, with all kinds of unrighteousness, Rom. i. 19, with drink, Eph. v. 18, with the measure of their fathers' sins, Mat. xxiii. 32; yea, so wretchedly vile are the lives of many, that they shew themselves to be filled with the devil himself, Acts v. 3; but the works almost of none are perfect, or filled before God, Rev. iii. 2.

Secondly, That there is something in grace or knowledge still wanting,—we 'know but in part.' Man's heart may be compared to a vessel, the means to a pipe, the Spirit of God to the wheel that beats the water into the pipe, the minister is the servant that opens the cock; and then the reason why we know but in part is, either the cock always runs not, or not always in the same measure; and sometimes our vessels are filled with other things, as the cares and lusts of the world, and so they run over; and usually our vessels run out, and lose what we receive by the means.

Thirdly, The knowledge of the will of God and spiritual things only can fill and satisfy the heart of man, all else is mere vanity and vexation of spirit, Eccles. i. 2. Earthly things cannot fill, neither the knowledge of them, nor the use or possession of them, because they are not infinite nor eternal; besides, there is nothing new, nor are they of a like nature with the soul; they are enjoyed with vexation and much satiety, for our affections will not love them still; yea, most an end the vanity of men's minds so turneth devices, concerning their knowledge or use, that death or loss takes them or us away, before they can find out that way of using of them that could satisfy and fill the heart.

Lastly, Nothing but the will of God binds conscience. The apostle of purpose layeth the foundation in the preface, concerning the knowledge of and resting upon God's will, that so he might the more easily beat down their traditions and philosophical speculations, of which he meant to entreat in the next chapter. Now, if this doctrine be true, as it is most true, then Apocrypha scripture, councils, fathers, and princes' laws do not bind further than they are agreeable to God's will; and therefore much less popes' decrees, traditions, and human inventions.

Thus of the object of knowledge.

In the next place it is described by the parts of it, in the next words, 'in all wisdom and spiritual understanding,' where the apostle shews that saving knowledge hath two parts, viz., understanding and wisdom. Concerning the difference between the two original words, in this place rendered *wisdom* and *understanding*, there is a great stir amongst interpreters. Some say that the one proceedeth out of the principles of the law of nature, and the other out of the principle of faith. Some take the one to be a knowledge concerning the end; the other, of things that are for the end. Some think by *understanding* is meant apprehension; and by *wisdom* is meant judgment or dejudication. Some think that *synesis*, rendered *understanding*, receiveth the will of God in the whole; and that *sophia*, *wisdom*, conceiveth it in the parts, and with weighing of all circumstances; by the first they consider what is lawful, and by the second what is expedient. Some say that the one of them conceiveth the object of felicity; the other, the means by which men attain it. Some think they differ thus: that the one understands of God absolutely, by scripture, as he is; and the other considers of God by relation, or comparison with the creatures, by experience, as he is tasted to be good. But the plainest and soundest difference is this: that understanding is contemplative knowledge, but wisdom is active knowledge; the one gives rules for practice, the other for judgment and contemplation. But before I consider of them apart, I observe two general doctrines:

First, That saving knowledge and wisdom is not natural, but from above, and had only by Christ; here it follows faith and love. It is wrought by the power of the gospel; it is prayed for; and lastly, it is plainly said to be spiritual. See more, James iii. 17, 1 Cor. ii. 14, 2 Cor. i. 30, Titus iii. 3; and it may serve for many uses.

First, It should enforce us to labour to become spiritual men, as we would desire to have anything to do with the knowledge of God's will; for if we be not more than natural men, it is certain we know not the things of God. Be sure, therefore, thou be no natural man.

Quest. How may a natural man be known?

Ans. He is a natural man: first, That hath in him only the spirit of the world, 1 Cor. ii. 12; secondly, That knows not that wisdom of God that is in a mystery, that is, his reconciliation and salvation by Christ, 1 Cor. ii. 7, x. 14; thirdly, That loves not God, ver. 9, as they do not that love not the word, people, and way of God; fourthly, That knows not the things given of God by the Spirit, ver. 12; fifthly, That accounts spiritual things foolish things, and religious courses foolish courses, ver. 14; sixthly, That hates sincerity, and walks after his own lusts, Jude 18, 19.

And it is worthy to be noted, that the apostle, when he foretells of these wicked loose persons and profane men living in the church, he saith, they make sects. And it is most sure that not only heretics and false teachers, that draw men out of the bosom of the church, to divide them from our assemblies, but even wicked men, that wallow in sin, make sects and schism, and division in the church, though they otherwise come to the word and sacraments as the people of God do; for the word is seldom effectual in the working of it in any place, but we may find the devil stirring up carnal and natural men, that strive by all means to pursue such as desire to fear God, lading them with reproaches, and blowing abroad slanders, and wilfully both disgracing them and shunning their presence; and when they have done, call them sectaries and other heretical names; them, I say, that excepting their care and conscience to walk uprightly with God and unrebukable amongst men, live in peace by them; but though men are deceived, God will not be mocked. These are the men that God means to indict for making of sects in the church, as well as heretics.

Secondly, Seeing true wisdom is from above, it should work in us a dislike both of hellish wisdom and earthly wisdom. By hellish wisdom I mean such wisdom as was in the priests when they killed Christ, 1 Cor. ii. 8; or that was in Pharaoh, who counts it to deal wisely to oppress God's people, Exod. i. 10. It is devilish wisdom to be cunning or artificial in hiding the practice of sin; it is devilish wisdom to have skill in defending sin; it is devilish wisdom that is used in the refining of sin; as, for example, drinking of healths began to grow to that detested head, and was accompanied with that filthy villainy and abomination, in respect of the excess of it, that certainly the devil should never have gotten the most men in a short time to have had anything to do with such a damned beastliness. Now the devil, not willing to lose his homage and sacrifice, inspires some men to bring in a liberty to drink in less glasses, and with allowance of choice of drinks or wines, and now the sin is refined, it goes current.

Earthly wisdom is of two kinds; for either it is a skill to get goods, or else it is human learning and policy, both allowable in themselves, but neither to be too much liked or trusted to; for as for the skill to get riches, 'what would it profit a man to win the whole world, and lose his own soul?' And the praise of human wit, learning, policy, &c., is much curbed by certain terrible places of scripture. The conceit of this wisdom makes the cross of Christ of none effect, 1 Cor. i. 18. And a man may have a great measure of it, and be famous, and yet be without God, without Christ, and 'without the covenants of promise, and without hope in the world,' Eph. i. 12; for 'not many noble, not many wise, hath God chosen,' 1 Cor. i. 26, 27. Yea, God many times hides the mysteries of the kingdom of grace from these great wise men, Mat. xi. 27, and sets himself of purpose to stain their pride, to destroy their wisdom, and to infatuate their counsels. Where is the scribe (learned in the scripture)? where is the disputer of this world (skilful in human learning and policy)? hath not God (to vex the very hearts of these men) tied conversion of souls, ordinarily, to the foolishness of preaching? 1 Cor. i. 19, and ii. 6.

Doct. 2. It is not enough to get piety unless we get wisdom also, 1 Cor. i. 24, 30, Acts vi. 3, Eph. i. 8, 17.

Use is: First, For confutation of those that hold all labour for the attaining of spiritual things to be folly, of most men those to be fools that make such ado about the use of the means of salvation. But it is certain that Christ, that gives godly men righteousness, gives them wisdom. Religion doth not make men foolish, but gives wisdom to the simple, Ps. xix. 7. Secondly, Professors should be advised to make conscience of discretion in their carriage as well as holiness; and to this end they should take heed: 1. Of pettishness and peevishness, a vice which should be only found in the bosom of fools, Job v. 2; 2. Of conceitedness, a foul vice, to be so wise in their own conceit that their own ways should always so please them that they think better of themselves than of 'seven men that can give a reason,' Prov. xii. 15, and xxvi. 12, 16; 3. Of rash meddling with other men's business, or prying into their estates, Prov. xvii. 24,—men's eyes should not be in every corner of the world; lastly, Of unadvised openness in all companies, without respect or heedfulness, to pour out all their minds, Prov. xxix. 11.

Thus of the general doctrines.

The first part of saving knowledge is here rendered *understanding*, and is contemplative knowledge.

Contemplative knowledge hath in it two things—apprehension and meditation; that is, the power to discern doctrine, and the power to meditate of it. Both are needful, and in both men are exceeding wanting, especially in the power of meditation. If you ask me what the object is about which we should meditate, it is answered before; it is the will of God, determining, approving, prescribing, and disposing. And it is no wonder that men get so little knowledge, or are so unable for contemplation, because every one is not capable of it. 'The scorner' may, in a passion, 'seek wisdom, but he cannot find it,' Prov. xiv. 6. Besides, the means must be used: especially in contemplation, it is exceeding hard to hold any course constantly, but the ground must be from matter of prayer, or hearing, or reading. Further, many things are required to fit a man to capableness and power of holy contemplation: First, Chastity of heart and affections; for such as are 'carried about with lusts,' are 'ever learning, but never come to the knowledge of the truth,' 2 Tim. iii. 6, 7. Secondly, Meekness, or rest of heart, from the hurry of disordered affections and troubled passions. Hasty affections and a foolish mind are inseparable. He that is passionate can lift up no holy thoughts, but he can easily 'exalt folly,' Prov. xiv. 29. Thirdly, A good mind, that is, an understanding not exercised in imagining and plotting of evil. Men of wicked imaginations are utterly disabled for contemplation. Fourthly, Humility, or a tender sense of one's own wants and unworthiness. The proud conceited man, for matter of meditation, is of an empty mind, unless it be that they 'dote about questions,' or 'strife of words,' or 'vain disputations,' that tend to nothing but strife or vain ostentation, 1 Tim. vi. 4, 5. Besides, a heart fatted and fleshed with presumptuous hopes, or profits and pleasures, and hardened through long custom and practice of sin, is almost wholly blinded in the things that belong to the kingdom of Christ: 'These men have eyes, and see not; and ears, and are as if they heard not,' Mat. xiii. 14.

To pass from this point of knowledge contemplative, I conclude only with the consideration of the 8th of the Proverbs, where it is the drift of the Holy Ghost to persuade men to seek to store their hearts with knowledge, both for sense and use. Wisdom cries to be heard. God would fain fasten knowledge upon all sorts of men. Now if any should ask why wisdom is so importunate, or wherefore they must set all aside to get her, there are three reasons given: first, Because we are naturally foolish, and not wise in heart, there is no inward substance of sound knowledge in us, ver. 5; secondly, The things to be imparted are the most excellent in heaven and earth, ver. 6; thirdly, No knowledge but this, but it is stained with error or lewdness. Now, in the scripture we are sure of two things—truth and purity.

Object. But the doctrine of religion, as it is revealed in scripture, is exceeding cross and contrary to our natures.

Sol. It is answered that 'there is no frowardness in it;' it is in us, not in the doctrine itself, ver. 8.

Object. But the study of saving knowledge is exceeding difficult.

Sol. That is answered, ver. 9: 'My words are

all plain to him that will understand, and straight to him that would find knowledge;' if there were a constant desire and endeavour in men, they would find great success.

Object. But it is not a profitable course, nor gainful.

Sol. That is denied, ver. 10, 11: 'Knowledge is better than silver, or gold, or precious stones;' and it is more thrift to get it than to get riches.

Object. But I see that many that follow sermons, and study the scriptures, are very indiscreet, and men of no reach nor parts.

Sol. It is answered, ver. 12, that 'wisdom dwells with prudence' or discretion, and finds forth knowledge and counsels: and if men were compared, in their present knowledge, with what they were before, it would appear that they have gotten more discretion, &c., than ever they had, and therefore it is a mere imputation.

Object. Many great professors are men of wicked lives.

Sol. Ver. 13, 'The fear of the Lord is to hate evil, as pride and arrogance, and the evil way, and a mouth that speaketh lewd things;' and, therefore, if any such be of wicked lives, they are hypocrites, thrust into profession by the devil, of purpose to shame the study and endeavour after saving knowledge.

Object. But the most that follow sermons and read the Bible so much are base persons, and men of no fashion in the world.

Sol. That is denied, ver. 15, 16. For the holy wisdom of the word hath been the fairest ornament, and help, and support to kings, princes, nobles, and judges: 'By me kings reign, and princes decree justice.'

Object. But this knowledge fills men with terrors and melancholy.

Sol. That is denied; for it is a lovely study: 'I love them that love me.' It is only terrible to such as so love their sins as they will not part with them.

Object. It is a knowledge never attained in any perfection.

Sol. That is denied too, ver. 17: 'They that seek me early shall find me.' Men get no ripeness in knowledge, because when they use the means their heads are full of cares or lusts, &c., or they wait not upon the opportunities and advantages of the means: they seek not early.

Object. But, at the least, it is an enemy to thrift, and a hinderance to men's outward estates.

Sol. That is false too, and he gives two reasons for it, ver. 18-20. For, first, The 'most durable riches' (that is, better than all gold or pleasure) 'is righteousness,' and this is gotten by the knowledge of the word; secondly, That that most an end impoverisheth men is the hand of God or of men; and sin usually and disorder is the original cause of all losses or poverty. Now wisdom causeth a man to walk in the ways of righteousness, and so to 'inherit substance;' and as God sees it meet for them to 'fill their treasures.'

Object. But a man can never observe the rules of holiness required in the word, and urged upon men by preaching.

Sol. The word doth not only shew men what they should do, but it gives power to do it: it 'causeth men to walk in the way of righteousness,' ver. 21. Lastly, to put all out of doubt—Knowledge: Why! It is the very glory of Christ, and dwelt with God in the very beginning of the world; yea, it was begotten from everlasting when there was no depths, nor the mountains settled, nor the earth framed, &c., ver. 22-32. The exhortation is in the end of the chapter, that as men would assure themselves to be God's children, or to be blessed in their ways, they should hear instruction in this point and be wise, and daily watch at the gates of knowledge, so should they get the life of grace, and obtain the favour of God, when others, that despise knowledge and the means of it, shall be so wounded in soul that they shall certainly die eternally, ver. 32-35.

Thus of contemplative knowledge.

Wisdom or active knowledge follows. The consideration hereof is exceeding difficult, for it lieth in the prescribing of the discretion in practice. Wisdom in practice stands principally in two things: first, In order of practice; secondly, In the specialties of good behaviour.

Wisdom's order lieth in the prescribing of rules concerning the priority and precedency of things in practice. She tells what must be first done, and chiefly: and thus she gives seven rules:

1. That heaven be sought for before the earth, and remission of sins in Christ before any other thing, Mat. vi. 33.

2. That men choose present affliction rather than future; rather suffer now with hope of reward in another world than take pleasure now to endure the pains to come, 2 Tim. ii. 3-8.

3. That God be served before man, whether it be other men or thyself. Thus it is wisdom to let God have the first place in the morning, before thou serve thyself in thy calling; thus it is wisdom to obey God rather than man, when the commandment of God and the commandment of man lieth before thee and are contrary one to another, Acts v.; thus, also, the duties of the first table are to be done before the duties of the second table in equal comparison, Mat. xxii. 38, 39.

4. That death be provided for before life: first, learn to die, and then it is easy to learn to live, Deut. xxxii. 29.

5. That opportunity be preferred before time. Work in harvest: walk while ye have the light; delay not whilst thou hast the means: seek God whilst he may be found.

6. That the first place in dignity over any be accounted the greatest place of service unto all, Mark x. 44.

7. That in duties to men, we first regard to practise the duties of the fifth commandment, Eph. vi. 3.

Secondly, concerning behaviour: wisdom binds the heart, the tongue, the conversation.

First, in binding the heart to good behaviour, she chargeth five things:

1. That in the dearness of affections and clearness of knowledge, in the purity of our thoughts, God be loved above all, Mark xii. 33.

2. That we draw weapon upon every imagination, or what else exhausts itself against contemplation, and the obedience of Christ, never ceasing till those inward sins be led away captive, 2 Cor. x. 4.

3. That we grow in meekness, as we grow in knowledge, James iii. 13; and that we be wise to sobriety, desiring the knowledge only that can profit us, Rom. xii. 13.

4. That we rest not till we be clearly resolved in religion, God's love, and our own salvation.

5. That the fear of God, throughout all our whole life, be our chief treasure, Isa. xxxiii. 6.

Secondly, in binding the tongue to the good behaviour, she chargeth:

1. That our words be few when we speak either to God or men, Eccles. v. 1. James i. 19.

2. That we do not so much as whisper against the Lord's anointed, Eccles. x. *ult*.

3. That we presume not to come near the sacred name of God to take it up in vain, Deut. xxviii. 58, Third Commandment.

4. That we censure not the just, nor justify and defend the wicked. It is not safe for the prince to smite with the tongue the meanest servant of God, Prov. xvii. 15.

5. That we answer not a matter before we hear it, Prov. xviii. 13.

6. That we judge nothing before the time, 1 Cor. iv. 5, and speak evil of no man, but be soft, shewing all meekness to all men. Titus iii. 2, 3.

7. That we seek a due season for good words, Prov. xv. 23.

Thirdly, in binding the conversation to the good behaviour, she chargeth:

1. That men walk exactly, accurately, precisely: it is translated *circumspectly*, Eph. v. 15.

2. That with all delight men set their hearts to keep God's commandments and do them, Deut. iv. 5, 6; and by good conversation men shew their works, James iii. 13.

3. That men meddle with their own business, 1 Thes. iv. 11.

4. That profit and pleasure give place to godliness, Ps. iv. 6, 1 Tim. vi. 6.

5. That men trust no fair pretences, but have some sure trial before we commit ourselves to any, John ii. 24.

6. That we fear and depart from evil before the cross come, Prov. xvi. 6, Isa. xxvii. 11. It is everybody's course to talk of repenting when misery is upon them; but a wise man will redeem his own sorrows, and fear God while the curse hangs in the threatening, though it come not yet into execution.

7. There is a special wisdom in knowing how to give place to the time, so far as may stand with keeping of faith and a good conscience. Thus

Paul forbears to speak directly against Diana of the Ephesians for three years, Acts xix. 10, 26.

8. That temporal things be ordered to conformity with God.

Hitherto of the parts of saving knowledge.

Ver. 10. *That ye might walk worthy of the Lord in all pleasing, being fruitful in all good works, and increasing in the knowledge of God.*

In these words the end of knowledge is at large set down. To this end we should fill ourselves with the knowledge of God's will, that our conversations might be rightly ordered, to the glory of God, the profitable pleasing of others, and the storing up of good fruits unto eternal life, in the salvation of our own souls. Neither doth he think it enough for those that have by the gospel gained much knowledge to do good or live well, but they must raise their endeavours to an eminence; and this he expresseth in three forms of speech:

First, They must *walk worthy of the Lord.*
Secondly, They must walk *in all pleasing.*
Thirdly, They must *be fruitful in all good works.*

And if any should ask how all this can be attained, he answers in the end of the verse, when he saith, *increasing in the knowledge of God.*

The doctrine out of the whole verse is, that the life of Christians ought to answer their profession, knowledge, and the means they enjoy. In the enlarging hereof I consider four things: 1. The motives to excite us to a holy endeavour after innocency; 2. The causes why so many men in the visible church, enjoying the means, have attained to so little innocency; 3. What we must do that we may thus walk; 4. The benefits would be gotten by a holy care of Christian innocency.

The motives are such as these:

1. We are not in our own power, to live to ourselves, but are tied 'to live to him that died for us,' 2 Cor. v. 15.

2. Our souls and bodies are destinate to incorruption in the heavens; and therefore we should set ourselves so to live, for this short space in this world, as we might deliver them up undefiled in the day of the Lord.

3. 'Have we ever found unrighteousness in God?' Jer. ii. 5. Shall we then serve Satan, that never did us good, and forsake the Lord our God? When our hearts are tempted to sin, we should say, Shall I thus requite the Lord for the innumerable benefits he hath bestowed upon me?

4. The long night of sin and ignorance, and hellish darkness and danger, by the light of the gospel, by the means of Christ our Saviour, is past, and a short season remains unto us to glorify God, and work out the assurance and fruition of our own salvation. Shall we not then arise from the sleep of sin, and now cast away the works of darkness? Is it not now time to arm ourselves against the sluggishness of our own natures, and the corruptions that are in the world, to walk honestly, as becomes this day of grace and favour? Rom. xiii. 11, 12.

5. The miserable events of serving the flesh might move us. If we have the means, and make a show, and yet live carnally and scandalously, we may deceive ourselves, but God will not be mocked; we shall reap as we sow—if we 'sow to the flesh,' we shall 'of the flesh reap corruption,' Gal. vi. 7, 8. And 'for these things the wrath of God cometh upon the children of disobedience,' Eph. v. 6. And therefore let no man deceive us with vain words; and if Jerusalem will not be instructed, my soul (saith the Lord) shall depart from her, and she shall be desolate, as a land that no man inhabiteth, Jer. vi. 8. And contrariwise, if we would sow to the Spirit, and not be weary of well-doing, nor faint or fail, in due season we should reap,—reap, I say, of the Spirit, even life everlasting, Gal. vi. 7, 8.

6. We should be much moved by the dreadful relation we stand in to God, to Christ, to the Holy Ghost, and to the church;—to God, for we are his servants, and therefore ought to be holy as he is holy, 1 Pet. i.; we are his children, and therefore ought to prove it by our obedience, Mat. i.;—to Christ, for he hath washed us in his blood, and shall we pollute ourselves again? he was in his own practice a perfect pattern of innocency, and shall we not learn of him? Mat. xi. 28; we are his members, shall we shame and dishonour our head? our Saviour is in heaven, and shall we be buried, like moles, in the love of sensual and earthly things? or rather, ought not our affections and conversations to be where Christ is, even in heaven, at the right hand of the Father? Col. iii. 1, Phil. iii. 20;—to the

Holy Ghost; we are his temple, and shall we defile God's holy place?—to the church, which is the city of the holy God, which he hath consecrated to himself, and therefore were it not wickedness to profane it with impurity? Let us live as the citizens of God, Eph. ii. 19.

Lastly, In the 1 Thes. iv., I find an exhortation to holiness, and it is enforced by five reasons: first, It is 'the will of God,' ver. 3; secondly, A holy life is an honourable life, ver. 4; thirdly, They are Gentiles, not Christians, that live profanely, ver. 5; fourthly, God is a certain 'avenger of all unrighteousness,' ver. 6; and, finally, We are 'called unto holiness,' ver. 7.

Secondly, If it be asked, how it comes to pass that such multitudes of people, living in the bosom of the church, are touched with so little care of holiness of life? I may answer divers things:

1. The veil of ignorance lieth upon their hearts, Isa. xxv. 7, and gross darkness still covers those people, Isa. lx. 2, 3. Though the light be come, and the glory of the Lord, yet for the most part these men abhor the light, Job xxiv. 13, and therefore are their ways dark and slippery, Ps. xxxv. 6.

2. Men's hearts go after their eyes, and men's senses are made masters of their lives, Job xxxi. 7; and therefore are their affections only stirred with carnal things; they take their directions from their own flesh, and walk in the way of their own lusts, Eccles. xi. 9.

3. Many times their brethren deceive them, Job vi. 15; I mean, they are misled sometimes by their own mistaking and misapplying of God's promises, and sometimes by the sinful daubing of wicked teachers, that set themselves to 'strengthen the hands of the wicked, and discourage the hearts of the righteous,' crying, 'Peace and safety,' where there is no peace.' Ungodly men these are, that gainsay the doctrine of those faithful men that would cure this sinful generation by a meet severity of doctrine.

4. The most men see no necessity of the restoring of their souls; they cannot be persuaded of the necessity of regeneration and conversion by the word, and when they come to the means, they seek not to God to lead them, Ps. xxiii. 3.

5. Men are double-hearted, and divide one part to the flesh and the world, and another to God. The more open part of their lives some pretend to direct with some respect of holiness; but the secret and inward part is full of all rottenness; and yet men will not see that God and sin, God and riches, God and the flesh, cannot be served both of one man at one time.

6. They are incorrigible, will neither be healed by the word, nor be forced by the works of God: 'They will not understand, though all the foundations of the earth be moved,' Ps. lxxxii. 5.

Thirdly, That we might attain unto this holiness of conversation:

1. We must grow out of liking with our own ways and our present carnal course, and forsake that way and return from it, Prov. ix. 6, Ezek. xviii.

2. We must get out of the way of sinners; for he that walketh with the ungodly will be like them, Ps. i. 1.

3. We must mightily labour for knowledge, and be much in contemplation, and to this end exercise ourselves in God's word day and night, and dwell in God's house. Coherence with verse before, and Ps. i. 2, Prov. viii. 20, and ii. 11, 12, Ps. lxxxiv. 4, 5, Isa. ii. 3; yea, we should by conference ask the way one of another, Jer. vi. 16.

4. We must get into Christ, for he is the way; and till we labour our ingrafting into Christ, and settle ourselves to seek a Saviour, even unto us by faith, all our works are in vain.

5. That our conversations might be more holy and unrebukable, we should first labour to get holiness into our hearts; for if grace be within, duties will be without; if corruption be mortified in the soul, which is the fountain, it will have no great sin in the life, which is the stream which flows from the heart. First, we should guide our hearts into the way, Prov. xxiii. 19, for thereout cometh life, Prov. iv. 23.

6. We must submit ourselves to God's corrections; 'learn obedience by the things we suffer,' Heb. v. 8; obey the checks of our conscience, and be contented to 'eat the bread of affliction,' Isa. xxx. 20; 'bear the words of rebuke and admonition,' 1 Thes. v. 13; for he that refuseth correction will certainly go out of the way of life, Prov. x. 17.

Lastly, we should 'commit our way to God,' and

by constant and daily prayer beseech him that he would shew us the way and lead us forth, Ps. xxv. 4; and then that he would stay our steps in his paths, that our feet do not slide, Ps. xvii. 5; and to this end that he would remove out of our way all impediments, and every lying way, Ps. cxix. 29; and that he would daily quicken us in the way against the sluggishness of our own natures, Ps. cxix. 37; and bend our hearts to his holy fear; but especially every morning we should beseech God so to assist us, and guide and strengthen us, to do the duties of the day, and that he would see to and defend the thing of the day in his day, 1 Kings viii. 58, 59, by the virtue of Christ's intercession and his words, which are near unto God day and night.

Fourthly, Thus doing, and endeavouring ourselves to know and do God's will:

1. The Lord would know us by name, and take notice of our ways, even with the knowledge of approbation, Ps. i. 6.

2. Our lives would be full of joy and cheerfulness; yea, they that have tasted of the joys of a crown, shall leave the throne and palace to seek the sweet delights of the faithful, and to sing their songs, Ps. cxxxviii. 5.

3. God would walk in the midst of us, Lev. xxvi. 11.

4. Yea, he would keep his covenant and mercy with us, 1 Kings viii. 23.

5. We would be protected against all hurtful troubles, being either preserved from them, or in them. If we walk in the day we shall not stumble, John xi. 8, 9; yea, though we went through fire and water, yet God's holy presence and strong arm would be with us, Isa. xliii. 3, Ps. xxiii. 3; yea, we might dwell with everlasting burnings—that is, within the knowledge of God's terrible presence and sight of his great judgments, when the hypocrites of the world would be afraid, Isa. xxxiii. 14–16.

6. Or if there were sorrows and griefs upon us in this world, yet heaven shall come, and we shall rest in the beds of eternal ease; whatsoever betide us, we shall not lie down in sorrow, Isa. lvii. 2, l. *ult.*

7. Thus to live is to rule with God, and to be faithful with his saints, Hosea xi. 12.

8. Thus shall we scape the vigour of the law, Gal. v. 18, and the flames of hell, Rom. viii. 1.

Lastly, If we continue faithful to the death, there is laid up for us a crown of life, Rev. ii. 10.

Thus of walking or holy conversation in the general; now, in particular, that we might walk in a holy eminency, three things, as is before noted, are here urged:

First, That we should 'walk worthy of the Lord,' that is, so to know and consider the singular mercies of God in Christ as to endeavour to express our thankfulness in the obedience of our lives, in such a measure as might become the mercies of God. Before I open the words further, I consider in the general two things:

1. That the obedience of the faithful is raised by the contemplation of the mercies of God; which should teach us, as we desire more to abound in good fruits, so to be more in the assurance and often meditation of God's love to us. More knowledge of this kind would work more obedience; and a confused knowledge of God's mercy is usually accompanied with an unconstant obedience. Besides, this reproves the dangerous and sinful abuse of God's mercies in the common people, that use to plead their safety, notwithstanding their sins, by the alleging of the mercy of God to sinners; whereas, it is most certain that the right knowledge of God's mercy would make men afraid to sin: 'there is mercy with thee that thou mayest be feared,' saith the psalmist, Ps. cxxx. 4; and it is the infallible sign of a true convert that he doth 'fear God and his goodness,' Hosea iii. 5. Every man can fear God and his justice, especially in some kinds of judgments; but a child of God doth never more tenderly fear God than when he hath greatest taste of God's mercies.

2. The papist would find merit of works in this verse, both because holiness of life is so much urged, as also because here is the word *worthy* used; as if the apostle should grant that they might be worthy of and merit the blessing of God.

My answer is: First, That merit cannot be founded upon scripture; and secondly, It cannot be founded upon this scripture. For the first, we cannot merit for many reasons in scripture; first, we are 'not our own' men, we are so tied unto God that gave us being in nature and grace, that when we have done all we can do, our own mouths must say 'we are but unprofitable servants,' Luke xvii. 10. Secondly, All our sufficiency to do any good is of God, not from ourselves, 2 Cor. iii. 5, Phil. ii. 13. Thirdly, God gains nothing by us: 'if thou be righteous, what givest thou to him? or, what receiveth he at thy hands?' Job xxxv. 7. Fourthly, Men talk of their well-doing, but what shall become of their sins? If the papists will first go to hell for their sins, and stay all that eternity there, then afterwards if God create another eternity, they may have hearing to relate what good they have done. The curse of the law will be first served; the punishment of Adam's one sin barred the plea for any reward for former righteousness. Fifthly, What comparison can there be between the glory of heaven and our works on earth? Rom. viii. 18. Sixthly, It is worthy to be observed, that it is mercy in God to set his love upon them that keep his commandments, Exod. xx., Commandment ii. Seventhly, We are so far from meriting, that we are taught to pray God to 'give us our daily bread;' we have not a bit of bread of our own earning. Eighthly, The sanctification of the most righteous is but begun in this life. Lastly, Unto all these reasons add the further testimony of these scriptures—Dan. ix. 9, Rom. iv. 5, and xi. 9, 1 Cor. iv. 4, Phil. iii. 8, 9.

Secondly, This place hath no colour for merit; for, to pass over that reason that the scripture requireth good works, therefore our works merit, as a most false and absurd argument, the words *worthy of the Lord* cannot be applied to merit by any means; for inasmuch as the Lord had bestowed many of his favours already upon them, and given his hand and writing and seal for the rest, they cannot by any works afterwards be said in any colour to merit what is past. They are urged, Mat. iii., to 'bring forth fruits worthy repentance.' Now it were absurd to think that the fruits afterwards borne should merit repentance which God gave before, for that is to affirm that not only a wicked man might merit his own conversion, but that he might merit it by the works he would do after his conversion, which I know not that any papist will affirm; and the like reason is there of the phrase here used.

Quest. But, letting the papist go, what is it to walk worthy of the Lord?

Ans. It is so to cleave unto God, that we refuse not, out of the holy estimation of God's free mercies, to forsake ourselves and the world, and to testify our obedience to the law and Spirit of God in uprightness with all thankfulness. But that this may appear more plainly, if we would walk worthy of the Lord:—

1. In general, our righteousness must exceed the righteousness of the scribes and pharisees, Mat. v. 20; we must be so far from resting in the custom and practice of the vile sins that abound in the world, that we must not be satisfied with this, that we be civil honest men, and well thought of in the world; for God's mercies challenge more at our hands than civil honesty.

2. In particular, if we would walk worthy of God:—

(1.) We must walk with God in the sense of God's presence, and in the light of his countenance, so knowing his love as we forget not his presence, Gen. xvii. 1. And because the wandering and unmortified heart of man is not easily brought to this, therefore we must humble ourselves to gain a better ability to walk with our God, Micah vi. 8.

(2.) We must set the law of God, as the only rule of our actions, always before us, Ps. cxix. 1; and by all means be careful to obey the motions of God's Spirit, even the law in our minds, that is, to walk after the Spirit, Gal. v. 21, and according to the Spirit, Rom. viii. 1.

(3.) We must labour to glorify God, by endeavouring by an open light to approve ourselves to the world, in shewing the power of God's grace in our works and the newness of our lives, James iii. 15, Mat. v., Rom. vi.

(4.) We must be contented to deny our own reason, wit, desires, delights, and profits, and to take up any cross God shall lay upon us, Luke ix. 24.

(5.) We should go beyond all civil honest men in this, that we would respect all God's commandments, and make conscience of every sin, by prayer and endeavour to avoid it, and to obey God both in our souls and bodies, and in every part of both.

(6.) Lastly, We should so admire God's love, in delivering our souls from death, and our feet from falling, &c., that we should seek God's face in the light of the living, and never to come empty-handed, but God's vows should be upon us, and we should ever be rendering praise. Thankfulness is all we can give to God, Ps. lvi. 12, 13.

In all pleasing. This is the second thing required in our conversation; we should not think it enough to live justly and religiously, but we must live pleasingly also. And this is true: 1. In respect of God— 'let us have grace that we may so serve God, that we may please him,' Heb. xii. 18, 1 Cor. vii. 31; 2. In respect of our own conscience, preserving the rest and goodness of the conscience; 3. In respect of men—thus the wife careth to please her husband, and the husband to please his wife, 1 Cor. vii. 33. It is not enough to be persuaded that that we do be good, but we ought to look to it that it be pleasing. So in all duties to God, and in our carriage to men.

Quest. But what should we do that we might so serve God as please him too?

Ans. This is answered in divers scriptures.

1. Be sure thou be not in the flesh, for no such can please God, Rom. viii. 8; and they are in the flesh that can relish nothing but fleshly things, that take no care to provide for the life of grace and peace of conscience, ver. 6; that will not be subject to the law of God, ver. 7; that have not the spirit of Christ, ver. 9; and that die not to sin, ver. 10.

Object. But there are many wise men to whom these signs agree; and may not they for their good parts otherwise be pleasing to God?

Sol. No; so long as they are fleshly persons, their wisdom, bred in the flesh, is so far from pleasing God, that it is enmity to God.

2. Thou must let the will of God, revealed in his word, be the rule of all thy actions, 'a light to thy feet, and a lanthern to thy paths;' for in the word is contained both what he requires and what will please him.

3. Thou must make conscience of little sins as well as great sins. If a man break the least commandment, and then by doctrine or defence maintain it to be a small matter, our Saviour Christ shews that this is not only displeasing to God, but it will cause God to cast men out of heaven with indignation; on the other side, whosoever shall make conscience to observe God's commandments in the things the world counts less matters, and shall constantly by doctrine or profession declare his sincerity herein, he shall be exceeding pleasing to God, and God will shew it by making him great in the kingdom of heaven, Mat. v. 19. What commandment could be less than the commandment about the not eating of blood, and yet with many words their obedience herein was urged, and that with this reason, as they would have all things go well with them and theirs, and do that which is pleasing or right in God's sight, Deut. xii. 23–26.

4. Thou must desire and pray for the best things; thou must so think of profits and pleasures of this world, as especially thy heart must desire and thy lips request of God the wisdom and grace that is from above. It did exceedingly please God that Solomon asked wisdom, and not riches or long life, 1 Kings iii. 9–11.

5. Thou must get a humble and contrite spirit, a heart able to see and hate sin, and mourn over it; and with a tender sense of thine own wants and unworthiness to implore God's favour, and the renewing of his mercies.

6. Thou must so profess respect of piety, as thou be careful in all things to deal justly and truly with men, delighting in all the occasions and means to shew mercy. He cannot please God that doth not endeavour to please men. Sacrifice is an abomination when men do not judgment and justice, Prov. xxi. 3; and God delights in men that will deal truly, Prov. xii. 22. If a man will deal justly, and love mercy, not be merciful only, and when he hath occasion to come to God in the duties of piety and worship, will come in all humility and contrition of heart, this is that, saith the prophet Micah, that is required; yea, that is good, that is exceeding pleasing and acceptable to God, Micah vi. 5–7.

Thou must be tender-hearted and merciful, to supply the necessities of the saints; for works of mercy are odours of sweet smell, sacrifices acceptable, well-pleasing to God, Phil. iv. 18.

7. Thou must take heed of such sin as God hates with a special hatred; for there are some evils, which a man being guilty of, God will at no hand be pleased with him; as First, The sins of the third commandment, swearing and cursing, and the like; for God hath told us before, that what sins soever he will bear with, yet he will 'not hold us guiltless if we take his name in vain,' Command. iii., Deut.

xxviii. 58. Secondly, Lukewarmness in religion, when men are neither hot nor cold; this is so exceeding loathsome upon God's stomach, he cannot be at rest till he have spued such persons out. Thirdly, For a man to bless his heart when God curseth, and to plead his hopes when God threateneth, Deut. xxix. 19. Fourthly, To fear God by men's traditions, Isa. xxix. 13. Fifthly, Presumptuously to break God's Sabbath, Jer. xvii. 27. Sixthly, Through impatience or unbelief in adversity to withdraw ourselves, Heb. x. 35, 36, &c., and without faith it is impossible to please God. Seventhly, To offer unto God the blind, the lame, and the sick, the torn, and the corrupt thing, Mal. i. 8-14. Eighthly, To be found in the fashions of the world, either in life or attire, Rom. xii. 2. Ninthly, Out of frowardness and malice, to cross and persecute such as fear God. God these please not, Thes. ii. 15, 16.

Thus of walking in all pleasing in respect of God.

Quest. 2. What must we do that we may walk pleasingly amongst men?

Ans. I consider of this first generally, then more particularly. That we may please men we must observe these rules:—1. We must be careful to please God, else it is just with God, that though we strive to please men yet we should not attain to it, because we are not in the first place careful to please God. 2. We must get that philanthropian love of men into our hearts, but especially philadelphian, the love of the brethren; for this engenders care and diligence to please, and makes the labour thereunto seem no baseness or burden. 3. In the general corruption of our callings we must live innocently. Samuel is much set by, and pleaseth the people, when he stands by Hophni and Phinehas, men so egregiously corrupt. 4. If we would please in conversing, we must learn to bear infirmities, Rom. xv. 2. 5. We must practise those virtues that especially win favour, as courtesy, meekness, candour, faithful dealing, though it be to our hindrance; we must give soft answers, overcome evil with goodness, be slow to wrath, and forgive, and not revenge. 6. We must hate those vices, and avoid them, which in conversation appear hateful amongst men, as backbiting, Rom. i. 29, 1 Tim. v. 13, Prov. xxvi. 20; discovery of secrets, Prov. xi. 13; bitter words, Eph.

v. 3, 4; boasting, Prov. xxvii. 1, 2; suspiciousness, Jer. xiii.; rashness in reproofs and admonition, offensive carriage, 1 Cor. x. 32; and the stirring of the infirmities of others, Gen. xiii. 8.

In particular, we must be careful to please in the family, in the church, in the commonwealth. In the family: 1. The governors must labour to walk in all pleasing; and to this end they must govern in the Lord, and cast the impression of religion upon the souls of their people, that the reason of their obedience may be the will of God; they must retain wisely their authority; it is not the way to please to loose the reins, and lose their authority; they must take notice of virtues as well as vices, and reprove in love, not in passion, and avoid that behaviour that irritates and provokes to wrath.

2. Inferiors, if ever they would please God, must be careful to please their masters, parents, and husbands, as bearing the image of God; and to this end they must pray God to make them able both to obey and please; they must be teachable, and not such as must be continually told of the same fault; they must avoid answering again, for as a sullen silence is hateful, so prating and haste to answer doth provoke, Titus ii. 9, 10. Lastly, They must avoid such sins as prove in their places specially hateful, as pride, lying, unfaithfulness, viz., to be such as cannot be trusted in anything, stubbornness, slowness, especially when they are sent upon business.

As in the family so in the church: ministers must walk in all pleasing; and to this end they must practise what they preach, and avoid envy, passion, contention, and partiality; they must be wise and gentle, apt to teach and instruct in meekness, though they be opposed. 2 Tim. ii. 24, 25; they must be vigilant, sober, of good behaviour, given to hospitality; they must not be pot-companions, or quarrelsome, or covetous, more desiring and delighting in the gain of the benefice than the profit of the people's souls; they must order their families as well as themselves, and keep their children in subjection and gravity, 1 Tim. iii. 2-4. Peace, peace, and daubing with untempered mortar, will not make them pleasing, though many strive to win applause by such daubing; for the conscience of the men that are so soothed doth secretly contemn these plausible seers.

The hearers also must strive to please their teachers, and that they may do so, they must yield them meet honour, and sufficient maintenance; but especially they must labour from the heart to yield obedience to the doctrine of their teachers, for that pleaseth a faithful minister more than all dignities or riches.

The magistrate must strive to be pleasing to the people; and, for that purpose, they must be men fearing God, Exod. xviii., studious of the scriptures, Joshua i. 9, lovers of the good, Micah iii. 2, just, hating covetousness, Exod. xviii., lovers of the commonwealth, industrious to acquaint themselves with the estate of their flocks, walking in and out before the people with all wisdom, courage, and gravity, careful to purge out those vices which, as evil humours, disease the public body, for this easeth and pleaseth the body afterwards. Such as will charge and remunerate as well as punish, countenance the good as well as restrain the evil. Such as in factions and emulations will cleave to neither side. Men that conceive a general care for the persons, goods, and good name of the subject, guiding them to holiness as well as happiness, to sanctity as well as safety.

The people, again, must strive to please their rulers, by reverencing them, and obeying them, though against their profit, with constancy and for conscience' sake. They must pray for them, and speak well of them. It was without doubt a great contentment to David, that whatsoever he did pleased the people, 2 Sam. iii. 36.

Thus of walking in all pleasing in respect of others.

Thirdly, We must walk in all pleasing towards our own consciences, providing by all means for the rest, peace, and contentment of our own hearts within; and that this inward peace and pleasing may be had, many things are profitable and available. 1. Sorrow for our sins; for this sorrow will be turned into joy, John xvi. 20; whereas the end of all carnal laughter will be sorrow and unquietness of heart, Luke vi. 25; and there is no peace to the wicked, and he is wicked that is not contrite in heart, Isa. lvii. 21. 2. The faith or belief of our justification in Christ; for being justified by faith our souls have peace, Rom. v. 1. We must seek the rest of our hearts in God's favour in Christ, for he is the Prince of peace, Isa. ix. 6. 3. The love of God's law, for 'great peace and rest have they that love God's law,' Ps. cxix. 165; yea, it is added, 'and nothing shall offend them.' 4. Diligence and constancy in the use of God's ordinances. It is a secret joy to the heart of every one that is a friend to the bridegroom to hear the bridegroom's voice, John iii. 29; and to be much in prayers is a way to be much in joy, John xvi. 24. 5. Meekness; while angry and wrathful persons fret themselves to their own singular evil, meek men shall delight themselves in abundance of peace, Ps. xxxvii. 8, 11. 6. Just dealing in all businesses with all men. For 'the work of righteousness is peace, and the effect of righteousness is quietness and assurance for ever,' Isa. xxxii. 17. Lastly, Would we attain that peace and pleasing contentment that passeth all the understanding of the carnal man, we must take heed of worldly care: ' in nothing be careful.'

Object. But we have so many crosses, how can we but care?

Sol. ' Let your requests be known to God.'

Object. We have prayed and are not rid out of them.

Sol. Add supplication to your prayers.

Object. We have prayed, and that earnestly, and daily, and with much importunity, and yet are disquieted still.

Sol. Be thankful for the mercies thou hast; unthankfulness hinders the restful success of prayer, Phil. iv. 6, 7.

Fruitful in all good works. The Son of man is ascended, and hath given authority and gifts unto men, and unto every servant his work. He calls for obedience, and detests sleeping, and requires all watchfulness to the speeding of all his works, and ' what he saith to one, he saith to all, Watch,' Mark xiii. 35–37. This is shewed unto all that turn unto God, that they must do works meet for repentance, Acts xxvi. 20; considering the season, that it is now high time to wake out of sleep; the night is far spent, and the day at hand, and therefore we should arm and address ourselves to cast away the works of darkness, and to labour in the light, Rom. xiii. 12, 13. Good works are the best apparel of Christians professing godliness, 1 Tim. ii. 10, and their most durable riches and treasures, 1 Tim. vi. 18, 19. To this end hath the light of the gracious and saving doctrine of God shined, that men might be familiarly instructed to conceive the necessity of doing all the works, both of piety, righteousness, and sobriety, Titus ii. 12. Yea, to this end did Christ give himself for us, and redeem us at so high a rate, that he might 'purify a peculiar people to himself, zealous of good works,' Titus ii. 14. We are 'the workmanship of God, created in Christ Jesus unto good works, which God hath ordained that we should walk in them,' Eph. ii. 10 ; and it shall be to us 'according to our works,' Rom. ii. 6 ; and therefore it should be our wisdom to 'shew by good conversation our works,' James iii. 13 ; and our love, to 'provoke others unto good works,' Heb. x. 24.

Concerning good works, I propound three things :
1. What works are not good works.
2. What rules must be observed to make our works good works.
3. What works are good in particular.

1. For the first, The works that are done to be seen of men are not good works, Mat. xxiii. 5. The works of persecutors are all naught, John viii. 39, 40. All works are naught that have not repentance going before ; for good works are the works of the penitent, Acts xxvi. 20. All the works that are done too late are thrust out of the catalogue of good works ; as to cry to God after a man hath stood out all the opportunities and seasons of grace, Prov. i. 28. It is a sign men's works are not good when they hate the light, and cannot abide to be reproved, John iii. 19, 20. And of the like nature are those works that are guided after the example of the multitude, of which men say, they do as the most do, Exod. xxii. Lastly, Doth not the world hate thee ? then suspect thy works, John vii. 7.

2. For the second, That we may have comfort, that God will account our works good works : 1. They must be warranted by the word of God. If we do truth, we must go to the light, that our deeds may be manifest that they are wrought in God, John iii. 21. 2. Our persons must be made good by justification, we must be created in Christ Jesus, Eph. ii. 10. Would we work the works of God, we must believe in him that God hath sent, John vi. 28, 29. 3. Our works must be finished, John iv. 34. 4. By mortification, we must purge ourselves that we may be meet for the Master's use, and prepared for every work we would have accepted as good, 2 Tim. ii. 21. Lastly, The ends must be good ; and the ends of all good works are : 1. The glory of God ; 2. The discharge of our obedience ; 3. The edification of our neighbours ; 4. The testification of our faith and thankfulness ; 5. The escaping of the punishment of sin, and the destruction of the wicked ; 6. The answering of our high calling in Jesus Christ ; 7. The obtaining of the glory of heaven.

3. For the third, In our conversation with men there are divers kinds of good works, some spiritual, some corporal. They are good works to instruct, admonish, encourage, reprove, and pray for others ; to pull an infant or weak man out of a flaming fire is a good work ; and such it is to recover a sinner by admonition, counsel, &c. It is a good work to cover infirmities, yea, a multitude of them ; and to forgive trespasses, and to overcome evil with goodness. So also they are good works to grieve with them that grieve, in giving honour to go one before another, to lift up the just praises of others, to lend to the needy, and to give liberally and cheerfully towards the relieving of the necessities of the poor, especially them of the household of faith.

To conclude, from the manner of phrase, *bearing fruit in every good work*, these things may be observed : first, That good works are fruits; for they are such things as shew our faith, prove our planting, and yield us comfort in God's acceptance of them ; secondly, That a religious mind will labour to get fruit of every sort ; he will not know a good work, but he will desire to carry some fruit of it ; thirdly, A Christian man carries his fruit, both because he carries the blessing of his well-doing, and because he is never without some fruit, as also he shall be sure his works will go with him, when all things else shall leave him.

Thus far of the eminency of Christians in holy conversation.

Increasing in the knowledge of God. Whereas a question might be asked, what should we do that we might attain to the holiness of life before described ? These words contain an answer to it, that they must increase in the knowledge of God.

The words in themselves stand of three parts : first, The grace, *knowledge;* secondly, The measure of it, *increase ;* thirdly, The object, *of God.* Of the grace itself I have entreated before, only from the repetition two things may be observed :

First, We had need to be often urged, and put in mind, and stirred up to seek knowledge. We are naturally so unapt to spiritual things, that 'line must be upon line, and precept upon precept,' Isa. xxix. Of ourselves there is none of us have any great mind to understand or seek after God, Ps. xiv. 2, or if we begin, we soon leave off to understand to do good, Ps. xxxvi. 3; and some of us are so wayward and wilful, that we know not, nor will not know, but walk on in darkness, though all the foundation of the earth be moved, Ps. lxxxii. 5.

Secondly, Men are not only to seek knowledge that they may be converted and sanctified and live a righteous life, but even after all these are attained we must still be industrious to get more knowledge, because knowledge enlarged gives the comfort and sense of grace received; else, a man may have faith, and yet for want of knowledge live without the comforts of it. Besides, it furthers the sanctification of our callings, and the creatures we use, 1 Tim. iv. 3. Further, it makes us able to discern things that differ, and in matters of salvation to trust our own faith, Phil. i. 10, 1 John iv. 1; and it keeps down corrupt affections; and in what measure we retain our ignorance, we retain fear and the spirit of bondage, Isa. xi. 7–9.

Increasing. The adjunct *increase* follows. Here are two doctrines :

Doct. 1. First, That we must increase in knowledge, else that we have will decay, and knowledge is given but in part, and not all at once. Besides, it is a special part of God's image, and therefore of great both necessity and honour. If men be never weary of seeking for wealth and riches, why should a Christian be weary of seeking wisdom, which is better than all treasures ?

Doct. 2. Secondly, That increase of knowledge is a great furtherance of holy life; the prevailing of sin in the life of the Jews was caused by the prevailing of ignorance, Isa. i. 3. Therefore there is no mercy nor piety in the land, because there is no knowledge of God in the land, Hosea iv. 1, 2. God shews his righteousness to them that know him, Ps. xxxvi. 10. And therefore neither the papists must tell men that ignorance is the mother of devotion, nor the common protestant so idly ask, what needs all this knowledge ?

More particularly, three questions may be here resolved :

Quest. 1. What are the lets of increase ?

Ans. There are many lets : 1. Ill opinions about knowledge, as that it is unprofitable, unnecessary, &c.; 2. Abuse of our callings; 3. The love of other things, Jer. ix. 23, 24; 4. The smothering of doubts, difficulties, and prejudice in the use of the means; 5. Security, when a man grows proud of what he doth know, and presumes of God's mercy for what he wants; 6. Presumptuous sin, as it hinders other graces, so it casts men behindhand in knowledge; 7. Resisting of God's Spirit pricking the conscience to get it awake, and smothering of terrors, Hosea vi. 1–3; 8. Internal evils nourished, as lust, 2 Tim. iii. 7, evil thoughts, Prov. xiv. 22, passion, Prov. xiv. 29, &c.

Quest. 2. How may we know when we increase in knowledge ?

Ans. We increase in knowledge : 1. If we increase in affection to the means, for God is never wanting in the success; 2. If we increase in the power of godliness. It is certain we grow in knowledge if we grow in grace; 3. If we grow staid and settled, and more resolved in the doctrine of God's grace and practice of holy life.

Quest. 3. What must we do that we may increase ?

Ans. We must observe these rules : 1. We must practise what we do already know, John vii. 17; 2. We must not be over-curious, or suffer ourselves to be drawn aside with fond questions, controversies, and speculations, but be wise to sobriety, Rom. xii. 3; 3. We must redeem the time, and watch to all the opportunities for the use of the means, Eph. v. 16; 4. We must use the world as if we used it not; 5. We must acknowledge, that is, confess and profess, what we know, lest God by our unthankfulness and fearfulness be provoked to scourge our spirits with a slumber or reprobate sense, Rom. i. 28; 6. We must mind our own way, Prov. xiv. 8; lastly, We must use God's ordinances, and all of them, and without interruption, constantly and cheerfully.

Thus of the grace itself, and the measure of it; the object follows :

Of God. Our knowledge must be of God four

ways: for first, It must be spiritual and divine knowledge, not human, natural, and earthly; 2. It must be of God; as he is the author of it, we must seek it from above by prayer; 3. It must be of God; as he is the end of it, it must draw us nearer to God; lastly, God must be the object of it; we must know God's name. In this last sense here are two things imported:

First, That even after regeneration there may be sometimes some working of the seeds of atheism. So wretched is the evil nature of man, that in this respect there is cause many times to hang down the head with horror, shame, and bitter mourning of heart, and confusion of face.

Secondly, That increase in holy conversation doth abate the movings of atheism; as any be more holy so they are more freed from the trouble of them. Be first holy, and then be an atheist, professed or resolved, if thou canst.

Concerning the knowledge of God four things are to be considered: 1. How he is made known; 2. Who they are that God chargeth with this, that they know him not; 3. How it comes to pass that man knows not his God; 4. What we must do that we may know God.

1. God is made known: 1. In his Son; in Christ God is, as it were, visible, John xiv. 9; 2. By his Spirit, 1 Cor. ii. 10, 11; 3. By his word, both by the testimony it gives of God, and by the relation of prophecies accomplished and miracles wonderfully wrought; it shews God, as it is a sacred treasury preserving the memory of wonderful things; 4. By his works; and that either in general, as God hath stamped upon them some marks of his invisible things, Rom. i., or in his particular works, as the founding of the earth, the hanging of the clouds, the spreading out of the heavens, the recoiling of the waters, leaving a habitation for man; terrors of conscience, plagues upon wicked men at their wish, answering of prayers, miracles, the soul of man, and state of devils.

2. There are many sorts of men, yea, even in the church, besides professed atheists, that are hated of God, and charged with this, that they know not God, as 1. All that keep not his commandments, Isa. i. 5, 1 John ii. 4; 2. All that hear not us, 1 John iv. 6; 3. All persecutors, John xvi. 3; 4. All that honour not such as fear God, 1 John iii. 1; 5. All that deny the natures or offices of the Son of God, 1 John ii. 23.

3. This wretched atheism, and ignorance of God, and evil thoughts of his nature, presence, attributes, &c., is caused: first, By corruption of our natures in the fall; second, It is increased by the custom of all sorts of sins; third, If it prevail, it may come by some special judgment of God, who, being provoked by other sins, doth leave men to a spirit of slumber, or, eternally rejecting them, doth leave them to a reprobate sense, or in the power of the sin against the Holy Ghost.

4. That we may know God, and increase in it, we must view his works, search his book, obey the motions of his Spirit, humble ourselves to seek the signs of his presence, and for the better success in all, labour for a pure heart, Mat. v. 6.

Hitherto of the object, parts, and end of knowledge; the cause followeth in these words:

Ver. 11. *Strengthened in all might, according to the power of his glory.*

In the words I note: 1. The thing itself, *strengthened;* 2. The manner of it, *in all might;* 3. The ground of it, *according to the power of his glory,* or *glorious power.*

Doct. 1. From the coherence I observe that we must be strengthened in grace before we can be filled with knowledge; till grace prevail evil motions and temptations grow many times too hard for the seeds of knowledge, and the devil steals away much of the seed.

Strengthened. Doct. 2. There are two sorts of Christians fearing God; some are strengthened with all might; some are feeble in the knowledge and grace of God. There are strong Christians and weak; infants and men of riper age. It is profitable more exactly to consider of both; and in the weak Christian I consider: 1. Who are weak; 2. What helps to make them strong in the might of God.

For the better understanding of the first, I propound three things: 1. What the infant or weak Christian wanteth, by which he discovers his weakness; 2. What he hath, notwithstanding his wants; 3. The happiness of his estate though he be weak.

They are but babes and infants in grace: 1. That

know not the love of Christ with particular, distinct, and full assurance, Eph. iii. 17, 19, 20; 2. That are not able to practise the more strong and purging duties of mortification, Mat. ix. 15, &c.; 3. That serve any passion and unruly affection, 1 Cor. iii. 1–3; 4. That are unsettled in the way of life, John xiv. 5, and tossed with the wind of contrary doctrine, Eph. iv. 14; 5. That stick at acknowledgment, and dare not stand out to the profession of the truth, Eph. iv. 13; 6. That cannot digest some truths of God, as being strong meat, and in their account hard sayings, John vi. 60, and xvi. 22; 7. That are inexpert and unskilful in the word of righteousness, Heb. v. 12, 13, especially if they be ignorant in the principles. Other signs may be gathered from the contrary estate of the strong Christian afterwards.

2. Yet the weakest Christian (whatsoever he wants) hath these things: 1. He discerns the season of grace, and the day of his peace and redemption, which the wise men of the world do not, Mat. xvi. 3; 2. Though in his own account he can do but little for the truth, yet he will be sure to do nothing against the truth if he may know it, 2 Cor. xiii. 8; 3. He is not in the flesh, he is more than a natural man, he is born again, 1 Cor. xv. 50, John iii. 5, Rom. viii. 8; 4. He hath an earnest appetite, and constant desire after the sincere milk of the word, 1 Pet. ii. 2; 5. He believes whilst he struggles with unbelief; 6. The strong man armed, which is the devil, is so cast out by Christ that he prevails not as he was wont; 7. He can deny his reason, pleasures, profits, and beloved sins, and take up his cross in some measure, Luke xiv. 26, 27, 33; lastly, Such a door may be opened to them that have little strength, as no man can shut; and such courage they may have, that they will stick to the word, and keep it as their best treasure, whatsoever they lose, and by no means be induced to deny Christ and his name, Rev. ii. 8, 9.

3. His case is happy though weak, for he hath such a High Priest and Saviour as knows how to have compassion on the ignorant, Heb. v. 2, and is touched with a feeling of his infirmities, Heb. iv. 15; and hath wrought the reconciliation of all his brethren, and was tempted himself, and therefore will succour the weak when he is tempted, Heb. ii. 18; and will see to it that more shall not be laid upon him than he is able to bear, 1 Cor. x. 13; it being his charge and office to provide that the bruised reed be not broken, or the smoking flax quenched, till judgment be brought forth unto victory. And at all times the weakest Christian may go boldly to the throne of grace, and obtain mercy to help in time of need, Heb. iv. 16.

The helps for strengthening of the weak are of two sorts: some without us, some to be used by us.

Without us there are many things that may strengthen, and encourage, and animate the weak: 1. There is proposed a glorious inheritance to them that overcome; 2. We have the example of all the saints; 3. We have a strong and sure foundation, 2 Tim. ii. 19; 4. We have a strong God, and his power is engaged to exercise itself in our weakness, and to keep us unto salvation, without falling, till he present us faultless before the presence of his glory, Jude 24, 1 Pet. i. 5, 2 Cor. xii. 9; 5. We have a strong word of God, able to build us up, and make us wise, and save our souls, Acts xx. 32, 2 Tim. iii. 16, James i. 21, as being God's arm, and mighty instrument of his power, 1 Cor. i. 18, Rom. i. 10; 6. The Spirit of God is a Spirit as of grace, so of power, 2 Tim. i. 7, and helpeth the weak, as in prayer, Rom. viii. 26, so in every duty and grace; 7. We have a strong Saviour; Christ doth strengthen and encourage the Christian three ways: first, By his own example, becoming a pattern to us to follow; secondly, By application, for unto all that lay hold on him by faith he is a priest after the power of endless life, Heb. vii. 16; the wisdom of God, and the power of God, 1 Cor. i. 24; thirdly, By operation, for he hath borne our infirmities—by his one offering he hath and doth consecrate and make perfect our persons and works in God's sight, Heb. ii. 10; he doth unite us to the Father, John xvii. 21, 23. He gives us his Father's glory, both in that he gives us such graces as will bring to glory, and in that he gives us credit where himself and the Father are in credit. Thus of the helps without us.

If any ask, in the second place, what we must do that we may be strengthened, I answer: 1. We must pray for knowledge and faith to discern and believe God's power and promise, Eph. i. 8, &c. And in the fourth of that epistle there are five things more to be done, that we may attain to a ripe age in Christ: 1. We must subject ourselves to be taught and wrought upon by such teachers as are set over us by Christ; 2. We must resolve and settle ourselves in the doctrine of the foundation and the principles of truth, that we be not tossed to and fro with every wind; 3. We must so be satisfied with the voice of Christ in our teachers, that we cast aside all respects of the voice of strangers, not opening our ears willingly to the sleights of cunning men, that will 'lie in wait to deceive us;' 4. We must take heed of personal discords with any that fear God, 'following the truth in love;' 5. We must mutually strive to yield and seek help, to and of one another, that every joint in this mystical body, 'according to the measure of the part,' may supply and make up the increase of the body, by virtue of union with the head and communion with the members, Eph. iv. 11-17. Besides, if we would increase in strength, we must 'let patience have his perfect work,' making conscience to mortify corrupt passions,—as worldly grief, anger, fretting, &c., James i. 4. And lastly, We must be careful to keep what God hath given us, 'that no man take away our crown.' Neglect of grace received is a great hindrance of strength and increase.

Thus of the weak Christian.

A strong Christian discovers himself by divers things: first, He is spiritual,—that is, such a one as not only hath a taste and desire after spiritual things, but is also ruled by the word and Spirit of God, that he restrains the evils of the flesh both in heart and life, so as he gives not occasion either of scandal to the weak, or of scorn to them that are without, 1 Cor. iii. 1. Secondly, He is able to be baptized with the baptism that Christ was baptized with, and to drink of the cup that Christ drank of. He is not only willing to bear ordinary wrongs and crosses, but is prepared for the worst the world or Satan may do to him, Mat. xx. 22, 23. Thirdly, He can 'bear the infirmities of the weak,' and in conversing deny himself, and please his brother in that that is good to edification, Rom. xv. 1, 2. Fourthly, He is full of goodness and knowledge, and is able to admonish, Rom. xv. 14, and comfort others with the comforts he hath found himself, 2 Cor. i. 4. Fifthly, He sins not in word, James iii. 2,— that is, he is able to govern his tongue with wisdom, meekness, grace, and truth. The ordinary faults of speech are not found in his tongue. Sixthly, He is not careful for his life, to take thought for what he shall eat or what he shall drink, nor doth he disquiet his heart about his body what he shall put on; for these outward things he can easily trust his heavenly Father, Mat. vi. 25, 30. Seventhly, He can love his enemies, endure wrongs without resistance or revenge; or if he use the help of the magistrate, he can seek it without malice or cruelty; he can 'bless them that curse him, and pray for them that despite him, and do good to them that hate him,' Mat. v. 38. to the end. Lastly, In faith he is strong, like Abraham, Rom. iv. 16 to the end. He can believe things to come as well as if they were present, ver. 17; he can believe above hope and under hope, ver. 18; he looketh not to the means, but to the promise, ver. 19; he vanquisheth doubts, ver. 20; he is as thankful for promises as others would be for performances, ver. 20, 21; for these things were not only true of Abraham, but may be true in us also, ver. 23, 24, who may have as great help from Christ as ever he had, ver. 25.

Thus of the strong Christian.

In all might. Note how the apostle presseth to perfection; before, 'in all knowledge,' 'all pleasing,' 'all good works;' now, in 'all might.' And we had need to be strengthened with all might, because not one part of the soul only is to be looked to, but the whole soul, spirit, and life throughout; nor have we one grace to tend, but all sorts of graces from God; nor doth there abide us one trouble, but calamities, indignities, and temptations of all sorts. We have not one adversary to encounter, but many, and of many sorts; inward, outward, visible, invisible, public, private, at home, and abroad. Neither do we stand upon our guard at one time, but must look to ourselves in all these respects at all times.

It must be all might that we should labour after in four respects:

First, It must be a might that extends to the strengthening of all the faculties of the soul, powers of the body, and duties of the life; our minds must be strengthened in the approving of truth and goodness, and in reprobating of evil and falsehood, 1 Cor. xiv. 20; our memories must be strengthened in retaining and recording the secrets and hid things of God which are committed to it; the will must be strengthened in the election of good and rejection of evil; and our affections need strength also. Thus we were to be strengthened in patience, James i. 4; joy, 1 Thes. v. 16; love, 1 John iv. 18; mercy, Col. iii. 12; hope and confidence, 1 Pet. i. 13; desires, Ps. xxvii. 4; in reverence, Heb. xii. 28; in hatred of sin, Ps. cxxxix. 22; contempt of the world, Phil. iii. 8, Isa. xxx. 22. So do we need strength to every duty of holy life.

Secondly, It must be a might that is gotten from the use of all the means; we must be strengthened in the power of every ordinance of God, and supported with the use of every help to make us strong.

Thirdly, It must be a might shewed in the use of all the armour of God. We must strengthen ourselves with every piece of armour, whether it be armour of defence, as, 'the girdle of truth, the breastplate of righteousness, the shoes of the gospel of peace, the shield of faith, the helmet of hope;' or armour of offence, as, 'the sword of the Spirit, God's word,' and the 'darts of prayer,' Eph. vi. 12.

Fourthly, It should be a might extended to all possible degrees and power of every grace and duty. Thus in mercy we should communicate in all good things, Gal. vi. 6; our service should be a hearty service, Eph. vi. 6; we must love the Lord with all our hearts, with all our souls, with all our might, Deut. vi. 5.

According to the power of his glory. In the handling of these words, I consider them: first, Apart; secondly, As they are joined together; and thirdly, The doctrines out of them.

Here are two things laid to pawn for the strengthening of the weak Christian, God's power, and God's glory.

Power is one of the attributes they call in schools *relata*. The power of God is infinite, both in respect of essence, for it is as large as the essence, yea, it is the essence itself; and in respect of objects; he hath not done so much, but far beyond our capacities he could do infinitely more; and so is it infinite in respect of continuance. Yet to speak of it according to our capacities, it is restrained: 1. By his will; he cannot do what his will is against. 2. By his glory; he can do nothing against his own glory. 3. By his nature, he cannot lie, &c., because it is against his nature. 4. In some respects, by the nature of the creature; so as whatsoever destroys the essential definition of the creature God cannot do; as God cannot make a man unreasonable, and yet he remain a man; he cannot make a body infinite, and it remain a body still. 5. Sometimes by the condition and qualities of the creature; as, 'Be it unto thee according to thy faith.' 6. By impossibility; I say by that which is simply impossible, for there are many things impossible in respect of us, which are not only possible, but easy to God. And therefore the common people reason foolishly, God can save me, therefore he will do it; and the papists as wilfully, Christ can be present in the sacrament, therefore he will. For besides that they will never prove his body can be in all places at one time, truly and locally present, remaining a true body, they also reason but absurdly till they find his will to be there in their manner.

The glory of God is taken sometimes for the sign of his presence, Exod. xvi. 10; for the means of his worship, 1 Sam. iv. 22; for praise and honour, 2 Chron. xxix. 11. But here it is taken for the excellency of God above all creatures as it may be revealed. God is more excellent than all creatures, in trinity of persons in one essence, in perfection of nature, in infiniteness of being, in eternity, in purity and singleness, in immutability of nature, will, and qualities, in understanding, in prescience, which absolutely falleth to no creature, in the idea of virtue, and in omnipotency. By reason of man's fall and custom in sin God's glory is much darkened; so as now man of himself cannot so conceive of the wonderful excellency of his creator.

God's glory is revealed unto man: 1. By his works, Ps. civ. 31, especially his dreadful and great works, Isa. xxiv. 16; 2. By the signs of his presence, Exod. xvi. 10; 3. By the means of his worship, 1 Sam. iv. 22, Ps. lxxxix. 7; 4. By the confession of guilty persons, Joshua vii. 19, 1 Sam. vi. 5, Mal. ii. 2; 5. By the praises of his servants; and therefore to give glory is translated, to give thanks, Luke xvii. 18; 6. By Christ, who is the Lord of glory, 1 Cor. ii. 8, the King of glory, Ps. xxiv., he maketh the glory of God, as it were, visible in his flesh, John i. 14; 7.

By man, 1 Cor. xi. 7; 8. By the spirit of revelation, Eph. i. 17; 9. By the gospel, 1 Tim. i. 11.

But if you ask who of all men see God's glory, I answer, only the saints in the brightness of it, Ps. lxxxix. 7, Isa. xxvi. 10, 11,—to wit, such as have the gospel shining in their hearts, 2 Cor. iv. 3, &c., Isa. lxi. 1-3; such as acknowledging God's threatenings, turn unto him by true repentance, Jer. xiii. 16; such as lead a holy and innocent life, Ps. cxxxviii. 5, &c., Isa. lxxx. 7-9; such as have a true and lively faith, John xi. 40, Isa. xlvi. 12, 13.

Thus of the words apart.

Power of his glory. There are four reasons why the power of God should be said to be the power of his glory, or glorious: 1. Because it will never leave strengthening till it bring to glory; 2. Because the power of all the means of salvation is from heaven, and therefore a glorious power; 3. Because God's glory sets his power a-work, inasmuch as by promise it lies engaged to his people; 4. It is a glorious power, because of the persons and things that are used in God's work, as God himself, the Son of God, the Spirit of God, ordinances that are of God, and men specially consecrated by God.

Doctrines. First, The perseverance of God's children is most certain; so long as there is power in God or glory, they cannot fall away by losing their happiness.

This point hath abundant and apparent confirmation out of the Old Testament, in these places:— Ps. cxlv. 10, 13, 14, Isa. xlii. 3, Ezek. xxxvi. 24-27, Jer. xxxii. 40, Hosea ii. 19. Out of the Gospels— Mat. xvi. 18, and xxiv. 25, John iv. 14, v. 24, vi. 39, x. 28, 29, and xiii. 1. Out of the Epistles also— Rom. vi. 8-11, viii. 30, and xi. 29, Eph. iv. 12, 17, Phil. i. 6, 2 Tim. ii. 19, Heb. vii. 16, 1 John ii. 19, and iii. 9. 1 Pet. i. 5, 13, 18, 20, 23.

Secondly, There is little reason of presumption in this doctrine; for, as power will preserve, so glory will revenge. If such as are in covenant with God return to sin, woe unto them, God's glory will not bear it; and he hath many ways to scourge them, for by their sins they may bring upon themselves crosses of all sorts, Ps. lxxxix. 22, Isa. xxx. 10, Zech. xiii. 7-9, Micah vii. 9, 18; terrors of conscience, Ps. li.; loss of many gifts, and want of sense of all grace, God's presence, and the joys of his promises and salvation, Ps. li., Cant. iii.; church censures, 1 Cor. v.; the want of many blessings, Jer. v. 24, 25; sore travail, and terrors upon their return again, Ps. li.; terrible buffets, both of the word and Spirit, &c.; and therefore we should 'work out our salvation with fear and trembling.' It is a fearful thing to fall into God's angry and scourging hand.

Hitherto of the object, parts, ends, and causes of knowledge; the effects follow, which in the end of the verse are noted to be three,—viz., patience, longsuffering, and joyfulness.

Patience. This is a virtue that well becomes a Christian, and a blessed fruit of the tree of life, much to be desired of man. Though it may seem troublesome to the flesh to endure crosses and afflictions, yet, if all things be considered, it is a virtue of great praise. God himself is magnified of men and angels for his patience and forbearance, Rom. ii. 4. It is the admirable glory of the Son of God that, in the great work of his Father about the gathering of the churches, in the midst of the oppositions of the world and evil angels, he should 'not cry, nor lift up, nor cause his voice to be heard,' and yet hold out 'without failing or discouragement,' Isa. xlii. 2, 4; yea, 'as the captain of our salvation, he was made perfect by suffering,' Heb. ii. 10. This is the praise of the saints, (which they may remember with comfort,) that they have endured many and great fights of afflictions, Heb. x. 32. The soldier cannot please his captain unless he endure hardness; nor he that striveth for masteries be crowned, unless he toil in the combat; nor the husbandman reap, unless he patiently endure the labour of sowing, and wait till harvest, 2 Tim. ii. 3, 5, 6. 'All that will live godly must suffer,' 2 Tim. iii. 12; the holy exercise of Christian patience is a good sign that men are good hearers of the word, and that they practise what they hear, Luke viii. 15. Men are not therefore miserable because they suffer much, Mat. v. 10. Christians need not be ashamed to suffer, 2 Tim. i. 12; they may be 'troubled on every side, yet not distressed; they may be perplexed, and yet not despair; they may be persecuted, and yet not forsaken; they may be cast down, and yet not destroyed,' 2 Cor. iv. 8, 9. Patience is a virtue full of good fruits; it appeaseth strife, Prov. xv. 18, xxv., it helps away the cross, (it is impatience and stubbornness that makes the father continue to beat his child,) it fits us for perseverance with comfort, as the coherence shews: 'The patient abiding of the poor shall not perish for ever,' Ps. ix. 18, but they shall receive, at the length, a crown of life, James i. 12. The worth of this grace appears by the hurt of impatiency; for impatiency exalts folly, Prov. xiv. 29; deprives a man of the possession of his own soul, Luke xxi. 19; dishonours all a man's gifts and graces, and all the good things he hath before done, Job iv. 6, &c. Let us therefore 'run with patience the race that is set before us.' Thus did Christ endure the cross, and now wears the crown, Heb. xii. 1-3. The things we commonly bear are nothing to that Christ and the martyrs have borne; we 'have not yet resisted unto blood,' ver. 4. By suffering we may reap the comfort that we are sons and not bastards, ver. 5-8, besides the profit of our sufferings, which God ever intends to the patient, —viz., the holiness of the heart, and fruitfulness of the life, ver. 9-11.

That we may be patient, first, we must get wisdom; and if we want it, ask it of God. It is ignorance makes men passionate; a great understanding is slow to wrath, Prov. xiv. 29, James i. 3-6. Secondly, We must get faith to believe our own reconciliation with God; our hearts need not be troubled if we believe in God the Father, in Jesus Christ, John xiv. 1. When the heart is possessed with peace in the assurance of justification by faith, then it is easy to be patient in tribulation, yea, to rejoice in affliction, Rom. v. 1, 2, 4, John xiv. 27. Thirdly, We must be much in the meditation of the comforts of another life. Fourthly, We must be often and constant in prayer, Rom. xii. 12. Fifthly, The hearing of the word faithfully and conscionably breeds a patient mind, and therefore is the word called a word of patience, Rev. iii. 10; the 'comforts of the scripture' beget both patience and hope, Rom. xv. 4. Sixthly, We must be temperate in the desires after and use of outward things; therefore are men unquiet under the loss, absence, want, or desire of earthly things about their bodies or estates, because they have not sobriety and temperance in their hearts and carriage, 2 Pet. i. 6. Seventhly, If we would have patience, we must be careful, by godly sorrow and confession, to cast off the sin that hangeth on so fast, Heb. xii. 1; it is our wretched corruption of nature that makes us so unquiet—it is nothing without us. Lastly, We must be diligent in our callings, and trust upon God, and cast all our care on him. Idleness and unbelief are the great nurses of impatiency.

Thirdly, We must exercise patience in seven things: 1. In bearing the common crosses that accompany our mortal estate of life, and therein to put on, as near as we can, Job's mind, and in all losses or wants to give glory to God, acknowledging that he hath as much right to take away as reason to give; 2. In bearing with the infirmities of such as are about us, with whom we converse, that shew themselves to be so, out of weakness, Rom. xv. 1, 3, 4; 3. In enduring persecution of all kinds for the truth's sake, 2 Tim. iii. 12, 2 Thes. i. 5, Rev. ii. 8, 1 Pet. iv. 12, &c.; 4. In tentations there is use of patience, both in waiting upon God for succour and issue, and in keeping the soul at as much rest and quietness as may be; it is the devil's desire to set us on a hurry, he knows his tentations will then work best, James i. 4; 5. In the expectation of the performance of God's promises and our spiritual happiness in Christ, Heb. vi. 12, and x. 35-38; 6. In the troubles of the mind and conscience, believing God's truth, and waiting for the appearing of his face, and the healing of the soul; 7. In perseverance in welldoing unto the end, Mat. xxiv. 13, Rom. ii. 7, Rev. ii. 2, Gal. v. 9, 1 John iii. 2.

Long-suffering. This virtue, in case of wrongs, must order us aright in ourselves and towards others; in ourselves it must restrain anger and desire of revenge; and great reason, for God himself suffers wrong, and that long too, Exod. iii. 4, 6, 1 Pet. ii. 22; and it is God's commandment we should suffer long, Mat. v. 21, 22, 45, Rom. xii. 21; besides, injuries befall us by God's providence, 2 Sam. xvi. 10; and revenge is God's right, Rom. xii. 19. Moreover, these raging and revengeful affections are great hindrances both to prayer, 1 Tim. ii. 8, and to the profit of the word, James i. 21. And lastly, Anger lets the devil into a man's heart, Eph. iv. 27.

Quest. 1. But how should I prevent it, being wronged?

Ans. First, Carry some of thine own sins always in thy mind, that being provoked thou mayest turn the course of thine anger thither; secondly, Avoid the occasions, which are both contentions, Phil. ii. 3, and contentious persons, Prov. xxii. 26; thirdly, Be daily jealous over thine affections, and keep them down by prayer.

Quest. 2. What if passion do suddenly surprise me?

Ans. 1. Conceal it, Prov. xxii. 16; 2. Depart from them with whom thou art angry, 1 Sam. xx. 34, Gen. xxvii. 43, 44; 3. Appoint at the least that bound unto thine anger, that 'the sun go not down upon thy wrath,' Eph. iv. 26.

Towards others we must shew the practice of this virtue thus:

In things that might displease us, but not hurt us, endure them without any notice at all; and in things that do hurt, if they be lesser injuries, see them and forgive them; and in the greater wrongs, thou must seek the help of the magistrate, and the law, after thou hast sought all private means, by entreaty, offers of peace, desire of arbitration, &c.; follow the law with love to thy adversary, without passion or rage, and in the issues be moderate, without shewing extremity,' Mat. v. 25 and xviii. 15, Rom. xii. 18, 1 Cor. vi. 5.

Joyfulness. A Christian estate is a joyful and comfortable estate. Saving knowledge makes a man live joyfully and comfortably. True joy is one of the fruits God's Spirit beareth in the heart of a Christian; yea, it is a chief part of that kingdom that God bestoweth on his people on earth. None have cause of joy but the children of Zion, and none of them but have great reason to 'shout for joy,' to 'rejoice and be glad with all their hearts,' Zeph. iii. 14. Is it not a great mercy to have all the judgments due unto us for sin taken away, and the great enemy of our souls cast out? Is it not a great honour that Jehovah, the King of Israel, should be in the midst of us, and that our eyes should not see evil any more? What sweeter encouragement than that the Lord should cause it to be said unto us, Fear not; and again, Let not your hands be slack! If we have great crosses, enemies, dangers, wants, temptations, &c., we have a mighty God; if there be none to help us, he will save; yea, he will rejoice to do us good; yea, he will rejoice over us with joy; yea, he so loves us that he will rest in his love and seek no further. Shall man be sorrowful when God rejoiceth? Shall the Lord rejoice in us, and shall not we rejoice in God? Zeph. iii. 14, &c. And if these reasons of joy be contained in one place of scripture, how great would the number of reasons grow, if all the book of God were searched! Such a joy and contentment is the joy of Christians, that crosses cannot hinder it. Life is not dear to a child of God, 'so that he may finish his course with joy,' Acts xx. 24. They suffer the spoiling of their goods with joy, knowing that in heaven they have a more enduring substance, Heb. x. 34; Yea, in many crosses they account it all joy to fall into temptation, James i. 2; they seem as sorrowful when, indeed, they are always rejoicing, 2 Cor. vi. 10.

Quest. What might we do to get this constant joyfulness, and unmovable firmness, and contentment of heart?

Ans. In general thou must be sure to be God's servant, Isa. lxv. 13, 14; a man justified and sanctified, Jer. xxxiii. 8, Isa. lxi. 10, and xii. 5; thou must know that thy name is written in the book of life, Luke x. 20, which cannot be without faith, 1 Pet. i. 8, Phil. i. 25, Rom. xv. 13.

In particular there are many things which have a sure promise of joy and comfort annexed to them.

First, Thou must lay the foundation of all eternal joys in godly sorrow for thy sins, John xvi. 20, Mat. v. 4, Ps. cxxvi. 5, 6.

Secondly, Thou must hang upon the breasts of the church, viz., the words and sacraments, continually, with trembling and tender affection, waiting upon the word of God; the law must be in thy heart, thou must buy thy liberty herein at the highest value, Isa. lxvi. 2, 5, 11, and li. 7, Mat. xiii. 44.

Thirdly, In thy carriage thou must be a counsellor of peace, Prov. xii. 20, and live in peace, as near as may, 2 Cor. xiii. 11.

Fourthly, Take heed thou be not insnared with gross sin, Prov. xxix. 6.

Fifthly, Wouldest thou reap joy? sow good seed; to be much in well-doing procures, as a blessing, a secret and sweet gladness upon the heart of man; a barren life is an uncomfortable life. Many would reap that will not be at the pain to sow, John iv. 36, Gal. vi. 7, 8. He that useth his talents to advantage, enters into his master's joy, a joy liker the joy of God than man, meeter for the master than for the servant, yet such a Master we serve, as will crown us with this joy, Mat. xxv. 21.

Sixthly, Be constant, bear fruit, and get the knowledge of the love of Christ, and abide in it, John xv. 10.

Lastly, In the 2 Thes. v. 16-24, there are seven things required in our practice, if we would always rejoice: 1. We must 'pray always;' if we be much in prayer we shall be much in joy. 2. We must 'in all things give thanks;' a heart kept tender with the sense of God's mercies is easily inflamed with joys in the Holy Ghost. 3. We must take heed of 'quenching the Spirit;' when a man puts out the holy motions of the Spirit, he quencheth his own joys. 4. We must, by all means, preserve an honourable respect of the word publicly preached, 'despise not prophesying.' 5. And whereas there be some things we hear do specially affect us, and concern us, we must be careful with all heedfulness to keep those things whatsoever we forget, 'try all things, but keep that which is good.' 6. In our practice we must not only avoid evil, but 'all appearance of evil,' else if we disquiet others with grief or offence of our carriage, it will be just with God we should find little rest, or contentment in ourselves. Lastly, We must endeavour to be 'sanctified throughout,' inwardly and outwardly, 'in soul, body, and spirit,' having respect to all God's commandments, and retaining the love of no sin; so shall we reap the blessing of all righteousness, and procure to our hearts the joys that are everlasting.

Hitherto of the preface.

Ver. 12. *Giving thanks unto the Father, which hath made us meet to be partakers of the inheritance of the saints in light.*

Hitherto of the exordium of this epistle, as it contained both the salutation and preface.

The second part both of the chapter and epistle followeth, and is contained in the 12th verse and the rest to the 23d. And it hath in it the proposition of doctrine. This doctrine propounded stands of two parts; for it concerneth either the work of redemption or the person of the Redeemer. The work of redemption is considered of in the 12th, 13th, and 14th verses; the person of the Redeemer is treated of from ver. 15 to 23. The work of redemption is two ways considered of: first, More generally, in the 12th verse; secondly, More particularly, ver. 13, 14.

In the work of our redemption, as it is propounded in this verse, three things are to be observed: 1. The efficient cause, *God the Father.* 2. The subject persons redeemed, *us.* 3. The redemption itself, as it is either in the inchoation and first application of it on earth, and so it lieth *in making us fit;* or in the consummation of it, what it shall be in the end. And so it is praised: first, By the manner of tenure, *inherit;* second, By the adjunct company, *saints;* thirdly, By the perfection of it, *in light.*

Giving thanks. The blessings of God upon every true Christian are such as they require continual thankfulness to God for them. Such, I say, for the worth of them, for number, for freeness of gift, for continuance, and as they are compared with what God bestows upon others in the world.

To the Father. A sanctified heart that hath sense of grace so sees God, the first cause of all blessings, through the second and next causes, that it maketh God the principal object both of prayer and praise. It is a great sin not to acknowledge the instrument by which we receive any good, but it is a great impiety not to give that which is due to the principal efficient.

The Father. Father, a term of relation, and is given sometimes to the whole Trinity, Mat. xxiii. 9, Luke iii. 38; sometimes to Christ, Isa. ix. 6; sometimes to the first person in the Trinity; so commonly, and so here.

God may be said to be a Father in this place two ways: first, In respect of Christ; secondly, In respect of the Christian.

1. In respect of Christ, God is a Father both by nature and by personal union; and in this sense two questions may be moved.

Quest. 1. Whether prayer is to be made to the whole Trinity, or but to one person?

Ans. It is to be made to the whole Trinity, Acts vii. 59, 1 Thes. iii. 2, 2 Cor. xiii. 13.

Object. But prayer is here made to one person.

Sol. Though but one person be named, yet the rest are included; for the persons may be distinguished, but severed or divided they may not be.

Quest. 2. Is the Father a Redeemer, in that redemption is here given to him?

Ans. The actions of God are twofold: some are inward, as to beget, to proceed, &c.; some are outward, as to create, redeem, &c. Now the outward actions are common to all the three Persons; they are distinguished only in the manner of doing. The Father begins, the Son executes, the Holy Ghost finisheth. As in the works of redemption, the Father redeems us, in that he begins it by devising this course and willing it from eternity, by calling, sanctifying, sending, and accepting of Christ in time; the Son redeems us, by taking our nature, and in obeying the law and suffering death, even the death of the cross for us; the Holy Ghost redeems us, by applying the merits and benefits of Christ to every believer.

2. In respect of the Christian, God is a Father, and the meditation hereof should serve for a threefold use: 1. For trial; 2. For instruction; 3. For consolation. For trial: for it stands us much upon to be assured of this, that God is our Father in Christ by adoption; for this is the foundation of true hope for what we want, and of true thankfulness for what we have. Now, such men as are born of God by regeneration, as well as of man by generation, are wont to be described in scripture by such marks as these. They have in them the spirit of adoption, both in the working and witness of it, Rom. viii. 15, 16, Gal. iv. 6, 7. They are separate from sinners; they cannot delight in the works of darkness, or in the wicked fellowship with workers of iniquity; they hate ungodly company, &c., 2 Cor. vi. 17, 1 John ii. 15. They have consolation and good hope through grace, 2 Thes. ii. 16. Christ is to them their way, the truth, and their life; and they love their Saviour more than any creature, and shew it in this, that they will rather obey his words than the commandment of any man or angel, John xvi. 6, 21. They are a people that, in respect of mortification, purge themselves by voluntary sorrows for their sins; and in respect of new obedience, 'come to the light, that their works may be manifest that they are wrought in God,' 1 John iii. 1-3, i. 6, 7, 1 Pet. i. 17, &c. They honour God with great honour, and tender his name more than their own credits, Mal. i. 16. They worship God, not for show, or with the adoration of the lips and knees only, but in spirit and truth, John iv. 23. They labour for the meat that perisheth not, and esteem it above their appointed food, John vi. 27. Lastly, they love their enemies, and pray for them that persecute them, and are willing to do good to them that hate them and hurt them, Mat. v. 45, &c.

Secondly, If God be our Father, it should teach us: First, To care less for the world, and the things thereof. We have a Father that both knows our wants, and hath all power and will to help us and care for us, Mat. vi. 32. Secondly, To come to him in all crosses, and make our moan to him that seeth in secret; for if 'evil fathers on earth know how to give good things to their children when they ask them, how shall not our heavenly Father give us whatsoever we ask in the name of Christ?' Mat. vii. 11; yea, it should teach us patience under, and a good use of, all crosses, Hosea xii. 9. Thirdly, To be willing to die and commend our spirits to God that gave them, seeing, in so dying, we commit them into the hands of a Father. This made Christ willing to die, and this should persuade with us also. Lastly, It should teach us to glorify God as a Father. We call God Father (many of us) and thus we speak, but we do evil more and more, and dishonour him, not living like the children of the Most High, Jer. iii. 4, 5. If he be our Father, let the light of our good works shine before men that they may glorify our Father, Mat. v. 6. Herein is God the Father glorified, that we bear much fruit, John xv. 8.

Thirdly, This point serves for consolation, and that many ways: first, Against the fear of our own weakness—'It is not our Father's will that one of the little ones should perish,' Mat. xviii. 14, 'none is able to take them out of his hand,' John x. 29; secondly, Against our doubts about prayer—'Whatsoever you ask the Father in Christ's name it shall be given you,' John xvi. 23; thirdly, Against all the troubles of this world—If he have been a Father of mercy to forgive thy sins, and give thee grace, he will be a Father of glory to crown thee in a better world in the inheritance of his sons, Eph. i. 17.

Who hath made us fit. Doct. We are neither

naturally happy nor universally so; not naturally, for we are made fit, not born so; not universally, for he hath made *us* fit—not all men. Christ died for his sheep only, John x.; for his church only, Eph. i.; not for the world, John xvii. And, therefore, when the scripture saith, Christ died for all men, we must understand it: first, In respect of the sufficiency of his death, not in respect of the efficiency of it; secondly, In respect of the common oblation of the benefits of his death externally in the gospel unto all; thirdly, As his death extendeth unto all the elect—*for all,* that is, for the elect; fourthly, *For all,* that is, for all that are saved, so that none that are justified and saved are so but by virtue of his death; fifthly, *For all,* that is, for all indefinitely—for all sorts of men, not for every man of every sort; lastly, He died *for all,* that is, not for the Jews only, but for the Gentiles also.

Quest. Are not all in the visible church, that are sealed with the sacrament of initiation, made fit?

Ans. No; for Nicodemus was circumcised, yet not as then fit for heaven; and Simon Magus was baptized, and yet perished in the 'gall of bitterness;' and many of the Israelites were signed with the same sacraments of righteousness, and yet were destroyed with fearful plagues, 1 Cor. xi.; the pharisees were baptized with John's baptism, and yet in great danger of wrath to come, Mat. iii.

There are five sorts of men that live in the church that are not made fit: first, Such as are in heart disjoined, so as indeed they care for the doctrine of no church, and thus atheists and epicures are unfit; secondly, Such as are in heart fastened to a false church, though in show they be members of the true: thus church-papists are not fit; thirdly, Such as receive religion and care for it, but only as it may fit the humours of such as are in authority, and may serve the current of the present times: and thus temporising politicians are not made fit; fourthly, Such as admit some parts of God's worship, and stand in professed enmity and dislike of the rest: and thus the common protestant, of all estates and degrees; they think if they come to the church to service, and be no papists, it will serve turn, though they neglect, yea, contemn, yea, commonly despise preaching, private prayer, true fasting, religious conference, and fellowship in the gospel;

fifthly, and lastly, Among the better sorts that are hearers, and constant hearers, there are many not made fit for the kingdom of God; for many hearers rest in a historical faith and external righteousness, either betraying the seed, by suffering the fiends of hell, those invisible fowls of the air, to take it away, or choking the seed by worldly cares, or if they get a taste of the good word of God, and of the powers of the life to come, by their wicked revolts and backslidings, they shew themselves not fit, nor worthy, the kingdom of God.

Who. Doct. God only can make men fit for his kingdom; he only can rescue us from the power of darkness and Satan; it is he only is the 'Lord of righteousness;' it is he only that can pardon our sins; it is he only can 'heal our rebellions,' and 'take away our iniquities;' he only is the fountain of all inherent holiness; he only is stronger than all to preserve us to the end, and crown us with glory.

Made fit. The word may be rendered either made *fit,* or *worthy,* so it be understood of the merit of Christ imputed to us, in whom only we are worthy of heaven.

We are made fit by redemption, by vocation, by adoption, by justification, by sanctification, and by glorification, for each of these adds something to our sufficiency. The use is to teach us to magnify God's exceeding mercy, that doth not only give us heaven, but makes us fit for heaven. The greatest king in the world, if he set his love upon a base slave or vassal, well he may give him an earldom or great office, but he cannot give him fitness for his place, and gifts to execute it; he may change his estate, but he cannot change his nature. But God doth not only give a kingdom to his servants, but he endues them with royal inclinations, desires, and behaviour.

The Rhemists upon this place note that we deserve salvation condignly; but we need not answer them, for Thomas Aquinas, the ordinary Gloss, and Cardinal Cajetan, upon this place cross them. Aquinas saith thus: *Dixerunt aliqui Deus dat dignis gratiam,* &c. Some have said God gives grace to the worthy, but not to the unworthy; but the apostle excludes this, because, whatsoever worthiness thou hast, God hath wrought it in thee; and to this end allegeth, 2 Cor. iii., 'We are not sufficient of ourselves to think a good thought.' The Gloss thus:

'He makes us worthy, not in the law but in light;' that is, through God, who is the light of light, by whose grace we are enlightened. Cajetan, thus: 'Worthy, that is, fit; by lot, that is, only by God's gift.' Note, only by God's gift, the papist saith.

To be partakers of the inheritance of the saints in light: or, as it is in the original, *verbatim,* Unto the part of the lot of the saints in light.

The lot of the saints is by some taken for the sufferings of the saints; by others, for their happiness, as it is had in this life, in the right or inchoation of it; by others, for heaven, and that as it is held by true title here in this world; so I take it here.

The word *lot* leadeth us, by allusion, to Canaan, and the division thereof; and the comparison holdeth in many things. As none had right to the land of Canaan but Israelites, so none have right to heaven but the saints; and as Canaan was furnished with buildings and all commodities, but not by the Israelites, Deut. viii. 7, &c., so heaven was prepared of old, before the saints entered it, Mat. xxv. The 'builder and maker of it' was not the saints, but God, 2 Cor. v. And as the Canaanites were thrown out that Israel might enter, so the devils were thrown out of heaven that the saints might enter. And as without a Joshua, though there were a land, there would be no lot, so without a Jesus, though there were a heaven, there would be no inheritance: and though the land were given by lot, yet it must not be possessed without a combat; they must first fight, and then inherit; so must heaven suffer violence, and before it be had we must wrestle with principalities and powers. And as all their lots were known to Joshua, so every Christian, in his standing, is known to Christ. As Joshua had what he asked, Josh. xix. 50, so our Joshua obtains what he asks, though he 'ask the ends of the earth,' Ps. ii. And as the comparison hath those things for information, so may divers instructions be gathered from hence also: and first, If we would have any lot in heaven, we must be sure we be true Israelites. Balaam seems a friend to Israel, but he is so far from inheriting with them, that he is destroyed by them; the sword of the Lord roots him out. This will be the portion of all hypocrites, Josh. xiii. 22. And we should labour for a particular warrant in the knowledge of our own portion: this would encourage us against all difficulties. Caleb dares fight with the Anakims if Joshua give him Hebron. Josh. xiv. 6, 11, &c.; and feeble and complaining Ephraim shall overcome and enlarge himself if Joshua particularly encourage him, Josh. xvii. And as no Canaanites ought to be left in the lot of Israel, so no wicked workers should be suffered to remain in the assembly of the saints, to be pricks and goads in the sides of the righteous. And as they that have their inheritance allowed them already must not rest, but fight till their brethren have rest, Josh. i. 12, so they that have comfort in their own conversion, must strengthen their brethren. And if any have too little room, the way is not to murmur and doubt, but to fight it out for more; so must Dan, Judges xviii.; so should weak Christians not give way to discontentment, but strive in the spiritual combat, till more grace and room for the enlarging of the heart be gotten. Lastly, As seven tribes are justly taxed and censured by Joshua for their negligence and sloth, in not seeking speedily to possess the land God had offered them, Josh. xviii. 2, so may the most of us be justly rebuked for grievous security about the heavenly Canaan. Many rest in the probabilities and hope of a title; nay, the most rest satisfied in such a condition as is without title and without hope, unless they amend; yea, the better sort, divers of them, have but a title, and therefore it justly falleth out that these are buffeted by Christ, as they were disgraced by Joshua; and as they must stand to the courtesy of the viewers of the land for the report of the goodness of their part, so must these secure Christians stand to the courtesy of their teachers for how much knowledge and comfort they shall think meet to impart unto them, concerning their inheritance in heaven and heavenly things.

Partakers of the inheritance of the saints in light. The happiness of the faithful is an inheritance, illustrated here, first, by the persons that must enjoy it: it is not common to all, but appropriated to saints; secondly, by the quality of it: it is in light.

Christ is the great heir of all things, Heb. i. 1, Ps. ii.; the Christian is co-heir with Christ. It is a doctrine that hath much comfort in it. A Christian holds by the fairest tenure, and firmest, and surest too; for though his life be changeable, and his days on earth must have an end, yet his inheritance endures for ever, and while he lives God will know him all his days for no worse a man than his own heir, Ps. xxxvii. 17, 18. And the consideration of the inheritance of the saints should teach us divers things: first, To pray that God would remember us with the favour of his people, and visit us with his salvation, Ps. cvi. 3, 4, Eph. i. 18, and that then he would open our eyes to see the glory of such an inheritance; secondly, To honour the righteous, and not despise poor Christians, seeing God hath made them his heirs, and 'rich in faith,' James ii. 5; thirdly, To endeavour with all care to walk worthy of such honour as to be made God's heirs; and, lastly, To be willing to suffer anything in this world for Christ, seeing in the world to come we must reign with him as co-heirs, Rom. viii. 17, 18.

Of the saints. Only saints inherit; and therefore be sure thou be a saint; be sure thou be more than flesh and blood, 1 Cor. xv. 50; be sure thou lie in none of the sins God hath threatened with the loss of this inheritance, Eph. v. 5, 1 Cor. vi. 9, Gal. v. 21; be sure of the imputation of the righteousness of Christ, Rom. iv. 13, 14, Titus iii. 7; be sure thou have in thee the spirit of the Son, Gal. iv. 7, Eph. i. 14; be sure to commit thyself to the word of grace, Acts xx. 32.

In light. The Christian's inheritance is said to be held in light in six respects:

First, Because he now obtains it in the times of the gospel, which times, in comparison with the times of the Old Testament, are called times of light—the light of the Jews being spread abroad among the Gentiles, and exceedingly enlarged by the rising of the Sun of righteousness.

Secondly, Because this inheritance can never be assured without the light of knowledge. In the understanding of man there is a three-fold light of knowledge—natural, evangelical, and celestial. The natural light is the light of reason, the evangelical light is the light of faith, and the celestial light is the light of heaven. Before we can see our inheritance in the light of heaven, we must first see it in the light of faith; and as for the light of reason, it will do no good for any evidence in this tenure.

Thirdly, Because this inheritance is held with true joy on earth and perfect joy in heaven; and joy is expressed by the word light in many places in scripture.

Fourthly, In respect of the admirable communion that a Christian hath with God and Christ, who is light of light, 'that true light,' John viii. 12.

Fifthly, Because of the certainty of this inheritance, it is said to be held in light. It is worthy the noting that Catharinus, a papist, writing upon this place, thus understands the meaning of light, and is much offended with those that plead for uncertainty of assurance.

Sixthly, In light—that is, in heaven; and the light of heaven is an excellent light, both for the perfection of it and the continuance of it. It is a perfect light, for there shall be on God's part a clear revelation, and on man's part a clear vision; and for continuance, that light shall never be overcome of darkness; nay, it shall never admit any mixture of obscurity, inasmuch as heaven is a city that 'needs not the sun or moon to shine in it; for the glory of God doth lighten it, and the Lamb is the light thereof,' Rev. xxi. 23. In the meanwhile, till God translate us to this light of heaven, let us labour to settle our hearts in the light of faith and certainty, and glad our hearts with the light of the Spirit and joy, choosing rather to die than to forsake the face and presence of God, the fountain of all true light both in earth and heaven.

Ver. 13. *Who hath delivered us from the power of darkness, and translated us into the kingdom of his dear Son.*

In this verse our redemption is considered more particularly; for as it is by inchoation in this life, it stands of two parts. The first is our deliverance from *the power of darkness*, and the second is our translating into *the kingdom of Christ*.

Darkness. This darkness imports the misery of unregenerate men, from which the children of God, in the days of redemption, are delivered; and it notes not only the darkness of Gentilism, proper to the pagans of that time, but also the darkness of sin, of ignorance, of infidelity, of adversity, of death, and of hell; for every unregenerate man is covered with a six-fold darkness: first, The darkness of sin, Rom. xiii. 13; secondly, The darkness of ignorance, which as a vail covers all flesh, John viii. 12, Isa.

xxv. 8, 2 Cor. iii. 17; thirdly, The darkness of infidelity, for as there is the light of faith in the regenerate, so there is a darkness of unbelief that possesseth every unregenerate man: all men have not faith: it is the gift of God: both the prophets and apostles have complained, 'Who hath believed our report?' Isa. liii. 1, Rom. x. 16; fourthly, The darkness of adversity, Isa. viii. 22, miseries of all sorts breaking in upon the soul, body, state, and names of men; fifthly, The darkness of death, for death is the house of darkness, and this is the wages of sin, Ps. lxxxviii. 12; lastly, The wicked man is in danger of utter darkness, even of the darkness of hell. Out of all this we may see the extreme misery of all carnal persons upon whom the kingdom of darkness breaks in, and prevails so many ways; and therefore accursed is their misery that can live in this estate, without sense, or remorse, or fear. If security, as a wretched lethargy, had not overgrown men's hearts, how could they eat, drink, sleep, marry, give in marriage, &c., when they find themselves in the power of such fearful and horrible darkness?

Power. This darkness gets power, and prevails over the world, by the unwearied labour of the prince of darkness; who, as he seduced our first parents, to extinguish the fair light in which they were created, (whence flowed a universal darkness upon all mankind,) so doth he still, as god of the unregenerate world, work effectually in blinding men's minds more and more, that the light of the gospel might not shine in their hearts, both by hindering by all the ways he can the means of light, and by leading man on from sin to sin, till custom have worn out sense, and bred a very liking of darkness more than light. And thus poor man runs from darkness to darkness, and from dungeon to dungeon, till he fall into the everlasting dungeon of utter darkness; and this would be the end of all flesh, were it not that God of his infinite mercy hath provided a means in Jesus Christ to deliver the elect from the power of this darkness.

Delivered. Every man hath great reason to think of this deliverance out of the kingdom of darkness, wherein naturally he is; for while he so continueth, he 'knoweth not whither he goeth,' John xii. 35, 1 John ii. 11; he 'hath no fellowship with God,' 1 John i. 6; his deeds are all evil, John iii. 19, 20; his ignorance will not excuse him, John i. 5; yea, it will be his condemnation, John iii. 19; his feet tread not in the way of peace.

Who hath delivered us. Here are four things: 1. What, *delivered*; 2. Whom, *us*; 3. When, *hath*; 4. Who, viz., God the Father.

Delivered. The original word, Ἐῤῥύσατο, doth not signify only to let out, or lead out, or buy out; but it noteth forcibly to snatch out. Man is not gotten so easily out of Satan's hands; nor will the world and flesh let him go without force, or without blows.

Quest. What must we do that we may be delivered from this power of darkness?

Ans. Believe in Jesus Christ, who is the true light, John viii. 12. Know that all true light is begun in the assurance of God's love to thee in Jesus Christ. Seek his knowledge. To this end, attend upon the preaching of the gospel, by which life and immortality are brought to light. And because this sun doth not always shine, 'walk in the light while you have the light,' John xii. 35. And because a man can never sincerely seek the comforts of God in Jesus Christ, or constantly love the word of the kingdom, the fountain of light, but that there will be great opposition from Satan and the world, therefore every one that is aweary of this darkness of ignorance and unbelief, and feels what darkness of adversity his sins have brought upon him, and fears the darkness of death and hell, must arm himself, resolve and prepare, and fight for his own deliverance, ' putting on the whole armour of light,' using all the means with faith and diligence, and then shall God's power be made known in his weakness, and the strong man armed, which is the devil, shall be cast out by him that is stronger than he, even by Jesus Christ.

At the time when this deliverance from the power of darkness is wrought, there are at the least these nine things in every one that is truly delivered: first, He seeks knowledge with great estimation of it; secondly, He is careful to amend his ways and to avoid sin; thirdly, He feels and resists temptations; fourthly, He renounceth the world, as being neither besotted with vanity, nor swayed with example; fifthly, He fights against his own flesh;

sixthly, He loves the word of God; seventhly, He forsakes evil company; eighthly, He mourns over, and prays against some special sins; ninthly, He loves all the children of the light. These are not all things that are wrought in man in the day his heart is changed and he delivered; but less than this can be in no man nor woman that is truly delivered from the power of darkness.

Who. **Doct.** It is God only that delivers us from darkness. This is needful to be considered of, both that carnal men may know they can never see the light if they use not the means God hath appointed, and that godly men might not despair under the sense of their wants; for as God hath called them to the light and given them means, so he is able to create light at his own pleasure.

Us. **Doct.** The saints, even the dearest of all God's children, have been ignorant, sinful, and miserable, as well as any other.

Hath. A question may here be asked, How it can be said that God's children have been delivered, seeing they are ignorant, sinful, fleshly, full of afflictions, and subject to die still?

Ans. They are delivered in respect of inchoation, though not in respect of consummation; though they be ignorant, yet the vail is not whole, but many pieces are torn off; though they be in a dungeon in this world, yet a great window is broken down and much light appears; though there be sin in them, yet it reigns not; though they must die, yet the sting of death is pulled out; though they endure the same afflictions that wicked men do for the matter, they are not the same for nature and use; they are not curses or punishments, but only chastisements and trials, or preventions.

The consideration of this, that we are not all at once delivered from the power of darkness, may defend often preaching, and the frequent use of all good means, public or private. This darkness will not away with one day's shining; these clouds will not be dispelled with one blast. What is the light of one candle, when the night hath enclosed the whole air?

And translated us into the kingdom of his dear Son. Or, as it is in the original, *of the Son of his love.*

These words contain the second part of our redemption on earth in this world. The redeeming of us is the translating of us; and this translation is amplified by the condition of life into which we are translated, which, for the excellency of it, is into a kingdom; and for the author of it, is into the kingdom of Jesus Christ, the Son of God's love.

Translated. The word is a metaphor, and the comparison is taken from plants in nature; and there are divers things signified unto us, concerning our redemption, in the similitude of translating plants. As trees are translated in winter, not in the spring, so commonly our redemption is applied in the days of special affliction and sorrow. And as the plant is not first fruitful and then translated, but therefore translated that it may bear fruit, so we are not therefore redeemed because God was in love with our fruits, but therefore translated out of the kingdom of darkness that we might bring forth fruit unto God. And as a tree may be truly removed and new planted and yet not presently bear fruit, so may a Christian be truly translated and yet in the first instant of his conversion he may not shew forth all that fruit he doth desire, &c.

In particular, *translating* hath two things in it: first, Pulling up; secondly, Setting again. The pulling up of the tree shadows out three things in the conversion of a sinner: First, Separation from the world. He cannot be in Christ that hath his heart rooted in the earth, and keeps his old standing amongst those trees, the wicked of the world. Secondly, Deliverance both from original sin in the reign of it, which is the moisture of the old earth, and also from hardness of heart; for *translating* hath removing of the mould and stones that were about the root. Thirdly, Godly sorrow raised by the sense of the strokes of the axe of God's threatenings, and by the loss of many sprouts and branches that were hidden in the earth. A Christian cannot escape without sorrow, for he hath many an unprofitable sprout of vanity and sinful profit and pleasure he must part with. The setting of the tree notes both our ingrafting into Christ by the Spirit of God through faith, and our communion with the saints—the fruitful trees in God's orchard; as also it notes our preservation by the infusion of the sap of holy graces.

And it is worthy to be noted that he saith *translated us*, to teach us that there remains in man the same nature after calling that was before, for our natures are not destroyed in conversion, but translated. There remains the same faculties in the soul, and the same powers in the body; yea, the constitution and complexion of man is not destroyed. As the melancholy man doth not cease to be so after conversion, only the humour is sanctified unto a fitness for godly sorrow, and holy meditation, and the easy renouncing of the world, &c.; and the like may be said of other humours in man's nature.

Into the kingdom. The kingdom of God is either universal, over the whole world, or spiritual, over the faithful souls on earth, or blessed souls in heaven, till the day of judgment; or it is both spiritual and corporal, over all the saints, after the day of judgment for ever. It is the kingdom of grace by inchoation in the way present here below that is here meant, not the kingdom of glory by consummation in our country above.

The kingdom of Christ here on earth, though it be not so visible and pompous as other kingdoms are, yet it excels all the kingdoms on earth; for when all other kingdoms are not only shaken, but translated, or removed, or dissolved, the kingdom of Christ will endure to the end; and in Christ's kingdom the number of possessors doth not diminish the largeness of the possessions of each, whereas in other states many kings make little kingdoms. Besides, wicked men may not only be subjects, but kings, in other kingdoms; but this kingdom, though it be everywhere, yet it is wanting to the ignorant and sinners. Christ reigns in this kingdom by his word and Spirit; and his government is taken up especially in two things: first, The collection of his church; and, secondly, The maintenance of it.

Great are the privileges of the saints under the government of Jesus Christ. They are qualified with eternal graces; they are comforted with the daily refreshings that flow from the sense of God's favour; they are confirmed in the assured peace with angels and good men; they are estated into an everlasting inheritance; they daily reap the benefits of Christ's intercession; they often sup with Christ, and are feasted by the great king; they live always in the king's court, inasmuch as they are always in God's special presence; they partake of the privileges, prayers, and blessings of all the righteous; and they have the Spirit of God in them, to unite them to God and Christ, to lead them in the paths of holy life, to comfort them in all distresses, to warn them if they go out either on the left hand or the right, and to help them in their prayers, making request for them when they know not what to pray as they ought.

Object. The world sees no such glory in the estate of Christians in this kingdom.

Sol. There lies a veil over the eyes of all worldly men; and besides, this kingdom, though it be in the world, is not of it; though it be here, yet it is not from hence; and the afflictions that commonly cover the face of the church, do hide from carnal men the beauty of it. And by reason of the opposition that is between the kingdom of Christ and the kingdom of darkness, though the world know the glory of Christians, yet they will not acknowledge it.

Object. The faithful themselves discern not any such excellency in their earthly condition.

Sol. We must distinguish of Christians. Some are but infants in grace, and babes. These may be entitled to great things, and yet have no great sense of it; as the child in nature hath no great discerning of the inheritance he is born to, or his own present condition wherein he excels others. A kingdom is never the worse because the infant prince cannot discourse of the glory of it. Some Christians fall away, for the time, into gross sin or error; and these are in matters of grace like the drunken man or paralytic in nature, their discerning is lost with their uprightness. Other Christians either want the means in the power of it, or are tossed with great afflictions, or are in the fit of temptation; and then they have but a dark glimpse of their felicity in Christ. But the strong Christian, that hath digested the assurance of God's love in Christ, and is exercised in the word of righteousness, sees such a glory in the kingdom of grace, and doth acknowledge it with such unmoveable firmness of heart, that all the powers of either earth or hell cannot alter his judgment in the high estimation of such a condition.

Use. The use of this doctrine concerning Christ's kingdom is:

First, For consolation. God's children should much

exult and rejoice in their estates: and inasmuch as Christ sitteth as king for ever, 'all that are in his temple should speak of his glory,' Ps. xxix. 9, 10. And if there were nothing else for a Christian to joy in, yet 'let all the children of Sion rejoice in their king,' Ps. cxlix. 2. Yea, the thought of this, that God is our king, should uphold us, and fence us against all crosses, Ps. lxxiv. 12; for Christ is 'a hiding-place for the wind, and a cover for the tempest; as rivers of waters in a dry place, and as the shadow of a great rock in a weary land,' Isa. xxxii. 2. And therefore let our eyes never grow dim in viewing this glory, or our ears grow dull in hearkening to the word of this kingdom.

Secondly, For reproof and terror unto all wicked men that harden their hearts and refuse to return. What greater loss than to lose Christ's kingdom? And what fairer service than to serve the Son of God? 'Who would not fear thee, O king of nations?' Jer. x. 7. Accursed is the estate of all such as subject not their necks to Christ's yoke; that refuse to let him reign over them by his word and Spirit; that come not up to do their homage in Jerusalem, even to worship this king, the Lord of hosts, Zech. xiv. 17. If Jesus Christ be a great king, then where shall they appear that say to the king, *Apostata?* Job xxxiv. 18. Even all such, I mean, that dare reproach the way of Christ, and deride the sincerity of such as desire to employ themselves in the business of the kingdom, &c. Is he a great king? How dare we then offer that unto him which they durst not offer to a mean king on earth? What mean the blind and the lame in God's house? Mal. i. 13, 14. How dare men so securely offer up their blind lip-service and lame devotions? It is a kingdom that is offered, why do we then trifle, why do they excuse? What means these fond excuses, 'I have married a wife, and cannot come; I have bought five yoke of oxen, and must go prove them; I have bought a farm, and must go see it'? I have this pleasure and that profit, and therefore cannot come? Will they lose a kingdom upon so silly a pretence, when thou needest not to lose either wife, farm, or oxen? God doth not bid thee leave thy wife, thy labour, thy calling, thy living, but only wills thee to attend thine own further advancement in the season of it. Seek

lawful profit, but seek grace first. Use thy lawful pleasures, but chiefly seek the pleasures of God, even these spiritual joys that are more worth than a kingdom.

Thirdly, For instruction. It should teach us above all things to seek our happiness in this excellent estate under the government of Jesus Christ. We should, in respect of the worth of it, 'forsake our father's house,' and the immoderate desire of any earthly thing, so that the king will please to delight in us, Ps. xlv. We should open our hearts wider, that the king of glory, by his word and Spirit, may come in, Ps. xxiv. 10. We should labour for all those graces by which an entrance is ministered into this kingdom, 2 Pet. i. 8, 11. And whatsoever we are uncertain of, we should 'make our calling and election sure.' And though we be never so many ways opposed, yet seeing we fight for a kingdom—nay, in a kingdom—we should hold it always 'a good light,' 1 Tim. vi., and continue constant and immovable. And if Christ lead us into his chambers of presence, Cant. i. 3, and delight us with the sweet joys of his presence, we should remember such princely love and joy in him alway. Let the Christian sing and make a joyful noise to the Rock of his salvation, and let him worship and bow down, let him serve with all reverence, and hear without all hardness of heart, Ps. xcv. 1, 3. Let no discontentment possess the heart of the true Christian; for to serve Christ is to reign, and all his subjects are kings, and the worst estate of the meanest Christian is a rich kingdom.

Of his Son. Quest. Why is it called the kingdom of the Son rather than of the Father?

Ans. Because God hath given all the power to the Son, and this kingdom is assigned over to him. The merit of this happiness is only in Christ, and the virtue that gathers us into this kingdom is only from Christ, and no man cometh to the Father but by Christ.

Son of his love. Christ is the Son of God's love: first, Because he is most worthy of all others to be beloved, as Judas is the 'son of perdition,' that is, most worthy to be damned; secondly, Because he was from everlasting begotten of the love of his Father, he is God's natural Son; thirdly, Because he is infinitely filled with the sense of his love, so they are said to be the children of the marriage that are full of joy in respect of the marriage; fourthly, Because it is he by whom love is derived into others, it is he that makes all other sons beloved; lastly, In respect of his human nature, he is that Son upon whom God hath showed his principal love in respect of the gifts with which that nature is admirably qualified. The meditation of this, that Christ our Saviour is the Son of God's love, is very comfortable, for he is like to speed in anything he requests the Father for us, and he will be sure to preserve us, that himself is a king's Son, yea, God's Son, yea, a king and God himself, and so infinitely beloved of the Father. It is an excellent thing to be Christ's member, seeing he inherits so great love: and if God gave us this Son so dear to him, how shall he deny anything, seeing never can aught be so precious, but that with Christ he will willingly give it?

Ver. 14. *In whom we have redemption, through his blood, even the forgiveness of sins.*

In the former verses our redemption is considered, as God the Father is the efficient cause of it. In this verse it is considered as Christ is the instrumental cause of it. In the verse four things are to noted: 1. By whom we are redeemed, viz., by *the Son of God's love,* implied in the first words; 2. Who are redeemed, *we,* that is, the faithful; 3. How we are redeemed, viz., *by his blood;* 4. With what kind of redemption; not by redemption from loss in estate, or servitude in body, but from sin in the soul.

In whom. Doct. The Son of God is the Redeemer of the sons of men. He that had no sins of his own did worthily cancel other men's: he that was in no debt paid our debts. In this work of redemption we may see piety itself beaten for the impious man, and wisdom itself derided for the foolish man, and truth itself slain for the lying man, and justice itself condemned for the unjust man, and mercy itself afflicted for the cruel man, and life itself dying for the dead man. None can redeem us but Jesus Christ; he only is God and man; he only was deputed hereunto; he only it is that is the firstborn, the brother, and the kinsman, Lev. xxv. Two things are required in a saviour and redeemer, viz., right and power; and the title or right must be either by propriety or by propinquity. In power and propriety the Father or Holy Ghost might redeem, but in propinquity Christ only is the next kinsman.

Secondly, It is to be noted that he saith *in whom,* not *by whom,* to teach us that the comfort of our redemption is not then had when Christ, as mediator, doth pay the price, but when, as our head, he receiveth us to himself. We must be in Christ before we can be pardoned: it is a vain thing to allege that Christ died for us, unless we can clear it that we are the members of Christ by conversion and regeneration; we must be in Christ before the devil will let go his hold; we must be in Christ before we can receive the influence of his grace, for that descends only from the head to the members; we must be in Christ before we can be covered with his garment; and if we be not in the vine we cannot persevere.

We. Quest. How could the obedience and sufferings of one man serve to redeem so many men?

Ans. It is sufficient, because he did all willingly; because, also, he was himself innocent and without fault; but especially because this obedience and suffering was the obedience of him that was more than man.

Again, it is to be noted that he saith *we,* not all men, have redemption, as the Universalists dream.

Have. Quest. Had not the fathers before Christ redemption in him as well as we?

Ans. They had, first, In predestination, because they were hereunto elect; secondly, In efficacy, inasmuch as they that did believe in Christ had the virtue of the redemption to come. Hence, that Christ is said to be 'the Lamb slain from the beginning of the world.'

By his blood. Christ shed his blood many ways: as when he was circumcised; in his agony in the garden; when he was crowned and whipped; when he was crucified; and when with a spear his side was pierced: but here it is by a synecdoche taken for all his sufferings.

There have been in former times four ways of redemption: first, By manumission, when the lord let his vassal voluntarily go out free; but thus could not we be redeemed, for the devil never meant to manumit us; secondly, By permutation, as when in the wars one is exchanged for another; and thus could not we be redeemed, for who should be changed for us? thirdly, By violent ablation, as Abraham redeemed Lot, by force rescuing him; but this way did not stand with God's justice; fourthly, By giving a price, and thus we are redeemed. But what price was given? not gold and silver, nor the blood of goats; not thousands of rams, or rivers of oil; not the sons of our bodies for the sins of our soul, Mic. vi. 4, 5; nay, if a whole thousand of us had been burned in one heap, it would not have expiated for one man's sin; but the price was the blood of Jesus Christ, 1 Pet. i. 19; and by this price we may see how hateful a thing sin is in God's sight, and we may resolve that we are not our own men any more to do what we list; neither ought we to be servants of men, Gal. i. 5. Besides, if there had been merit in the work of the law, the Son of God needed not to have shed his blood; and seeing it is shed, we need no other mediator, nor works of satisfaction or supererogation.

Forgiveness of sins. The doctrine of remission of sins is many ways comfortable. It is a comfort: 1. That sins may be remitted, 1 John ii. 1; 2. That this remission may be applied particularly; thou mayst have it and keep it for thyself 1 John i. 9; 3. That if our sins be once forgiven they can never be laid to our charge more, they return not, Isa. xliii. 25, Mic. vii. 19, Ps. xxxii. 1; 4. That where God forgives one sin he forgives all sins; 5. That where God forgives sin he heals the nature, where he justifies he sanctifies. An earthly prince may forgive the felon, but he cannot give him a better disposition; but God never forgives any man but he gives him a new heart also, Ezek. xxxvi. 26, 27; 1 John i. 9 and ii. 1, 4; 6. That where God forgives the sin he forgives the punishment also, Acts v. 31, Ps. xxxii. 4, Mat. ix. 2, 5; lastly, That by remission of sins we may know our salvation, 1 Luke i. 77.

Secondly. As it is a comfortable doctrine to faithful men, so it is a terrible doctrine to wicked men, and that many ways: first, All men's sins are not forgiven; secondly, All need remission of sins; thirdly, If sin be not forgiven, it makes men loathsome to God, which the word *cover* importeth, Ps. xxxii. 1; it sets the soul in debt; it separates between God and us, and hinders good things from us, Isa. lix. 2; it defiles, Ps. li. 1; it remains upon record, written with a pen of iron, and with the point of a diamond, Jer. xvii. 1; it causeth all the disquietness of heart, Ps. xxxviii. 3; it is the cause of all judgments; it brings death, Rom. vi. 23.

Thirdly, A question is here to be considered of, viz., What should a man do that he may get a comfortable assurance that his sins are forgiven him?

Ans. He that would be assured of remission of sins, must do these things: First, He must forgive other men their trespasses against him, else he cannot be forgiven, Mat. vi. 14. Secondly, He must search out his sins by the law, and mourn over them in God's presence, striving to break and bruise his own heart with grief in secret, in the confession of them to God, Luke iv. 18, 1 John i. 9, Hosea xiv. 3, Zech. xii. 12 to the end, and xiii. 1. Thirdly, We must take heed of the sin against the Holy Ghost, which, beginning in apostasy, is continued in persecution of the known truth, and ends in blasphemy, and is therefore a sin unpardonable, because the sinner is utterly disabled of the power to repent. And howsoever all sins against the Holy Ghost are not unpardonable, but only that sin that hath the former three things in it; yet the man that would have evidence of pardon, must take heed of all ways of offending against God's Spirit, and therefore must take heed of speaking evil of the way of godliness, of contemning the means of grace, by which the Spirit works, and of tempting, grieving, or vexing of the Holy Ghost within his own heart or others. Fourthly, He must daily attend upon the preaching of the gospel, till the Lord be pleased to quicken his own promises, and his heart to the joyful application of the comforts of God's love, contained in his word. And when men come to God's presence to seek so great a mercy as the pardon of sin, they must, above all things, take heed of wilful hardness of heart, lest their unwillingness to be directed by God's word be required with that curse that God should grow unwilling that they should repent, and he should forgive them, Mark iv. 11, 12, Acts xxvi. 18. Fifthly, The prayers of the faithful are very available to procure the pardon of sin, James v. 16. Sixthly, He must, with due preparation, be often in receiving the sacrament of the Lord's Supper, which is to the worthy receiver a worthy seal of remission, Mat. xxvi. 28. Seventhly, He must amend his life and believe in Jesus Christ, Mark i. 4, Acts v. 31, x. 43.

Ver. 15. *Who is the image of the invisible God, and the first-begotten of every creature.*
Hitherto of the work of redemption ; now followeth the person of the Redeemer, who is described as he standeth in relation :
1. To God, ver. 15.
2. To the universe or whole world, ver. 15-17.
3. To the church, ver. 18, 19, &c.
In all the verses in general may be observed the evident proof of his divine nature. For, as the verses before, when they mention redemption in his blood, prove him to be man, so these verses, ascribing to him eternity, omnipotence, &c , prove him to be God. That our Saviour is God may be further confirmed by these places of scripture : Gen. xix. 24, Judges ii. 1, 4, 14, Ps. xlv., Prov. viii. 22, Job xix. 25 ; Isa. vii. 14, ix. 6, xxxv. 2, 4, xl. 3, 10, 12, xliii. 10, 11, 23, xlv. 22 ; Jer. xxiii. 5, 6 ; Hosea i. 7, xii. 4 ; Mic. ii. 12, iv. 1 ; John i. 1, &c. ; 1 John v. 20, Rev. i. 6.

Besides, the apostle's drift is to extol the excellency of Christ, by whose blood we are redeemed. Howsoever he appeared in form of a servant, yet he exceeded all monarchs that ever were on earth ; for Christ is the essential image of God, whereas the greatest monarchs are God's image but by a small participation. He is the Son of God by generation ; they are so only by creation or regeneration. He is the first-born ; they are but younger brothers at the best. He is the Creator ; they are but creatures. All things are for him, whereas they have right and power over but few things. He is eternal ; they are mortal. Things cannot consist without a Redeemer in heaven ; but so they may without a monarch on earth. He is a mystical head, and by his Spirit uniteth all his subjects to him, and by influence preserveth them ; but so can no political heads do their subjects. Other things I might instance in the verses following, but these shall suffice.

The first thing in particular by which the Redeemer is described in his relation to God in these words, *who is the image of the invisible God.*

Here three things are to be considered : first, The person resembling, *who ;* secondly, The manner how he resembleth, viz., by the way of *image ;* thirdly, The person resembled in his nature, *God,* in the attribute of his nature, *invisible.* For the first, if we be asked of whom he here speaketh, it is easily answered out of the former verses ; it is the Son of God, ' the Son of his love,' ver. 13. And thither I refer the consideration of the first point.

Image. Our Redeemer resembles God by the way of image.

There is a difference between the image of a thing and the similitude of it. The sun in the firmament expresseth God by similitude ; for as there is but one sun, so there is but one God. And as no man can look upon the sun in his brightness, so no man can see God with mortal eyes, &c. But yet the sun is not therefore God's image. God's image is in men, and in Christ.

God's image is in man three ways : First. By creation ; and so it is in all men, even worst men, inasmuch as there is in them an aptitude to know and conceive of God, &c. Secondly, By recreation ; and so it is in holy men, that do actually and habitually know and conceive of God, &c., but this is imperfectly. Thirdly, By similitude of glory ; and so the blessed in heaven conceive of, and resemble God, and that (in comparison with the two former) perfectly.

But there is great difference between the image of God in man, and the image of God in Christ. In Christ, it is as Cæsar's image in his son ; in man, it is as Cæsar's image in his coin. Christ is the natural image of God, and of the same substance with God, whom he doth resemble ; but the Christian is God's image only in some respects, neither is he of the same nature with God. Man is both the *image of God,* and *after the image of God.* The image of God because he truly resembles God ; and after the image of God, because he resembles him but imperfectly. But Christ is the perfect image of God, and not after his image. Some express the difference thus : Christ is the image of the invisible God, but man is the image of the visible God, that is, of Christ.

Christ is the image of God three ways : 1. In operation, because it is he that worketh God's image in us; 2. In apparition, because he appeared for God to the fathers in the old law; 3. In person, and that in both natures, both as God and man; for the most perfect image of God is Christ God, the perfect image of God is Christ man, the imperfect image of God is man.

That Christ is the image of God, as he is God, is apparent by that place, Phil. ii. 6, and Heb. i. 4. And here two things are admirable: first, That this image is an infinite image, like the thing resembled; secondly, That the image is the same in number, not in species only, with the thing resembled.

Christ as man is the image of God, 1 Tim. iii. 16, and that three ways: first, As the Godhead dwells in Christ bodily, in respect of the unutterable presence of the divine nature; secondly, As by his miracles and great works he manifested the divine nature, and showed God in the world; thirdly, As his human nature is qualified with knowledge, righteousness, purity, and other gifts; for if man be God's image in respect of this, Christ is so much more. To conclude, Christ, as he is God, is not only the image of the invisible God, but the invisible image of God; but as man, he is the visible image of the invisible God.

Use. The considerations of this doctrine, that Christ is the image of the invisible God, may serve for six uses: First, To teach us the admiration of that God whose image is of so admirable praise. Secondly, To show the fearfulness of their estate that 'turn the glory of the incorruptible God into the image of corruptible creatures,' Rom. i. 23. And this is the sin not only of the Gentiles, but of the papists also. Thirdly, It should wonderfully quicken us to all the duties of humbleness of mind and meekness, and make us ready in all things to serve one another, without wrangling or contention, in love; seeing he that was in form of God, equal with God, put upon him the form and image of a servant, Phil. ii. 1, 2, 3, 6. Fourthly, We may hence learn that if we would know God, we must get into Christ; for in him only is the Father known: 'he that hath seen Christ hath seen the Father,' John xiv. 9; 2 Cor. iv. 4. Labour, then, in the business of mortification and justification, and then that knowledge of God, which is impossible to nature, will be possible to grace. They have the firmest apprehension of God, not that have the most wit or learning, but that have the most grace in Jesus Christ. One may be a great scholar, and yet a great atheist. The surest way is to know the Creator in the Redeemer. Fifthly, Seeing it is Christ's honour to be God's image, let it be our honour to be Christ's image, which we can never be, unless we 'put off the old man and his works,' Col. iii. 9, 10, and see to it that the light of the gospel be not hid from us by the god of this world, for the gospel is the gospel of glory, 2 Cor. iv. 4, and iii. 18, 19, &c., Gal. iv. 19. Now, we may be framed like to the image of Christ in three things: 1. In knowledge, Col. iii. 10; 2. In sufferings, Rom. viii. 29; 3. In holiness and righteousness of heart and life, Eph. iv. 21, 24; lastly, Shall the devil make men worship the image of the beast, Rev. xiii., and shall not we for ever honour this everlasting image of our God?

Invisible God. God is invisible, John i. 18, 1 Tim. vi. 16, John ix. 11, &c., and xxiii. 9, 10. God cannot be seen, because he is a spirit, not a body; and because of the exceeding thinness and purity of his nature, and because of the transplendency of his glory; and lastly, because of the infiniteness of his essence.

The use is: first, To teach us to walk alway in fear and trembling, seeing we serve such a God as sees us when we see not him, Ps. lxv. 5, &c.; secondly, This should check the secret and beastly discontentment of our hearts, which are many times moved to vexation, because our God is not visible; whereas, we should therefore the more admire him that is so absolutely perfect. Yet were imperfection to be visible. And yet notwithstanding, though God be not visible to sense, he is visible to understanding; and though nature cannot see him, yet grace can. Now, if any ask what he might do that he might see God, I answer, that he that would see God: First, He must look for him in the land of the living; seek for him amongst true Christians. He must first know and love his brother, and then he shall know and see God, 1 John iv. 12. He that would know the Father, must be acquainted with the child. Secondly, He must with fear, and reverence, and constancy, wait upon the manifestation of God in his house; in that light we shall see light.

We must eat at God's table, and it must be our contentment to taste of the fatness of his house, and to drink out of the river of those pleasures, if we would with clear light see God, Ps. xxxvi. 8, 9. God is to be seen in Zion, Ps. lxxxiv. 5, 7, 8; God's goings are seen in the sanctuary, Ps. lxviii. 24. Thirdly, He must learn God's name; for he that knows his name, sees his nature. When God would show his glory to Moses, he proclaims his name to him, Exod. xxxiii. 19, and xxxiv. 6, &c. Fourthly, He must be sure to get into Christ by faith, being born of God by regeneration, John vi. 46, and xiv. 7. Lastly, He must be pure in heart, Mat. v. 8; he must specially strive against the corruptions inward in his thoughts and affections. Thus of the second use.

Thirdly, The consideration of this, that God is invisible, should encourage us to well-doing, even in secret, seeing we serve such a God as can see in secret, Mat. vi. 4.

Hitherto our Redeemer is described as he stands in relation in God. Now, in the second place, he is described as he stands in relation to the creatures. And Christ is in relation to the creatures five ways: 1. As the *first-begotten* among them; 2. As their *Creator*; 3. As the end of them, *all for him*; 4. In respect of eternity, as *he is before all things*; 5. As *all things in him consist*. All things depend upon Christ as their preserver, as their ancient, as their end, as their Creator, and as the first-born.

The first-begotten of every creature. Two things are here to be considered of Christ: 1. That he is God's Son by generation; 2. That he is the first-begotten.

For the first: God hath sons by nature and by grace; Christ is born as man, and begotten as God. Things are begotten three ways: 1. Metaphorically, only by comparison, or in some respects; 2. Corporally; 3. Spiritually. Some things do beget without themselves, as bodies do; but this is more ignobly and basely; some things beget within themselves, as doth the spirit or soul, more perfectly. But the most perfect and unutterable glorious generation is the begetting of the Son of God by God. The way of God in eternity who can find out? and his generation who can tell? His ways are not as our ways; yet a glimpse of this great work we may reach to two ways:

1. By way of negation, as they say in schools.
2. By way of comparison.

First, By denying that unto God which hath imperfection in it. In the generation of the creatures we may see something into the generation of the Son of God. There are eight things in the generation of the creatures which are not in this begetting of the natural Son of God: 1. The creatures beget in time, because themselves are first begotten; but this is not in God. Christ is *of the Father*, but not *after the Father*. There is here a priority in order, but not in time. 2. The creatures beget by affection; this is imperfection, but God begetteth by nature. 3. The creature begets without himself, so as sons are diverse and divided from the father, because they are finite. We are of like nature to our fathers, but not the same nature, ὁμοιουσιοι, not ὁμοουσιοι; but it is not so in God, for Christ is not divided from the Father, as he is the natural Son of God. 4. The generation in the creature is not without corruption or diminution of the nature of the begetter; but here God the Father begetteth without corruption or diminution, by a way divine, unenarrable, and incomprehensible. 5. Our children are less than their parents; but Christ is as well co-equal as co-eternal. 6. The creature communicates but a part of his substance, but God communicates the whole. 7. The father and son, among the creatures, are two in number, one in species only, but in God it is not so; for the Son of God is another, but not another thing, *alius*, but not *aliud*; he is another, viz., in person, but not another thing in essence. Lastly, The creature begets mortal creatures, and propagates but a being for a time, but God begets a Son immortal by nature, such a one as can never die in the nature so begotten.

Secondly, This generation is shadowed out by some comparison with creatures: The river and the spring are two, yet not divided; so is the sun and the beams of it. The savour and the ointment are together, and yet the ointment is not corrupted. But the principal comparison is in the mind and the word: The mind begets the word naturally, without passion or corruption within itself; so as the word begotten remains in the mind, the word afterwards, clothed with a voice, goeth into the ears of men, and yet ceaseth not to be still in the mind. This in many things, as you may see, is like to the generation of Christ by the Father. But all these are but shadows; the glory of the thing itself cannot be expressed by any words of man or angel.

The consideration of this doctrine should inflame us to the love of such a Son, who being, as he was, co-equal and co-eternal with the Father, yet was pleased to delight himself in God's earth, which is man, Prov. viii. 22, 31, 32. And we should for ever hearken and attend to the words of this wisdom of God, who teacheth us the secrets of the very bosom of his Father. And seeing this is the Son, of whom God hath spoken to the dreadful astonishment and wonder of heaven and earth, woe unto them that sin against the Son and provoke him to anger. How shall they be broken to pieces like an earthen vessel? Ps. ii. 5, 7, 9, 11, 12. But blessed are all they, that with all fear and trembling, and with all reverence and affection, subject themselves to the sceptre of his kingdom, and trust in the love of the Father, through the merits of the Son. Thus of the consideration of Christ, as he is begotten of God: it is here added that he is first-begotten.

First-begotten. Christ is the Son of God, John i. 14; he is the only-begotten Son of God, John i. 18; he is the natural Son of God, Rom. iii. 8; and here is termed the first-begotten Son of God. He is first-begotten, as God, two ways: 1. In time; he was before all other things. Of this afterwards. 2. In dignity; he is the foundation of all that respect by which others are made sons. He is first-begotten as man, not in time, but in dignity and operation: first, In respect of the miraculousness and wonderfulness of his birth and conception,—so are none other born; secondly, In respect of his resurrection, in which God did, as it were, beget him again,—thus he is afterwards said to be the first-born of the dead; thirdly, In respect of pre-eminence; as he hath the right of the first-born, being made heir of all things.

The use is divers: First, 'Let all the angels of God worship him,' Heb. i. 6. Secondly, It should kindle in our hearts godly sorrow for our sins. If we can mourn for the death of our first-born, how should we be pierced to remember that our sins have pierced God's first-born? Zech. xii. 12. Thirdly, We should never think it strange to suffer in this world, seeing God spared not his own first-born, Rom. viii. 29. Lastly, It may be a great comfort to Christians, and that two ways: first, Because they shall be accepted with God, in, and for Christ, who is the first-born, and hath received a blessing for all the rest; secondly, Because in Christ they themselves are accounted as God's first-born in comparison of other men: God will use them as his first-born, Exod. iv. 22, Heb. xii. 23, Ps. lxxxix. 27. By this God's children are made 'higher than the kings of the earth,' Ps. lxxxix. 27; and therefore woe shall be to them that wrong God's first-born, Exod. iv. 22. And therefore also every Christian should so esteem his birth-right as by no means, with profane Esau, for any lust, profit, or pleasure, to sell it, Heb. xii. 16.

Ver. 16. *For in him were all things created that are in heaven, and that are in earth, visible or invisible, whether they be thrones or dominions, or principalities or powers. All things were created for him and by him.*

In this verse four things are to be considered: first, Concerning creation itself in the general; secondly, Who created? thirdly, What was created? fourthly, The distinctions of creatures.

Created. God works not as the creatures do; God works in an instant. Angels work suddenly; nature works by little and little, and by degrees. There is a threefold effusion of the goodness of God: 1. By generation; 2. By spiration; 3. By creation.

The works of God are either internal and emanent, and are in the essence of God by an act internal and eternal,—and thus predestination is God's work,—or external and transient, passing to the creatures by an act external and temporal. And these works are either works of nature, or works of grace. The works of nature respect her, either as she is in making *qua est in fieri*, or as she is made *qua est in facto*: the latter works are works of providence, the former are works of creation.

A difference must be made between creating, generating, and making. A thing comes into being, of nothing, by creation; of something, by making; and of a substance, by generation. Creation is of God, by himself; generation is of nature according to God.

Doct. The world, even this whole frame of all things, was created and had a beginning. This we may know by faith, out of scripture, Gen. i., ii.; Ps. xxxiii. 6-9; Job xxxviii. 39; and by reason, from the state of creatures; their alterations, subordinations, debilities, and expirations, prove a beginning, and that they are not eternal.

Object. This drowns our thoughts, that we cannot conceive of eternity, what it was before the world was.

Sol. It is not meet we should account ourselves able to judge of eternity. What do plants judge of sense? what do the beasts judge of reason? how canst thou be fit to judge of eternity, that thyself hast no certain continuance in time?

Thus of creation in general; the second thing is, who is Creator?

In him, or by him. The whole Trinity did create the world; because it is a rule that the works of God that are without are undivided; so as that which one person doth, all the three persons do. Yet there is difference in the order: for the Father moves and wills it, the Son works it, and the Holy Ghost finisheth it. Creation is given to the Father, Acts xvii. 24; to the Son, John i. 3; to the Holy Ghost, Gen. i. 2, Ps. xxxiii. 6.

But in this place, the honour of the work is specially given to the Son. And it is to be noted, that the original hath more than barely *by him*, for it is said, *in him*, &c. The creation of the world was in Christ in two respects: First, It was in him as in an exemplar; the frame of the world to be made was in him as the image of the Father's understanding; for, in the building of a house there is a double frame, the one in the head of the carpenter, the other the frame external of the house, built after the pattern of that that was in the carpenter's head; so is it in the creation of the world. Secondly, It was in him, as that decreed and fore-appointed head and foundation, in which all the other things should be placed and consist; thus he is said to be 'the beginning of the creatures of God,' Rev. iii. 14.

This work of creation ascribed unto Christ proves his deity, eternity, and omnipotence. Thus of the Creator.

Thirdly, It follows, what was created? viz., *all things.* The whole world. By the world I mean not the frame of all things, as it was in God's essence from eternity, nor man only, which is called a little world, but this whole universe and great building, consisting of all sorts of creatures. Concerning this creation of all things, I only note two things: first, How they were created; secondly, The errors that sprung up against this doctrine.

Now, *all things were created:* First, Most freely, without any necessity that impelled God thereunto, Ps. xxxiii. 9, cxv. 3. Secondly, Without any labour, motion, or mutation of himself, with a beck only, and by his omnipotent word, Ps. xxxiii. 9. Thirdly, Of nothing. Of nothing, I say, negatively, in the creation of the first mass of all things; and of nothing privatively, in the second creation of things out of the first mass or chaos; for though in the order of nature, and by men, nothing is made of nothing, yet this extendeth not to God and the first creation. Fourthly, Most wisely, so as there flowed in the creation a goodness to every creature, so as they were all good in God's account, Gen. i. 31. This goodness in man and angels was God's image in them. Fifthly, In time, with time, in the very beginning of time, Gen. i. 1. Sixthly, In the space of six days, not at one time only; and this shewed the creature's disability, that could not form itself when the first matter was created. Herein God also shewed his power, and that he was not tied to second causes, as he declared when he gave light to the world, while yet there was no sun.

Then herein he teacheth men to dwell long upon the meditation of the creation, seeing God himself did prolong the creation for so many days, which yet he could have despatched in an instant.

There were four errors about the creation. Some said the world was eternal; some said, though it were not eternal, yet it had a material beginning, it was made of something; some said God made the superior creatures himself, and the inferior by angels; some made two beginners of things,—they imagined that one beginner made things incorruptible, and another made things corruptible. The very first verse of the Bible confutes all four errors. The word *in the beginning* shews the world was not eternal; the word *creation* notes that it was made of nothing. When he saith, God created all, he excludes angels; and lastly, when he saith, God created heaven and earth, he shews he was the only beginner of all sorts of creatures.

Fourthly, The distinction of the creatures follows.

Here they are distinguished three ways: 1. By place,—some are things *in heaven*, some things *in earth;* 2. By quality,—some are *visible*, some are *invisible;* 3. By a subdivision of the invisible,—some are *thrones*, some are *dominions*, &c.

Thrones, or dominions, or principalities, or powers. These words are diversely interpreted. Some think there is no necessity to understand them of angels, but in general of all empire, and of the order of economy among the creatures, in marriage, laws, or governments in heaven or earth. Some restrain the words to order amongst men only; some understand by thrones the palace of God's majesty and the seat of blessed immortality, and the rest of the words they interpret of angels; but the commonest opinion, and most ancient, is to understand all the words of angels only. But in this there is no agreement; for some think the apostle speaks by way of concession, as if he should say, Be it so that angels are thrones and dominions, &c., as the Jews and false apostles affirm when they go about to persuade you to angel-worship; yet if that were granted, Christ only were to be worshipped, because he made all those, and what excellency they have, they had it from him. Others think that the apostle reckoneth up the excellent things in human government, and gives them to angels, to shadow out their glory, and consequently the glory of Christ that made them. I think there is no hurt in their opinion that give all these words unto angels. And they are called thrones, dominions, principalities, and powers; because God by them governs the nations, and, as some think, moves the heavens, restrains the devils, works miracles, foretells things to come, protects the faithful, and exerciseth his judgments upon the world; yet so as these names may be given to all angels, in divers respects, and upon occasion of divers employments. Or they may be given to some angels for a time, and not for ever; or if it be yielded that those names do distinguish the divers sorts of angels and their orders, yet it will not follow that we can tell their sorts, as the bold Dionysius and the papists have adventured to do.

Thus of the doctrine of creation; the uses follow, and they are: 1. For reproof; 2. For consolation; 3. For instruction.

1. The doctrine of creation cannot but be a doctrine of great reproof and terror to wicked men; because those goodly creatures, being God's workmanship, will plead against them, and make them inexcusable in the day of Christ, inasmuch as they have not learned to know and serve God with thankfulness and fear, that shewed his wisdom and power, and other the invisible things of God, in the making of all those creatures, Rom. i. 19. And besides, from the great power of God, in the creation of themselves and other creatures, they may see that they are in a woful case that by sinning 'strive with him that made them,' Isa. xlv. 9, for he hath the same power to destroy them.

And further, if God made all, then he knows all, and so all the sins of the sinner. And in that he made all, he hath at his command, as Lord by creation, all armies, to raise them against the wicked for their subversion.

2. Secondly, The doctrine of the creation may comfort God's children many ways: First, It may comfort them in the faith of the world's dissolution. It is he that created heaven and earth that will accomplish it, 'that time shall be no more,' Rev. x. 6. I mean not times of mortality, sin, labour, infirmity, &c. Secondly, It may comfort them in the success of Christ's kingdom on earth. Though it be a great thing to gather men again into covenant with God, and to open the eyes of men, blind with ignorance, and to deliver the souls of men that have long lain in the prisons of sin and misery, yet we may be assured that God, by the ordinances of Christ, will accomplish all the great things of this spiritual kingdom, because he was able to create the heavens and earth. And God himself doth remember his power in the creation, to assure his performance in our regeneration, Isa. xlii. 5, 6. Thirdly, It may comfort us in our union with Christ; for what shall separate us from his love? Inasmuch as he is unchangeable himself, nothing else can, for they are all his creatures, and must not cross his resolved will, Rom. viii. Fourthly, It must needs be a comfort to serve such a God, as hath shewed himself in the creation to work so wonderfully. Blessed is he that can rejoice in God and his service, and is refreshed with the light of his countenance, and assured of his love, Ps. lxxxix. 11, 15. Fifthly, The wonders of the creation serve to shew us how

wonderful the works of grace are, in the working of which the Lord useth the very term of creating. To regenerate a man is as glorious a work as to make a world, Eph. ii. 10, and iv. 24, 2 Cor. v. 17, Gal. vi. 15. The protection of a Christian hath in it also divers of the wonders of the creation. The peace that comes into the hearts of Christians, as the fruit of the lips, is created, Isa. lvii. 19. A clean heart is a rare blessing, for it is created also, Ps. li. 10. Sixthly, It is a comfort against the force of wicked men and their wrongs. The wickedest men are God's creatures: 'he created the destroyer to destroy, and the smith that bloweth the coals, and him that bringeth forth an instrument;' and therefore 'all the weapons that are made against God's children cannot prosper.' And it is a part of the Christian's inheritance to be protected against the malice of the wicked that would destroy him, Isa. liv. 16 and xliii. 1-3. Lastly, It may comfort God's children in the expectation of their salvation; for God hath promised as certainly as he hath created the heavens he will save Israel, though it should be as hard a work as was the spreading out of the heavens, Isa. xlv. 15, 17-19.

Thirdly, The doctrine of the creation should teach us divers duties :

First, The admirableness and variety of God's works should provoke us to contemplation : 'How dear are thy thoughts unto me,' Ps. cxxxix. 17.

Secondly, In affliction, we should willingly commit ourselves to God, and trust in him, though our means be little or unlikely; for he is a 'faithful Creator,'—his love to us affords him will to do us good, and the creation proves his power, 1 Pet. iv. 19, Isa. xlv. 12, 17, 22.

Thirdly, The greatness of the works in creation should imprint in us reverence and fear, and force us to the duties of the adoration and worship of God, Rev. iv. 11, and v. 13, Ps. civ. 31, and c. 3.

Fourthly, The knowledge of the glory and greatness of the Creator should inflame in us indignation against idols and the worship of the creature, Jer. x. 3-16, Rom. i. 25.

Fifthly, The remembrance of our Creator and creation should work in us an abatement of our pride and jollity, and dull the edge of our fierce appetite to sin, Eccles. xii. 1.

Sixthly, The consideration of our equality in our creation should keep us that we transgress not against our brethren : 'We have all one Father, and one God hath created us,' Mal. ii. 10, Job xxxi. 14, 15. Thus of the creation.

The third thing in Christ's relation to the creatures is, that *all things are for him.*

For him. In divers respects : first, As it is he only in whom the Father is well pleased, and so the love of God to the world is for his sake; secondly, As all the creatures do serve to point out the Son, as well as the Father, and that because they shew Christ as the wisdom of the Father; and besides, their changes and corruptions do cry for the liberty of the sons of God in Christ; and further, they are all at command for the propagation and preserving of the kingdom of Christ; thirdly, As he is heir of all things, they are for him—that is, for his glory; so as he is not only the efficient, but the final cause of all things. The carpenter makes his house, perhaps for one more honourable than himself, but not so Christ in making this great house, the world. The consideration of this point, that all things are for Christ, should teach us divers things.

Uses. First, We should less doat upon the world and the things thereof, inasmuch as these things were principally made for Christ, and not for us; and secondly, We should use all these things as helps to lead us to Christ; thirdly, In the use of the creatures we should be careful to express the glory of Christ, by giving thanks, by magnifying his wisdom, power, goodness, &c., and by distributing them according to his appointment, as to the poor, and to the maintenance of the worship of God; for seeing they are his, and for him, we should dispose of them as he requires; lastly, It should keep us from the use of all ill means; for seeing it is for Christ, we should not lie, deceive, use false weights, run to witches, or take any other ungodly course; for he needs not our lie, nor desires to be helped by any sinful course.

The fourth thing which Christ is commended for is his eternity:

He was before all things. The immensity of Christ's divine nature hath four things in it : first, Infiniteness in respect of itself; secondly, Incomprehensibleness in respect of our sense and understanding;

thirdly, Incircumscriptibleness in respect of place; fourthly, Eternity in comparison of time. That Christ is eternal these places prove: Prov. viii. 22, &c.; Micah, v. 2, 4, &c.; Rev. i. 8, 11, xxi. 6, and xxii. 13.

The eternity of Christ may be thus defined: It is a pleasant and at once perfect possession of endless life; and hereby may the eternity of Christ appear to differ from the eternity of all other things. The heavens have an endlessness of essence, but they want life: the devils have an endless, not only being, but life, but it is not a pleasant life: the saints in heaven have a pleasant life till the day of judgment, but they have not whole possession: the angels in heaven have a whole possession, but it is not at once, but successively, both in revelation and joy; I say it is whole in them, because their whole nature or essence is possessed of pleasant and endless life: and lastly, Christ's eternity differs from all eternity of all the creatures, because no creature hath the former things absolutely perfect; that is, such a possession of endless life as unto which nothing is wanted, for they want many of the perfections that are in Christ, though they be perfect in their own kind.

Seeing Christ was before all things, we should prefer him before all things,—we should acknowledge his title as heir of all things,—as the eldest among all things, we should willingly hear him speak, and honour his words,—we should trust in him, and live by faith, &c.

And in him all things consist: that is, he upholds, rules, and governs all things by his providence; and this is the first thing by which our Redeemer is described in relation to the world. That providence is given to the Son, as well as creation, these places prove: Heb. i. 2, 3; Prov. viii. 15; John v. 12. Christ is not like the carpenter that makes his house, and then leaves it; or like the shipwright, that frames his ship, but never after guides it. All things are said to consist in him, in respect of *conservation,* in that he keeps all things in their being; in respect of *precept,* in that from him are prescribed the laws by which nature, policy, and religion are governed; in respect of *operation,* in that all things move in him; in respect of *ordination,* in that he appointeth all things to their end; in respect of *disposition of the means* to the end; and lastly, as the *universal cause* of nature, and natural instincts in all creatures, by which they further their own preservation.

Object. But we see the means by which all things are wrought and preserved as by their causes.

Sol. The means notwithstanding, all things consist in Christ: first, Because Christ useth not the means necessarily; secondly, He ordains the means as well as the end; thirdly, The means is many times evil, in matter or form, yet the work is made good by Christ; fourthly, He is not tied to the means, but he can work either with, without, or against the means; fifthly, All means hath his efficacy from Christ. But the words would be particularly weighed.

In him. All things consist in Christ, both in general, as he is God, and in special, as he is Redeemer. Four ways all things consist in or by Christ, as he is God: first, In respect of *ubiquity*—he comprehends all things, and is comprehended of nothing, 'the nations are but a drop of his bucket,' and time itself is but a drop of his eternity; secondly, In respect of *power*—in his power this whole frame stirreth; thirdly, In respect of *omniscience* and wisdom, for all is within his knowledge, and receiveth order from his wisdom; fourthly, In respect of *decree*—for the world to be made did from everlasting hang in the foreknowledge and pre-ordination of Christ.

As Christ is Redeemer, all things consist in him three ways: first, Because he is that atonement which kept the world from being dissolved for Adam's sin; secondly, Because the respect of him and his church is that that keeps up the world to this day: if his body were once complete, the world would not stand one hour; thirdly, Because the promise made to man, concerning his prosperity in the use of all creatures, are made in Christ.

All things. Even all things which are, or are done, in earth or heaven; things visible or invisible, which have either being, life, sense, or reason, past, present, or to come, adversity as well as prosperity, &c., Acts xvii. 25.

Consist. This word notes four things: order, continuance, co-operation, and immutability.

First, The creatures consist, that is, by an excellent order, agree together, in a glorious frame:

for God is the God of order, and not of confusion.

Object. There be many miseries, evils, and mischiefs in the world, and therefore how can there be order in all things?

Sol. First, There may be order in respect of God, though not in respect of us; secondly, It followeth not that there is no order, because we see none, 'O the depth,' &c., Rom. xi.; thirdly, Many of the reasons of the fearful miseries that are in the world are revealed, as the justice of God in punishing of a sinful world, either whole nations or particular persons, the humbling of his children, and the preparing of them for heaven, and such like; fourthly, There may be order in respect of the whole, though not in respect of every part.

Object. 2. There be many sins in the world, and those consist not in Christ, neither tend they to order.

Sol. The truth is, that those come into the world by the devil and man, and they are, by the providence of God, not effective, but permissive, yet so as there is operation in four respects about the sins of the world: for first, Christ is the author of the motion in general, though not of the evil of the motion; secondly, Christ worketh in that he withdraweth grace, being provoked thereunto; thirdly, He worketh in determining or setting a measure unto sin, that it pass not his bounds; fourthly, He worketh in converting the sin to a punishment of the sinner, or in working thereout an occasion of humiliation, and of grace in the penitent.

Secondly, Consisting notes the continuance together of the creatures; for by the providence of Christ it is that no substance *in specie* that was at first made ever ceased, but there are still as many creatures as ever were; and the very singulars of every sort do consist *in individuo*, as long as pleaseth Christ; and the like may be said of the essential qualities of all the creatures.

Thirdly, Consisting notes the co-operation of the creatures, so as by the providence of Christ all things work together for his glory; and all things are ready at Christ's will and command by joint moving, &c.

Fourthly, Consisting notes immutability in the providence of Christ.

Thus of the doctrine: the uses follow.

Uses. And first, the meditation of the providence of Christ serveth for great reproof of wicked men's security in sin, who carelessly add sin unto sin, so it may be hid from men; as if they were of the mind of those that thought God did not see, or had forsaken the earth and the care of men's actions below. But seeing all things consist in Christ, wicked men cannot stir but Christ discovereth them as plainly as anything that is in his own heart. Yea, seeing all things consist in Christ, it checketh the doubtfulness and mistrustfulness that is in the hearts of God's children, as if in their crosses God did not care for them, or that they should be helpless. This is at large reproved in these places: Isa. xl. 27, and xlix. 14, &c., and liv. 7, &c.

Secondly, Seeing all things consist in Christ, it should teach us to trust in Christ, and not in the second causes; and it should make us less careful for our preservation, never asking 'what we shall eat, or what we shall put on,' Mat. vi. Yea, seeing he rules all things, let us willingly subject ourselves to his sceptre, and let him be 'our guide unto death,' Ps. xlviii. 14.

Quest. But what must we do that it might go well with us by the providence of Christ?

Ans. First, We must be saints, if we would have Christ to keep us and preserve us; that is, such men as hide not their sins, but confess and forsake them, and live innocently, 1 Sam. ii. 9; Isa. xlviii. 17, 18; Ps. v. 8; Hosea xiv. 9; Prov. xxviii. 13. Secondly, True prosperity must be learned out of the word; we must be taught to profit. And the next way to get Christ to bless us in our houses is to wait upon his direction in his house, for all prosperity depends upon God's promise; and if we would prosper, we must do such things as are of promise, Ps. i. 3, and xxxiii.; Isa. xlviii. 13. Thirdly, We must, in true humility and sense of our own unworthiness, rest upon the providence of Christ. It is just if I prosper not in my estate if I will not trust God with it. Fourthly, We must pray God to 'direct the works of our hands' continually, Ps. xc. 7. Fifthly, We must take heed of cruelty, and despising and backbiting of God's poor afflicted servants, Ps. xli. 1-3, and cxl. 11-13.

Lastly, If all things consist and are preserved in

Christ, then much more the righteous are preserved with a special preservation and in a peculiar safety. In the 37th Psalm, this point is excellently and at large handled, both by direct proof, and by answer to all the usual objections against their safety. That they shall be preserved is affirmed, ver. 3, 17, 23, 25, 32. The objections answered are many.

Object. 1. Wicked men flourish.

Sol. A righteous man should never grieve at that, for 'they shall soon be cut down like the grass, and wither as the green herb,' ver. 12.

Object. 2. Righteous men are in distress.

Sol. Ver. 6. The night of their adversity will be turned into the light of prosperity; and as surely as they can believe when it is night that it shall be day, so surely may they be persuaded, when crosses are upon them, that comfort and deliverance shall come.

Object. 3. But there are great plots laid against the righteous, and they are pursued with great malice, and their intended ruin is come almost to the very issue.

Sol. Ver. 12–15. The Lord sees all the plots of wicked men, and laughs at their spiteful and foolish malice; while they are busy to destroy the righteous, and hope to have a day against them, 'the Lord seeth that their own day is coming upon them,' even a day of destruction, a day of great judgment and eternal misery; 'their bow shall be broken, and the sword that they have drawn shall enter into their own heart.'

Object. 4. But the just have but small means.

Sol. Ver. 16, 17. 'A little that the righteous hath is better than the riches of many wicked; for the arms of the wicked shall be broken, and the Lord upholdeth the just.'

Object. 5. Heavy times are like to befall them.

Sol. Ver. 19. 'They shall not be ashamed in the evil time, and in the day of famine they shall have enough.'

Object. 6. But the wicked wax fatter and fatter, and they prevail in vexing the righteous.

Sol. Ver. 20. Indeed the wicked are fat, but it is but 'the fat of lambs;' their prosperity shall soon melt; and as they be like smoke in vexing the godly, so shall they be like smoke in vanishing away.

Object. 7. But the righteous do fall.

Sol. Ver. 24. Though he do fall, yet he falls not finally, not totally; for he is 'not utterly cast down;' and besides, there is an upholding providence of God in all the falls of the righteous.

Object. 8. We see some wicked men that do not so fall into adversity, but rather are in prosperity to their dying days.

Sol. Ver. 27. Though they do, yet 'their seed shall be cut off.'

Object. 9. But some wicked men are strong yet, and in their seed spread also.

Sol. Ver. 35, 36. Note also, that those 'spreading bay-trees' many times 'soon pass away;' and they and their houses, are sometimes 'utterly cut off.'

Object. 10. But upright men are under many and long crosses.

Sol. Ver. 37. Yet, 'his end is peace.'

Object. 11. But nobody stands for the godly when they come into question.

Sol. Ver. 39, 40. 'Their salvation is of the Lord;' he is their strength, he will help them and deliver them, &c.

But if we would be thus delivered, observe—

1. That we must not unthankfully fret at God's providence, ver. 1; 2. We must 'trust in the Lord and do good,' ver. 2, 3; 3. We must 'delight ourselves in the Lord,' and not place our contentment on earthly things, ver. 4; 4. We must 'commit our ways to God,' ver. 5; 5. We must get patience and humble affections, ver. 7–11; 6. We must be of 'upright conversation,' ver. 14; 7. We must be merciful, ver. 25, 26; 8. We must 'speak righteous things,' and get 'the law into our hearts,' ver. 30, 31; 9. We must 'keep our way,' and 'wait on God,' and not use ill means.

Ver. 18. *And he is the head of the body, the church; he is the beginning and first-born of the dead, that in all things he might have the pre-eminence.*

Our Redeemer is described before, both in his relation to God, and to the world. In this verse, and the rest that follow to the 23d, he is described as he stands in relation to the church; and that two ways: first, In relation to the whole church, ver. 18–20; secondly, In relation to the Church of the Colossians, ver. 21, 22.

The praise of Christ in relation to the whole church is first briefly propounded, and then more largely opened. It is propounded in these words: *And he is the head of the body, the church.* There is great odds between the world's subjection to Christ, and the church's; for the faithful are subject to Christ as the members are to the head; but the wicked are subject as vile things under his feet, Eph. i. 22.

Great are the benefits which come to the church from Christ, as her head. I instance in six, viz., love, sympathy, audience, advocation, union, and influence: first, Infinite love,—no man so loves his wife as Christ loves his church, Eph. v. 27; secondly, Sympathy, by which Christ hath a fellow-feeling of the distresses of all his members,—that which is done to them, he takes it as done to him, whether it be good or evil, Mat. xviii. 5, and xxv. 40, 45, Heb. ii. 17, and iv. 15; thirdly, Audience and willing acceptance of all the desires and prayers of all his members,—the head hears for the body; fourthly, Advocation,—no natural head can so plead for its members as doth our mystical head for us; fifthly, Union,—we as members are honoured with the union of essence, in that he hath taken our nature; with the union of office, so as the members are anointed kings, priests, and prophets in their kind, as well as Christ; and also with the union of virtue and benefits, by which union we partake of his righteousness, holiness, and glory. By virtue of this union with Christ, the faithful have the everlasting presence of Christ to and after the end of the world, Mat. xxviii. The last benefit is Influence; influence, I say, both of life, (for the second Adam is a quickening spirit, 1 Cor. xv.,) and light, (for Christ is the fountain of all true wisdom, 1 Cor. i. 30: the head seeth for the body, and the body by and from the head,) and grace, (for of his fulness we receive all grace,) and motion, (for all good desires, feelings, words, and works, come from the working of the head in us.)

The political head is the glory of the world, and the mystical head is the glory of the church; yet the mystical head excels the political many ways. For:

1. Christ is the head of such as are not[1] together in the being of nature or grace.

[1] Qu. 'knit'?—Ed.

2. Christ is a perpetual head; the other but for a time.

3. Christ is a head by influence; the other but by government.

4. Christ is an absolute head; the other but subordinate to Christ, and his vicegerent.

That Christ might become our head, we must consider what he did in fitting himself thereunto; and secondly, what he doth in us. For himself he took the same nature with his church, else had the church been like Nebuchadnezzar's image; yet as he took our nature, so we must know that he bettered it. The head differs in worth from the body, because therein is seated the mind, which is the noblest part of man; so in the human nature of Christ dwells the Godhead bodily; and by expiation in his own person, Christ takes away the sins of the church, which else should have letted all union. And lastly, he exalted his suffering nature, and seated himself aloft, as meet to have the preeminence, and become head of all the faithful; and as the head is thus fitted, so are the members: for, 1. They are collected out of the world by the sound of the gospel,—let them lie hidden in the world that mean to perish with the world; 2. They are framed, formed, proportioned, and begotten, by daily hearing; 3. They are ingrafted in an unspeakable and invisible union, presently in truth, afterwards in sense.

Church. This word is diversely accepted. It is taken sometime, in evil part, for an assembly of wicked men; and so there is the 'church of the malignant,' Ps. xxvi. 5, Acts xix. 32, 41; sometimes for the faithful in heaven, Eph. v. 27; sometimes for Christians on earth, 1 Tim. iii. 15, Acts v. xi., and this not always in one sense; sometimes for the pastors of the church, and governors, as some think, Mat. xviii. 17; sometimes for the people and the flock, 1 Pet. v. 2, Acts xx. 28; sometimes for particular churches; and lastly, sometimes for all the elect of God, that have been, are, or shall be, so Mat. xvi. 18, Eph. i. 23, and v. 23, and so here.

The church of Christ is glorious in three praises: 1. She is *one*; 2. She is *holy*; 3. She is *catholic*.

She is *one*, in respect of one head and service; in respect of one spirit and binder; and in respect of one faith and constancy in doctrine. She is *holy* by segregation from the sinful world; by the inchoation of the grace of Christ, and by imputation of his righteousness. She is *catholic*, especially in the New Testament, in respect of place, the elect may be in any place; in respect of men, for it is gathered of all sorts of men; and in respect of time, for it shall continue unto all times, even till time be no more.

Thus of the doctrine concerning Christ and the church. The uses follow.

Uses. The first use is for confutation: and that three ways:

First, In vain do the wicked enemies of the church pride themselves in the greatness of learning, power, means, &c., thinking to suppress the being or glory of Christ's church on earth, for 'the stone that the builders refused will prove the head of the corner.'

Secondly, In vain do the papists go about to maintain their ministerial head; for the church is neither without a head nor many-headed. And it is absurd to excuse it, that the pope is but a head under Christ: for the body were monstrous that had two heads, one above and another under.

Thirdly, In vain do carnal men plead their hopes in Christ, when they can yield no sound reason to prove they are Christ's members. They are not members of this body, under this head, that want faith; that have not the spirit of Christ; that are not quickened with the life of grace; that are not wrought upon by the word of Christ, nor built upon the foundation of the prophets and apostles; that feel no influence of graces from Christ; that want the knowledge of prophets, or mortification of priests, or victory over the world as kings; that either pride themselves in their own civil righteousness, or can fall away wholly and for ever.

The second use is for instruction: and first, As Christ is considered to be our head, we should:

1. Pray that God would open the eyes of our understanding, that we might with sense and affection see what the hope of our calling is, Eph. i. 19, 22, &c., to become members of such a body, under such a head.

2. Take heed of all pollutions that might any way tend to the dishonour of our head, whether it be of flesh or spirit, 2 Cor. vi.

3. Consider our place in this body, and under this head, and not presume to know above what is meet, Rom. xii. 4, 5.

4. Use all means to grow in this body, and not pull it back, or shame our head by spiritual security or unprofitableness: and to this end we should stick fast to the words of the prophets, and not suffer ourselves to be 'carried about by every wind of doctrine,' and 'follow the truth in love,' without pride or discord, Eph. iv. 14-16.

5. Obey as the members do, in union with the head by faith; in communion with the fellow-members by love; and with a natural, voluntary, and not extorted obedience.

Secondly, If the church be the body of Christ, and we members of this body, we should learn to carry ourselves one towards another in all humbleness of mind, and long-suffering, supporting one another, and keep the bond of peace in the unity of the spirit, Eph. iv. 2-5. And we should labour to profit one another with the gifts God hath bestowed upon us, that our graces, as holy ointment, may run down from member to member; and all our love should be without dissimulation, in giving honour, going one before another, inasmuch as what honour one member receiveth, is done in some respect to all, Rom. xii. 6, 9. And we should willingly distribute to the necessities of the saints, and rejoice with them that rejoice, and weep with them that weep, Rom. xii. 10-16, out of the sympathy of members; by all means shunning to give offence in the least thing, especially not censorious, or contentious in matters of indifference, 1 Cor. x. 24.

Lastly, All discontentments with our place or calling, or estimation in the body, and all contempt, or envy at the gifts or place of other Christians, should be banished out of our hearts, 1 Cor. xii. 15, 22, 23, 26.

Thus of the excellence of Christ, in relation to the church, as it is briefly propounded: the explication follows.

The head hath three privileges, or excels all the members in order, perfection, or virtue, and efficacy. The pre-eminence of Christ is three ways considered: first, In respect of the dignity of order, ver. 18, of order, I say, toward the members; secondly, In respect of perfection in himself, in the fulness of grace, ver. 15; thirdly, In respect of virtue, efficacy, and influence toward the whole body, ver. 20.

The primacy of Christ, in order or relation to the members, is twofold: first, In the estate of grace 'he is the beginning;' secondly, In the respect of the state of glory 'he is the first-begotten of the dead.'

He is the beginning. Christ may be said to be the beginning in three respects: first, As he is the first-fruits, for whose sake the rest are accepted and blessed; secondly, As he is the repairer of the world, decayed by man's sin; thirdly, As he is the beginning of the good things that are in the church, He is both the object and efficient cause of faith; mortification flows from his death, and new obedience from his resurrection; justification is wrought from his obedience.

Uses. And this shows the misery of all carnal men that are not members of Christ; in respect of the life of grace they are dead; in respect of faith they are infidels; in respect of justification they are without God; in respect of repentance they walk in trespasses and sins; in respect of communion of saints they are strangers from the commonwealth of Israel. There can be a beginning of no true felicity without Christ. Christ is said to be 'the beginning of the creation of God,' Rev. iii. 14; and from thence is inferred a most severe reproof of man's lukewarmness in matters of piety, repentance, and grace, Rev. iii. 15-17. And if Christ be the author and beginning of faith and grace, it should teach us to persevere in the faith, and contend for the truth, and keep that which is committed to us, with all patience, wisdom and constancy, Heb. xii. 2. And, inasmuch as he is Alpha, he will be Omega, as he is the beginning so he will be the end; and therefore 'blessed are they that do his commandments;' and 'let him that is righteous be righteous still,' and let profane men, that will not by faith and repentance seek unto Christ, 'be filthy still,' Rev. xxii. 11, 13, 14.

The first-begotten of the dead. Christ, as head of the church, holds his relation both to the living as their beginning, and to the dead as their first-begotten.

There is a threefold primogeniture of Christ. He is the first-begotten: first, In respect of eternal generation, as he is the Son of God,—of this before; secondly, As he is born of the Virgin Mary, for she is said to bring forth her 'first-begotten Son,' Mat. i.; thirdly, When God raised Christ out of the grave he is said to beget his Son, for so the the words of the second Psalm, 'Thou art my Son, this day have I begotten thee,' are applied to the resurrection of Christ, Acts xiii. 33. In that Christ is said to be the first-begotten of the dead, three things may be noted, as implied here, concerning the members of Christ, and three things concerning Christ himself as head:

First, Concerning the members, these things may be gathered:

1. That not only wicked men, but the true members of Christ die, Heb. ix., Ps. lxxxix., 2 Sam xiv. The consideration of this, that the godly must die, may serve for many uses: first, 'Why doth vain man die then without wisdom?' Job iv. 21; secondly, How shall wicked men escape? Job xxi. 32, Isa. xxviii., their covenant with death must needs be annulled; thirdly, It should cause us deeply to digest the vanities of this life, Eccles. ii. 16, 17; fourthly, It should cause us to take heed of Eve's *lest ye die,* for it is out of all question die we must, and therefore meet it were we should provide for it, without mincing or procrastinating; lastly, We should encourage ourselves, and die like the members of Christ, with all willingness, faith, and patience.

2. The government of Christ reacheth as well to the dead as to the living members. This the faithful were wont of old to note, when they would say a man were dead, they would say, he was 'joined to his people.' This should be a great encouragement unto godly men to die.

3. From coherence, that if we would have Christ to be the first-begotten to us when we are dead, we must subject ourselves to his ordinances, that he may be the beginning of true grace to us while we live.

Secondly, Concerning the head, these three things may be noted:

1. That he was among the dead, and this was good for us; for thereby he dissolved the power the devil had to inflict death, or the fear of it, upon his members, Heb. ii. 17, ix. 15; and thereby he finished the expiation of all our sins; thereby he ratified God's covenant; thereby he kills the power of sin in us; and

thereby he takes away the curse of our natural death.

2. That he was not only among the dead, but he was begotten among the dead, that is, raised from death to life; and this also was profitable for us, for he 'rose to our justification,' Rom. iv. 23, 24; to our vivification, Rom. vi. 4; to our 'deliverance from wrath to come,' 1 Thes. i. 10.

3. That he is not only begotten, but the first-begotten among the dead, and that in three respects: first, As he was more excellently raised than any of the dead are, for he carried no corruption to the grave, and he 'saw no corruption' in the grave, and he was but a short time under the power of the grave; secondly, In respect of time, he was the first that rose from the dead, Acts xxvi. 23; thirdly, In respect of efficacy, it is he by whose power all the rest rise, 1 Cor. xv. 20, 22, John v. 21, xi. 28.

This must needs be a great comfort to us while we live, against the time our bodies must go into the house of darkness, the darksome lodging in the grave; only let us seek the virtue of the resurrection of Christ in this world, and the experiment of the vigour of it first upon our souls, in plucking us up out of the grave of sin, to walk before God, in newness of life, Phil. iii. 9.

That in all things he might have the pre-eminence. These words are added for further amplification or explanation of the former. They give unto Christ a primacy and pre-eminence in all things, first over both living and dead, as he is the beginning to the living, and the first-begotten to the dead. Christ then hath the pre-eminence, he is first in all things, Mat. xxviii. 18, Rom. iv. 9, Phil. ii. 9, Eph. i. 23. He is first many ways: first in time, as before all things; first in order, he hath a primacy of order; he is the first to be reckoned and admired in the church; first in the dignity of person, he excels in both natures all that is in the church, or ever was; first in degree, John i. 5; first in government, Mat. xx. 27; first in acceptation with God, Mat. xvii. 5; lastly, he is first effectively, as the cause of all the respect, order, and excellency in others; he is the root out of which springs all the glory in the church.

Uses. The use is, first, for terror to all those that sin against Christ's pre-eminence, as they do in a high degree, that having 'begun in the Spirit, will end in the flesh,' such as having 'known the way of righteousness,' afterwards turn from the holy course, 'with the dog to the vomit, and with the swine to the wallowing in the mire,' 2 Pet. ii. 20, 22, Rev. ii. 4, 19. Secondly, The consideration of Christ's primacy and pre-eminence should learn us to take heed of climbing in the church; it is dangerous to desire to be chief; it is almost the sole power of the head of the church, Mat. xx. 27, Mark ix. 35, x. 44, John ix. 10. Lastly, Let it be our care, both in heart and life, to yield Christ the pre-eminence, which we shall do, if we labour to know nothing more than Christ crucified, if we mind the things of Christ's kingdom more than the things of this life, if we make him our chief refuge by faith, for all happiness and reconciliation, if we make him our joy, rejoicing more in Christ than carnal men can do in the world, (for a discontented life denies Christ the pre-eminence,) if the zeal of God's house can eat us up, if, in all our actions, we perform the worship of God first, if we stick not to confess and profess Christ, if we honour the faithful, and contemn the vile, and join ourselves to such as fear God, though they be despised in this world, and, lastly, when we can in all things rather choose to please God than men:

Ver. 19. *For it pleased the Father, that in him should all fulness dwell.*

There is great reason Christ should be acknowledged head, as in the former verse by reason of his primacy and pre-eminence, so in this verse by reason of the plenitude that dwells in him. No natural head so full of senses as he is full of grace.

It is to be noted in the general, that the head should excel the members in gifts; and therefore it is a fault in cities when the people choose unto themselves unmeet men to be their heads. God may choose Saul following his father's asses, because if he make princes, he can give spirit unto princes: but it is not so with men; they may give the office, but they cannot give the gifts to execute it. And it is likewise a great shame to such rulers of the people as are so far from repressing disorders, that they are disordered themselves and their households. So domestical heads likewise, if they would not see swearing, lying, whoring, passions, idleness, &c., in their children and servants, they must be free from ill example themselves, and be as heads excelling the rest of the family in gifts and good behaviour.

It pleased. The moving cause and foundation of all the grace shewed to the creature, is the good pleasure of the will of the Creator, Eph. i. 5; 2 Thes. i. 11. Why is Israel planted? Ps. xliii. 3; why are the great mysteries of God hidden from the wise, and revealed to babes? Mat. xi. 25; why hath the little flock a kingdom? Luke xii. 32; why hath God mercy on some and not on others? Exod. xxxiii. 19; why hath Job riches, and why are they taken away? Job i.; why is judgment and righteousness in a forlorn world that deserved nothing? Jer. ix. 24; why is Judah as potter's clay? Jer. xviii. 6; why is the world saved by preaching? 1 Cor. i. 21; why are some predestinate to be adopted? Eph. i. 5; why is the mystery of God's will opened now and not before? Eph. i. 9. To conclude, why is all fulness in the head, or any grace in the members, but only because 'it pleased him'?

Uses. The use of this is: first, To teach us to do likewise, that is, to do good without respect of desert; it is royal, yea, it is divine; secondly, It should teach us, if we would get any grace or blessing from God, to examine ourselves whether we be in his favour, and to labour in all things so to serve him as to please him; thirdly, To subject our reasons and affections to God's will, though he should show us no other reason of his doings but his will; for we must always know that things are always just, because he willed them; fourthly, In our troubles, and under crosses, it should teach us patience, Ps. xxxix. 9, and to labour to pacify God, by prayer and humiliation, in the name of Christ, and to acknowledge the sovereignty of God, referring ourselves to his pleasure for deliverance, Ps. xl. 13; not trusting upon the means, Ps. xliv. 3, 6; lastly, It may be a comfort that nothing can befal any Christian but what pleaseth God.

Doct. 2. God is well pleased in Christ, Isa. xlii. 1; he loves him infinitely; he can be content he have anything, yea, all things; and therefore it should teach us to fly to Christ for help, and hear him, Mat. xvii. 5, 2 Pet. i. 17; and we should never seek nor acknowledge any other mediator or advocate, seeing God is well pleased in him.

That in him should all fulness dwell. Doct. There is a fulness and absolute completeness in Christ: 1. In respect of members; so the church is the fulness of Christ, Eph. i. 23; 2. In respect of the inhabitation of the divine nature in the human, for 'the Godhead dwells in him bodily,' Col. ii. 9; 3. In respect of power; so all power and fulness of authority was given to him over all things in heaven and earth, Mat. xxviii.; 4. In respect of merit; for here is great fulness, if we consider either who merited, not man only, but God also; or when he merited, viz., from the very moment of conception; or for whom, not for himself, but for millions of others; or what he merited, viz., remission of all sins, graces of all kinds, glory that will last for ever; 5. In respect of grace; there is a completeness of grace in Christ, not only in respect of the grace of personal union, or of office, or of adoration, but in respect of habitual graces, or gifts, and endowments of his soul. The last is here meant; all fulness of gifts dwell in him.

Uses. The uses follow:

First, 'Great is the mystery of godliness; God manifested in the flesh, justified in the Spirit,' &c., 1 Tim. iii. 16; secondly, This is joyful news to all Christ's members, for 'of his fulness they receive grace for grace;' thirdly, This confutes papicolists in the opinions of their head; he cannot be a head in whom there is not fulness to serve the whole body, and therefore the pope can be no head of the whole church; lastly, Let the rest of Christ be glorious to our souls, Isa. xi. 10; he hath the words of life, whither shall we go from him? Thus in general.

This fulness hath increase of praise three ways:

1. It is *all* fulness;
2. It is *in him;*
3. It *dwells* in him.

For the first, there is in Christ *all* fulness, both in respect of the member[1] of graces, Isa. xi. 2, and in respect of the measure of them, John iii. 34; and therefore let the Christian rejoice in the Lord, 1 Cor. i. 30; and in all wants of the soul seek to him by prayer in faith, for from him and out of his ful-

[1] Qu. 'number.'—ED.

ness may be had wisdom and sanctification, 1 Cor. i. 30, counsel and strength, Isa. xi. 2, joy and gladness, Isa. lxi. 3; yea, a Christian should be covetous, seeing here is enough to be had, and therefore should labour to be full of knowledge, Isa. xi. 9, and of the fear of God, Prov. xix. 23, and of good fruits, James iii. 17, Phil. i. 11. This also reproves the justiciaries and sanctieolists, pharisees and saint-worshippers. A fulness is nowhere to be had but in Christ, and there is so much as needeth no supply from saints or angels. It shews, also, that the common protestant serves an idol instead of Christ, inasmuch as he gets in his relation to Christ no more joy, grace, and holiness. The true Christ hath all fulness, not only in himself, but by influence, for the good, and according to the state of his members.

For the second, this fulness is *in Christ*; and this hath matter of great weight, for thereby is implied the misery of all unregenerate men. There is no fulness, completeness, sufficing felicity wheresoever to be had out of Christ. And besides the emphasis imports great comfort to the true convert; for this fulness is in Christ. God doth not look to have the members actually absolute in themselves, it will serve turn that all fulness be in the head. And inasmuch as the perfect bliss of a Christian is in his Christ, it is well for his safety against the malice of Satan, who now may bite the heel, but cannot touch the head. And from hence we must learn, if we would ever get, by participation and influence, any grace from Christ, we must by faith and effectual calling get into Christ.

Thirdly, In that he saith, this fulness *dwells* in Christ, it notes the continuance of it; the personal union shall never be dissolved, and therefore the habitual graces of Christ shall never be abolished: and these graces had need continue in him, for in him rests the calling of the elect, not yet gathered, and the perseverance of the saints.

Uses. The rivers must needs be empty if the fountain be dry. This is comfortable; we may now beseech him to help our unbelief, as well as the man in the Gospel. We may find joy and victory in Christ crucified, as well as Paul; his grace will still be sufficient for us. There dwells in him still fulness of wisdom to keep us from error, fulness of grace to keep us from apostasy, fulness of joy to keep us from despair, fulness of power to preserve us against all evil men and evil angels; only, refuse not knowledge when he offers the means, wink not when the sun shines, shut not the door when he knocks, fight when he gives thee weapons, and 'cast not away thy confidence,' and 'let no man take thy crown.'

Hitherto of the plenitude in the head.

Ver. 20. *And by him to reconcile all things to himself, and to set at peace, through the blood of his cross, both the things on earth, and the things in heaven.*

In these words the Redeemer is described as a head by influence; the apostle shews us the good that comes from Christ as our Mediator; and the sum of all is, that he reconciles us to God.

In this verse are eight things to be noted:

First, *Why*, or the moving cause; and that is, *it pleased him*—for that must be supplied out of the former verse, as the copulative *and* sheweth. Secondly, *By whom*, or the instrument; *by him*. Thirdly, *What; to reconcile*. Fourthly, *Whom*; in general, *all things*. Fifthly, *To whom*, or to what end; viz., *to himself*. Sixthly, The effect; *making peace*. Seventhly, The means of merit; *by the blood of his cross*. Eighthly, *What* in particular; viz., *things on earth, and things in heaven*.

The principal point in the whole verse to be observed is, that man hath then attained the chief good when his soul is reconciled to God. This is the sum of all that which Christ hath procured for his church: 'Blessed are the people whose God is the Lord.' Others may be more rich than they, but none more happy; for hereby man is joined to the fountain of all good, and not only hath interest in his favour, but reapeth unspeakable benefits by communion with his attributes, word, works, holiness, and glory. Our reconciliation with God gives us a title to a better happiness than ever Adam had —it estates us in the possession of eternity, and frees us from immortal woe.

Uses. All this should encourage with all care and constancy to seek God's favour, and forsake our sins, that we may be reconciled, whatsoever it cost; sparing no labour or tears, till we 'see the face of God with joy,' Jer. l. 5. This shews, also, the woful estate of such men as are left to themselves, and have this peace and reconciliation hid from their eyes. And of all judgments, it should most grieve us to be separate from God. If to be reconciled be our greatest happiness, to miss the comforts of God's presence and love cannot but be an extreme affliction. And to this end we should beseech God to deliver us from a blind or stony heart, or a sleepy conscience, or impure affections; for these, if they reign in us, hinder the vision of God.

And. This carrieth us to *it pleased the Father* in the former verse. Whence we may note that our reconciliation stands with the everlasting good pleasure of God's will; and therefore it follows: 1. That our reconciliation cannot be hindered or altered; 2. That it ariseth from no sudden motion in God, but is anciently decreed; 3. That we are not reconciled for our merit, for it was decreed before we had done good or evil; 4. That the reasons of the rejection of some, and the gathering of others in time, are just, though not always expressed, because there is no decree without God's counsel; 5. That if ever we would have the comfort of our election, we must make sure our reconciliation; we can never know God's eternal love to us till we find the experience of his favour in our reconciliation. The prisoner knows not what favour is in the king's breast till his pardon comes.

By him. Doct. Christ is the instrument of our reconciliation. The first Adam took God from us, the second Adam restored God to us. Man would needs become God, and therefore lost God from us. God out of his love becomes man, and restores us again to God. The world is now restored by the same wisdom it was first made.

God's image is restored in us by him that is the eternal image of the Father. The middle person in the Trinity is the mediator between God and man; the natural Son makes men sons by adoption. It is Christ that both can and ought to reconcile us. He could not do it if he were not God; he ought not to do it if he were not man—1 Tim. ii. 5, Rom. iii. 25, 1 Cor. i. 3, 1 John ii. 1, 1 Cor. iii. 11, Acts iv. 13.

Uses. This doctrine yields us matter of admiration of the love of Christ, if we consider what either he was, or what we were. The Lord, in the form of a servant, procures the salvation of the servant; he that was the beginning of God's works repairs him that at best was the last of them. God descended from heaven to earth, that man might ascend from earth to heaven. God is made the Son of man, that man might be made the son of God. He that was rich became poor to make us rich; the immortal became mortal to make us immortal. He is a physician to us sick, a redeemer to us sold, a way to us wandering, and life to us dead. Secondly, This should teach us in all suits to God to seek to Christ the Son of God; it is he must offer up our prayers, procure our pardon, and make our peace; yea, it is he and none other. Thirdly, We should seek the testimony of Jesus, as well as his ransom. If he witness to our reconciliation, we need never doubt of it; if he give no witness, we can have no assurance. The testimony of Jesus is given partly by the promises of the word, he putting spirit and life into them for our particular comfort, and partly by the witness of the Spirit of adoption in the unutterable feelings and joy of our hearts—1 Tim. ii. 6, Isa. lv. 6, 1 Cor. i. 6.

Reconcile. The word imports a restoring of one to amity, from which he was by his own fault fallen. There is a threefold estate of man; there is the estate: 1. Of innocency, and here the man is at amity with God; 2. Of corruption, and here is mortal enmity between God and man; 3. Of grace, and here they are made friends, and the league renewed. Into the first estate we came by creation; into the second by propagation; and into the third only by regeneration. The distinct knowledge of this threefold estate of man clears God's justice from the blame of all those plagues [which] broke in upon mankind through corruption; and it should scare wicked men out of their wretched condition, as they are by nature servants of corruption. And it greatly commends the mercy of God, that could love us when were enemies.

In the performance of this work of reconciliation or mediation, there are six distinct things done by Christ: the first is discretion or dijudication of the cause,—he takes notice of the state and business of the church; secondly, He doth report the will of God, the covenant and conditions of agreement with God to the church; thirdly, He makes intercession for the offending party; fourthly, He satisfies and expiates for sin; fifthly, He applies that satisfaction; sixthly, He conserves the elect in the state of reconciliation. Discretion and relation belong to the prophetical office; intercession and satisfaction to the priesthood; application and conservation to his regal office. Inquire, then, whether thou be reconciled to God in Jesus Christ. I consider it negatively. Thou art not reconciled, if thou be not enlightened and inspired with the Holy Ghost to lead thee into all truth. For if Christ did reconcile thee as a prophet, he must teach thee both by his word and Spirit. Again, thou art not reconciled, if thou hast not consecrated thyself to kill the beasts, thy sins, in sacrifice before the Lord, and by the Spirit of intercession, to pour out thy soul in God's sight. When Christ reconciles as a priest, he pours upon man the spirit of compassion and deprecation, Zech. xii. 12. Thou art not reconciled if Christ beget thee not by the immortal seed, or rule thee not by the sceptre of his word, or conserve thee not in uprightness with respect of all God's commandments.

All things. That is, the church or elect of God—all the faithful. The elect are called all things: 1. Because of their number, there is a world of them, 2 Cor. v. 19; 2. Because there is for their sakes a reconciliation with all the creatures in general, for corruption is taken from the whole, though not from every part; 3. Because God doth not receive their persons into favour, but all things that belong unto them that may concern their felicity; 4. Because whatsoever they have, in heaven or earth, comes by virtue of this reconciliation.

Uses. The use is: 1. To teach us to take notice of the world's vanity. What is all the world if God's children were out of it? Nothing. The elect are all things, worth all, better than all. Kingdoms and sceptres and all the glory of the earth is nothing in God's account. And all is now corrupt with sin. God would have it known he stands not bound to any in the world, or the whole world, but only to the elect. 2. It should teach us to 'know no man after the flesh,' 2 Cor. v. 16; that is, not to respect men for their lands, apparel, titles, parentage, &c., but for grace. 3. We should not much wonder at the disorders which are in the world; for were it not for the elect it would soon appear, by the ruin of all, how little God cared for rebellious reprobates. 4. It is a great comfort no one of the elect shall perish, for all things be reconciled. 5. It should teach us to make much of them that fear the Lord. Let them be instead of all things in our account. Lastly, Seeing all things are reconciled, now let us keep the peace, even 'the unity of the Spirit, in the bond of peace,' Eph. iv. 3.

To himself. Some read *in him.* There is difference between for Christ, by Christ, and in Christ. *For,* noteth the meritorious cause; *In,* noteth the conjunction with the head; *By,* noteth the instrument.

Doct. We are reconciled in Christ or unto Christ. This is true four ways: 1. As he is the person by whom we are reconciled; 2. As his glory is the end of our reconciliation; 3. As his glory and holiness is the pattern after which our happiness and holiness is proportioned; 4. In respect of his love, providence, custody, and protection, unto the which we are received.

The use of all may be to teach us: 1. To take heed of opposing, disgracing, or persecuting of such as are reconciled to God, for he that toucheth them toucheth the apple of Christ's eye. Note, he saith *to himself.* 2. In the use of all things, to carry ourselves so as we provide to give account, and give the things to God which are God's; and, as good stewards, dispose all things in that time, and according to those rules, Christ hath appointed. 3. Seeing we are now brought so near unto God, we should humble ourselves to walk before him in all reverence and fear; and to this end we should labour for purity of heart, that we might see God, Mic. vi. 8; Mat. v. 7; Heb. xii. 29; 1 Sam. vi. 20. Yea, we should hate all spiritual pollutions, and be zealous in all good works. And seeing God hath chosen us to himself, we should set up the Lord to be our God, to serve him with our whole heart, and have respect to all his commandments, 1 Pet. ii. 9, 11, 12; Tit. ii. 13; Deut. xxvi. 16, 17. And to this end we should labour for special sincerity in the profession of religion: an ordinary care will not serve the turn: if we will live with the multitude, we may perish with the multitude. But let us cleave to the Lord with a perpetual covenant, and resolve to receive him as our guide unto the death, Jer. l. 5, Ps. xlix. ult.

Set at peace. The effect of our reconciliation is peace. Concerning this peace, I propound five things:

1. Who made it. No other can set a peace among the creatures but he that reconciles men to the Creator: he is the 'Prince of peace,' Isa. ix. 7; 'the chastisement of our peace was upon him,' Isa. liii. 5; 'he is our peace,' Eph. ii. 14.

2. With whom the faithful are at peace. They are at peace: First, With themselves: peace rules their hearts, Col. iii. 15. Secondly, With good angels, Ps. xxxiv.; Heb. i. 14. Thirdly, With the seed of Abraham, the Jews; the partition wall is broken down. Fourthly, With God's ordinances; God creating peace, or else the word would always be goring and smiting with the strokes of war and words of vengeance, Isa. xi. 4, and lvii. 19. Fifthly, With the godly, Isa. xi. 6, 7. Sixthly, With all creatures, Job v., Heb. i. 18, Ps. xci. 13. Only there can be no peace: first, With the powers and principalities, —for after the two strong men have fought, there is no more peace, Eph. vi. 12; secondly, With the world,—the world hath hated the Master, and therefore the servants may not look for better entertainment, John xv. 18.

3. The effects of this peace, which are principally two: first, The restitution of sovereignty and dominion over the creatures; secondly, The safety of the Christian in all estates, for from this peace flows great security and protection, even to the poorest Christian. either from or in dangers, Job v. 15, &c.

4. That we may attain the sense of this peace, we must be reconciled to God, Hosea ii. 18; we must be sincere worshippers, Hosea ii. 17; we must keep us in our ways, Ps. xci. 13; we must get a meek and quiet spirit, Ps. xxxvii. 12; we must in nothing be careful, but in all things shew our requests unto God, Phil. iv. 7; we must love God, and shew it by the love of the knowledge of his name, Ps. xci. 14.

First, God's children should know this privilege for themselves; it will be a preservation against sin. Secondly, Hence we may gather the miseries of all carnal persons that are not reconciled to God. They want the protection of angels; they are under the government of 'the god of this world;' the creatures are armed against them; they are stript of the royal privileges arising from the communion with saints; yea, God fights against them, in and by themselves, as by terrors of conscience, and by unquiet affections and passions, giving them over to an unruly heart. What are envy, malice, lust, and rage, but so many weapons to fight against the soul? Yea, God fights against the sinner by the deadness of his heart, which both afamisheth the soul in spiritual things, and takes away the contentment of outward things.

By the blood. Here he notes how we are reconciled, viz., by the blood of Christ. This is that 'blood of sprinkling,' Heb. xii. 24; the blood of the immaculate Lamb, 1 Pet. i. 19; the blood of the everlasting covenant, Heb. xiii. 20; Christ's own blood, Heb. xiii. 12.

Many are the fruits and effects of the blood of Christ: 1. We are elected through it, 1 Pet. i. 2. 2. It ratifies the covenant of God, Luke xxii. 20, Heb. ix. 18. 3. It is that reconciliation justifying us from our former sins, Rom. iii. 25, and v. 9, Eph. i. 7, Job i. 7, Rev. vii. 14. 4. It joins Jew and Gentile together in one city, yea, in one house, Eph. ii. 13, &c. 5. It purgeth the conscience from dead works, Heb. ix. 14, and x. 4. 6. It turns away wrath, and saves us from the destroying angel, Heb. xi. 28. 7. It makes intercession for sins after calling, Heb. xii. 24. 8. It makes perfect in all good works, Heb. xiii. 20. 9. By it the faithful overcome the dragon, Rev. xii. 11, and antichrist, Rev. xix. 21. Lastly, It opens the holy of holies, and gives us an entrance into heaven, Heb. ix. 7, and x. 19.

Uses. The use is: first, To teach us to take heed of sinning against the blood of Christ, for if it be thus precious, it must needs diffuse a horrible singuiltiness upon such as transgress it. If Abel's blood, wronged, cried so fearfully, and the blood of Zacharias, what shall the blood of Christ do? Mat. xxiii. 30, 35, Luke xi. 50. And men sin against Christ's blood: 1. By resisting the means of application of Christ crucified; 2. By profane swearing and cursing; 3. By ascribing remission of sins to the works of the law, Rom. iii. 20, 21, 25; 4. By committing the sin against the Holy Ghost, Heb. x. 26, 29; 5. By returning to the lusts of our former ignorance, 1 Pet. i. 14; 6. By profane and unworthy receiving of the sacraments, 1 Cor. xi. And in the sacraments men offend against the blood of Christ: first, When they come to it with an opinion of real presence, either by transubstantiation or consubstantiation, for thereby they deny the truth of the blood of Christ by consequent, and open a gap to the adoration of Christ in or before bread or wine; secondly, When men use the sacraments but as bare signs, not discerning spiritually the presence of the blood and body of the Lord; thirdly, When men come thither unbidden, being not called, nor within the compass of the covenant by conversion; fourthly, When men come to eat this Lamb, but without the sour herbs of godly sorrow for their sins and repentance; fifthly, Such as come without faith (by which they lay hold on Christ) and love (by which they are joined to Christians.)

Thus of the first use.

Secondly, The consideration of the dignity of Christ's blood should teach Christians to esteem their new birth. It is better to be born of the blood of Christ, than of all the bloods of men, John i. 13. Seeing by his blood we have the atonement, we should rejoice in God, Rom. v. 11; and comfort ourselves in this great prerogative, that our many sins and infirmities are done away in the intercession of Christ, his blood speaking better things than the blood of Abel, Heb. xii. 24.

Thirdly, We should never be much perplexed for the ordinary troubles which befall us; for if we look upon 'the author and finisher of our faith,' he endured the shame and contradiction of sinners, yea, and shed his blood too; whereas 'we have not yet resisted unto blood,' Heb. xii. 2, 4.

Fourthly, It should inflame us to a desire of all possible, both thankfulness, giving glory to him that shed his blood for us, Rev. i. 5, and obedience, striving to walk worthy of the effusion and application of such precious blood, Heb. xiii. 20, striving after perfection in all well-doing.

Of his cross. It was needful our Saviour should be upon the cross, that so he might be the accomplishment of what was signified by the heave offering and the brazen serpent, and that so he might bear the special curse of the law for us; of all deaths, the death on the tree being, by a special law of God, made accursed.

The consideration of this, that Christ suffered on the cross, should teach us both humiliation and humility. We should be pricked in our hearts to think of it that our sins caused him to be pierced, Zech. xii. 12; and we should put on all humbleness of mind, when we see him that was equal to God abasing himself for us in the form of a servant, to die on a tree, Phil. ii. 8, &c.; yea, the more baseness he suffered, the more we should glory and rejoice in his sufferings. Nothing should glad our hearts more than Christ, and him crucified, Gal. vi. 14.

Further, Christ died on the cross to break down the partition wall, and to slay hatred, Eph. ii. 16, 1 Cor. i. 13. And shall enmity and discord live when **Christ is dead**? Shall he be nailed, and shall not our vile affections be nailed down with him? Besides, it should be our care to see to it, that 'the cross of Christ be not made of none effect,' 1 Cor. i. 18; which is, when by faith it is not applied; when the doctrine of Christ is not God's power in our souls; when our flesh is not crucified with the lusts of it, Gal. v. 24; and when we take not up our cross to follow Christ, Mat. x. 38; and, lastly, when we are so bewitched that we cannot obey the truth, Gal. iii. 1.

By him. This is repeated in the original, though the translation express it not, for four reasons: First, To show how hardly men are drawn to ascribe from their hearts their happiness unto Christ. Secondly, To shew the necessity of it. It is not possible to be saved, but by the imputed righteousness of Christ. Thirdly, To shew that all things in Christ's action and passion were meritorious, lest men should superstitiously doat or dream upon his blood, or the wood of the cross, or the sign of it, or the like. There is no merit in blood, but as it was in him. Fourthly, To conclude, the worship of angels, which abuse began then to grow among the Colossians.

Both the things upon earth. This *all things*, by a distribution, is again repeated, to medicine the doubtfulness of God's children which question it, whether Christ's merits extend unto them; as also to inflame us to an admiration of the virtue of his death, by considering how far it extends.

On earth. Note here two things: First, That

eternal life is begun in this life. We should never see God's face in heaven if we taste not of his favour on earth. And if this must be begun on earth, why do men defer so great a work as their reconciliation, as if it belong to heaven rather than to be done on earth? yea, this taxeth the slowness of heart, and discontentment of God's children. This knowledge, joy, affection, &c., is the same thou must have in heaven. And we should learn hence to live on earth like the citizens of heaven. Citizens will not live so rudely as the country swains; much more odds ought there to be between Saracens and Hagarenes, if I may so say; much difference between them that dwell in Sion and those that have no portion but in Sinai. God's children are the sons of the free-woman, and citizens; wicked men are the children of the bond-woman, and foreigners and strangers from the commonwealth of Israel.

Secondly, Where he saith, *upon* the earth, and yet *in* heaven, I might note the uncertainty of our abode on earth. We have nothing to possess but the outside of the earth, which is ready to shake us off daily.

All things in heaven. For the meaning of these words we know that there are in heaven both angels and saints. And it may be questioned whether angels be reconciled in Christ or no. Though angels sinned not, yet angels have gained by Christ a more perfect adhering to God, and establishing in their standing, increase of knowledge, Eph. iii. 9, and of joy, Luke xv. 10; yea, the angels are reconciled by Christ thus,* that is, they are made friends with us, with whom they were at enmity. Yet I think this is not meant here, but the saints only are intended; because it seems he entreateth here of Christ, not only as head, for he is head of angels, but as mediator between parties fallen out. Whence we may note two things: First, That the very saints now in heaven once needed the merits of Christ. None come there but were first reconciled; which may be a comfort to the afflicted spirits of mourning and drooping Christians, if they consider that the greatest saints did need remission of sins as well as they. And besides, it pounds to pieces merit of works, inasmuch as these saints came not into heaven but by the merits of Christ. Secondly, We may learn that Christ merited not only our persons, but our grace and glory.

Ver. 21. *And you hath he now also reconciled, that were in times past strangers and enemies, because your minds were set in evil works.*

Hitherto of the description of the Redeemer, as he stands in relation to the whole church. In these two verses he is described by relation, in particular, to the church of the Colossians. In this description consider two things: first, The misery the Colossians were in without Christ; secondly, The remedy in Christ. Their misery is both propounded and expounded. It is propounded to stand in two things, viz., alienation and enmity. It is expounded in two things, viz., that they were thus miserable: first, In their minds; secondly, In their works. The remedy follows in the next verse.

Before I come to consider of their misery, there are certain words of coherence to be weighed, viz., 'And you hath he now also reconciled.' Where observe: first, The word of connexion, *and;* secondly, The benefit repeated, *reconciled;* thirdly, The person whom, *you;* fourthly, The time when, *hath now;* fifthly, The person who, *he.*

From the general consideration of the matter contained in this verse and the next, with the coherence, six things may be observed.

First, That Christ is a true head to every particular church.

Secondly, That then is any people happy, and not before, when the gospel gathers their souls to God.

Thirdly, They cannot be miserable that cease to be strangers and enemies to God, whatsoever their outward estate be.

Fourthly, Doctrine must be applied: for the humiliation of God's servants; so to David: for the convincing of the wicked; so to Ahab: for the trial and detection of the temporary faith; so to Herod: for the hardening of the reprobates and their rejection, and cutting down by the sword of God's servants; and for the special consolations and directions of God's servants. And therefore ministers should employ themselves in application, and to that end should study for power of matter, as

* Qu. 'to us?'—Ed.

well as form of words, and turn themselves into all forms, requesting, beseeching, reproving, &c., with all diligence and sincerity. The people also must know that their profiting lies in application; and to this end they should attend, meditate, repeat, pray, strive against security and objections, keeping alive the sparks that are kindled in their souls. When a man can conscionably apply the word, it shows he truly hates sin, and is a true hearer.

Fifthly, Men may know particularly they are reconciled, 1 Cor. ii. 11; which both checks security in not labouring for this knowledge, and confutes papists and drowsy protestants that say it is presumption to think so.

Sixthly, Experience gives sure testimony to the doctrine of the gospel. Then we know profitably when we know the doctrine in our own case, as the Colossians here their reconciliation. We need not wonder then if we see that the most powerful parts of practical divinity have little or no testimony, or if it be, it is dark, and seldom from the most men, yea, from many churchmen. The cause is, they never had experience themselves. And we should learn to esteem their judgment most that do draw religion most into practice; for God will 'shew the humble his way.'

And you. In the gathering of souls God works beyond desert, and many times beyond probabilities. If we respect the men, they were Gentiles, hardened by hundreds of years in custom of sins; if we respect the means, it is Epaphras, none of the greatest of the apostles. Which should teach us to live by faith, and use God's ordinance with confidence; as in the business of conversion, so in matter of preservation, knowing that God is not tied to desert or means.

Also. Doct. The church and kingdom of Christ is in this world still in progress. Christ hath not done when he hath conquered Rome spiritually, that had conquered the world before corporally; but here is a fresh increase and a new—you also. And thus it will be still till the end of the world; and therefore we should every one do what we can to help forward the kingdom of God, and the adding of such souls as yet belong to the vocation of Christ. And this we may do, both by furthering the gospel preached, and by seeking a holy seed, getting within the covenant ourselves, and by education labouring to amend what by propagation we have marred. Yea, the consideration hereof should much encourage us in the combat against sin and the world; for in the war soldiers use to gather spirit and valour upon the tidings of new supplies.

Now. Men are not reconciled till redemption be applied. Christ died before, but they were not reconciled till now. It is not safe for men to rest in the historical belief of Christ's death. Either learn to die to sin, to crucify thy flesh, and to take up thy cross daily, or else forbear to mention Christ; for it is in vain, thou hast no part as yet in Christ.

Hath. Though sanctification, while we tarry in this world, be imperfect, yet reconciliation is past so soon as a man is turned to God. God's rich favour may stand with the many wants and infirmities of man; but then we must remember it is free and gracious; for if we be perfectly reconciled and yet not perfectly sanctified, then it must needs follow we are not reconciled from our own works.

He. That is Christ, which being again mentioned, shows: 1. That he is God, seeing reconciliation is here given to him, which was before ascribed to the Father. 2. It proves that in the one essence of God are more persons than one. 3. It proves that Christ died willingly; he is not only the means, but the undertaker of our reconciliation, Heb. ix. 14; he is not only the sacrifice, but the priest also.

Reconciled. The repetition or application of this word and work to the Colossians shows that there is one constant way that God holds unalterably with all his people. No sort of men can be happy until they be reconciled. If men will not mind their peace, and sue out their pardon in Christ, their hope will fail them; there is no other way to be saved.

Thus of the words of coherence: there remains both their misery in this verse, and the remedy of it in the next verse.

Strangers and enemies, &c. In general we may first observe, that it is profitable for men to know and meditate of their natural misery, though men be never so unwilling to it; yea, though they be already delivered from it; for the consideration hereof shows men the need of a Saviour, and, as a schoolmaster, trains them up to Christ. It mollifies the stony hearts of men, it breeds watchfulness over our nature, when we know it is so poisoned and corrupted; it makes us compassionate over others in their distress or infirmities; it sets a high price upon spiritual things, and makes us account God's favour our greatest joy; it makes us cleave to God in a perpetual covenant. To omit many other commodities that arise hereof, it reproves the seldom teaching and learning of the doctrine of man's natural miseries.

Strangers. Unregenerate men are strangers in five respects: 1. In respect of heaven, not only pilgrims here, but without promise of a better life, so continuing. 2. In respect of God, 'without God in the world.' 3. In respect of God's people, not fellow-citizens, but foreigners, Eph. ii. 12. 4. In respect of the special providence of God, 'strangers to the commonwealth of Israel.' 5. In respect of the life of God, Eph. iv. 18. And that if we consider either the rule of life, they account the law a strange thing, Hosea viii.; or the fountain of life, viz., regeneration, they are dead in sin, Eph. ii. 1; or the obedience of holy life, their imaginations are only evil continually, Gen. vi.

But if any ask how this strangeness comes, the word in the original seems to note it, for it is *estranged*, which is more than *strangers*, for it imports they were not so created, but made so. They were made so: 1. Originally, by the transgression of the first man, from whence flowed the first strangeness between God and man; man running from God, and God refusing to delight in the sons of men. 2. By their own actual sins, which separate between God and them, Isa. lix. 2. Alienation is to the workers of iniquity, Job xxxi. 3.

Quest. But what hurt is it to carnal men to be thus estranged?

Ans. There is no safety against dangers, where God is not to protect men; there is no comfort in affliction, where one can neither look to God nor the saints for succour and comfort.

The god of this world doth rule effectually in all the children of disobedience; they are in bondage to the world, they are in bondage to their own flesh, even to a passionate, blind, hard heart, and rebellious nature. They want the delightful refreshing of all the blessings of God, his ordinances, graces, and outward favours. All glory is departed from men when God is gone; besides, obstinacy may cast them into a reprobate sense, and eternal death may swallow them up.

That we may be delivered from this strange estate of separation, the blood of Christ must be applied, we must become new creatures, our peace must be preached, access must be had to God by prayer, we must be joined to God's children, we must be built upon the foundation of the prophets and apostles, and our souls must become temples for the Holy Ghost to dwell in. All this is set down in the second of the Ephesians, from verse 13 to the end of the chapter.

And to this end we must take heed of working iniquity, Job xxxi. 3; of ignorance, Eph. iv. 17; of an uncircumcised and an unmortified heart, Ezek. xliv. 7; of strange doctrine, Heb. iii. 9; of the strange woman, Prov. vi.; of strange fire, that is, will-worship; and of the manners of strange children; for all these by effects will estrange.

Lastly, If it be so great a misery to be estranged, woe be to them that lie in this misery and regard it not; the less sense the more danger; and most faulty is that frowardness in any that profess to fear God's name, that voluntarily bring a curse upon themselves by estranging themselves from the society of the faithful. But let all that know God's mercy in their reconciliation, rejoice in their deliverance from this misery.

Enemies. Unregenerate men are enemies both actively and passively. Actively, they are enemies to their own souls, for he that loves iniquity hates his own soul. 2. To holiness of life; they hate to be reformed, Ps. l. 3. To God's children, for it is certain they shall be hated of all carnal men for Christ's name's sake, John xv. 18. 4. To the light; he that doeth evil hates the light, John iii. 21, Amos v. 10. 5. One to another; they 'are hateful and hating one another,' Titus iii. 3. 6. To God.

Object. Sure no man hates God.

Sol. Many men do hate God, as appeareth by the threatening in the second commandment; and the scripture elsewhere notes such as in God's account hate him; such are these: 1. Such as withstand the truth, and labour to turn men from the faith, Acts xiii. 8. 2. Such as are friends to the world, James iv. 4. 3. The carnal wise men of the world, whose wisdom is enmity to God, Rom. viii. 7. 4.

All workers of iniquity, Ps. xxxvii. 18, 20, and xcii. 9. 5. All scoffers that reproach God's name, truth, or people, Ps. lxxiv. 18, 22. 6. All that hate God's children, Ps. lxxxi. 14, 15, and lxxxiii. 2, 3, and cxxix. 3, 5, John xv. 18, 23. 7. All those that refuse to subject their souls to the sceptre of Christ, and will not be ruled by his ordinances; these are called his enemies, Luke xix. 27. And among other, such are those loose people that live under no settled ministry. Lastly, All epicures, 'whose god is their belly, and mind only earthly things, and glory in their shame,' Phil. iii. 17, 18. Passively, they are enemies to God, who hates them, Ps. v. 4; to God's ordinances, which smite, and pursue, or threaten them, Ps. xlv. 4; to all the creatures, who are in arms against the sinner, till he be at peace with God; and in particular to the saints, who hate the company and assemblies of the wicked, Ps. xxvi. 4.

And all this shews the great misery of wicked men; and how can they but be miserable that are in the estate of enmity? All severity will be accounted justice; all their virtuous praises but fair sins; stripped they are of all the peculiar privileges of the saints; and that which men would desire to do to their enemies, God will certainly, by an unavoidable providence, do to them. All the creatures are against him; a wicked man is as he that should always go upon a mine of gunpowder; either by force or by stratagem the creatures will surprise him. Oh, that men would therefore labour to mortify active hatred in themselves, that the passive destroy them not, and seek to Christ, in whom only this enmity can be removed!

Again, this makes against merit, for what could we merit that were enemies? And let such as are delivered, and have felt the bitterness of this enmity, take heed of secret sins after calling unrepented of, lest God return and visit them with the strokes of an enemy, Job xiii. 24, &c., Jer. xxx. 14, Isa. lxiii. 19.

In the mind. It greatly matters in the business of man's happiness how the minds of men are ordered: 1. Man makes it the fountain of all his actions; it is his privy councillor; he speaks first with his mind; he obeys his mind, Eph. ii. 3; it is the shop whence he frames all his engines against God and man. 2. The devil especially labours to be possessed of this fort, and to have it in his custody, 2 Cor. x. 4. 3. The godly man repenting, first labours to be renewed in his mind, Eph. iv. 23. 4. God especially looks after man's mind, which appears in that he gave a law to the mind, Rom. vii., setting as it were a guard to rule and appoint it; and the inward worship of God is here performed. We must love God with all our mind, Mark xii., and pray in mind, 1 Cor. xiv. God makes a special search after men's minds; it is his special glory to search the heart and mind of man; and if God be enraged, the strength of the battle is directed against the mind, and his worst strokes light there. One of his last curses is a reprobate mind.

The consideration hereof may serve for reproof of the great carelessness that is in the most for the mind and the inward man, and the purity thereof. Thought is not free, as many fondly think. He will never truly repent for evil works that doth not first care to repent for evil thoughts, and such like corruption in the mind. There should man begin his repentance, where God begins the discovery of our misery.

And let us learn to be more watchful against the sins of our minds, and be more grieved for the dross and corruption we find there, and learn more to hate the sins of the mind, such as are ignorance, distracted service, false opinions, emptiness of holy meditations, evil, dishonourable, impure, and unchaste thoughts against God or man, pride, malice, frowardness, vanity, security, and unbelief.

Doct. 2. There is in unregenerate men a strange minding of sin; they 'imagine mischief;' they have a 'spirit of fornication,' 'profound to decline,' deeply set; they 'trust in their own ways,' so as many times they regard neither God's word, nor the rod, nor the threatenings of God, or rebukes of man; neither can they be stirred with the four last things. This shows, as man's misery and death in sin, so the wonderful mercy of God in forgiving such sins. It is a comfort that sins of set knowledge may be forgiven. And hence may be gathered a difference between the sins of the regenerate and the sins of the unregenerate; for the godly sin not with a full mind, they are not set in evil; sin rebels in them, but not reigns. Lastly, this may let us see how little cause we have to stand upon our minds, or reason, or natural parts, in matters of hope and salvation.

In evil works. If the dependence, and the words themselves, be duly considered, we may here gather five things: first, That the evil works of the sinner cause the strangeness and enmity aforesaid; secondly, That a wicked man can like himself well enough, though his very works and outward behaviour be evil,—he can 'bless himself in his heart, when his iniquity is found worthy to be hated,' Ps. xxxvi. 2; thirdly, That where the life is evil the mind is evil,—the heart cannot be good where the works are naught; fourthly, That he that allows himself in one sin will pollute himself with many sins; fifthly, When God looks upon the works of evil men they are all evil: note a difference; if the carnal man look upon his own works, they are all good; if a godly man look upon them, they are partly good and partly evil; but if God look upon them, they are all naught, because his person is naught, his heart is naught, his end is naught, the manner is naught, &c.

Hitherto of their misery, both as it is propounded and expounded.

A question may be asked, How it comes to pass that men have so little sense of their misery, and are so loath to take notice of it? For answer hereunto, we must understand that this comes to pass because the god of this world, having possession, blinds their eyes, and men do not examine themselves before the law of God. And they are withdrawn by the deceitfulness of sin, which in particular they have allowed themselves in; neither do men remember their latter ends, or the judgment of God before their death. Their eyes are not anointed with eye-salve; a number have not the word to direct them, and some are deceived by false teachers, which 'cry peace, peace, where there is no peace.' And the most are deceived with false opinions and conceits; for either they think that such like places as this are true of Gentiles, and not of them; whereas unregenerate Israel is as Ethiopia unto God, Amos ix. 7; or they fear that this knowledge will make men melancholy. Yea, some are so foolish, they say this course drives men out of their wits; thus Paul is mad, and Christ hath a devil; or they think late repentance will serve the turn, and then they may have time enough to consider.

Thus of their misery.

Ver. 22. *In that body of his flesh, to present* (or make) *you holy, and unblameable, and without fault in his sight.*

In this verse the remedy of their misery is set down, where observe: first, The means; secondly, The end. The means is 'by that body of his flesh, through death;' the end is 'to present us,' &c.

In that body of his flesh, through death. Here are two things: 1. The nature of Christ; 2. The sufferings of Christ. But first in the general I observe two doctrines:

First, There is no remedy for the sinner but the death of his Saviour. How foolish mankind hath been distracted about the cure for their misery, is lamentable to consider: Adam gets fig leaves, and Israel a foolish cover, Isa. xxx. 1. As for death and hell, men are at a point; they have made a covenant with them. Or they think they are helped of their misery if they can forget it; they can bless their hearts that they will not feel the smart of any curses, Ps. xxxvi. 2, Deut. xxix. 19; or they will make satisfaction; the sons of their body shall serve for the sins of their souls, Micah vi.; or else 'the temple of the Lord,' their going to church, must make God amends, Jer. vii. Others cover all with the garments of their own civil righteousness; others put their trust in the wedge of gold, and say to it, 'thou art my confidence.' But unto us there is no name by which we can be safe but the name of Jesus Christ. He must rescue us that first created us; he makes us partakers of love, that was the Son of God's love; he makes us adopted sons, who himself is God's natural Son.

Secondly, It is profitable to be much in the meditation of Christ's sufferings, that it might sink into our minds that we must go out of ourselves for happiness; and such meditations open a way to godly sorrow, Ezek. xii. 12. They tend to the mortification of sin, and they incline the heart of a Christian to be willing to suffer with him; for he suffered as the master, we are but servants; he suffered for others' sins, we deserve more than we can suffer by our own sin; he suffered all sorts of crosses, and infinite much, we suffer but light affliction. And the thought of his sufferings may make us willing to contemn the world, seeing hereby we discern that his kingdom is not of this world. Yea, we owe unto Christ the remembrance of his sufferings. It is a small thing he requires of us, when he wills us to think on him often, what he hath endured for us.

In that body of his flesh. These words note Christ's nature; yet we must consider which nature. In Christ there were two natures in one person, personally united—his divine and human nature. His divine nature was from eternity, immutable, immortal, impassible. His human nature was conceived and born in time, mutable, mortal, passible, one and the same; without time begotten of the Father, the Son of God, without mother; and in time born of the Virgin, the Son of man, without father; Son to both, natural and co-substantial. These natures are in one person, for that God and man might become one in covenant, one is become God and man in person. These natures are personally united; this union is personal, but not of persons; and it is a union of natures, not natural.

In these words the apostle speaks of the nature assumed, namely, his human nature. And there are two things to be noted in these words: first, That he saith, *that body,* not *the body*; secondly, That he saith not simply *his body,* but *that body of his flesh.*

That body. Here he points out a special excellency in the body of Christ above all bodies in heaven and earth; for his body was without sin, formed by the overshadowing power of the Holy Ghost, so is no man else; 2. It is assumed into personal union with the divine nature; 3. It was honoured with special prophecies, types, and sacrifices; 4. This body was offered up as a full expiatory sacrifice; 5. It is to be remembered to the end of the world in the sacrament.

Body of his flesh. To note that it was a true body like unto ours, and to distinguish it from his sacramental and mystical body. In two things Christ's body was not like ours, and in three things it was like. It was not like: 1. In the manner of subsisting; it was not independent or a person of itself. 2. in the vicious accidents of the substance of it; no sin either could or ought to infect it—could not.

because original sin was restrained by the Holy Ghost; ought not, because in it a purgation for our sins must be made. In three things it was like ours: 1. In substance; he took our whole nature; he was the seed of the woman, of Abraham, of David, the Son of man, &c.; and he took the parts of our nature, both soul and body. 2. In properties; and thus he assumed both the properties of the whole nature, in that he was finite, and create; and in the parts, as in the soul, he assumed understanding, will, memory; and in the body, figure, quantity, and circumscription, &c. 3. In infirmities; for he assumed not only our nature but the infirmities of nature; but we must know that he took the defects or infirmities they call miserable, not those they call damnable.

Thus of the doctrine of his nature; his sufferings follow.

Through death. The death of Christ doth reconcile us, inasmuch as it ratifies the covenant, and takes away the guilt of the sins of the former testament, and the virtue of it eats down the power of present sins, and destroys the power of our natural death.

Christ's death differs from the death of all the elect in three things: first, In that in death he sustained not his own person, but dies as our surety, and so is a sacrifice for sin; secondly, He was in death a whole burnt-offering, for as he died in body, so his soul was an offering for sin, inasmuch as he sustained the sense of the infinite wrath of God in his agonies; thirdly, In that his death was the death of him that was the Son of God. Hitherto of the doctrine of the nature and sufferings of Christ; the uses follow.

First, For instruction. The consideration of all this should teach us: 1. To value reconciliation, with all the graces that flow from it, according to the worth of the means by which they are procured. If there were no other way to know the worth of God's favour, knowledge, spiritual refreshings, and graces, yet by the price paid for the purchase of them we may discern they are worth more than all the world. 2. Is it not possible for us[1] to hate sin, upon the consideration of so pregnant an example of the odiousness of it, when the imputation of sin brought the Son of God on his knees, to his death? O the

[1] Qu. 'Is it possible for us not to hate'?—ED.

soul's lethargy, that hath overgrown us. 3. That we may have the profit of the incarnation and passion of Christ in his natural body, we must be careful to get into his mystical body. 4. The apostle useth the meditation of Christ's humiliation to the death as an argument to persuade us to compassion, mercy, fellowship in the spirit, unity, humility, clemency, and meekness of mind, Phil. ii. 1–9.

Secondly, Wicked men may here see what smart they are like to feel from the impartial justice of God. Doth he not spare the body, the flesh, the blood, the life, of his own Son, when he became but a surety for sin? How shall ungodly men, ever enemies, and never sons, that themselves have committed sin, escape when the day of wrath shall come?

Thirdly, Godly men may here see great reason of comfort, not only by considering the great love of Christ, and the great benefits must needs flow from his death; but if two things be weighed: first, The honour done to our nature, in that in the humanity of Christ it is joined to the divine nature, 1 Tim. iii. 16, Phil. ii. 6, 7—this makes amends for that breach that is made by the damnation of millions in our nature; secondly, The great certainty of God's covenant of grace and mercy—for a man's covenant, if it be once confirmed, no man abrogates it, or addeth, or taketh from it, Gal. iii. 15; therefore, much more God's covenant shall stand unchangeable, being ratified and confirmed by the death of Christ.

Thus of the means.

The end follows in these words, 'To present you holy, and without spot, and unblameable in his sight.' And in these words, is both the presentation and the sanctification of Christians to be considered.

To present you. The original word is very significant, and diversely accepted; it signifies to restore, so Acts ix. 41; to assemble, Acts ii. 26; to make present, so Acts xxiii. 23; to make ready, furnish, purge, or make clean, Acts xxiii. 24; to make acceptable, 1 Cor. viii. 8; to make manifest, 2 Tim. ii. 15; to prove evidently, Acts xxiv. 13; to assist and stand to, Rom. xvi. 2, 2 Tim. iv. 16; to offer by way of dedication or gift to God, 2 Cor. xi. 2, Luke ii. 22, Col. i. 28.

It is true that Christ restores us, collects us, brings us into God's presence, cleanseth us, makes us acceptable, assists and defends us, and manifests us to be holy. But I take it principally in the last sense: he presents us by dedication to God. Thus Christ shall present us holy, both at the day of judgment, and in the day of death, when he shall deliver the soul to God, Rom. xiv. 10. Thus also, Christ doth present us in this life: first, When, by the preaching of the gospel, he severs and segregates us from the world, and brings us into God's household; secondly, In justification, when, clothing us with his own righteousness, he becomes our justification; thirdly, In new obedience, and that two ways: (1.) When he presents our works, covered with his intercession; (2.) When he causeth us to present ourselves to God, both by prayer and consecration of ourselves to God's service, and holiness of life. It must be every man's care, then, to seek his presentation from Christ, and to that end, by covenant, prayer, and practice, devote himself to a subjection to all the ordinances of Christ.

Thus of presentation; sanctification follows.

Holy, unblameable, and unreproveable in his sight. At the first sight I should incline to understand these words either of justification, or our consummate holiness at the day of judgment, but that the sway of interpreters force me to expound them of sanctification. It is greatly to be weighed, that a man in this life should be here said to be holy, unblameable, and unreproveable, or as the other translation hath it, without fault in his sight. For the better conceiving of it, we must compare with these words other scripture, wherein is given unto the godly that they have clean hands and a pure heart, Ps. xxiv. 4; that they are pure, Prov. xxi. 8; upright in heart, Ps. xcvii. 11; sanctified throughout, 1 Thes. v. 23; perfect or undefiled in their way, Ps. cxix. 1; perfect, 2 Cor. xiii. 11, Phil. iii. 15, Mat. v. 48; faultless, Jude 24; without spot, and blameless, 1 Pet. iii. 14; walking in all God's ways, 1 Kings viii. 58; and that they keep God's covenant, Ps. xxv. 10, lxxviii. 8, 10, cxxxii. 22. Thus Noah is said to be perfect, Gen. vi. 9; Hezekiah walked before God with a perfect heart, Isa. xxxviii.; David's heart was perfect, 1 Kings xi. 4; Zacharias and Elizabeth were both righteous before God, and walking in all the commandments of the Lord blameless, Luke i. 6.

The question is, how those sayings should be

true, and in what sense they are meant? And for the clearing of the doubt, the way is not simply to reject the propositions, as impious, and untrue, and heretical, as some ignorant and malicious persons do; but seing they are the sacred words of scripture, to consider what it is may be attained, and what God requires of us. To think with the papists or anabaptists that any mortal man can perform the obedience required in the moral law perfectly, so as never to commit sin against the law, is a most blasphemous, detestable, and cursed opinion; for there is no man that sinneth not; the best of the saints have had their thousands of sin. But those places are to be understood of the righteousness of the Christian, as he is considered to be under the covenant of grace and the gospel; not of legal perfection, but of an evangelical innocency and uprightness. Not as their works are in themselves, but comparatively, either with the works of wicked men, or as they are in their desire and endeavour, and as they are presented in the intercession of Christ, who covers the imperfections that cleave to the works of the faithful. Sometimes the faithful are said to be perfect, that is, strong men in Christ, compared with the weak Christian and infant in grace; so that we see what a Christian in this life may attain unto; the rigour of the law being taken away in the covenant of grace, and the imperfections of his works and frailty being covered in Christ's intercession.

Holy. This word *holy* is the general, and comprehends the other two. For holiness is either internal, and that is expressed by the word ἀμώμους, unblameable, or external, and so it is expressed in the word ἀνεγκλήτους, unreproveable. Holiness is given to God, and so essentially, Luke i. 49; to the Spirit of God, and so effectively, because it works it in others; to Christ, as he derives it by influence to his members, Acts iii. 14, Luke i. 35; to angels, Mat. xxv.; to sacrifices, by way of type; to the covenant of God, as it promiseth holiness to the faithful, Luke i. 71; to the prophets, as teachers of holiness, Acts iii. 21; to the scriptures, as the rule of holiness, Rom. i. 2; to places, for the holiness of the subject; but here it is a glorious adjunct, conferred upon the faithful by Christ.

Concerning holiness of heart and life in general, there are here four things to be noted: 1. The necessity of it; we can never be reconciled or glorified without it, Tit. ii. 12, 13; 2. The difficulty of it; less than the power of Christ crucified cannot make men lead a holy life; 3. The meritorious cause of it; holiness is merited by Christ, as well as salvation; 4. The order; men must first be reconciled to God, before they can get holy grace, or lead a holy life.

Unblameable. Christian perfection hath two things in it: first, Uprightness of heart, noted by this word; secondly, Uprightness of life, noted by the word following. Internal perfection or holiness must have these things in it: first, The stain of former sins must be washed away with the tears of repentance, Jer. iv. 4. Secondly, the inward worship of God must be set up in the heart; some impressions men have of an external worship; but of the inward worship, men are naturally almost wholly ignorant. God is inwardly worshipped by the constant exercise of grace from above, as love, fear, trust, delight, desire, &c. Thirdly, There must be in us an assurance of God's favour, Heb. x. 22, Acts xv. 9. Fourthly, There must be a freedom from prevailing evils in the mind or affections; in the mind, as ignorance, wicked thoughts, errors; in the affections, as impatience, lust, servile fear of men, Prov. xix. 2, Ps. xli. 12, James i. 4; malice, &c. Fifthly, Hypocrisy must not reign; our desire must be more to be good, than to seem so, Ps. cxxv. 4. Sixthly, Our whole heart must be set upon God's whole law, to have respect unto all God's commandments; God abhors a divided heart, Hosea x. 2, and a double heart, James iv. Seventhly, The mind must be set upon heavenly things, and converse in heaven, Col. iii. 1. Where these things are happily attained unto, there the heart is upright, whatsoever defects or infirmities be in it. These things are different in Christians, in the degrees; for there is an infancy and weakness in sanctification, as well as faith.

The signs of an upright heart are these: first, It desires perfection, Phil. iii.; secondly, It will not cease well-doing for crosses, Job ii. 3; thirdly, It will serve God though alone, Josh. xxiv. 15; fourthly, It will not follow the eye, is not sensual, Job xxxi. 7; fifthly, It rejoiceth in the love of Christ above all things, Cant. i. 3; sixthly, It will smite for lesser sins, as David's did, 2 Sam. xxiv.; seventhly, It is constant, Ps. lxxviii. 37.

That we may attain an upright and unblameable heart. In general, we must get a new heart, Ezek. xxxvi. 27. In particular: 1. We must by mortification circumcise our hearts, Deut. x. 16; 2. We must get God's law written in our hearts, Jer. xxxi. 33; 3. We must seek and love purity of heart, Prov. xxii. 11; 4. We must keep our hearts with all diligence, Prov. iv. 23; lastly, We must walk before God, Gen. xvii. 2.

Motives to inward holiness: first, We shall never see the righteousness of God imputed till we be upright in heart, Ps. xxxvi. 10; secondly, A pure heart is one of the clearest signs of a blessed man, Mat. v. 6; thirdly, God searcheth to find what men's hearts are, as well as what their lives are, 2 Chron. vi. 30; fourthly, ' The eyes of the Lord behold all the earth, to shew himself strong, with all them that are of a perfect heart,' 2 Chron. xvi. 9; fifthly, ' Light is sown for the righteous, and joy for the upright in heart,' Ps. xcvii. 11; lastly, The whole 125th Psalm incites hereunto.

Unreprovable. This word notes the external uprightness, or Christian perfection of life. External innocency must have in it divers things: 1. We must be free from the gross sins of every commandment; 2. We must cease from our own works, Heb. iv. 10, keep us from our wickedness, 2 Sam. xxii. 23, and not turn after the ways of our own heart, Isa. lvii. 17, that is, we must be sure to cease from our particular beloved sins; 3. Our families must be well-ordered, both for peace, labour, and piety, Tit. i. 6, 7; 4. We must be free from idolatry, Deut. xviii. 13, from the customary sins of the tongue, James iii. 2, from the reign of hardness of heart, from hasting to be rich, for he that hasteth to be rich cannot be innocent, as the proverb is, Prov. xxi. 29; lastly, We must love our enemies, Mat. v., *ult.*; that we may attain hereunto, we must walk in the way of good men, Prov. ii. 20, we must set God's laws ever before us, and let them be our warrant, 2 Sam. xxii. 23; we must not be destitute of heavenly gifts, 1 Cor. i. 6-8.

In his sight. These words may be referred either to our presentation or to our sanctification. And whereas some would think that they overthrow the former sense of the words, and prove that he entreats here of our holiness in God's sight by justification, they are deceived, for they may find these words given to sanctification ordinarily in scripture, as Luke i. 6, 7, Heb. xiii. 21, 1 John iii. 22, Rev. xiv. 5.

The words being referred to sanctification, import four things:

First, That what we are or do is in his presence; so the words used, Luke ii. 18, and xiii. 26, Acts x. 33.

Secondly, That God is a witness of all we do; so the words used, Luke viii. 47, 2 Cor. vii. 12, Gal. i. 20.

Thirdly, That God accepts of what is truly good in any measure, Luke i. 75.

Fourthly, That God highly prizeth all that is good in the good, Luke i. 25, 2 Tim. ii. 3, and v. 4, as the words there used shew.

Ver. 23. *If ye continue grounded and stablished in the faith, and be not moved away from the hope of the gospel, whereof ye have heard.*

The second part of the epistle, viz., the proposition of doctrine, hath been handled hitherto from the 12th verse unto these words. In these words and those that follow to the end of the second chapter, is contained the third part of the epistle, viz., matter of exhortation, wherein he both persuades and dissuades. The persuasion is contained in this verse and the rest, unto the 8th verse of the next chapter. The dissuasion is from verse 8th of chapter second to the end of the chapter.

In the persuasion, the apostle exhorts them to perseverance, both in faith and hope. Where is to be observed: 1. The matter to which he exhorts in the beginning of this verse, and the reason to enforce the exhortation in all the verses following. The matter to which he exhorts is twofold: first, To perseverance in faith, in these words: ' if ye continue grounded and stablished in the faith;' secondly, To perseverance of hope, in the next words: ' and be not moved from the hope of the gospel, whereof ye have heard.' From the coherence and general words of the exhortation, we must observe, that God's children, after they have gotten true grace, and are comforted in their reconciliation, must look to their faith and hope. It is not enough once to get faith and hope, but after they are conceived in us they must be daily looked to, for 'the just must live by his faith,' Hab. ii. 4, Heb. x. 38. It must be to him according to his faith, not according to his friends, money, labour, means, &c. By faith he must draw virtue out of all God's ordinances, Eph. iii. 16. By faith he must purge his heart of his daily sins, Acts xv. 9. By faith and hope he walks with God, and overcomes the world, 1 John v. 4, 2 Tim. iii. 15. This may greatly reprove man's carelessness. Men look to their grounds, cattle, shops, &c., but who looks to their faith and hope?

If you continue grounded and stablished in the faith. Here are two things: first, The manner of the propounding of the exhortation, viz., with an *if;* secondly, The exhortation itself. Where note: 1. The duty, 'continue;' 2. The manner of the duty, 'grounded and stablished;' 3. The object, 'in faith.'

If. The apostle propounds this exhortation with an *if*, because he speaketh to a mixed multitude, among whom were many that would not continue, and thereby shew they were not truly reconciled. Yea, it was needful that the godly amongst them should have it thus doubtfully set down, that so they might be more careful to settle and establish themselves in the faith, that they might hold out in it.

As this *if* looks upon the wicked, it shews that in places where the gospel gathers souls to God, many that for a time were forward and greatly affected will afterwards fall away. And therefore God's servants, both ministers and people, should look for apostasy, and not to be overmuch troubled when they see any fall away.

It is not amiss to consider by what means or motives men are plucked away from the love of the truth. Some fall away for hard sayings, John vi. 30, 42, 52, 60, 61, &c. Some cannot follow Christ long because of their carnal friends. Others are corrupted with lewd company. Others cannot bear the reproofs of their faults; and if they be reproved, either they will lift Amos away from Bethel, or they get themselves away from hearing Amos. Some hear this sect everywhere so ill spoken of that they will be better advised ere they settle upon such courses; and the rather, because they do not see the multitude set out with them, or great men yield any countenance to such strict courses. Others are seduced by time-serving, flattering, false, or corrupt teachers, who, labouring to hinder the efficacy of the doctrine of painful ministers, hope to accomplish either the stopping of their mouths, or the increase of their bonds, or at least their disgrace with the people, Ezek. xiii. 19-22, 2 Tim. iii. 12-14. Others are ensnared with the earthly things, and forsake the sincerity of the truth, to embrace this world, with Demas. Many fall away for the cross, and all are caught with the deceitfulness of some sin, Heb. iii. 12, 13.

Quest. But may the faithful fall away and not continue?

Ans. The faithful may lose, and fall from: 1. Some degrees of innocency of life; 2. Some degrees of the working and efficacy of God's Spirit; 3. Some degrees of communion with Christ,—their communion may be lessened, though their union cannot be dissolved; 4. From faith, of which he makes mention here. And thus they may fall in respect of sense, in respect of some degree, in respect of some acts of faith, in respect of some doctrine of faith, and, lastly, in respect of the means of the doctrine of faith. But there are seven things from which the elect can never fall: first, Eternal life, John x. 29; secondly, Confirming grace in some measure, Ps. xiv. 5; thirdly, Remission of sins past, Isa. xliii. 25; fourthly, The seed either of doctrine or grace, 1 John iii. 9; fifthly, The spirit of sanctification; sixthly, The habit of faith, Luke xxii. 32; seventhly, Union with Christ, John xvii. 22, 23, 26.

Continue. Three things I propound concerning perseverance: first, Some reasons to move us to labour, to hold out, and continue; secondly, Rules to be observed that we might continue; thirdly, The helps the faithful have to further their perseverance.

For the first: Unless we continue we shall never have the full truth of God, nor be made free by it, nor have sound comfort that we are the disciples of Christ, John viii. 31, 32. Neither is any man 'fit for the kingdom of God, that puts his hand to the plough, and looks back,' Luke ix. 6. 'The branch cannot bear fruit except it abide in the vine,' John xv. 4. And, 'if they continue not with us, it is because they were not of us,' 1 John ii. 19. 'It had been better (for men) never to have known the way of righteousness, than after they have known it, to turn from the holy commandments delivered unto them. For if after they have escaped the pollutions of the world through the knowledge of Jesus Christ they be again entangled and overcome, the latter end will be worse than the beginning,' 2 Pet. ii. 19, 20. Yea, the very children of God by backsliding may fall into a miserable condition; the powers of hell may assault them, Ps. xlvii. 11. They may go to the grave with unrecoverable affliction; yea, they may lose some graces, without all restitution in this world, as the joy of their salvation, plerophory, or full assurance, &c.

For the second: If thou wouldst continue, thou must observe eight rules: first, Thou must get a continuing faith; get thee an infallible assurance of God's favour, arising from the wise application of God's promises, and the sure witness of God's Spirit, John vi. 40. Secondly, Thou must at first be thoroughly cleansed of all thy filthiness, making conscience to repent of all sin, and 'have respect to all God's commandments;' and thou must be sure thou get a new heart, for the old heart is deceitful, and will not hold out in anything that is good, Ezek. xxxvi. 26, 27. Thirdly, Thou must continue to use the means of preservation: thou must still hear, pray, read, confer, meditate, and receive the sacraments: for the spiritual life is preserved by means, as well as the natural. Fourthly, Thou must join thyself to such as fear God in the society and fellowship of the gospel. The affections and desires of many are blasted, and soon vanish, like a morning cloud, for want of communion with such as are able to direct, comfort, admonish, or encourage them, Jer. xxxii. 39, 40, Phil. i. 5, 6. Fifthly, Thou must see to it that thou get knowledge as well as affection, Hosea ii. 9, 20, and affection as well as knowledge, Ps. clxv. 20. Sixthly, Thou must so receive the truth of the doctrine of Christ as thou be also ready and willing to confess it, and profess it, amidst the different opinions and humours of men, Mat. xvi. 16. Seventhly, Thou must be a sheep—meek, tractable, profitable, sociable, innocent; for boisterous, conceited, perverse, unteachable natures will never hold long, John x. 28.

Lastly, Thou must be ever wary, and take heed of cross teachings and the puffs of contrary doctrine; and withal, take heed of coldness in following the truth, and of discord with such as fear God. Many times personal discords work, through men's singular corruptions, apostasy from the truth once received, Eph. v. 13, 14.

The sum of all is, that if we get a justifying faith, and be once assured of God's favour; if we at first make a thorough reformation; if we daily stick to, and wait upon, the means; if we converse with God's children; if we have wise affections, that are warmed with piety and shewed with discretion; if we make a sound profession of the sincerity of the truth; if we be meek and teachable, and follow the truth without coldness or contention, we shall never fall, but continue as Mount Zion that cannot be moved. And out of all this we may discern the cause of the backsliding of many,—either they were deceived by a temporary faith, or neglected the constant use of God's ordinances, or were slightly in mortification, or they forsook the fellowship of the saints, or they were tossed with contrary doctrine, or they were people of unruly affections, or were seduced by secret lusts.

For the third, Though it be a hard work to continue by reason of the infirmities within us, and the impediments from without us; yet a Christian hath great helps to further him in perseverance. He hath helps: first, From the saints, and is furthered by their example, by their exhortations, and by their prayers, Heb. xii. 1, x. 24, 1 Tim. ii. 1. Secondly, From the immortal seed which is within them, which hath as great aptness to grow as any seed in nature, and is as seed that is sown for continuance, even for eternity itself, 1 John iii. 9. Thirdly, From the easiness and grace of the covenant in which they stand in favour with God. And here it would be observed how the words of the covenant run; for when God saith, he will make his everlasting covenant, his promise is, that he will not turn away from them to do them good, and his fear he will put in their hearts, that they shall not depart from him, Jer. xxxii. 40. And in another place he saith, he will not only cleanse them, but he will give them a new heart, and take away the stony heart out of their bodies, and put his Spirit within them, and cause them to walk in his statutes and to do them, Jer. xxxvi. 26, 27. Fourthly, From the Spirit of God, which is in them; for the Spirit sets the soul at liberty, 2 Cor. iii. 17; and furnisheth it with graces, Gal. v. 22; sealeth up unto the day of redemption, Eph. i. 14; strengtheneth the inward man, Eph. iii. 16; shows the things given of God, 1 Cor. ii. 12; is a perpetual comforter, John xiv. 16; leadeth into all truth, John xv. 13; frees from condemnation and the rigour of the law, Rom. viii. 1, 3; is life for righteousness' sake, ver. 10; mortifies the deeds of the flesh, ver. 13; bears witness that they are the children of God, ver. 16; is a Spirit of prayer to cause them to cry Abba Father, ver. 15; helps their infirmities, and makes request for them, ver. 26. Fifthly, From Christ, for from Christ they have protection, John x. 18; influence, John xv. 1, 4, 5; intercession, by which he covers their sins and infirmities, presents their works in his merits, and moveth the Father to keep them from evil, &c., John xvii. 9, 11, 15, 17, 22. Sixthly, They have helps from his ordinances, for by prayer, when they ask according to God's will, they may be sure to have anything, 1 John v. 4; and by the sacraments faith is confirmed and sealed, and grace nourished.

And by the word they are many ways furthered. I take but only the 119th Psalm to show how our continuance is helped by the word: It redresseth our ways, ver. 9; it keeps from sin, ver. 11; it strengthens against shame and contempt, ver. 22, 23, 143; it quickens and comforts, ver. 25, 28, 50, 54, 93, 111; it makes free, ver. 45; it makes wise, ver. 98, 100; it is a lantern to our feet, ver. 105, 130; it keeps from declining, ver. 102, 104, 118, 155, 160, 165. Lastly, they are helped by the promises that concern perseverance, and preservation, and falling away; such as are contained in such scriptures as these: John xiii. 1, 1 Cor. x. 13, Rom. viii. 29, Ps. lxxxiv. 12, 1 Tim. iv. 18, Rev. ii. 25, 26.

Grounded and stablished in the faith. It is not enough to get faith, and continue in it, but we must be grounded and stablished. And when he saith stablished in the faith, we must understand the doctrine, profession, exercise, assurance, and effects of faith. And this establishing and grounding of our hearts hath in it particular knowledge, certainty, resolution, and contentment.

To be thus established would fortify us against all the changes and alterations of estate or religion in after-times; and as the coherence imports, it would much further us in the attainment of an unstained and unrebukeable life; whereas of doubting can come nothing but the shunning of God, the liberty of sin, and desperation, and the like. Besides, this grounded establishment in faith would free our profession from the dishonours which an unsettled or discontented faith or life doth cast upon us. Atheists, papists, epicures, and belly-gods, if this were in us, would be astonished to see the power of religion in our resolved contentment, and to consider how immoveable we were, so as the gates of hell could not prevail against us. Besides the unsearchable solace that a peaceable and restful conscience would breed in us.

That we might be thus grounded and stablished divers things are carefully to be observed: 1. We must be founded on the prophets and apostles, Eph. ii. 20; we must be daily conversant in the scriptures. 2. We must be much in prayer; but in practice of prayer we must nourish the hatred of every sin, and daily labour to increase in the reformation of evil. And it is a great help to be much with such as fear God, and call upon God with a pure heart. It would much establish us to see the faith, affections, fervency, and power of God's Spirit in others in prayer, 2 Tim. ii. 19, 22. 3. There is a secret blessing of God, in settling a man's heart, follows upon well-doing; so as to be abundant in God's work is a great means of steadfastness; whereas a fruitless and barren life is both uncomfortable and unsettled, 1 Cor. xv. 58, 1 Tim. vi. 19. 4. We must pray God to give us a free and ingenuous spirit, Ps. li. 12; we must pray to God to give us a mind cheerful, speedy, full of incitations to good, glad of all occasions to do good, free from the stain of the sins of the time, nation, or calling, and from the reign of former lusts, inclinable to serve God and our brethren by love, fearing the gospel more than the law, and God's goodness more than his justice. 5. We must set an order in faith and life. It is exceeding behoveful in matter of opinions to deliver up our souls to some sound frame of doctrine, in which we will ever quietly rest; and in matters of life to gather out of the commandments a platform of living that might fit our own case, Prov. iv. 26. We are not usually settled and soundly stablished till we have been shaken with affliction, and have gotten the experience which the cross learns us, 1 Pet. v. 10. Lastly, We must consecrate ourselves to God, endeavouring daily to practice what we daily hear; for 'he that cometh to Christ, and heareth his sayings, and doeth them, is like a man which hath built a house, and digged deep, and laid the foundation on a rock; and when the flood arose, and the stream beat vehemently upon that house, it could not shake it, because it was founded on a rock,' Luke vi. 48, 49.

Quest. What should be the reason why many, after long profession and much hearing, and some comfortable signs of assurance at sundry times conceived, should yet be unsettled and distracted, and shew so much perplexity and want of firmness either in contentment or practice?

Ans. This is occasioned diversely: first, Sometimes for want of a distinct direction or careful examination about the application of the signs of God's favour. Some Christians have not the signs clearly and distinctly collected; others that have them, and know the use of them, grow slothful and negligent, and are justly scourged with the want of the glory of this establishment.

Secondly, Sometimes it comes to pass for want of using private means more conscionably, as reading, prayer, or conference.

Thirdly, It is so sometimes with Christians, because of some sin they lie in without repentance. There may be some sin which they too much favour, and are loath to forsake, whether it be secret or more open.

Fourthly, Untruthfulness and barrenness in good works may cause it; for if faith did bear fruit upwards, it would take root downwards.

Fifthly, Many are grievously pressed under legal perfection, being not able distinctly to discern the benefit of the covenant of grace in freeing them from the curse and rigour of the law. The ignorance of this one point hath and doth cover the faces and hearts of millions of God's servants with a perplexed confusion and fear without cause.

Sixthly, Many professors live in much unrest for want of discerning things that differ, and the right use of Christian liberty.

Seventhly, There is a kind of lukewarmness in practice after hearing, which is in many scourged with the withholding of this rich grace of spiritual steadfastness. I say lukewarmness in practice; for it may be observed that many hear with great affection, and continue to be stirring in expressing their liking of the word, and yet are exceedingly negligent in the conscionable and daily practice of such rules as in the ministry of the word they seem to receive with admiration and great liking.

Eighthly, This comes by reason of the want of patience and a meek spirit. Some Christians are froward, passionate, transported with violent affections, either of anger or worldly grief; and these seldom or never gain any long rest or continual contentment. Troubled affections greatly hinder settledness even in the best things.

To conclude, Many professors revolt to the world, and give themselves to an unjustifiable liberty in following either their profits or their pleasures; and therefore no marvel though grace and true religion thrive so slowly in them, when they eat up their hearts and lives with these cares and delights of life.

Hitherto of faith; now of hope.

Be not moved away from the hope of the gospel, whereof ye have heard. Though by faith we are interested in God's favour, and our souls garnished on earth with divers graces as the fruits of faith, and our lives protected with celestial privileges, yet the glory of our kingdom is neither of this world nor in this world. Hope must guide us to future things, as well as faith to present; and therefore the apostle Peter doth with great reason teach us to bless God for 'begetting us again to a lively hope,' 1 Pet. i. 3. Our whole happiness may be branched out into these two parts: first, What we have already on earth; and secondly, What we look to have hereafter in heaven. The one, faith procures; the other, hope assures. Now in that we have not all our happiness here, but hope for it elsewhere, it should teach us divers things:

First, We should effectually pray unto God to

give such sound wisdom and revelation by his word and Spirit that we may indeed know the hope of our calling, Eph. i. 18.

Secondly, In all troubles we should be the more patient, seeing we hold our full and final deliverance (when we shall feel no more troubles or crosses) by hope. Perfect salvation is had here only by hope, Rom. viii.

Thirdly, When our friends go out of the world, such as were dear unto us in the bonds of grace, we should not mourn immoderately for them, for that were to proclaim our want of knowledge, or want of sense and feeling, in the thoughts of the happiness of another world, 1 Thes. iv. 13.

Yea, fourthly, Seeing the greatest part of our happiness is yet to come, we should learn to place our joys in the contemplation of heaven, according to the apostle's direction, who biddeth us 'rejoice in hope,' Rom. xii. 12.

And lastly, We should prepare for death, and wait when the time of our changing should come, that we might enjoy the glorious liberty of the sons of God.

Not moved away. Doct. It is not enough to have hope, but we must get to be unmoveable in it: for as the author to the Hebrews shews, we should be diligent to get 'and have a plerophory, or 'full assurance of hope to the end,' Heb. vi. 11. We must 'hold fast the confidence and rejoicing of hope,' Heb. iii. 6. This is our sure and steadfast anchor, to which we should in all storms have our refuge, to hold fast by it, Heb. vi. 18, 19.

The use is twofold: First, It may reprove that unsettledness and discontentment which is found in men in the times of their affliction, when every cross can move them away from their confidence. We would think him a strange man that in time of peace would walk up and down with a helmet on him, and when he were to go into any battle or fray, in the midst of the fight, when it was at the hottest, would take his helmet and throw it off him. And yet so strange are we. In prosperity we outbrag all men with our hope in God, and our strong confidence; but when the devil, or the world, begin to deal their blows, and to molest us with sharpest assaults, then we grow heartless or impatient, and throw away our hope, when we have most need of it. Secondly, It should teach us to labour after this unmoveableness of hope; which, that it may the better be done, two things are to be looked to: first, That our hope be a true hope; secondly, That we use the means to make this hope unmoveable.

And for the first, we must consider three things: first, What hope is not true hope; secondly, What persons have no hope; thirdly, What are the effects or properties of true hope. Some things of many, in each of these, shall be instanced in.

First, There is a hope of which men shall one day be ashamed: such is men's hope in their riches, Ps. lii. 7; in the arm of flesh, Jer. xvii. 5; in oppression, vanity, and sin, Ps. lxii. 10; in the instruments of deliverance, as the bow or sword, Ps. xliv. 6, &c.; in the deceitful conceits of their own brains, Isa. xxviii. 15; or in their civility of life. This is to trust in Moses, John v. 45. All these, and other such like hopes, are egregiously vain.

Secondly, There are many sorts of men in the world, concerning whom it is plain in Scriptures, they have not hope; for in the general, there is no hope in any unregenerate man, 1 Pet. i. 3, Eph. ii. 12; and in particular it is clear there is no true hope: first, In the ignorant, Ps. ix. 10; secondly, In profane men that make no conscience of sin, Ps. cxv. 11; thirdly, In the presumptuous that bless their hearts against the curses of the law, Deut. xxix. 19; fourthly, In the hypocrite, for though he have woven to himself, out of the bowels of his poisonous breast, a fair web of hope, yet it shall be as the house of the spider, Job viii. 13, one sweep of God's besom shall easily lay him and his hope in the dust of misery; lastly, It is not in workers of iniquity that make a trade of sin, and every day plod about mischief.

Thirdly, True hope is most stirring in affliction, and then it shows itself by four things:

First, By profession, it will not only know, but 'acknowledge that truth, which is according to godliness,' Tit. i. 1, 2. It will confess and profess; whereas the common hope seldom or never at any time holds it convenient to be so forward.

Secondly, By abnegation; for it will endure scorns, losses, temptations, oppositions, &c. It is not moved away by the carnal reasons of the flesh, the disdain of carnal friends, the violence of unreasonable adversaries, or the like; the chain will not fear it, nor the reproach shame it, 1 Tim. iv. 10; it will be busy, though he have no thanks for his labour, Acts xxviii. 20; and it will not haste to ill means to get out of distress, Isa. xxviii. 15, 16. Whereas the common hope is frightened with the noise of a chain, and put out of countenance with a scoff of disgrace; it will speak Christ fair, but lose nothing for his sake; it likes preaching well, but it will never believe it is so as the preacher says; it loves God above all, but yet it must have a care to see to it, at any hand, that such and such friends be not displeased; it will be better advised than to be in danger of such and such troubles. And if it be hard bestead, it will venture to send to a wizard, to use now and then a lie, or an oath, or a little fraud, and false-dealing, &c.

Thirdly, By mortification; 'he that hath this hope purgeth himself, that he may be pure as Christ is pure,' 1 John iii. 3. It stirreth up to much prayer, confession, sorrow, fasting, and spiritual revenge. He that hath most hope is most in the humiliation of his soul. It is not, as the world conceives, that mortification is the way to desperation; but the common hope hath no hands to do good works, nor eyes to shed these tears, nor stomach to abide this fasting; nor flesh to endure this revenge, nor tongue to speak this language.

Fourthly, By perseverance; it will not cease from yielding fruit, Jer. xvii. 8. Job, guided by this hope, resolves to trust still in God though he kill him, Job xiii. 15; but the common hope will be sure then to fail when there is most need of help.

Now that we might be unmoveable in this hope, we should wait patiently upon God's ordinances, that we might abound in the comforts of the scriptures, increasing in knowledge and wisdom, Rom. xv. 4, Prov. xxiv. 14; but especially we must stick to the word preached, and never give it over, Eph. i. 1-4; nourishing every grace of Christ, 2 Thes. ii. 16; and we must be much in prayer, Ps. lxii. 8, and lxi. 2, 3; and soundly careful to deny all ungodliness and worldly lusts, Tit. ii. 12, 13, Job xi. 14, 15.

Thus of the duty and the object, *grace*; now of the means by which it was wrought, which was the gospel preached.

Of the gospel. *Doct.* The gospel is the ordinary means to breed hope in a man's heart, 2 Tim. ii. 10, Rom. i. 16; and therefore it is called 'the gospel of the kingdom,' and the 'gospel of salvation,' Mat. iv. 13, Eph. i. 13. And the gospel breeds hope, as it shews us the doctrine of our reconciliation with God; and as it contains the promises of the covenant of grace; and as it shews our deliverance from the rigour and curse of the law; and lastly, as it shews Christ crucified, with all merits.

Of which ye have heard. *Doct.* The gospel is then most effectual when it is preached; and more particularly what efficacy is in preaching may appear by these scriptures following: Ps. li. 8, Isa. lv. 4, Luke iv. 18, Rom. x. 14, 1 Cor. i. 21, &c., Acts x. 36, 42, and xv. 21, 2 Cor. i. 19, 20, Gal. iii. 1, 1 Tim. iii. 16, Titus i. 3.

Again, in that the apostle allegeth the efficacy of the doctrine they heard, to prove that they ought not to be moved away from it, we may note that that doctrine which converts souls to God is true, and men ought to continue in it. The apostle, 2 Cor. iii. 2, proves his doctrine to be true by this seal of it; and this must comfort faithful teachers against all the scorns of men, if they gather souls to God and breed hope in God's people. And the people must hence confirm themselves in their resolution to stick to their teachers, when God hath given this testimony to their ministries. Thus of the exhortation.

The reasons follow:

1. From consent of the elect, ver. 23.
2. From the testimony of Paul, ver. 23, 24.
3. From the testimony of God, ver. 25.
4. From the excellency of the doctrine of the gospel, ver. 26.
5. From the excellency of the subject of the gospel, ver. 27.
6. From the end, or profitable effect, of the gospel, ver. 28.
7. From the endeavour of Paul, ver. 29.

Which was preached unto every creature under heaven. These words contain the first reason, and it stands thus: Inasmuch as the doctrine taught you is the same doctrine that hath been taught to and received by all the elect, therefore ye ought to continue in it, and never be moved from the grace wrought by it.

Quest. But was the gospel preached to every creature under heaven?

Ans. Some understand the meaning to be this: that the apostle intends to note, by the preaching of the gospel to every creature, only thus much, that it was now no more confined in Judea, but was published to Gentiles as well as Jews; and so it was preached to every creature, inasmuch as all mankind had as much interest as the Jewish nation. Others think the speech imports no more but that the fame of the gospel was spread by the merchants and other that lay at Rome, Jerusalem, and other great cities, unto all known countries of the world. Others think it is no more than if he had said it was published far and wide; as in John they say, 'the whole world goeth after him;' but they mean a great multitude, an usual hyperbolical speech. Lastly, others think that when he saith it was preached, he meaneth it should be preached to every creature, the time past being put for the time to come, to import that it shall as certainly be done as if it had been done already. But I take it is meant of the preaching of the gospel by the apostles and evangelists in the conversion of so many nations to the faith of Christ.

There may be seven observations gathered out of this speech of the apostle: *First*, That doctrine only is true which is agreeable to the doctrine of the apostles, by which the world was converted to God. *Secondly*, We may see that no power is like the power of the word of God; here it converts a world in a short time; and our eyes have beheld that it hath almost in as short a time restored a world of men from the power of antichrist. *Thirdly*, We may by this phrase be informed that the words *all* and *every one* are not always in scripture to be understood universally of all the singular persons in the world, as the universalists conceive. *Fourthly*, They were but a few fishermen that did this great work, and they were much opposed and persecuted, and in some less matters they jarred sometime among themselves. Whence we may observe, that doctrine may be exceeding effectual, though : 1. But few teach it; 2. Though they be but of mean estate and condition; 3. Though it be opposed by cross and contrary teaching; 4. Though it be persecuted; 5. Though the people be indisposed and muzzled in sin and superstition, as the Gentiles were; 6. Though the preacher be often restrained; 7. Though there be some dissension in less matters. The *fifth* thing that may be gathered hence is, that in the conversion of sinners, God is no respecter of persons. Men of any age, nation, sex, condition, life, or quality, may be converted by the gospel. And *sixthly*, It is plain here that preaching is the ordinary means to convert every creature, so as ordinarily there is none converted but by preaching. *Lastly*, If any one ask what shall become of those nations, or particular persons, that never yet heard of the gospel, I answer, the way of God in divers things is not revealed, and his judgments are like a great deep. It belongs to us to look to ourselves, to whom the gospel is come.

Thus of the first reason.

The second reason is taken from the testimony of Paul, and he gives a double testimony : first, By his ministry ; secondly, By his sufferings.

Whereof I Paul am a minister. Out of these words many things may be noted :

First, In that the apostle, notwithstanding all the disgraces and troubles that befell him for the gospel, doth yet lift up the mention of his ministry therein as an inducement to the Ephesians; it may teach us that the glory of God's truth is such as no man need to be ashamed to teach or profess it; nay, there can be no man or woman to whom it may not be their chiefest glory, whatsoever carnal worldlings or timorous Nicodemites conceive of it.

Secondly, In that so great an apostle doth not disdain to yield his testimony, of purpose to shew that Epaphras, their preacher, had taught nothing but what he had likewise taught; it sheweth that it is the property of faithful and humble ministers to strengthen the hearts and hands of their brethren, though they be their inferiors; and then it will follow, that they are proud, and envious, and malicious persons, that by cross teaching labour to increase their bonds whom God hath honoured with success in their labours in the gospel. Such are they that in many places strive to pull down as fast as others build, making havoc in the church, and bending their whole might in their ministry to hinder the sincerity of the gospel and the conversion of sinners.

Thirdly, In that the apostle urgeth his own testimony, *I Paul*, it sheweth that the testimony of one apostle is better than a thousand others, one Paul opposed to many false teachers; which should teach us to converse much in the doctrine of the apostles and prophets, which are of like authority. And the rather because the best of other men may err, nay, have erred; and therefore a heap of human testimonies should be of no value against one scripture. And as the people should try the spirits by this witness, so should preachers make conscience of it, to take more pains to inform the consciences of the people by the testimony of the word than by human authority of what sort soever.

Fourthly, In that here is but one Paul, that comes in to confirm the truth of the gospel, it shews that many times the soundest teachers are the fewest in number. Here it is so in the best times of the church, so it was before; there was but one Michaiah for four hundred false prophets. So in Christ's time there was a swarm of pharisaical, proud, vainglorious, hypocritical, silken doctors, that loved the chief room, and sought pre-eminence, teachers of liberty and strife, defenders of traditions, and their own glory and greatness, when Christ and his disciples were by their envy scorned as a few precise, singular fellows.

Fifthly, In that the apostle styleth himself by the name of Paul, and not of Saul, it may intimate that men truly regenerate hate the vain name of their unregeneracy. It is a foul sign when men can glory in the titles and names of their lewdness and sin past.

Lastly, In that the apostle termeth himself a deacon—for so the word translated *minister* is in the original—it notes his great humility. It was a happy time in the church when the apostles called themselves deacons; and then began the church to decay in true glory when deacons would needs be apostles.

Thus of the second reason and the 23d verse.

Ver. 24. *Now rejoice I in my sufferings for you, and fulfil the rest of the afflictions of Christ in my flesh, for his body's sake, which is the church.*

These words contain the apostle's second testimony, and it is taken from his sufferings for the gospel; and he conceiveth that they have great reason to persevere in the love of the truth, since he hath with joy endured so many things for the confirmation of the doctrine he had taught.

In these words I note two things: first, The apostle's joy in affliction; secondly, The reasons which moved him unto his rejoicing. His sufferings in which he doth rejoice he amplifies by the time, *now*, and the divers sorts of crosses he endured, which he expresseth indefinitely, when he saith plurally, *my sufferings*, as also by the use of them, *for you*, that is, for confirmation of your faith and encouragement. The motives are four: first, Because they are *the afflictions of Christ*; secondly, Because they are laid upon him by the decree of God; his measure is set him, and he hath almost done his task, he is ready to die; thirdly, Because they are but *in his flesh*; fourthly, Because they were for the good of *the church*.

Now rejoice I in my sufferings. Doct. God's children have much joy; even in affliction they are cheerful, and with great encouragement they bear their crosses, Rom. v. 3, James i. 2, 2 Cor. vii. 4, viii. 2, Heb. xi. 37, 2 Cor. i. 5, &c.; and if any ask the reason why they are so glad in their affliction and trouble, I answer, God's servants are the more cheerful under crosses, because they know: first, That the 'the Prince of their salvation was consecrate through affliction,' Heb. ii. 10; secondly, That their Saviour did therefore suffer that he might succour them that suffer, Heb. ii. 18, John xvi. 33; thirdly, That the sting is taken out of the cross, and therefore it is not so painful to them as it is to the wicked men; fourthly, That 'the same afflictions are upon their brethren that are in the world,' 1 Pet. v. 9; fifthly, That the way to life is such a kind of way, a strait and narrow troublesome way, Mat. vii. 14; sixthly, That after all their troubles are a while borne in this world, they shall have rest with the blessed in heaven, when the Lord Jesus shall be revealed, and better and more enduring substance than any here they can want or lose, Heb. x. 34, 2 Thes. i. 6, 7; yea, that their afflictions are to be accounted a part of that treasure that they would lay up against the last day;

seventhly, That God will in the mean time comfort them in all their tribulation, 2 Cor. i. 4; eighthly, That their manifold temptations serve for great use, as for the trial of their precious faith and refining of all graces, with the purging out of much dross and corruption in their natures, 1 Pet. i. 6, 7; ninthly, That no afflictions can separate them from the love of God in Christ; with many other reasons, which I might instance in, besides those mentioned in the end of this verse. If any yet ask, how God's servants have attained to such joy, since there are worlds of people that in their troubles could never be induced to conceive of such contentment by any reason could be brought them, I answer that there are divers things in God's children which are not in wicked men, which are great causes and helps to joy in tribulation: as, first, They will receive the light, and treasure up holy knowledge, which they find singular use of in their troubles, whereas an ignorant mind is usually attended with a distempered heart, Heb. x. 32, 34; secondly, They have faith in God, and carry about in their hearts the warm and inflamed love of Jesus Christ, and are, therefore, able to trust in God's providence in any distress, 1 Pet. i. 7, 8; thirdly, God's children hold such a course as this, when as παθήματα, the sufferings, which are *mala pœnæ*, evils of punishment, do fall upon them, they presently run and revenge themselves upon those inward παθήματα, *mala culpæ*, evils of sin, even their secret passions and affections; and by crucifying them, they work their peace and tranquillity within themselves, for no man would be hurt by his afflictions without if he would mortify his passions within, Gal. v. 24; fourthly, They are much in prayer, and keep a good conscience in an upright, innocent, and sincere conversation, 2 Cor. i. 5, 11, 12; and lastly, the word is a continual fountain of joy in all troubles, which keeps them from discouragement or unquietness, Ps. cxix.

For you. These words may be referred either to *rejoice* or to *sufferings*. It is true God's servants do feel great joy one for another, 1 Thes. iii. 7. And to think of the grace or prosperity of other of God's servants is many times a great comfort in trouble. But I rather think the words are to be referred to *sufferings*, and then the sense may be *for you*, that is for the doctrine, which, as the apostle of the Gentiles, I taught you; or for the confirmation of your faith and encouragement to like patience; and the rather, because the offering of him up for the sacrifice and service of their faith was as the consecration of the first fruits to God, upon which followed a greater blessing upon the whole church.

Uses. The consideration hereof should teach God's people, not to faint at the troubles of their teachers, since they are for them (though to carnal reason it seems contrary); yea, the apostle, Eph. iii. 13, saith, it is their glory. Which also shows the vain pains that wicked men take when they persecute faithful teachers; for though they think thereby to plague the people that so greatly rely upon them, yet, indeed, God turns all for the best, that those sufferings are for them and not against them. And if wicked men were thus persuaded, they would spare such wicked labour; and if the godly could believe this it would make them unmoveable in trouble; for what shall make against them if this kind of troubles make for them?

And fulfil the rest of the afflictions of Christ. Some of the late papists gather from these words that Christ did not suffer all that was needful for man's deliverance from sin, but left a deal to be suffered by his members, especially men of principal note; and hence grew their supererogation, satisfactory pains, and indulgences. But that this cannot be the meaning of this place is clear: first, Because that doctrine is contrary to other scriptures, as Isa. liii. 4, 12, John xix. 30, Heb. x. 1, 15, Heb. ix. 14, 25, 26, 2 Cor. v. 14, 1 John ii. 1, Ps. xlix. 7; secondly, Themselves being judges, this sense brings in a gross absurdity, for if the words be understood of the suffering Christ left to his people to endure for satisfaction for sin, then it will follow that Paul suffered all was wanting, and so there should remain none for any other to suffer; for he saith, he 'suffered the rest of the sufferings of Christ;' thirdly, Calvin and Fulke say that none of the fathers did here thus understand the words, and it is plain that St Augustine is flat against this sense when he saith, (August. Tract 84 in Johan,) 'Though brethren die for brethren, yet no blood of martyrs is shed for remission of sins: this Christ only hath done.' And Leo, a pope, could say, the just receive, not give, crowns. And out of the fortitude of the faithful arise examples of patience, not gifts of righteousness; fourthly, The next verse cleareth this, for he did thus suffer, 'according to the dispensation given him of God.' Now, he was given to edify, not to redeem the church; fifthly, Their school divines are against them: the Gloss hath it thus, *Pro vobis, i.e., Confirmandis in doctrina evangelii.* Aquinas doubts not to say, that to affirm that the passions of the saints are added to make up or fulfil the passion of Christ, is heretical. Cajetan refers the word *quæ desunt* unto *in carne mea.* The plain meaning is, that the apostle did endure that measure of afflictions that God in his counsel had appointed him to endure for the name and gospel of Christ, and the good of the church, in the confirmation and encouraging of men's minds in the truth of the gospel.

Of Christ. His sufferings may be said to be the sufferings of Christ, either as Christ is taken for the whole mystical body, which is not strange in scripture, for by *Christ,* in 1 Cor. xii., he meaneth the body of Christ, or as he is the head of the church; and so the afflictions of God's servants may be said to be his sufferings; either because they be such as he should suffer himself if he were on earth, or because they were laid upon him by Christ for the church's good; or because they were for Christ and his doctrine; or because they deserve nothing, but all the praise is Christ's; or because of the sympathy of Christ with the Christian, who accounts them as if they were his sufferings. And in this latter sense, I think, chiefly these words are to be taken, for it is certain Christ doth so feel the miseries of his people, that he accounts them in that respect to be his own miseries, as these places shew: Heb. iv. 15, Rom. viii. 17, Mat. xxv. 42, &c., Phil. iii. 10, 1 Pet. iv. 13, 2 Cor. i. 4, Acts ix. 4. Hence grew that witty division of Christ's sufferings into προπαθήματα and ὑστερήματα; so as the first should be understood of the sufferings he endured in his own person, and the latter of the sufferings he felt in his members.

Uses. The consideration of this, that Christ accounteth the afflictions of his members to be his own, may serve for divers uses: for, first, It shews that they be in a woeful case that have aught to do against Christ's ministers or any of his servants. They would easily grant it that the Jews were brought into great distress by the wrongs they did to Christ himself; then must it also follow that they cannot escape scot-free that despise, revile, traduce, or any way abuse the messengers or servants of Christ, since he accounts it as done to himself. Secondly, This may be a wonderful motive to stir us up to be industrious in well-doing, and in helping and relieving the poor members of Christ, since we are sure to have thanks and reward from Christ himself, as if we had done it to him. Lastly, In all our sufferings we should strive that we might be assured that our sufferings are his sufferings. And that it might be so, we must be sure of two things: 1. That we be 'found in him,' Phil. i. 9, 10; for unless we be the members of Christ we cannot have the benefit of this sympathy; 2. That we suffer not for ill-doing, 2 Pet. iv. 15, &c.

Rest of his sufferings. Doct. So long as Christ shall have a member on earth there will rest something for him to suffer in his members; and therefore we should learn not to promise ourselves rest and ease while we are in this world.

To fulfil. The word signifieth either to do it instead of another, as if the soldier fight in the captain's room, or to do it in his own course or turn, according to the appointment of his governor, and in such proportion as is required; and thus I think it is taken here. It is certain that all the afflictions of the members of Christ come from God's decree, and the continuance and measure of them is appointed of God, Rev. ii. 8, 10, Isa. xxvii. 7-9, 1 Thes. iii. 3, 4. And therefore it should encourage every Christian the more cheerfully in his course, and when his turn comes to take up his cross and follow Christ, and never stand much upon the malice of men, or the rage of devils, but to look principally to God, with this assurance, that God will deliver him when his measure is full.

In my flesh. Doct. 1. God doth afflict the flesh of his servants, he spareth not the best of his servants herein.

Use is to teach us, therefore, not to pamper our flesh, but to be resolved to suffer it willingly to be used like the flesh of Christ and the saints. But especially we should take heed of taking care for the flesh, Rom. xiii. 14, or serving the flesh, Gal. vi.

T

It is an unseemly thing in a Christian to make very much of his flesh, but it is worse to spend his cares about it, but worst of all to let his whole husbandry be only for his outward man.

Secondly, Great things may be suffered, and yet the soul be untouched; as here the apostle's sufferings, which were exceeding great and manifold, reach only to his flesh; they enter not into his soul. And the reason why some of God's servants are so unmoveable in their crosses is because they converse in heaven, and their spirits walk with God, and so are without reach of these earthly perturbations. Besides, when a man's heart is settled and grounded in the truth, and in the assurance of God's love, what should disquiet his soul, that knoweth nothing to mourn for but sin and the absence of God? and nothing joyous, but what comes from the light of God's countenance?

Thirdly, He that hath felt the troubles of the soul for sin is not much troubled with the crosses that are but outward.

The use is, for great reproof of carnal Christians, that are seldom observed to grieve but when somewhat aileth their flesh, but, on the other side, are not at all touched with the miseries of the soul. As also we should learn of the apostle, in all outward crosses, to say with ourselves, why should I be troubled or disquieted? or rather, why should I not be joyous, since what I endure is but in the flesh? and since the Lord doth spare my soul, let him do whatsoever pleaseth him.

Lastly, We may here note the wonderful love and compassion of Christ, that pitieth not only our souls but our flesh, accounting what we suffer to be as his sufferings. Is it not enough that he should accept of the contrition of our souls, but that also he should regard the sorrows and troubles of our flesh?

For his body's sake, which is the church. Sufferings are of two kinds: either *of the church* or *for the church*. Of the church are also of two kinds: either chastisements or trials. Sufferings for the church are likewise of two sorts: either expiation, and so Christ only suffered; or martyrdom for confirmation of doctrine, or encouragement in practice, and so the saints have suffered for the church.

The principal doctrine from hence is, that the particular sufferings of God's servants, especially the ministers, serve for the good and profit of the whole body.

The use is manifold: first, We should hereby be informed to mind the good of the church, and to seek the advancement of religion and the good of religious persons, above our own estate. Our care should be most for the body of Christ, and we should rejoice in any service we could do to the church of God. Secondly, Such as are called to suffer should labour to show all good faithfulness, zeal, constancy, and holy discretion, seeing their sufferings concern more than their own persons. Thirdly, This should stir us up to pray for such as are in trouble for good causes, since their afflictions are some way for our sakes, 2 Cor. i. 11. Fourthly, This may encourage poor Christians that complain they have not means to do good. They may be hence informed that if God call them thereunto they may do good, yea, to the whole church, by their sufferings. No wants can hinder, but that the poorest Christian may profit others by prayers, fastings, counsel, admonitions, comfort, and suffering. Fifthly, Since the sufferings of the righteous are for our confirmation and encouragement, we should use the meditation of such sufferings when we find ourselves inclineable to discouragement, or impatiency, or doubting. Lastly, This greatly reproves carnal Christians, which are so taken up generally with the care of their natural bodies, that they have utterly neglected the care and service of the mystical body. And inasmuch as men are generally so barren in doing good, it is a plain sign there is no hope that ever they would suffer for God.

Secondly, Further hence may be noted, that the doctrine or sufferings of the saints are no privilege or benefit to any but the true church, and therefore papists have no cause to boast of Peter and the saints, so long as they remain a false church.

Thirdly, We may also observe hence, that they only are of the true church who are of the body of Christ; and therefore we must be sure we be members of Christ before we glad our hearts with our privilege in the church. And a member of Christ thou art not unless: 1. Thou believe the remission of thy sins, for we are engrafted only by faith; 2. Unless thou have had in thy soul an influence of holy graces from Christ, as from the head ; 3. Unless thou work the works of Christ, and bring forth the fruits of a reformed life, for thereby thou must try whether thou be a true plant in this vine; and lastly, If thou be of this body thou hast some room in the affections of God's children, or else it will be hard to prove that thou art a fellow-member.

Fourthly, Here we may see that seldom comes there any good to the church but there is suffering for it; it cannot be redeemed but Christ must die; and if the merit of this redemption be applied, Paul must die. It is an ill sign thou hast no true grace when thou sufferest nothing for the grace thou trustest to. It is an ill sign that God is not with the watchmen of Ephraim when they suffer nothing for the efficacy of their doctrine. Neither may any think this may be prevented by meekness or wisdom; for the treasures of both these were in Christ, and yet he was a man full of sorrows.

And for conclusion: Out of the whole verse we may gather together a number of arguments against the cross: 1. Paul suffers; 2. One may rejoice notwithstanding afflictions; 3. The longer we bear the cross the better able we shall be to endure it,—this may be gathered out of the word, *now*; 4. They are such as Christ accounts his; 5. They come from the decree of God; 6. Their measure is set by God; 7. We bear them but in our course, others have gone before us, and after us must others follow; 8. Christ suffered the great brunt of God's wrath, our sufferings are but small relics, or parcels, that are left behind; 9. The measure will once be full, and that shortly; 10. They are but in the flesh for the most part; 11. Christ respects the troubles of our flesh as well as the affliction of our spirit; 12. We may profit the church by our sufferings.

Ver. 25. *Whereof I am made a minister, according to the dispensation of God, which is given to me for you, to fulfil the word of God.*

In this verse is contained the third general reason, and it is taken from the testimony of God; wherein he shows that they ought to continue in the doctrine they had received, because God, by a special dispensation, had ordained him and the rest of the faithful teachers, by their ministries, to serve to the good of the members of Christ, by fulfilling and accomplishing thereby whatsoever concerns the salvation either of Jew or Gentile.

In this dispensation I consider five things : first, Who is the author of it? God; secondly, What kind of dispensation it is, viz., a household administration, for so the word οἰκονομία importeth; thirdly, What he dispenseth, viz., the service of his ministers; fourthly, How he dispenseth, viz., by granting out a commission to them in particular, 'unto me is given;' fifthly, To what end, viz., ' to fulfil the word of God.'

From the coherence with the 23d verse, I note: That if men would be established in faith and hope, they must be subject to the power of the ministry of God's servants. From the coherence with the former verse, I note : That if the ministers of Christ do find that their service is available and powerful to profit the souls of the people, they must not think it strange that they fall into many tribulations.

From the general consideration of the whole verse, I observe both the dignity and the restraint of the ministry. The dignity of a minister stands in three things: first, That he is God's ambassador; secondly, That by his commission he is sent unto God's people, who are the only worthies of the world; thirdly, That a great part of the efficacy of the word rests, by God's appointment, upon him and his office. The restraint is likewise in three things : first, He is a minister or servant, not a lord or saviour; secondly, He receives his commandment from God, he must not run of his own head, nor hold his office by mere human ordination; thirdly, The word of God must be his ground and rule for all his dealing in dispensing the things of God.

Of God. God is the dispenser of all good things to the church, but in special of the ministry of his servants, both in respect of his embassage, and the calling of the ambassador; and in respect of the efficacy of the embassage, both in the preparation and power of the teacher, and in the hearts of the hearers.

Uses. Which should teach us especially two things : first, In the church's want of able ministers to seek to God, the great Lord of the harvest, to send forth more labourers ; and secondly, We should reverence God's ministers, inasmuch as they are the ' dispensers of God's secrets,' 1 Cor. iv. 1. Ministers also may hence learn to execute their commission with all diligence, 2 Tim. iv. 1, 2; 'in the declaration of the truth approving themselves to men's consciences, in the sight of God,' 2 Cor. iv. 2, ii. 17; with discretion, Mat. xxiv. 45, xiii. 52; as becomes servants of God, Titus i. 7, &c.; rebuking sin with all zeal and power, Micah iii. 8. Lastly, hence ariseth the woeful estate of such ministers as preach not the gospel, 1 Cor. ix. 16, and of such people as hear not God's ministers, 1 John iv. 6, either for want of means, or through wilful unbelief, Luke xvi. 31.

Thus of the person dispensing.

This kind of dispensation is οἰκονομία. God governeth his church with a household government, as a father governeth his family; not as a tyrant that rules what by right he owns not; nor as a monarch that knows not the thousandth part of what he rules; nor as a captain that trains his soldiers only to labour and danger, while their treasures are at home; nor as a schoolmaster that rules children that are not his own : but as a most provident and loving father, that keeps none but he owns them, and knows them particularly, and provides for them, and all at home, Mat. xx. 1, Gal. vi. 10, Eph. iii. 16, ii. 19.

Uses. The use is: first, For instruction. If we would have God to rule us with this most familiar and fatherly providence, we must then be sure that we be of his household; and that we may try: first, By the manner of God's taking possession of us; for before he comes thus to rule us, there is a strong combat between Christ and 'the devil, that strong man,' Mat. xiii. 27, xxi. 33; and if sin and Satan rule still in our hearts, the Lord is not there, neither can we serve two masters, Mat. xii. 29, Luke xvi. 13. Secondly, By our affection to God's glory and his people. If we be right 'the zeal of God's house will eat us up.' Thirdly, By the gifts of God's Spirit, as namely, by the spirit of prayer; for God's house is a house of prayer, and all his household can and do pray. Fourthly, By the privilege of the house; for if we be admitted of God, ' the Son doth make us free,' John viii. 35. Fifthly, By the sovereignty of Christ, for as many as have this honour, they do submit themselves to be ruled by the word and spirit of Christ,' Luke i. 33. If the Son cannot rule us, the Father will not own us. And further, if we find ourselves to be of this household, we should live in the household of God, showing all faithfulness in using our talents, and carefulness in dispensing those earthly things that God hath entrusted us withal, and also observing the orders of God's house, and not receiving appointment from the example, will, customs, or traditions of men, Gal. iv. 8, 9.

The third thing is, what he dispenseth, viz., the ministry of his servants, *whereof I am a minister*. The church hath great need of ministers.

Quest. But what good do they to us ?

Ans. They are God's ambassadors, to reconcile us to God, 2 Cor. v. 20; they are the arms of the Lord, to collect us out of the world, 2 Thes. ii. 14, Isa. liii. 1; they are the light of the world, Mat. v. 15; and the salt of the earth, Mat. v. 13; they are our spiritual fathers, to beget us to God, 1 Cor. iv. 15, 1 Pet. i. 23; and nurses after we are begotten, 1 Thes. ii. 7; they are our intercessors to God, being our mouth in public and in private, rising up in the gap, praying to stay God's anger; they are stewards over God's house, Luke xii. 41; and the keys of heaven are delivered to them, Mat. xvi., John xx. 23, Mat. xviii. 18. All which should stir us up to honour and love them with a singular love for their work's sake.

Which is given to me. Ministers must be called by special commission from God, as well as by outward calling from man.

To fulfil the word of God. Divers things may be hence observed : First, The word is that special treasure, and the chief portion that God hath left, both to ministers and people. Secondly, Whatsoever the word seemeth to be unto carnal men, yet it is certain God will see to it, that all that is in it shall be fulfilled. Thirdly, The preachers of the gospel are the means to set the word a-working; and therefore, no wonder though troops of people that are not subject to the ministry of the word find little power in it. Besides, it evidently confutes those that think, by reading at home, to get enough both for knowledge and salvation; for it is preaching that, by God's blessing and ordination, doth put life into the word, and brings it into accomplishment. Fourthly,

Quest. How may we conceive of it, that God's ministers do fulfil the word ?

Ans. The word is said by them to be fulfilled four ways: 1. If we respect preaching itself; 2. If we respect the manner of preaching; 3. If we respect the suffering that follows preaching; 4. If we respect the efficacy of preaching.

For the first: Paul may be said to fulfil the word, in that he doth preach as he was by his commission appointed; he was charged by God to preach, and in obedience to God's word or will he did preach it. It is not enough for ministers to receive commission to preach, but they must fulfil it; and therefore woe to those loiterers and non-residents, that care more to fill their barns than to fulfil their ministration.

For the second: Ministers are said to fulfil the word when they execute their commission in a due manner; and this they do: first, When they preach with all diligence; secondly, When they hold out to the end, not taking pains for a sermon or two, or a year or two, till they can get preferment, but with all constancy, persevering in the labour and work of their ministry, till their course be ended, and the fight finished, 2 Tim. iv. 8; thirdly, When they reveal all the counsel of God that is needful for their hearers,—thus Paul fulfilled the word, Acts xx. 18.

Thirdly, Ministers fulfil the word by afflictions, for thereby they confirm the hearts of their hearers; as also, thereby is fulfilled upon them that which is in scripture so oft foretold should befal the faithful dispensers of the word, 2 John xv., xvi., xvii.

Quest. Can all ministers show their bonds for the gospel?

Ans. Nay, some can show the livings they have lewdly gotten, their ease, their dignities, their resisting of the word faithfully taught by others, the disgraces they have cast upon their brethren; but alas! their pains or sufferings may easily be reckoned. But woe unto them; for, for all the evil they have done, they have brought evil upon their own souls; the Lord Jesus consume them with the breath of his coming!

Lastly, In respect to the efficacy of the word, it is fulfilled by them; for many great things threatened or promised in the word were to be accomplished by them, some extraordinary, some ordinary. The extraordinary were bound to certain times, such as were heretofore, the calling of the Gentiles, and the induration or obstinacy of the Jews; and such as are now in doing, or to be done, as the reclaiming of the world by the everlasting gospel, the downfall of antichrist, and the gathering of the Jews. These things have been promised in the word, and have, are, and shall be wonderfully fulfilled by the ministry of preachers. The ordinary are fulfilled in the church at all times; and thus the word is fulfilled in the elect and in the reprobate. In the elect, ministers fulfil the word: 1. In converting those by the word, which were foreordained of God, Rom. i. 16, xv. 19. 2. In conveying Christ to their souls; so as the word is not a bare history of the merit and grace of Christ, but is fulfilled in the application of Christ, Rom. viii. 4, 2 Cor. ii. 14, 1Cor. i. 17, Gal. iii. 1, 3, 5. 3. By dividing the word amongst them, as the food of their souls, to preserve them. 4. By the application of the promises, which are effectually in the ministry fulfilled in the hearts of the hearers, Luke iv. 21. Lastly, In causing the elect to fulfil the word, both in obeying the word, Rom. xv. 18, and in persevering in the doctrine to the end. In the reprobate, they fulfil the word: 1. In hardening them, 2 Cor. ii. 15. 2. By making them inexcusable by illumination. 3. In occasioning many sins through their own wilful corruption, Rom. vii. 8. 4. In slaying them, or by sentence cutting them off, Isa. xi. 3, Mat. xvi. 16, 2 Cor. x. 6.

The use of all this is: 1. To show the necessity of continual preaching, seeing by it the word must be fulfilled; many are still to be converted, and all to be comforted, directed, strengthened, reproved, &c. 2. To justify the continual travail of faithful ministers, that will never give over to exhort, reprove, convince, &c. They are enjoined to see the word of God fulfilled, and therefore no wonder though they will not let men rest in their sin and security. 3. To teach us in all temptations or afflictions to run to the word preached, for thereby God will certainly perform all needful consolation, or direction, or humiliation. 4. To inform ministers that they must add indefatigable pains, since so much is to be fulfilled by them. 5. To admonish stubborn sinners to take heed of provoking God, for if the word may not be fulfilled in their salvation, it shall be fulfilled in their induration.

Ver. 26. *Which is the mystery hid since the world began, and from all ages, but now is made manifest to his saints.*

These words are the fourth general reason, taken from the excellency of the gospel, which is here described in four things: 1. By the nature of it, a *mystery.* 2. By the antiquity of it, *since the world began*, or *from ages and generations.* 3. By the time of the full revelation of it, viz., *now*, in the new world by Christ. 4. By the persons to whom it is revealed, viz., *the saints.*

The mystery. The gospel is a great mystery, 1 Tim. iii. 16; a hidden mystery, Rom. xvi. 25; hidden in God, Eph. iii. 9, 2 Tim. i. 9; because it was a secret in the purpose and grace of the Father before the world began. Hidden in Christ, because he was that store-house in which the Father laid up all his treasures that concern man's life and immortality, Col. ii. 3, and because he was the meritorious cause of all our happiness. Hidden in the word, Rom. xvi. 26; because the scriptures of the prophets and apostles are the sacred fountains of knowledge, and originals, from the bowels of which flow the comforts of the gospel to the church. Hidden also in the dark shadows of the ceremonial law. Hidden from Adam himself in paradise, so long as he acknowledged his happiness by the covenant of works. Hidden from the Gentiles many hundred years, while they served dumb idols, and had not the sun of righteousness shining among them. Hidden from the Jews in part and comparatively, because in a manner all the Jews were ignorant of the manner of Christ's kingdom, and of the calling of the Gentiles, and such like; comparatively, in respect of us, they had the light of a candle, but we have the light of the sun; and therefore John is said to be least in the kingdom of God. Hidden from the natural man still, who cannot perceive the spiritual things of God, 1 Cor. ii. 7, 14; no, though otherwise he abound with wit and learning. Hidden also from the very faithful, comparatively, in respect of what they shall know in the kingdom of glory; and in respect of the differences of degrees among themselves now.

Quest. But why is the doctrine of man's happiness so obscure to many, even in the church, in these days?

Ans. Man is by nature covered with the veil of original blindness, Isa. xxv. 8; and besides, he is bewitched with the deceitfulness of his actual sins, Heb. iii. 13; the god of this world, with his wiles and subtilties, his deepness and his methods, blindeth many thousands to their destruction, that he may hide the gospel from them, 2 Cor. iv. 3, Eph. vi., Rev. ii., 2 Cor. x. 4. Also evil thoughts, nursed and fortified as thick clouds, hide the light from divers. To some in judgment Christ speaks in parables, Mat. xiii.; others shall never have the light was offered, because they used not the light they had. The envious man in many places sows the tares of corrupt doctrine. And unto many congregations, for want of sincere preaching, immortality and life is not yet brought unto light, 2 Tim. i. 10, Tit. i. 3, besides the transplendency of the doctrine itself is such as exceeds the capacity of the most.

Quest. But how comes it that even the godly themselves in all places attain to so small a measure of knowledge in the gospel?

Ans. There are remnants of natural blindness even in the best; and the sin that hangs on so fast is not without pollution, and an obscuring property. Faith also, that should have principal use in conveying this light, is not without some mixtures of doubts and other dross. Affections are not without their fumes which becloud the understanding; sometimes they want the means, sometimes they are negligent in the use of them; and to see perfectly is the only privilege of the New Jerusalem that is above.

Uses. The uses are for reproof, for information, for instruction, and for consolation.

First, It reproves the horrible profaneness of those that so securely contemn the gospel, so sacred a mystery; and fearful is the curse with which God doth avenge the quarrel of his word, even this, that unto these men the Scriptures, both read and preached, are a sealed book, Isa. xxix. 11. And is the gospel a mystery? Then singular is their dotage and madness that say they know as much as any of them all can teach them.

Secondly, We may hereby be informed concerning the necessity of preaching. The greater the mystery is, the greater need of laborious and studious men, that are thereunto set apart to make manifest those secrets of the kingdom; for this is the 'appointment of God our Saviour,' that by preaching committed to certain men thereunto sanctified, as the apostle saith, 'the word promised before the world began should be manifested in due time,' Tit. i. 2, 3.

Thirdly, This should teach us divers duties: 1. Let every man account of faithful teachers, as 'the ministers of Christ, and such as dispense the mysteries of God,' 1 Cor. iv. 1. 2. We must bring faith to the gospel, else it will not profit, Tit. i. 1, 3, Heb. iv. 2. Reason and sense are no competent guides or judges in these divine mysteries. And the Lord hath commanded these secrets to be manifested and revealed by the Scriptures for the trial of his elect, and for the exercise of their obedience in believing as well as in doing, Rom. xvi. 25, 26. 3. As we should bring a resolution to believe God's word in all things, though it be never so contrary to sense and to common reason of the world, so when the Lord doth reveal his promises and statutes to us, we should hide them in our hearts as great jewels and worthy treasures, meet to be kept in our secretest remembrance, and the very bowels of our affections, Jer. xxxi. 34. 4. This doctrine urgeth the necessity of observing the rules of preparation; and to this purpose we may find five things charged upon us, all drawn from this consideration of the mystery of the gospel: First, We must be sure we be turned to the Lord by true repentance, for till then the veil cannot be taken away, 2 Cor. iii. 16. Though the word were never so plain in itself, yet we cannot discern it, by reason our understandings are covered with a veil, and no man can look upon this bright sun till his eyes be anointed with eye-salve, Rev. iii. 18. Secondly, Inasmuch as the book is sealed with seven seals, and no man nor angel is able powerfully to unfold and open God's eternal comforts to the conscience of man for his salvation, save only the Lion of the tribe of Judah, which is also the Lamb slain, having seven eyes, which are the seven spirits of God; therefore, in acknowledgment of his wisdom and power, we must go unto him, importunately begging this blessing for his glory that the book may be opened, even to enrich us, Rev. iv. 1, 3, 12; and that to this end he would make acceptable the odours of our desires and prayers to God. Thirdly, We must remove lets; for if it be a mystery in itself, we had not need to bring hardness of heart with us, or worldly cares, or troubled affections, or a sluggish spirit, or prejudicate opinions, or inordinate lusts, or any such impediments. Fourthly, We must bring with us the loan and advantage of former doctrine communicated to us; for 'to him that hath,' for practice and increase, 'shall be given; but from him that hath not,' for employment and conscionable use, 'shall be taken away that which he hath,' Mat. xiii. 11, 12. Fifthly, We must bring a pure conscience, as a holy vessel, to receive this mystery of faith in, 1 Tim. iii. 9; and the conscience is then pure when it is purified by the blood of Christ, and doth daily excite the desire of purity of heart and life, bearing with the love and liking of no sin.

Ministers must also here learn, with all reverence and painfulness, to behave themselves as becometh those great mysteries; they must not only be clean themselves by holiness of heart and life, but must, in compassion to the people, and the holy fear of the majesty of God's truth and presence, teach with power, frequency, perspicuity, and authority, and since the Lord hath made them his stewards of his mysteries, and holy jewels, and treasures, 'it is required of them that they be faithful,' 1 Cor. iv. 1, both in applying them to the right owners, and in setting them out according to their truth.

Lastly, The meditation hereof may serve for singular comfort to all those that find mercy from the Lord in the revelation of his mystery: 'blessed are their eyes that see it, and their ears that hear it,' Mat. xiii. 16; they are more happy than many millions of men besides.

Hid since the world began, and from ages. Ἀπὸ τῶν αἰώνων καὶ ἀπὸ τῶν γενεῶν. The first of these words is diversely accepted. Sometimes it is translated from eternity, as Ps. lii. 1, 'The goodness of the Lord hath endured from all eternity,' as Beza thinks, writing on Luke i. 70; sometimes, since the world began, as Luke i. 70, Acts iii. 21; sometimes it signifieth but of old, or a long time ago, as the

Hebrew word, which is thought to answer it, is rendered, Ps. cxix. 52; sometimes it is taken for the space of a man's life, as Peter said, 'thou shalt not wash my feet,' εἰς τὸν αἰῶνα, that is, never while I live; and in Eph. iii. *ult.* there is such a phrase as this, 'glory to God, &c.,' εἰς πάσας τὰς γενεὰς τοῦ αἰῶνος τῶν αἰώνων, as if it should be rendered unto or throughout all the generations of the world of worlds, that is, of the world to come; and 2 Pet. iii. *ult.*, he saith, 'glory to him,' καὶ νῦν καὶ εἰς ἡμέραν αἰῶνος; that is, henceforth to the day of eternity. There is unto man two worlds; the one begins with his life, the other with his death. But some would have it thus, ἀπὸ τῶν αἰώνων, *a seculis, i.e., a filiis sceuli hujus,* from the men of this world. Sometimes the word notes the state of things in the world, as Rom. xii. 2, μὴ συσχηματίζεσθε τῷ αἰῶνι τούτῳ, 'be not conformed to this world;' and Eph. ii. 2, κατὰ τὸν αἰῶνα τοῦ κόσμου τούτου, 'according to the course of this world;' but others render it *ages;* and so *from ages* may note the time of the Gentiles, or the time since the world began; so that is well rendered in the last translation, *hid from ages and from generations;* and if any will have the two words distinguished, then it may be from ages, *quoad tempora;* from generations, *quoad successiones hominum;* but howsoever it is, it fully imports the great antiquity of the gospel. If the papists will plead antiquity, let them have recourse to the word; or if their trumpery will not bear the trial of this antiquity, it is because there is no truth in them; and let this be a sufficient stay to all godly minds, that our doctrine is grounded upon the doctrine of the prophets, patriarchs, and apostles, which are the best ancients; but this is general.

Ages and generations. From the particular consideration of these words, divers things will arise:

First, The transitory estate of the world may here be noted. The things of the world, in their best frame, are so mutable, that they expire and are altered with varieties, and the men of the world have but their short time, and then they go out and leave their rooms to their succeeding generation; which may serve for divers uses, if it be seriously thought on: First, It should cause us to fear him that can not only change us, but mow down with his scythe whole generations of men, 'before whom the nations are but a little dust of the balance, or drop of the bucket;' and we should also magnify and adore that God that is of himself subject to no change, and lives for evermore, Rev. iv. 10. Secondly, It should make us in love with the world of worlds, and to admire the blessed estate of such as shall be accounted worthy to obtain that world and the resurrection from the dead, Luke xx. 35, to such an angelical and unchangeable condition; and to this end we should be quickened to a serious preparation for the world to come, seeing we have but our turn and course upon earth; we should 'not fashion ourselves to this world,' Rom. xii. 2; we should refuse to square our actions according to the lusts and humours of men, 1 Pet. iv. 2: let us serve, not time nor the fancies of men, but the king of times, 1 Tim. i. 17. Secondly, We should look to it that neither the cares of this world choke, nor the god of this world hide or take from us, the word of the kingdom, Mat. xiii., 2 Cor. iv. 4. Thirdly, And if we must not serve the men of the world nor the things of the world, much less may we serve sin; for if any man be a servant to sin, he shall not abide in the house to the next world, John viii. 34. Fourthly, This may abate the great opinion of the wisdom of this world; for what shall it profit me to have great skill to get money and means for this life, if I have no skill or wisdom for the saving of my soul? What shall it advantage me to have a nature and carriage tilled and fitted for the winning of friends for this world, if I know not how to make me friends for a better world? What availeth it to have gifts for an eminent place in man's commonwealth, and for want of grace be not acknowledged of the 'commonwealth of Israel?' To what purpose is it to be a 'disputer of this world,' and in the day of Christ to be swallowed up with amazed silence, as not having a word to say for thy poor soul. And yet providence for our future estate may be learned from these children of this world. For if the children of sin be so industrious to make shift for their time, how much more should the hearts of the children of eternity be enlarged to an inflamed care of large provision for their immortal estate. Fifthly, This should embolden us to a willing forsaking of ourselves in the worst of all outward trials, which is, to forego even all for Christ's sake and the gospels, if we be put to it. What great thing is it to part with that little *all* that we have in this world, seeing it could serve us but for a little time, and at length we must leave all? And besides, by a voluntary abnegation, we shall be advantaged in the gain of an eternal recompense of reward a hundredfold better.

Again, in that the gospel is hid from whole ages and generations of men, we may see that whole multitudes may be in a miserable estate; and that it is no privilege for any in sinning that many are such sinners. Neither is multitude or succession of men in one mind for matters of religion any note of the true church; for here are whole ages, and many successions of men, that all lived and died without the knowledge of the gospel. It is a slender prop for faith to rest on to say our fathers and forefathers lived and died in this or that mind or opinion. Further, we may observe hence the infectiousness of sin; how naturally it will spread, even to the poisoning of whole worlds of men. If sin but once get a fountain, if the Lord stop it not, into what rivers of contagion will it diffuse itself! Also, we may see how fearful a thing it is to fall into the hands of an angry God, since the lives of so many millions cannot find pity or pardon with him. And the insensibleness of sinners may hence be noted also. When would those ages and generations of men have awaked out of their idolatrous sleep, if the Lord, by the voice of his Son and his servants, had not awaked them? Moreover, it may be manifest from hence, that the Lord, in dispensing his grace, is not moved by any outward things; for what can any person or people have to commend them by to God, which those nations had not? Lastly, we may here see it verified that God's judgments are like a great deep: it is not for man to conceive that he should be able to search into them. Yet, lest any should stand still, and be swallowed up with amazement at the fall and ruin of those worlds of men, let him consider of these things following: first, That these people were instructed by the creatures, and had a law written in their hearts, Rom. i. and ii.; secondly, That these terrible desertions and exquisite judgments were deserved by an infinite measure of horrible sins, which, if we could soundly consider of, our objections about their falls would be much dulled; thirdly, That it is God that prescribes and describeth justice, and therefore things are just because he doth them, not that first man must pronounce them just and then God will do them; fourthly, That the reasons of this dealing may be just, though not expressed unto us; fifthly, That Christians are charged to be wise to sobriety,—they may not let their thoughts run as far as they will, but must let God alone with his secret judgments; sixthly, That the things are now strange and obscure shall be more fully revealed in the day of Christ, when all shall be cleared and made manifest.

Object. But some papist may say, it is plain by these words that the scripture is hard, and not fit for the common people, seeing it is called a mystery.

Ans. 1. This place cannot help them; because it is said that now it is revealed; and so their cavil comes out of season. 2. Because it is and was hidden from carnal men, not from God's servants: we do not wonder though the scriptures be as a sealed book unto such carnal wretches as they are.

Now revealed. God hath revealed the mystery of his will divers ways: first, By dreams, by day-visions, by types and sacraments, by angels, by prophets and extraordinary men, by Christ appearing in our nature, by his Spirit, by the scriptures, and by the ordinary preaching of the ministers. Dreams, visions, and types were peculiar in a manner to the Old Testament. The ministry of Christ in his own person, of the prophets and extraordinary men and angels, is now ceased; so as unto us this mystery is revealed by the Spirit, in the ministry of God's servants, and in the use of the scriptures.

Quest. But was not the gospel revealed till now since Christ?

Ans. Yes, it was, as these places may prove: John viii. 56, Abraham saw his days, and Moses wrote of him; all the prophets gave witness unto Christ, Acts x. 43, Rom. i. 2; Christ is the same yesterday, and to-day, and for ever, Heb. xiii. 8. But the gospel was hidden in respect of the time of the manifestation of the glory of Christ, (especially to the Gentiles,) and divers things in the manner of Christ's kingdom were not revealed unto them, 1 Pet. i. 10: as also in respect of clearness of revelation, and the more ordinary life and power of the graces of the Messias, and the more plentiful effusion of the gifts of the Spirit. Fifthly, That it was not revealed before, viz., as it is now: they had before Christ ἐπαγγελίαν, that is, the promise of the Messias to be exhibited, and we have ἐυαγγελίαν, the tidings of the Messias exhibited. Two things may be here observed:

First, That God's servants may know their own particular blessedness, for he saith it is revealed to the saints.

Secondly, That the seasons of the revelation of the gospel, in the power of it, are singular privileges, and greatly to be heeded; and therefore woe is to those souls that neglect such days of grace; it is double condemnation. It is damnable to sit in darkness, and have no means of life; but it is much more the condemnation of these worlds of profane persons, that light is come into the world, John iii., yea, into the country, yea, even to their own towns and congregations, and yet they will love darkness rather than light. And on the other side, it should teach men that know the time of such visitation, both to bear witness to the light by presence, countenance, maintenance, and establishing of it for them and theirs, and also to walk as the children of the light, even as a people exceedingly privileged and blessed of God.

To his saints. The word *saint* is sometimes given to Christ, Ps. xvi. 10; sometimes to angels, Job xv. 15; sometimes to the blessed in heaven, Mat. xxvii. 52; sometimes to the faithful on earth, Ps. xvi. 3. The pope hath his saints, and such are the choice of the most desperate traitors, as he ordereth his canonisations in our days; and the world hath his saints too, and they are civil, honest men; but here by saints he meaneth the faithful on earth. And they are saints that are holy by the righteousness of faith, Acts xxvi. 18; that have the spirit of sanctification, 1 Cor. iii. 16, 17; that are separate from sinners by a holy calling, Rom. i. 6, 1 Cor. i. 2; that are reformed from the principal evils of their former conversation, 1 Cor. vi. 11; that call upon the name of the Lord, 1 Cor. i. 2; that are consecrate to God in special holiness of life.

Quest. But if a man live civilly in the world, will not that serve the turn?

Ans. It will not; our righteousness must exceed the righteousness of the scribes and pharisees. And it may be profitable oft to recount the defects of the civil, honest man. First, He wants sincerity in the first table; secondly, He sticks not at the inward corruptions of the second table; thirdly, His praise is of men in his best actions, or else some other corrupt ends; fourthly, He is wholly void of the inward worship of God, and in the outward he is either secure or superstitious; fifthly, He never travailed in the new birth for his honesty; sixthly, He wants the righteousness of faith; seventhly, For the most part his heart is not sound nor upright in his family, especially for matter of God's worship.

Ver. 27. *To whom God would make known what is the riches of his glorious mystery among the Gentiles, which riches is Christ in you for hope of glory.*

These words contain the fifth general reason, taken from the excellency of the subject the gospel in the preaching of it propounds unto men, and that is Christ. And in this revelation of Christ consider: 1. To whom, viz., *to the saints;* 2. By whom, viz., *God;* 3. What is the cause, viz., the will and *good pleasure of God—he would;* 4. The manner: (1.) If we respect the unregenerate world, it is in a *mystery;* (2.) If we respect the grace communicated, it is a *glorious and rich mystery;* (3.) If we respect the place where Christ as a Sun of righteousness riseth, it is *in you,* that is, in the heart of man; (4.) If we respect the persons he makes choice of, it is the miserable Gentiles—*amongst the Gentiles;* (5.) If we respect future things, he is revealed as *the hope of glory.*

To whom. Of the persons to whom, I have spoken in the end of the former verse; only this doctrine may be added, that only the saints, that is, holy men, find treasures and riches in the power of the glorious gospel of Christ. The Lord's secret is only with them that fear him, Ps. xxv. 14. Till faith be revealed, men are shut up as in a dungeon or prison, Gal. iii. 23. The Lord speaks peace only to his people and his saints, Ps. lxxxv. 8. The righteousness of God is revealed to the just man that will live by faith, Rom. i. 17. Flesh and blood, till there be a new birth, is not capable of this revelation, Mat. xvi. 17. Men that hate to be reformed have nothing to do with God's covenant, Ps. l. Hence we may see where the fault is when men be so averse and unteachable. When people have the means and cannot understand to profit and do good, it is only in their own hearts' lusts and wickedness of life; and therefore let every one that would grow rich in knowledge, labour to be abundant in practice, for the saving knowledge of this mystery increaseth as grace and holiness groweth.

God. *Doct.* God is the author of all saving knowledge; he is 'the Father of lights.' The use is, therefore: first, 'If any man lack wisdom, let him ask it of God,' James i. 5. Secondly, Let all that would have knowledge use good means. Those people that are too wise to use reading, hearing, conference, and prayer, are but in a miserable case; those they account silly people, even as babes and sucklings, Mat. xi. 25, in comparison of them, carry away the blessing, while they live and die in their sins. Thirdly, In the ministry of men, we must believe them no further than they bring warrant from the word of God. It is God's word, and not men's sayings or precepts, must be our guide. A fear of God, bred by man's precepts, will be in vain, Mat. xv. Fourthly, We should prize every dram of true knowledge got from the word at a high rate, even to excel all other things, as being the peculiar gift of God.

Would. The reasons of the dispensation of spiritual favours in Christ are not in us, neither in will nor work, but in the good pleasure of God's will; which should teach us with so much the more thankfulness to express our admiration of God's love, that could find nothing in us but cause of hate, even for ever. What are we, or what are our fathers' houses, that we should be thus exalted in the courts of our God ! And withal we should in all things resign ourselves over to God's will, as the highest cause of all things. We should rest in his approving will as our chiefest happiness, and obey his prescribing will as the absolutest and perfectest form of holiness, and be subject to his disposing will, being patient in all trials and troubles, because he did it, Ps. xxxix. 9. Lastly, This might break to powder carnal hopes. How canst thou plead, thou hopest that God will save thy soul, seeing there is simply nothing in thee that the Lord cares for, and thou hast not sought his grace by sound repentance and true faith?

Make known. Divers things have been noted before concerning this manifestation and revelation of the gospel; that which only I will here add is the effects of it. The proper effect of the powerful publication of the gospel is to 'bring life and immortality to light,' 2 Tim. i. 10. But the accidental effect is to make variance and oppositions amongst men. When Christ comes in this manner, he comes not to bring peace; as the fan scattereth the chaff from the wheat, so is the word powerfully preached. I need go no further than this city for an instance. Though matters of controversy have been wholly forborne, and differences in matters about church government and ceremonies have not been so much as touched with public preachings; and that matter of regeneration, faith, and sanctification hath been almost only urged; yet see what stirs, what differences of censures, what indignation at the reformation of any souls that have been wrought upon by the word. What invectives, what strange reports, what abominable lies and slanders have been almost weekly raised and divulged throughout all the country round about!

What is the riches of the glory? The apostle's variety, and effectual terms, are to be noted; though he has spoken much, yet he is not drawn dry, but speaks still with great feeling and efficacy, both of words and matter. And, indeed, as any men are more holy, they have the more deep and tender affections in the meditation of the glory of the things of the gospel. This holy man cannot fall upon the mention of the gospel but his affections burst out into great terms of admiration, as if he thirsted after variety of words to express his inward estimation; and as it is a sign of a sanctifying disposition to be so affected, so when we see holy men striving for words to express the glory of spiritual things, it may secretly condemn the coldness and barrenness of our dull spirits, that usually, through the deceitfulness of sin, prove to have the dullest affections, where we should be most stirred; and the apostle doth well in seeking these affecting terms, that so he might excite affection and appetite in the hearers; for people will no longer profit by the word than they admire it, and long after it with estimation; and therefore it should be a holy discretion in ministers to study by all means to teach in such a manner as might most stir affection and just admiration at the power and fitness of the word.

But here a question may be asked. Say that we have gotten a great affection to the word, and that we do highly esteem of it, and long after it, what must we do to keep this appetite, that we lose it not, and that it die not in us by little and little? I answer, Thou must look to thyself in five things: first, Take heed of evil company; the people that cried out, for very admiration, 'Hosannah, blessed be he that cometh in the name of the Lord,' when they were gotten among the scribes and pharisees, had altered their note into 'Crucify him, crucify him.' Secondly, Thou must purge often, that is, thou must, by mortification, be oft in humbling thy soul, by confession and sorrow to God in prayer, else fulness and satiety will overcharge this appetite; for so must he do that hath a stomach apt to be filled with ill humours, as experience both in body and soul shews. Thirdly, If thou wouldst not despise prophesying, thou must 'try all things, and keep that which is good;' which thou doest if thou observe these two rules: 1. If in hearing such ministers as have either their hearts or the doctrine unsound, thou separate the precious from the vile; 2. If in hearing the best men thou be especially careful to keep that part of doctrine as did particularly touch thee, and so was in a special manner good for thee. Fourthly, Thou must look to thyself that the profits, pleasures, or lusts of the world, steal not away thy heart from communion with God in the means. Whoredom and wine, and the cares of this life, &c., will take away any man's heart, Hosea iv. 11, Luke xxi. 34. Fifthly, Thou must exercise thyself in the rest of God's ordinances, else disuse in one will in time breed contempt of all; and God will not have all the honour given to one of his ordinances, and doth of purpose many times withdraw his blessing (which is the bellows of affection and estimation) from one of his ordinances, because he will be sought in all.

Again, out of the apostle's terms we may observe the great excellency of the gospel: for wit it is a mystery most deep; for worth it is riches; and for credit it is glory.

Riches. Doct. The true knowledge of Christ is a rich knowledge. Hence the Corinthians are said to be rich in knowledge, 1 Cor. i. 5; and Paul compares it with, and commends it beyond, all earthly riches, Phil. iii. 9; and it is so both in respect of the object, which is Christ, the fountain of all treasure, and in respect of the nature of it, being a part of eternal life, John xvii. 3, and in respect of the effects, because it makes a man rich in grace. And it appears by the contrary; for to be blind is to be poor, and naked, and miserable, Rev. iii. 17; and therefore they are far wide that think all this studying of the scriptures, and following sermons, will make men beggars: they remember not that to take the gospel from Jerusalem was to leave their houses, as well as God's house, desolate, Mat. xxiii. 37–39; and the want of the knowledge of God in the land was the cause the Lord contended with them by so many judgments, Hosea iv. 1, 2. And if any nation under heaven may avouch the truth thereof, this English nation may; for we may well say the gospel hath been a rich gospel unto us; it hath brought us peace and prosperity within our walls, and abundance into all the quarters and corners of the land. Hence also we may gather a trial of our faith; for if we have faith, we are careful to seek, and as glad to find, saving knowledge, as the carnal man is to find his earthly wealth. Parents also may hence know which way to go about to make their children happy, even by stirring up in their hearts the instruction and nurture of the Lord.

Glorious. Doct. This mystery is glorious, and it is so: first, If we respect the original of it; it was begotten and conceived in the bosom of eternity. Secondly, If we respect the persons employed in the ministry of it, viz., God himself, Christ, angels, and the choice of men. Thirdly, If we respect the effects, it brings glory to God; for upon the opening of the book by the Lamb there followeth hymns to God, Rev. v. It brings a glorious rest to the hearts of Christians, when they are satisfied in the assurance of the tidings of God's love, and purged of those unruly affections that so turmoiled their hearts before, Isa. i. 10; besides the glorious privileges which, after men are called out of darkness, they enjoy in this marvellous light, 1 Pet. ii. 9. Finally, It shows a Christian the glory of heaven. This should comfort God's servants against the scorns of the world and troubles of life. The gospel, with disgrace and much want, is a great portion; and it matters not how we be esteemed in the eyes of the world, if we be made glorious by the gospel in God's eyes, and in the eyes of the saints; they are glorious times when the gospel works openly in the life and power of it.

Among the Gentiles. In the calling of the Gentiles we may inform and instruct ourselves many ways.

First, It should settle us in the assurance of the truth of God's promises. Never any promises more unlikely; and besides they lay dead for a long time. That which Noah foretold is come to pass, for Japhet is persuaded to dwell in the tents of Shem, Gen. ix. 27. That sea of knowledge which Isaiah spake of is likewise gloriously accomplished among the churches of the Gentiles, Isa. xi. 9. Jeremiah said the Gentiles should come unto God from the ends of the earth, and it is fulfilled, Jer. xvi. 19. The concourse to the preaching of the word, which Micah and Zechariah foretold, is likewise verified, Micah iv. i., Zech. viii. 20.

Secondly, We may hence see that the word will make great alterations where it comes.

Thirdly, That God is tied to no place nor people: if the Jews will not bring forth fruits worthy of the gospel, but despise it, the Lord will provoke them to envy, even calling to himself a people that sought him not.

Fourthly, That they that are last may be first, and that they that now are not under mercy, may go to heaven before us.

Fifthly, That as any people are more sensible of their misery without grace, they more see the riches of their calling. The Gentiles that wallowed in sin and wickedness see a wonderful glory in religion when by the gospel they are converted. And that may be the reason why publicans and sinners are so deeply affected and inwardly touched, when civil, honest men are scarcely moved with any sense of the need of their conversion.

Sixthly, Their conversion may assure us that none are so miserable but the gospel can make them happy.

Seventhly, We may see cause to bewail the hardness of our hearts. Can the gospel conquer so mightily and effectually these worlds of people to the obedience of faith, and such a tender sense of the glorious riches thereof, and are our hearts no more melted and stirred within us? Though the Lord cry and roar, and stir up himself in his jealousy as a man of war, yet are we deaf and hear not, and blind and see not.

Eighthly, In that he saith that this mystery is glorious among the Gentiles, it shews that the monarchy of Christ over these conquered Gentiles is truly glorious. Which may justly confound our statists and politicians, that can see no glory but in earthly kingdoms.

Ninthly, Let us that are abjects of the Gentiles, that have no true honour but by God's covenant, ' draw water with joy out of these wells of salvation,' Isa. xii. 3.

And *lastly*, Our calling, that are Gentiles by nature, should make us, in compassion of the Jewish nation, pray heartily for their restoring, since ' they were cut off that we might be grafted on,' Rom. xi., and ' the law came out of Sion, and the word of the Lord out of Jerusalem,' Isa. ii.

Which riches is Christ in you. Out of these words four things may be observed:

First, That there is one and the self-same happiness conferred by the gospel to all the faithful; the same, I say, in nature and quality, though not the same in quantity, ' the same spiritual meat, and the same spiritual drink;' the same God and Father, the same Christ and Saviour; the same means and the same merits, the same graces and the same glory. Which may serve for good use. For if the Lord give us the same wages he did his best servants, we should strive to do the same work. We should bewail our sins with the same sorrow, and watch over our lives with the same care, and abound in the same fruits of righteousness, and live by faith in all trials and tentations as they did. And again, it may be comfortable for penitent sinners. For the same God that had mercy on David will confirm unto them, if they truly desire his favour, and will forsake their own imaginations, ' by an everlasting covenant, the sure mercies of David,' Isa. lv. 1, 4, 8. And if by faith we prove ourselves the children of faithful Abraham, we shall be blessed with Abraham, Rom. iv. 24, Gal. iii. 9, 12.

Secondly, That Christ is the only true riches of the Christian, 2 Cor. viii. 9, Eph. i. 7, ii. 7, iii. 8,

Heb. xi. 26. This may serve for divers uses: 1. To warn us that we despise not poor Christians, seeing they are made rich in the faith of Christ, and heirs of the kingdom, James ii. 5: they are truly rich men, though they be never so mean in the world. 2. Let us all look to ourselves that we 'despise not this riches of the bountifulness of God,' when in the gospel it is offered unto us: though we may go on with the hardness of our not repenting hearts, yet if by speedy repentance we prevent not our ruin, we shall heap up wrath against the day of wrath, even the day of the declaration of the just vengeance of God upon such obstinate and secure sinners, Rom. ii. 4–6. 3. Let not worldly rich men glory in their riches, Jer. ix. 24, but rather use their outward riches as helps to further them unto this true treasure, else their riches shall not shelter them in the day of God's wrath against the woes denounced against them, Job xxxvi. 18, 19, Luke xvi. 22. Lastly, Would any man know some sure way how to thrive with great success in these spiritual riches? let him then, amongst other things, especially remember to pray hard, for the Lord is rich to all them that call upon him, Rom. x. 12.

Thirdly, Christ is in the faithful, 2 Cor. xiii. 5; he lives in them, Gal. ii. 20; he dwells in them, Eph. iii. 17. But that this doctrine may be more fully understood, I propound five things:

1. How Christ is conveyed into the soul of the faithful.

2. By what effects he discovereth himself to be there.

3. What they get by his coming.

4. What entertainment they ought to give him.

5. Who have not Christ in them.

1. For the first there is this order: first, God secretly gives Christ to the believer, and the believer to Christ, Rom. viii. 32, Isa. ix. 6, John xvii. 6. Then Christ begins to manifest himself, riding in the chariot of the word, 2 Cor. ii. 14. The word that before was a dead letter receiveth life by the presence of Christ, and that both in the law and the gospel. The law being made alive, attacheth the particular sinner, and playeth upon him the part of a sergeant, accuser, jailer, or judge. And the sinner putting in bail, the law brings him to Christ, and will not let him go to another, Gal. iii. 24. Then the gospel gets alive, and crucifies Christ before his eyes, Gal. iii. 1; and propounds variety of sweet promises. The sinner, being beaten and wounded almost to death before he would yield to the arrest of the law, seeing now whither he is brought, laments with unspeakable groans his own sins, and the horrible torments he sees the Son of God put to for his sake. And at the same time, the Spirit of the Son working faith, a wide door is opened, Christ enters in with invaluable joys wrought in the heart of the sinner.

2. Now, if you ask by what effects Christ discovers himself to be there? I answer, there is a light when Christ comes in that 'gives the knowledge of the glory of God in the face of Christ,' 2 Cor. iv. 6, and being ravished, they 'behold as in a mirror the glory of God, and are transformed into the same image,' the Spirit of God making them suddenly 'new creatures,' 2 Cor. iii. 18; 2. The convert now finds a savour of the things of the Spirit, and his heart is bowed to be subject to the law of God, Rom. viii. 5, 6; 3. He is baptized with the fire of zeal and holy affections and desires, Mat. iii. 11; 4. There appears a battle and combat in the soul, and much lusting on either side, the Spirit resisting with tears and strong cries; 5. In this combat, Christ, undertaking the battle, sends out by his ordinances his arrests, and apprehends, one by one, every imagination that rebelliously puts itself forward in the opposition, and exalts itself, and will not leave till it be brought in subjection, so as the obedience of Christ may have the upper hand, 2 Cor. x. 5; 6. The Spirit of the Son discovers himself as a Spirit of supplications, by which the tender infant begins to learn with holy desires and secret encouragements to speak in God's language, and by prayer to make known his griefs and wants in the best manner, uttering his affiance in God as a Father, Gal. iv. 6, 7; 7. The love of God and of Christ, and of God's word and God's people, is shed abroad in his heart, and it now constraineth him to holy duties, Rom. viii. 1, 9, 2 Cor. v. 14; 8. The 'body grows dead in respect of sin, and the Spirit is life for righteousness' sake,' Rom. viii. 10—resolution more and more increasing both for reformation of sin and new obedience; 9. He finds himself proclaimed free, the prison doors set open, his fetters knocked off, his wounds made by

the law healing apace, his debts paid, and himself in a new world, enjoying a true jubilee, 2 Cor. iii. 17, Isa. lxi. 1, 2; 10. He lives thenceforward by the faith of the Son of God for salvation, for justification, and for preservation, Gal. ii. 20, 2 Cor. xiii. 14; 11. The heavenly dews of spiritual joys often water and refresh his heart, in the use of the means, with delightful peace and tranquillity in his heart and conscience, Hosea xiv. 6, Rom. xiv. 17; lastly, In a holy covenanting with God, his daily purposes and desires are to cleave unto God, devoting and consecrating himself and his vowed sacrifices unto God, in the mediation of Christ.

3. Thirdly, The benefits he hath by the inhabitation of Christ are such as these: 1. 'God is in Christ, reconciling him, not imputing his sins,' 2 Cor. v. 19; 2. Christ is 'made unto him wisdom, sanctification, righteousness, and redemption,' 1 Cor. i. 30; 3. All 'the promises of Christ are to him yea and amen,' having the earnest given in the Spirit, and the same sealed by the same Spirit, 2 Cor. i. 20, 22; 4. He is not destitute of any heavenly gifts, 1 Cor. i. 6, 7, but hath the seeds and beginnings of all saving graces; 5. The grace of Christ shall be sufficient against all temptations, 2 Cor. xii. 9, by the power of Christ that dwells in him; and as his outward afflictions do abound, so shall the consolations of Christ abound also, 2 Cor. i. 5; 6. Paul is his, and Apollos is his, yea, all things are his, as he is Christ's, 1 Cor. iii. 22, 23; he hath his interest in all the means of salvation; 7. God hath given him Christ, 'how shall he not with him give him all other things also?' Rom. viii. 34, 35; finally, Eternal life is the gift of God, in and with Jesus Christ, Rom. vi. 23.

4. For the fourth, If you ask what you must do when you find Christ in your hearts? I answer, 'if you live in the spirit, walk in the spirit,' Gal. v. 24; let 'old things pass, and all things be new;' for 'if you be in Christ Jesus, you must be new creatures,' 2 Cor. v. 16, 17; the old conversation in times past will not now serve turn, but the old man with his deceivable lusts must be cast off, Eph. iv. 22. Now thou must learn also to live by faith, and not by sense and carnal hopes, as thou hast done; for Christ keeps his residence in our hearts by faith, Eph. iii. 16: for in that we 'henceforth live in the flesh,' we must resolve to 'live by the faith of the Son of God that liveth in us,' Gal. ii. 20, being assured that in him are all treasures of holiness and happiness. And to this end thou must pray constantly to God that thou mayest be able to discern the length, breadth, depth, and height of this love and loving presence of Christ, Eph. iii. 18; for otherwise it is a knowledge passeth all natural understanding, and his working in us is above all we can ask or think. Why should a Christian fear any want, that carrieth a mine of treasure within his own breast? And what a shame is it that we grow not exceeding rich, seeing there is nothing but faith and prayer will get it, Rom. x. 12; and why should we fear either tribulation, or persecution, or pain, or peril, seeing this our victory, even our faith, and we are assured that in the end we shall be in all these things more than conquerors, through him that loveth us and lives in us? Rom. viii. 35, 37.

Further, doth the spirit of meekness and of Christ dwell in thee? Oh, then, above many things learn lowliness and humility, Mat. xi. 29; and if the Lord give thee a tender and a harmless heart, watch with all carefulness that thou be not beguiled from the innocent simplicity that is in Christ Jesus, 2 Cor. xi. 3. Lastly, Thou must labour for inward sincerity, both of thoughts and affections. Thy heart is Christ's chamber of presence, where he always resides; and as thou art careful to look to thy behaviour because of man's presence, so must thou much more look to thy heart, to keep it clean, and pure, and chaste, and every day to dress it new, since the King of glory is come in to dwell with thee. Men would be very careful to look to that room where they would give their best entertainment. Alas! we have no better room than our hearts to welcome our Saviour into;—and shall not we keep them with all diligence? Woe be to us if we tempt or grieve him by our inward uncleanness.

5. Now for the fifth point: There are seven ill signs that Christ dwells not in a man's heart:

First, When a man savours nothing but carnal things.

Secondly, When a man hath, or desires, or esteems, or labours after no other knowledge but what is ordinary or natural.

Thirdly, When a man makes no conscience of inward sins.

Fourthly, When a man hath no zeal in God's worship, or holy affections towards God and his people, and his word.

Fifthly, When a man hath not a faith that he can live by.

Sixthly, When a man never feels the heavenly joys of Christ in his heart.

Seventhly, When a man can live in any gross sin without trouble and anguish of spirit, or desire and endeavour to break it off by repentance.

The hope of glory. The riches of a Christian are either in this life, and so it lies in the grace of Jesus Christ; or else in the world to come, and so it is glory, even a most glorious and admirable excellency of felicity, which shall have in it eternal righteousness and the continual blessed vision of God, eternal joys, and perfection of all things round about, everlasting honour, and singular esteem, most sweet society with holy angels and blessed saints, with unspeakable peace and rest, together with that admirable clarification of the very bodies of the righteous.

Uses. The consideration hereof should allure us to the continual thought of heaven, and to a fervent affection after it, striving to express our hope of heaven by a conversation that tends to glory and immortality; and to this end we should be importunate with the Lord to show us this glory by the spirit of revelation, that we may be able profitably to solace our souls in the midst of the tentations and afflictions of this world, with a serious contemplation of our right in Jesus Christ to this admirable glory that is to be revealed. And the meditation of the glory poor Christians shall one day have should teach us to honour them now, and receive them into our hearty and inward society, and to use them as such, as we are assured are the heirs of more glory than this world is worth. And lastly, do we look for glory from God in another world? then we should seek to glorify God in all things with all our might in this world.

Secondly, We may in these words note that where Christ will glorify in another world, there he is the hope of glory in this world. A Christian holds his glory by this tenure. Now, concerning this hope, many things have been noted already upon the fourth verse, and upon the twenty-third verse, and, therefore, thither I refer the reader.

Ver. 28. *Whom we preach, admonishing every man, and teaching every man in all wisdom, that we may present every man perfect in Christ Jesus.*

In this verse is contained the sixth general reason, taken from the end and profitable effect of the gospel. If they continue constant, by the power of the word, they will be made fit to be presented in some measure of ripeness and perfection unto God in Jesus Christ.

Two things are in the verse to be observed: The means and the end;—the means is *preaching,* which is amplified by the parts of it, *admonishing* and *teaching,* and by the manner of it, *in all wisdom.*

Whom we preach. The reason why the apostle falls so often into the mention and praise of their preaching is to rescue it from the contempt under which many times it lay disgraced.

There are four things may be observed here which tend to express the honour of the ministry in this place: 1. They are, as it were, the Lord's high treasurers, to dispense the riches of the kingdom of Jesus Christ. And if such an office be in such request under earthly princes, what is it to be so honoured of the Prince of all princes? All the world is beholding to the ministry, for they show that mine of incomparable treasure; they dig it up, they offer it as spiritual merchants; yea, the Lord by them doth, as it were, particularly enrich all Christians. 2. This honour of publishing the gospel is now taken from the very angels, and given to them; now we, not the angels, preach unto you. 3. They have the best subject that ever men had to entreat of; all other sciences are base in comparison of them. They entreat of Christ, and grace, and glory for ever by him; nay, 4. Herein differs preaching from all other relations whatsoever, that they do not preach *of Christ,* but they preach *Christ,* that is, they give what they speak of.

And these three little words express diversely the duty of ministers. 1. They must preach, that is plain. 2. They must preach diligently, which may be gathered from the expressing of it in the present tense. It was not a sufficient excuse, we have preached as diligently as any in our young times, or before we came to such preferment. No; this must be the comfort of a minister, and his continual plea, we do preach, not, we have preached. 3. They must preach Christ, that is, that part of divinity that concerns redemption, justification, and sanctification. 4. They must labour, in preaching, to express, as much as lies in them, consent ; consent, I say, with the prophets and apostles, and consent with their fellow-ministers; we, not I; there is one only truth for all ministers to teach. 5. They must resolve to win the honour and reputation of their ministry, for the work of it, not from the reward of it; they must get their credit by preaching, not by their great livings.

And from hence also is impliedly to be collected the just reproof of many ministers:—

1. Such as preach not. Some would preach and cannot ; some can preach but will not; some neither can nor will. All shall be judged accordingly in the day of Christ, when he shall call for an account of their stewardship.

2. Such as preach, but not Christ; and these are not all of a sort : for, 1. Some preach themselves, not Christ, or if they paint out Christ, it is in their own likeness, so as under his name they commend themselves to the world. 2. Some preach, but it is beside Christ, in raking together men's inventions ; and surely that so great affecting of human authorities in preaching, when it is with a kind of neglect of the search of scriptures, as if they wanted wit or power, cannot be justified. 3. Some preach, but it is against Christ; and such are they that care not covertly to contradict the main doctrines of Christ, or else bend themselves in their whole ministry to 'strengthen the hands of the wicked, and make sad the hearts of the righteous.'

3. Such as preach Christ; but it is for envy, and to increase the bonds and disgraces of others ; or it is not diligently, or they preach not Christ crucified, (they teach not soundly the doctrine of mortification,) or they preach not Christ risen again; they teach so coldly, so barrenly, so insufficiently, as if Christ were still in the grave. Some there be that preach of Christ, but it is chiefly of his crown and sceptre ; they are never kindled till they get into questions of church-government ; they teach their hearers the doctrine of reforming of churches, when they had more need to teach them how to reform themselves and their household.

Admonishing and teaching. There is some ado among interpreters to put the difference between these two words. Some thus : admonishing them that are out of the way; teaching them that are in the way. Some thus: admonishing them that are ignorant ; teaching them that have knowledge. Some thus : admonishing those that teach false doctrine or contradict the truth ; teaching such as are desirous to learn the truth. Some thus : admonishing about things to be done ; teaching about things to be known. Some thus : admonishing to stir affection ; teaching to inform the understanding. But I think there is no necessity thus to restrain the senses ; so as it may be thus. Admonishing, that is, checking, rebuking, warning the ignorant, wandering, wayward, slothful, dull, or profane hearers, both about things to be done and known, and teaching the rest the whole doctrine of Christ.

Admonishing. From this word these things may be observed :

First, Preachers must intend to rebuke sin, as well as to direct or comfort, Isa. lviii. 1, 2 Tim. iii. 17, Heb. ix. 10, Acts xx. 31, 1 Thes. v. 11.

Secondly, Men commonly never care for instruction to grow in Christ till they be touched with the rebukes of the word for sin.

Thirdly, Preaching may be said to admonish in divers respects : 1. The very sending of the word preached to any place, is a warning to men to look to themselves and repent, Acts xvii. 30; for then is the axe laid to the root of the tree, Mat. iii. 10. 2. Because preaching doth set before us such examples as do admonish, 1 Cor. x. 11. 3. Because by it Christ secretly smites the earth, that is, the consciences of carnal men that are so glued to the earth, Isa. xi. 3 ; many a time is their hearts smitten that the world little knows of ; but especially by preaching are the public abuses in the lives of men publicly reproved.

Every man. Every one needs to be rebuked and admonished ; and there is no man nor woman but they are bound to stoop to the rebukes of the word, whether they be rich or poor, learned or unlearned, Jew or Gentile, young or old, in authority or under authority, converted or unconverted.

x

Uses. The use of all should be to teach us to know them that are over us, and admonish us in the Lord, 1 Thes. v. 12. Now there are divers reasons to persuade men to be willing to suffer admonition: 1. It is noted to be in God's account a beastly quality to rage or to be senseless when we are rebuked; therefore, David saith, ' be not as the horse or mule,' Ps. xxxii. 9.   2. If we will not be rebuked, sin lies at the door, Gen. iv. 12; and we know not how soon we may be arrested with judgment.   3. Thou mayest by stubbornness provoke the Lord so much, that in his very judgment he may set a continual edge upon the word to rebuke thy conscience, so as rebukes being now turned into a punishment, the Lord may consume thee by them, eating upon thy conscience as a moth, Ps. xxxix. 11, till he have wearied thee with his secret buffets and terrors, and then in the end cast thee off into a reprobate sense. Woe is unto man, when the Lord in his word, or by his Spirit, sets himself to disgrace and vex him.   4. ' Instruction is evil only to him that forsaketh the way, and he that hateth correction shall die,' Prov. xv. 10. It is a brand of a scorner to hate him that rebuketh him, Prov. xv. 12; and a man that hardeneth his neck when he is rebuked shall suddenly be destroyed, and cannot be cured, Prov. xxix. 1.   5. The Lord may be so much incensed by sins of this kind, that at length there will be no remedy, as he was by the Jews, 2 Chron. xxxvi. Lastly, Great is the profit of admonition to such as are wise to make use of it, as these places shew: Ps. cxli. 5, 6, Job v. 15-17, xxxvi. 8-16, Prov. xxviii. 13.

Teaching. This is the second part of preaching: this also is absolutely necessary. We shall not partake of Christ's riches, or be fit to be presented to God without it. Now that we may profit by public preaching we must pray God by his Spirit to lead us into all truth, John xiv., and we must strive to be truly humble, for the Lord will teach the humble his way, Ps. xxv. 9, and we must be much in confessing our own sins unto God in secret, Ps. cxix. 26, 2 Chron. vi. 26-30; we must take heed of forwardness in trusting to our own reasons, and wills, and affections, and bring faith to the word, glorifying it in what we understand, and waiting upon God for what yet we want, mourning for our own unteachableness, and praying God to be with the mouth of the teacher, opening to him a door of utterance.

Every man. This is again added, and not without reason, for it imports: first, That every man is bound to live under some teaching and admonishing ministry; secondly, That the people, yea, all God's people, must be instructed; contrary to the doctrine of the papists; thirdly, A right persuasion of this, that the word will admonish and teach every man, would make men more quiet under rebukes, and more willing to be taught. He saith not you, but every man, to import that the word hath not a particular quarrel at some one man, but will find out the sins of all men, &c. We see by experience that this is the sore in many minds, that either the preacher should meddle with nobody, or not with such as they: he must not meddle with great men, or not with scholars and learned men, &c.

In all wisdom. These words may be understood either of the subject-matter taught, or of the instruments, the teachers, or of the effect in the hearers.

For the first, The word of God is well called wisdom, either as it is the pattern, or image, or resemblance of God's everlasting wisdom, which from all eternity in his counsel he had conceived; or as it portrayeth out Christ, who is the natural Wisdom of God; or as it unfoldeth the depths of God's wise providence, especially in his church; or comparatively, with all the forms of doctrine conceived by the wisest of the Gentiles, or any carnal men.

For the second, These words may be referred to the teachers, and then the sense is, they must teach in all wisdom. They are called wise men, Mat. xxiii., and that they may teach in all wisdom: first, They may be sure they teach truth and not errors —neither errors of doctrine nor errors of fact. It is a grievous shame for preachers out of the pulpit, of purpose to disgrace some kind of men, to report of them things utterly untrue, especially to fail often or usually this way. Secondly, They must labour to express the power of the Spirit, as well as a sound form of doctrine. Thirdly, They must make use of all opportunities and advantages to work upon the people when a door is opened. To preach wisely is to preach seasonably. Fourthly, They cannot preach in the wisdom of God if they hunt after and effect that which the apostle calls the wisdom of words, 1 Cor. i. 17, or excellency of words, 1 Cor. ii. 1. Fifthly, There is a special wisdom in fitting doctrine to the state of the hearers, to give every one his own portion.

Thirdly, It may be said to be in all wisdom by effect in the hearers, as being such a preaching as tends to work true wisdom in the hearers, as well as other graces; a wisdom, I say, by which they understand their own way, Prov. xiv. 8, 9, 15, 16, and deny their own reason in the things of God, becoming fools that they may be wise, 1 Cor. iii., and know their days of peace, and accordingly gather in summer, Prov. x. 5, even in the seasons of grace, while it is yet called to-day, walking with the wise, Prov. xiii. 20, preferring spiritual things above all earthly, as things that are truly excellent, Phil. i. 10, carefully watching over themselves, and with all preciseness or circumspection, Eph. v. 15, avoiding even the lesser evils, redeeming the time, with all discretion, labouring to avoid all occasions of just offence; and, lastly, considering and providing for their latter end, Deut. xxxii. 22, Job iv. *ult.*

Quest. But can all wisdom be attained?

Ans. He saith, all wisdom, either comparatively with the knowledge of the heathen or carnal men; or else by all wisdom he meaneth all necessary to salvation; or else he meaneth wisdom of all kinds, though not perfect iu every kind.

That we may present every man. The hearers are said to be presented to God by their teachers in divers respects: first, As they gather them out of the world into the profession of the faith of Christ; secondly, By framing and working upon the hearts of their hearers, fitting them for Christ, even in the presence of Christ, in his ordinances; thirdly, By forcing men, through the strength of terror or comfort, to run and present themselves to God; fourthly, They may be said to do it in respect of their prayers, carrying the suits of the people unto God; fifthly, They shall present them at the day of judgment, when every teacher shall say, 'Here, Lord, I am, with the children thou hast given me.'

Uses. This should teach the people so to order themselves towards their ministers that they might have encouragement to go to God, either for them or with them. To this purpose they should honour them, maintain them, obey them, shew their hearts and states to them, &c. And woe is unto them that despise God's ministers or discourage them; that hate their doctrine or shun their society, howsoever they account of them. Yet these are the men should have made way for them to Christ, they are of his privy chamber, and the dust of their feet shall witness against contemners; yea, the time shall come when they would be glad to have them excuse them to Christ, but it shall not be granted, Luke xiv. 18, 19. And ministers also may from hence both be comforted, considering the honour Christ hath done them, and instructed to look carefully to their flocks, and to go to God for them, and by all means to carry themselves so as they that must once give an account for their people.

Perfect. The word τελειον is not in the text in some copies; but Stephanus hath it in, and it is acknowledged of the translators and expositors, both old and new, and therefore perfection cannot be denied, only the sense must be inquired into.

The faithful are said to be perfect: first, Comparatively with wicked men, or the Gentiles unconverted. Religion will make a man perfect in comparison of that which by nature man can attain unto. Secondly, They may be said to be made perfect, that is, to want nothing that is absolutely necessary for salvation. Thirdly, In righteousness there is perfection, and so they shall be absolutely perfect at the day of judgment, and are already perfect in respect of justification; yea, this word here used is given to the sanctification of the faithful, and that two ways: first, As *to be perfect* notes nothing else but to be a strong man in Christ, so Heb. 5, *ult.*: secondly, As *to be upright* is accepted with God for perfection, by the benefit of the covenant of grace, and the intercession of Christ. Thus, I think the very word is used in these places: 1 Cor. ii. 6, Phil. iii. 15, James i. 17, Heb. vi. 1, 12, 13; thus, there is perfection in doctrine, Heb. vi. 1; in faith, James ii. 22; in hope, 1 Peter i. 13; in love, 1 John iv. 18, John xvii. 23; in understanding, 1 Cor. xiv. 20.

Quest. But who is a strong man in Christ, or a perfect man, as here?

Ans. First, He that is a strong man in Christ can forgive his enemies, and pray for them, and do good to them, Mat. v. 48; secondly, He doth finish his work, he doth not begin slightly, and work for a spirit, but perseveres.—the word used in that sense, John xvii. 4; thirdly, He doth hold a constant amity and holy communion with God's children, 1 John iv. 12, John xvii. 23; fourthly, He hath renounced the world, denying himself, and consecrated his life to God, Rom. xii. 12; fifthly, He will not be carried away with every wind of doctrine, but will acknowledge and follow the truth with all constant unmoveableness, Eph. iv. 13, 14; sixthly, He presseth after perfection, forgets what's behind, and looks to the mark of the high prize of his calling, labouring to find out the virtue of Christ's death and resurrection, Phil. iii. 13-14, x. 9; seventhly, He hath a plerophory or full assurance of the will of God towards him, Col. iv. 12; eighthly, He can digest the stronger doctrines of religion, Heb. v. 14; ninthly, Patience hath in him her perfect work, James i. 4; tenthly, He sins not in word, James iii. 12; eleventhly, He keeps the word, 1 John ii. 5; twelfthly, He is settled in the love of God, and hath not fear, but boldness, 1 John iv. 17, 18.

Every man. Every true Christian might be made a strong Christian; which may serve for great humiliation to such as, having the means, have neglected so great grace or measure of it. What knowledge, what power or gifts, what abundance of fair fruit we might have had and borne if we had attended the means, and seriously laboured to redeem the time! We might many of us have been teachers, that now need to be catechised.

In Jesus Christ. All that supposed perfection that is out of Christ Jesus is not worth seeking after. Whatsoever carnal men propound unto themselves concerning the worth of their own projects, yet all in the end will prove vanity that is not in Christ Jesus. And contrariwise, all true perfection is in Christ; which should so much the more comfort fearful Christians, seeing their perseverance and the perfecting grace begun is in him,—it is his office to see it performed, and it will be accomplished by his power, as it is given for his merits; and it should teach all the faithful to make much of communion with Christ; to keep their hold, and not let go their confidence; to preserve by all means tenderness in a holy intercourse with Christ; for if once Christ absent himself, the work of grace will stand still. Thirdly, This shows how perfection can be attributed to Christians; namely, as in Christ Jesus the evil of their works is covered by him, and what is good is presented by him to the Father. Lastly, It should teach us in all our wants to seek to Christ, in the use of all means appointed by him to give or confirm grace, waiting upon him with faith and prayer.

Ver. 29. *Whereunto I also labour and strive, according to his working that worketh in me mightily.*

In this verse is contained the seventh reason to enforce the exhortation, and it is taken from the great pains of the apostle, and the great success the Lord was pleased to give to his pains.

Whereunto. Some read *in whom*, viz., in which Christ, that is, by whose assistance, and blessing, and protection, &c. But I take it as it is here, *whereunto*; and so it may be referred either to the exhortation in the three and twentieth verse, or to perfection in the verse before. It is sure that the perfection of ministers' labours should be the perfection of their hearers. It is not enough to know how to preach sermons, but it must tend not only to beget men unto Christ, but also to build them up, which is a wonderful hard work, and few ministers are well skilled herein; and therefore ministers should much consult with God, and the people should pray constantly and earnestly for their teachers.

Labour. An effectual ministry is a painful ministry: the Lord's work must not be done negligently, 2 Tim. iv. 1-3, 1 Thes. v. 12, which may justify continual and daily preaching.

Quest. But what needs all this preaching?

Ans. It is exceeding needful, for it is the ordinary means to save men's souls and to beget faith; and inasmuch as there are daily still to be added to the church, therefore still the means is to be used, besides the secret judgment of God in the induration of the wicked, and leaving them without excuse. And as there needs daily food for the body, so doth there for the soul; and the Lord by his word doth heal the daily infirmities of his people, Ps. cvii. Men think it needful the exchequer should be open all the year that their law-cases may be determined; and more need it is the Lord's spiritual exchequer should stand open for the daily determining of the cases of conscience which arise in the souls of God's people: and we need a daily light for our paths and lantern for our feet, Ps. cxix. What shall I say? Our very calling needs direction out of the word, and our crosses and temptations cause us to feel a daily need of the comforts of the word to be applied to us; the godly are to be encouraged in well-doing, and that continually; and we all need to be called upon daily for reformation and prevention of sin. Grace will not hold out without means, and knowledge must be increased; and a daily ministry is of singular use to prepare us for death, and wean us from the world. These and many other be the reasons of daily preaching, which should greatly reprove such ministers as labour not, either for want of gifts or plurality of places, or distraction of business, or for very idleness, or unwillingness to take pains. Woe unto them, for as they provide evil for their people's souls, so they reward evil to their own souls.

According to his working that worketh in me mightily. Before I consider particularly of these words, I note how feelingly the apostle speaks of God's providence, and with what affection he sets out the observation he made of it, which greatly shames the most of us, that are so excessively dull in apprehending, and so affectionless in the thought of things. Now if any would know what should be the reason we are so dull, and the apostle so tenderly sensible of God's power and providence, I may answer that a number of us are not thoroughly persuaded of God's particular providence; besides, he was excellently acquainted with the word of God, and thereby he saw lively how every promise or threatening came into execution. There could hardly anything fall out, but he remembered some scripture that foretold or foreshewed it. And no question he knew how unable the means was to work without God's blessing. Further, it is certain that such holy men as he sought God's blessing by prayer, and, therefore, now they were affected when they observed what followed their prayers. And besides, the apostle did walk with God in a great measure of sanctity and holy care in all things to keep his communion with God, whereas we are estranged by our corruptions, and for the most part negligent in a daily walking with God. Lastly, he was humble, and not conceited of his own gifts, and had consecrated himself, and devoted his life to God's glory, and, therefore, he was sensible of the glory of God in his working providence.

But the main particular doctrine is, that in the ministry of the gospel there is God's special working; for it is God's work to raise up men that will labour in the gospel, considering the ill-success in many hearers, and the infirmities in themselves, and the strange discouragements from the world; and when the Lord hath gotten him labourers, it is his working that they can get fit meditations and affections into their hearts in private, and fit utterance in public. It is not art and learning alone that will furnish them with powerful matter. And, thirdly, it is God's working to extend the power of the word to the hearers, so as the heat of it go out before it kindle in the people's hearts. What shall I say? It is God's mighty working that the people are preserved and daily built up by the word in grace. All which should teach us to place our faith, not in men, but in the power of God. And let wicked men be advised, lest by resisting the ministry they be found fighters against God; and it may be a great comfort to a minister too, for if God work for us and by us, it matters not who be against us. And lastly, Christians should make much of, and be thankful for, and greatly admire all knowledge and grace gotten from the word, for it was wrought by the very finger of God.

THE ANALYSIS OF THE SECOND CHAPTER.

TWO things are contained in this chapter: first, The continuation of the exhortation begun in the 23d verse of the first chapter to ver. 7; secondly, A dehortation, from verse 8 to the end.

The exhortation is continued two ways: first, By alleging more reasons, ver. 1–3; secondly, By prolepsis, removing sundry objections, ver. 4–7. There are three reasons to press them to care of perseverance in the doctrine they had received. The first reason is taken from the care of the apostle for the delivery and defence of the gospel, in these words, 'I would you know what great fighting I have for your sakes, and for them of Laodicea, and for as many as have not seen my face in the flesh,' ver. 1.

The second reason is taken from the effects of the gospel, and they are two: 1. Consolation, 'that your hearts might be comforted;' 2. Love, 'and knit together in love.'

The third reason is taken from the adjuncts of the gospel, and they are three: first, Certainty, 'unto all riches of full assurance of understanding;' 2. Sublimity, 'to the acknowledgment of the mystery of God, even the Father, and of Christ,' ver. 2; 3. Perfection, in these words, 'in whom,' or 'in which, are hid all the treasures of wisdom and knowledge,' ver. 3.

Thus of the reasons; the answer of objections follows:

Object. 1. Why doth the apostle urge us so largely with this exhortation?

Sol. 'This I say, lest any beguile you with enticing words.'

Object. 2. But how doth he know our estates, being absent?

Sol. To this he answereth, that though he were 'absent in the flesh, yet he was present in spirit.'

Object. 3. But is it charity to entertain surmises of us?

Sol. He saith he did 'rejoice in their order and steadfastness' present; but he wrote this to warn them to take heed.

Quest. Tell us at once what you would have us do.

Ans. Ver. 6, 7. Two things are to be done. The first concerns holy life, the second faith. Concerning holy life, there is, first, A precept, 'walk on;' secondly, A rule after which that precept is to be squared, viz., 'as ye have received the Lord Jesus Christ.' Concerning faith there is: first, A precept —they must be 'rooted, built up, and stablished;' secondly, A rule—'as they have been taught.'

And thus of the exhortation, the dehortation follows, from ver. 8 to the end. There are three parts of the dehortation: first, He setteth down the matter from which he dehorts, ver. 8; secondly, He gives six reasons to confirm the dehortation, from ver. 9–16; thirdly, He concludes, and that severally, from ver. 16 to the end.

In the 8th verse he sets down three things from which he dehorts: 1. From 'philosophy,' which he calls 'vain deceits;' 2. From 'traditions of men;' 3. From the ceremonies of Moses, which he calls the 'rudiments of the world.'

The reasons are: 1. Because they are not after Christ, ver. 8; 2. Because in Christ there dwells all the fulness of the Godhead bodily, ver. 9, where note an excellent description of Christ: 'In him,' he notes his person; 'the Godhead,' his divine nature; 'corporally,' his human nature; and 'dwells,' the union of both; and for the measure, it is 'in all fulness.'

3. Because we are complete in Christ, without any of these things, ver. 10. Here note the persons, *ye;* the time, *are;* the benefit, *complete;* the author, *Christ;* the limitation, *in him.*

4. Because we are circumcised without hands, and therefore need not circumcision made with hands, and consequently no ceremonies. This reason is propounded ver. 11, and confirmed by prolepsis, ver. 12.

Concerning circumcision without hands, five things are to be noted: 1. The persons, *ye;* 2. The time, are; 3. The manner, set down negatively, *without hands:* 4. The form of it, affirmatively, *putting off the body of the sins of the flesh;* 5. The efficient cause, *the circumcision of Christ.*

Object. But it follows not, We are circumcised without hands, therefore need not circumcision with hands.

Sol. It follows to us now in the New Testament, because we have baptism instead of circumcision with hands, we are 'buried with Christ by baptism.'

Object. But was not circumcision a more lively sign?

Sol. It was not, which he shews to be true, both in respect of mortification, *buried with him,* and in respect of vivification, *raised up together with him by baptism,* which is amplified by setting down what is required in them to whom baptism is thus effectual, viz., *the faith of the operation of God.*

5. Because none of these can help us in misery, nor further to happiness when we want it, ver. 13. The words in themselves express a twofold estate of Christians: first, What they are by nature, and so: 1. They were *dead* in actual *sins;* 2. They were in the *uncircumcision of the flesh,* in respect of original sin. Secondly, What they were in the state of grace: 1. They were *quickened;* 2. They were *forgiven all their sins.*

6. Because Christ hath cancelled the *chirography* that was against us, which were these ceremonies, ver. 14, 15. Concerning these two things may be noted: 1. What the ceremonies were in themselves; 2. How the church was discharged of them.

For the first, they were for honour *ordinances* of God; for use, *handwriting;* for effect, they were *against us.*

For the second, Christ on the cross cancelled them, fastened them, and took them out of the way; yea, he spoiled the devils, and triumphed over them openly, who had the power to serve execution for forfeitures, ver. 15.

Thus of the reasons: the conclusion follows from ver. 16 to the end. The conclusion hath three branches; for first, He concludes against ceremonies, ver. 16, 17; secondly, Against philosophy. ver. 18, 19; thirdly, Against traditions, ver. 20 to the end.

In the conclusion against ceremonies, note: 1. The things which are named to be abrogated, viz., the respect of *meats and drinks;* 2. Of times, which are threefold: (1.) *Days;* (2.) *Months;* (3.) *Sabbaths:* these are the things, ver. 16. The reason is, ver. 17, because these are but *shadows of things to come, and the body is Christ.*

In the conclusion against philosophy, note, first: The thing which in special he reasons against, viz., angel worship; secondly, The reasons by which he condemns them that brought it in: 1. They did it hypocritically, under pretence of *humbleness of mind;* 2. They did it ignorantly, *advancing themselves in things they never saw;* 3. They did it proudly, *rashly puffed up in their fleshly mind;* 4. They did it dangerously. Their danger is laid down and amplified—laid down in these words, *not holding the head;* amplified by a digression into the praises of the mystical body of Christ: 1. For ornament, *furnished;* 2. For union, *knit together by joints and bands;* 3. For growth, *increasing with increase of God.*

In the conclusion against traditions, observe: first, The matter condemned, *why are ye burdened with traditions,* amplified by the kinds, *touch not, taste not, handle not,* ver. 21; secondly, The reasons: 1. *Ye are dead with Christ,* ver. 20; 2. Ye are dead from the *rudiments of the world,* therefore much more from traditions; 3. They are *burdens;* 4. The matter of them is light, and vain, and idle, ver. 21; 5. They all *perish with the using;* 6. They are *after the commandments and doctrines of men,* ver. 21.

Object. But there seemeth to be a depth in them.

Sol. He confesseth that they have *a shew of wisdom,* and that in three things: 1. In *voluntary religion;* 2. In *humbleness of mind;* 3. In *not sparing the body.* But yet he censures them two ways: 1. It is but *a shew* all this; 2. It withholdeth the honour due unto the body, *neither have they it in any estimation to satisfy the flesh,* ver. 23.

THE METAPHRASE UPON THE SECOND CHAPTER.

Ver. 1. For I would ye were thoroughly informed of it, what great care, conflict, strife, and fighting I have for your sakes, and for them of Laodicea, and for such as I never knew, but only hear of to be such as embrace the gospel which we preach; and to this end I tell you of my care and fighting, so to move you to be much the more resolute in persevering in the faith and hope of the doctrine you have received.

Ver. 2. Great are the benefits which you and all those that believe in your parts receive from our pains in the gospel, for hereby both your hearts are comforted with true refreshings, and besides you are hereby knit one to another, and established in brotherly love; and as the benefits of the adjuncts of the gospel should much move you to stick still to it, if you consider how rich God hath made you, in the infallible and full persuasion of understanding which you have felt, and withal what admirable desires there are in the doctrine of the gospel concerning God the Father and Christ.

Ver. 3. Or lastly, if you consider the perfection of the doctrine of the gospel, either as it contains the treasures of wisdom and knowledge, or as it shews us Christ, in whom are all admirable perfections of all sorts of rich knowledge.

Ver. 4. Now, if you ask me why I am so tedious in urging these things? I answer, it is only for fear lest any should, by plausible and probable enticement of speech, beguile you from the simplicity that is in Christ.

Ver. 5. And if you say I know not your estate, I answer, though I be absent from you in the flesh, yet I am present with you in the spirit; and if you think that this discourse implies that I dislike you, know that I do truly rejoice to hear of your good order of life, both public and private, and how steadfast your faith in Christ.

Ver. 6. Now, if you ask me at once what is the sum of all I would have you do? I answer, that as concerning holy life, I would have you walk on in the same manner as ye have received Christ hitherto.

Ver. 7. And for matter of faith, I would have you by all means to seek to be further rooted and built up and established in the assurance of faith accordingly as you have been taught; but by any means remember to abound in all thankfulness to God for the happy estate you are in; and thus for what I have to exhort you to in matters of doctrine.

Ver. 8. Now I must enter upon matter of dehortation: take heed lest any man, of what gifts or profession soever, make a prey of your souls, and carry them away as a spoil; and, in particular, look to it in three things: first, In philosophy, not simply in the doctrines of philosophy, but in such devices and vain fancies as, under colour of such speculation, or from the authority of philosophers, are brought in by any; secondly, Take heed of traditions of men; and, thirdly, Of the ceremonies of Moses, which were things at first brought in to be as the A B C, or alphabet to train up the people of God in the principles. But now this and the other are not to be regarded, for many reasons, whereof the first is, they are not after Christ.

Ver. 9. Besides, there is such an infinite fulness in Christ, by reason of the divine nature that dwells by an inexpressible union in the human nature, that we need not seek to anything else but only unto Christ.

Ver. 10. And you yourselves in Christ have all completeness and sufficiency, by reason of your mystical union with him; and such is the fulness of Christ, that the very angels, those excellent and potent creatures, are subordinate to him, and acknowledge him as their head, which, by the way, shews that they are not to be worshipped.

Ver. 11. And to speak yet more expressly, what should you do with circumcision or any part of the law ceremonial, seeing in Christ ye have received that which was signified by circumcision? for in him you are circumcised, not with the hands of men, as they were under the law, but by the finger of the Spirit of God, which stands in the mortification of that body of sins which ye were guilty of while ye were in the flesh, and this ye have by the virtue of Christ's circumcision.

Ver. 12, 13. And if you say that Abraham had the circumcision without hands, and yet was circumcised in the flesh, I answer, that we have baptism instead of that circumcision, and therefore need it not; and the rather, because baptism doth so lively set out our spiritual burial and resurrection with Christ, which all they attain unto that have the faith of God's operation—that is, that can believe that God by his power will do what he promiseth in baptism, grounding their faith upon the resurrection of Christ from the dead.

Ver. 14. And further, this should move you to disregard those things, because they neither could help you when you were miserable, nor confer the benefits upon you which you enjoy without them, for in your estate of nature you were dead in actual sins; and in respect of original sin, you lived in the uncircumcision of the flesh; and since you were quickened by true regeneration, you have obtained the forgiveness of all your sins, and therefore what would you have more from these things?

Lastly, The ceremonies, though they were ordinances of God at the first, yet they were hand-writings against us, and now Christ hath cancelled them, and fastened the obligation upon the cross, and so taken them out of the way, and therefore you should never more have mind to them.

Ver. 15. And the rather because our Saviour hath not only cancelled them, but he hath spoiled the devils which had power to execute the forfeitures of these bonds. I say, both in himself on the cross, and in us daily, he hath and doth spoil them, and triumph over them, and make an open shew of them, so as we are freed from the danger of their arrests.

Ver. 16. Now therefore I come to the conclusion; which I direct distinctly, first, against the ceremonies; then against philosophy; and, lastly, against traditions: First, I say, let no man condemn you, (or if they do, care not for it,) condemn you, I say, for any of the ceremonies, whether it be about meats or drinks, or about the ceremonial days, or months, or sabbaths, that were required in that law.

Ver. 17. For these and all the rest were but shadows of things to come, and now in Christ we have the substance and body of them.

Ver. 18. The like I say against philosophy, and in special against angel-worship, let no man bear rule over your consciences, for they that bring in this doctrine do it hypocritically, upon pretence that it tends to make men humble, and they do it very ignorantly, for they never saw the kingdom of angels, nor what is done in heaven, and most proudly do they advance themselves, swelling in the vain conceits of their fleshly minds.

Ver. 19. Yea, they that bring in this doctrine fall from the foundation, and hold not Christ, who is the head of the church, of whom every member doth depend, and the whole body is excellently furnished and indissolubly knit together, and increase with the increasing of God.

Ver. 20. And lastly, for traditions: I wonder at it you would be clogged with them, seeing you are delivered from them in the death of Christ, and they are not so honourable as the ceremonies of Moses, but are vile burdens.

Ver. 21. Think but with yourselves how vainly they impose upon you when they say, touch not, taste not, handle not.

Ver. 22. Besides, all these are perishable things, and fit nothing at all to eternal life; and further, they are evidently the common documents and devices and doctrines of men, that never had warrant in the word of God.

Ver. 23. It is true they find out many fair pretences to blind men's eyes withal, as that hereby we shew special zeal to God in doing more than he commandeth, and these things seem to tend to humility and the taming of the flesh; but all these are but shows, and therefore naught, whatsoever they say, because they yield not a due respect even to the body of man.

CHAPTER II.

VER. 1. *For I would ye knew what great fighting I have for your sakes, and for them of Laodicea, and for as many as have not seen my person in the flesh.*

The exhortation, begun in the 23d verse of the former chapter, is continued in the first seven verses of this chapter, wherein the apostle propounds three other reasons for confirmations, and answers divers secret objections. The reasons are in the three first verses, and the answer to the objections in the four next.

The first reason is taken from the care the apostle took for them in the work of his ministry in this verse. The second reason is from the effects of the gospel, viz., consolation and love, ver. 2. The third reason is from certain adjuncts of the gospel, viz., certainty, sublimity, and perfection, ver. 2, 3.

Object. But what needs all this ado? might some of the Colossians say. Why are we thus tediously urged, and with so many reasons?

Sol. Ver. 4. 'This I say, lest any man beguile you.'

Object. But you are a stranger to us, and absent from us, how know you our estate?

Sol. Ver. 5. 'Though I am absent in the flesh, yet I am present with you in the spirit.'

Object. But it is uncharitableness to entertain such conceits of us, as if we were a people corrupt and fallen away.

Sol. Ver. 5. For your present condition, 'I rejoice in your order,' being fully ascertained of your present 'steadfastness of faith in Christ.' But I write this to keep you as you are, that you may not be drawn away.

Quest. But what would you advise us? Tell us briefly, and at once, what you would have us to do?

Ans. 'As you have received Christ Jesus the Lord, so walk in him,' &c., ver. 6, 7.

Thus we see the order and general meaning and dependence of all these first seven verses.

In this first verse, the apostle would stir up the Colossians to constancy in the gospel received, by shewing his great care and daily strife for them and their good.

It is not unlawful, in some cases, to praise a man's self; the apostle here doth it. Nor is it unlawful to use rhetorical insinuations, to win and excite affection in the people. Paul would persuade, by shewing his own care for them. But sure it is, ministers shall hardly ever profit the people, or powerfully persuade with them unto constancy, in receiving and retaining the care of their doctrine, unless they shew their own care in teaching, and their own love to the people they would persuade.

What a great conflict. Paul shews his great love to them; he fighteth for them, and this he did when in all likelihood he should employ his cares for himself, being now in such straits, as it were in the midst of death, and the rather they should be affected with this proof of his love in them, because they were absent from him.

For. This *for* shews an aitiology; for it points to a dependence upon the last verse of the former chapter. There he had shewed what pain he took, and how mightily the Lord had shewed his power in working through his ministry. Now he tells of a fight and combat, which evidently imports that when the gospel works upon men's consciences, and the ministry of God's servants proves effectual and powerful, there will follow some stir and opposition, there will be a conflict and strife.

Yet hence also may be gathered, that the grace

of the gospel is excellent, and worthy the having, else there would not be so much ado to hinder it.

What great conflict or fighting. 'Αγωνα, the original word, is diversely rendered; some render it care or solicitude, some danger; sometimes it signifies a race, as Heb. xii. 1; sometimes it signifies only to strive; but here and in divers places, it is fitly rendered a conflict, or fighting, or wrestling. But leaving the signification, the matter is plain, that if ministers execute their offices sincerely, they must look for a battle and opposition. Indeed, the life of faithful ministers is but a continual battle; they must look to suffer, and be 'shamefully entreated,' 1 Thes. ii. 2; if they be bold to speak the gospel of God, it will be 'with much contention;' if they discharge the trust God hath put in them, 'not pleasing men, but God that trieth the heart,' 1 Thes. ii. 4, war they must. This is their comfort, it is 'a good warfare,' 1 Tim. i. 18, and a good fight, 2 Tim. iv. 7: to undertake the ministry, it is to go a warfare, 1 Cor. ix. 7.

If any ask how this fight should grow, I answer: first, It is manifest the devil is the enemy of all goodness, and will cross the gospel what he can. Besides, the flesh, both in ministers and people, will lust and strive against the spirit. A minister should have something to do to 'beat down his own flesh,' 1 Cor. ix. 27. And in the apostle's times, tyrants with their civil, or rather uncivil, sword, did fight against the truth; so did heretics with the tares and poison of their infectious doctrine; so did the infidels also, with slanders and outrages. And though these cease, yet opposition will rise from other sorts of men; for in general, all men of wicked life will be 'contrary to sound doctrine,' 1 Tim. i. 10; and particularly both worldlings and epicures, do in all places discover their dislike of the faithful and diligent preaching of the gospel, inasmuch as the word would restrain the excess of their pleasures and cares of life; yea, the civil honest men of the world, though they give heaven good words, and can be long more quiet than the former, yet let once their inward corruption be ransacked, or their special evils powerfully unmasked, they will become like horses and mules, they will strike at all that crosseth the praise of their quiet estate. And for temporisers, it is wonderful evident that in all places they hold it a point of their care to see that sound preaching be disgraced. For howsoever, by God's singular mercy amongst us in this nation, by the laws of the kingdom preaching is both established and protected with honour, yet because in practice people of all degrees tend to liberty, and many great ones like not that preaching that should discover or restrain the grievous excesses of the time, hence it is, that such as serve the humours of men, and run in the current of profaneness, do everywhere take all advantages to disgrace painful and godly preachers and preaching. Besides, such is the hellish spite and rage of papists and popish persons in all places, that, in imitation of their 'holy father,' who is noted to 'oppose and exalt himself,' 2 Thes. ii. 4, they, especially the 'locusts' among them, are as 'horses prepared to the battle,' Rev. ix., as soon as the gospel begins in any place to be sincerely taught. Lastly, This opposition many times is made by corrupt teachers, men that either are poisoned with unsound opinions, or otherwise be of corrupt and ambitious minds; 'as Jannes and Jambres resisted Moses, so do these resist the truth.' 2 Tim. iii. 8, and 'withstand the words' of faithful men, and 'do much evil,' 2 Tim. iv. 14, 15; these, 'by cunning craftiness, lie in wait to deceive,' Eph. iv. 14. So that there are twelve opposites that set against the sincerity of the preaching of the gospel.

Now, if any ask how Paul, and so every faithful minister, doth fight against these? I answer, that as the adversaries are divers, so their fight is divers also; for against their own flesh they fight, by renouncing the world, and the care or confidence in worldly hopes, making profit and credit stoop to the calling of God.

2. Against the temptations of Satan, and the many objections by which he labours to discourage or hinder them, they fight by care; that is by a daily study, devising how to advantage the good of the churches, devoting their best desires for the people's good.

3. They fight by apology and just defence, and so both against corrupt teachers and the calumnies and slanderous reproaches of the wicked.

1. They fight against the corruptions and abuses

of the time, by reproofs and the denunciation of the threatenings of God's word.

5. They wrestle and fight even in prayer to God, Col. iv. 12; and so they fight by complaining against the injuries of wicked men, or else by striving with God himself to overcome him by importunity.

6. They fight even by their sufferings; they win many battles by their very patience and faith in affliction, by enduring the 'fight of affliction.'

The consideration of this fight may first awaken careless ministers, inasmuch as they proportion out such a course of preaching as they can escape blows, it gives just cause of suspicion that they are combined with the enemies, in that they are let alone and not opposed.

Again, this may both sound an alarm to all faithful ministers to arm and prepare for a fight; and it may comfort them in that this hath been the case of the best of God's servants; and withal the people may learn how to be affected to their godly teachers. Do your ministers so many ways labour and strive for you, and shall not you strive for them, by apology, prayer, care, and all ways of just defence?

I would you knew. Quest. Why was the apostle so desirous they should know his care, patience, fighting, &c. for them?

Ans. There might be great cause of it: 1. To remove all conceit that he did not respect them; 2. To encourage them to constancy in that doctrine for which he suffered so much; 3. It might arm them with patience to suffer, if they should be called to it, considering his example; 4. That so they might be stirred up the more earnestly to pray for him. In general this shews that it is not enough that we love one another, but we must manifest it; especially affection between the minister and his people should not be concealed.

For you and for them of, &c. There were two sorts of godly men in the apostle's time: 1. Such as were converted immediately by the apostles in their own persons; 2. Such as were converted by others sent of the apostles. The apostle here shews he loves these latter as well as the former.

There is a communion with the absent members of Christ, even with such as we never saw in the face; a communion, I say, in the same head, and in the same spirit, and in the same privileges of a regenerated life. And we see here we are bound to desire and endeavour the good of the absent saints as well as the present; we may fight for the absent by prayer, by apology, by our sufferings, and by using the means of consolation or information; yea, herein is a lively trial of our true love to the brethren, if we can love them we never saw, for the grace of God we hear to be in them.

For them of Laodicea. Though there were many cities of this name, yet I think this is the Laodicea mentioned Rev. iii. If the estate of these Laodiceans be well marked, as it is there described, we may observe, that in matters of religion and God's worship, they were neither hot nor cold; that they thought they had as good hearts to God as any; that they were in love with no saving grace; that they were utterly ignorant of the doctrine of their misery; that they would take no pains either about justification or santification, &c.; yet, no doubt, God had his remnant among these. Christ was *Amen* in this church, he did faithfully perform his promises, and they were such as by a new creation of God were begotten again, even amongst so careless a multitude. The general security of a people doth not simply dissolve the covenant with a people, and the gospel is with all care to be taught, though but the tithe of men be wrought upon by it.

And for such as never saw my face. Two things may be here further noted:

1. That we have the profit of the prayers and holy endeavours of such as we never saw in the flesh.

2. That it is a great benefit to enjoy the presence of those that are eminent in God's service, for that is implied in the words. Certainly it is one thing should make us willing to die, because then we shall see the worthies of the Lord face to face. If so much grief, Acts xx., because they should see Paul's face no more, then what joy shall it be when we shall sit down in the kingdom of heaven, with Abraham, Isaac, and Jacob!

Ver. 2. *That their hearts might be comforted, and they knit together in love, and in all riches of the full assurance of understanding, to know the mystery of God, even the Father, and of Christ.*

In the beginning of this verse is contained the

second reason, taken from the effects of the gospel, which are two: the first, Consolation; the second, Establishment of their hearts in brotherly love. The rest of the words of this verse belongs to the third reason, as shall appear afterward.

This is the fruit of the care and earnest strife of godly teachers in their painful labours of the gospel, that it breeds much comfort in the hearts of God's people, and likewise greatly confirms them, and settles them in the mutual love one of another—it knits their hearts together. And contrariwise we may generally here note the hurt and mischief that false and corrupt teachers bring upon men; they hinder the consultations of God's people, in that they draw them away from God the fountain of all consolation; and likewise they withdraw them from the society and fellowship with the saints. But this is but general. I consider distinctly of these effects.

That their hearts might be comforted.

Doct. 1. The people whose hearts are not effectually wrought upon by the gospel, are void of the consolations of God; they are in comfortless distress. A natural heart is a comfortless heart; and they must needs be without comfort, for they are without God and Christ, and the promises, and communion with the godly, which are the wells of comfort. Besides, by reason of the veil of ignorance, their souls sit in darkness. And what comfort can they have in such a continued spiritual night of darkness? Neither will the disorder of their affections, passions, or lusts, suffer their hearts to enjoy any true ease, or rest, or joy; and how can comfort dwell where evil angels have their throne? The powers of hell prevail in every child of disobedience, and the joys of the Holy Ghost are altogether restrained from them. Neither can there arise any true consolation from outward things, for in their own judgments most an end they are at a want of contentment, they are daily fretted with the interruptions befall them; and vanity and vexation of spirit are the inseparable companions of earthly things, or if they were not, what were the possession of all things if they be set before the thoughts of death, or God's wrath, or the last judgment, or hell? Imagine a man driven out of the light by devils, where he should see nothing but his tormentors, and that he were made to stand upon snares or gins with iron teeth ready to strike up and grind him to pieces, and that he had gall poured down to his belly, and an instrument raking in his bowels, and the pains of a travailing woman upon him, and an hideous noise of horror in his ears, and a great giant with a spear running upon his neck, and a flame burning upon him round about; do you imagine this man could be solaced in this distress with bringing him straws or trifles to play withal? Alas, alas! this is the estate of every wicked man, if he had eyes to see what belongs unto him, and what is his danger, as these places shew, whence these comparisons are taken: Job xviii. 18, vii. 8, xx. 24, 25, xv. 20, xxi. 26, 30. Certainly heaven and earth shall pass away before one jot of these miseries shall be removed out of the way, so as they should not fall upon wicked men, being impenitent; and, alas! what then can outward things do unto them? Oh, then, shall not men be warned and awaken, and stand up from the dead, that Christ may give them light? and shall not our bowels turn within us, to think of this comfortless distress of so many thousand souls? And will the rebellious world still rise up against the messengers of God, that give them warning of their miseries? shall he still be made to sin in the word, and be taken in a snare, that reproveth in the gate? Oh, the inexpressible senselessness and slumber that possesseth the hearts of some men! But I come to the second doctrine.

Doct. 2. This is a main end of the gospel, to bring men to true consolation and contentment. The gospel brings joy, because it brings knowledge, which refresheth the mind, as the light doth our senses; it comforts as it revives God's favour in Christ. How can it be but comfort, when it gives the Spirit, which is the Comforter; and it is a daily refreshing against the guilt of sin and the afflictions of life; it shews mortality and the hope of glory to come; it discovers the mines of treasure that are in God's promises, and it shews us also our right in earthly things, as it is conferred upon us in Christ.

Uses. The use is first for confutation; it doth not make men desperate and melancholy, but contrariwise it easeth and solaceth the hearts of men.

2. All that are in any distress, either inward or outward, may here be directed whither to go for heart's ease and comfort, viz., to the word, and though any use of the word in sincerity hath much

life, yet is the power of the word most available in the sincere preaching of it. In the 19th Psalm this is one evident fruit of the word, that it rejoiceth the heart. Now, if we seriously consider the praises of the word in that place, we shall perceive, not only that this truth is maintained, but many objections are answered too; only this we must know, that where the word hath this effect, it must first convert us to God; for to the unregenerate mind it doth not so work, but where men's hearts are turned to God, it is perfect, it is of excellent and exquisite use, it is good for all occasions, it will direct in all our ways, and comfort in all distresses.

Object. But may a man trust upon it, if he subject himself to the word, and wait upon God in it, that he shall be directed and comforted?

Sol. Yes; for 'the testimonies of God are sure,' they never fail.

Object. But might one say, it may be great learned men might find so much good by it, but, alas! I am unlearned and simple.

Sol. It 'makes the simple wise.' The word can help the unlearned as well as the learned.

Object. But can it be that the word should fit my turn, to serve for my particular occasion, of need, of direction, and comfort?

Sol. Yes; 'the statutes of the Lord are right,' and out of the fitness they have to our estates, they greatly 'rejoice the heart.'

Object. But I am much troubled with evil thoughts and continual infirmities and weaknesses, besides many outward faults.

Sol. 'The word of the Lord is pure,' it is so by the effect; it will make thee pure; it will purge out those evils, and greatly help thee against those corruptions that molest, and trouble, and annoy thee.

Object. But I cannot tell how to do to order my course for hereafter, if I were now comforted.

Sol. 'It gives light to the eyes;' it will teach us what to do.

Object. But yet there are many evils that I am by nature so addicted to, or by custom so entangled in, that I fear God will never take any delight in me, &c.

Sol. 'The fear of the Lord is clean.' That word of God which tells us how to fear God, is clean by effect, it will pull down and master any sin, and cleanse our hearts and lives of it.

Object. But how may I know it will work this in me, though others have found it so; because I know not how I shall persevere and hold out?

Sol. The fear of God 'endures for ever.' That word, I say, which works in us the true fear of God, will never cease to be effectual, and there is as much force in it now as ever was in it. No time can ever wear out the efficacy of God's word in the hearts of such as fear God. If it have wrought the true fear of God in thee, thou mayst be assured thou hast right to the directions and comforts contained in it, and it will still be of force to thee, if thou wait upon God in the true use of it.

Object. But I see many are otherwise minded, and some teach otherwise.

Sol. Yet 'the judgments of the Lord are true.' God's word must and will stand, howsoever we are minded.

Object. But may a man find help against any sin from the word, and direction in all things?

Sol. Yes; for 'God's judgments are righteous altogether.' They are exactly sufficient to make a man a godly man, complete in all his ways, and to order him in all that justice he should perform, either towards God or man.

Object. But might not the hearts of men be delighted with other things, and men's estates made happy with other treasures?

Sol. No; it is 'more to be desired (the word is) than fine gold, yea, than much fine gold, sweeter also than honey and the honeycomb.'

Object. But if I should devote myself thus to the word, the world would account me a very fool, and that I would grow to strange simpleness.

Sol. 'By them is thy servant made circumspect.' Nothing teacheth men true discretion but God's word, and if many hearers be not circumspect, it is either because they attend not to the word, or because they are not God's servants.

Object. But what profit will come of all this?

Sol. In the sound practice of the directions of the word 'there is great reward.'

Thirdly, This may comfort God's servants in their choice; they have chosen the better part, in that they have set their hearts upon the word, howsoever the world think of them.

Fourthly, We may here see the state of scorners and contemners of the word implied; let them mock on, but this they shall have, they shall never taste of the joys of God.

Fifthly, God's servants should be admonished from hence to express the power of the word in their carriages, that the world might see and know there is wonderful comfort and contentment in following the word.

Lastly, This may serve for the humiliation of all such as have long heard the gospel, and yet have not gotten any sound contentment.

Now, that men may not be mistaken, it will not be amiss to discover the true causes of this want of contentment in many that enjoy the gospel. It is true that the proper effect of the gospel is to comfort; but it is true also that it comforts only God's servants, Isa. lxv. 15. Again, if men have not mourned for their sins, no wonder though they be not comforted, Mat. v. 4, Isa. lxi. 1–3. Besides, many do not lay up the word in their hearts, and then how can it comfort their hearts? We must be a people in whose heart is God's law, Isa. li. 7, if we would feel this inward joy and consolation. Many also are ensnared with gross sin, whereas only 'the righteous sing and rejoice,' Prov. xxix. 6. Many want assurance, and therefore no wonder though they rejoice not with those unspeakable joys which are companions of faith and the love of Christ only, 1 Pet. i. 8, 9. Besides, many have but little joy, because they use but little praying; we must pray much if we [would] have our joy full, John xvi. 24. Further, some through unbelief resist comfort, Ps. lxxvii. 3.

There are seven inconveniences of an uncomfortable heart : 1. It is exceeding liable to temptations ; 2. It is under the reign of continual unthankfulness ; 3. It is easily perplexed with every cross, and turned out of frame and quiet ; 4. It is a daily let to the efficacy of all God's ordinances ; 5. It is accompanied with strange infirmities in doing good duties ; 6. It is usually barren in the very disposition to do good ; 7. It provokes God to anger, Deut. xxviii. 47.

Being knit together in love. Love is in God, in Christ, in angels, in saints glorified, in godly men converted, and in carnal men also. In the Trinity it is infinite ; in Christ, without measure ; in angels and men glorified, perfect, but measured ; in godly men on earth, imperfect, but holy ; in carnal men unholy, yet natural ; in the other creatures without reason, by instinct.

It is a religious and holy love amongst the members of Christ that is here meant.

The author and fountain of this love is God, 2 Cor. xiii. 11. The bond internal is the Spirit, external is the gospel ; the subject or seat of it is the heart, yet not every heart, but a pure heart, 1 Tim. i. 5. The effects are a heavenly comfort in the gospel, with all the fruits of it.

If thou ask whom thou must especially love? I answer, the saints ; that is, such as thou seest to strive after holiness of life, making conscience of their ways. These, and all these, are to be loved.

Neither will bare affection to them serve, but thou must seek to have fellowship with them in the gospel, Phil. i. 5, and ii. 1. If thy love to God's children be right : 1. It is diligent, 1 Thes. i. 3 ; 2. In things indifferent it doth not willingly offend, Rom. xiv. 15, Gal. v. 13 ; 3. It will cover a multitude of sins, 1 Pet. iv. 8, and it will forgive great offences upon repentance, 2 Cor. ii. 7, 8 ; 4. It is compassionate and liberal, 1 John iii. 17, 2 Cor. viii. 24 ; lastly, It hath the properties mentioned, 1 Cor. xiii. 4–7.

That this holy and religious love might be preserved amongst Christians, divers rules must be observed : 1. Men must not so much respect their own earthly things, Phil. ii. 4 ; 2. Men should labour with all meekness for union in judgment, without all contention and vain-glory, Phil. ii. 2–4 ; 3. Men must take heed of rejoicing in the evils one of another, 1 Cor. xiii. ; 4. Men must get more patience to suffer longer, and upon more occasion, 1 Cor. xiii.; 5. We should with all possible care endeavour to increase in knowledge and sense of God's love, for that inflames to the love one of another, Phil. i. 9 ; 6. We must study to be quiet and meddle with our own business, 1 Thes. iv. 11 ; lastly, We must much and often think of our living together in heaven, for the hope of heaven and the love of the saints are companions.

Yet, that we may not mistake, there are divers

sorts of people with whom we may not hold open and professed love, and union, and amity, and society: 1. With such as are open enemies to the truth, by infidelity or idolatry, 1 Cor. vi.; 2. With men that live in notorious wickedness and profaneness, such as are atheists, swearers, drunkards, adulterers, usurers, &c., Ps. xxvi. 5, 6, Eph. v. 6, Phil. iii. 18; 3. With scandalous brethren, that make shows of religion, and yet are lewd in conversation, 1 Cor. v.; 4. With corrupt teachers and seducers, that would draw men from the sincerity that is in Christ, and speak evil of the way of righteousness, Phil. iii. 2; 5. With those members of the synagogue of Satan, whose tongues are set on fire with the fire of hell, in respect of slandering and disgracing such as truly fear God. Rev. ii. 9; 6. With such professors of religion that live idly, and in that respect walk inordinately, and will not be reclaimed, but in that respect live offensively, 2 Thes. iii. 6; 7. With such as openly refuse to obey the sayings and censures of God's servants, 2 Thes. iii. 14–16.

As the knitting together of God's people is wonderful comfortable, and a gracious effect of the gospel, so to disturb the love and unity of the church and people of God is most execrable and abominable. It is a grievous sin to disquiet and disjoin God's servants. Now if we observe in our own times who they are that are disturbers of the church and unity amongst true Christians, we shall find four sorts of men may be justly taxed with this grievous fault: 1. Papists and half-papists; these in all places labour to hinder the progress of the gospel and the unity of the church. 2. Ambitious temporisers, Diotrephes had his hand deep in this sin. Too many there are that scarce know any readier way to cover their damned simoniacal practices, and to advance their own aspiring ends, than to blaze and enlarge, and with bitter exasperations proclaim, that heavy rent and dissent of opinion that hath divided the sons of the same mother. 3. Men of flagitious and wicked life; for wicked men disturb God's church, both by their sins vexing the righteous, and by their railing opposing the truth, and cause God by his judgment to afflict his own Israel. 4. Sectaries and humorous persons, that out of their hellish pride despise all the assemblies of God's people, because they favour not their fantastical projects. These many of them divide from us both in church and habitation.

Thus of the affection itself. But I must more specially yet consider of the manner in the words 'knit together.'

Knit together. The original word, συμβιβασθέντων, when it is taken properly, it signifies to set in a frame of building: but, usually, it is taken in the New Testament in a borrowed sense. Sometimes it is to demonstrate a thing by evident testimony, Acts ix. 22; sometimes to assure, Acts xvi. 10; sometimes to instruct, 1 Cor. ii. 16; but most frequently to knit together as the members are knit in a body, Eph. iv. 16; and so it may well be taken here; and so we are considered as joined together in the mystical body of Christ. And we may hence observe: 1. That our union one with another must be sanctified in one head; if we be not joined to Christ, we do in vain plead our love to men; 2. Our affections must carry us to a thirst and constant desire to procure the good of the body; the body of Christ must be dearer to us than our particular good; 3. That we must respect all that fear God, and not contemn the meanest Christian. We are knit to the whole body, and not to some one member only.

Thus of the second reason, viz., from the effect of the gospel.

And unto all riches of the full assurance of understanding. The third and last reason is taken from the adjuncts of the gospel, which do more and more appear by the power of it in the pains of God's faithful servants. And these are three: 1. Certainty; 2. Sublimity; 3. Perfection. The first is in these words.

The gospel is certain two ways: 1. In itself; 2. In the infallibility and steadfastness of the persuasion of the elect. In itself, the apostle had good reason to say so, for it was no new device, lately broached, but long before from the beginning propounded to God's servants, and confirmed in all ages by the prophets, &c. But in this place it is considered in the certainty of the persuasion of the godly, by faith laying hold upon it and believing it. This he expresseth in the word full assurance, or plerophory. The fulness of a Christian is either general or special. The general is that fulness which every member hath in Christ, their head, and by influence from him;

z

the special is that fulness wherein some members excel. Thus, some are full of the Spirit, Eph. v. 18, of love, 1 Thes. iii. 12, of joy, Rom. xv. 13, 2 Cor. vii. 4; some in obedience and good works, Acts ix. 36, Phil. i. 11, Rev. iii. 1, 2 Cor. x. 6; some in faith and knowledge. So Rom. xv. 14. So here.

Quest. But is full assurance essential unto true faith?

Ans. Some seem to say so, but I see no reason so to think. And experience shows us many worthy in the praises of the gospel, and yet have not gotten full assurance. Full assurance is in the greatest faith, but faith may be true in the least measure, though it be not so confirmed; it is essential to a strong faith, not to a little faith.

Quest. May this plerophory, or full assurance, be had in this life?

Ans. It may without all doubt, as these scriptures evidently prove: 1 Thes. i. 5, Heb. vi. 11, x. 22, Rom. iv. 21.

Quest. But are we bound to labour for this full assurance?

Ans. We are. Heb. x., he saith, 'let us draw near in the full assurance of faith;' and in the sixth chapter they are exhorted to 'shew their diligence unto the full assurance of hope to the end.' We make no question but we ought to make sure our houses and lands, &c., and shall life and happiness lie unassured?

There are seven things wherein this assurance hath been employed: 1. There is a full assurance of the things done by Christ, mentioned Luke i. 1; 2. There is a full assurance required in the knowledge of our liberty in things indifferent; 3. There is a full assurance requisite unto the persuasion of the truth of their ministries to whom we subject our souls, as the original word imports, 2 Tim. iv. 5, 17; 4. We must be fully assured of the doctrine of the religion that we profess; 5. There is a full assurance of the hope of a better life, Heb. vi. 12; 6. There is a full assurance sometimes in special and particular persons, as that to Abraham about his son, Rom. iv. 21; lastly, There is a full assurance of faith in God's favour, upon the warrant of God's word and Spirit. This is chiefly to be laboured for.

Now there are seven properties or signs of a plerophory, or full assurance of faith: 1. It will receive the word in affliction with much joy, 1 Thes. i. 6; 2. It will not be 'carried about with every wind of doctrine,' Eph. iv. 14; 3. It is industrious and laborious in the duties of love to God's children, Heb. vi. 11, 12; 4. It is unrebukable, and full of innocence and integrity of life: it cannot possibly stand with any presumptuous sin, Heb. x. 22, 23; 5. It will give glory to God against all sense and reason, Rom. iv. 20; 6. It mortifies and extinguisheth all headstrong affections, Isa. xi. 7, 9; 7. It is carried with full sails unto holy duties, (for so the word signifies,) and is fruitful in good works; 8. It is able to admonish, Rom. xv. 14.

If we would obtain this plerophory we must be much in hearing and prayer, for they do both exceedingly settle faith; especially we must attend much unto the promises of God, and the testimony of the spirit of adoption; and we must get calm and quiet affections; we must grow in grace, and strive to be strengthened in the inner man. But especially we must beg it often of God by prayer, and strive against hardness of heart and unbelief, carefully discerning and rejecting the objections of Satan and the flesh; consulting daily with such as have the oversight of our souls.

Use. The consideration hereof may both confute the papists, that plead so earnestly against the assurance of faith, and it may serve also to scourge the wanton distempers of carnal protestants, that, against a principle of their own religion, will so commonly disgrace the assurance of faith, by saying men cannot be so certain of their own salvation. And it may excite all that fear God to labour after it, and the rather considering the worth of it, as the word 'riches of full assurance' imports.

Riches of full assurance. There are two sorts of rich men: there is a worldly rich man, and a spiritual rich man. Now our spiritual riches lie: 1. In the word of Christ dwelling in us, Col. iii. 16; 2. In the Spirit of Christ, Titus iii. 6; 3. In works of mercy and liberality, Eph. ii. 4, 2 Cor. viii. 1, ix. 11; 4. In sufferings and patience; 5. In prayers, Rom. x. 11; 6. In good works, 1 Tim. vi. 18; 7. In utterance and all holy knowledge, 1 Cor. i. 5; lastly, It lies in our faith, James ii. 5; and so the more full assurance we have the more rich we are. Now this in general may inform how to conceive of rich men, and who are to be accounted indeed great rich men. And it may lesson worldly rich men not to swell in the thoughts of their greatness, but rather rejoice that God hath made them low; and withal it should teach them to think more highly of poor Christians, that have the true grace of Christ, whom God hath enriched with the faith and holy graces of his Spirit.

Worthily is full assurance of faith called riches, for it doth all that riches can do unto men. It comforts the heart, it defends from dangers, much better than outward riches can, for the just live by their faith. It gains the godly more true reputation than houses, or land, or money could do. It abounds more to spiritual mercy and well-doing with more sufficiency than outward riches can, and it buys for the soul all necessaries. It is unto God's servants according to their faith, and unto faith all things are possible; yea, it doth that that all the riches in the world cannot do, for it will settle a man's heart against all earthly mutations; yea, it will make a man stand undaunted against the rage of tyrants, yea, of death itself; yea, in some sense, it will fence a man against the weapons of God himself; though God kill Job in the battle, yet he will not let go his hold, but he will still trust in him; yea, the Lord is pleased many times to yield the victory to the wrestlings of faith, and accounts it no disparagement to be overcome of the faith of his servants, and to let them bind his hands, that he should not do what otherwise he might and would have done. How can it be but great riches, when it brings a man the assured pardon of all his offences? And how doth it establish the heart of a man in his religion, more than ten thousand arguments or volumes of controversies?

Thus of the adjunct certainty; the sublimity of the gospel follows.

To the acknowledgment of the mystery of God, even the Father, and of Christ. The gospel is a divine mystery, both for the admirable depth of it, for it is a secret only God can reveal, and for the excellency of the subject it entreats of, which is God the Father, and Christ.

How the gospel is a mystery, and to whom, hath been shewed in the former chapters, only let us, from the repetition of it here, be confirmed in this, never to trust to the judgment of carnal persons in matters of godliness and salvation, for they pronounce of things they never effectually understand, they cannot perceive the things of God; and withal we should be excited to a daily care of faith, for reason will not reach here.

Further, we may here observe, that when the Lord doth reveal this mystery unto us, we must not only believe it, but we must acknowledge it, even by an outward profession of our faith in Christ, and our consecration of ourselves to the worship and knowledge of God. The world wonderful hardly brooks acknowledgment; most men ask, What needs this profession? They will not understand that we must bear about, and hold out the light of the truth received, labouring to win glory to God by the power of confession and obedience.

Of God, even the Father, and of Christ. Divers things may be from these words particularly observed.

1. We may see here the glory of the gospel, and the studies of Christians. They have the only excellent subject in the world; other sciences consider of the creature, but theology of the Creator.

2. Here is a plain proof of the divine nature of Christ, for God is said to be the Father of Christ.

3. From coherence we may know, that as men grow in faith and love, so they will be more and more settled in the doctrine of the persons of the Trinity. It is such a mystery as is revealed by degrees, as holiness and other saving knowledges increase in us.

4. That we never rightly know God till we know Christ, Mat. xi. 27, 1 John ii. 23.

5. We may hence observe the misery of all unregenerate men; they neither know God nor Christ aright.

6. That howsoever we be ignorant in many other knowledges, and that of matters of religion too, yet it is glorious riches to know God to be our Father in Christ, and to be fully assured of God's love in Christ.

Ver. 3. *In whom are hid all the treasures of wisdom and knowledge.*

In whom. In quo, is referred either to Christ or the gospel; it is true either way; or rather both are conjoined together in one sense. In Christ, who is the subject of the gospel, is all treasures, &c., or in the gospel, as it entreats of Christ, is all treasures,

&c., so that these words contain a third adjunct of the gospel, and that is singular perfection of wisdom.

Note here with what feeling the apostle speaks, when he falls upon the mention of Christ and the gospel. He abounds in powerful affections and admirations of these things; which may wonderfully abase and humble us, for our barrenness both in thoughts, and affections, and words, when we have to deal with the things that belong to the kingdom of God.

Again, if there be any such treasures in Christ and the gospel, we may conclude it is not in vain to devote ourselves to the knowledge of Christ in the gospel, though it cost us never so much pains, or care, or cost, and though we be never so much opposed by the flesh and the world.

Further, we need not doubt but that all things needful to salvation and happiness are contained in the word. Here are treasures of wisdom and knowledge; we need no traditions nor inventions of men, nor decrees of popes, &c.

The ubiquitaries abuse this place to prove a real communication of the properties of the divine nature to the human. Now, for answer to their cavil, divers things may be propounded:

1. If the words be understood of the gospel, then their conceit wholly falls to the ground. 2. If they be understood of Christ, yet there is no necessity to understand them as these treasures are in Christ himself only, but as they are in his members by communication. 3. If as it is in him, yet it is not necessary to understand it of all knowledge in general, but of that which is needful for the salvation of the elect. 4. If of all knowledge, yet the apostle saith not that it is in the soul of Christ, but in Christ. 5. If in the soul, what wisdom? not increate and infinite, but created wisdom.

Thus in general.

In whom. Wisdom and knowledge are in Christ, in angels, in men; but indifferently:[1] in Christ by union; in angels by vision; in men by revelation. There are divers gifts conferred upon the human nature of Christ, the gift of personal union, the gift of office of mediator, and head of the church, the gift of adoration, with his divine nature, and the gifts they call habitual, which above the measure of men or angels are conferred upon him.

[1] Qu. 'differently'?—ED.

Which may comfort us against all our defects in ourselves, for though we have so many wants, yet we have a head in whom we have all fulness; and it should be our course to make use of this doctrine, by stirring up ourselves daily to lay hold upon Christ for the supply of our wants out of the riches of his grace.

Are hidden. The admirable excellencies of wisdom and knowledge in Christ are said to be hidden: 1. In respect of our apprehensions, because we can never reach to the depth of them. 2. In respect of the cross that followed Christ and his members; for the cross, like a veil, obscured the glory of Christ's perfections, both in himself and the communication of his gifts to his members.

And may not this teach us singleness of heart and humility, even more to seek to be good than to seem to be so? Christ was contented his treasures should be hidden, and shall we fret ourselves when our drops of grace are not admired? shall it not be enough to us that we shall appear in glory when his glory shall be revealed?

All treasures. Wisdom and knowledge in Christ is called treasures, not for the quantity only, but for the worth also, for grace and knowledge are the best treasures.

Which may shew the misery of all wicked persons, for inasmuch as they are not of Christ, they are destitute of the treasures of God; and contrariwise, they are most happy that have Christ, for in him they find all true treasure and riches, he cannot be poor that hath Christ, nor can he be rich that wants Christ.

Quest. But what is the cause that so many Christians want treasures, and yet profess Christ?

Ans. Either they want workmen to dig for the mine, through want of preachers; or else they dig for this treasure in a wrong earth, by seeking it, but not in the scriptures; or else men know not the mine when they find it; or else they let the earth fall upon their work after they have begun, through negligence in slightly working in their entrance.

Of knowledge and wisdom. The different terms may note but the same knowledge in Christ, but for our capacities varied; it is true that there is in Christ a most admirable perfection, both of the knowledge of contemplation, and of the wisdom and direction of working and practice; and thus it was in him in his own obedience, and is still by participation to his members, to make them wise and discreet, as well as full of understanding and judgment; sure it is that Christ would be rich unto us in the gift of holy discretion, as well as in the gift of holy understanding, if we would seek it of him, for he is 'made unto us of God wisdom,' 1 Cor. i. 30; neither can true wisdom be found in any men under the sun that have not the true grace of Christ; neither can any Christian he found without the grounds of heavenly wisdom; such wisdom, I mean, as none of the wisest men in the world could ever attain; for though it be true that there may be and are many deficiencies in such as otherwise truly fear God, yet if the best wisdom be inquired after, the meanest and simplest Christian doth exceed the greatest and exactest politician or disputer of this world. For what wisdom can it be for a man to have exceeding skill to know the secrets of nature, or the order of civil affairs, or the ways to advance his own outward estate, and yet know no certain and safe way how to save his own soul?

Ver. 4. *And this I say, lest any should beguile you with enticing words.*

Whereas the Colossians might ask why the apostle is so large in urging them to constancy, he shews in this verse that it is to prevent the enticements of seducers.

1. It is the duty of every minister to labour by all possible means to preserve his people, that they be not beguiled. It is not enough to teach them true doctrine; but they must be watchful, that neither Satan nor evil men infect and corrupt them.

2. It is the usual practice of the devil, when the word hath wrought with any power in any place, to essay by all means to draw away and deceive the minds of the people. Let men look to themselves, and not live securely, for certainly the devil will attempt them with all cunning and fraud.

3. If these words be compared with the apostle's exhortation in the 23d verse of the former chapter, it will appear manifestly that one reason why many are deceived is their unsettledness in the doctrine of faith and hope. If they had been established in their assurance of God's favour in Christ, and the hope brought by the gospel, they could not have been so deceived and beguiled, or not so easily.

4. The way by which men are in points of religion deceived, is not by apparent falsehoods, but by probabilities of truth. The apostle calls them paralogisms of pithanology, $\~{\iota}\nu\alpha$ $\mu\eta\tau\iota\varsigma$ $\upsilon\mu\~{\alpha}\varsigma$ $\pi\alpha\rho\alpha\lambda o\gamma\iota\zeta\eta\tau\alpha\iota$ $\dot{\epsilon}\nu$ $\pi\iota\theta\alpha\nu o\lambda o\gamma\iota\alpha$. *Pithanology,* which the apostle condemns, is a speech fitted of purpose, by the abuse of rhetoric, to entice, and, by tickling the affections of men, to please and seduce. And herein properly lies the abuses of logic or rhetoric in matters of divinity, when, out of affection and some subtle purpose to deceive, vain and false arguments are varnished and coloured over, and made probable to the minds of the simple; yea, though the matter taught be sometimes truth, yet many minds are beguiled from the power and profit of it, by placing their respects and affections upon the wisdom of the words, and the affected artificial frame; otherwise there is singular use both of logic and rhetoric, when they are applied to set out the wisdom of God in his word, upholding the hidden depths of the power of the word of God. The very preaching of the gospel is exceeding effectual when without affectation men use their art to express the native force and life of the words of the Holy Ghost in scripture; but the chief thing in general, is for us hence to learn, that heresy and error was never so unclothed but it was presented to the world with great colours and probabilities. Many simple people wonder that papists or Brownists should be able to say so much for their idolatry or schism; but we must know, that any heretics that ever were have brought great probabilities for their heresies as well as they. The devil were wonderful simple if he should think to bewitch men so far as to believe with any confidence things that had manifest appearance of falsehood; that cannot be. Thus in general.

Now, in particular, concerning the corrupting or deceiving of the souls of men, we may consider three things: 1. The miserable estate of the soul that is deceived, or beguiled, or corrupted; 2. How the soul is corrupted; 3. The means to prevent it.

1. For the first, look what the carcase is when it is putrefied; such is the soul when it is corrupted. It is spiritually loathsome, and wonderfully unpleasing unto God, and cast out of his sight; and the more

is the misery of such souls, because to plead that they were deceived will not serve turn. We may deceive or be deceived, but God will not be mocked.

2. For the second, if we ask by whom or how the soul is deceived or corrupted, it is to be answered, generally, we must take notice of it to beware. The two great deceivers are the devil and antichrist, 2 Cor. xi. 3, 2 Thes. ii. It is true that by the malice of Satan and frowardness of wicked men, God's faithful servants are everywhere called deceivers, 2 Cor. vi. They that most labour to preserve men's souls from corrupting are most charged with seducing; but these are so called, and are not.

The most ordinary deceivers are: 1. Carnal friends; 2. The profits and pleasures of life; 3. Evil company,—this corrupts like leaven; 4. Carnal reason; 5. Sin, Heb. iii. 13; 6. But especially corrupt and false teachers, Jer. xxiii. 14, Ezek. xiii. 10, Micah iii. 5, Gal. v. 9.

3. Thirdly, If we would not be beguiled and deceived, we must look to three things: 1. We must get a steadfast faith in Jesus Christ. Plerophory or full assurance of God's favour is a wonderful preservative against corruption of doctrine or life. 2. We must constantly cleave to the means, unto which God hath given testimony by the power of his presence and blessing. We should get under the shelter of a powerful ministry, and this will be a rock of defence. 3. We must preserve uprightness of life, and our care of innocency in what we know to be required; contrariwise, so long as we are unsettled, and want assurance, especially if we live not under the power of the word, we are in continual danger to be drawn away. And so it is with us too, if we fall into the love of any sin of knowledge; for corruption of life is many times scourged with corruption of doctrine and opinions.

But if we would have more abundant caution for our preservation, then I will follow the similitude of beguiling amongst men, from whence by comparison we may learn many things for our caution and observation.

Men that would thrive in their estates, and would not be beguiled in the world or wronged, observe most an end these rules: 1. They will buy such things as are durable, not toys or trifles; so should we, we should set our hearts upon eternal things, and not mind earthly things, which will last but for a short time; and when death comes, if we trust upon earthly things, we shall find ourselves deceived. 2. They will know their commodities themselves that they sell or buy; so should we, both for the sins we would part with, and the opinions or duties we would purchase. 3. They will know the persons with whom they deal; so should we try the spirits. 4. They will have all the security may be had; so should we see all warranted by the scriptures, for other security we cannot have put in that is sufficient, if the devil, or the world, or corrupt teachers tempt and entice us; we must put them to it, to put us in security from the scriptures, which because they cannot do, we must wisely reject them. 5. Men that deal for much are glad to seek the protection of great men; so should we seek the protection of the great God. 6. If men doubt in anything about their estate, they will presently consult with their friends, and in difficult cases they will have opinions of lawyers too; so should we do if we would have our states safe; we must propound doubts one to another, especially to our teachers, that they may resolve us out of the word of God.

Ver. 5. *For though I be absent in the flesh, yet am I with you in the spirit, rejoicing and beholding your order, and the steadfastness of your faith in Christ.*

These words depend upon the former, as the answer of two objections: first, They might say, How doth he know our estates? To which he answers, in the first words, that though it were true that he were absent in respect of the flesh, yet it was also true that he was present in the spirit, both in that his affection carried him to a daily thought of them, and so to a willingness upon all occasions to take notice of their estate; and besides, as some think, he was acquainted with their estate extraordinarily, by revelation of the Spirit. And thus also he secretly gives them notice to look to their ways; for he takes notice of all that passed amongst them. How careful should we be in all our courses, as well as they! for we have the Spirit of God in us, and the people of God round about us. Here also ministers may take notice of their duties: their spirits should cleave to their people, and their daily thoughts and cares should run upon them; they should still observe them, and watch over them in the Lord.

Object. 2. But, might some one say, is it charity in the apostle, being thus absent, to entertain surmises and hard thoughts of us, as if we were falling away, &c.? Now to this he answers, that though he wrote this to exhort them and to warn them, yet he did greatly rejoice to know so much as he did of their order of life, and steadfastness of faith. Many are so diseased, that they think if a man reprove them or admonish them, that then he hates them altogether, and likes nothing in them; but the apostle, to prevent that, acknowledgeth the praise of their life and faith. A holy mind can rejoice in the good things of those he warneth or reproveth.

Your order. Order hath original in God, he is the God of order, 1 Cor. xiv. 33, as all disorder and confusion is of the devil. Order is that wonderfully commends whatsoever it is in. There is a kind of seed of order sown in the creatures. This order in man is their eutaxy, or well disposing of themselves.

The apostle might commend their order generally, both in relation to the commonwealth, and to the church, and in their families, as also in their particular conversation.

That there might be order in commonwealths, God hath set man in authority, (for by him kings reign and have their power,) Prov. viii., Rom. xiii.; and hath communicated a part of the honour of his own divine laws to their civil laws, viz., that they should bind men's consciences so far as they are not disagreeing from his word. Besides, he hath recorded threatenings against the disobedient, and acknowledgeth magistrates to bear his image, to be as it were gods by representation, and he guides them by his Spirit for the time, many times qualifying them with gifts, and guiding their mouths in judgment, (for a divine sentence is in the mouth of a king,) yea, he himself drew a platform of rules for commonweals, to give them a taste of government.

Now that men may attain to this eutaxy and good order in commonweals, they must read the law of God, and let that be a general guide to them, and they must propound sanctity as well as felicity, as the end of their government; and in calling to office, they must be careful not to set the feet where the head should be, but to choose men that fear God and hate covetousness, and are men of courage. The fear of God and courage is wonderfully wanting in all sorts of magistrates. And as for courage in respect of the people, what are they the better if they have a good man that will do no good, than if they had evil men that would do no evil? Yet in truth, magistrates, whether good or evil men, do much evil by suffering evil to be unpunished. But to return to the point, magistrates that would preserve order, must give good example themselves, and mend the disorders of their own households, and bring such a sympathy and love of the people, as they should both preserve their authority, and yet remember that they rule their brethren. And in their government, they cannot observe order, unless they punish vice, as well as command or provide for virtue and wealth. Besides, they must take away the persons or places that are occasions of disorder, and they must charge and remunerate, as well as punish. Finally, the people out of the obligation of conscience, must strive to live in order, with reverence and fear, yielding ready obedience and furtherance to those that are placed in authority over them.

There is order also in the church; and thus there is order in doctrine; for milk must be propounded before strong meat, or with sufficient reference to the parties to be taught. There is order also to be observed in the time, places, and manner of celebration of God's worship. There is order also to be respected in the use of things ecclesiastically indifferent. There is order in the subordination of persons in the ministry, some to rule, some to teach, some to exhort, some to distribute. There is order also to be observed in the discipline of the church, proceeding by degrees with offenders, so long as they are curable.

Neither may our families be without order; order, I say, not only in the duties that concern the maintenance of the family, but also in the exercises that concern religion and the service of God in the family. In families there must be a care also of reformation, especially that openly profane persons, only for temporal advantage, be not retained or admitted there. In the family also, there must be a daily exercise of patience, humility, knowledge, and all other Christian graces that concern mutual edification. What should I say? There is a mutual relation in all the members of the family one to another, and the discharge of their several duties one to another is charged with a daily care of order.

But I think the apostle commends the order of holy life, unto which every Christian is bound. It is certain we can never soundly proceed in godliness without a care of a settled frame and order of living. We may not live at a venture in religion. It is not enough to do good now or then, by flashes. There is an order in holy conversation. We must walk by rule, Gal. vi. 16. There is a holy disposing of our ways required, Ps. 1. ult. It is required of us that we should ponder the paths of our feet, Prov. iv. 26. We must order our affairs with discretion, Ps. cxii. 5; this is called the way of prudence or understanding. There is a guiding of our feet unto the ways of peace, Luke i. 79. It is a wonderful curse to be left to our security, to walk in dark and uncertain ways; and contrariwise the vision of the salvation of God, is promised to such as dispose of their ways aright, Ps. 1. ult. And to be careful of an orderly course of life, is to keep our souls, Prov. xix. 16, and peace shall be unto such. But alas! men have corrupted their ways, and their understandings are darkened, and they are strangers from the life of God; neither will men cease from their rebellious ways. The civillest men walk after the way of their own hearts, yea, the most men hate those that are right in their ways, and are like Dan, that would bite the heels of such as endeavour to walk in sincerity. Some hypocrites there are that will know the way of the Lord, and ask of him the ordinance of justice, as if they would be careful to please God; but alas, they were never washed from their old sins, and they quickly return with the dog to their vomit, and corrupt their ways, being of purpose set on by the devil to make a clamorous profession, that so their fall might more dishonour the glory of an exact and circumspect conversation. Alas! what should I say? There is wonderful want of order in the very lives of God's children. Scarce the tithe of professors in sincerity of the gospel that have gathered a catalogue of holy duties, and observed out of the word that frame and order of settled holy conversation.

There are ten helps of order in holy life: 1. Knowledge; 2. Uprightness, that is, an unfeigned resolution to shew respect to all God's commandments; 3. Constant diligence; 4. Watchfulness; 5. Contemplation or meditation; 6. Prayer; 7. Reading the word daily; 8. Frequent hearing of the gospel preached in the power of it; 9. A tender conscience; 10. Society and fellowship with gracious Christians in the gospel.

There are many impediments of an orderly conversation: 1. Men are not reconciled to God, and so not being in Christ they receive not influence of grace from Christ to enable them to walk in a holy course. 2. In others it is negligent mortification; the stain of former sins being not washed away, there remains in them an ill disposition to sin. 3. Many are ensnared with evil opinions, either in doctrine, (and so error of life is the scourge of error in opinion,) or else about practice, as that such strictness is not required, or it is impossible, or none do live so. 4. Many know not what order to appoint unto themselves. 5. Many are confirmed in a heart accustomed to evil, and they love some one sin, wherein especially they break order. 6. Satan strives above all things to keep men in a dead sleep, that they might not awake to live righteously, or express the power of godliness. 7. Many are so set in the way of the ungodly, that their very evil society chains them down to a necessity of dissoluteness. 8. Many are put out of all order by their daily distempers and disorders in their families. Lastly, Some fail and fall through very discouragement, received either from opposition, or contempt, or scandal.

Now, if any be desirous to know in general what he should do to bring his life into order, I shall profitably advise four things: first, That he do resolutely withdraw himself from the sins of the times, and keep himself unspotted of the world in respect of them. Now the sins of the times are apparent: pride of life, contempt of the gospel, coldness in faith and religion, swearing, profanation of the holy Sabbath, domestical irreligion, contention, usury, whoredom, drunkenness, and drinking, oppression, and speaking evil of the good way; secondly, That he observe the more usual corruptions of the calling of life he lives in, and with all heedfulness shun them, whether he be magistrate, minister, or private person; thirdly, That he especially strive against and subdue the evils that by nature he is most prone unto; fourthly, He shall do wonderfully profitably, if he would get a catalogue of duties out of the whole law that directly concern himself in particular, which is very easy (especially by the help of some that are experienced) to be distinctly gathered, labouring to shew all good faithfulness in duties of piety as well as righteousness, and to strive for inward piety as well as outward, resolving to continue as well as once to begin. Hence it is, if we mark it, that the Holy Ghost, in divers scriptures, draws to keep the people of those times divers catalogues, either of grace which specially tended to their praise, or of duties that most fitted their state, or of sins that they must most carefully avoid, as being most commonly committed; yea, it could not but be of excellent use, if we did task ourselves to the more strict observation of some of those catalogues, either of grace, or sins, or duties, as we might perceive they most fitted us.

But if ever we would go about the order of our lives, we must in general: 1. Labour to weaken the love of earthly things; 2. We must resolve to keep our hearts with all diligence,—I mean we must with all care and conscience strive against inward sins; 3. We must put on a mind to live by faith whatsoever befall us; 4. If we fall we would speedily recover ourselves by confession and prayer, and not accustom ourselves to sins either of omission or commission.

Uses. Upon the consideration of all this, what should we do, but even pray the Lord that he would make his way plain before our face, Ps. v. 8, and direct the works of our hands, Ps. xc. *ult.*, and hold up our goings in his paths, Ps. xvii. 5, that our steps do not slide. And to this end we should every one be piecing and amending his ways. making his paths straight, being ashamed and confounded for all the disorder of our lives past. But if thou go about this, be not δίψυχος, a man that hath two hearts, for then thou wilt be unstable in all thy ways; either go about it with all thy heart, or else let it alone. What shall I say but this, let us all learn the way of God more perfectly.

Thus of order.

The second thing he commends is their faith, which he praiseth for the steadfastness of it.

The steadfastness of their faith. Concerning steadfastness of faith, I propound five things to be considered of: 1. That it may be had, and ought to be sought; 2. What the nature and properties of it are; 3. What is the cause why the faith of many is not steadfast; 4. What we must do to attain it; and, lastly, Concerning unsteadfast faith.

1. For the first, That it may be had is manifest; for God, that giveth the earnest of his Spirit, and sealeth and anointeth us in Christ, doth stablish us in him, 2 Cor. i. 21, 22. There is a sure foundation of God, 2 Tim. ii. 19, Mat. vii. 24, upon which we may found our alliance. And God, 'willing more abundantly to shew unto the heirs of promise the immutability of his counsel, interposed himself by an oath to confirm his promise, that by two immutable things, in which it was impossible for God to lie, we might have strong consolation, which flee for refuge to lay hold upon the hope set before us; which hope we have as an anchor of the soul both sure and steadfast,' Heb. vi. 17, 18. And we are commanded to resist steadfast in the faith, 1 Pet. v. 9. And wavering is secretly threatened and disgraced by the apostle James, after he had charged that we should pray in faith without wavering, James i. 6.

2. Now, for the second, There are many excellent properties and praises in a steadfast faith; for a man that is indeed settled and steadfast in his faith knows both the truth and the worth of the love of Christ, Eph. iii. 17-19; he is able to contemn and deny the allurements, examples, customs, and glory of this world, 1 John v. 4, Gal. vi. 14; he can bear adversity with singular firmness of heart, without hasting to evil means, Rom. v. 4, Isa. xxvi. 16, or limiting God for the manner, or time, or instruments of deliverance; he can stand in the combat against frequent and fiery tentations, and go away without prevailing infection; he can believe without feelings, Rom. iv. The promises of God are not yea and nay, 2 Cor. i. 18, 19, but always a sure word and undoubted. He hath a kind of habitual peace and contentment in his conscience, with easeful delights and refreshing in the joys of God's favour. He hath a kind of spiritual boldness and confidence when he approacheth to God and the throne of his grace. Lastly, He can look upon death and judgment with desire to be dissolved.

3. And for the third thing, The reasons why many

men shew not this unmovableness, and steadfastness, are divers; some have not faith at all, 2 Thes. iii. 2; some have not a true justifying faith, but either rest upon common hope, or a historical or temporary faith. In many the presumption of certainty doth hinder steadfastness itself. Some want powerful means that should establish them; and some, having the public means, are justly blasted in their faith because of their daily neglect of the private means. And this reason may be given also why some of the better sort are not yet established, namely, because they are so hardly excited and persuaded seriously to try their own estates by the signs of God's favour and marks of salvation. And for the worser sort they shun trial, because they know beforehand their state is not good, and besides they live in some one master sin or other, which they cannot be persuaded to forsake, and therefore resolve at least for a time to live at a venture, and refer all to the unknown mercy of God.

4. If we would be established in believing: 1. We must be much in the meditation of the promises of God; 2. We must be much in prayer, and the acknowledgment of secret sins, observing the comforts of God's presence, and keeping a record of the wonders of his presence, and striving to retain constantly the assurance we sometimes feel in prayer; 3. We must cast about how to be more profitable in welldoing. An orderly life, especially fruitfulness in our places, doth marvellously, though secretly, establish and settle a man's heart in faith, 1 Cor. xv. 58, whereas it is almost impossible that a barren life should have much steadfastness of assurance. Again, would we yet further know how it comes to pass that some men get such a steadfastness above many others? Observe, then, and you shall find, that when they find the pearls of grace, and the means, they will sell all to buy them. Now the love to the means is like death or jealousy, that cannot be resisted; there is in them a constant coveting of the best things, with a true hunger and thirst after them; and if they offend God, they cannot be quiet till they return and confess their sin and get favour. They will not live days and weeks in a voluntary neglect of communion with God, and therefore reap this unmovableness as the fruit of their daily conversing with God.

Thus of steadfastness in itself.

5. Now, in the contrary, concerning an unsteadfast faith, I propound two things to be considered: 1. The effects or consequences, and concomitants of it; and then the kinds of unsettled faith.

Not scripture only, but usual experience, shew the many inconveniences that attend such as are not stablished in the faith.

1. They want the many comforts the steadfast faith feeleth; 2. They are disquieted with every cross; 3. They are tossed with the wind of contrary doctrine, yea, the very truth is sometimes yea with them and sometimes nay; sometimes they are persuaded and sometimes they are not; 4. They find a secret shunning of the ordinances of God when any approach should be made unto God; 5. The fear of death is almost inseparable; 6. They are sometimes frighted with fears of perseverance, besides their daily danger to be foiled by the baits of Satan and the world.

Unsteadfastness may be considered three ways: 1. As faith is weak; 2. As faith is weakened; 3. As steadfastness is lost.

For the first, in the first conversion of a man unto God, while they lie yet in the cradle of godliness, they are assailed with much doubting and many fears, &c.

Quest. But what, might some one say, How can faith then be discerned in the midst of so many doubts and fears?

Ans. The truth of their faith and grace appears: 1. By their earnest and constant desire of God's favour; 2. By the tenderness of the conscience in all their actions, and their daily fear of sinning; 3. By their frequent complaints of unbelief and secret mourning for it; 4. By the lowliness of their carriage, even towards the meaner sort of those that truly fear God; 5. By their desire after the sincere milk of the word; lastly, By their endeavour to walk inoffensively.

Quest. But seeing their faith is true, what is the cause of the unsettledness of it?

Ans. They are unsettled, partly because they have yet but a small measure of saving knowledge, and partly because they discern not the consolations offered to them, and partly for want of application of particular promises that belong unto them; and sometimes it is for want of some of the means, and in some it is because they see a greater power in some of their corruptions than they think can stand with true grace.

Now, for the remedies of this unsettledness: This weak faith will grow settled more and more if they continue upright in the use of the means; especially as their reformation and victory over sin increaseth, and as they grow more and more confirmed in the divorce from the world and carnal company, and they grow more expert in the word of righteousness, especially after the Lord hath refreshed them with the frequent comforts of his promises and presence, besides conversing with the faithful and established Christians. And all this the sooner, if they do propound their doubts, and by asking the way seek daily direction, especially if they resign over their souls to the ministry of some faithful and merciful man of God, who as a nurse shall daily feed them with distinct and particular counsel and comfort.

Thus of the unsteadfastness that accompanieth faith weak.

Now there is an unsteadfastness accompanieth faith weakened, that is such a faith as was sometimes stronger. For the clearer understanding hereof, I consider three things: 1. The causes of this weakness of faith; 2. The signs to discern it; 3. The remedies.

There may be divers causes or means to weaken strong faith: 1. Loss of means; 2. Secret sins ordinarily committed, not lamented nor reformed; 3. Presumptuously to use ill means to get out of adversity; 4. Relapse to the love of the world.

The signs to discern it are: 1. The sleepiness of the heart; 2. Fear of death; 3. Constant neglect or secret contempt of fellowship with the godly; 4. The ceasing of the sensible working of God's Spirit within; 5. Reigning discontentment; 6. Security under known sin.

The remedies are: 1. A serious and sound examination of the wants and faults which by this weakness they are fallen into; 2. A constant and daily judging of themselves for their corruptions till they recover tenderness of heart, and some measure of godly sorrow for them; 3. It will be expedient that they plant themselves under the droppings of a daily powerful ministry; 4. The meditation of their former feelings; 5. The use of the sacrament of the Lord's supper—this is a means to confirm faith both weak and weakened; lastly, They must hold a most strict watch over their hearts and lives till they be established in a sound course of reformed life.

Thus of faith weakened.

3. Steadfastness may be lost; note that I say steadfastness of faith may be lost; I say not that faith may be lost, that is true faith. This steadfastness was lost in David, Solomon, and it is likely in Job too.

The causes of this loss of steadfastness are divers: in some it is the inundation of afflictions, violently and irresistibly breaking in upon them, especially raising the fierce perturbation of impatience; thus it was in Job. 2. In some it is some horrible sin; I say horrible sin, either because it is some foul transgression, as in David and Solomon, or made horrible by long continuance in it.

Now into this evil estate some fall suddenly, some by degrees; commonly it begins at spiritual pride, and proceeds after from the careless use of the means to the neglect of them, and from thence to a secure disregard of the inward daily corruptions of the heart, joined with a bold presumption of some unfolded mercy of God, till at length they fall into some special sin or wilful relapse.

The effects and concomitants of this relapse and loss of steadfastness are divers and fearful, as: 1. The ceasing of the comforts of the Spirit, the Spirit being asleep and in a manner quenched; 2. The heart is excommunicated from the power of God's ordinances, as they may feel when they come to use them; 3. Spiritual boldness or encouragement to come unto God is lost with it; 4. They are secretly delivered to Satan, to be whipped and buffeted with tentations, many times of blasphemy or atheism, or otherwise through his spiritual wickedness held in internal vassalage; 5. Most an end the outward providence of God is changed towards them, yea, sometimes they are scourged with horrible crosses; 6. Many times they are given over to be punished with other sins.

Yet for the more full understanding hereof, it will be profitable to consider of some distinctions, both of the persons, and the cause, and the effects. For of these that fall from their steadfastness some are sensible of it, some are insensible. Those that have their hearts wakened after this loss, do usually feel a strong conflict of terrors, the conscience being wearied with the tortures that their wounded spirit is tormented withal under the sense of God's fierce anger, and in many of these their terror is renewed upon every cross, yea, almost at every word of God, so doth the conceit of God's fighting against them prevail with them.

Now, in the insensible, the special effect is a spiritual slumber or lethargy, with the rest of the ill effects before in common propounded.

Secondly, A distinction must be made of the cause, for the sin is sometimes secret, sometimes open. Now the consequents or fruits of open falling by open sin is divers. Usually 'the fall thereof is great;' it makes a wonderful noise in the church; besides, it wounds the hearts of God's children, and breeds exceeding great distaste in them. Further, their falls make them wonderful vile before the world; the mouth of every beast will be open to rail against them; wicked men will keep the assize for them; yea, the banks of blasphemy in wicked men will be broken down, so as they will with full mouth speak evil of the good way of God. Besides, it cannot be avoided but many will be defiled by it, and wonderfully fired and confirmed in sinning.

Again, we must distinguish of effects or consequents, for some are ordinary, some extraordinary; for sometimes, besides the ordinary events, the Lord scourgeth those falls with satanical molestations, either of their persons or houses, yea, sometimes they are smitten with death.

1. *Quest.* But do all these come always for sin?

Ans. Not always; but where sin is presumptuous they do.

2. *Quest.* But do all these things befall all such as fall into presumptuous sins?

Ans. The judgments of God are like a great depth, and he afflicts how he will; but these are his rods; he may use all of them, or any of them, as pleaseth him.

3. *Quest.* But are these things found in those that lose their steadfastness by the violence of crosses?

Ans. Though many of them are, when the cross hath a mixture with any special impatience, as in Job's case; yet properly they are rods for presumptuous sins.

Object. But is it not better, may some say, to continue as we are, than to acknowledge and make profession, and be in this danger to fall into so evil an estate?

Sol. Is it best to live and die a beggar because some one great heir, through his own default, hath ruined for a time his house? Or is the condition of a beggar better than of a prince, because Nebuchadnezzar was seven years like a beast?

4. *Quest.* But if his losses be thus many and miserable, is there anything left in him?

Ans. There is: 1. His seed abides in him, the holy seed of the word can never be rooted out of him wholly; 2. He hath faith, though it be in a trance; 3. Grace is alive in him, though he be in the state of a palsied man, or as one that hath a dead palsy, and yet is alive; 4. He hath the Spirit of God in him, but he is locked up and taken prisoner.

Now, for the remedies of this loss of steadfastness, they must know that there is required of them a special humiliation; note that I say a special humiliation; for they must in private afflict their souls before the view of their special sins and God's fierce wrath, with strong cries and sighs unspeakable making their moan before God: they must 'cry unto God out of the deep,' as the psalmist saith. Besides, they must shame themselves openly by making themselves vile before the people of God; so did David, and Solomon, and Paul: yea, they must voluntarily resign over themselves unto God's scourging hand, being so desirous to be cleansed of their sins as to be contented God should wash them thoroughly, though it were with many crosses. And further, they must be revenged of their own flesh, by straitening and curbing themselves in their lawful desires and delights. Thus of their special humiliation. Now, secondly, They must take special pains to recover their faith in God, and to get pardon of their sins. They must cry daily unto God, they must search again and again in the records of God's promises, especially waiting upon the preaching of the gospel, to see when the Lord will return and have mercy, by reviving of their hearts with the comforts of his presence. And for this they must be wonderful careful of the Spirit of grace, to stir it up by daily prayer, and to observe with all watchfulness the stirring of it, resolving with all thankfulness to acknowledge any measure of the reviving of the Spirit.

Lastly, When they are in any measure recovered, they must look to two things: 1. They must forsake all appearance of evil; 2. They must use a continual watchfulness, and, with fear and jealousy, look to their hearts, even in their best actions, lest Satan beguile them, and they revolt again, and then their case of residuation be worse than the former: 'Blessed is the man that feareth always.'

Thus of the loss of steadfastness, especially as it is in the curable; for there is a loss of steadfastness, and the joy of God's salvation, even in the elect, which in this life is incurable. Of this I can say little, because the scripture is in this point exceeding sparing, and because the judgments of God, especially of this kind, are exceeding deep. Who can wade into them? Only a word or two of it. This loss is incurable two ways; sometimes in the cross or judgment it brought upon the offender, sometimes in the unsteadfastness itself; for sometimes, though the Lord restore inward joy and assurance, yet he will not remove the outward sign of his wrath; sometimes he draws back the outward affliction, but doth not restore the inward comfort, or not in so great a measure; so as some of God's children may die without the sense of the joy of God's salvation till they come to heaven; yea, they may die in great terror and despair: yet the Lord may be reconciled, and they may truly repent, though these terrors or judgments be not released; because God many times will thereby purge the public scandal and clear his own justice. Besides, such spectacles do give warning to a careless world, to let them know that God hath treasures of wrath for sin if they repent not. Thus of the doctrine of steadfastness of faith, and unsteadfastness also; now briefly for some uses of it.

Uses. It may serve for great reproof of the great neglect of seeking this steadfastness of faith. We may complain as well of the common protestant as of the papists herein, for they are alike adversaries to the assurance of faith. Let such as are touched with fear of God and desire to believe travail more and more for attainment hereof, and to this end cleave to the sure word of the prophets and apostles, and labour in the practice and exercise of all holy and Christian graces.

And for particular consideration of the troubles and losses of God's children, we may note: 1. That it is a wonderful fearful thing to fall into God's hands, and that the promises of God yield no protection to a willing offender. Woe unto profane beasts! If sin make God angry towards his own children, and make them also vile before men, then where shall those beasts that wallow in sin appear? If they be justly abased that fall once into one sin, what shall be the confusion of face and heart in those men, when all the sins they ever committed shall be revealed before God's angels and men at the last day? 2. They that stand have great reason to take heed lest they 'fall from their steadfastness,' and be 'carried away with the error of the wicked,' Ps. lvi. 9, and cxvi. 7. 3. We should be wonderful thankful if God hath kept us from falling; it is his singular grace to 'keep the feet of his saints.'

Ver. 6. *As ye have therefore received Christ Jesus the Lord, so walk ye in him;*

Ver. 7. *Rooted and built up in him, and stablished in the faith, as ye have been taught, abounding with thanksgiving.*

In these two verses the apostle concludes the exhortation begun in the twenty-third verse of the former chapter; for whereas after all these reasons, and the answer of sundry objections, they might finally have said, tell us then at once what it is you would have us to do? The apostle answers summarily, that concerning holy life, he would have them walk as they have received the Lord Jesus Christ; and concerning faith, he would have them to be rooted and soundly edified and established in the faith, especially to abound in thankfulness to God for their happy estate in Christ Jesus.

The sixth verse contains a precept concerning holy life, viz., to walk on in Christ, and a rule by which that precept is to be squared and determined, viz., as they have received Christ Jesus the Lord.

As ye have received Christ Jesus the Lord, &c.

These words may be diversely urged upon them, according to the divers senses may be conceived of them. For:

1. To walk as we have received Christ, may bear this sense, namely, to frame our obedience according to the measure of the knowledge of Christ we have received; it shall be to us according to what we have. To whom God hath given much, of them he requireth much; and judgment certainly abideth for him that hath received the knowledge of his Master's will and doeth it not. If our practice be according to the knowledge we have, this may be our comfort, God will accept of us; and otherwise they are but in a miserable case that are barren and unfruitful in the knowledge of our Lord Jesus Christ, 2 Pet. i. 9.

2. Such a sense as this may be gathered, viz., so live with care of a godly life, as ye neglect not to preserve the doctrine concerning Christ ye have received. Certainly it ought to be the care of every godly mind to do his best to preserve the purity of the doctrine he received together with Jesus Christ; great is the general neglect of many sorts of people herein.

3. Or thus: Let the doctrine you have received from Christ Jesus be your only rule both for life and manners; so live and walk as you have received. The apostle commandeth to 'separate from every brother that walketh inordinately, and not after the traditions which they had received of the apostle,' 2 Thes. iii. 6. By tradition he meaneth the holy word of God delivered by lively voice unto the churches while yet it was not written, even the same which now is written. The elect lady and her children are commended for 'walking in the truth, as they had received commandment of the Father,' 2 John 4. Yea, so must we stick unto the word received, as if any man teach otherwise he should be 'accounted accursed,' Gal. i. 9, 1 Cor. xv. 1, 2. For the apostles received it 'not of men, but by the revelation of Jesus Christ,' Gal. i. 12; and as they have 'received of the Lord, so have they delivered' unto us, 1 Cor. xi. 23. Therefore we must conclude with the apostle, 'These things which we have learned and received, and heard out of the holy word, those things we must do,' Phil. iv. 9.

4. The sense may be thus: As ye were affected when ye first received Christ, so walk on and continue. At first men receive Christ with singleness of heart, with great estimation of the truth, with wonderful joy, with fervent love to God's children, with a longing desire after spiritual things, with endeavour to bear fruit, and without the mixture of men's traditions and inventions.

Now then they are exhorted to take heed that they 'lose not what they have wrought,' 2 John 9, but preserve those holy affections and desires still; striving against the witchcrafts of Satan and the world, that they be 'not beguiled from the simplicity that is in Christ Jesus.'

The doctrines hence to be noted are:

1. That Christians do receive Christ, and that not only publicly into their countries and churches, —which yet is a great privilege, for Christ bringeth with him many blessings, and stays many judgments, brings a public light to men that sit in darkness and shadow of death, and raiseth immortality as it were to light and life again,—but privately, and particularly into their hearts and souls. This is the happiest receiving of Christ, Phil. iii. 9. Oh, the glory of a Christian in receiving Christ! for he that receiveth Christ into his heart, receiveth excellent illumination, unspeakable joy, 1 Pet. i. 8, sure atonement, Rom. v. 11, and iii. 25, hid manna, Rev. ii. 17, eternal graces, 1 Cor. i. 6, and iv. 7, yea, the very Spirit of Christ, Rom. viii. 9, to make him know the things given of God, to set the soul at liberty, 2 Cor. iii. 17, to mortify the deeds of the flesh, Rom. viii. 13, to be a spirit of prayer, Zech. xii. 12, to give answer concerning our adoption, Rom. viii. 15, to furnish the soul with gifts, Gal. v. 22, to seal us up to the day of our redemption, Eph. i. 14, to be an eternal comforter, John xiv., to be life for righteousness' sake, Rom. viii. 10, to help our infirmities, Rom. viii. 26, and to raise up our dead bodies at the last day, Rom. viii. 11. Lastly, He that receiveth Christ, receiveth with him the promise of an eternal inheritance, Heb. ix. 15, into which he is presently acknowledged an heir, yea, a co-heir with Christ Jesus, Rom. viii. 17.

2. The second doctrine. It is not enough to receive Christ, but we must walk in him. To walk in Christ is not only so to live as we be sure that Christ liveth in us, Gal. ii. 20, or to walk after the appointment of his will expressed in his word, but

it is chiefly to continue a daily care of holy perseverance in the graces and duties of holy life, holding fast our communion with Christ; this the apostle thinks wonderful needful to be often urged and pressed by all means upon us, so shamefully do many fall away, and so cursedly is the sincerity that is in Christ Jesus pursued by the devil, and the flesh, and the world, and so necessary is the endeavour to preserve the glory of perseverance in all well-doing to the end. Oh, this perseverance, it is a wonderful thing! and where is the man that doth not lose something of what he had? Oh that we could be soundly awakened to the care of it, or that we had minds that would be willing to do anything we could to further it! but alas! there is not a heart in us; there are divers excellent directions in the word to confirm us herein, if we were not overcome with sluggishness.

There are divers things which, if they were looked to at our first setting out, we were sure to hold out and continue walking in Christ. As:

1. If men did at first put their hearts to these questions of abnegation, so as they would be thoroughly advised, if thou hadst asked thine own heart these questions: Canst thou take up thy cross and follow Christ? Canst thou suffer adversity with the righteous? Canst thou profess Christ amidst the different opinions of multitudes of men? Canst thou be content to deny profit and reason, and thy desires, and pleasures, and credit, and all for Christ's sake? If not, thou wilt certainly fall away, and therefore better never begin.

2. At men's first setting out they must take heed they be not slightly in their reformation and mortification; but do it thoroughly, not sparing to afflict their souls with sensible and sound godly sorrow; for else they will afterward repent of their repentance; whereas if it were done with sound advice and serious humiliation, this would be an unmovable foundation of rest and encouragement to faith and well-doing. It is a great question whether such will hold out, that come in without sorrow for sins.

3. Men must at first look to their kind of faith. We see many are grossly deceived. Temporary faith maketh such a show, that unless it be thoroughly tried, it will deceive many; and there is a marvellous loathness in our nature to abide the trial, though we know it be plainly here required, 2 Cor. xiii. 5; whereas if we did get a continuing faith at first, we might have the more assurance of holding out.

4. It would much further perseverance if we did at first endeavour that knowledge and affection might be inseparable twins; not to be much proud of knowledge without affection, nor to trust much to zeal without knowledge: either of these may be alone in men that will fall away shamefully.

5. When men go about reformation they should do it thoroughly, and be sure their hearts are renewed; for the old heart will not hold out long to endure the hardship of a reformed life; and if some sins have been favoured and spared, though they lie still for a time, yet afterwards they will revive and shew themselves. We see in some what ado there is to leave some corruptions and faults; they are seven years many times before they can be persuaded to forget them, resting in the reformation of other faults; whereas there is no assurance that they walk with a right foot in the gospel, till they make conscience of a ready reformation of every known sin; and till they reform thoroughly they are like to fall away, whatsoever fair show of zeal and forwardness they make.

6. In particular, divers men are to be warned of passion and violent affections. If thou mean to prosper in thy persuasion of reformation, then speedily 'cease from anger, and leave off wrath,' else there will be little hope that thou wilt not rereturn 'to do evil,' Ps. xxxvii. 8, 9; the promise of constant protection is with such as are sheep, John x. 28, and are so far humbled as they have left their wolfish qualities and passions.

7. To make thy standing more sure, acquaint thyself with such as fear God, and join thyself to them by all engagements of a profitable fellowship in the gospel. There is a secret tie unto constancy in the communion of saints, Jer. xxxii. 39, 40. He is not like to walk long that walketh alone, especially if he might walk with good company; and this is a clear mark of temporary faith in such as for many things go far, when men see they shun society with the godly.

8. It is an excellent help, also, at first to strive by

all means to get the testimony of Jesus confirmed in us, 1 Cor. i. 6, 1 Tim. ii. 6. Christ gives testimony especially three ways: 1. By the promise of the word; 2. By the graces of his Spirit; 3. By the witness of the spirit of adoption. Now if we did study the promises diligently, especially recording such as we had interest in upon our conversion to God, and did withal try ourselves diligently and particularly concerning those saving graces which are marks and signs of regeneration and salvation, and did also beg the witness of the Spirit, waiting for those unspeakable and glorious joys of the Holy Ghost, and with all thankfulness acknowledging God's seal for our confirmation, when he is pleased so to set it to, methinks this threefold cord could never be broken. Oh, the heavy slumber and sluggishness of our natures! How wonderful 'rich is God in compassion!' How ready is he to forgive and 'multiply pardon!' How willingly doth he 'lift up the light of his countenance' upon us! and yet men have not the heart answerably to wait upon him, or to be at the labour of this confirmation. How are many, that seem somewhat unto many,—how are they, I say, bewitched with security, so as they cannot be fired out of it, but live at a venture, and neither seek nor esteem the testimony of Jesus.

9. Would we be set in a safe condition, and stablished? Then we must strive for a free spirit, remembering David's prayer, 'stablish me with thy free spirit,' Ps. li. 12. Now, if any ask what a free and ingenuous spirit is, I answer: 1. It is a mind that will not be in bondage to the corruptions of the times; it acknowledgeth no such bonds or relations to any as to sin for their sakes. 2. It is a mind that apprehends liberty in Christ; a mind that will not be in bondage to legal perfection, but discerns his release from the rigour and curse of the law; it will not be subject neither to a corrupt conscience, nor yet to a conscience erring or over-busy, but sees his prerogatives he enjoys in Christ, either in the hope of glory, or sense of grace, or use of outward things, or his liberty in things indifferent. There is a kind of servileness or spirit of bondage in many, that wonderfully holds them down, and if they be not better lightened of their daily fears and burdens, the flesh will lighten itself by rebellion and apostasy. 3. It is a mind not chained down to the love of or lust after earthly things. 4. It is a mind ready pressed to do good, full of incitations to good things, and careful to preserve itself from the occasions of evil; as resolved to stand upon the sincerity of his heart, as rather to lose his life than his integrity; as neither caring for those things which the common sort seek after,—as praise, profits, outward shows, &c., nor fearing their fears.

10. Men must at first labour to get a sound and hearty love of the truth, desirous to store and furnish themselves with the treasures of holy knowledge. If the law be written in the hearts and bowels of men, Jer. xxxi. 33, Ps. xxxvii. 31, they will hold out to the end.

Lastly, Men must be sure that they be good and true in their hearts, Ps. cxxv. 1, 2, 4. as the psalmist saith, for then they shall be 'as the Mount Sion that cannot be moved,' and the Lord will always do well unto them.

Now the signs of a good and true heart are such as these: 1. A true heart is a new heart; that must be taken for granted, else in vain to inquire any further, if there be not a newness of the heart to God; 2. It loves God with unfeigned and undivided love; though it cannot accomplish all it would, yet it hath holy desires, without hypocrisy, after God above all things; 3. It labours for inward holiness as well as outward, both seeking the graces that should be within, and mourning for inward sins as well as outward; 4. It will smite for small sins, as well for numbering the people as for murder and whoredom; he hath not a good and true heart that is vexed only for great evils and offences; 5. A true heart is a constant heart, it is not fickle and mutable, as many are in all their ways, but that it is once it desires to be always; 6. It desireth the power of godliness more than the show of it, and is more affected with the praise of God than of men; 7. It quickly finds the absence of Christ, and cannot be at rest till he return; 8. It constantly pronounceth evil of sin and sinners, and well of godliness and good men.

Now, on the other side, the reason why many fall away, was because they were not true in their hearts at first; they set up a profession of repentance, with carnal ends, and through hypocrisy beguiled themselves and others.

Secondly, If men find that they have been rightly

formed in the womb and birth of their change, then there are other directions for them to observe throughout their lives, that they might continue in this holy walking with God and his saints. Wouldest thou be sure not to fall away? Then look to these things.

1. Be sure thou continue in the careful use of the means: as the word, prayer, conference, and sacraments; else know that when once thou givest way to a customary hardness of heart in the use of the means, or neglect of them, thou art near either some great sin or temptation, or some great judgment and apostasy; and therefore, concerning the means, principally look to two things: 1. Preserve appetite; 2. Practise that thou hearest without omission or delay.

2. If thou discern any spiritual weakness or decay, or feel any combat with the flesh, or the temptations of Satan, be sure thou complain betimes and resist at the first, for then the grace of God will be sufficient, and the weapons of our warfare mighty through God; prayer will easily master sin at the first through the victory in Jesus Christ.

3. Resolve with thyself not to let go thy assurance, or cast away the confidence of thy hope, whatsoever befall thee, Heb. x. 35; or at least, not till thou mayest see wonderful evident reason. It is a marvellous great fault to call the love of God into question upon every occasion, whereas men cannot glorify God more than to live by faith, and to be immovable in it; God takes little delight in a soul that will withdraw itself upon every occasion by unbelief. Are they not strangely foolish that will wear their helmets when there is no stir, and as soon as they see an adversary, or any blows towards, then to cast away their helmets and do it so usually? Such are we and worse that stand bragging of our faith and hope in prosperity and ease, and when affliction and temptation comes, then most childishly we cast away both faith and hope, and till reason and sense are satisfied we will not be persuaded.

4. Set perfection before thine eyes to strive after it, Phil. iii.; and to this end acquaint thyself with the rules of holy life, and consider the examples of such as have walked therein, and the woeful events that befall the contrary-minded, especially think much of the great recompense of reward, even the price of our high calling in Jesus Christ.

5. Take heed of the occasions of falling, such as are spiritual pride, known hypocrisy, desire to be rich, discord with the godly, and vain janglings without discretion, neglect of our particular callings, and ungodly company.

Hitherto of perseverance in life. Now in the next verse he entreateth of perseverance in faith.

Ver. 7. *Rooted and built up in him, and stablished in the faith, as ye have been taught.*

In these words is both a precept and a rule; a precept to be rooted, built, stablished; a rule, as ye have been taught. The substance of the precept is but to counsel them to increase more and more that they might be steadfast in the assurance of God's favour in Jesus Christ. Of this steadfastness I have at large entreated in the fifth verse. Only we may here again be instructed and informed.

1. Of the necessity and excellency of steadfastness. The apostle would not thus often peal upon it, but that he knew it to be of singular worth in the life of man, and of great necessity unto our consolation; besides, it implies that people are, for the most part, slow-hearted herein, and hardly drawn to the unfeigned and diligent labour after the establishing of their faith and assurance.

2. That all this steadfastness of assurance is not the work of a day; a great tree is not grown or rooted but successively; a great house is not built all at once; we must be every day adding something to God's work, that the building of grace may be in due time finished; none are so established but they may grow in faith; none have such great roots but they may take root yet more; many men strive hard to make their trees shew in branches and leaves—I mean in outward profession in the world— but alas! what should this great bulk, and so many branches and leaves do, unless there were more roots within? Yea, many dear children of God mistake wonderfully; they every day carry together heaps of precepts for life, but alas! poor souls, so great a building will not stand unless they lay their foundation sure—I mean that they get their faith in Christ —the only sure foundation—more confirmed and established.

As ye have been taught. Note here the apostle's candour. He doth not arrogate the glory of their establishment to himself, but sendeth them to their minister, and teacheth them to depend upon him, to wait upon the blessing of God upon his labour, and to acknowledge the good they have, to have been received by his ministry.

Here divers things may be noted:

1. That the people should labour for a reverent estimation of the doctrine they receive from their faithful teachers.

2. That as faith cometh by hearing, so doth the establishment of faith also.

3. That it is wonderful dangerous to neglect either the charge of our teachers when they urge us to assurance, or the rules by which they guide us out of the word of God for the attainment of it; if we would go about it when our teachers call upon us, the Lord would be with his ordinance to bless it to us; we should be afraid to delay, when we are taught how to confirm our souls in faith and grace.

4. That faithful ministers do greatly labour to establish their hearers in the assurance of God's favour, and the duties of holy life.

Abounding therein with thanksgiving. In these words the apostle shuts up all, wherein his intent is to stir them up to thankfulness, that as they did thrive in the mean or matter of faith and holy life, so they should glorify God by all possible thankfulness for it; as he would have them abound in faith and holiness, so also in thankfulness to God. This may wonderfully smite our hearts; for if we observe our wretched evil dispositions, we may find that we are wonderfully bent to the very habit of unthankfulness; and therefore it is just with God many times that we do no more thrive in victory over our corruptions, or in the power of divers graces, or in the progress of duties, because we do not more tenderly and constantly acknowledge the goodness of God we have had experience of. Oh that it were written upon our hearts, and graven deep in our memories, that nothing becomes us more than to abound in thankfulness, no fairer sight than to see the altar of the Lord covered with the calves of our lips! Never can the estate of a child of God be such but he hath exceeding great cause of thankfulness for his happiness in Christ.

Ver. 8. *Beware lest there be any man that spoil you through philosophy and vain deceit, through the traditions of men, according to the rudiments of the world, and not after Christ.*

Hitherto of the exhortation. From this verse to the end of this chapter is contained the dehortation, wherein the apostle labours to dissuade the Colossians from receiving any corrupt doctrine, or any vain observations, either borrowed from philosophy, or from human traditions, or from the abrogated law of Moses.

The dehortation hath three parts:

1. He setteth down the matter from which he doth dehort, ver. 8.

2. He gives seven reasons to strengthen the dehortation, to ver. 16.

3. He concludes against the things from which he dehorts, and that severally, from ver. 16 to the end.

In this verse he dehorts from three things:

1. From philosophy,—that is, doctrines taken out of the books of philosophers not agreeing to the word of God, which, though it had a show of wisdom, yet indeed was but very deceit.

2. From traditions,—that is, observations, and external rites, and vain superstitions concerning either ordinary life or else God's service, devised by men, whether learned or unlearned, and imposed as necessary upon the consciences of men.

3. From the elements of the world,—that is, from the ceremonies of Moses, now abrogated, and so from Judaism.

In general, we see in the church of God men must bear the words of dehortation as well as of exhortation. Men are in a strange case that love to eat poison, and yet cannot abide to receive any antidote.

Again, from the coherence we may note that the best way to be sound against the hurt of corrupt doctrines or traditions is so to cleave to the doctrine of the gospel as we grow settled in the assurance of faith, and experienced in the way of a holy life. He cannot be hurt that minds holiness and assurance.

Beware. When we find these caveats in the scriptures, we must think of them as more than bare notes of attention, for they shew some great evil or deceivings; and withal, it imports that we of ourselves are inclinable to fall,—as in this place this *beware* imports that men naturally are inclined to falsehood more than truth, to evil more than good, to wise men more than the wise God, to traditions more than the written word, to their own devices more than God's precepts, to false teachers more than the true apostles, to ceremonies more than the weighty things of the law.

Any man. See here the vanity and levity of man's nature. Many men, either by word or example, cannot reduce unto order or unto truth, yet any man may seduce unto sin and error. All sorts of men may be fountains of evil; but in case of returning, an obstinate sinner or superstitious person is usually wiser than seven men that can give a reason.

Spoil you. This word is various in signification; it signifieth, as some take it, to make bare, or to prey upon, or to circumvent, or to deceive, or to drive away as a prey, or to lead away bond and captive, or as here, to spoil; it is so to seduce or to carry away as a spoil. For the matter expressed in this word we may note:

1. That a Christian stands in danger of a combat, and if he look not to himself may be spoiled and carried captive; for the word seems to be a military word, and so imports a battle.

2. That there are worse losses may befall us than the loss of goods or children. A man is never worse spoiled than when his soul suffers spiritual losses. Job's losses by the Sabeans was great, yet theirs were greater (1.) That lost the good seed sown in their hearts, Mat. xiii.; (2.) That had those things taken away that sometimes they had in spiritual things, Mat. xiii.; (3.) That lost their first love. Rev. ii.; (4.) That lost the kingdom of God in losing the means of the kingdom, Mat. xxi.; (5.) That lost what they had wrought, 2 John 10; (6.) That lost the presence of God, Hosea v. 15; (7.) That lost uprightness and sincerity; (8.) That lost the taste of the powers of the life to come, Heb. vi.; (9.) That lost the joys of their salvation, Ps. li.; and lastly, Much more theirs that lose their crown, Rev. iii. 11.

3. We may here see that corrupt opinions mar all and spoil the soul, and make it into a miserable prey to evil men and angels.

4. That matters that seem small things and trifles may spoil the soul, and bring it into a miserable bondage, such as those traditions might seem to be.

You. This word noteth the persons spoiled, and so gives us occasion to observe two things:

1. That we may be in the sheepfold of Christ and yet not be safe. You, yea, you Christians. The devil can fetch booties even out of the temple of Christ.

2. When he saith you, not yours, it shews that howsoever it be true that most an end false teachers seek theirs, not them,—that is, seek gain, not the souls of the people; yet it sometimes falls out that even the most dangerous and damned seducers may be free from seeking great things for themselves. It is not any justification to the popish priests, nor proof of the goodness of their cause, that they can deny their own preferments and liberty on earth to win proselytes to their religion. There have always been some even in the worst professions of men that have at least seemed outwardly to care for nothing but the souls of the people.

Through philosophy. This is the first kind of corruption here condemned.

Quest. But is philosophy naught and here rejected?

Ans. It is not simply condemned, but in some respects, namely, as it doth not contain itself within its bounds, or is not to the glory of God, or as it is 'vain deceit.' So that vain deceit may be here added interpretatively; it explains the sense.

Quest. But how became philosophy to be vain deceit?

Ans. It is vain deceit four ways: 1. When it propoundeth and teacheth devilish things, as the philosophy of the pagans did; as in their magics, when they taught the divers kinds of soothsayings, conjurings, casting of nativities, and a great part of judicial astrology. 2. When the *placets* and opinions of philosophers that are false are justified as true; as their doctrine of the world's eternity, or the soul's mortality, or the worship of angels, or their Stoical fate and destiny, or their wild opinions about the chief good. 3. When the principles of philosophy, that in the ordinary course of nature are in themselves true, are abused to deny things propounded in the gospel above nature: as those maxims,

'That of nothing nothing is made,' and 'That of a privation to a habit there is no regression,' and 'That a virgin cannot conceive.' The first is brought against the creation of God, whereas it is true of the second cause only; so the second is brought against the resurrection, whereas it is true only in the ordinary course of nature. 4. When the truest and best things in philosophy are urged as necessary to salvation, and imposed as meet to be joined with the gospel.

Philosophy may yet be used, so as she be content to be a servant, not a mistress. If, when God's word reveals anything absurd in her, that then she will humble herself, and acknowledge her blindness, and be admonished by divine light. And, on the other side, men may be corrupted with philosophy, and that divers ways: 1. If men use any part of philosophy that is devilish, as too many do; 2. If men neglect the study of the scriptures, and spend their time only in those human studies; 3. When men measure all doctrine by human reason and philosophical positions; 4. When men depend not upon God, but upon second causes; 5. When men strive to yoke men's consciences with the plausible words of men's wisdom. Hence, also, we may note that false doctrine may be supported with great appearance of wisdom and learning, as was the corruption of those false teachers. We may not think that papists are fools, and can say nothing for their religion; but if the Lord should let us fall into their hands to try us, we must expect from divers of them great shows of learning and colours of truth.

Thus of philosophy.

After the traditions of men. The word 'tradition' hath been used three ways: Sometimes to express the doctrine of God's servants by authority from God, delivered to the church by lively voice, but afterwards committed to scripture; so the doctrine of Christ and the apostles, and of the patriarchs before the law, was first delivered by tradition. Sometimes to signify such opinions as are in scripture, but not expressed; they are there, but not spoken therein,—that is, are drawn but by consequence or impliedly. Sometimes to express such observations as were never anyway written in the word, but altogether unwritten in the scripture, as being devised merely by men. So it is taken ordinarily, and so traditions are to be condemned.

There is another distinction about traditions, and that is this: 1. Some things are founded upon scripture, and did always tend to further godliness, and are therefore apostolical, and to be observed; as all the doctrines of the word, and the public assemblies of prayer and preaching; 2. Some things were founded in scripture, and were sometimes profitable, but now are out of all needful use, and therefore, though they be apostolical, yet they bind not, as the tradition of abstaining from things sacrificed to idols, and strangled, and blood; 3. Some things have not foundation in the word, yet may further piety if used without superstition, and therefore not unlawful, as the observation of the feast of the nativity of Christ, and such like; 4. Some things have no foundation in scripture, nor do at all further piety, but are either light or unnecessary, or repugnant to the word: those are simply unlawful.

Traditions were both in the church of the Jews, and in the churches of the Gentiles; the Jewish traditions were called the traditions of the elders, not because they were enjoined them by their Sanhedrim, or college of elders, but because they were brought in by their fathers after the captivity, the most of them after the rising of the sect of the pharisees. For among them was that distinction of the law written, and the law by word of mouth; this law by word of mouth is the cabalistical theology, a divinity so greatly in request amongst the pharisees; but how well our Saviour Christ liked those traditions may appear, Mat. xv.

The traditions in the churches of the Gentiles, may be considered two ways: 1. As they were in the times of the primitive church; 2. As they were in the times after, under antichrist.

In the primitive church they had by degrees, one after another, a great number of traditions, such as these—to stand and pray every Sabbath, from Easter to Whitsuntide; the sign of the cross; to pray towards the east; the anointing of the baptized with oil; the canonical hours; Lent and divers kinds of fasts; the mixing of water with wine; the addition of divers orders in the church, as canons, exorcists, ostiaries; holidays, &c.; to sing hallelujah at Easter, but not in Lent, and such like.

Now, if any ask what we are to think of those and the like traditions then in use, I answer: 1.

That the church had power to appoint traditions in indifferent rites, so that the rules of the apostles for indifferent things were observed, as that they were not offensive, nor against order, or decency, or edification,—as to appoint the time and place of public prayer, to set down the form of it, to tell how often the sacraments should be administered, &c.

2. We must understand that the word 'traditions' used by the fathers did not always signify these and such like things devised by men, but sometimes they did mean thereby such things as were warranted by scripture, though not expressly,—as the baptizing of infants, the observation of the Sabbath, &c.

3. There were some traditions in some churches, in the first hundred years, that were directly impious,—as the invocation of saints and images.

4. Some other things were then used that were not every way impious in their own nature, and yet not greatly justifiable in their use, and such were divers of the afore-named observations.

5. That divers things at the first brought into the church with good intent and to good purpose afterwards grew into abuse,—as, for example, in the primitive order of monks.

6. The worser traditions were brought in by false teachers, and too pertinaciously observed by the people, the fathers bewailing it, and sometimes complaining of it.

7. The fathers themselves in some things shewed levity and unconstancy of judgment; sometimes, to please the people, approving things; and again, sometimes standing upon the sole perfection of the scriptures.

Lastly, It cannot well be denied but that the liberty taken in the primitive times to bring in traditions opened a door to antichrist.

Now, concerning the traditions in popery under antichrist, their doctrine is abominable, for they say that the word of God is either written or unwritten; and they say their unwritten verities are necessary as well as scripture; yea, that they are of equal authority with scripture. And those traditions they would thus exalt are, for number, many; for nature, childish, unprofitable, impious, and idolatrous. But that we may be fully settled against their impious doctrine of traditions, we may profitably record in our memories these scriptures, Deut.

xii. 32, Rev. xxii. 18, Mat. xv. 1, Pet. i. 18, Gal. i. 9, Isa. viii. 20, 2 Tim. iii. 16, Jer. xix. 5, Col. i. 28, Luke xvi. 29, 1 Cor. i. 5-7.

Object. 1. But our Saviour told his disciples, 'I have many things to say unto you, but ye cannot bear them now; but the Spirit, when he is come, shall lead you into all truth,' John xvi. 12, 13. *Ergo*, it seems there are divers truths of Christ which were not revealed in scripture, but by the Spirit uttered by tradition after.

Sol. This may be understood of the gifts of the apostles, and of the effects thereof, and not of doctrine; for of doctrine he had said in the chapter before, 'All things that I have heard of my Father, I have made known unto you,' John xv. 15. 2. If it were understood of doctrine, yet he doth not promise to lead them into any new truths, but into the old, and those Christ had already opened, which should be brought to their mind, and they made more fully to understand them. For so he saith of the Comforter, in the 14th chapter, 'He shall teach you all things, and bring all things to your remembrance, whatsoever I have said unto you,' John xiv. 26. 3. Be it he had not revealed all as yet, what, did he therefore never reveal it? Why, the very text is against it, for he said, 'I have yet many things to say unto you,' John xvi. 12; therefore he did say them, namely, after his resurrection, Acts i. 3. 4. Let it be noted that he saith, 'Ye cannot bear them now;' the things he had to say they could not then bear; why should we think that they could not then bear these grave traditions, as the anointing and christening of bells and such like? Lastly, Let them prove it to us that those toys are the things Christ promised to reveal, and then they say somewhat.

Object. 2. But in the 20th of John, he saith, 'There were many things which were not written which Jesus did.'

Ans. He saith that 'the things which are written are to this end written, that we might believe, and believing, might have eternal life,' John xxi. 25, xx. 30; so that what is needful to faith and eternal life is written. 2. He saith there were other things not written; he saith other things, not things differing from these; other things in number, not in substance or nature, much less contrary things.

Object. 3. But the Thessalonians are charged to 'hold the traditions they had been taught.'

Sol. The scriptures were not then all written. 2. The apostle understands not traditions as the papists do. For in the same place he calleth the things written in scripture traditions, as well as those that were not yet written.

To conclude this discourse concerning traditions, we must further understand that the traditions in any church, though they be things indifferent in their own nature, become unlawful if they be such as be taxed in these eight rules.

1. If they be contrary to the rules of the apostles concerning such things ecclesiastically indifferent; 2. If they be urged and used with superstition; 3. Or as any parts of God's worship; 4. Or with opinion of merit; 5. Or as necessary to salvation; 6. Or if they be equalled with the law of God, or the weighty things of the law neglected, and those more urged; 7. If they be light and childish; lastly, If by their multitude they darken and obscure the glory of Christ in his ordinances. Thus of the second thing.

The third thing from which he doth dehort is the rudiments of the world.

The rudiments of the world. By the 'rudiments of the world,' he meaneth the laws of Moses, especially concerning meats, washings, holidays, garments, and such like ceremonial observations.

Those laws were called 'rudiments' or 'elements,' as some think, because the Jews and false apostles held them as needful as the four elements of the world; or else because in their first institution they did signify the most choice and fundamental principles of the gospel, that were necessary for all to know that would be saved; but it is most likely they are called so by a grammatical relation to the abcedaries, that as little children begin at the alphabet, and so go on to higher studies, so did the Lord give those laws as the A B C of the Jews to be their pedagogue in the infancy of the church.

Now they might be said to be 'of the world,' because they were external rites, and subject to the sight and sense; and because they consisted of a glory that was more worldly than spiritual, and because worldly men do most stand upon that which is external.

It is the drift of the apostle to dissuade from the observation of those rites, because now the law of Moses was abrogated. Abrogation is a plausible doctrine in popular estates. Proclamation concerning immunities from tributes and taxations, or concerning isonomy,—that is, indifferent liberty for all to be competitors for honours or free for profits of a commonwealth, those were wont to be wonderful grateful to the multitude. And such is the doctrine of abrogation in divinity; yet because it may be abused by epicures, it is to be more carefully opened.

The law may be said to be abrogated divers ways: 1. When it is antiquated or obsolete, so as men are neither bound to duty nor punishment, and thus the ceremonies are abrogated; 2. When the punishment is changed, only the obedience still remaining in force, as in the law of stealth; 3. It is abrogated to the guilty, when the punishment is transferred on another, so as the law cannot exercise her force upon the guilty person; 4. It is abrogated when it is weakened and enervated by transgressors. To break the law is to loose or dissolve the law. Thus wicked men by their lives abrogate it.

Quest. But is the whole law of Moses abrogated?

Ans. No; for though Moses be said to give place to Christ, that doth not import a change of the law, but of the lawgiver. Moses gave three kinds of laws, moral, judicial, ceremonial.

For the moral law, it may in some sort be said to be abrogated as: 1. In respect of the curse and malediction, as it did work anger, and made execrable; for so 'there is no condemnation to them which are in Christ Jesus,' Rom. viii. 1, 2. Inasmuch as 'the law of the spirit of life hath freed them from the law of sin and death.' 2. In respect of the inexorable rigour and perfection of it; for we are 'not now under the law, but under grace,' Rom. vi. 14. 3. In some sense it is abrogated in respect of justification; for now it is no more required of the godly that they should seek justification by the law, but by Jesus Christ. Again, we must distinguish of the persons; for the law still lieth on the neck of the unregenerate, but in the former respects is abrogated to the faithful; for 'against them there is no law,' Gal. v. 23; but the law is given to the unrighteous, 1 Tim. i. 9.

Now, for the judicial laws of Moses, they were, as it were, civil laws, concerning magistrates, inheritance, order, and process of judgments, contracts, marriage, bondage, divorce, vows, usury, and trespass between man and man.

These judicial laws must be considered two ways: 1. As they bind the Jews as they were men,—that is, in a common and general right; and so those laws are perpetual in the nature and equity of them. 2. As they bound the Jews as they were Jews in a personal, national, or singular right; and thus where the reason of a law is particular, there the law is so, and binds not other people, but as it may fit their commonwealths.

The ceremonial laws did concern sacrifices, and sacraments, and other holy things, and ritual observations. Divines have a saying, that the judicials are dead, but the ceremonials are deadly. That the ceremonies are abrogated was signified by the rending of the veil of the temple: yea, the temple itself is destroyed, as will more fully appear when I come to the 15th verse.

And thus of the rudiments of the world. Hitherunto also of the matter of the dehortation. The reasons follow.

And not after Christ. These words contain the first reason against philosophy, traditions, and ceremonies. They are not after Christ, and therefore to be avoided, lest our souls be spoiled. These things were not after Christ: 1. Because they no way tended to the furtherance of heaven and reconciliation with God, which in Christ we should principally look to. 2. Because they were no way warranted, or approved, or commanded by Christ. Christ, when he came, imposed no such things. 3. Because they do now no way lead us after Christ, but from him rather, inasmuch as we rest in those things done, and neglect the commandment of God. Lastly, They feed the humours of carnal men, and draw away men's minds from the spiritual worship of God in Christ.

Hence we may note an answer to that question, Whether the Gentiles may not be saved without Christ by philosophy? The apostle determines that the soul is spoiled by philosophy, if it be not after Christ.

Again, hence we may learn a note of trial concerning the truth of religions. That religion which is not after Christ is a false religion; for this is a foundation, that everlasting happiness must be expected from Christ alone.

Lastly, Here we may note that sins against Christ will be accounted for, though they were not forbidden in the moral law. We have now another law in the gospel, so as whatsoever is not after Christ is a great transgression; neither may we think that we sin not against Christ but only by traditions and ceremonies; for there are many other ways of offending against him,—as, to live without Christ and communion with him, Eph. ii. 12; to be an enemy to the cross of Christ, Phil. iii. 18; to make the doctrine of redemption an occasion of liberty to the flesh, 1 Pet. ii. 16; to live after the lusts of men, and not after the will of Christ, 1 Pet. iv. 1, 2; to harden our hearts against the doctrine of reconciliation, 2 Cor. v. 20; to hold false opinions concerning the person or office of Christ; to pervert the gospel of Jesus Christ, Gal. i. 7; to persecute or despite Christ in his members; to trust in the merit of our own works, Rom. x. 3, 4; to deny him before men, Mat. x. 33; to reproach the servants of Christ, Heb. xi. 26; not to believe the report of his messengers, Isa. liii. 1, Rom. x. 16; not to imitate his graces, Mat. xi. 29; to offend one of Christ's little ones, Mark ix. 42; to make division or schism, 1 Cor. i. 12; not to discern his body in the sacrament, 1 Cor. xi. 28; to build again things destroyed, Gal. ii. 17-19; to break our vows, 1 Tim. v. 11, 12; to fall away from the doctrine of Christ, 2 John 9; to grieve the Spirit of Christ, Eph. iv. 30; to be beguiled from the simplicity that is in Christ Jesus, 2 Cor. xi. 3; to cast away their confidence, Heb. x.; or to fashion ourselves to the lusts of our ignorance, 1 Pet. i. 14.

Thus of the first reason.

Ver. 9. *For in him dwelleth all the fulness of the godhead bodily.*

These words contain the second reason; and it stands thus: If in Christ there be all divine fulness and sufficiency, then there needs no supply from human inventions, either for doctrine, or worship, or manners; but in Christ there dwells all fulness, even from the ocean of all perfection; and therefore, let no man spoil you through philosophy, traditions, or ceremonies, &c.

For the explication of the minor, we may conceive of the words of the text thus: There is in Christ all fulness of wisdom as the prophet of the church, therefore there needs no philosophy; 2. There is all fulness of merit in Christ's satisfaction as priest of the church, therefore there needs no expiating ceremonies; 3. There is all fulness of power and efficacy in Christ as king of the church, therefore there is no need that we should help him with inventing traditions to uphold the lives or godliness of Christians, or any way to further the ordinances of Christ.

This verse contains in itself an excellent proposition concerning Christ, viz., that the godhead is in the body,—that is, in the human nature of Christ; and this is amplified: 1. By the manner of presence, he 'dwelleth' there; 2. By the measure, in all 'fulness.'

The word 'corporally' hath been diversely interpreted. 'Corporally,' that is, truly and indeed. 'Corporally,' that is, not in show or shadow only, but completely, in comparison of the shadows of the law or prefiguring signs. He dwelleth not in Christ as he did in the temple. 'Corporally,' that is, according to flesh. 'Corporally,' in respect of the manner of his presence, not as he is in all creatures by efficacy or power; nor as he is in the saints by his grace; nor as he is in the blessed by glory, but corporally,—that is, by union with the person of the Word. But I think it is safest and plainest to take it in the third sense, viz., corporally,—that is, in his human nature.

Christ is commended in the praise of his relation: 1. To the godhead, in this verse; 2. To saints and angels, ver. 10.

'In him' notes his person; 'godhead' expresseth his divine nature; 'corporally' imports his human nature; and 'dwells' tells us of the union of the natures.

The sum of all is, that inasmuch as the Lord hath saved us by so wonderful salvation in Christ, and in that our Saviour was true God as well as man, as being the second person in Trinity, therefore we should wholly rest upon him, and not distract our thoughts, or faith, or services with either philosophy, or traditions, or ceremonies, as supposing that our salvation should be anyways furthered by those. Now, in that the Holy Ghost is so careful to teach the divinity of Christ, we should also learn to be affected with the wisdom of God that hath designed the second person in the Trinity to be our Mediator. Think of it often, and weigh with yourself the glory of God's wisdom herein. Who is fitter to restore the world than he that made it? John i. 1, Col. i. 15. Incarnation is a mission: now it was not fit he should be sent by another, that was not of another; as the Father was not. It is wonderful suitable that the natural Son should make sons by adoption, John i. 11. Who fitter to restore the image of the Father lost in us than he that was the eternal image of the Father? Col. i. 15, Heb. i. 3. Who was fitter to break open the fountain of God's love than he that was the Son of his love? Col. i. 13. The personal Word became the enunciative Word to declare unto us his Father's nature and will: he that is the middle person in the Trinity is fittest to be the middle man or mediator between God and man.

Is our Saviour God then? Then he is eternal, Rev. i. 7; omnipresent, Mat. xxviii. 21; omniscient, Rev. ii. 23; and omnipotent, Phil. iii. 21.

The consideration of the divinity of Christ may and ought wonderfully to comfort us against the greatness of our sins and God's wrath, remembering that the Lord Jehovah is he that is our righteousness, Jer. xxiii. 6, Mat. i. 21, and justification from all our sins; as also against the greatness of the enemies and adversaries of our souls, and the truth or true grace of Christ in us. Our Saviour is the mighty God, Isa. ix. 6, 7, and therefore can and will easily subdue all our enemies under our feet: besides, hereby we are assured of the supply of all our wants, seeing he that hath all the fulness of God in him hath undertaken to fill all things in the church, Eph. i. 23. And as this may comfort, so it should instruct: why should we not come 'willingly at the time of assembly,' Ps. cxx. 3, seeing we serve the God of heaven, and have all our service done in the name of the Son of God, and presented by his mediation to the Father? And further, shall we not account unbelief to be a monstrous sin, considering how little cause we have to fear or doubt? But especially, shall we not learn humility of him that, being in the form of God, humbled himself for our sakes to take upon him the form of a man, and to be subject to the very death? Ps. ii., Mat. xi. 29. Lastly, shall we not learn hence the hatefulness of sin, and the odious filth of it? We may commit sin, but God must remit it, and become a sufficient propitiation for sin.

Corporally. Quest. How can the whole divine nature be said to be in the human, seeing the one is infinite, the other finite?

Ans. 1. It is no more than to affirm that the human nature is united to the divine in the fulness of it; or, 2. That it is incorporate, or made flesh, incarnate, or hath a body joined to it; or else, 3. Let it be granted of the inhabitation in the flesh of Christ, yet it followeth not that therefore it is there included; for it is so in the flesh whole, that without the flesh it is everywhere. For the divinity is not only immense that it can be everywhere, but also most simple, that it can be, and be everywhere whole, as the soul in the body, and the light is in the sun, and yet not included there, yet truly and whole there.

Quest. But since this text plainly affirms that Christ had a body, and so by synecdoche a true human nature, it may be here inquired whether his human nature was like ours, and the rather since the godhead did dwell in him bodily?

Ans. That this may be clearly resolved, we must know that, what is said in this verse notwithstanding, Christ in his human nature was like unto us. But for evidence, I shew briefly in what he was like, and then in what he was not like. He was like: 1. In that he took a true body, not fantastical; 2. He took a true human body, and not a celestial body, and he was endued with a reasonable soul; 3. He had the essential faculties of both; 4. He had the very infirmities of our nature, I mean such as were not sinful. Now, Christ was unlike us in body, in soul, in both. In body: 1. In his conception there was a difference, for we are *of* Adam, and *by* Adam, but he was *of* Adam, and not *by* Adam: for he was not begotten, but made, and so original sin was avoided, and some think his very body had all the parts at the first conception formed; 2. His body was not corruptible, it saw no corruption. In soul he differed two ways: 1. In that it was without sin; 2. In that it was endued with gifts above men and angels. In both there was difference; for, 1.

They subsisted from the beginning in the divine nature, and did not make a person of themselves; 2. They are admitted unto the grace of adoration, so as now Christ-man is worshipped, though not properly as he is man.

Thus of the natures of Christ; the union of them follows in a double consideration: 1. Of the manner, in the word *dwell;* 2. Of the measure, *in all fulness.*

Dwell. There are two kinds of unions in Christ: 1. Of the soul and body; 2. Of both those with the person of the Word; the latter is here meant.

There are two questions about union in theology, that are wonderful full of difficulty: 1. The union of three persons in one nature; 2. The union of two natures in one person. This latter is in Christ, he is begotten as God, created in respect of his soul, and born in respect of his body.

There are divers unions: 1. Substantial in the trinity; 2. Natural in soul and body; 3. Carnal in man and wife; 4. Mystical in Christ and the church; 5. Personal in Christ, for in him as soul and body are one man, so God and man are one Christ.

It is much easier to tell how this union in Christ is not, than to tell how it is. Negatively thus:—

Things are united three ways: some things are compounded and made one, yet the things united are not changed, mingled, or confounded, but remain perfect, as many stones united in one building; 2. Some things united are perfect, but yet changed, and not what they were, as the body of a man made of the union of the four elements; 3. Some things remain whole and not changed, but imperfect of themselves, as the soul and body of themselves apart. Now this union of Christ is not after any of these ways.

Again, this union in Christ is: 1. Not by bare assistance or presence; 2. Not by habitual union, either by affection, as friends are one, or by grace, as the saints are one with God; 3. Not by worthiness or authority; 4. Not by harmony or consent of will or opinion, as the angels are one with God, and as the saints shall; 5. Not by joint authority, as two consuls are one; 6. Not by homonomy or giving of the same name to each nature; 7. Not of pleasure only, as if it were so only because God would have it so; lastly, Not by bare inhabitation.

for the Word is made flesh; and therefore, though the Holy Ghost use the similitude of dwelling here, to note the continual residence of the divine nature in the human, yet that similitude doth not express this union clearly, for the householder and the house cannot be fitly called one.

The effects of this union may be considered either as they are in Christ or to usward.

In Christ from this union flows:

1. The predication of the things of each nature to the person, and that truly and really, as when his blood is said to be the blood of the Son of God, Acts xx. &c.

2. The enriching of the human nature with admirable gifts, as great as could possibly be in a created nature; in respect of which he came the nearest unto God of any that ever was or could be. Nay, if all the goodness of man and angels were conferred on one creature, yet it were not comparable to that that is one Christ.

These gifts in Christ were either natural or supernatural. By natural gifts I mean as these: In the mind, the best wit or memory, and such like faculties, better than ever were in any man,—I except not Adam himself. In the body, most fair form and divine face; his very countenance did express a divinity in him. The very temperament also of his body was such as nothing could be better tempered or more excellent, as being formed by the Holy Ghost.

His supernatural gifts were either in body or mind: In body, as that he could with his eye pierce the heavens, and see there what he would; for Stephen could see into heaven, as is recorded, Acts vii., much more must we believe of our Saviour, for in Stephen there was but a small parcel of divine light. Now, I say, those gifts were above nature in Christ, but yet not against nature. In mind there was in him exceeding holiness, goodness, wisdom, and all the gifts of the Spirit.

But all these supernatural gifts, both in soul and body, must be considered in Christ two ways: 1. In the state of humiliation; 2. In the state of exaltation. Such gifts as he received in the state of humiliation were properly the effects of this union, the other were given in respect of his obedience unto death.

Of the first sort, I propound these: 1. In the whole soul, so great holiness as can be imagined to befall a creature; 2. In the mind, most exquisite wisdom; 3. In the heart, such bowels of charity, love, and compassion, as was never in any man or angel; in the whole man, wonderful power.

Now, amongst all these, I only consider of his wisdom and power.

There was a twofold wisdom in Christ: increate, and that was only in his divine nature; and create, and that was in his human. This created wisdom in Christ was threefold: 1. Knowledge by immediate vision, Mat. xi. 27; 2. Knowledge by heavenly habits infused, Isa. xi. 3; 3. Knowledge gotten by experience, Luke ii. 52. By the first knowledge he knoweth immediately the Word of God, to which his human nature is united, and in God as in a glass he sees all other things. Thus he sees God face to face, and this is a certain created light in the soul by participation of divine light.

Concerning this first sort of knowledge in Christ strange things are said by divines, but the sum of all is this: 1. That the soul of Christ by this created light and vision sees God; and that first, whole; secondly, perfectly; 2. That in this vision he sees all things.

Object. Then might some one say, the knowledge of Christ in his human nature is made equal to his divine.

Sol. Not so: for, 1. Though he see God whole, yet he seeth him not wholly, that is, not so much as can be seen by God himself, though more than any creature can attain unto; 2. Though he know the things that are and shall be, yet he knows not such things as shall not be, and yet God can do them; 3. What he doth know by this finite light, he knows not so plainly as the Word doth; 4. It seeth not things at one view or altogether, but one thing after another. Thus of his immediate or blessed knowledge.

The second kind of knowledge is habitual or infused knowledge. By this knowledge he knows all that can be known of man or angels, yea, of all of them together. Of this he speaks, Isa. xi. 3. There are four words to express it, *wisdom, understanding, knowledge,* and *counsel.* By the first, He understandeth celestial and divine things; by the second, Things separate from matter, as the angels; by the third, things natural; and by the last, Things to be done.

But this knowledge is much inferior to the former, for thus he knows not the divine essence. Of experimental knowledge the Holy Ghost spake, Luke ii. 52, when he said, Jesus 'increased in wisdom,' and that must needs be in such knowledge as he got by observation by degrees in the world. Thus of the wisdom of Christ.

Concerning the power of Christ, many things are controverted in other churches, and I have spoken of it before; more than men of wrangling natures and corrupt envious minds did well take, though no more than what is ordinary in the writings of learned men; I shall not need, therefore, to say much of it in this place. The power of Christ is twofold,—increate and create. Increated power is the power of his divine nature, and so he is omnipotent. Created power is an admirable force in the human nature of Christ, above man or angels, to accomplish that unto which it is directed. By his divine power Christ worketh divine things, and by his human power he worketh human things; thus is he powerful above all creatures, in understanding, memory, will, and in acting whatsoever the law of God can will.

Hitherto of the power of Christ; and so of the gifts in the state of humiliation.

In the state of exaltation, there befell Christ four things: 1. A wonderful excellency of glory; 2. The grace of adoration with the divine nature; 3. The power of administration of all things in heaven and earth, Mat. xxviii.; 4. A judiciary power, viz., to be the judge of the whole world, Acts xvii. 30.

Thus of the second effect.

The third effect of this union in Christ was his mediatorship, in remaining perfect God he became man; so without any mutation of himself, he is by this union become perfect mediator between God and man, the true high priest, and the only head of the church.

The fourth and last effect of this union is the communion of the effects. There are divers operations of both natures, yet they meet in one work done. The worker is the person; the fountains of operation are the two natures according to their properties; the actions are some proper to the divine nature, some to the human; yet the outward fact, or thing effected, is the work of both natures. Thus of the effects of this union in Christ.

Now, the effects that flow to us from hence are either in Christ for us, or in us by Christ. In Christ for us, there are two effects, expiation and reconciliation to the Father. In us by Christ, are three effects, justification, sanctification, and glorification.

In all fulness. The ubiquitaries do abuse this place, for they allege that this place proves that the essential properties of the divine nature are communicated really to the human, and so they say Christ is in his human nature omnipotent, everywhere present, and omniscient; this they fall upon to establish his real presence in the sacrament. But that this place cannot fit their turns, may appear by these reasons: 1. He saith 'in whom,' that is, in which person the Godhead dwells, &c. Now it is not doubted by any, but that the person of Christ is omnipotent, everywhere present, &c. 2. Be it 'in which body' the Godhead dwells, &c., yet this proves nothing for them, for so he dwells in the saints, and yet they do not say they are everywhere present. 3. When he saith 'all fulness,' this fulness notes the essence as well as the properties. Now I hope they will not say the essence is wholly communicated to the body of Christ; 4. 'All fulness' imports all attributes as well as some. Now all attributes are not communicated, as for example, the body of Christ was not eternal. Lastly, the same was cleared before; the fulness of the Godhead is there, as the light is in the sun.

Uses. From the consideration of all which doctrine, we may see cause to be abased and confounded in ourselves, that we should not more admire the wonderful glory of the person of Christ; and for the time to come, we should heartily strive with God by prayer, and the use of all good means, that he would be pleased to 'reveal his Son in us,' and show this rich mystery of 'God manifested in the flesh.' Lastly, this should confirm us in the faith of all the good things promised in the Messiah, seeing hence we know how infinitely complete he is in himself. Thus of the ninth verse.

Ver. 10. *And ye are complete in him, who is the head of all principality and power.*

The third reason of the dehortation, is taken from our perfection in Christ. We need not go to traditions, or philosophy, or ceremonies, seeing we are so complete in ourselves as we are in Christ.

Observe in the first words: 1. The persons, 'ye;' 2. The time, 'are;' 3. The benefit communicated, 'complete;' 4. The author, 'Christ;' 5. The limitation, 'in him.' In general, we may observe, that Christ doth derive of his fulness to his members, 'of his fulness have we all received grace for grace,' John i. 16; 'out of his fulness he filleth all in all,' Eph. i. 23; he 'ascended far above all heavens, that he might fill all things,' Eph. iv. 10.

Now, if any ask wherein Christians are complete, or what it is Christ doth derive unto Christians out of his fulness? I answer, he maketh them complete, or filleth them out of his fulness with knowledge, Mat. xi. 25, Rom. xv. 14; grace and truth, John i. 16; peace, power, Acts vi. 8; joy and righteousness, Rom. xiv. 17; strength against temptations and death, Heb. ii.; abundance of blessings in the gospel, Rom. xv. 29; and he supplieth all their necessities out of the riches of his glory; but especially they are complete in the imputation of his most perfect righteousness.

Thus of the author and the benefit. Where he saith, 'ye are complete,' teacheth them that there must be a particular application of this fulness of Christ. Though there be water enough in the sea, or in the river, or fountain, yet it helps not us, unless it be derived to us by conduits, &c.; though there be food enough in the market, yet we are not filled with it, unless it be brought and dressed, and taken by us.

Now for the time; when he saith 'ye are complete,' he shews that it is not enough that men's hearts have been full of Christ, but they must be so still.

Quest. How can they be said to be already filled and complete in Christ, seeing many things for their perfection are not yet given, and there is a difference of fulness in the children of God?

Ans. That this point may be more clearly understood, I consider of this completeness more exactly, both in what it is, and what it ought to be, for they may be said to be complete, in that they ought to labour after it.

The faithful are complete, or implete rather, either comparatively or positively; comparatively in this sense, because they are in the absolutest estate that any kind of people are in, and far more happy than all the world beside; for the earth is cursed to all other men, the felicity they would desire cannot be had, or if it were, yet the wrath of God for their sins lieth like fire in the midst of all, and who knows when it will burn? How can there be any completeness in their estate, seeing the unregenerate heart cannot be filled, and the things they can get serve but for the flesh and bodily life? Thus they are comparatively complete. Now positively, they are so four ways: 1. In respect of the fulness of the body mystical; it is a glorious well-compacted complete body, Eph. i. 23, iv. 16; and so the church is 'the fulness of Christ.' 2. In respect of justification, and that two ways; for every child of God hath whole Christ given him, and his whole righteousness imputed; and besides, he hath forgiveness of all sorts of sins, original, actual, of infirmity or presumption, &c. 3. In respect of sanctification; 4. In respect of glorification.

Now for glory. We must understand, that though they are not yet in heaven, yet they have it in respect of promise, Heb. ix. 15, and in hope, Heb. vi. 14, and in the means, 2 Tim. iii. 16, and in the beginning of it, John xvii. 3; and for sanctification and grace, it must be considered according to the threefold degrees of it: 1. In inchoation; 2. In ripe age; 3. In perfect consummation in heaven.

Now for the first, even the weakest babes and infants in grace are complete four ways: 1. They have complete and perfect promises, even of completeness itself, Ezek. xxxvi., Jer. xlii. 39; 2. They are complete in respect of the means of sanctification, for first, they have full liberty to use them as they have opportunity, and they may make their best profit of them; besides the respect of the efficacy of the means, their God is the holy one of Israel, Christ is the head in all fulness of virtue, &c., they may pray for what they will and be heard, and the word is the arm and power of God to salvation; 3. They are complete in respect of the parts sanctified, they have grace in every part, though not in every degree; 4. They are complete in their desire and respect to all God's commandments.

Thus of weak Christians and their completeness.

Now the strong Christian's completeness may be considered negatively; and so they are not complete that are not full of knowledge, that cannot bear hard sayings, that hath not a plerophory of assurance, that is not filled with contentation, that cannot live by faith, or is not filled with the fruits of righteousness.

The last thing is the limitation, 'in him.'

In him. Nothing will be had by Christ till we be in Christ, 1 John v. 20. Things are said to be in Christ: 1. In respect of creation, all things were 'created in him,' Col. i. 16; 2. In respect of preservation, all things 'consist in him,' Col. i. 17; 3. In respect of the mystical union, and so the church only is in him.

In him we are elected, Eph. i. 4; in him 'the righteousness of God is revealed from heaven,' Rom. i. 17, 1 Cor. v. 21; in him 'all promises are yea and amen,' 2 Cor. i. 20; in him we are made rich, 1 Cor. i. 5; in him Jews and Gentiles are made one, Eph. ii. 6; in him the building is 'coupled together and grows,' Eph. ii. 20; in him we have life, 1 John v. 11.

Now men may know whether they be in Christ, if they examine themselves whether they be new creatures or no, 2 Cor. v. 17; and whether they have the Spirit of Christ, Rom. viii. 9; and whether they love the appearing of Christ, 2 Tim. iv. 8, 2 Thes. iii. 5, 2 Pet. iii. 12; whether the world hate them, John xv. 18, 20; whether they love the brethren, 1 John iii. 14, Eph. iv. 16, 17; and whether they walk in the light in all desire of holy conversation, 1 John i. 6, Heb. ix. 14, 1 John iii. 6.

Who is the head of all principality and power. It is true that magistrates be in great place on earth, and have principality and power, and may be so called justly; but that is not meant here. These principalities and powers are the angels, and so these words contain the fourth reason. Christ is the head of angels, therefore whatsoever they have they have it from Christ, and therefore what should we do to go to angels to help us when Christ the head is given to be our mediator?

The angels are diversely called in scripture: they are called spirits, to express their nature, and angels, to express their office, as messengers sent of God; they are called sons of God, Job xxxviii.; they are called cherubims, Gen. iii., from the form they appeared, viz., like youths; they are called seraphims, Isa. vi., for their order and fierceness in the execution of God's anger; they be called stars of the morning, Job xxxviii. 7, from their brightness of nature; they are called watchmen, Dan. iv. 10, they are in heaven as a watch-tower, and they keep the world; they are called flaming fire, Ps. civ., because God useth their help to destroy the wicked. Here they be called 'principalities and powers,' which are words of greatest excellency amongst men, and are used here to shadow out the glory of those heavenly creatures. Angels are most spiritual creatures without bodies; they move like the wind irresistibly, easily without molestation, and in an unperceivable time. And, for their number, I am not of their fond opinion that think they are meant in the parable of the ninety and nine sheep, as if they were so infinite beyond the number of mankind; yet, without question, their number is exceeding great and almost incomprehensible, and cannot be known of us in this world, Dan. vii. 10, Hosea xii. 24, Mat. xxvi. 53. They wonderfully excel in knowledge, and that natural and supernatural and experimental. But to speak a little more expressly, I consider in the angels: 1. What they are in themselves, here called principalities and powers; 2. What they are in relation to Christ, who is said here to be their head; 3. What they be in reference to the body of Christ.

The angels in themselves are principalities for their excellency of nature and estate. They are called powers for their wonderful force they have over other creatures at God's appointment. The words do not import any hierarchy among the angels, for howsoever we are not to think there is any ataxy among those glorious creatures, so it hath been bold presumption in those, either Jews or schoolmen or papists, that have travailed in it, to describe a fantastical number of orders amongst them. For their excellency of nature, as they are here called principalities, so elsewhere they are called stars of the morning, sons of God, yea, gods, *Elohim*. And for their power it is exceeding great over the creatures: as when an angel could destroy all the first-born of Egypt; and to overthrow so many thousands in Sennacherib's army. An angel set Peter out of prison; an angel carried Philip in an instant,—they can strangely wind themselves into men's imaginations, so as they can appear to men in their dreams, Mat. i. As evil angels can suggest tentations, so do good angels holy motions. They have power over the devils to restrain them, but work miracles they cannot but by the power of God. The angel, in the 5th of John, could move the waters, but he could not of himself cure the sick.

Thus of angels in themselves.

In relation to Christ, so they are implied to be of the body, and Christ to be their head. Now we may not marvel at it, that Christ should be the head of angels, for there be divers distinct benefits which angels from thence do receive, which by natural creation they had not: 1. It is a benefit that they are vouchsafed a place in the mystical body under Christ, that they might be received, as it were, into the new order in Christ. 2. A peace is made between them and man in Christ. 3. The rooms of angels fallen are supplied by the elect, the society of angels being much maimed by their fall. 4. They are refreshed with singular joy for the conversion of the elect; besides the enlarging of their knowledge, that they are vouchsafed the understanding of the secrets of the gospel. 5. They receive from Christ confirming grace, and so assurance that they shall never fall, which is their chief benefit. 6. Their obedience in its own nature is imperfect, Job iv., though not sinful, and therefore may need to be covered by Christ's perfections.

Thus of the relation to Christ. Now, if any ask what relation they have to the body of Christ, and what they do unto it? I answer, by propounding both what service they do to the body, and in what manner. For the first, They are like masters and tutors, to whom the great King of heaven sends out his children to nurse. God out of the rabble of best men doth adopt children to himself, and after commit them to be kept by those most noble citizens of heaven, Ps. xxxiv. Besides, they execute judgment upon the enemies of the church. They attend us at the hour of death, and carry our souls to heaven, Luke xvi. They shall gather our bodies together at the last day, Mat. xxiv. Lastly, For the accomplishment of all designments for our good, they stand always looking on the face of God to receive commandments, Mat. xviii. 10. Now, for the manner; in the Old Testament they are reported to have sometimes appeared unto men, sometimes in their dreams,

sometimes in visions,—the prophets being ravished into an ecstacy,—without true bodies, but not without the form of bodies. Sometimes they appeared in true bodies, either such as were for the time created of nothing, or else formed for the service of some pre-existing matter, or else they used the bodies of some living creatures. For if the devil could speak in the serpent, why might not some good angel use other creatures, as some think the angel spake in Balaam's ass? But for this kind of declaring themselves to men, in the New Testament it is ceased, especially since the primitive times, so as now we cannot describe how the angels do perform their service to the church.

Now for the use of the whole, inasmuch as Christ is the head of principalities and powers, we may comfort ourselves divers ways. If Christ fill the angels, how much more can he out of his fulness fill us in the supply of all our wants? Again, shall we not rejoice in the grace here is done to us, in that we are united into communion with angels under our head? yea, and that such glorious creatures are appointed to be our attendants, why should we fear when Christ and his angels will be so ready about us? Further this may also instruct us, we need not be ashamed of Christ's service, seeing the very angels follow him and depend upon him. A prince that kept great princes to be his domestic servants, were like to be much sought to for preferment of such as would follow him. Oh! how should we long after Christ who is head over such glorious creatures as the angels are!

Ver. 11. *In whom also ye are circumcised with the circumcision made without hands, in putting off the body of the sins of the flesh by the circumcision of Christ.*

Here is the fifth reason, and is peculiarly addressed against those Christians of the Jews which joined the law with the gospel, as necessary to salvation. By circumcision they were initiated to the law of Moses; and if circumcision can add nothing to us, nor perfect us any way in Christ, then neither can the law itself. We have that in Christ of which circumcision and the law were signs; we are circumcised in the spirit, and therefore need not to be circumcised in the flesh, and in Christ we have the accomplishment of what was shadowed in the law.

Object. Might some one say, The consequence is strange: we are circumcised in spirit, therefore we need not be circumcised in the flesh. Why, Abraham was circumcised in spirit as well as we, yet he needed to be circumcised also in the flesh.

Sol. For answer hereunto, we must know that in the time of the Old Testament, this consequence was of no force; yet now in the New it is exceeding strong. For now we have not only accomplished what was signified by circumcision, but Christ hath appointed another sign instead of it, viz., baptism; especially this is clear amongst the Gentiles, which never were circumcised in the flesh.

There is imported unto us in this verse a twofold circumcision: 1. The circumcision made with hands; 2. The circumcision made without hands. The one external, in the flesh by Moses; the other internal, in the spirit by Christ.

Concerning circumcision made in the flesh, there is an observation of a fourfold time: 1. There was a time wherein it was not, viz., from the creation till Abraham's days; 2. There was a time wherein it was necessary, viz., from Abraham till Christ; 3. There was a time wherein it was tolerable, viz., for some few years after Christ; 4. There was a time wherein it was intolerable and utterly unlawful, viz., since the apostles' times to the end of the world, Gal. v. 1.

Circumcision had a double significance, for partly it looked to Christ, and partly to the members of Christ. As it looked to Christ it signified: 1. That they should have a Saviour that was circumcised, that is, free from all sin. 2. That he should come of the seed of Abraham. 3. That he should satisfy for sin by effusion of blood, for all blood in the Old Testament was typical. Now as it looked to man, it signified: 1. That by carnal generation we were unclean, and out of covenant with God. 2. That the faithful have interest in the blessed seed. 3. That our hearts must be circumcised, by the painful mortification of sin, and the painful casting away of sin, as a wretched foreskin; and that we should suffer affliction of spirit for sin, till our hearts were as sore as the Shechemites' bodies. 4. That we are adopted into God's favour and communion with saints, and distinguished from all other men. 5. That all holiness of life and forgiveness of sin must be had in society with the seed of Abraham. 6. That through bearing the cross, the first-fruits of our blood should be ready to be offered for him that died for us.

The ends why circumcision was appointed were: 1. To teach them by signification the things before mentioned. 2. To be as a sacrament initiatory to let them into the church. 3. To be a partition-wall between them and the Gentiles, and as fetters to restrain them from society with them. 4. To bind them to keep the whole law, Gal. v. 3. 5. To be a seal both of the righteousness of faith, Rom. iv. 11, and of their right and possession of the land of Canaan as a type of heaven, Gen. xvii. 7.

There were three sorts of citizens in the old church of the Jews,—Israelites, proselytes, and religious men. Israelites were of the seed of Abraham, those were bound to circumcision necessarily, Gen. xvii. 12-14. Proselytes were Gentiles converted to the Jewish religion; those for the strengthening of their faith did subject themselves also to circumcision and the ceremonial law. Now there were certain religious men of the Gentiles converted, and embraced the covenant of God, but were not subject to circumcision: such were Naaman, and the eunuch, and others.

Now this circumcision after the coming of Christ was abolished: 1. Because all effusion of blood must cease when Christ's blood was shed. 2. The partition-wall was now taken down, and therefore there needed no sign of difference. 3. The priesthood was changed, and therefore the rites belonging to it also.

Object. But Christ himself is said to be the minister of circumcision, Rom. xv.

Sol. That was true: 1. As he was given to the Jews by expiation to perform what was promised to their fathers. 2. He was a minister, not of the law, (which he abolished and fulfilled in his coming,) but of the Jews among whom he was conversant; for he preached not to the Gentiles. He was a minister of circumcision, that is, he was a preacher among the Jews, as Peter was the apostle of circumcision. Thus of circumcision made with hands.

Now concerning circumcision made without hands, five things in this verse may be noted: 1. The persons circumcised, 'ye;' 2. The time 'are;' 3. The mannor negatively set down, 'without hands;' 4. The form of it, 'putting off the body of sins of the flesh;' 5. The efficient cause, 'the circumcision of Christ.'

In general we may note that the case of the Gentiles is not worse than the Jews. We want sacrifices, types, oracles, circumcision, &c., but we have the thing signified; before the law they had the shadow, under the law they had the image, after the law we have the body.

Quest. But what should be the reason that the Holy Ghost in this place and in divers others useth such hard phrases and dark kinds of speech?

Ans. The Lord of himself in many places of scripture doth use allegories or dark sayings. 1. Thereby to execute upon wicked men a strange and secret curse; he speaks to them in parables, Mat. xiii., Isa. vi. 2. The majesty of the matter sometimes denieth to be expressed in more ordinary terms. 3. In allegories the Holy Ghost doth not only tell the thing, but explicate it by comparison, as here. 4. The hard places of scripture are God's chests, wherein he hides his treasure from wicked men. 5. God hereby provides for the constant nourishment of the faithful, that though now they find a sweet relish in the word, yet if they come again to the same word, there is such depth in it, they may find more food in it. 6. God somewhat aims at the humbling of the proud heart of man, and will hereby make him see his wants, and many ways buffet him. 7. To excite in us so much the more diligence. 8. Some parts of scripture are for an appointed time, Heb. ii. 3, and till then they are sealed up. So a veil is yet drawn over some parts of the revelation in things not yet accomplished; so it was in Daniel's time, Dan. xii. 8. Thus in general.

Circumcision without hands is a wonderful work of the Spirit of grace, wrought by the word upon the members of Christ, upon their receiving into the mystical body, by which corruption of nature is wounded, beloved sins cast away with sorrow, and the sinner received into an everlasting communion with God and his saints. Now that there is such a work as this in every child of God is apparent by these places of scripture: Deut. x. 16 and 30, Jer. iv. 4, Rom. ii. 26, and this text.

The first thing here to be considered is the persons, both in themselves, 'ye,' and in their relation to Christ, 'in whom,' and to other gifts mentioned before, and imported in the word 'also.'

Ye. What graces we hear to be in Christ's members we must look to it that they be in us. It was no comfort to the Colossians that others were circumcised with circumcision without hands, unless it might be truly so said of them also. Which serves for great reproof of many that neglect the power of all doctrine, which is the application of it to themselves; but this comes to pass either for want of faith, Heb. ii. 1, or through prejudice, Ps. ii. 3, 2 Kings ix. 11, Jer. xxix. 26, or the slumbering of the spirit, or the love of secret sin; yea, many lose the power of the doctrine by wondering observation how it may suit unto others.

In whom. Circumcision without hands is only found in such as are actually in Christ; they only wound corruption of nature, and cast away beloved sins with sorrow: this is the difference between temporary faith and justifying faith. There are three sorts of hearers in the city: Some wholly profane, such as will mend nothing, nor like to hear of mending; some openly sincere, professing constantly this circumcision without hands; a third sort, partaking of the properties of both the former, for they agree with the best in these things: 1. In the love of the ministry and ministers that preach faithfully; 2. In the taste of the powers of the life to come, finding the word often of singular power, so as they receive it with joy and great admiration; 3. In the defence of the truth they seem as forward as any. These are near the kingdom of God, as the scribe was; these are more than half persuaded, as Agrippa was; these are fired with desire many times to know what to do to be saved, as the young man in the Gospel was. But, alas! all this brings them within the compass of none of God's promises, and if they look not to it, fearful apostasy will be the end of all this, and they may prove most spiteful adversaries to the same ministry they admired, and proud contemners of the same remorse with which themselves were often smitten, and so their latter end be ten times worse than their beginning.

Quest. But what do these men want, or what are their defects, that they should be right for all this, having such great affection to the word, yea, even when it is most sincerely taught?

Ans. Alas, there are divers things too apparent in their estate: for, 1. They join not themselves with such as fear God in fellowship in the gospel. 2. They shun by all means the cross for righteousness' sake. 3. They respect not all God's commandments; there are some sins they will not leave; there are some corruptions they are so engaged unto that they will at no hand leave them. 4. Some of them forsake not the very sins they seem to detest, and sometimes to cry out against; they cry out upon swearing, and yet (vile beasts as they are) they will swear still, yea, and that most fearfully, yea, after many remorses of conscience for it. 5. They will not be persuaded to use all God's ordinances; indeed, they hear constantly, and, to any man's thinking, with great attention, but they pray not in their families; they will not use the help of conference; they read not the scriptures with any order or conscience, &c. 6. You see they are not careful of their company; they neither shun the appearance nor the occasions of evil; they give not over their going nor their resort unto ungodly company; they have not been truly humbled by godly sorrow for their sin. Lastly, They have sincerity in respect of persons; in some they like it, in others they do not like it; they love not all the saints.

Also. This 'also' leads us to the former privileges in Christ, and imports that the circumcision without hands here mentioned is to be accounted a marvellous grace of God, and worthily; for our judging of ourselves frees us from the condemnation of the world, and our days of mortification are, as it were, the wedding days of the soul, and godly sorrow is accompanied with the spirit of prayer, and a fountain of grace is opened when our hearts are opened with true contrition. Thus of the persons.

Are. This word designs the time of this spiritual circumcision: the time for the putting away and cutting off of our beloved sins is in this life; it must be now done or never done; besides, till this be done, we can feel no profit or benefit from Christ.

Quest. The Jews in the law did know directly when they should be circumcised in the flesh. May not we also guess at the time of the circumcision without hands, when God would have us go about it, beyond which time it may not be deferred without singular danger?

Ans. There is a time, and it may be known, and it is wonderful dangerous to stand out that time. In general, the time to humble ourselves by mortification for our sins, and so to set about this spiritual circumcision, is when God grants us the means of salvation, Luke xiv. 17; more especially when we are pressed with God's judgments, Joel ii. 12; or when the months of God's servants are in a special manner opened unto us, and their hearts made large, 2 Cor. vi. 2; or when God dispenseth other graces, as temporary faith, love to the word, and joy, &c., 2 Cor. vi. 2; or when we are smitten with the axe of God's word, and remorse for sin is wrought in us, Mat. iii. 10; or when hearing hath kindled in us a desire and thirst after the best things, Isa. lv. 1, 6; or lastly, when we first set out to make profession of our being in Christ, John xv. 2.

Quest. But may not any man repent at any time?

Ans. No: 1. A man may tarry so long till he commit the sin against the Holy Ghost; 2. Men that go not so far may yet by obstinate impenitence provoke God to cast them into a reprobate sense, Rom. i., xi. 8-10, Isa. vi., Mat. xiii. 13. We see by experience that the most men that pretend to mend afterwards, yet do not, but troops of men that forget God go into hell, Ps. ix.

Object. But the scripture saith at what time soever a sinner repenteth him of his sin from the bottom of his heart, God will forgive him, &c.

Sol. 1. Mark the words, they have a limitation, thou must repent from the bottom of thy heart, or else they comfort not thee. 2. For the extent of the time, in so many precise words; the text in Ezekiel is not at what time soever, but in the day that a sinner repenteth, which is not so universal but that it may admit the exceptions before, and though some men may and do repent at their latter end, yet neither all nor the most.

Object. But yet the thief repented on the cross.

Sol. Shall one example make thee presume? Why, thou mayest know that worlds of people when they came to die did not repent as he did;—why shouldest not thou more fear the example of so many not repenting? what is one to thousands? 2. Thou readest that the other thief upon the same cross died without repentance. 3. Thou must know that an ordinary rule cannot be drawn from an extraordinary instance. His conversion was miraculous, one of the seven wonders wrought by Christ in his death. Christ made Peter walk on the sea—will he make thee do so too? will he, for thy pleasure, darken the sun, or shake the earth, or cleave the rocks? &c. Thus of the time.

Without hands. Two things may here be noted: 1. That that is not circumcision which is outward, made with the hands of man, but that is true circumcision which is inward. Hence there is two sorts of Israelites: the one is a carnal Israelite, one outward; the other is a true Israelite, for he is one inward in his spirit. As it was then, so it is now; the carnal Israelite hath the name of Israel, and the sign of true circumcision; as then, the circumcision in the flesh, so now baptism; and besides, they profess to be the seed of Abraham, and they speak fair of God and heaven.

Quest. But what are the principal defects of the carnal Israelite?

Ans. 1. He rests in the work done; he bears himself upon the external work of holiness; he served God, for he was at church; he is regenerated, for he was baptized; he hath prayed to God, for he stretched out his hands. 2. His praise is of men, and not of God. 3. He wholly neglects the power of godliness, and the exercises thereof. 4. He is disordered in his life, laden with iniquity. 5. He is senseless or incorrigible under public judgments. 6. He usually opposeth and pursueth him that is born after the spirit.

2. We may note here that God is not tied to means, he can work without hands. What is then the estate of wicked men? No hands of men or angels can make them happy, it is a work done without hands. Oh, how honourable is the work of mortification of a sinner! It was a glorious work to make those huge heavens, and this mighty earth without hands. Such is the glory of our spiritual circumcision. We see also here how little beholden the kingdom of Christ is to this world; their hands will not be gotten to set it up, God must do it without hands. Lastly, We should learn in all estates to live by faith, and rest upon God, whether in affliction, or temptation, or mortification of sin; though we see not means, yet let this comfort us—God can can help us without hands. And thus of the instrument of circumcision, as it is here set down negatively.

Putting off the body of the sins of the flesh. Here is the form of this circumcision without hands; it lies in the mortification of the body of sins that are in the flesh. Where note: 1. The matter to be mortified, *the body of sins;* 2. The manner, it must be *put off.*

The flesh. The flesh is one of the three great enemies of God and man's salvation; it is a treacherous domestical enemy. As it is treacherous, so it is tyrannical; it will not be pleased unless it reign. A most secret enemy, for she sits at the fountain and poisoneth all. Most falsely she lets in the devil, and permits him to set up his holds and fortifications in the minds of men; and is never quiet till it bring the soul into actual high treason against God. It is the flesh that causeth whoredoms, murder, drunkenness, and all disorders. She opposeth all the ways of goodness, both by objecting against them, and by making evil present. She 'savours not the things of God,' nor 'can understand them.' It is she that makes the law impossible to us. What with her veil of ignorance, and the slowness and hardness she diffuseth upon our hearts and spirits, she makes the service of God to seem almost always evil unto us. Yea, if she get into her throne, she dare exalt herself against God, and judge even God himself, and his will, counsel, providence, and people: her very wisdom is enmity against God. And so infectionsly vile is she, that she diffuseth her poison to our very posterity, so as we beget a very race of rebels; and in all this she fortifies herself by all advantages, from evil example, or by riches and worldly greatness, or carnal wisdom, or success in sinning; yea, rather than she will be subdued, or much pursued, she will entrench herself under the very colours of Christ, making her pretence of following him in words, that she may the more securely follow her own lusts in deed. This she doth, and thus spoils the image of God in us, and makes us most filthy and loathsome, and so opens the door of our soul unto Satan, that our hearts are made a very sty for unclean spirits to dwell in; and thus she will do if she be not mortified, till she bring men to hell, and eternal condemnation there.

Now, for the taming of the flesh, God hath taken divers excellent courses: 1. He hath laid a necessity of mortality upon it; all flesh must know it is but grass, Isa. xl. 6. 2. To cross the glory of the fleshly, the Lord, of purpose, when he chooseth heirs of salvation, will not take many of those the flesh commends for mightiness, or nobleness, or wisdom, or the like, 1 Pet. i. 2, 4, 1 Cor. i. 3. God hath set a standing curse upon the chief things desired by the flesh, so as they cannot be used but with a kind of experience of their vanity, and loathing and vexation of the spirit. 4. He hath enacted terrible decrees against such as walk after the flesh, and gives proclamation that he will certainly judge men for all the practices of the flesh, 2 Pet. ii. 9, 10, Eccles. xi. 9. 5. He placeth his Spirit within us to lust against the flesh. 6. He sent his Son to take the similitude of sinful flesh, that in the flesh he might subdue the flesh, Rom. viii. 3. Lastly, He hath shewed us ways what we must do that we might tame and subdue the flesh, as when he tells us: 1. That we must be sober,—that is, moderate in meat and drink, and recreation and apparel, and what else may hamper the flesh; 2. That we must put no confidence in the flesh; 3. That we must mortify it by confession of sin, and godly sorrow, with strong cries calling upon God for help against it; 4. That we must search the records of God's promises, and by faith lay hold upon him. For till we can shew a better draught of happiness than the flesh doth, we do in vain go about to charm it; 5. We must silence it, not suffer it to object, or excuse, or extenuate, or deny.

Hitherto in general of the flesh and the mortification of it. Now, more specially, we must consider here: 1. The matter to be mortified, viz., the 'body of sins;' 2. The manner, in the words 'put off.'

Sins. Two things may be here noted: the one is implied, the other is expressed. That which is implied is, that God doth not require this circumcision in other things, but only in sins. 1. Regeneration doth not oppose the flesh in the substance of it. We are not required to cut off any parts of the body, nor to destroy any faculties of the soul; and the same I say of the complexion or constitution of the body; it doth not require the melancholy man should be made sanguine. 2. This circumcision reacheth not to the natural desires of the flesh, I mean such as are needful to the being of nature, as to eat, sleep, &c.; 3. Nor to the moral projects; 4. Nor to the remainders of spiritual light, as sparkles of God's image; 5. Nor to the outward necessary helps of life, as house, land, friends, &c., only it restrains those when they are hindrances to godliness. The use is therefore wisely to discern between the mere natural defects arising from the constitution of our bodies, and the sins and disorders of our souls; for this spiritual circumcision will not cure men's bodies, but only sanctifies men's minds.

Again, we should learn of God here how to deal with our enemies. He distinguisheth between nature and the sin of nature: so should we; we should oppose their sins, but love their persons.

The second thing here to be noted, is, that our sins are from the flesh; yea, if the flesh did not by defect, action, approbation, or consent, give way to sin, the devil and the world could fasten no sin upon us. Divers persons should be informed herein; when they fall into grievous evil, they cry out of their ill luck, or of ill counsel, or ill company, or of the devil; but they should indeed cry out of their own ill nature, for the rest could not have hurt them, but by the wickedness of their own dispositions; and we should all grow suspicious of the flesh and his motions, reasons, desires, &c., and in time to mortify her, with all her lusts.

Body of sins. He saith not only that there are sins in the flesh, but a body of sins, that is, a huge mass or lump of sins linked together as the members of our body are. The sins of the fleshly may be called a body in divers respects.

1. In respect of that harmony and union of sins one with another in practice, so as if one sin be practised, many will accompany it; as in Adam's sin, the sin was to eat the forbidden fruit, but that would not be alone, but was attended with doubting of God's word, with faith in the devil, with most inordinate pride or desire to be like God, with discontentment with their present condition, with

vile ingratitude, with apostasy from all righteousness, with profanation of the sacrament, with wilful murder of all their posterity, and evil concupiscence. Cain was angry that God did not accept his profane sacrifice, but would this sin be alone? No, for there follows it the hatred of his brother, the falling of his countenance, the rejecting of God's admonition, coloured hypocrisy, murder, and blasphemy. When desire of gain infects the hearts of tradesmen, we see by experience it will not be alone, a number of transgressions grow with it, as love of the world more than God, neglect of sincerity in the use of God's ordinances, swearing, breach of Sabbath, rigorous dealing with inferiors, unmercifulness to the poor, selling by false weights and measures, usury, if not otherwise, yet in selling time, deceit, lying, oppression by engrossing of wares or encroaching upon the trade of others.

2. In respect of union in continuance after they are committed, thy sins committed vanish not; but by adding sin unto sin, thou makest up a very body of sin, and so in God's sight they stand compacted together as the very limbs of a monster.

3. These sins may be called a body, because they are committed by the body, as the external means of them.

4. The mass of sin in the fleshly man may be called a body of sins, for that it hath many things like unto the body of man; or many comparisons may be taken from the body of a man to express the sins of the flesh. As the body of man is a fair substance made of base matter, so sin in itself is most vile, though it be coloured over by the devil or the world with the fair proportion of profit or pleasure. And as there be many members in the body, so there are in the sin of the fleshly man. As some members in the body are outward, some inward, so are our sins. As men would be ashamed of their bodies were it not for their clothing, especially if there be any deformity, so would men of their sins, were it not for their great places or fair excuses and wretched shifts they have to hide their deformities. And as the body of a prisoner in a dungeon is alike a true body with his that sitteth on the throne, so sins that are secret, that are never so closely committed, are sins as well as such as are openly done. As his body is a true body that yet wants a leg or an arm, so is it in some, though they be not murderers or adulterers, yet they may have a body of sin in them. As the natural body cannot live if you take away food and clothing, so neither would sin if we did not love it, approve it, defend it, excuse it, and if we take away carnal reason and ill company. And as the body of princes is better clad than the bodies of poor men, yet it is alike a body of clay and corruption, so are the sins of great men, though men do not speak so openly of them.

Uses. Now for use of all: first, Here we may see a difference between the sins of the regenerate and the sins of the unregenerate. In the godly after calling there is not a body of sins; the nest of sin is scattered, sin is not in his full strength, he doth not give his members as servants to unrighteousness.

Secondly, Here men may try the truth of their repentance. That is not true repentance that mortifies some one or few sins, but that which mortifieth a whole body of sins.

Thirdly, This shews the greatness of God's mercies, that can forgive or take away a whole body of sins and transgressions.

Lastly, This may be a great comfort to afflicted consciences, that cry out of the multitude of their sins. If thy sins were as many as the joints of thy body, and as strong as the body of Goliah, yet the Lord can forgive, and true repentance will pull them down. This is the matter to be mortified; the manner follows.

Put off. Sin must be put off as the beggar puts off his rags, and as the master puts off his false servant, and as the porter puts off his burden, and as the husband puts off his vicious wife, and as the serpent puts off his skin.

There are four things in mortification distinct. The first is the dislike of sin, the second is the confession of sin, the third is the godly sorrow for sin, the fourth is forsaking of sin. This last is here meant by putting off of sin. And this the Lord stands upon as a thing he will never dispense with the want of it, as these places shew: Prov. xxviii. 13, Isa. lv. 8, Jer. vii. 3, 4, Isa. i. 16, 17, Ps. cxix. 9, Eph. iv. 22, &c., 1 Pet. iv. 1-4, Ezek. xviii. 33. And there are exceeding comfortable promises made to such as are upright in the desire and endeavour hereof, Prov. xxviii. 13, Isa. lv. 8, and xxvii. 9, Joel ii. 12, 13, Isa. i. 18.

Quest. But can the flesh be so mortified, and sin so put off, that it shall cease to be any more, in this life?

Ans. No; for even in the children of God the flesh will raise infirmities. It will let the understanding, it will be framing evil thoughts, it will lust against the spirit, it will not always allow what good is done or to be done, it will present evil when good is to be done, it will rebel against the law of the mind, yea, sometimes the soul of the poor sinner is led captive for a time by his imperious flesh.

Quest. But how can it then be said to be put away?

Ans. Sin is put away, first, If it reign not, nor hold a constant dominion over us. It may be put away, even when it leads us captive, if it be an unwilling captivity, if the power of it seem unto us as a most base servitude. It is put away if men take no care to fulfil the lusts of it. Secondly, If there be a constant combat in some degree against it; if we find a striving and constant fighting against the corruptions of our nature; if we pray against it, judge ourselves for it, and mourn over it with an unfeigned desire to forsake it. This desire to be put off, is one true degree of forsaking of sin.

That this may yet be better understood, we must know that sin is put off five ways even in this life: 1. Sacramentally; in the sign, covenant, and seal, that is, in baptism. 2. In the guilt of it, though not in the act of it; thus God puts off by not imputing. 3. In act too, by inchoation, though not perfectly. 4. Perfectly; though not in us, yet in Christ our head it is already put away, in his person though not in ours. 5. It is put away in hope, in that we do by hope wait for an absolute and full redemption from all sin and misery. Thus of the form of this circumcision; the efficient cause follows.

By the circumcision of Christ. There is a twofold circumcision of Christ: first, That which he suffered in himself; secondly, That which he works in us. The virtue of the first is a great cause of the second.

Quest. But why was Christ circumcised, seeing there was no cause of circumcision in Christ? for nothing could be signified by it, seeing he was the Messias himself, perfect God and man, nor was there any impurity in him, the amputation whereof should thereby be signified; he was a Lamb without spot, a High Priest separate from sinners; the covenant of the promised seed was in him fulfilled, and he came to abolish circumcision; and lastly, it is he that circumciseth the hearts of others.

Ans. 1. Christ was circumcised, thereby to shew himself to be true man. 2. Thereby to honour the institution of circumcision, as he had done other parts of the law. 3. That the Jews might not cavil and say they would not receive an uncircumcised Christ. 4. To commend the virtue of obedience by his example. 5. That he might bear the burdens of them that, being under the law, were not able to bear the burdens of the law. God by this sign, as by an initiating rite, did subject himself to the law, he hereby professing himself a servant to the law to make us free. 6. He was circumcised and baptized, to signify his union with both churches, both of the Old and New Testament, and that he 'came of twain to make one.' 7. To ratify and sanctify the circumcision of the fathers, as his baptism now sanctifieth ours. 8. To signify the cleansing of our nature, especially by bearing of the imputation of our impurities. 9. He did in his circumcision begin to satisfy God by those first-fruits of his blood; it was as an earnest or pledge of his blood, to be more plentifully poured out; it was a part of his humiliation, and of the price of our sins. Lastly, He was circumcised, that our hearts, by the virtue of it, might be circumcised; for as his death killeth sin in us, and his resurrection raiseth us up to newness of life, so doth his circumcision circumcise our hearts.

Hence we may gather comfort against the difficulties of mortification, for Christ will be pleased to derive virtue from his own circumcision; yea, it is a pledge to assure us, that as certainly as he was circumcised himself, so he will see to it that our hearts be circumcised. If we will cast ourselves upon him, and by faith come unto him, there is no sin so linked but in Christ we may have some deliverance from it. On the other side, it shews the misery of all such as live in the love of their sins, and mind not mortification; this shews they are not in Christ yet, for they cannot be in Christ except they be circumcised. Lastly, it may serve for instruction at once to all that hope for freedom in Jesus Christ, to shew the proof of their interest by their circumcision spiritually; and to speak distinctly of it, we must understand that the Lord that requires this circumcision of us, extends his precept both to the heart, Jer. iv. 4, and the ears, Jer. vi. 10, and the tongue; and contrariwise complaineth of uncircumcised both heart, and ears, and lips, Exod. vi. 3. In the heart we must especially look to the circumcision or mortification: 1. Of ignorance; 2. Of wicked thought; 3. Immoderate care; 4. Profaneness of God's service in a wretched security, or a neglect of inward worship; 5. Disordered affections, as lust, anger, suspicion; 6. Discontent with our estate; 7. Unbelief. Now, for our ears, they must be circumcised: 1. In the unpreparedness, or want of attention, in hearing the word; 2. In receiving tales; 3. In communicating with the sins of others, by a willing hearing of their wickedness. Lastly, look to the circumcision of the tongue, and that in the care to avoid: 1. The polluting of God's name, either by swearing or blasphemy; 2. Rash censuring; 3. Rotten speech; 4. Lying; 5. Bitter and furious words, and the spirit of contradiction; 6. Flattery; 7. Tale-bearing; 8. Idle and vain words. And thus much now of the spiritual circumcision and of the 11th verse.

Ver. 12. *In that ye are buried with him through baptism, in whom ye are also raised up together through faith of the operation of God, which raised him from the dead.*

In the former verse the apostle hath laid down the first reason, and directed it principally against Judaism. We have spiritual circumcision in Christ, and therefore we need not carnal circumcision, and so by consequent none of the ceremonial law. Now in this verse he meeteth with objections.

Object. 1. The reason seemeth not to follow, they were spiritually circumcised, therefore needed not the outward; for so was Abraham, yet he received outward circumcision.

Ans. The reason is of no force now in the New Testament, because Christ hath appointed another sacrament instead of it; for we are 'buried with Christ by baptism.'

Object. 2. But was not circumcision a more lively sign?

Ans. It was not; which he sheweth to be true, both in respect of mortification and in respect of vivification, baptism lively representing and sealing unto both.

Quest. But have all that are baptized these things signified by baptism?

Ans. They are offered to all, but they are enjoyed only by such as have faith in the operation of God.

Quest. But how may our faith be supported in believing those things shadowed out in baptism?

Ans. Two ways: first, If we consider 'God's operation;' secondly, If we consider Christ's resurrection. This is the brief order and dependence of this verse; so that here he entreats of baptism, both by the effects and by the causes. The effects are spiritual burial and spiritual resurrection; the causes are three: faith, the operation of God, and the resurrection of Jesus Christ.

Buried together with him. Three things may be here noted: 1. The burial of Christ; 2. The burial of the Christian; 3. The union of both. For the first, that Christ was buried, was storied by the evangelist, John xix., and foresignified by Jonas as a type, Mat. xii. 39, 40, and foreprophesied of by Isaiah the prophet, Isa. liii. 9. He was buried in Jerusalem, the place where the dying sacrifices had given warning of his death; but it was without the city, both to answer the type, Lev. xvi., and to signify that his sufferings belonged to Gentiles as well as to Jews. He was buried in Calvary, the place commonly appointed for condemned men, and not in Hebron, where some think Adam was buried, to note that his death was to be available for the condemned men, of Adam as well as for Adam himself. He was buried in another man's grave, to signify that he died for other men's sins.

Now, for the second, viz., the burial of Christians, they may be said to be buried even while they live, —for the burial of the body he cannot mean here,— in divers respects:

1. In respect of disgrace and reproach. The

throats of wicked men are often 'an open sepulchre,' Ps. v., into which, if the names of the godly fall, they are buried for the extremity of disgrace and reproach with which they cover them.

2. In respect of abnegation, or the denial of the love and care for earthly things; and so we are buried to the world when like dead men we care not for it, but devote ourselves to the contemplation of heavenly things.

3. In respect of mortification of our sins. The scripture, by divers metaphors, expresseth the divers degrees of mortification. For, first, there is the wounding of sin, when the sinner is pricked with remorse by the law. Secondly, The condemning of sin, when the sinner, keeping a spiritual assize, doth examine, confess, and judge himself guilty before the Lord. Thirdly, The crucifying of sins, when the sinner racks his own soul by godly sorrow, driving in the nails of God's threatenings, with acknowledgment of his own deserts, and restraining his flesh through a spiritual revenge, not caring to expose himself to the shame of the world, so that in Christ he may find atonement for his sins. Fourthly, The killing of sin, when the sinner puts off the body of sins, and forsaketh his evil ways. Now, then, after this followeth the last degree, and that is here the burial of sins. Certainly there remains even after true repentance in the very godly a great deal of hidden corruption of nature, inward wanderings, and distractions after the world, sudden evil propositions against God, or his word, or providence, or presence, or promises, or people; impatience, secret pride, and sometimes hypocrisy; a frequent rebellion within against good duties, unthankfulness, frequent omissions, either of holy duties or the care of the power of them, hastiness or anger, impure desires, thoughts of revenge, besides a great deal of disorder, he may find in himself both at home and abroad. Now it is not enough, nor may he rest in the former repentance, but he must proceed even to the removing of these remainders of corruption. Death commonly ariseth out of the disease of some one part, but burial covers all. The work of reformation and repentance many times begins at the care of some few principal sins; but we must never be quiet till we bury the whole old man with his works, so that in one sense the burial of sin is nothing else but the progress of mortification. Again, after we have forsaken our sins, to bury them is to keep a diligent watch over our nature, and to take down our flesh, yea, sometimes with refraining of lawful delights or pleasures. Further, the burial of sin, it may import our care, after we have left our sins, to remove them out of sight: both out of God's sight, by suing out our pardon, and out of the sight of our consciences, by quieting them in the application of the blood of Christ and the promises of grace, and out of the sight of others, so far as our sins were scandalous also, by shewing forth our repentance and care to avoid all appearance and occasions of like sinning. Great is the glory and happiness of Christians that have attained to this burial of sin, for these serve God in a near acquaintance with him; these have 'overcome the world,' these can stand before death and judgment unappalled, these are mighty in the power of God's ordinance, these know 'the secrets of the kingdom of God,' these are without the reach of the law, and feel not the stings of crosses; these are had in singular honour with God and the holy angels of heaven, and the providence of God is usually eminent towards these.

Now, for the third, might some one say, What hath the Christian's burial to do with Christ? how is there any relation between them?

Ans. Our spiritual burial in the progress of mortification depends upon Christ divers ways: 1. In that he hath required and made gracious promises to it; 2. In that the efficacy of the means by which it is wrought comes from Christ; 3. In that it is accepted of God only for Christ and through his intercession; 4. In respect of example—he was buried as well as we. But chiefly in respect of virtue, our burial of sin is wrought by a virtue arising from Christ's burial in the grave.

Uses. The uses of all this follows: first, For information. Here we may see how God stands upon mortification, and that men must not think always they have done enough when they have left their faults; and withal we may see how dangerous a course they take that so soon give over the exercises of mortification, for by this means we cause the old sins many times to break out again, and their consolations are small and seldom. Crosses daily trouble them, and the heart is often grieved and griped with fear and terrible doubts, or else they are quickly overgrown with a spirit of slumber.

Secondly, For instruction, to be careful to bury our sins. But here take heed of the dissimilitude, for in some things the comparison cannot hold. As here in two things: For first, When we bury the bodies of our friends, we bury them in hope they shall rise again; and secondly, We mourn because we must part with them; but both these must be denied here. It is the property of the wicked to part with their sins with sorrow, because they must leave them, or else with hope that at length they may return to them again. But let all such as fear God be otherwise minded; especially let us learn from this comparison of burial to advantage ourselves in what we may in mortification. If the master be buried, we know all his servants will attend the funeral. So it is with us in the mortification of sins, if we light upon the master sins and drag them to the grave, we shall be sure of all the attendants, they will follow to the funeral. The Jews' manner was to bury with odours: so should we, our odours and sweet smelling prayers offered up in the mediation of Christ. And howsoever this work may seem difficult, yet God many times strangely relieves our infirmities. After Jezebel was cast down and dead, they had not been long within, but sending out to bury her, they found nothing but the skull, and her feet, and the palms of her hands. So many times would it be with us, if we cast down the Jezebels, our sins, when we come to finish our mortification, we may by the strange help of God find the body of the master gone we know not how, so as we shall not be troubled, unless it be with some skull, or feet, or palm of sin. But certainly though this kind of burial be somewhat difficult, yet it is the true burial-place of kings, the most noble funeral that can be.

Thus of the first effect; the second is in the next words.

In whom ye are raised up together. Christ is said to raise men up divers ways: 1. When he awaketh men out of their natural lethargy, or spiritual sleepiness and security in matters of religion, thus Eph. v. 14; 2. When he brings forth the minds of men out of the dungeons of ignorance, and shews them the light, Isa. lx. 1, 2; 3. When he cures men of discouragements and discomforts under their crosses, Ps. xli. 10; 4. When he recovers the church from security or relapses, either ordinary or extraordinary, Cant. ii. 10, 11, &c., v. 3, 5, Prov. xxiv. 15, 16; 5. When he encourageth men to holy duties, Cant. vii. 12. But principally there is a fourfold resurrection: the first is out of desperate crosses, Isa. xxvi. 19; the second is the lifting of men up some special callings in the church, Mat. xi.; the third is the resurrection of our bodies at the last day; and the last is the resurrection of the soul unto holy graces and duties: this is called the first resurrection, and is meant here in this place, and Rom. vi. 4; but most usually we say there is a twofold resurrection, the one from the corruption of the flesh, the other from the corruption of sin. This latter is here meant, and this belongeth to vivification.

Now this first resurrection must be considered either in itself or in the union or relation of it. In itself, and so there is a double resurrection: first, The resurrection of graces; secondly, The resurrection of duties. For the first, there are certain graces, which are not in the heart of man by nature, which by the mighty power of Christ are wrought in the hearts of such as are truly converted, and are actually the members of Christ: as first, A holy inquiry after God, Hosea ii. 5, Jer. l. 4; secondly, A holy wisdom in spiritual things, James iii. 17; thirdly, A lively faith in the favour of God in Christ; fourthly, A holy delight and meditation in the word of God, Ps. cxix. 10, 11, 128, and xxvii. 4; fifthly, A lively hope of an eternal inheritance, 1 Pet. i. 3; sixthly, A holy love of God's children, 1 John iii. 14, such as is required, Rom. xii. 9-11; seventhly, Godly sorrow for sin, 2 Cor. vii. 10; eighthly, Unspeakable and glorious joy even in affliction, Rom. v. 2, 1 Pet. i. 7, 8; ninthly, A holy contempt of the world, and sin, and sinful persons, Ps. xv. 4, 1 John ii. 19; tenthly, A holy reverence and fear of God and his goodness, Hosea iii. 5; eleventhly, A holy zeal and fervency of affections, especially in the service and worship of God; twelfthly, A holy love even of enemies; and lastly, A holy desire to be dissolved and to be with Christ. Now for the effecting of these, the Spirit of Christ is called, in respect of wonderful working, the Spirit of God and of glory,

1 Pet. iv. 14; the Spirit of power, of love, and of a sound mind, 2 Tim. i. 7; the Spirit of prayer or deprecation, Zech. xii. 12; and the Spirit of revelation, Eph. i. 17.

Thus of resurrection of graces; now concerning resurrection of duties.

We must know that there are divers duties which the natural man will never be brought unto, in which lieth the very power of godliness, and the experience of all sound and saving consolation. Now these duties may be three ways considered : 1. As they respect holy life in general; 2. As they respect piety to God; 3. As they respect righteousness to men. For the first, there are four things wherein the lives of God's children differ from all others: 1. In the manner; 2. In the matter; 3. In the means; 4. In the ends of holy life. For the manner, three things are eminent : 1. That they are devoted and consecrated to holiness, Rev. xii. 1; 2. That they delight and love to be God's servants, Isa. lvi.; 3. That they have their conversation in simplicity and godly pureness, 2 Cor. i. 12, xi. 3.

For the matter, they have respect to all God's commandments, Ps. cxix. 31, and do endeavour after inward holiness, Mat. v. 6, as well as outward. Besides, they live by faith in some measure, Rom. i. 17, which is a way of holiness altogether unknown in the practice of wicked men. And for the means of holiness, the godly have a recourse to a threefold fountain of sanctity, with such a sincerity and constancy as no wicked man can attain it, viz., the word, Ps. i. 2, Luke viii. 15; prayer, Gal. iv. 6; and the Sabbath, Isa. lvi. And for the end of their obedience, their praise is of God and not of men, Rom. ii. 29, having a main respect always to exercise themselves so as they may have a conscience void of offence towards God or towards men, Acts xxiv. 16.

Thus of holiness of life in general.

Now in respect of piety to God, it is a very resurrection through the power of Christ to bring a man to acknowledge God and his truth and glory, against reason, profit, or pleasure; to make a man walk with God, setting the Lord always before him; to bring the will of man to a holy subjection to God's will in crosses, temptations, wants, &c.; but especially to create in man that sincerity of worshipping God in spirit and truth without hypocrisy.

And as for righteousness, in that part of it that concerns either men's own souls or the souls of others, how is all the unregenerate mankind dead? It is the work of a godly man only to serve the brethren by love. Only the members of Christ can in their calling deny profit and pleasure, and make the particular calling serve the general : but especially in the combat against concupiscence, only the godly do make conscience of it.

And howsoever in the matter of holy duties there are strange imperfections in the very godly, yet their desire, prayer, purpose, and endeavour, is to approve themselves to God herein; and they do attain to it, in some comfortable beginnings, and they go on with a holy increase both of strength and desire. Whereas it is evident by divers scriptures that wicked men are dead men in the former respects, as would appear if we should examine particularly. For they seek not God, Ps. xiv. 1. They respect not the word of God aright, Jer. vi. 10; nor can they love the brethren, John xv. 19. Though they be smitten, yet they will not sorrow after God, Jer. v. 3. And for the most part they are lukewarm, without true zeal, Rev. iii. Their minds are covered with a veil, Isa. lii. 8. They are without hope, Eph. ii. 12; neither have all these men faith, 2 Thes. iii. 2. And for the want of holy duties it usually seems evil unto them to serve the Lord. They are strangers from the life of God, Eph. iv. 18. They call not upon the name of God with a pure heart, Ps. xiv. 4; neither take they heed of God's Sabbaths. But it were too long to run to particulars in matters of duty, seeing the scripture everywhere points out the ill lives of all wicked men.

In whom. *Doct.* The virtue by which Christians are raised is from Christ.

Quest. But what is there in Christ which distinctly causeth this resurrection in the Christian, or plucketh up his heart to the care of holy graces or duties ?

Ans. 1. The virtue of Christ; 2. The Spirit of Christ; 3. The example of Christ; 4. The intercession of Christ; 5. The loving invitations and allurements of Christ; 6. The resurrection of Christ; and lastly, The second coming of Christ is like a loadstone to pluck up the desires and affections of Christians unto the study of heavenly things.

Thus of the doctrine of the Christian's resurrection.

Use 1. Hence may presumptuous, secure, wilful sinners gather secret terror and anguish. Where is thy spiritual burial in this life? Where is the first resurrection? It is most certain, if this work, this strange work, be not wrought in thee, thou art in the power of the second death, without God, without Christ, without hope. And here thou mayest see the vanity of all thy shifts, for dost thou say thou seest no such wretchedness in thy sinful course? Why, this doctrine tells thou art dead while thou livest, and how canst thou discern thine own wretchedness? Dost thou think that this will serve thy turn, that thou intendest to mend hereafter? Consider what is here implied, the work of true amendment is a true but spiritual resurrection. It is, then, like that resurrection that shall be of our bodies; and thou knowest when God shall raise our bodies at the last day, when the trump shall blow, it will be a silly pretence to say, Oh, let me alone now, I will rise hereafter. So it is with thee; the trumpet of grace now bloweth, Christ is now coming in the Spirit, the dead in sin must now be raised, Christ's voice still reacheth unto thee. Now, if thou confirm thyself in that spiritual grave of sin, dost thou think thou hast reason to believe that Christ will tarry thy leisure, and put off till thou appoint the time?

Use 2. Here is singular comfort for such of God's children as are afflicted in spirit, especially about the greatness of the power of sin, and the difficulties of well-doing; they should here consider not only that it is Christ's work to make them holy, but that he is pleased to resemble it to the resurrection of the body. And can it be a harder thing to put down thy sin, or to quicken thee in all well-doing, than to raise thy body out of the dust of the earth? Neither ought their terrors to amaze them, for it is Christ's manner to bring us down to the grave that he may raise us up. The fear of hell now afflicteth thee that thou mayest not be hurt hereafter. Besides, sin doth so cleave to us that it will almost kill us before we kill it.

Object. But I do not see either the graces or duties mentioned to be wrought in this resurrection.

Ans. 1. There may be grace though thou see it not. 2. If one saving grace be in a man's heart, it is a sign the rest be there, though not so easily discerned. 3. The spiritual age of a Christian must be distinguished: thou must not think that the graces of God's Spirit, or the power of holy duties, will appear so freshly or so strongly in thee while thou art but an infant in grace, as they will do when thou comest to be of riper years. Lastly, Thy endeavour in Christ and desire is accepted and taken for the deed: what graces thou unfeignedly desirest, and constantly usest the means to attain, thou hast; so the sin thou strivest against thou hast not.

Thus of these effects, as they are in themselves; now as they are in their sign, which is here called baptism.

By baptism. Baptism is a holy memorial of Christ baptized in the seas of God's wrath for us. It is a badge of distinction from unbelievers. It is a certain initiating rite by which we enter into the visible church. It is a seal of the righteousness of faith. It is a sign to teach us by representation both our deliverance and sanctification.

Quest. But what hath baptism to do here with our mortification and vivification, or spiritual burial and resurrection?

Ans. Baptism stands in a threefold relation or respect unto them: 1. In signification, baptism doth represent them unto us, setting out our dying to sin, and rising to newness of life; 2. By seal, for baptism is a seal of God's covenant, assuring us that in Christ we shall be buried to our sins, and raised up with him; 3. It is a band, it ties us to the desires and endeavours after the beginning and finishing of these.

There are many other benefits signified and assured unto us by baptism than these here mentioned, for baptism doth signify and seal unto us: 1. Our deliverance from the seas of God's wrath, Mat. iii. 8, 1 Pet. iii. 21; 2. The resurrection of our bodies, 1 Cor. xv.; 3. Our communion with the whole Trinity, Mat. xxviii.; 4. Our adoption, Gal. iii. 27; 5. Our communion with the saints, 1 Cor. xii. 13; 6. Remission of all sins, Acts ii. 38, 39.

Baptism is available for these respects: When we amend our lives and confess our sins, Mat. iii. 8; and gladly receive the word, Cant. ii. 14; and lay hold upon the promises of grace, Mark xvi. 16; especially when the conscience maketh request unto God, 1 Pet. iii. 21, for the application and fruition of the things signified by baptism. Hitherto of the effects. The causes follow: 1. Faith; 2. The operation of God; 3. Christ's resurrection.

Through the faith of the operation of God. The faith that is mighty through God to make baptism effectual, and to raise us up after the burial of sin, is neither historical nor temporary, nor of miracles, but that which is in scripture called the faith of God's elect, and by divines justifying faith. Nor is it enough to bring hither the persuasion of God's mercy in Christ, which is the first and chief act of justifying faith; but we must believe the power of God in the particular success of the means for effecting both of mortification and vivification, which, as I suppose, is here meant, where he calleth it, 'the faith of the operation of God.'

Quest. But shew us how faith hath to do in baptism or in sanctification.

Ans. In baptism faith is needful, not only the faith of explication, but also the faith of application; for we are bound not only to believe that those things there shadowed out are so as they import, but that also they are fulfilled, not only to the faithful in general, but to my own soul in particular.

And for sanctification faith must needs be of great use, for without faith nothing we do can please God, Heb. xi. 6; and by faith Christ lives in us, Gal. ii. 20; it quencheth the fiery darts of the devil, Eph. vi. 16; it lighteneth our darkness, John xii. 46; it purifieth the heart, Acts xv. 9; it overcomes the world, 1 John v. 4; it breeds joy and consolation, Rom. v. 2; and love to God's children, Gal. vi.; it maketh the scripture available to salvation, 2 Tim. iii. 15; and, lastly, our prayers to be such as God cannot deny.

Quest. How may we attain to it to believe that baptism doth signify and assure these things to us?

Ans. 1. Labour to express that which on thy part is required, that is, set up the confession of thy sins and amendment of thy life; 2. Then go unto God, and let thy conscience make request for the answer of the Spirit of adoption, by which the Lord may assure thee, that, in the mediation of Jesus Christ, thy baptism is given to thee as a particular seal of God's covenant and grace.

Quest. But how may I do to be assured that my sins shall be subdued, and that I shall be raised up in holy graces and duties?

Ans. 1. Acquaint thyself with God's promises of this kind, and grow skilful in them; 2. Cry strongly to God for the testimony of Jesus in thy heart, that by his Spirit he would settle thee in this persuasion; 3. Wait upon the word and prayer till God do effect it; 4. Strengthen thyself both by the experience of others, as also with due observation of success in the subduing of any sin, or the exercise of any graces or duties.

Uses. The uses may be divers. First, For information. We may here see how vain the common faith of the common protestant is: shew me thy faith by thy fruits; how canst thou believe aright, and yet thy sins not mortified, and thy heart and life unsanctified? Again, we see we have not comfort of our baptism till the power of holiness in some measure appear in our lives.

Secondly, For instruction. We should all examine ourselves whether we have faith or no; and while we have means of assurance, make use of all advantages to settle our hearts in the faith; and to this end we should deliver up our souls to be nursed up in the words of faith and wholesome doctrine.

Lastly, We might here be greatly comforted if we had true faith. We see God can deny nothing unto faith. It should be to us, in the sacraments, in mortification, and in graces and duties, according to our faith.

Of the operation of God. The doctrine of God's power and working is of singular use in the church. Great is the interest of God's servants in his power, and therefore great cause they have to rest upon it. The elect only can reason from God's power to the effect: he is able to do it, therefore he will do it. But then these three things must be noted:—

1. They must be believers that look for this privilege; 2. They must bring a particular faith to draw out this power of God into operation; 3. It will not be set a-work about everything, but such things for which there is promise or meet examples in the scriptures.

Now, it is a matter of singular weight to know in

what things we may have warrant to bear ourselves upon the power of God. The power of God is engaged for operation in four things for the benefit of the faithful: first, In their afflictions; secondly, In their temptations; thirdly, In the difficulties of holy life; fourthly, In his ordinances.

In afflictions, God hath bound himself to shew his power: 1. In giving strength to endure them, Phil. iv. 13, Isa. xli. 10; 2. In moderating the afflictions to their strength, Isa. xxvii. 7; 3. In guiding them to the right ends, Job xvi. 22, Isa. xxvii. 11, Zech. xiii. 9; 4. In deliverance out of them, Ps. lxxi. 20, Isa. xliii. If we look upon the enemies of the godly in particular, God shews his power: 1. In restraining or disappointing them, Job xii. 16, Isa. liv. 16, 17; 2. In rewarding and overthrowing them, Exod. xv. 6, 7, Isa. xlii. 13, xli. 15.

So likewise in temptations, the power of God; though it be secret, yet it is wonderful in dissolving the works of the devil, and in upholding his servants, and destroying the strongholds and fortifications of Satan, 1 Cor. x. 12, 2 Cor. xii. 9, Isa. xxvii. 1.

Thirdly, In the difficulties of holy life, the Lord useth his power: 1. In making his servants able to walk in his ways, both by giving them power and strength, Ezek. xxxvi. 28, Isa. xxvi. 12, and by relieving and reviving their strength daily, and renewing it, Isa. xl. 29–31, and lvii. 15; 2. In keeping them from evil, 2 Tim. iv. 18; 3. In establishing them that they may persevere and hold out, Phil. i. 6, Jude 24, 1 Pet. i. 5, 1 Sam. xxix.

Lastly, God's operation is wonderful in the use of his ordinances, and this is that is meant in this place. In respect of this the psalmist saith, 'God is greatly to be reverenced in the assembly by all them that are round about him: O Lord God of hosts, who is a strong God like unto thee?' Ps. lxxxix. 7, 8. Thus the Lord is mighty through the ministry of his servants, Gal. ii. 8, Col. i. *ult.* Thus the Lord performeth the counsel of his messengers, Isa. xliv. 26; his word returneth not to him in vain, Isa. lv. 11; yea, his ordinances are his power unto salvation, Rom. i. 16, 1 Cor. i. 18; they are all mighty through God, 2 Cor. x. 4. Thus it is in particular in the sacraments: though for their outward show they do not promise much, yet, by the marvellous operation of God, they are available in effect for all that is promised in them, only if we could get this faith in this operation of God here mentioned.

Uses. The use of all is: first, For information. We may here take notice of the difference between hypocrites and the godly. In matter of godliness they can know nothing but the form of it, the other have experience of the singular power of God in all the passages of holy life, both in the use of the means, and in his preservation.

Secondly, For instruction. We should observe and seek out 'the working of the Lord,' Ps. cxi. 2, and daily ascribe power unto God, and pray for the experience of it, and that he would 'establish that which he hath wrought in us,' Ps. lxviii. 28.

Again, it may teach us not to despise the weak Christian, for 'the Lord is able,' through his operation, 'to make him stand.' And it should encourage us all to the works of righteousness, Heb. xi. 35, seeing God's operation is so ready to be found; and for hereafter in the use of all the means 'our faith should be in the power of God,' 1 Cor. ii. 5. Thus of the operation of God.

Through the resurrection of Jesus Christ. Many are the benefits which we reap from the resurrection of Jesus Christ. As first, The resurrection of our bodies, 1 Cor. xv. 16, 20; secondly, The accomplishment of the promises made unto the fathers, Acts xiii. 33; thirdly, Justification and forgiveness of sins, Rom. iv. 25; fourthly, A secret virtue unto the ordinances of God, 1 Pet. iii. 21; fifthly, Regeneration; sixthly, Lively hope of an immortal inheritance, 1 Cor. xv. 14, 1 Pet. i. 3, 4; seventhly, The power of vivification and raising of us up to new obedience. And this last is acknowledged in this place.

Ver. 13. *And you, being dead in your sins and the uncircumcision of the flesh, hath he quickened together with him, forgiving you all your trespasses.*

The sixth reason of the dehortation is contained in this verse, and it stands thus: That which cannot help us when we are in misery, nor further us to happiness when we want it, is not to be followed nor rested upon; but such things are philosophy, traditions, and ceremonies; they cannot heal the corruptions of our natures, nor raise us out of the graves of sin, nor any way procure us the pardon of our transgressions. Or thus, If in Christ we be delivered from the power of our sins by his quickening grace, and from the guilt of them by the free pardon which is to be had by his means, then we need not go any whither else, neither to philosophy nor traditions, &c.; but so it is, and so the very Colossians found it in their case, as the words of the text express, *ergo*.

The words in themselves express the twofold estate of Christians in this world, what they are by nature in their unregenerate estate, and what they are by grace in the estate of grace.

In the state of corruption two things are true of them, and are true of all men: 1. They were dead in actual sins; 2. They were then in the uncircumcision of the flesh, and likewise dead in it. In their estate of grace he puts them in mind of two benefits: 1. Regeneration; 2. Remission of sins.

Thus of the coherence and order of the words.

Divers things may be noted in the general.

1. We may from hence be informed of the fruitlessness of philosophy, traditions, or ceremonies of Moses: they cannot make a miserable man happy, they cannot infuse the least spark of spiritual life into any.

2. We see the apostle thinks it meet to put men often in mind of their misery by nature; and great reason, for it exalts the praise of the riches of God's grace in Christ. And it may serve to humble men for their falls after calling, and to keep them still suspicious and watchful over a nature that hath been so prone to sin and security in sinning; it may serve to eat down the proneness of our nature to vain boasting and confidence in the flesh; and it should much excite men to the love and care of godliness and piety, with all life and power, seeing they have been so long slaves to sin.

And lastly, The apostle rips up this matter of purpose to withdraw their minds from traditions and philosophical dreams.

Dead in sins. They were dead in sins, both if you respected their public estate, or each particular person. If you look upon public estates before they are framed and reformed by the word, what are they but heaps of men dead in the graves of sin, and senseless in their sinful courses? And thus it is with every particular person; the words import that he is guilty of many sins, and he is dead in them also. Naturally every man is guilty of secret atheistical conceits, of unbelief, of ignorance, of hardness of heart, of swarms of evil thoughts and affections, of hurtful passions and lusts, besides his defects of the knowledge of God, and that warmth of the holy affections of love, fear, trust, and joy in God. Who can sufficiently rip open the unthankfulness, lukewarmness, hypocrisy, inconstancy, and presumptuous profaneness that is in our hearts by nature, in matters of God's service? How do men daily offend, either by not calling upon the name of God, or by taking it up in vain? Who can number the oaths, lies, reproaches, curses, flatteries, and filthy communication, hath and did daily infect the mouths of men? Oh, the world of sins we are actually guilty of against God, or men, or our ownselves; public, private, secret, open, inward, outward, in prosperity, and adversity, in the church or family, or abroad in men's conversation! Alas! we can discern but a glimpse of that sin and guiltiness that is in us by nature; and this is the increase of their misery in all their sins, they are dead in them.

Dead. There is a fourfold death: temporal, corporal, spiritual, eternal. The state of man being in misery, he is dead temporally, Isa. xxvi. 19. The body of man being in the grave, he is dead corporally; the soul of man lying in sin, is dead spiritually; and both soul and body being cast into hell, are dead eternally.

The Colossians were dead spiritually; there is a death *to* sin, and a death *for* sin, and a death *in* sin: a death to sin, and so the godly die by mortification; a death for sin, and so malefactors die by execution; and a death in sin, and so every natural man kills himself by enliving his sin.

The spiritual death in sin is an unutterable loss of the life of God, by which the sinner is senseless and careless in extremity of misery, unto his own everlasting ruin, if the Lord prevent it not by regeneration. Now, that men are in this case by nature, these scriptures prove: Eph. ii. 1, 2; Mat. viii. 22; John viii. 25; Rom. viii. 10; Luke xv. 32; Rev. iii. 2; Jude 12; 1 Tim. v. 6. Neither let any deceive themselves about their estate, for a man may be dead in sin, and yet be alive in the flesh; yea, thou mayest be a wise man in the flesh, Rom. viii.

7. or a prince of this world, 1 Cor. ii. 9, 14; yea, thou mayest have a name that thou livest spiritually, Rev. iii. 2; and yet be stark dead.

Now this spiritual senselessness is called a death: 1. Because it is a privation of spiritual life from the soul, as the natural death is from the body; 2. Because it tends to eternal death.

The use may be fourfold: 1. For information. No wonder wicked men can come and go from the word of God and not be touched. Alas! they are dead men: and so is it with them in respect of the judgments of God. Alas! if thou couldst roll a mountain upon a dead man, he would not feel; so is it with a man dead in sin. And further, we may here observe, that to live, yea, to die quietly, is no sign of a man in a happy case; for if this death in sin be not cured, thousands of people may die quietly, because they die senselessly; they feel no more of the fear of hell, or judgment, or God's anger, than, if they were already dead in their bodies, they would feel outward extremities. I know that God many times can lay terror upon the flesh of wicked men, and make their spirits drink in of the bitter anguish arising from the fervency of God's burning displeasure; but I say if God let them alone, usually the most would die in a wretched senselessness and inconsideration, being neither able nor willing to entertain the thoughts of what must presently and necessarily befall them.

2. This may serve for confutation; and so (1.) Of the papists about their free will. How can there be this free will in a dead soul? We are dead in sin, and therefore of ourselves move not unto life till God quicken us by his word and Spirit. (2.) Of the carnal protestant, that bears himself so strongly upon his supposed 'covenant with death and hell.' His 'agreement must be disannulled;' nay, his very security imports his unavoidable destruction, if it be not removed by the power of Christ.

3. For instruction: Art thou a man that hearest this, that hast lived all thy time without remorse for thy sins, and never yet entertained the care of reformation of thy life? Be here warned of thy misery; let it be enough thou hast been dead in sin; do not lie still rotting in the graves of iniquity, but rise so soon as thou hearest the trumpet of the gospel, the voice of Christ sounding in thine ears, and piercing thy heart.

4. Lastly, Here is consolation implied unto weak Christians. If thou canst feel thy misery, and struggle in any measure of true constancy against the corruption of nature and the transgressions of thy heart and life, thou art not dead, there is some breath of life in thee, there is motion, and therefore life.

Thus of their actual sins.

Their misery in respect of original sin is expressed in these words:

And in the uncircumcision of the flesh. These words be diversely interpreted. Some thus: in the uncircumcision of the flesh, that is, in the flesh which is uncircumcision, that is, a thing hateful to God. Some make these words to be the sign of their death in sin; as if he would say, Your very uncircumcision, that is, in your flesh (which are Gentiles), is a token that you are strangers from the life of God. Some thus: And you hath he quickened which were dead in respect of your sins and carnal life, which ye lived in the uncircumcision—that is, in your estate of Gentilism. Some make these words express the cause of their death in sin. Thus, in the uncircumcision of the flesh—that is, for your fleshly vices which caused that death in sin. But I think with those that understand by the flesh original sin, and by the uncircumcision, their misery in respect of it, implied in the allusion to the circumcision literally taken.

Original sin is called flesh, because the flesh is the instrument by which it is propagated; 2. Because it is the subject in which it is; 3. Because it is the end it drives us to, viz., to satisfy the flesh, and to seek fleshly things.

This original sin here called flesh is a spiritual kind of disease—gall, leaven, and poison, which daily diffuseth itself throughout the whole man, and still infecteth it, though this be not the whole nature of the sin; for to speak distinctly, in original sin there are three things: 1. The guiltiness of Adam's fact derived unto us by just imputation; 2. The want of that original justice was in us in the creation; 3. The depravation and corrupt disposition of our natures.

Here the word uncircumcision imports our misery in respect of our very corruption of nature, for it imports: 1. That we are hateful to God, children of wrath; 2. That we have no portion in the heavenly Canaan; 3. That we have no fellowship in the communion of saints; 4. That we have no part in the promised Messias;—for all these were shadowed out by the want of circumcision in the time of the law.

Uses. The uses follow: First, From hence we may inform ourselves in divers things; as, first, we may see why the fair works of wicked men, as their alms, prayers, tears, sacrifices, prophesyings, preaching, fasting, and professing, are not accepted of God; for the fountain is poisoned, the flesh infects all; it puts to either ill ends, or ill effects, or ill means; besides that, it keeps the person still loathsome to God. Oh, what cause have civil, honest men to know that though they come to church, and pay every man his own, and be no drunkards nor adulterers, &c., yet their case cannot be good, for though they lived never so honestly outwardly, yet the very uncircumcision of the flesh makes them miserable; the inward corruption of nature is an abomination to God, who 'searcheth the hearts and reins!' yea, what cause have all men to be humbled and abased in themselves, considering how unclean a beginning they have! How can men be so quiet, and yet be so diseased with so filthy a leprosy as is original sin? If this disease were in the body, as it is in the soul, how would men lament their distress!

Hence, also, may we see what a woeful estate all wicked men are in that take care for the lusts of this leprous flesh, and sow to it. What should I say? May we not see hence the necessity of regeneration? Assuredly 'except we be born again, we can never enter into the kingdom of heaven:' this impure, poisoned nature of ours may not enter into God's holy place.

Secondly, We may here discern the fountain of all actual transgressions. When we fall into evil courses we must not cry out of our ill fortune, or of ill company, or of the devil only, but especially we must lay the fault upon our ill natures; 'twas thy wicked disposition made thee so to sin.

Lastly, From hence we may learn to know ourselves, and accordingly to keep a narrow watch over our wretched natures, and daily strive and struggle against this infectious corruption and disease that hangs so fast upon us, Heb. xii. 1; yea, we should by confession and contrition endeavour the daily crucifying of our wicked flesh, with the lusts thereof, Gal. v. 24, condemning ourselves by a daily verdict and sentence, as we are men according to the flesh, 1 Pet. iv. 6, so suffering in the flesh that we may cease from sin, 1 Pet. iv. 1; yea, we should learn constantly to deny ourselves, and not to give way to the reasons, or objections, or desires, or excuses, or delays of the flesh; yea, and to this end we should be willing to suffer afflictions, and to endure any hardship, rather than the flesh should prevail in us.

You hath he quickened. Hitherto of man's misery and the state of corruption; now of God's mercy in the state of grace. In two things is their happiness here described: 1. In their quickening; 2. In their forgiveness.

We are quickened two ways: 1. In Christ; 2. In ourselves. When our head Christ Jesus was raised from the grave, we were quickened in him. In ourselves we were quickened three ways: 1. Sacramentally, in baptism; 2. By inchoation in our conversion; 3. Perfectly, by hope of perfection in heaven: by baptism, by conversion, by hope. The quickening he here speaketh of is the quickening of conversion, when we are begotten to God.

This life is called the life of God, Eph. iv. 17, the life of grace, the life of Jesus, 1 Cor. iv. 16, the life of immortality.

It is begotten in us by the whole Trinity: the Father calleth up these generations, Isa. xli.; the Son giveth this life, Heb. vii. 16; so doth the Spirit quicken also, John vi.

The means by which we are quickened is ordinarily only the word, and that preached also, which is therefore called 'the word of life,' Ps. xix. 8, 1 Pet. i. 22, Phil. ii. 15, John v.

The necessity of this quickening is such as without it we cannot possibly enter into the kingdom of heaven, John iii. 5.

They that are thus quickened and converted are styled by divers names or titles: they are called the holy seed, Isa. vi.; the called of Jesus, Rom. i. 6; the children of the Most High, Luke vi.; the brood of immortality; they that follow Christ in the regeneration, Mat. xix.; and the heirs of eternal life, Titus iii. 7.

Many are the singular prerogatives of such as are converted and quickened in Jesus Christ; 'godliness,' in general, 'hath the promises of this life and the life to come.' In special: first, great is the honour of their birth, greater than if they were born of the greatest bloods of men, John i. 13. These prolong the days of Christ upon earth, being begotten by the travail of his soul, Isa. liii. 2. They are sweetly comforted and tenderly used in the healing of all their sorrows, Jer. xxxi. 25, Hos. xiv. 5, Isa. lvii. 15, 16, lxi. 1-3, Micah vii. 18, Ezek. xi. 19, Isa. l. 4, Acts iii. 19. 3. All their sins are forgiven, as the coherence shews, and these scriptures further confirm: Isa. xliv. 22, Eph. i. 6, 7, Rom. iii. 25, 1 Cor. vi. 11, Heb. viii. 12, 1 John i. 7. 4. They are in great account with God, Isa. xliii. 4, Rom. i. 7. 5. They are delivered from this present evil world, Gal i. 4; even from bondage under the custom of it; from the practice of the vices of it; from the fellowship with the men of it; and from the plagues that belong unto it. 6. They are blessed with the seeds of all spiritual blessings in heavenly things, Eph. i. 3, Isa. lxi. 10. 7. They are happy in their heavenly relations, to God, to Jesus the mediator, to the angels of God, to the spirits of the just, and to the faithful everywhere, Heb. xii. 22. 8. They are assured of the success of all the means of salvation, Isa. xii. 3, lxv. 15-23, and lvi., 1 Cor. iii. 22, 23, Isa. lv. 6. 9. They have great promises of comfort, audience, protection, and deliverance out of all their troubles, Isa. iv. 5, 6, Rom. viii. 17, &c., 2 Cor. i. 3, 4, Isa. xli. 12, xlii. 13, and xlix. 14. 10. The Spirit of God is poured upon them, to assure them of God's loving presence, Ezek. xxxix. 29; to bring them forth unto liberty, 2 Cor. iii. 17; to enlighten them, 2 Cor. iii. 18; to sanctify them, Rom. i. 3; to make intercession, and that by making them pray, Gal. iv. 6; and by producing mighty success in prayer, Rom. viii. 26, Hosea xii. 5, 6; and to make them fruitful both in graces and duties, Ezek. xxxvi. 27; and to be the seal and earnest of the inheritance purchased, 2 Cor. i. 22, Eph. i. 13, 14. Lastly, They have an assurance of a most glorious inheritance reserved for them in heaven, prepared from the foundation of the world, 1 Pet. i. 3, 4.

Now, if any enamoured with these privileges ask how we may know whether we be converted and quickened or not? I answer, it may be known by divers signs. Of these signs, some agree to the weak Christian, and some to the strong Christian. The first sign that usually breaks out in a convert is affliction of conscience, which is such an inward pricking in the heart, Acts ii. 41, as causeth him voluntarily to remember his evil ways, Ezek. xx. 43, and judge himself daily for it, Isa. iv. 4, mourning for his sinful life, Isa. lxi. 2, 3, and confounded in himself for his ways, which were not good. The second is, affection to the word; such an affection it is as esteemeth the word above all treasure, Mat. xiii., and longs daily after it, Job xxiii.; it makes them fly as the dove to God's house, and as doves to the windows, Isa. lx. 8, yea, their affections to it are such as heaven suffers violence, Mat. xi.; they feel a savour of life in the word, 2 Cor. ii. 14; Christ's words to them are spirit and life, John vi., yea, such is their affection to the word, they can be content to receive it with patience and much afflictions, 1 Thes. i. 6; and if they obtain a sanctuary of God, they will endeavour their own daily sanctification by it, Ezek. xxxvii. 28; they will practise the word and be exercised by it. The third sign that discovers itself in them is their love to such as fear God, 1 John iii. 14, which they shew by their admiration of them, Isa. lxi. 7, and by their delight in their fellowship, Phil. i. 5, and by a willing communicating to them in all ready service and well-doing, Acts xvi. 14, 15, Heb. vi. 9, 10, Isa. xxiii. 18. The fourth sign is their ceasing from sin, even their daily endeavour to subdue and forsake all sorts of sins, inward as well as outward, secret as well as open, lesser as well as greater, yea, not sparing their most pleasing, gainful, or beloved sins, 2 Tim. ii. 19, Ps. xiv. 6, 4, Isa. lv. 8, Mat. xviii. 8. The fifth sign is a holy constant desire after God's favour, and remission of sins, as the greatest happiness, rejoicing in all the hopes and signs of it, Isa. lv. 1. The sixth is, that they can love and forgive their enemies, Mat. v. 6.

Now, there are other signs in stronger Christians, such as these: 1. A full assurance of faith in Jesus Christ. 2. A longing and constant desire of death, and love to the appearing of Jesus Christ in a sensible and ardent measure, and that in prosperity. 3. A great conquest and victory in overcoming the world and the flesh. 4. The spirit of prayer, and such like.

Uses. The use of this point concerning the quickening of the godly by true conversion to God is divers: First, Since this is the first and common work, without which we can never get out of our natural misery, here may the cursed and damnable waywardness of the most be reproved, who live snorting in sin, as if they needed no conversion to God. How hath a very spirit of spiritual fornication intoxicated men, and besotted them that they cannot mind to return, Hosea v. 4.

Three sorts of men grievously transgress against this doctrine:

1. The careless, that freeze in their dregs, and consider not whether God will do good or evil; 2. The inconstant, whose righteousness is as the morning dew, that by flashes and fits only think of turning to God; 3. The profane scoffer, that speaks evil of the good way of God, and reproacheth by consequence the very blood of Christ, without which he can never be saved.

2. Here is an excellent comfort to weak Christians. Note that the text saith *quickened*, not *born*, to assure the weak that though their strength be but as the child's when it lieth in the womb and is first quickened, and not so much as the strength of a child new born, yet they are accepted with God. The first springings in the womb of grace is precious before God, though everything be not yet so clearly performed; yet if grace be but conceived in them, God knows them, and owns them, and will not deny his own works, but annexeth here forgiveness of sins, even to this first sprouting and forming of true grace.

3. How should the consideration of this work, and the glorious privileges belonging to it, even compel all men to 'awake and stand up from the dead,' and never give over till 'Christ be formed in them!' labouring above all things to be made new creatures; resolving to beg this quickening at God's hands, till by his word he be pleased to beget it in them.

Lastly, How should they walk in newness of life that are born again of God! There is a path and it is called holy, and they must walk in it, Isa. xxxv. 8. Seeing this grace hath appeared, how should they deny ungodliness and worldly lusts, for ever resolving to live 'soberly, and godly, and righteously in this present world,' Titus ii. 12. And they should 'give all diligence to make up their assurance of their holy calling and election,' 2 Pet. i. 10, Heb. vi. 12, 'girding up the loins of their minds, that they might trust perfectly on the grace that is brought unto them, in the revelation of Jesus Christ,' 1 Pet. i. 13. And since they are in so happy an estate, they should 'always rejoice,' and 'let their moderation of mind be known to all men, being in nothing careful, but in all things making request unto God, with prayers and supplications, and giving of thanks;' so should 'the peace of God that passeth all understanding, keep their hearts and minds,' Phil. iv. 6, 7.

And for our carriage towards others: first, We should for ever in all places, acknowledge such as are born again of God, 1 Cor xvi. 10, 2 Cor. i. 14; secondly, We should 'exhort one another, and provoke one another to love and good works,' and, 'not forsake the fellowship of the saints,' Heb. x. 24-26; praying one for another, that God would 'fulfil the good pleasure of his will, and the work of our faith with power, that we might abound in love, and be established in holiness before God, in the coming of our Lord Jesus Christ with all the saints,' 1 Thes. iii. 12, 13.

Thus of our quickening; only we may observe that he saith, we are quickened together with him, which is true divers ways. Men are quickened together with Christ: 1. Because we are quickened as well as he; 2. Because, being quickened, we are united unto him; 3. Because we are quickened by the same Spirit and power that raised him from the dead. All which may increase our consolation in this gracious work, and confirm us unto the end.

Forgiving you all your trespasses. First, for the meaning of the words: the word 'forgiving,' as it is in the orginal, signifieth to acquit them *gratis*, and as a free gift of his grace, to send them the news of their pardon; the word rendered 'trespasses,' usually is understood of actual sins. But yet we must not think that original sin is not forgiven; for either it is a synecdoche, and so one sort of sins is named instead of all; or else he speaks according to the feelings of many of the godly, who even after forgiveness are marvellously troubled with the flesh and the wicked proneness to daily sins.

But for the matter itself, we may here note:

1. That God doth certainly forgive men their sins, when he gives them repentance, and converts them by his word.

2. That where God forgives our sins, he heals our natures too, therefore quickening and forgiving are here joined together; and herein God's pardons differ from all the pardons of kings. Men may forgive the treason or felony, but they cannot give a nature that will offend no more; but now if God forgive a man, he will certainly give his good Spirit to mend his nature, and cleanse him from his sin.

3. That howsoever justification go before sanctification, yet it is sanctification first appears, therefore quickening first named.

4. That it is a singular happiness to obtain of God the forgiveness of our sins.

5. That if we were used according to our deserts, God must never forgive us; it is his free grace.

The use of all may be, first, for great reproof of the general carelessness of the most men, that will take no pains at all to get the pardon of their sins, but wholly neglect the seeking of the assurance of it. Now this monstrous neglect of so admirable a benefit comes: 1. From ignorance. Men know not their woeful misery in respect of their sins. 2. From the hardness of man's heart; and their hearts in this point of neglect of remission of sins are hardened both by the effectual working of Satan, and by the example of the careless multitude, and by the entertainment of false opinions about it, as that it need not be sought, or cannot be known, or hereafter will be time enough to inquire; or else men are conceited in false acquittances. Either they rest in this, that Christ died for them, or that God makes promises of forgiveness in scripture, or that their civil course of life, or their works of mercy or piety, will make God amends, &c. Again, this neglect ariseth from the forgetfulness of man's latter end. If men knew the time of the day of the Lord, they would get their pardon confirmed if it were possible, lest it should come upon them unawares. Lastly, this comes from the love of sin. Men are loth to leave their sins, and therefore not careful to seek forgiveness of them.

2. Here is a confutation of merit of works; for if we pay the debt, then it is not forgiven us; and if it be forgiven us, then certainly we pay it not: besides the word denotes that it is freely done, as hath been shewed before.

3. Shall we not be stirred up to seek forgiveness of sins?

Quest. What should we do that we might be confirmed in the assurance to obtain the forgiveness of sins?

Ans. 1. Thou must forgive men their trespasses, Mat. vi. 16; 2. Thou must acknowledge thy sins, 1 John i. 9; 3. Thou must pray, and get others to pray, for the forgiveness of thy sins, James v. 16; 4. Thou must often receive the sacrament of the Lord's supper, for this is God's seal of forgiveness of sins, Mat. xxvi.; 5. Thou must bewail thy sins, Zech. xii. 12, 13, and xiii. 1, and beg the witness of the Spirit of adoption in the intercession of Jesus Christ, till those unspeakable joys of the Holy Ghost fall upon thee, and seal thee up unto the day of redemption.

And thus far of the thirteenth verse.

Ver. 14. *Blotting out the handwriting of ordinances that was against us, which was contrary to us, and took it out of the way, nailing it to his cross.*

This verse and the next contain the seventh reason of the dehortation. It is laid down in this verse, and amplified in the next. The argument may stand thus: If the ceremonies were a chirograph or handwriting against us, when they were in force, and if now Christ have cancelled that writing, then we ought not to use them again; but such they were, for they were a handwriting against us, and Christ hath removed them by fastening them upon the cross, therefore we ought not to revive them again. Or thus, If the debt be paid and the obligation cancelled, then is it a fond course to cause the obligation wilfully to be of force again.

Handwriting. This handwriting is by divers diversely referred; for some think it to be referred to the covenant with Adam. All mankind in him was bound to God. This obligation he brake, and so the forfeiture lay still upon our necks till Christ paid the debt, and cancelled the obligation. Some refer it to the law of Moses in general, and say the people did bind themselves unto it, Exod. xiv., by the rites they used. The bond was forfeited by the Jews, and lay upon them. Some refer it to the moral law in special, and therein we did enter into bond, which was called the covenant of works. The rigour and curse of this law lieth upon all mankind, and when God sues out this bond, men are carried to prison, even to the prison of hell. Some refer it to the conscience of men, and say that an evil conscience is a chirograph, a bill of debt, and it accuseth by ordinances, that is, it taketh conclusions from the law of God to arrest or condemn the sinner. But most usually it is referred to the ceremonial law. By some of them, men did enter into bond, as by circumcision. So saith the apostle, 'He that is circumcised is bound to keep the whole law,' Gal. v. 5. By others of them men made bills of debt. Circumcision confesseth corruption of nature by propagation. The washings were open confessions of the foulness of our lives; in the sacrifices men subscribed to their own death and damnation, for they confessed they had deserved to die instead of the beast.

The words may be true of all, but most principally of the ceremonial law. In general he here entreateth of deliverance from the ceremonies of Moses. Then two things may in particular be noted: 1. What the ceremonies were in themselves; 2. The manner or means how the church was discharged of them. For the first, if we require what they were; they were: 1. For honour, 'ordinances' of God; 2. For use, 'handwritings;' 3. For effect, they were 'against us,' or contrary to us.

Ordinances. Some read 'for' ordinances, some read 'by' ordinances, some 'with' ordinances, and some 'of' ordinances. They that read 'for ordinances,' say the handwriting was for ordinances, that is, either in favour of the decrees that were against us, or for the better assuring of the keeping of the ordinances; it was 'by ordinances,' viz., evangelical, for they say the decrees of Christ did evacuate the laws of Moses. They that read 'with ordinances' say that the handwriting was the debt of death which Christ took away with the ordinance, that is, the external rites and rudiments of Moses. But I think the sense is clear as it is here rendered, *of ordinances.*

And so the point to be observed is, that the ceremonies imposed upon the Jews were God's ordinances, which may shew us that God did take upon him the right to bind the conscience of men by ceremonies; 2. Seeing Christians are freed from them by God himself, therefore the apostle would have them stand to their liberty; 3. This should exalt the praise of the moral law; if they were bound to observe the very ceremonies, because they were God's ordinances, then much more should we be careful to keep the moral.

Handwritings. This word notes their use; because men are by nature wonderful slow to acknowledge their misery, therefore the Lord in all ages did drive men under their hands, as it were openly, to make profession of their own sin-guiltiness and fall, that so God's justice might be cleared. Therefore were the sacrifices required presently after the fall, and baptism now is of like nature, to shew us our natural uncleanness that needs to be washed.

Against us. In effect they were against us. The ceremonies were against us, that is, against the Jews, four ways: 1. As they were bills of debt; 2. As they told the longing wife that her husband was long after to come; 3. As they proclaimed God infinitely hating sin, so as he must have atonement in blood, and that daily; 4. As they were transgressed in respect of the right manner of observing them.

Now, though these ceremonies belong not to us Christians, yet we are in the same debt by nature that they were, though we have not that way of expressing our debt.

Quest. But how could that which God commanded them to do be against them?

Ans. Many ways. 1. When they failed in the matter, as when they offered strange fire, or sacrificed their sons. 2. When they did anger God by omissions or delays, as when Moses trifled out the circumcision of his son. 3. When they did it for wrong ends, as when the whore would sacrifice to colour her whoredoms, Prov. v., or when men did think thereby to make amends for their sins, Jer. vii., or when they used them for the hurt of God's children, as Balaam used his sacrifice. 4. When they mingle their own inventions with God's ordinances, and their fear towards God was taught by the precepts of men. 5. When they did use them as a burden, and it was a weariness to them. Lastly, when they that used them were wicked men, and did use them without knowledge, or faith, or repentance for their sins, or the care of the due manner, as many places of scripture shew. And thus may the very law of God be against us still, as well as against them.

The use of all this chiefly may be to shew the misery of every impenitent sinner. His sins are upon record; there is the handwriting against him. Let him look upon sacrificing Jews, and there he may behold man daily, in effect, saying thus: thus must it be done to the man that repenteth not of his sins; the obligation lies forfeited, and the Lord may call upon him for his debt of ten thousand talents when he hath not a farthing to pay, and then he will be cast into prison.

Again, when he saith 'us,' he shews that this is the estate of all men by nature; there was a handwriting against the very apostle himself, and such as were in the visible church, therefore he saith 'against us.' Thus of what the ceremonies were in themselves. Now of the discharge from them, these two things may be noted: 1. The manner, Christ 'put them out,' 'took them away,' 'fastened them;' 2. The means, viz., 'the cross.' The sum is, that Christ Jesus, by his sufferings on the cross, paid our debt, and freed us from the handwriting that was against us; the anger of God conceived against us for the forfeiture was thereon, by the blood of Christ, appeased, Rom. v. 9, and forgiveness of sins and debts therein merited, 1 John i. 7. And by the blood of Jesus, the faithful overcome the devil, Rev. xii. 11, Heb. xi. 28; that had power to destroy, by reason of the forfeiture; and because none of the former agreements would serve by reason of man's weakness, therefore God makes a new covenant, and seals it by the blood of Christ upon the cross, Zech. ix. 11, Heb. ix. 18; and if we would be assured of our release in particular, first, for the forfeiture in paradise, we receive an atonement in the blood of Christ, Rom. v. 11, 12, 17; and he that, from the curse in paradise, had power over death, was now by Christ destroyed, Heb. ii. 15. And for the law of Moses, we are by Christ delivered both from the rigour of it and from the curse of it, his own sacrifice being the propitiation to still the cry of the law, and to hide it from the eyes of God's justice. And as for the writing of the conscience, the blood of Christ cleanseth it from dead works, Heb. ix. 14, and quieteth it in the declaration of forgiveness, Eph. i. 7, 8; and it maketh intercession for sin after calling to keep it quiet, Heb. xii. 14. And as for the ceremonial handwritings, they were both fulfilled, Col. ii. 17, and abolished in the sacrifice of Christ on the cross, he himself saying, 'It was finished.' And the more to assure us of our safety from these forfeitures, he useth those divers phrases, of 'putting out,' 'taking out of the way,' and 'fastening it to the cross.'

Uses. The use of all is: 1. For information. We may see what a case sin sets us in by nature, and how hateful the nature of sin is: if we have any thing to do with God, why, our sins lie like so many blocks in our way, and Christ Jesus only can lift them out of the way. And can our wretched hearts delight in sin, seeing they nailed Christ to the cross? It is an easy thing to rend an obligation amongst men, but it was not so easy to get ours cancelled; it could be rent in no place but on the cross; Christ Jesus himself must be fastened to the tree, that he might fasten our cancelled handwriting thereto. And if God spared not his own Son, when he came about this business of cancelling the handwriting, what think we shall be the case of all wicked men that die in their sins, and must suffer the whole forfeiture to fall on their necks? If what Christ endured on the cross were so painful, they must not think to escape. Hence also we may see what wonderful cause we have to love the Lord Jesus, that hath done all this for us. Oh, how precious should his memory be amongst us! Finally, here the faithful should gather singular comfort against the law, sin, death, and hell, seeing here they may be informed all these were nailed upon the cross, and Christ hath openly declared that he hath cancelled whatsoever might be to shew against us, for any forfeiture or debt of ours whatsoever. And shall not we take heed of running in debt again by sinning, after the sprinkling of the blood of Jesus Christ? Or shall we wretchedly bind ourselves to the law again, by pleading our justification before God, by the works of the law?

Ver. 15. *And having spoiled principalities and powers, he made a shew of them openly, triumphing over them in it.*

These words are an amplification of the former,

wherein he sheweth that, not only the bill in which we were made infinitely indebted was cancelled, but the devils also (who had power to serve executions upon us, and prove from the ceremonial law, as is before declared) mightily conquered by Christ, and therefore to revive again the ceremonies was to renew the bond, and so stand still in danger of the devil's executions.

The words are a most portly and deep allegory, and they carry news of a remarkable victory. The battle was fierce, cruel, prodigiously difficult, bloody on the best side; and if Christ had been a jot less than he was, there had been no remedy nor hope. The battle was first fought between Satan and man, with a depth of fraud and cruelty, and hellish invisible spite; the day was lost, man with the woeful issues of the conquest was either cast down wallowing in blood, or scattered with pursuing cruelty; no sooner sprouting in the life of nature, but smitten with the venom of spiritual infection, plagued with the bondage of more than cruel servitude, not pitied, not helped; more forfeitures laid upon him than he could find words to acknowledge. Now one man cometh into the field in the right of millions, (that could not stand their own quarrel,) challengeth the victors, with singular compassion calleth back the scattered, raiseth a mighty expectation, exposeth himself to the danger, with incredible fury is encountered, one with millions or legions of devils, of incomprehensible rage, and long-beaten experience; and the infinite anger of God was kindled against this one man as a surety for the rest.

Now in this text is a report of the happy success of the battle; news of a most victorious conquest; the devils spoiled, the elect restored, with unutterable hymns attend the conquest; the wretched spirits are in chains, exposed to infinite shame, and dragged after the chariot of triumph, as he ascended into the New Jerusalem.

In general two things may be observed: first, That Christ is God; he was brought in before, quickening, pardoning, filling, circumcising the heart, now here spoiling the devils, and triumphing over them.

2. We may here comfort ourselves with this, that the devil shall never have success against Christ and his kingdom. God hath cursed all his ways; and yet we find by experience the devil will not give over, though he hath never so ill success from day to day; which may awaken many wicked men, who are herein like the devil,—no ill-success can make them give over their ill courses. Again, would we not be spoiled and crossed in the success of that we take in hand, and be made like the devil in ill-success, then let us take heed of his qualities, be not like him in cruelty, in fraud, in lying, in accusing, or envying the children of God; for if thou be, thou art sure, with the devil, to be accursed and rebuked of God.

Now for the particular opening of these words, we must understand that they have been three ways interpreted: first, Some papists say this battle was fought in hell, when Christ fetched the fathers out of Limbus. This interpretation I reject, not only as a fond conceit obtruded upon the world, but because the most popish writers could see no such thing in this place, but expound it otherwise.

Secondly, Some orthodox writers say this battle and triumph was both begun and ended before Christ's death. The devils encountered Christ two ways upon the cross: visibly and invisibly. Visibly, by inspiring wicked men with vile provocations to vex him, and molest him; as the impenitent thief, Luke xxiii. 38; the rulers of the Jews, Luke xiii. 38; and the soldiers, Luke xxiii. 37. Invisibly, the devils themselves, with all might, fury, malice, and slight encountered him upon the cross, in the sight of God and the holy angels.

The victory is described in this verse, and it is said first he 'spoiled' them, which is diversely read and referred; for some understand it, he spoiled the devils; some of the fathers put in a word, and read it, 'after he had spoiled himself of his flesh,' and so it is a comparison borrowed from wrestlers or runners, that first put off all might hinder them; and so Christ, that he might overcome, first laid down his flesh upon the cross. And where the text saith, he made a show of them openly, the Holy Ghost alludeth to the trophies of great victors. Their manner was, in the place where they did overcome, either to cut down the arms of great trees, and thereupon hanged the spoils or weapons of the vanquished, or else they built some stately pillars, and there painted or wrote upon, the conquest, with other monuments of victory; so did Christ openly serve the devils, openly before God, angels, and the world he defeateth them, and by a new way, by suffering, gave occasion to all to see the shaking of the hellish kingdom. Where he is said to triumph over them, therein is an allusion to the third degree of victory. They were wont to lead their captives after the chariot of triumph into the city with great pomp; thus did Christ to the wicked spirits, either upon the cross, or in his resurrection.

Quest. But might some one say. What appearance was there of any victory when Christ suffered?

Ans. Great every way; for if we observe it in every branch of the process, there is evident signs of victory. For do they attach him? why, first the officers are smitten to the ground with a very word, and Judas, the chief leader, is made to go and hang himself; the ear of Malchus was miraculously cured, and they are suffered to do no jot more than will fulfil the scriptures, Mat. xxvi. 26. Will they arraign him in the consistory? why, there sits a high priest that was made whether he would or no to prophesy of Christ's death for the people, John xi. 50, with xviii. 14; and Christ casts a spirit of giddiness upon the witnesses, so as their testimonies could not agree; yea, he there foretells them of his most glorious and terrible second coming in the clouds of heaven, and then miraculously recovers Peter, a lapsed sinner. Will they arraign him in the common hall? why, there he overcomes by patience; no indignities could stir him; and the judge's wife from a dream gives warning that he was a just man, yea, the judge himself was compelled to pronounce him innocent. Will they have him to the cross? there are wonders of victory,—a thief without means saved, the veil of the temple rent, signs in heaven and earth, and a title of victory superscribed by his very adversaries, 'This is the King of the Jews;' besides his incorruption in the grave, and glorious resurrection, and visible ascension to heaven.

All this being considered, where is the ignominy of the cross, seeing the devils erected a cross for themselves when they plotted to crucify Christ? And why should we be afraid of sufferings, seeing the cross is Christ's triumph? and let us resolve also to overcome by sufferings, Rom. viii. 34. It is an excellent and lofty praise to overcome by suffering.

Lastly, Let us never judge of Christ or Christians by their outward show; great things may be done in the kingdom of Christ, which are not discerned by carnal reason. Here we see a great ado, trophies, triumphs, yet the world took no notice of it; so is there incomparable glory, even in this world, in the souls and lives of Christians, which the blind multitude never takes notice of.

And thus much of the second interpretation.

The third and last interpretation is of those that limit not the time of this victory to the cross, but consider it generally, and instead of the words 'upon the same cross,' read 'in himself;' and thus do the most interpreters, new and old, read it; and so this victory is understood not so much of what Christ did attain in his person, as what he doth in us. By the conversion of sinners, by the gospel, he daily spoils principalities and powers, and triumphs over them, &c.; and so these words are a consequent of the putting out of the handwriting mentioned in the former verse.

Four things are in these words to be considered: Who, whom, what, and by what means. For the first: It is the second Adam that undertakes this battle, he that is God and man, he of whom the prophecies ran, he that by a voice from heaven at his baptism was acknowledged the only champion, it was he that sent the challenge by his forerunner John Baptist, he it is that foiled Satan in many monomachies, this is he that now comes forth in the gospel in the several ages of the church to spoil these principalities and powers.

Now for the second: The spoiled are called principalities and powers.

Principalities and powers. These terms are given to the good angels, Eph. iii. 10, and to great magistrates and princes on earth, Eph. i. 23. In effect they are given to Christ, Isa. ix. 6, 7; but usually they are restrained to evil angels, and so they are called, either considering them as they were before their fall, or, as it is usually conceived, it notes their estate even since their fall.

The two words note two things in the evil angels: excellency and ability; excellency, so they are principalities; ability, so they are powers. Their excellency is two ways to be considered: 1. In themselves; 2. Their sovereignty over the world. In themselves and their own nature, ever since their horrible fall, they are creatures of wonderful knowledge, swiftness, discerning, and such like.

And in respect of the unregenerate world they have a principality: hence called worldly rulers, Eph. vi.; the prince of this world, John xii.; yea, and the god of this world, 2 Cor. iv. 4. We may observe here in the Holy Ghost a wonderful pattern of candour, he praiseth what is praiseworthy even in his enemies; and it may wonderfully comfort God's children in their acceptation with God; for if God can yield these titles, and acknowledge that is yet good in the very devils, sure, then, it cannot be he should not like what he finds good in his own saints, though they have many wants and sins, seeing they sin not of malicious wickedness, as the devils do.

As they are called 'principalities,' so for their ability and force of working, they are called 'powers.' The wonderful power the devils have may be considered either in the world or in the church.

In the first race of men before the flood, how soon had they drawn away Cain's race into apostasy, and not long after Seth's, till they had chased the light of sincerity within the walls of one house, and not all sound there neither. After the flood the world is no sooner filled again, but, together with the building of Babel, a most dreadful confusion was wrought by the devils, even the beginning of a general falling away into Gentilism and idolatry, which will never be utterly recovered again while the world stands, all the families making apostasy in the beginning of the Babylonish monarchy, and such an apostasy, as they continued in for many hundred years in the generality of them, so as there was only a little light left in the race of Shem.

Now leaving the whole world lying under this powerful wickedness, come to Abraham, a brand taken out of the fire of the Chaldeans, in whom the light shined with great glory, see the power of these wicked spirits over his race. The Ishmaelites went quickly off to Gentilism; then the Edomites were easily gained after; then in Egypt the light that did remain was almost put out, the bondage of the Israelites being as great in soul, as it was in body, Ezek. xx.

In Moses' time the light was diffused in that people all abroad again, and a kingdom of priests was raised up to God. This light held with various increase and decrease till the captivity, after which time it waxed dimmer and dimmer, till Christ, the day-star, arose, and filled heaven and earth with the brightness of his coming.

After, in the very first hundreds of years, these cursed spirits not only persecuted religion by incredible tyranny, but infected it with the tares of strange errors, and prodigious superstitions and heresies, till all grew together in one body in antichrist.

Under antichrist all sincerity was again almost universally put out, the face of religion corrupted, and idolatry brought into the churches 1260 years. Lastly, In our own days, when the prophecies were accomplished, and the everlasting gospel published again, alas! yet consider the state of the world! One part of the world lieth in paganism, another in Turcism, another in Judaism, another in papism; and in all these four these wicked spirits reign, and hold the world captive at their pleasure.

Come we to the visible assemblies of the true churches of Jesus Christ, and consider there their power. How mighty it extends; for there they have secret atheists, church-papists, persons excommunicate, witches, and such like diabolical practisers, hypocrites, apostates, the unmerciful troops of the ignorant, besides the swarms of vicious livers and profane persons, such as are swearers, drunkards, filthy persons of all kinds, liars, usurers, railers, and such like workers of iniquity.

It is true worlds of men feel not this power of theirs; but, alas! this war is spiritual, these enemies are invisible, their sleights are of infinite depth, their souls are already in their possession, and all is covered with gross darkness, and done in a spiritual night, and wicked men are like dead men in their sinful courses, senseless, and secure.

Uses. The use is to shew the misery of all impenitent sinners, though they go in brave clothes, dwell in fair houses, possessed of large revenues, abound in all pleasures of life, &c., yet, alas, alas! for their woeful estate with all this. Oh, the devils, the devils are their masters, and rule over them as effectually as ever did tyrant over his slave! Oh, if men have ears let them hear, and awake and stand up from the dead, and not dare to continue in so woeful a condition! and let the righteous leap and sing for true joy of heart, whatsoever their outward estate be in the world! Oh, let them praise the rich grace of God, that hath 'translated them out of this kingdom of darkness, and given them a lot among the saints!'

The third thing is the victory, expressed in three degrees.

He spoiled them. This is to be understood in the behalf of the faithful, for whose sake he hath and doth daily smite them with his great sword, Isa. xxvii. 1. He reproveth them, and rebuketh them, Zech. iii. 1–3; he casteth them down like lightning, Luke x. 20; he breaks their head, Gen. iii. 15; yea, and sometimes treads them down under the feet of his saints, Rom. xvi. 20; making them in many tentations and tribulations more than conquerors, Rom. viii. 34; pulling down their strongholds, which they had within, 2 Cor. x. 4. When they compass the righteous with their tentations, he ever openeth a door for issue, and delivereth the righteous, 2 Pet. ii. 9; sending succours, Heb. ii. 18; and making his servants often to lead Satan captive.

He spoiled them by taking from them the souls of the righteous, which they possessed as their booty, Acts xxvi. 18; he spoiled them by loosing the works of Satan, 1 John iii. 8; he spoiled them by taking from them altogether the power they had over death, Heb. ii. 14, so far as concerns the righteous. He hath so far spoiled them that they are not only judged by the word of the saints in this life, John xvi. 11, but the saints shall also sit upon them to judge them at the last day, 1 Cor. vi. 3.

Uses. And all this may serve for constant comfort unto all the godly, each word being a well of consolation if we wisely apply it. And withal it may encourage them against the remainder of the power of evil spirits. It is true they accuse still, they hinder the word what they can still, they will steal the seed still, they will raise trouble and oppositions still, they sow tares still, they will be casting their snares still, they buffet them by tentations still; but yet the same God and our Lord Jesus Christ that hath thus far subdued them will prosper his own work, and make us 'stand in all the evil days,' so as we will 'put on the whole armour of God.'

Now, whereas he saith he hath spoiled him, it is true of the time past: 1. In the person of Christ himself; 2. In the merit of our victory; 3. In our justification he is perfectly spoiled; 4. In our sanctification he is spoiled by inchoation.

And made a show of them openly. These words contain the second degree of victory, and are true in a double sense: for first, He hath made a show of them in that he hath discovered them, and made them known to the church. This is a dragging them out of their cells of darkness in the light of observation, by shewing their natures and practices, by unmasking them to the view of the soul. Thus are they displayed in the doctrine of the gospel, and the souls of the righteous behold this detection of Satan from day to day by the word with as much admiration as ever the Romans did behold any great rebel, or barbarous rebel or monster, subdued, and in triumph brought into Rome. Neither may this detection of Satan seem to be the least part of Christ's victory; for it is certain it is a work that evil men or evil angels never hear but are vanquished. There is a hot opposition in all places before Satan will abide this.

Secondly, He made a show of them—that is, as some think, he made them to be for examples, and that three ways: 1. In shame, making detestation to be their portion; 2. In confusion, and an inexplicable kind of astonishment, and benumbedness, and blindness; 3. In torments and punishments, 2 Pet. iv. 5, Jude 9.

Use. The use may be for increase of consolation; we see Christ will never cease till he hath finished this victory. Why should we, then, fail through unbelief, or faint in the resisting of the devil? The Lord will more and more make a show of them, and give us increase of experience of the power of his word and presence herein. Here also men's waywardness may be reproved, that cannot abide to hear talk of the devil or his courses. This is but a work of Satan in them to hinder their salvation; for to make an open show of them is one part of Christ's victory.

The word rendered 'openly' signifieth sometimes eminently, John vii. 4; sometimes without authority, Acts iv. 29; sometimes with confidence and undaunted resolution, with assurance or plerophory,

1 John v. 14; sometimes with plainness and evidence, John xvi. 25, 29; sometimes with liberty, 1 Tim. iii. 13. But I rest in the word 'openly,' here used.

And triumphed over them. Here is the third part of the victory. This triumph was first begun in the resurrection and ascension of Christ, Eph. iv. 7. 2. It was continued in the publication of the gospel, 2 Cor. ii. 14, (which is news of victory,) and in the life of Christians; for what is the life of every Christian but the show of a brand taken out of the fire, or of a soul preserved out of darkness? The soul is mounted in the chariot of the word, prayer, and holy living. This chariot is followed with the applause of angels, and the approbation of the saints: the place is in the New Jerusalem on earth, in the temple of their God. The chariot is drawn with white steeds, sincere teachers; it is provoked and driven on by the Spirit of God; and the effect of all is a heart inspired with heavenly joys and refreshings. 3. As it began in Christ, and is continued in the life of a Christian, so this triumph shall be perfected in death, and consummated in the resurrection, to the eternal dissolution and confusion of all wicked men and devils.

Use. Now for the use of this. 1. What just cause is there to take up bitter lamentations for the wonderful frowardness of the natures of the most men, who had rather be miserable and serve the devil still than be made glorious by conquest in repentance for their sins. They had rather be his prisoners, than such princes; rather slaves to Satan, than sons to God; rather dragged into captivity with the devil, than carried in the chariot of triumph with the saints.

2. If such honours be done to Christians, and such joys had in a Christian estate, oh, then, let it be the prayer of every godly man daily to God, as Ps. cvi. 4, 'Remember me, O Lord, with the favour of thy people, visit me with thy salvation,' &c.

Lastly, How should it excite in us a desire to walk worthy of such a victory! yea, how should it inspire us with spiritual magnanimity to resist Satan, and with a holy scorn to disdain his filthy temptations, and in all estates to demean ourselves so as might become men that know and believe that Christ hath spoiled principalities and powers for us! &c.

4. For the means of this victory, it is added in these words:

In himself. So it is read in the Greek, and in the most interpreters; and this 'in himself,' either it notes his mystical body, or else it notes Christ himself alone; and in this latter sense it is continually taken. And so we may here learn that it is the Lord Jesus Christ alone, even himself alone, that hath wrought this victory for us; there was none other able to stand in the field against the adversary; there is no name else under heaven by which we can be saved; and therefore we should give all the glory to Christ alone, and not to any man or angels, for they never fought for us, nor were they able to stand in this battle of our redemption.

Ver. 16. *Let no man therefore condemn you in meat or drink, or in respect of an holiday, or of the new moon, or of the sabbath-days:*

Ver. 17. *Which are but a shadow of things to come; but the body is in Christ.*

Hitherto the seven reasons of the dehortation. The conclusion follows in these words and the rest to the end of the chapter; and it hath three branches: for 1. He concludes against Judaism in these words; 2. Against philosophy, ver. 18, 19; 3. Against tradition, ver. 20 to the end.

In these words is contained both the conclusion itself, ver. 16, and the reason, ver. 17; and the drift is to shew that the ceremonies of Moses are abolished, and therefore they should not receive them, or hold themselves bound unto them. This was foretold, Dan. ix. 17—it was signified by the rending of the veil; and these ceremonies were solemnly and publicly laid down in the first council which was held by the apostles at Jerusalem, Acts xv. And they were then so laid down that the apostle after gives order to the church that those ceremonies should never be used, nor any other devices, but such as might be to edification, order, and decency, and were without offence.

The ceremonies named in the text are the difference of meats and drinks, and the observation of times, concerning which he writes more sharply. Gal. iii. 1, 3, iv. 10, v. 9, and vi. 12.

In the law there were three sorts of meats that legally were required: first, The meat-offerings;

secondly, The shewbread; thirdly, The clean beasts. The meat-offering was a type of Christ, our nourishment; the shewbread was a type of the church in her mystical union; and the clean beasts (known by chewing the cud and dividing the hoof) were types of the Christian's both meditation and discretion in the means of his holy conversation. And for the confirmation of this place, the apostle elsewhere shews evidently that the difference of meats is taken away, 1 Tim. iv. 1-4.

The difference of times in the law is here said to be threefold: of days, of months, of sabbaths.

In respect of an holy day. The original and most translations word for word have it thus: 'in part of a holiday,' but in divers senses: some say, in part of a holiday—that is, in partition of a festival day from a not festival day, as well in days, as in months, or sabbaths. Some say, 'in part,' for they could not observe all ceremonies, being absent from Jerusalem. Therefore the apostle would have them to receive none at all, seeing they could not receive them all. Some say in part of a holiday—that is, in that part of them which concerns days, &c. But it is more plainly as it here rendered.

Or of the new moon. They did observe the calends, or first days of every month.

Or of sabbath-days. There were divers sorts of sabbaths: of days, of years, of sevens of years. The sabbaths of days were either moral, viz., the seventh day, which God did choose, or ceremonial. The ceremonial sabbaths were either more solemn, such as were the three great feasts, passover, pentecost, and tabernacles; or less solemn, such as were the feasts of blowing the trumpets, Lev. xxiii. 24, and the feast of expiation, Lev. xvi. 32-34. The sabbath of years was every seventh year, Lev. xxv. 4, 6-11. The sabbath of sevens of years was the jubilee, which returned every fifty years. We see here, then, that the apostle shews that we are delivered from the bondage of the observation as before of meats, so now of sabbaths.

Object. But is the sabbath-day that was moral abrogated?

Sol. No; the apostle speaks here of the ceremonial law, not of the moral; and of ceremonial sabbaths, not of the moral sabbath: the word is in the plural number.

The manner of propounding the conclusion is to be observed.

Let no man condemn you. These words may be referred either to God's children or to false teachers. In the first sense it is thus: let none condemn you—that is, do not shew such love to these ceremonies hereafter that thereby you incur justly the blame and censure of God's children. And if they be referred to false teachers, then it is thus: let no man whatsoever persuade you that you are condemned or judged of God for omitting the observation of the ceremonies; care not for their censures; never trouble your consciences about it.

Which are shadows of things to come. Here the apostle with full sail drives into the haven, by shutting up with this unavoidable argument. These ceremonies are but shadows of that substance which now we have, and therefore it is a foolish thing to strive about the shadow when we have the substance.

Ceremonies were shadows in divers respects: 1. In respect of certainty of signification: the shadow is a sure sign of the body; so was this of Christ to come. 2. In respect of causation: the body causeth the shadow, so is Christ the cause of all ceremonies. 3. In respect of the obscurity of signification: a shadow is dark, so were the ceremonies. 4. In respect of cessation: a shadow is quickly gone, so were the ceremonies; they were not to last for any long time. Lastly, They were shadows as they were types: so the lamb was a shadow of Christ, and the ark of the church, &c. They were shadows not given to justify, but to shew justification by Christ.

It is added, 'of things to come,' to keep off the blow from our sacraments, which are no shadows of things to come, but of things past.

But the body is in Christ. The words are diversely interpreted. Some refer the words to the next verse, but without reason; some supply a word, 'body,' and read, 'but the body is the body of Christ:' but the plain meaning is, that the truth and substance of all the ceremonies is now enjoyed by the church in and by Christ, in whom all is now fulfilled; and therefore heaven should now suffer violence, and 'the children of Sion should now rejoice in their King;' and Christians should 'stand fast in the liberty' that is brought unto them in Christ Jesus.

Ver. 18. *Let no man bear rule over you by humbleness of mind and worshipping of angels; advancing himself in those things he never saw, rashly puffed up with his fleshly mind.*

Ver. 19. *And holdeth not the head, whereof all the body, furnished and knit together by joints and bands, increaseth with the increasing of God.*

In these two verses he concludes against philosophy, and therein specially against angel-worship, a device like the old doctrine of the Platonists concerning their *dæmones tutelares*. The divines also that first broached this apostatical doctrine in the primitive church were philosophers; and if the papists will persist in angel-worship, they must bear it to be accounted better philosophers than divines.

The apostle makes four observations upon those that bring in this worship of angels: 1. That they attribute that to themselves which is proper to God, namely, to bear rule over the consciences of men in matters of religion, though they pretend to bring in those things because they would have men think humbly of themselves; 2. That they thrust in for oracles, not things they have seen and heard, but devised of themselves; 3. That those things were founded on no other foundation than the opinions of men immoderately pleasing themselves in their own devices; 4. That this course tends to the high derogation of the honour of Christ, who only deserves all glory, and by whom alone all the sins of the church are despatched. The men, then, that urge these things are: 1. Hypocrites, they pretend one thing and intend another; 2. They are ignorant persons; 3. They are proud and insolent in self-conceit; 4. They are profane, without Christ.

Let no man bear rule over you. The original word, καταβραβευέτω, hath troubled interpreters, but is for the most part rendered, either bear rule over you, and so play the part of a judge or rector, or else defraud you of your prize. It is granted by all to be a word taken from the manners in the Olympiads or other where, who run for prizes; among whom there was one they called *Brabeutes*—that is, one that by appointment did sit as judge, and gave the prize to the winner.

If it be taken in the first sense, viz., 'let no man bear rule over you,' then the apostle's meaning is to warn them, for the reasons above rehearsed and herewith adjoined, not to suffer their teachers to lord it over them in their consciences, as before he had charged them not to let them carry away their souls as a prey, ver. 18, or to condemn them, ver. 19. This may teach the ministers of the gospel to know and keep their bounds, and the people likewise not to suffer any to bear rule over their consciences with their own devices. It condemns also the hellish pride and imperiousness of the popish clergy, in playing the judges over men's consciences at their own pleasure, seeing we have no judge nor lawgiver but only Jesus Christ, to whom the Father hath given all power.

Quest. But have not the ministers of the gospel power, upon observation of the runners, to be as judges to assign the crown to them that run well?

Ans. They have, and therefore are called the 'disposers of God's secrets,' and 'watchmen,' and 'overseers;' but yet they must be true ministers, and they must give judgment by warrant from the word.

Let no man defraud you of your prize. That is, seeing you have begun to run so well, and have run so long, let no man now beguile you of your prize, the crown of glory.

The church is like a field; the race is Christian religion; the runners are Christians; the feet are faith and love; the goal or mark is death in Christ; the *brabium*, or prize, is the possession of eternal life. Now the doctrine hence implied is:

Doct. That men may run and come near the goal, and yet lose the prize. Many run, yet one obtaineth, 1 Cor. ix. 24. Many receive the grace of God in vain, 2 Cor. vi. 1. Many come near the kingdom of God, with the scribe, and yet lose, Mark xii. 34. Many lose what they have wrought, 2 John 8. Hence that exhortation, 'Let no man take away your crown,' Rev. iii. 11.

The use may be, first, for reproof of such as do wrong, either the judges or standers-by, by a wrong applause, such as give away the honours of God's children to such as never run in the race, or not aright, and give the titles of the church and Christianity to wicked men; but especially this reproveth those men that having run well for a time, Gal. v. 7, suffer themselves to be hindered, and so lose the prize. Many are the ways the devil hath to hinder men in running: sometimes by raising up adversaries, Phil. i. 29, and outward molestations, Rev. ii. 10; sometimes he casts shame in their way, and names of reproach, 1 Thes. ii. 2, Acts xviii.; sometimes he injects tentations, James i. 12; sometimes he leaves them by keeping them in bondage, to the defence or love of some lesser superstitions or smaller sins, as the world accounts, Gal. v. 7, 9; sometimes he hinders them by the domestic enemy, the sin that hangeth so fast on, Heb. xii. 1; sometimes he casts men into a dead sleep, and they lie along in the middle of the race.

2. This may serve for instruction, to teach us with all heedfulness to look to ourselves after we set out in the race of Christian profession, that no man take our crown; and to this end we must consider, both what to shun and what to follow. If we would not lose our crown we must shun: 1. The sin that hangs on so fast, Heb. xii. 1; 2. Profane babblings and oppositions of science falsely so called, 1 Tim. vi. 20; 3. Scandal, Phil. ii. 15, 16; 4. The profits and pleasures of the world, so as our hearts be not set upon them, 1 Cor. ix. 25, 1 Tim. vi. 11. 12; 5. Self-love and trust in our own judgment, when we think ourselves wise enough to order our race without advice, Gal. ii. 2; 6. Uncertain running, 1 Cor. ix. 16. Now for the second, That we may run successfully, divers rules must be observed: 1. We must watchfully stop the beginnings of sin, and when we feel ourselves begin to halt, we must seek a healing, lest we be turned out of the way, Heb. xii. 13; 2. We must follow peace with all men, so far as may stand with godliness, Heb. xii. 14; 3. We must keep the faith; 4. We must labour for the love of the appearing of Christ; 5. We must continue and resolve not to give over till we have finished our course: these three rules may be gathered out of 2 Tim. iv. 8, 9; 6. We must pray that the gospel may run more freely, 2 Thes. iii. 1; for that, like a mighty wind, helps wonderfully in the race; 7. We must order riches so as they be no hindrances, 2 Tim. vi. 18; 8. We must use the advice of the best that can be had for skill or experience, Gal. ii. 2; 9. We must faithfully discharge the duties of our calling, 1 Pet. v. 4,—we must so resolve upon the race, that we labour to be undaunted and every way resolved against all afflictions and trials whatsoever that may befall us, accounting it all happiness to fulfil our course with joy, Acts xx. 24, arming ourselves with this mind, that we will take up our cross, and endure any hardship, 2 Tim. ii. 5, James i. 11.

At their pleasures. This is added as an aggravation. The word notes they did it not ignorantly, or by frailty, but they did wrong the conscience of men, with desire, willingly, wilfully. It doth greatly increase the guilt of sin when men do it willingly and wilfully, where men do it because they will do it. So some men go to law because they will go to law, Mat. v. 40; so some will be great, Mat. xx. 26; some will do the lusts of their father the devil, John viii. 44; thus are men daily doing the wills of the flesh, Eph. ii. 3. The like waywardness may be observed in the negative: men will not be gathered, Mat. xxiii. 37; men will not come to the wedding, Mat. xxii. 3; in some things they willingly knew them not, 2 Pet. iii. 5; and it is charged upon the idle they will not work, 2 Thes. iii. 10; hence those conditional speeches, 'if ye will receive it,' Mat. xi. 14, and 'if any man will save his soul,' Mat. xvi. 25.

The use may be for terror to stubborn offenders. God takes notice of it that they sin at their pleasures; they sin because they will sin, and therefore let them be assured he will be froward with the froward, Ps. xviii., and therefore he will have his will upon them irresistibly. Hence these threatenings: he will take account, Mat. xv. 23; he will quicken whom he will, John v. 21; he will give to the last as to the first, Mat. xx. 14; it shall not be after the wills of the flesh, John i. 13; the Spirit shall blow where he will, John iii. 8; the mystery shall be made known to whom he will, Col. i. 27; and he will not have sacrifice, Heb. x. 5.

Secondly, Comfort is here implied: for if there be so much infection in a will to sin, then there is hope God will accept a will to be and do good; he will accept of the will in prayer, John xv. 7; and the will to resist corruption of nature, Rom. vii. 15–17; and of the will to live honestly, Heb. xiii. 18, John vii. 17.

Hitherto the apostle hath charged them generally: now in the words that follow he enforceth his speech more particularly, both for matter, pointing out 'angel-worship,' as the doctrine he would conclude against, and for manner noting four things in those that brought in that worship: 1. That they brought it in hypocritically, pretending 'humbleness of mind;' 2. That they did it ignorantly, 'advancing themselves in things they never saw;' 3. That they did it proudly, 'rashly puffed up,' &c.; 4. That they did it dangerously, 'not holding the head,' &c.

Worshipping of angels. The main matter the apostle strives to beat down is the worship of angels: as a philosophical dream, as a superstition that defrauds men of heaven, as a hypocritical and ignorant worship, charging them to be proud and fleshly persons that use it; yea, he avoucheth they cannot hold the head, which is Christ, if they maintain or practise such a worship. All these reasons are in the text and coherence against it.

Which may serve for confutation of papists, who at this day still maintain it, not only without commandment or any approved example in scripture, but directly against the prohibition of the scriptures, as in this place, and so Rev. xix., the angel forbids John to do it.

The papists offend in their doctrine about saints and angels three ways: 1. In giving unto them what may be attributed only to Christ and to God; 2. In adoring them; 3. In invocating and praying to them; and all three contrary to scripture.

For the first, they attribute unto them: 1. Intercession; 2. The knowledge of all things that concern us; they rob Christ of his intercession, and God of his omniscience. Now in all this we have a sure word of God to trust to. For, for intercession, it is plain we have none in heaven with him, Ps. lxxiii. 25; there is 'one Mediator betwixt God and man, the man Christ,' 1 Tim. ii.; we 'offer up spiritual sacrifices acceptable to God by Jesus Christ,' 1 Pet. ii. 5. Let us, therefore, saith the apostle, 'by him offer the sacrifices of praise always,' Heb. xiii. 15. Note the words, 'by him' and 'always;' and whereas they object the angel, Rev. viii., that offered the prayers of the saints; we answer, that angel was Christ, who only hath the golden censer, and who only is meet to bring incense to offer upon the golden altar. The endeavour of Peter for their good after his decease, was performed while he lived, as is apparent by comparing the 13th verse with the 15th of 2 Pet. i.

And whereas they give the knowledge of all things unto them, they rob God of his glory, who only is the knower of the hearts of men, 2 Chron. vi. 30; and it is granted, Isa. lxiii. 16, that Abraham knew them not, and Israel was ignorant of them. And whereas they object that Abraham, in the 16th of Luke, is said to know that they had Moses and the prophets' books, we answer that that is spoken parabolically, not historically; they may as well say that Lazarus had fingers, and Dives a tongue, &c. But were that granted, yet it followeth not, because the doctrine of the church was revealed unto him, therefore he knew all things.

The second thing they give is adoration, contrary to the flat prohibition of the angel himself in the Revelation, who chargeth, 'Worship me not,' Rev. xix. 10; and without all example in scripture, or the least syllable of warrant for it; besides we see here angel-worship in express words condemned.

The third thing is invocation, praying to them; which likewise is contrary to scripture, for 'how shall we call on them on whom we have not believed?' Rom. x. 14; and we are exhorted to 'go boldly to the throne of grace,' with the help of our High Priest, 'to obtain mercy and find grace to help in time of need,' Heb. iv. 16; for Christ is 'the propitiation for the sins of the whole world,' 1 John ii. 2. Why then should we give his glory to any other? And invocation is a part of the forbidden worship of angels, as well as adoration.

In humbleness of mind. It was the practice of Satan, and pretence of false teachers, to thrust in this corruption of angel-worship under this colour, that it tended to keep men in humility, and to make men to know their duties to the great majesty of God, and to acknowledge their gratitude to the angels for their service. This hath been the devil's wont, to hide foul sins under fair pretences, and vice under the colours of virtue.

This may serve notably for the confutation of the papists about their saint and angel worship; for is not this their smoothest pretence, to tell us by comparison, that men will not go to great princes directly with their suits, but will use the mediation of some courtiers; and so they say they must do to God. This you see was the old deceit in the primitive church, and therefore worthily we may say to the people, let none of the popish rabble defraud you through humbleness of mind.

Again, is the devil ashamed to show sin in his own colours? Doth he mask it under the colour of virtue? Then where shall those monsters appear that declare their sins as Sodom, and are not ashamed of open villanies and filthiness? Such are they that will constantly to the alehouse, and never be ashamed of it. Such are our damned swearers. Such are those filthy persons that know they are known to live in whoredom, and yet never blush at it, nor learn to repent. Such are these, in this city, that live in open contention, who care not, against apparent right, to maintain continual suits and wranglings, though they know all men detest almost the very sight of them for their wicked profaneness and unjust contentions; yea, though the hand of God be apparently upon them, and they know not how soon the Lord may turn them into hell. Such also are the open and wilful sabbath-breakers; and many more of all sorts of presumptuous offenders.

Again, if vice masked in virtue's colours can so please and allure men, how much should virtue itself ravish us? If counterfeit humility can be so plausible, how should true humility win to the admiration and imitation of it?

Lastly, This may warn men to avoid counterfeit gestures, and all pretended insinuating shows of devotion, such as are open lifting up of the eyes to heaven, sighing, and all pretended tricks that are used only to pretend what is not. And thus of their hypocrisy, their ignorance follows.

Advancing themselves in things they never saw. Two things are here to be noted: first, Their ignorance, in things they never saw; and secondly, Vainglorious self-liking, which the word *Embateuon* expresseth.

For the first, There are some things cannot be seen with mortal eyes while we are on earth, as the nature of God, angels, and what is done in heaven; 2. There are some things we ought not to see though we might, and therefore he prayed, 'Lord, turn away mine eyes from seeing vanity;' 3. There are some things we may and ought to see, as the glory of God in his works; 4. There are some things we may and so ought to see, as it is a great curse if we see them not, as the favour of God and spiritual things, in respect of which to be blinded in heart is a miserable judgment, Isa. vi. 10; of the first sort are the things done in heaven.

There is a contrary waywardness in the nature of wicked men; sometimes men are wilful and will not be persuaded even in the things which yet they see; sometimes men are stiff-hearted and will not be removed in opinions about things which they never saw; and so here.

Ignorance is of divers kinds. There is a natural ignorance, and that is of two sorts: for there is an ignorance of mere negation, and so Christ knew not the day of judgment; so it is no sin in a husbandman if he be ignorant of astronomy or physic, &c. There is a natural ignorance which is of corrupt disposition, as to be blind in our judgment in spiritual things from our birth; this is sinful, but not here meant.

There is a profitable ignorance, and that is likewise of two sorts, for it is either profitable, absolutely and simply, or but only in some respects. It had been simply profitable and good for the Jews if they had never known the fashions of the Gentiles; so it had been good for Samson if he had never known Delilah. But it had been profitable for the Pharisees, but in some respects, not to have seen or to have had so much knowledge, John ix. 41. So the apostle Peter saith it had been good for apostates if they had never known the way of truth, &c., 2 Pet. ii. 21.

There is willing ignorance, and that is of two sorts: of frailty or of presumption. Of frailty, when men neglect the means by which they should know, either in part or in some respects. Thus men fail that see a wide door set open for comfort and direction, and yet through carelessness or willing slackness neglect great riches of knowledge, which might have been attained if they had made use of opportunities. Presumptuous ignorance is when men not wittingly only, but wilfully, contemn true knowledge; 'They will none of the knowledge of God's ways,' Job xxi. 14.

Presumptuous ignorance is likewise of two sorts: 1. When men refuse to know God's revealed will, needful to their salvation; 2. When men wilfully embrace fancies and superstitions in opinion, especially in such things as they neither do nor can understand; and such is the ignorance here condemned.

Doct. But the main doctrine is, that it is a great sin and a hateful vice to be rash and adventurous to venture upon opinions in matters of religion, either that concern worship or practice, where men are not first well-informed in judgment by true grounds of knowledge. Hence men are advised to 'take heed how they hear,' and to 'try the spirits, and to be wise to sobriety,' Rom. xii. 3, and to beware of fables, 2 Tim. ii. 16, 23, iv. 3, 4, 1 Tim. i. 4, iv. 6, 7, vi. 20, Titus i. 14, iii. 9, 2 Pet. i. 16. This condemns the strange coining of opinions, without all warrant of the word, in the papists, that so confidently tell us of the rooms in hell, and of the queen of heaven, and how many orders there be of angels, &c. And, withal, it may restrain such as profess the fear of God and reformation of life, to be well advised in their opinions, and not pitch resolutely upon opinions in things the word doth not warrant. Blind zeal hath no more allowance than superstition hath to coin opinions to tie men's consciences withal.

Advancing himself. The word signifieth to take possession, and to go proudly and to search hidden things with deep insight. As it is here applied, it may note in their sin three things: 1. A deep insight or out-reaching into a thing beyond ordinary knowledge; 2. A mighty approbation or very possessing of a man's self in a peculiar content arising from his own invention; 3. An external advancing or vain-glorious priding of a man's self in his fancy. There is a strange corruption in the nature of all sorts of men, a secret inclination to devices and reaches both in opinion and life. The scripture gives warning of the 'doctrines of men,' Mat. xv. 9; of 'opposition of science,' 1 Tim. vi. 20; of 'the deepness of Satan,' Rev. ii. 24; of transformation in evil ministers into ministers of light, &c., 2 Cor. xi. 14. And thus are men in their practice: though they commit the same foul evils they condemn in others, yet they have such devices with which they please themselves, that they are called 'counsels,' Ps. v. 10, and they are said to 'seek deep to hide their counsels,' &c. They have their 'turning of devices,' Isa. xxix. 15. Every man almost thinks he hath some conceit which others have not, &c., such as these: either they may do it though others might not, or the manner is different, or the issues will not be alike, or he will repent at such a time when he hath tried so far, or he will make amends, or it shall not be known, or God is merciful, or his fault is not so great as others, or the scripture doth not condemn it in express words. These and such like conceits in themselves are dull and silly. But where the love of sin hath warmed the heart, and the devil hath put life into them, it is incredible to conceive how miserably pertinacious men will shew themselves to be; and so do men approve of their own devices, that usually there is no error or sin so vile but men can bless themselves against any terror or threatening: and if men find their devices to have any entertainment, they will advance themselves wonderfully, and not only swell in great thoughts of themselves, but outwardly vain-glory will overspread their carriage, words, and actions.

The consideration hereof should teach us to trust more in God and less in men, Ps. xcii. 8, 9; and to labour for plainness of heart and simplicity, Prov. xii. 5, xxi. 8; and to long to hear God speak, and shew us the secrets of his wisdom, Job xi. 5, 6; and to suspect ourselves when we feel a self-liking or an inclination to boast of our device; especially we should pray that the Lord would keep us from desire of vain-glory; and accordingly we should endeavour to do nothing through strife or vain-glory, but rather set our glory and boasting in knowing God, and in the cross of Christ, and in the hope of the glory of the sons of God, daily examining ourselves, and proving our own works, lest we think ourselves something when we are nothing. Thus of their ignorance.

Rashly puffed up. These words are a taxation of their swelling pride, described: 1. By the nature of it, 'puffed up;' 2. By the effect, 'in vain,' or 'rashly;' 3. By the cause, 'in the mind of their flesh.'

Puffed up. What is pride but a wind? a wind to fill, and a wind to torment. Men may be spiritually swelled both in life and opinion. There is a swelling for abundance of riches, there is a swelling behaviour in men's carriages, there is a swelling in sin, but here is a swelling for opinions. Oh that we could learn to abhor pride and swelling, by considering how much the Lord abhors it, as many scriptures shew, Prov. viii. 13, xvi. 5, 19, Job xl. 6, Hab. ii. 5, Mal. iv. 1, and many such like. Oh that we could be in love with a meek and quiet spirit, in the hid man of the heart! But let us observe the effects of pride.

Rashly. The word is εἰκῆ, and it signifies either 'rashly,' or 'in vain.' Sure it is a great fault to be rash, light, sudden, in opinion or practice. It is a great fault to be rash in reproving, in praising, in dispraising, or taking or mistaking doctrine, in judging or censuring; and we should pray that the Lord would give us a staid spirit, and a mind not easily hurried into distemper.

If we read it 'in vain,' it notes fitly that pride always is in vain. In vain, I say: first, In respect of God, who resisteth it, James iv. 7, Luke i. 51; secondly, In respect of other men, who will not regard it, Prov. xi. 2, Ps. ci. 5; thirdly, In respect of themselves, who inherit nothing by it but folly, Prov. xiv. 18, 1 Tim. vi. 4. Our hearts' desire then should be, that the Lord would hide our pride, and mortify our natural corruption herein.

In the mind of the flesh. Here he shews whence all this stuff and swelling comes; it came from the mind of the flesh, even from the fairest part of the soul. The mind of the flesh is that *acumen*, that sharpness of wit, that perspicacity that is in men; and so we may see that wit, sharpness of understanding, carnal reason is in vain, (whatsoever men savour of themselves,) a mere puff of wind, a very vanity, whether it be in opinion or in life; the very wisdom of the flesh is enmity with God, our own very minds are so defiled and corrupt. Which should teach us to 'gird up the loins of our minds,' and restrain what self-conceit might arise from the pride of our own minds or carnal reason, we should (as the apostle shews) 'become fools, that we might be truly wise,' 1 Cor. iii. 18. Again, it should teach us not to rest upon the wisdom of men, nor to think of any above what is written, or be puffed up one against another. Thus of the third thing.

Ver. 19. *And not holding the head, whereof all the body, furnished and knit together by joints and bands, increaseth with the increase of God.*

These words note the fourth thing, viz., their danger; they did it not only hypocritically, and ignorantly, and proudly, but also dangerously. Their danger is both laid down and amplified in this verse; it is laid down in these words, 'not holding the head,' and amplified by a digression into the praises of the mystical body of Jesus Christ, for the union and increase thereof.

Not holding the head. These words shew that they that believe and practise such things are themselves out of Christ, and by this kind of worship they draw men from Christ. Four things may from hence be observed:

1. That angel-worship razeth the foundation, so that the churches that practise it fall from Christ, and are not the true churches of Christ; and this evidently proves the church of Rome to be no true church, because, besides many other heresies and idolatries, they maintain the worshipping of saints and angels.

2. That hypocrisy, ignorance, and pride are inseparable companions of apostasy from Christ.

3. That there is a difference between sin and sin, error and error; every sin or every error doth not cut us off from Christ: there be some sins be sins of infirmity Gal. vi. 1; some sins be such as there remains no more sacrifice for them, Heb. vi.; there be some ceremonies may be borne withal, Rom. xiv.; some ceremonies that abolish from Christ, Gal. v. 3; there be some errors of mere frailty and ignorance, Ps. xix.; some errors that altogether corrupt the mind, and make men destitute of the truth, 1 Tim. vi. 4. And therefore we should learn with all discerning to put a difference, Jude 24.

4. That it is an utter misery not to be joined unto Christ; which imports a singular feebleness in the hearts of men, that cannot be stirred up with all heedfulness to make sure their union with Christ.

Head. The dream of Catharinus, that the pope should be here meant, is to be scorned, not confuted. The words note the relation that is between Christ and the church.

The creature stands in relation to Christ: 1. More generally in existence, and so all things are in him, Col. i. 16. More especially in union, and so man only is joined to Christ; but this union is threefold, for it is either natural, or sacramental, or mystical. In the union of nature, all men are joined to Christ. In the union of sacrament or sign, all in the visible church are joined to Christ. In the mystical union in one body, only the faithful are joined to Christ. And this is here meant.

And so we have here occasion again to take notice of this truth, that the church of Christ is joined unto Christ in a most near union, even to Christ as her head. The doctrine hath been largely handled in the former chapter; only from the renewing of the meditation of it, we may gather both comfort and instruction; comfort if we consider the love, presence, sympathy, influence, and communication of dignity with which Christ doth honour us as our head; instruction also, for this may teach us to be careful to obey Christ willingly, as the member doth the head, and to carry ourselves so godly and discreetly, that we dishonour not our head.

From which all the body, &c. Hitherto of the danger as it is laid down: now followeth the aggravation by a digression into the praises of the church, the mystical body of Christ. In general three things may be observed:

1. That by nature we are wonderful blind in the contemplation of the glory of the mystical body of Christ, and therefore we had need to be often put in mind of it.

2. That one way to set out the fearfulness of sin, is by the fairness of the blessings lost by it; the fairness of the body of Christ shews the foulness of lumps of profaneness and apostasy.

3. Digressions are not always and absolutely unlawful. God's Spirit sometimes draws aside the doctrine to satisfy some soul which the teacher knoweth not; and sparingly used, it quickeneth attention. But I forbear to plead much for it, because though God may force it, yet man should not frame it; and it is a most happy ability to speak punctually, directly to the point.

But in particular, in these words the church, which is the body of Christ, is praised for four things: 1. For her original or dependence upon Christ, 'of whom;' 2. For ornament, 'furnished;' 3. For union, which is amplified: 1. By the parts, 'knit together;' 2. By the means, 'joints and bands;' 4. For her growth, 'increasing with the increase of God.'

Of whom. Doct. All the praise of the church is from her head; for of herself she is black, Cant. i., she is but the daughter of Pharaoh, Ps. xlv.; she was in her blood when Christ first found her, Ezek. xvi.; she needed to be washed from her spots and wrinkles, Eph. v.; and therefore we should deny ourselves, and do all in the name of Christ, who is our praise.

All the body. Doct. The care of Christ extends itself to every member as well as any. Observe these phrases in scripture: 'Every one that asketh,' Mat. vii. 8; 'every one that heareth these words,' Mat. vii. 24; 'every one that confesseth Christ,' Mat. x. 32; 'every one that is weary and heavy laden,' Mat. xi. 29; 'every one that the Father hath given him,' John vi. 37; 'every one that calleth on the name of God,' 1 Cor. i. 2; and the like.

Use is, first, for comfort: 'Let not the eunuch say, I am a dry tree; or the stranger say, The Lord hath separated me from his people,' Isa. lvi.; 'nor let the foot say, I am not the eye,' &c., 1 Cor. xii.; and, secondly, We must learn of Christ to extend our love also to all saints.

Body. It were to no purpose to tell that there are divers bodies, terrestrial, celestial, natural, spiritual, a body of sin, a body of death: it is Christ's body is here spoken of. Christ hath a body natural, and a body sacramental, and a body mystical; it is the mystical body is here meant. The mystical body of Christ is the company of faithful men, who by an unutterable union are everlastingly joined to Christ; though they are dispersed up and down the world, yet in a spiritual relation they are as near together as the members of the body are. If we be faithful there can be no separation from Christ and Christians, whatsoever become of us in our outward estate.

This body of Christ is commended for three things: ornament, union, and growth; and well are all put together, for not one can be without the other, especially the first and the third cannot be without the second. It is no wonder Christians cannot grow nor be furnished if they be not knit to Christ; they may be near the body, but not of the body. There is great difference between our best garments and our meanest members; the worst member of the body will grow, yet the best raiment, though it fit never so near, will not. So is it between wicked men professing Christ, and the godly that are members of Christ indeed.

Of these three, union is of the essence of the

body; the other two are adjuncts; the one needful to the being, the other to the well-being of the church. First, therefore, of this union:

This union is two ways here set forth: 1. That it is, in these words, 'knit together;' 2. How it is, in these words, ' by joints and bands.'

Knit together. The faithful are knit together: 1. With Christ; 2. With Christians.

Great is the glory of Christians knit to Christ, for from that union with him flow many excellent privileges, such are these:

1. The communication of names,—the body is called sometimes by the name of the head, viz., Christ, 1 Cor. xii., and the head by the name of the body, viz., Israel, Isa. xlix.; 2. The influence of the virtue of the death and resurrection of Christ, Rom. vi.; 3. The inhabitation of the Spirit of Christ, Rom. 8; 4. Intercession, 1 John ii. 2; 5. The communication of the secrets of Christ, 1 Cor. ii. 16; 6. The testimony of Jesus, 1 Cor. i. 5; 7. Expiation, as he is the sacrifice and passover offered for us, 1 Cor. v. 7; 8. Consolation in affliction, 2 Cor. i. 5; 9. Power against tentations, 2 Cor. xi. 9; 10. The anointing or power of office to be prophets, kings, and priests unto God, 2 Cor. i. 21; 11. Universal grace, not in respect of persons, that it reacheth to all the members only, but in respect of parts, that he being the fulness that filleth all in all things, Eph. i. 27; 12. Sympathy in all miseries, Heb. ii. 15; 13. The sanctification of all occurrents in life or death, Phil. i. 21; 14. The resurrection of the body, both for matter, Rom. viii. 11, and priority, 1 Thes. iv. 16; lastly, The opening of heaven, Heb. x. 24, a lease whereof is granted and sealed, and earnest given in this life, Eph. i. 14. Thus of union with Christ.

From their knitting with Christians also arise excellent advantages and prerogatives, for hereby they have right to the external privileges of Zion; they stand in relation to all saints, they receive the benefit of the prayers of the whole body, and from the known saints they have the light of example, fellowship in the gospel, outward blessings for their sakes, assistance in the fight against the world, sympathy in afflictions, the profit of spiritual mercy, counsel, consolation, admonition, &c., and, lastly, a part in their lot.

By joints and bands. The meaning is that God's servants are tied together by as near, certain, and sure means as any member in the body can be joined to the rest by joints and bands.

We are tied to Christ both by his Spirit, and by faith, and hope, and holy desires; we are tied to the church in one spirit, in one head, in the freedom and use of his ordinances, the word and sacraments; in affection, in subordination of callings, and in the covenant of grace, and in the same lot of inheritance.

The uses of all follow: first, If we be thus tied to Christ by joints and bands, then they are to be reproved that like it so well to be still chained in the bonds of iniquity, and seek not this holy union; let them take heed they be not reserved unto everlasting bonds. But especially the meditation hereof should work in us a hatred of fornication and that filthy coupling with a harlot, 1 Cor. vi. 15; and we should take heed of offending, wounding or wronging the brethren, for thereby men sin against Christ himself to whom they are united, 1 Cor. viii. 11, 12; and it should separate us from sinners, 2 Cor. vi. 15; and cause us to strive to shew ourselves new creatures, 2 Cor. v. 17; and to seek those things that are above, where our head and Saviour is, Col. iii. 1. Here also is great comfort, for our union with Christ may assure us that we shall not be destitute of any heavenly gift, needful for this life or the appearing of Christ, for present sanctification or future preservation, for 'God is faithful who hath called us to this fellowship with his Son.' And seeing we are tied with such joints and bands, 'who shall separate us from the love of Christ?' Rom. viii.

Again, are we united to Christians and knit together as fellow members? Then we should be faithful in the use of our own gifts, and diligent in our callings for the common good, Rom. xii. 6-8; to all well-doing, to do it with love, sincerity, and brotherly affection, ver. 9, 10; yielding honour to the places and gifts of others, ver. 10; with all uprightness, diligence, and respect of God's glory, ver. 11; with hope, patience, prayer, ver. 12; with mercy, sympathy and humility, ver. 13-16. Thus of union; ornament follows.

Furnished. The church is furnished with unsearchable riches, Eph. iii. 9, with all sorts of spiritual blessings in heavenly things, Eph. i. 3; she is cleansed by the blood of Christ, Heb. ix. 14; Christ is her wisdom, righteousness, and sanctification, and redemption, 1 Cor. i. 31; she is not destitute of any heavenly gift, 2 Cor. i. 6; and this he took order for when he ascended on high and led captivity captive, Eph. iv. 7. Oh, then, that the love of Christ could constrain us, and that the Spirit of Christ would enlighten us, to see the riches of our calling, and the glorious inheritance of the saints! Thus of ornament; growth followeth.

Increasing with the increase of God. Growth is a marvellous glory to Christians.

The body of Christ groweth: 1. In the number of parts or members, men being added daily to the church; 2. In the powerful use of the means of salvation; 3. In grace, 2 Pet. iii. 18, as knowledge, and the like, Col. i. 9-11; 4. In practice of holy duties, Phil. i. 11; 5. In the strength of Christ, Eph. iii. 16.

There are many lets of the growth of grace and holiness in Christians; some are secret, some open. The secret are: 1. Want of the true grace; 2. A profession advanced for ill ends, inward hypocrisy; 3. Errors, and wicked opinions, either concerning the doctrine of godliness, or the practice of it, 2 Pet. iii. 17, 18; 4. Want of knowledge how to perform holy duties, and faith to believe God's acceptation; 5. Strong affections, 1 Cor. iii. 3, Eph. iv. 30, 31; 6. Spiritual pride, 2 Cor. xii. 6, 7; 7. Love of ease, or loathness to endure either the labour or the trouble of the power of godliness; 8. Want of internal order in digesting the comforts or directions of God, and unsettledness in assurance; and lastly, Some secret corruptions which they favour and will not forego.

The open and external lets are: 1. Want of public powerful means, Eph. iv. 12, &c.; 2. Discord with the members of Christ, Eph. iv. 16; 3. Neglect of private means; 4. Want of order of life, Col. ii. 5, 6; 5. Unfaithfulness in other bonds, 1 Pet. iii. 7; 6. Secret detractors and backbiters; 7. Ungodly company; 8. Living without a particular calling, or not diligently in it; 9. Worldliness, as in Demas; lastly, Resisting of counsel and admonition.

There are divers motives even in this text which may persuade us to strive after increase: 1. It will be a sign thou art far from fundamental errors in opinion or worship, and from pride and hypocrisy; 2. Thou shouldst do it for thine head's sake,—dishonour not thine head by thy not increasing; 3. Increase for the good and glory of the body; lastly, It is the increasing of God, and so it is four ways: 1. In respect of kind, it is not a thriving in estate or temporal things, but in the things of God; 2. As he is the efficient cause of it, God only is the author of all holy increase; 3. In regard of the worth of the matter, it is a divine thing to increase; 4. In respect of the end, it tends to God's glory.

That we may increase we must look to three things: 1. That we often purge our hearts by godly sorrow, and humiliation for our sins; 2. That we love brotherly fellowship; 3. That we willingly resign ourselves to the ministry of the gospel, to be subject, and obey it in all things.

And thus far of the conclusion against philosophy; the last branch of the conclusion follows.

Ver. 20. *Wherefore if we be dead with Christ from the ordinances of the world, why as though ye lived in the world are ye burthened with traditions?*

Ver. 21. *As touch not, taste not, handle not.*

Ver. 22. *Which all perish with the using, and are after the commandments and doctrines of men.*

Ver. 23. *Which things indeed have a show of wisdom in voluntary religion, and humbleness of mind, and not sparing the body, which are things of no value, since they appertain to filling of the flesh.*

In these words is contained the third branch of the conclusion, and it is enforced against traditions. Here I observe both the manner of propounding, and the matter: For the first, it is to be observed, that whereas he condemned the former by way of advice, he condemns these by bitter and tart expostulation, 'why are ye burthened with traditions?' as if he should say, Were there not a singular proneness of nature to corruption, could they be so blinded as to suffer false teachers to impose traditions upon them?

In the matter consider: first, What he condemns, viz., traditions, explicated in the kinds, ver. 21; 2. The reasons why he condemns them; and these are six: 1. Ye are dead with Christ, and therefore ye ought not to be subject to traditions,—of the force of this reason afterwards; 2. You are dead from the rudiments of the world, that is, from the ceremonial laws of Moses, which yet were as rudiments or ways of instructing the world in the principles of the kingdom of God, and therefore much more should you now give over traditions; 3. They are burdens, and the greater by how much the less sense you have of them; 4. The matter of them is light, and vain, and idle, ver. 21; 5. They are all corruptible, and perish with the using; 6. They are after the accounts and doctrines of men, ver. 22.

Object. But there seemeth to be a depth in these traditions.

Sol. Ver. 23. He confesseth that they have a 'show of wisdom,' and that in three things: 1. 'In voluntary religion;' 2. 'In humbleness of mind;' 3. 'In not sparing the body,' which he censures two ways:

1. It is but a show or flourish, no true substance either of worship or sanctity; 2. It withholds the honour due to the body.

Now that the whole may be better understood, we must distinctly consider what he meaneth by tradition, which will appear if it be considered negatively, with comparison with the two former.

1. They are not things required by scripture any way; for all such were condemned under the first kind, viz., ceremonies, which though now abrogated, were once required.

2. They are not such rites besides scripture, as are practised with opinion of worship, for they are condemned under the second kind, viz., philosophy.

So then the traditions here condemned are such rites, customs, or observations, as men bind their consciences to observe or practise in the civil life of man. Besides the instances in the text, such are the observation of evil days, or hours to be born in, or to marry in, or to set out on a journey in; the rules observed about infants unbaptized, as that they must not be washed, or they must lie in a sieve, or such like about women that lie in; such is the not marrying with kindred at the font, as they call it; such are the observation of signs of ill luck, or of death, gathered from the crying of birds, or the running of beasts; such is praying at the lighting up of candles, and the burning of candles over the dead corpse, or the naming of children with names that agree to men and women, to make them live the longer; such is not burying on the north side of the church, and the like silly trash with which simple people abound more than is ordinarily observed.

Thus of the general.

Wherefore if ye be dead with Christ. In these words divers things may be observed:

1. Here we see the necessity of our union with Christ; the apostle will not be done with it, he remembereth it still.

2. When he saith, 'if you be dead,' it implies that men may make a fair show, and profess long, and live in true visible churches, and yet it is a question whether they be in Christ or no, 'if ye be dead with Christ.'

3. Note here the praise of a mortified life; for when he saith, 'if ye be dead in Christ,' it imports that to be so is an excellent condition; to be truly mortified with Christ is a rare happiness; to die with Christ is better than to live with the world.

4. Penitent sinners have life and death, joys and sorrows, &c., common with Christ.

5. In special they have death common with Christ. They die with Christ: (1.) Because Christ's death was theirs. When Christ died they died, because his death was for their sakes, and for their benefit. (2.) Because when their bodies die they die in union with Christ. (3.) Because the virtue of Christ's death is derived to their souls; whence flows death to the law, that is, a release from the rigour and curse of it; 2. Death to sin, that is, a power to mortify sin, conveyed in the ordinances of Christ, and applied by the Spirit of Christ; 3. The presence of Christ in all the duties of mortification; though they be done never so secretly, yet Christ is with them.

The use may be both for trial and comfort. For trial: art thou not dead with Christ in respect of the mortification of thy corruptions? then art thou not in Christ. For comfort to the mortified: thou art in Christ, and he will never leave thee nor forsake thee, till he hath raised thy body and cured thy soul. Thus of the words in themselves. They are also to be considered as they are here used against traditions, and so they are two ways:

1. Christ is dead, and in his death ye are freed from all bondage of soul to anything but the will of God, and therefore it is a dishonour to Christ's death and

the freedom purchased in it to make ourselves servants to traditions.

2. You are dead with Christ, that is, you are mortified persons; and these things are too light for any grave and penitent person to take up his thoughts or cares about them; fleshly persons are only capable of this trash; mortified persons without teaching suspect them.

Thus of the first reason.

From the rudiments of the world. The second reason stands thus: If by the death of Christ ye be freed from the ceremonies of Moses, which were then rudiments, or, as it were, the first grounds of instruction, then much more are you freed from traditions, which are but beggarly observations, that nobody can tell whence they came, or what good they do. This should be of force to prevail with us against the multitudes of idle traditions that reign amongst the people.

Why, as though ye lived in the world, are ye burdened? &c.

Quest. Do not the faithful live in the world, that he saith with such a salt interrogation, 'as though ye lived in the world!'

Ans. 1. They live in the world corporally, yet not in the world in respect of their profession of spiritual and celestial life; so Christ's kingdom was not of this world. 2. In respect of subjection to all the frame of rites and observations of the world: they live not as men that are tied and vowed to the service of the world in whatsoever observations it shall propound.

Burdened. Traditions are a grievous burden to the soul, and the worse the less they are felt. Men will not willingly suffer unjust impositions in their freeholds in the world, nor should men suffer the world to impose burdens upon their souls.

The word also notes the audacious liberty of the imposers: before they pestered the church with the ceremonies of Moses, then they corrupted God's worship with philosophical dreams, such as was the worship of angels; now they proceed further, they clog the civil life of man and his private affairs with imperious observations.

Thus of the third reason.

As touch not, taste not, handle not. These words must be understood to be uttered *mimeticos*, in a kind of scorn. See the wicked subtlety of the devil, he turns himself into all forms to ruin us. Once he destroyed the world by tempting man to eat, now he goeth about to poison men's souls with restraining them from eating.

Some observe that the haste of the words, without copulatives, notes their eagerness in pressing these things, and persuading men to the care of them. Sure it is, men of corrupt minds are more eager about these than about weightier matters.

Some learned render 'touch not' by 'eat not,' and so note a gradation: first, they would not have them eat; then not so much as taste; and when they had gotten them to that, then not so much as to handle. Ambrose runs against the stream of all interpreters to understand these words to be the commandment of the apostle.

Thus of the fourth reason.

Which all perish with the using. These words are two ways interpreted:

1. They bring destruction to the users; they are a doctrine of the devil's, and make men the children of hell. This is true, but not the truth of this place.

2. They are of a perishable nature, and therefore men ought not to load their consciences with necessity of observing them.

This is the nature of all outward things; they perish with the using; all is vanity; the glory of the flesh is but as the flower of the field, Isa. xl.; rust or moth doth corrupt them, Mat. vi.; even crowns are corruptible, 1 Cor. iv. 24. Here we see a clear difference between earthly things and spiritual. Earthly things, not only in the abuse, but in the very use, are either worn out or less regarded, or have less vigour, fairness, power, &c.; but clean contrary with spiritual things. Why should we not then moderate our love to these outward things? Why should we not strive to 'use this world as if we used it not,' no more 'trusting in uncertain riches'? This should also stir us up to the care of spiritual graces and duties that never perish, that we may attain that 'uncorruptible crown of righteousness' which 'God will give to all that love his appearing.' The very daily perishing of food and raiment are types of thine own perishing also.

Thus of the fifth reason.

And are after the commandments and doctrines of

men. The reason stands thus: whatsoever hath no better warrant than the commandment and doctrines of men is to be rejected as a burdensome tradition. But these things are such, therefore why are ye burdened? See the wretched disposition of men's natures, how ready men are to prescribe, and how easy men are to be led on in these foolish vanities. But are the commandments of God so easily obeyed? Are the doctrines of God's word so willingly embraced? Alas! alas! men's examples or counsel will easily pass for laws, but the Lord is as if he were not worthy to be heard in the practice of the most.

Thus of the six reasons.

Now follow the objections. Though these things were not commanded in the word, yet they were wisely devised by our fathers, and therefore are to be observed.

Sol. Ver. 23. The apostle grants that there were three things alleged to approve the discretion of the founders of these things, and instanceth in one kind, viz., abstinence or fasting, for that he confesseth had a show of voluntary, not co-acted or forced religion; 2. Of humbleness of mind; 3. Of the taming of the body. But when he hath granted this, he doth dash all as it were with thunder and lightning, when he saith: 1. This was but the show of wisdom; 2. This sparing did withhold the honour due unto the body.

Observe here that it is a fair property to use candour and ingenuous inquiry after the truth, and willingly to acknowledge what they see in the reasons of the adversaries. We see the apostle fairly yields the full of the reasons, not mangling them, but setting them out distinctly, and then confutes them. It were happy if there were this fair dealing in all reasonings, public and private, in print or by word of mouth, in all that profess love to the truth especially.

Show of wisdom. There is a wisdom only in appearance, and in men's account, in name only. Some men have wisdom, others have the praise of wisdom. But in matters of conscience and religion, it is dangerous for man to lift up himself in his wisdom, or to admit the varnish of carnal reason. The wisest worldly men are not always the holiest and most religious men. Oh that there were a heart in us indeed, to acknowledge and to seek the true wisdom that is from above!

The colours cast upon their traditions were three: 1. Voluntary religion; 2. Humbleness of mind; 3. The taming of the body. All these, as base varnish to smear over men's insolent wickedness, are here rejected. Which may confirm us in the detestation of popery, even in that wherein it makes the great show. What are their works of supererogation, their vows of single life, their canonical obedience, their wilful poverty, and the like? What can be said or shewed in their praise, which was not pretended for these traditions? The apostle here gives warning: let not men be deceived; these fair pretences of our papists are but the old objections of the false apostles, new varnished over again by the pope and his vassals. Oh that our seduced multitude would consider this! then would they not be thus led to hell with their fair shows.

The last thing in this verse is the apostle's reason against these colours.

They have it not in estimation to satisfy the body or flesh. That is, they yield not due honour to the body. The body of man is to be honoured, for, first, the Son of God (as the fathers say) made it with his own hands in the likeness of the body he assumed. 2. The soul, a divine thing, is kept in it, and helped by it in great employments. 3. The Son of God took the body of a man into the unity of his person. 4. He redeemed the body by his blood, and feeds it with the sacramental body. 5. The body is the temple of the Holy Ghost. 6. It is consecrate to God in baptism. 7. It is a part of the mystical body of Christ. Lastly, It shall be gloriously raised at the last day. Then let men know, they must give account that dishonour their bodies, and if these superstitious persons must reckon for it that punish their bodies without commandment from God, where shall these beasts appear that sin against their bodies by gluttony, and drunkenness, and lust, and whoredom, and cruelty, and murder? Oh, the condemnation that abides these impenitent men, that glory in their shame, and mind only to fulfil the lusts of the flesh!

Thus of the dehortation. Thus also of matters of faith.

Thus also of the second chapter.

THE LOGICAL ANALYSIS OF THE THIRD CHAPTER.

HITHERTO the apostle hath entreated of matters of faith; now he entreateth in these two chapters of matters of life, prescribing rules for conversation.

These rules are either general or particular. The general are from ver. 1 to 18; the particular are from ver. 18 of this chapter to ver. 2 of the fourth chapter.

The general rules concern: first, The meditation of heavenly things, ver. 1 to 5; secondly, The mortification of vice, ver. 5 to 10; thirdly, The renovation of life, ver. 10 to 18.

The exhortation to the care and study of heavenly things is propounded, ver. 1; illustrated, ver. 2; confirmed by reasons, ver. 3, 4.

In the proposition of this exhortation to the study of heavenly things, two things are to be observed: 1. The duty required, 'seek those things that are above;' 2. The reasons, which are four: 1. Ye are risen with Christ; 2. These things are above; 3. Christ is above; 4. Christ is exalted there, and sits at God's right hand.

This exhortation is illustrated, ver. 2: first, By repetition, in these words, 'Set your affections on things which are above;' secondly, By the contrary, 'and not on things that are on earth.'

The confirmation is set down by two motives; the one from the condition of the faithful in this world; the other from their glory in the end of the world.

In this world two things should incite them: 1. Their distress, they are 'dead;' 2. Their hiding of the happiness they have, their 'life is hid with Christ in God,' ver. 3.

In the end of the world they shall appear in glory when Christ shall appear, ver. 4. Thus of the meditation of heavenly things.

The mortification of evil follows; and so he entreats: first, Of the mortification of vices that concern ourselves most, ver. 5–7; secondly, Of the mortification of injuries, ver. 8, 9.

In the first there is both the matter to be mortified, and the reasons.

In the first there is two things: 1. The proposition of mortification, 'Mortify therefore your members that are on earth;' 2. The catalogue of vices to be mortified, which are either against the seventh commandment, 'fornication, uncleanness, inordinate affection,' or against the tenth commandment, 'evil concupiscence,' or against the first commandment, 'covetousness, which is idolatry.'

The reasons are taken: first, From the evil effect, which is the 'wrath of God,' amplified by the persons on whom it falls, 'the children of disobedience,' ver. 6; secondly, From experience, 'in which ye also walked when ye lived in them,' ver. 7.

Thus of the mortification of vices.

The mortification of injuries follows, where observe: 1. The exhortation itself; 2. The reasons of it.

In the exhortation there is two things: 1. The charge in general, 'put away all these things;' 2. The catalogue of injuries to be put away are either the sins of the heart or the sins of the tongue: the sins of the heart are 'anger, wrath, malice;' the sins of the tongue are 'cursed speaking, filthy speaking, lying.'

The reasons are three: first, Ye have put off the old man and his works, ver. 9; secondly, Ye are renewed, which is explicated by showing that this new birth is in general the putting on of the new man in particular, it is the renewing of the mind with knowledge, and of the whole man with the image of Christ, ver. 10; thirdly, God is no accepter of persons, without grace he will respect none, and with it he will disregard none, for 'with him there is neither Grecian nor Jew, circumcision nor uncircumcision, barbarian, Scythian, bond, free: Christ is all in all things,' ver. 11.

Hitherto of the second thing needful to holy life, viz., the mortification of vices. The third follows, viz., the exercise of holy graces and duties, from ver. 12 to 18; and here the rules concern either: 1. The matter of holiness, ver. 12 to 16; or, The means of holiness, ver. 16; or, The end of holiness, ver. 17.

For the first, he gives in charge nine graces, but first proposeth three motives: 1. The election of God, 'as the elect of God;' 2. Their sanctification, 'holy;' 3. The love of God to them, 'and beloved.'

The graces are of three sorts; some of them have their greatest praise in prosperity, viz., 'mercy, kindness, meekness, humbleness of mind;' some of them concern the times of adversity principally, viz., long-suffering and clemency in forbearing and forgiving, ver. 12, 13.

Some of these graces ought to reign at all times, and these are three:—

First, Love, which is set out both by the dignity of it, 'above all put on love,' and by the use of it, it is 'the bond of perfectness,' ver. 14.

Secondly, Peace, amplified by the author, 'of God;' by the power of it, 'let it rule;' and by the seat of it, 'in your hearts.' To which he exhorts by two reasons: 1. From their vocation, 'to which ye are called;' 2. From their mutual relation, 'as members of one body,' ver. 15.

The third is thankfulness or amiableness, ver. 15. Thus of the matter of holiness.

The means follows, which is the word.

The exhortation to the use of the word: 1. Concerns the word in general; 2. The psalms in special. For the first, he propounds three things: 1. The author of it, 'the word of Christ;' 2. The manner of entertaining the word, 'let it dwell in you plenteously in all wisdom;' 3. The end or use it should be put to, viz., to teach in what we know not, and to admonish in what we do not.

The second part concerns the psalms in particular, where he sets down the sorts, 'psalms, hymns, and spiritual songs;' and the right manner of singing of psalms, 'singing with grace in your hearts to the Lord.' Thus of the means of holiness, ver. 16.

The third thing is the end, which is considered two ways: first, As the end of intention that we aim at, and so he exhorts to it in these words: 'whatsoever ye do in word or deed, do all in the name of the Lord Jesus;' 2. As the end of consummation that finisheth our works, and so they must 'give thanks to God, even the Father by him.'

And thus of the rules of holy life that concern all men as they are Christians.

Now follow particular rules fitted for particular callings, and that in the family. In the family there are three couples: wives and husbands, children and parents, servants and masters; and to these he giveth rules distinctly.

First, The wife's duty is laid down and enlarged; laid down in these words, 'wives be subject to your husbands;' enlarged, first, by a reason, 'it is comely;' 2. A limitation, 'in the Lord,' ver. 18.

Secondly, The husband's duty is propounded: 1. By exhortation, 'husbands love your wives;' 2. By dehortation, 'be not bitter to them,' ver. 19.

Thirdly, The duty of children is laid down in these words, 'children obey your parents;' and amplified: 1. By the extent, 'in all things;' 2. By reason, 'for this is well pleasing to the Lord,' ver. 20.

Fourthly, The duty of parents is expressed by dehortation, in these words, 'parents provoke not your children to anger;' and confirmed by a reason taken from the ill effect, 'lest they be discouraged.'

Fifthly, In setting down the duty of servants, there is first the exhortation, ver. 22, 23; the reasons, ver. 24, 25. The exhortation is both briefly laid down in these words, 'servants be obedient to them that are your masters;' and explicated: 1. By provisos about their obedience; 2. The manner how they must obey.

The provisos are two: one restrains masters, they are their servants but 'according to the flesh;' the other extends the duty of servants, they must obey 'in all things.'

The manner how they must obey is set down: first, Negatively, 'not with eye-service, not as men-pleasers;' secondly, Affirmatively; and so they must obey: 1. 'With singleness of heart;' 2. With 'fear of God;' 3. 'Heartily, as to the Lord.'

The reasons are two: first, From the certain hope of reward from God, ver. 24; secondly, From the certain vengeance of God upon them that do wrong.

THE METAPHRASE UPON THE THIRD CHAPTER.

VER. 1. Hitherto you have been taught, exhorted, and dehorted in matters that concern faith and opinions. Now it followeth that I should stir you up in such things as concern your carriage, both general, as you are Christians, and particular, as you are of several conditions of life. And the first thing you should be careful of in the right order of your lives, is to raise up your thoughts and affections to the study and contemplation of heavenly things; for hereby you do effectually prove that you are risen up in the first resurrection with Jesus Christ. And heavenly things are above, and therefore for their worthiness fitting your contemplation; and for their difficulty, they cannot be reached without seeking, and diligent study and inquiry. Besides, is not Christ above your head and Saviour, and where should your hearts be, but where your treasure is, yea, where Christ is, there in singular glory, advanced above all men and angels, next in glory and power to God himself? Oh, then, how should your minds run upon him; and to contemplate of these things is to ascend after him.

Ver. 2. And when I exhort you to seek the things that are above, my meaning is that you should study about them, and with all wisdom raise up not your thoughts only, but your affections also to the love of heavenly things; and this you cannot do unless you withdraw your affections from things on earth, whether they be traditions, or worldly things, or the works of the flesh.

Ver. 3. Now there are excellent reasons by which I may briefly stir you up hereunto, both from the consideration of your present estate in this world, and from the meditation of your future condition in the day of Christ. In this world two things should much move you: First, That ye are but dead men; for both you profess the forsaking of the world, and the world accounts of you but as dead men; and your affections drown and overwhelm you many times. Secondly, The spiritual happiness which you have, which is the life of your life, is hid always from wicked men, who have no judgment or discerning in spiritual things; and sometimes by the violence of temptation yourselves discern not your own happiness. Yet be not discouraged; it was so with Christ while he lived; and though it be hid, yet is it hid with God; it is in him, it is in his power, and he will preserve it.

Ver. 4. But especially, if you think of the coming of Jesus Christ, you should be stirred to the love and study of heavenly things; for then shall there be an end of all earthly felicities, then shall men make accounts of all their actions and studies, then will not riches avail in that day of wrath, then will the incomparable gain and glory of godliness be discovered. Oh, the invaluable dignity of heavenly-minded Christians in that day! And thus of the meditation of heavenly things.

Ver. 5. The second main part of my exhortation shall concern the mortification both of vices and crimes. First, I would hence observe those special sins which are most hateful to God in your former course of life, and then have been most prone to. When I say mortify, I mean that you should use all the means indefinitely that serve to kill the power and practice of those sins, never giving over confession and godly sorrow till you find the power of them abated and deadened. And this I would have you do, not only in outward sins, but any sin, though they were as dear to you as the very members of your bodies, yet you must cut them off. Now some of the sins that I would have you studious to avoid or mortify are these: first, look to the filthiness condemned in the seventh commandment; not only avoid whoredom, but all kinds of wicked fleshly filthiness and uncleanness; yea, look to that internal burning or the flames of lust within, that habitual effeminateness and passions of lust; and more than all this, see that you make conscience of evil thoughts, and that contemplative wickedness which may be in your minds without consent of the will to practise it; for even those thoughts are filthy in God's sight. Now the last sin I will name is covetousness, which is a kind of vile idolatry in God's sight.

Ver. 6. For these and such like sins bring down the fearful judgments of God upon the offenders, and they wonderfully vex God; and besides, to live in these sins, and love them, and continue in them, is a manifest sign that they are but wicked men, children of disobedience, whatsoever they seem to be, or what shows or profession soever they make.

Ver. 7. And the rather should you be for ever careful to keep yourselves from these evils and the like, or speedily to subdue them and forsake them, seeing you have felt by experience, in your unregenerate estate, what it is to have sin like a monster to live and reign in the heart or life.

Ver. 8. You must also make conscience of injurious dealing with others, and that not only of the gross acts of injuries, but of doing wrong in your very words; yea, in the passions of your heart; yea, to approve that now ye walk not in sin, shew your uprightness by putting away even everything that might tend to the injury of others. To express my meaning, I will instance in divers sins the unregenerate would make no conscience of. And first, in the heart there is inward fretting, and that passion that discovers itself by outward signs, and that inveterate anger called malice; these you must make conscience of. Besides, in the tongue, there are three vices you must also avoid, viz., cursed speaking, filthy speaking, and lying.

Ver. 9. There are three weighty considerations should move you thereunto: first, When you repent of sin you profess to put off the old man and his works; this old man is the old tempter of your natures, and his works are such as these fore-mentioned passions, and distempers in the tongue.

Ver. 10. Secondly, You are now in the state of grace; you are new men, and therefore must not live after the old manner; you are renewed in knowledge to discern these things to be evil, and therefore ought to shew it in your practice; and you are renewed after the image of Christ. Now there was no guile found in his mouth, nor any of these wretched perturbations in his heart, and therefore how suitable soever they be to the harmony of the most men, yet for that reason you must keep yourselves far from them.

Ver. 11. Thirdly, God is impartially righteous and just. If men will not be reformed of those old corruptions, he cares not for them, though they were Jews, circumcised, free; and contrariwise, if men strive after that holiness they see in Christ, and mortify these corruptions that abound in the world, he will accept them though they were Grecians, Scythians, bounden. Thus of the second main thing needful to holy life, viz., the mortification of vices and injuries.

Ver. 12. The third thing you must be careful of is the exercise of holy graces and duties; and here I shall put you in mind of three things: the matter, the means, and the end. For the first, there are nine graces should principally be remembered in your practice; and that you may be quickened thereunto, be much in the meditation of three things: 1. God's election; 2. Your own sanctification; 3. The love of God to you.

Ver. 13. The graces are: 1. Tenderness in all sorts of injuries; 2. Courtesy; 3. True and hearty humility and lowliness; 4. Quietness and meekness, and tranquillity of heart; 5. Long-suffering in respect of crosses.

And sixthly, Clemency, which stands in two things: in forbearing and forgiving. Forbearing in respect of wrongs and infirmities, and forgiving freely one another. And this forgiving must be extended to every man, and it must be as Christ forgave us, and that is though they be our inferiors, and though they have done us great wrong, and so as we forget as well as forgive.

Ver. 14. But seventhly, Above all others, be sure you clothe yourselves with love; for this will knit us together perfectly, and by this all the saints, and all the graces of the saints, tend unto perfection.

Ver. 15. Eighthly, Get peace, that peace, I mean, that God only gives, and let it rule and prevail with you; and if you cannot be at peace in your life, yet let it be in your hearts still, how unreasonable soever men be; and the rather should you be careful hereof, both because you are called of God to it, and besides you are all members of the same body. Lastly, Add unto all these, amiableness and thankfulness one to another. And thus of the matter of holiness.

Ver. 16. Now, I must also stir you up to a due respect of the means of holiness, which is the word. And so both the word in general, and the Psalms in special. For the word in general, you must remember it is the word of Christ, both as the subject and the cause of it; and you should never be satisfied till you grow familiar and plentiful in it, through the daily use of it, both in your hearts and houses also, and that with all judgment and discretion, not seeking or using it coldly, perversely, carnally, or indiscreetly; and this word you must employ, both to teach you and one another what you know not, and to admonish you and others for what you do not. And in special, be careful of the Psalms, remembering that they also are the word of Christ, and the rather, considering the exquisite variety of sweet matter in them; but in singing, observe these rules: first, Exercise the graces of the heart according to the matter of the Psalm; secondly, Do it with attention and understanding; thirdly, Respect God's glory in it, and his holy presence.

Ver. 17. Lastly, Be careful of the end of all your actions, both that all be done to the glory of God in Christ, (all, I say, both in word and deed,) beginning with calling on the name of Christ, and ending with the sacrifice of thanksgiving, which must be offered unto God in the meditation of Christ, as well as your prayers. Thus I have briefly laid before you the rules that concern holiness, as you are Christians in the general.

Ver. 18. Now, I think it meet to propound some duties that are more particular; and I will only instance in the family; and there I begin with wives, whose word is 'be subject,' an epitome of their duty, and a thing God most stands upon, and which women most fail in. And great reason, for here lieth the true comeliness and beauty of a wife; it is not in her face and garments, but in her subjection to her husband. And the rather should you be subject, because God hath provided you shall not be pressed but in the Lord, not in anything against the word.

Ver. 19. Now for husbands, their word is 'love,' as that God most stands upon, and they most fail in. And in particular, I give them warning to look to one vice above many, and that is, that they be not bitter to their wives.

Ver. 20. And for children, their word is 'obedience;' and they must know that God so enjoins it, that he will have it done thoroughly; they must obey in all things, and submit their wills and desires to their parents; for this is a thing that will not only keep and increase their parents' love to them, but it is also wondrous well-pleasing to God himself.

Ver. 21. Parents also must take heed they sin not against their children, not only by too much indulgence, but also by provoking them, and that not only to sin, but to passion, by unjust precepts, or contumelies and disgraces, or hard usage, or immoderate correction; and that as for other reasons, so lest they be discouraged either from love of well-doing, or of obeying them.

Ver. 22. You that are servants must also with great care attend your duties; your word also is 'obedience;' and the rather because your masters have authority, but only over your flesh, not over your consciences. But in your obedience see to it, it be in all things that concern the subjection of the outward man. But let not your service be only when your masters look on, or fitted only to please men, but obey even in the singleness of your hearts, as in God's presence, where you should fear to displease.

Ver. 23. Neither let what you do be done out of

a slavish fear, but from the heart, with all willingness, as doing therein service to God, and not to men only.

Ver. 24. Knowing infallibly that if men would not reward you for your pains and faithfulness, yet God will, who will not use you as servants, but provide for you as sons and heirs to him. For in all this labour, God accounts you as the servants of Christ, and will reward all as if all had been done to him.

Ver. 25. And contrariwise, he that doth wrong, be he master or servant, shall receive of the Lord for the wrong that he hath done; for God is no accepter of persons.

CHAPTER III.

VER. 1. *If ye then be risen with Christ, seek those things that are above, where Christ sits at the right hand of God.*

Hitherto of Christian doctrine, now followeth Christian life. The apostle hath before discoursed of matters of faith, now he intends to entreat of matters of life, and to prescribe rules of conversation. And these rules belong either to our general calling as we are Christians, or to our particular callings as we are people of such or such condition or state of life.

The general rules are set down from the 1st verse of this chapter to the 18th, and the particular rules begin at the 18th verse, and continue to the 2d verse of the next chapter.

The rules of the first kind may be referred to three heads; for either they concern, first, The meditation of heavenly things; or, secondly, The mortification of vice; or, thirdly, The renovation of life. The meditation of heavenly things is urged from ver. 1 to the 5th, the mortification of vice is urged from ver. 5 to the 10th. Renovation of life is generally laid down ver. 10, 11, and more specially opened ver. 12 to the 18th.

The exhortation to the care and study of heavenly things is thus digested: first, It is expounded, ver. 1; secondly, It is illustrated, ver. 2; thirdly, It is considered[1] by motives and reasons, ver. 3, 4. And thus for the order of the whole chapter, and the general frame of this first part.

Before I open the words more particularly, there are divers things may be noted from the coherence and dependence of these words with the chapter before and the matter following in this chapter.

From the coherence with the former chapter, I observe these things:—

[1] Qu. 'confirmed'?— ED.

First, That there can be no holiness of life without faith; and therefore the apostle first instructeth them in matters of faith. It is a true rule, 'whatsoever is not of faith is sin,' Rom. xiv. 23, and may be extended further than things indifferent. While we are out of God's favour, and know not our reconciliation and justification in Christ, our best actions are but fair sins, for 'without faith it is impossible to please God,' Heb. xi. 6.

Secondly, That the terrestrial blessedness of man is, in respect of sin, two ways principally assaulted: first, With errors of opinion; secondly, With corruptions in manners. And against both we should learn from the apostle in the latter part of the former chapter, and the first parts of this, to be armed and furnished with holy directions and meditations.

Thirdly, That these men that are so superstitiously earnest and so zealously forward for ceremonies and the traditions and observations of men, whatsoever they protest, or pretend, or seem to be, are indeed void of true devotion and fervent affection to heavenly things, Eph. ii. 10.

Fourthly, That he that is by faith made a new creature, must resolve to be at God's appointment for his whole carriage in his general and particular calling.

Thus of the coherence with the former chapters; from the order of doctrine in this chapter two things may be noted:

Doct. 1. First, That before a man can be good in his particular calling, he must first be good in his general. Thou mayest be painful and diligent, but thou canst not be every way a faithful and sound-hearted husband, wife, servant, child, &c., till thou be a good man or good woman, in respect of grace and godliness; and therefore we should 'first seek the righteousness of God's kingdom.' And it may serve for direction unto such as choose wives, or servants, or the like. If they be not faithful to God, how canst thou be assured they will prove faithful to thee? Moreover, wouldst thou have thy servants or children to be amended? then bring them to the powerful preaching of the word, and call upon them to get into the fellowship of the godly, that they may learn to be good abroad in matters of religion, and then thou mayest hope to find them by proof and daily experience trusty and faithful in thy business. Finally, this reproves both the sinfulness and folly of many carnal parents and masters; they never care, so their servants do their work, though they altogether neglect God's work. And many times they restrain their servants and children, and will not let them hear sermons, or come into godly company, as if that were the way to make them idle and careless, whereas we see the clean contrary to be true.

Doct. 2. Secondly, That men are never likely to hold out and prove sound in the reformation and new obedience of their lives till they fall in love with heavenly things, and grow in some measure weary of the world and the things thereof.

Thus of the general observations from the twofold coherence. Now followeth the particular opening of the words.

In the proposition of the exhortation to the study of heavenly things laid down in this verse, two things are to be considered: first, What, or the duty required, viz., 'seek those things which are above;' secondly, Why, or the reasons to enforce the duty, and they are four: first, Ye are 'risen with Christ' in the first resurrection; secondly, These things are 'above,' and not attained without seeking or study; thirdly, Christ is above in his bodily presence; fourthly, Christ sits at the right hand of God, exalted in the glory of his Father. Each of these strongly conclude the exhortation, as will further appear in the particular handling of them.

If ye be risen with Christ. There may be conceived to be a threefold resurrection of a Christian. The first is sacramental, and thus we rise again in baptism; the second is corporal, and so we shall rise again in the day of Jesus Christ, in our bodies, out of the dust of the earth; the third is spiritual, and so we must rise in this life, in soul, from the death of sin, or else we shall never be delivered from the second death. Of this spiritual resurrection, called elsewhere the first resurrection, Rev. xx. 6, he here entreats. And it is a work of the Spirit of grace, delivering us from the power of sin, by which we are quickened to the heavenly desires and endeavours of holy life, by virtue of the resurrection of Jesus Christ, applied unto us by faith in the effectual use of God's ordinances. It is a work by which we grow 'conformable to Christ,' being risen again, Rom. vi. 4, 5; by which also we 'taste of the powers of the life to come,' and are 'born again to a lively hope of an eternal and incorruptible inheritance,' 1 Pet. i. 3, 4; the earnest of which we have received, and shall shortly receive the whole possession purchased, Eph. i. 14, though for a time we be absent from the Lord. This first resurrection carrieth with it a similitude or resemblance of Christ's rising again, so as every Christian in this work bears the image of Christ, and in him Christ riseth before our eyes, not only because the Lord Jesus doth in this gracious work give us a daily and fresh remembrance of his resurrection, by renewing such fruits of it, but also because he imprinteth a secret kind of heavenly-mindedness, the Christian in some weak measure living as Christ did in the interim between his resurrection and ascension, waiting always for his exaltation into heaven.

Now, the consideration of this work is here used by the apostle to persuade unto the meditation of heavenly things, and that fitly; for if we be risen as Christ was, then we must be minded as he was. Now we know that after he was risen again, he was not encumbered with this world, nor did he converse with the men of this world, but lived with the Lord, as it were, immediately, in a heavenly manner, waiting for heaven. So should a Christian do; he should every day be striving to get up his heart, by faith, and prayer, and meditation, and voluntary abnegation, by all means begging and seeking the virtue of Christ's resurrection, that being enabled to forsake the world, and the unnecessary society with worldly men, he might have his heart and conversation in heaven, every day 'waiting when the time of his changing should come.'

Quest. How may a man know whether he be risen with Christ?

Ans. This question may be resolved both negatively and affirmatively. For first, They are not risen with Christ that are in bondage to traditions, as the coherence with the latter end of the former chapter shews; nor they that are drowned and made senseless with the cares of this life, or the pleasures of voluptuous living, Luke xxi. 34; nor they that, confirming themselves in a dead presumptuous common hope, plead the abounding of God's grace, to avouch their continuance in sin, Rom. vi. 1, 4, 5, 1 Pet. i. 3. For the apostle in the Epistle to the Romans, useth a reason taken from our conformity to the resurrection of Christ, to confute this vicious and profane plea of careless men. Further, they that 'worship the beast,' (the great antichrist of Rome,) and receive his mark upon their foreheads or their hands, are reckoned among the dead men, that have not their part in this first resurrection, Rev. xx. 4-6. Also the prophet Isaiah seems to say, that such men as will not see God's high hand of judgment, nor will learn to do uprightly in the land of uprightness, nor can be allured to godliness, though mercy be shewed them, are to be accounted among the dead men that shall not live, Isa. xxvi. 9, 10, 14. Lastly, They are not risen with Christ that do not believe in Christ, John xi. 25. Now for the affirmative. They may have comfort in the first resurrection, that have felt a divine power in the voice of Christ, quickening their hearts with effectual desire and endeavour to rise out of the graves of sin, John v. 25, and to stand up from the world of the dead, Eph. v. 14. 2. That are constantly affected with a holy estimation of the knowledge of Christ crucified and risen again, (an effectual knowledge I mean,) valuing the means and signs of it above all earthly things, Phil. iii. 9, 10. 3. That find their hearts changed from the cares and delights of this life, to a constant desire of the second coming of Christ, to translate them to the presence of glory in heaven. 4. That shew a daily care to walk in newness of life, yielding their members as weapons of righteousness, striving to crucify the old man, and destroy the body of sin, as they that are alive unto God, Rom. vi. 4-6.

2. Again, in that the apostle saith 'if ye be risen again with Christ, seek those things that are above,' we may note, that it is as hard a thing to get up the hearts of men to the study of heavenly things, as to lift up a massy corpse out of the grave and to inspire it with the desire of life; there is need of the Spirit and power of Jesus to do it. And therefore we should not wonder to see natural men so heartless; nor should we attribute it to any inefficacy in the means, if carnal men be not persuaded; for a man may long persuade a dead man to rise before he will get up; and it should touch us with all thankfulness to acknowledge God's mercy if he have given us a mind to heavenly things, to desire them and delight in them.

Thirdly, In that he saith, 'if ye be risen,' speaking not only conditionally, but doubtfully, it imports that one should be exceeding careful to search and try whether they have their part as yet in this first resurrection, and withal implies that many a man may seem to himself and others to be delivered from the kingdom of darkness, and yet lie buried still in the graves of sin.

Seek those things which are above. Here the apostle enters upon the proposition of the first main exhortation, or rule of new life. Now, before I bring in the apostle urging this duty, imagine with thyself how far the Christian (thus now to be instructed for order of life) hath already proceeded by faith; for before a man can be truly capable of direction of life, there be divers things requisite in the preparations of faith. And these things are necessarily to be presupposed: 1. That faith hath plucked him out of the world of sinners or dead men; so that he is already withdrawn from the society of the wicked. 2. It hath shewed him God's favour and joined him to Christ. 3. It hath shewed him in some measure such things in the kingdom of Christ, as his natural ear never heard, or his natural eye never saw, or his natural heart never conceived, 1 Cor. ii. 9. 4. It hath joined him to the living saints, so as he now with great desire and delight converseth with them. 5. It hath made him to suffer in the flesh for his sins, and withal hath refreshed his spirit, and cured him of his distrustful and solitary sorrows. 6. It hath garnished his soul with new budding graces, and opened for him a fountain and spring of grace within him, even in his bowels,

John vii. 38, 39. 7. It hath raised in him a true and constant desire of new obedience of life, with a secret resolution not to depart from anything the Lord shall command, all the days of his life.

Now, presupposing the Christian to be thus far proceeded, the apostle comes in, and to begin his institutions of manners, he first chargeth him with this rule: 'seek those that are above;' teaching us, that the first main thing to be laboured after in the reducing of our lives into a holy order is to strive by all means to get up our hearts to a constant seeking and minding of heavenly things, according to that serious charge of our Saviour Christ, 'first seek the kingdom God and the righteousness thereof,' Mat. vi. 33.

That this rule may be more clearly understood, and more carefully practised, it will be profitable to consider distinctly what things are above, and how they are to be sought. And so the things that are above may be distinguished into eight sorts. First, God is above; for he 'dwells in the high and holy places,' Isa. lvii. 15, and he must be sought, Hosea iii. 5. And if you ask what we must seek in God, I answer, we must seek the true knowledge of his nature, Ps. xiv. 1. 2. We must seek his favour, and the pacification of his just anger for our sins, Zeph. ii. 3; we must seek his face and presence, Ps. xxiv. 6, Ps. xxvii. 8; we must seek his honour and glory, John v. 44; and we must seek his salvation, Ps. cv. 4, lxx. 4. And if you ask how we must seek God, I answer, we must seek God with acknowledgment of our faults, Hosea v. ult., with weeping and repentance for our sins, Jer. l. 4, Isa. xxi. 12; with the desire of our hearts, Isa. xxvi. 7; with prayer and supplication, Mat. vii. 7; with fear of his mercies, Hosea iii. 1; with meekness, Zeph. ii. 2, 3; and in the way of holy life, Ps. xxiv. 4, 5.

Secondly, Christ is above; for so he saith to the Jews, 'ye are from beneath, I am from above; ye are of this world, I am not of this world,' John viii. 23; and he is the Lord whom every Christian ought to seek, Mal. iii. 1. Now Christ is two ways sought principally: first, In the sincere and constant use of all his ordinances, both public and private, that by them we might find his presence of grace on earth, and thus the church sought him in the Canticles, Cant. iii. 1, &c.; secondly, In the desires, prayers, and preparations for our own dissolution and his appearing, Phil. i. 21, Rev. xxi. 20, 2 Tim. iv. 8, 2 Pet. iii. 12.

Thirdly, The New Jerusalem is above; for so the apostle to the Galatians expressly saith, Gal. iv. 26, even that heavenly society of glorious spirits in illustrious splendour. And these are to be sought two ways: 1. By the constant desire of their presence and to be gathered to them; 2. By the imitation of their graces and virtues which they shewed when they were on earth.

Fourthly, Heaven is above; for it is the prize of our calling that is above, Phil. iii. 14. and the glory of that eternal and immortal honour is to be sought, Rom. ii. 7, and that five ways: 1. By prayer for preparation, and that daily; for so our Saviour hath taught us in the second petition of his prayer, Mat. vi. 10. 2. By seeking the assurance of faith and hope, and the pledges and earnest of it, Heb. xi. 1, Eph. i. 14. 3. By meditation and contemplation, striving to express our desires and sighs after it, 2 Cor. v. 2. 4. By carrying ourselves as strangers and pilgrims in this world, weaning our hearts and retiring our lives from the world, confessing and professing our travels towards a better country that is above, Heb. xi. 13, 14, 16. 5. By continuing in well-doing, Rom. ii. 7, striving to live a citizenlike life here, Phil. iii. 20, in all things provident, to send our works and prayers to heaven before us, as our provision and treasure, Mat. vi. 14.

Fifthly, Holy graces are above: for St James saith, 'Every good giving and every perfect gift is from above, and cometh down from the Father of lights,' James i. 17; and it is apparent that they are part of the kingdom of heaven, and they tend to heaven, and therefore the prophet Isaiah calls grace by the name of glory, Isa. iv. 5; and they come down from heaven, which will also appear in the particulars. Wisdom is from above, James iii. 17; so is zeal, for it is the zeal of God's house, Ps. lxix. 9; so is lowliness, so is faith, so is peace and joy, and all the rest. And that these are to be sought many scriptures evidently prove, 1 Cor. xiv. 1, Zeph. ii. 3, 2 Cor. xiii. 5, Rom. xiv. 17, 38; and if you ask how they are to be sought, it is shortly answered, by prayer, and the use of the means which the Lord hath appointed as holy vessels and instruments, and as it were wombs to conceive, convey, and derive grace unto us.

Sixthly, The means of salvation themselves are things above, for they are called 'the kingdom of heaven,' Mat. iii. 2; and the kingdom of heaven is said to be taken away when the means is taken away, Mat. xxi. 43; and these we must seek, Isa. xli. 17, 18; though it cost us much travail, if there be a famine. Amos viii., or much cost, if the Lord give us to find such pearls of instruction or comfort in the field of any church or congregation, Mat. xiii. 45.

Seventhly, Holy duties are many of them from above, for the wise man saith, 'the way of life is on high to the prudent, to avoid from hell beneath,' Prov. xv. 24, and that because both the will that enjoins them, and the power to do them, and the success or effects of them, are all from above. And, therefore, the author to the Hebrews, when he would discourse of doing of God's will, quoting the place in the Psalms, seems to intimate that the true speech of such duties is to speak from above, Heb. x. 8, 9; and these good things are to be sought, Prov. xi. 27; we must seek the old and good way, Jer. vi. 16; we must seek judgment and righteousness, Isa. i. 17.

Eighthly, Many of the privileges of Christians are from above, as the righteousness of God's kingdom, Mat. vi. 33; forgiveness of sins, 1 John i. 7; deliverance from this present evil world, Gal. i. 4; both in respect of the contagions and punishments of the same; all spiritual blessings in heavenly things, Eph. i. 3; the revelation of hid mysteries, 1 Cor. ii. 9, Col. i. 26; the Spirit of the Son, Gal. iv. 6, 7; the influence of Christ's death and resurrection, Phil. iii. 9, 10; the word with all the treasure of it, Ps. cxix. 94; and the honour which is above, John v. 44; these are to be sought. Thus of the particular things that are above and we must seek.

Use. The consideration of all this may much abase and humble us for our deadness of spirit, and egregious slowness of heart, in these things that so greatly concern us. The devil takes more pains in seeking to destroy us, 1 Pet. v. 8, than we either do take, or are willing to take, to save our own souls, by seeking these things, all of them so worthy to be sought. The worldly man is more industrious to seek riches, and the ambitious man more to seek honour, and the luxurious man to seek his sport, lust, or pleasure, than Christians are to 'seek those things that are above,' though never any truly sought but did find, Mat. vii. 7, and never less was found than either the evidence or the possession of a kingdom, Luke xii. 32, and that of God. Nay, nay; how have every one of us sought out all ways and all inventions, while we lived in the service of the flesh, and had no fruit or wages, but that of which we are now ashamed, Rom. vi. 21, and yet are seldom or never weary of such unprofitable and shameful labour. But I refer the urging of motives till I come to the next verse; it followeth:

Where Christ sitteth at the right hand of God. These words contain the latter reasons, and comprehend a principal part of Christ's exaltation; the meditation whereof is here used to excite us to the love of heavenly things, seeing our Saviour Christ, that so entirely loves us, not only is in heaven, but is there in great favour, and honour, and majesty, and power.

There is a fourfold presence of Christ: for, first, He is everywhere as God; secondly, He is in the hearts of the faithful only, by his Spirit of grace and regeneration; thirdly, He is by representation in the sacrament; fourthly, He is bodily in heaven.

Quest. But is not Christ with his church on earth still?

Ans. He is as God, but not as man. I say not as man locally, for else he is present in his members that bear the image of his true human nature, and his very body is present sacramentally; he is present by the imputation of righteousness, and by mystical union.

'The right hand of God' hath divers significations in scripture: sometimes it signifieth the power and help of God, Ps. xliv. 3, Acts ii. 33; sometimes the place of eternal rest in heaven, Ps. xvi. 11; sometimes it notes the majesty, and authority, and sovereignty of God, Ps. cx. 1, Heb. i. 3; to 'sit,' signifieth to abide or dwell, Luke xiv. 49; and to govern, 1 Kings i. 30, Prov. xx. 8, Isa. xvi. 5. Here to sit at God's right hand comprehendeth three things: first, An exceeding glory above all creatures, even the very angels, Heb. i. 13, Acts vii. 55; secondly, Full power of government, Eph. i. 20; thirdly, An equality in majesty and sovereignty, even with God the Father, in his person, Phil. ii. 6, 7, 9.

Object. But Stephen saith he saw him 'standing' at God's right hand, Acts vii. 75.

Sol. Divers gestures for our capacity are attributed for divers ends: first, He stands to shew his watchful eagerness and readiness to take notice of wrongs to his members, to come to their succour; secondly, He sits, to note majesty and sovereignty.

Object. But to sit at God's right hand, seems to import the real communication of divine attributes to the human nature, so as in his very body he is everywhere, &c.

Sol. It doth not. Christ's human nature is here reckoned under the name of things above. And, besides, in the Epistle to the Ephesians, the apostle saith expressly, he 'sits at God's right hand in heavenly places,' Eph. i. 20.

Use 1. The use of Christ's sitting at God's right hand follows. And first, it may be a notable terror to wicked men if they do but consider that he whom they daily pierce by their sins, Rev. i. 7, and despise by contemning his ordinances, by which he would rule them, Luke xix. 14, is exalted to such glory, that he hath all power to subdue his enemies under his feet, Ps. cx. 1. But sure it is if they will not now fear and repent, the time shall come when all they that said, This man shall not rule over us, shall see him 'sitting at the right hand of the power of God,' Mat. xxvi. 64, and 'coming in the clouds,' to render vengeance on all those his adversaries, that would not obey his gospel, 2 Thes. i. 8, but strive to break his yoke, and cast his cords from them, Ps. ii. 2, 3.

Use 2. Secondly, It may serve for singular comfort to all God's servants; for from his session at God's right hand flow unto them many singular blessings, as the places of scripture quoted in the margin will shew. First, The casting out of all accusations of Satan, Rom. viii. 34, Eph. i. 20; secondly, The filling of the church with all needful fulness of grace and blessings, Heb. i. 13, 14; thirdly, The service of angels ministering to the heirs of salvation; fourthly, Speed in all suits, 1 Pet. iii. 22; fifthly, The providing of a place for us, John xiv. 2; sixthly, Intercession, Heb. vii. 26; seventhly, Power to subdue our enemies, Ps. cx. 1. As the consideration of the several places of scripture alleged will manifestly shew; yea, his exaltation may be our comfort, because in a sort we sit together with him, Eph. ii. 6; not only because this honour is done to our nature in his flesh, but also because by our mystical union it is done to our head; and moreover, he doth in part communicate this honour to us; for as Christ is at the right hand of the Father, so is the church at the right hand of Christ, Ps. xlv. 9. Finally, In the second coming of Christ, his glory shall be more fully and openly communicated, when all the faithful shall be set on his right hand, Mat. xxv. 33, to hear that most gracious sentence, 'Come, ye blessed of my Father, inherit the kingdom prepared for you before the foundations of the world.'

Thirdly, The session of Christ at God's right hand may teach us: first, To mind a spiritual worship, seeing he hath taken his body out of the way; secondly, To 'go boldly to the throne of grace to seek help in time of need,' Heb. iv. 16, seeing we have so sure a friend to procure both audience, acceptance, and success; thirdly, To wait with patience under all sorts of wrongs, for it is sure that 'he that shall come will come' in his due time, 'and will not tarry,' and then he will make all his enemies to be his footstool, Heb. x. 12, 13; lastly, The apostle here useth the consideration of this doctrine as a motive to stir us up to mind heavenly things. And surely if we do seriously weigh it, it should continually draw up our thoughts to think of heaven, whither so loving and so glorious a Saviour is gone before; yea, it should do us good to look up towards these visible heavens, remembering that one day we shall be carried to that blessed place of rest and holy joys that is above them, even to the heaven of heavens, to reign with Christ for evermore. And thus of the proposition.

Ver. 2. *Set your affections on things which are above, and not on things which are on the earth.*

The exhortation in the former verse propounded, is in this verse illustrated and expounded: first, By repetition; secondly, By the contrary. The repetition is in these words: 'Set your affections on things which are above.' The contrary, from which he doth dehort, is in these words: 'And not on things which are on earth.'

Repetitions in scripture are not without their

use; for thereby the Holy Ghost usually imports our slowness and dulness of capacity in conceiving, and backwardness in practice; and besides thereby enforceth both the necessity and the excellency of the matter so repeated. And surely all three may be applied to this repetition; for the contemplation and desire after heavenly things is a most gracious ornament to a religious life; and without some measure of holy affections, it is impossible to get rid of the power of sin, or to practise with any success or acceptation the duty of a renewed life; and if in anything we are backward, or wanting, or decaying, or languishing, it is in this rule here given by the apostle.

Set your affections. The original word varieth in signification. Sometimes it is rendered, to study; and it is, out of question, our duty to study and contemplate of heavenly things. Sometimes it signifieth, to try by tasting; and it is sure that if carnal people had but once tasted of the sweetness of godliness and religious duties, they would not so securely neglect the provision for eternity; but especially, they would see that they have spoken evil of what they knew not. Sometimes it is translated, to be wise about a thing; and certainly a Christian should be wise in the matters of his religion and profession, and shew it by forecast and diligence to compass what may be gotten of this true treasure, and by serpentine discretion in the manner and circumstances of well doing, and by stayedness in a Christian course, void of passion, rash zeal, and fickle inconstancy, growing more and more skilful and cunning in the soundness of knowledge, how with more power and spiritual advantage to practise every duty, or exercise every grace. Sometimes it signifieth, to savour of a thing; and it is true that all the carriage and dealings of Christians should savour of the things above; but I take it as it is here rendered.

Set your affections. And so it manifestly teacheth us that we must get not minds or thoughts only, but sound affections to heavenly things, which may both serve for reproof and comfort: for reproof, I say, both of the loathsome lukewarmness of the most, Rev. iii. 19, and of the dangerous loss of first love in the better sort, Rev. ii. For comfort; for it is certain if thou canst find thy heart upright in affections and constant desire after heavenly things, thou mayest be assured of three things: 1. That God will accept thy will for the deed: he will bear with many wants and weaknesses, where he sees a man or woman come to his service with hearts desirous to do their best, and tenderly affected. 2. That thou art not in danger of falling away; for apostasy never discovers itself to hurt us or endanger us, till it hath stolen away our hearts and the care of affections in holy duties. 3. That to that thou hast, more is and shall be given, Mat. xiii.; as thy affections grow and continue, so doth true knowledge, grace, and godliness grow also. And thus of the repetition.

And not on the things that are on earth. From the coherence and general consideration of these words, three things may be observed:

1. That a man cannot both at once seek and affect earth and heaven, for they are here disjoined and opposed; a man 'cannot serve God and mammon,' Mat. vi.; 'the love of the world is the enmity of God,' James iv. 4; but this is thus to be understood, if the world be sought in the first place, and with chief affection and care.

2. Nay more, this dehortation implies that it is hard for a man to deal with the world, but a man's affection will too much run after it. It is hard to be much employed about profits and recreations, but a man shall love them too much; not that it is simply unlawful to use the world, but that we should be very jealous of ourselves, to watch our own hearts that our affections be not set on the world.

3. To be crucified unto the world, able to neglect and contemn the glory and pleasure of it, is a notable sign that one is risen with Christ.

Thus in general.

The things on earth. The things on earth here meant by the apostle are either traditions, mentioned in the former chapter, or worldly things in themselves lawful, or the works of the flesh, simply in themselves unlawful.

Traditions and man's inventions, which the apostle hath before taxed, may well be called things on earth: 1. Because they spring from the earth and earthly-minded men; they were never inspired from God, nor devised by heavenly-minded men. 2. Because they hinder them that are devoted to them from looking up, or attaining any insight in things that are above. 3. Because these by effect make men more earthly and sensual; but of these in the former chapter.

The works of the flesh and the corruptions of life to be avoided and not affected are the third sort of things on earth; but of that also afterwards in the second part of the general duties, especially in the fifth verse. So that the second sort of things on earth remaineth to be more largely considered; those are profits, honours, pleasures, friends, health, and long life.

There be eight reasons to persuade not to affect earthly things.

The *first* may be taken from the condition of man on earth; for we are here but pilgrims and strangers, Heb. xi. 13; and therefore being but in a strange place, to what purpose should we trouble ourselves with more than what will serve our present need, and the rather knowing that when we come into our own country these things will serve us for no use? Besides, our present lot lieth not in those things, but the kingdom of God and righteousness is our portion even in this life, all other things are but cast upon us as additaments.

The *second* may be taken from the disability of earthly things. For, first, They cannot so much as fill or satisfy a man's heart; 2. They cannot fence a man against any of the trials of God when the hour of temptation comes, Rev. ii. 10; 3. They cannot all of them redeem one soul, Ps. xlix. 7.

The *third* reason may be taken from the inconveniences that follow the love of earthly things. For, first, 'The cares of the world choke the word,' that it can never prosper, Mat. xiii.; 2. They breed excuses and shifts in men's minds, and alienate by degrees a man's heart from the use of the means, Luke xiv. 17; 3. To seek after the world is to sorrow after the world, for to the most the world is a cause of much sorrow and vexation; 4. The amity of the world, as the apostle saith, is the enmity of God, James iv. 4, 1 John ii. 15, and that both actively and passively, for it both makes us hate God, and it makes God hate us; Fifthly, The lust after worldly things fills the world with corruptions and sins, 2 Pet. i. 4; Sixthly, These earthly things thus sinisterly affected, may one day witness against us, James v. 1, &c.; Seventhly, Many a man is damned and gone to hell for 'minding earthly things,' Phil. iii. 18.

The *fourth* reason may be taken from the sovereignty that God hath over all earthly things, and the power he hath given to Christ over them, Ps. xxiv. 1, Mat. xxviii. 18. Now why should we turmoil ourselves with care about these, seeing they are in God's hand in Christ, to have them and dispose of them as may be for his glory and our good?

The *fifth* reason may be taken from the baseness of the nature of all these things; for they are not only on the earth, but of the earth; and if they be compared unto the soul of man, for which we ought chiefly to provide, the whole world is not worth one soul; which may appear both by the price of a soul, and the disproportion between the gains of the world and the loss of one soul: it is no profit to win the whole world and lose a man's own soul, Mat. xvi.; and besides, if the whole world laid on one heap would have been a sufficient sacrifice for the redemption of the soul, the Lord Jesus would never have abased himself to such a suretyship. But because there could not be found, neither in heaven nor earth, any other name or nature by which we could be saved, therefore 'he humbled himself, and took upon him the form of a servant, and was obedient unto the death, even the death of the cross,' Phil. ii.

The *sixth* reason may be taken from the example of the Lord's worthies, who in all ages have been tried with all kind of trials, and 'wandered up and down in sheep-skins and goat-skins, being destitute, afflicted, and tormented, wandering up and down in wildernesses, mountains, and dens and caves of the earth, whom the world was not worthy of,' Heb. xi.; all these seeking another country, and willingly professing that they expected no abiding-place here.

Seventhly, It is somewhat to persuade us that our Saviour Christ professeth of purpose to hinder and interrupt our rest and ease in the use of those things, when he saith, that he came not to send peace, as knowing that much peace and liking of earthly things was unprofitable for us.

Lastly, We may be moved by the consideration of the fleeting condition of all earthly things: riches have wings, Prov. xxiii. 5, and the fashion of this world passeth away, 1 Cor. vii. 31, 1 John ii. 17; yea, heaven and earth shall pass, the earth with the works thereof shall be burnt up, 2 Pet. iii. 10.

But that we may be the more deeply affected with the contempt of the world, I further add these reasons:—

1. Of Solomon, the wisest of all sinful men.
2. Of Christ, the wisest of all men.

Solomon, in his book of Ecclesiastes, is exceeding plentiful, and indeed not without cause; for such is the strength of the rooted love of earthly things in many men, that they had need to be encountered with an army of reasons; and if I single out some of the chiefest out of divers chapters, I hope it will appear tedious to none but such as will hear no reason.

In the first chapter, among other things, these may be noted: 1. That after a man hath travailed to get what he can, how small a portion in comparison of the whole hath he achieved, so as he may say to himself, when he hath done, 'What now remaineth to me of all my travail which I have suffered under the sun?' Eccles. i. 3. 2. If a man could get never so much, yet he cannot live to enjoy it long, for the elements of which man was made are more durable than man himself, for 'one generation passeth and another cometh, but the earth remaineth still,' ver. 4-6. The like may be shewed of the air and water. 3. 'All things are full of labour, no man can utter it,' ver. 8; and certainly many times earthly things gained answer not the labour spent about them. 4. Earthly things possessed will not satisfy; 'the eye will not be satisfied with seeing, nor the ear with hearing,' ver. 8. 5. A man can compass nothing that is new, for 'there is nothing new under the sun: is there anything of which one may say, behold this is new, and never was before?' ver. 9, 10; they have been already in the old time that was before us. 6. The Lord, in wonderful wisdom and righteousness, permits in the nature of man those cares, that they may be travails to humble and break the heart of man, ver. 13. 7. The best of these will not make a crooked thing straight, ver. 15; they will not mend the perverse manners of men: a man may be and continue vicious for all these things, or for aught they will do unto him.

In the second chapter we may observe these reasons: first, Let a man procure unto himself the fullest and fairest use of all sorts of earthly things: pleasure, laughter, great houses, gardens, orchards, waters, fruit-trees, woods, servants, cattle, silver and gold, treasures, and music, yet all these will not deliver a man from satiety, loathing, and vexation of spirit, so as he may truly say there is no profit in them, chap. ii. 1, 12; 2. In these things there is one condition to all, it befalleth to the wise man as it doth to the fool, ver. 14, 15; 3. Let a man excel never so much, yet within a short time all will be forgotten, 'for all that that now is, in the days to come shall all be forgotten,' ver. 16; 4. When thou hast gotten all thou canst together, thou knowest not whether he shall be a wise man or a fool that shall enjoy them after thee, ver. 19; 5. To attain those things men usually spend their days in sorrow, travail, and grief, and their hearts take no rest in the night, ver. 23.

In the third chapter, ver. 1-9, these further reasons may be noted: first, All things are swayed with the swing of their seasons and times, so as nothing is steady, though it be born, and now plant, and build, and laugh, and dance, and embrace, and sow, and love, and live in peace; yet there will be a time to pluck up, and break down, and weep, and mourn, and cast away, and hate, and mourn, and die too. Secondly, Though the Lord should set the world in a man's heart, yet he might spend all his days and never know the full nature of these things, ver. 11. Thirdly, All things are subject to God's unavoidable disposing: let man get what he can, yet God will have the disposing of it; and whatsoever God shall do, it shall abide; to it can no man add, and from it can none diminish. And this God will do that man may fear him, ver. 14. Fourthly, Such is the state of the children of men, that they may lose all they have at the very place of judgment, ver. 16. Fifthly, Yea, the very state of mortified men, in the reason of carnal men, because of these oppressions and uncertainties, seems little better than the state of beasts, ver. 18.

In the fourth chapter, ver. 1-3, note first, that when a man hath set his heart upon these earthly things, if ever he lose them, he is filled almost with unmedicinable tears and sorrow, so as he would 'praise the dead above the living,' and wish he had never been born. Secondly, They are occasions of a man's envy, ver. 4. Thirdly, The eyeing of these things infatuates many a man's heart; so as we may see many a man that hath neither son, nor daughter, nor brother, and yet there is no end of his travail, and he hath not the judgment to say with himself, 'For whom do I travail, and defraud myself of pleasure?' ver. 8. Fourthly, A man may get much with sore travail, and live to see himself despised of him for whom he provideth them, so as they that shall come after him will not rejoice in him, ver. 15, 16.

In the fifth chapter there are also seven other reasons, ver. 8 : first, These earthly things lead the greatest men into bondage by dependence; for 'the king cannot consist without the tilling of the field.' Secondly, 'He that loveth silver shall not be satisfied with silver, and he that loveth riches shall be without the fruit thereof,' ver. 9. Thirdly, When goods increase, they are increased also that eat them, and what good cometh to the owners thereof but the beholding of them with their eyes? ver. 10. Fourthly, Many times the servant sleepeth when the master can get no sleep, ver. 11. Fifthly, There is an evil sickness, often seen under the sun, that riches are kept for the owners' ruin, ver. 12. Sixthly, Or else they will perish while the master looketh on, ver. 13. Seventhly, But certain it is, he can carry nothing out of the world when he goeth, but must leave them where he found them, ver. 13–15.

In the sixth chapter there are these reasons, ver. 1–7: first, A man may have all abundance, and yet not have a heart to use them, and so be worse than an 'untimely fruit.' Secondly, What needs all this ado? for 'all is but for the mouth,' and nature is content with a little; and, therefore, to have a soul so insatiably greedy of having is a prodigious madness, ver. 7. Thirdly, The having of all these things makes not a wise man better than a fool : and what wants a poor man, if he knows how to carry himself with the wise? Fourthly, All cannot make thee cease to be mortal; for it is known man cannot strive with him that is stronger than he, ver. 12.

In the seventh chapter there is this reason : A man may spend all his days before he can come soundly to know (after many trials) what is the best use to put these earthly things to.

And for honour, in the eighth chapter three things are worthy noting : first, A man is not lord of his own spirit, to keep himself alive in his honour, ver. 8. Secondly, Many men rule to their own ruin, ver. 9. Thirdly, Men after death are quickly forgotten. They that come back from the holy place remembereth them not long; yea, a man may be quickly forgotten in the city where he hath done right, ver. 10.

And in the ninth chapter, two reasons more are added, ver. 1 : first, No man can know the love or hatred of God by these things. Secondly, They are not gotten always by help of means; for the race is not always to the swift, nor the battle to the strong, nor riches to men of understanding, nor favour to the wise; which makes the atheist and epicure conclude that time and chance cometh to all things.

The sum of all that Solomon can say is, 'vanity of vanities, all is vanity.' And now that we have heard Solomon, let us in the next place hear a greater than Solomon.

Our Saviour Christ, in the sixth of Matthew, divides the care of earthly things into two sorts. For either men are greedily transported with the desire of getting treasures, that is, abundance and superfluities; or else they toil their hearts with distrustful and distracting cares about necessaries, as what they shall eat and what they shall put on. From the first kind of care, he dissuades with four reasons : first, All treasures are subject either to vanity or violence, either the moth will eat them, or the thief will steal them, Mat. vi. 19, 20. Secondly, These things bewitch and steal away men's hearts, ver. 21. Thirdly, The minding of these things darkeneth the eye of the soul with greater darkness than can be expressed, ver. 22, 23. Fourthly, A man cannot serve God and riches, ver. 24.

From the second kind of care he dehorts with eight reasons : first, The life is more worth than meat, and the body than raiment, ver. 25. And if the Lord have given the greater, why should he not be trusted for the less? Secondly, God provideth for the very fowls that have not such means as man hath; and will he not provide for man? ver.

26. Thirdly, All thy care will not add one cubit to thy stature, ver. 27, but if thou wouldst swell thy heart out, it is God only must increase thy strength or health. Fourthly, This care is a sign of little faith, ver. 30. Fifthly. It is for Gentiles that know not God, nor the covenant of his grace and mercy in Christ, to seek after these things, ver. 32. It is a gross shame for any Christian to be so heathenish. Sixthly, Doth not your heavenly Father know all that you need? ver. 32. If he be a Father, hath he not will, and if he be in heaven, hath he not power, to help? Seventhly, You have a flat promise, that if you seek the kingdom of heaven and the righteousness thereof, which should take up your chiefest care, all these things, without such carking, so far as is needful, shall be cast upon you, ver. 33. Lastly, Hath not every day his evil? and is not the grief of the day great enough? ver. 34. Why, then, dost thou distract thyself for to-morrow? Assure thyself the time to come will afford thee matter of grief and trouble enough; thou needest not disquiet thyself beforehand.

Use. The consideration of all this, as it may be a comfort against all wants and crosses about these base earthly things, so it may greatly reprove those that 'bury their talents in the earth,' that is, spend all their gifts about earthly matters. But especially we may hence learn divers lessons. And first, since we have heard Solomon's opinion, after long discourse, that all is vanity, we should learn of the same Solomon, therefore, to 'fear God, and keep his commandment, for this is the whole duty of man, and the end of all,' Eccles. xii. 13. 2. Let the place of the sanctuary, where we may get the best things for our souls, be as a glorious throne exalted, Jer. xvii. 11, 12. 3. Let us 'use this world as if we used it not. Let them that rejoice be as if they rejoiced not, and they that weep as if they wept not, and they that buy as though they possessed not,' 1 Cor. vii. 30, 31. 4. If the Lord give us but a little portion in these things, let us esteem his mercy, and live with contentedness, resolving that 'better is a handful with quietness, than two handfuls with labour and vexation of spirit,' Eccles. iv. 6. And fifthly, we may hence be confirmed to take the more liberty to use these earthly things for our own joy and refreshings; they are none of the things the Lord would have us with such ado keep; but he allows us to 'eat and drink, and delight ourselves with the profit of our labour,' Eccles. ii. 24. Lastly, we should improve them and use them as means to do what good we can with them in this life. 'I know,' saith the wise man, 'there is nothing good in them, but to rejoice and do good in his life,' Eccles. iii. 12. And to this end we should 'cast our bread even upon the waters, for after many days we may find it; and give our portion to seven, and also to eight,' Eccles. xi. 1, 2. The best use of these riches is to be rich in doing good with them.

Thus of the illustration; the confirmation follows.

Ver. 3. *For ye are dead, and your life is hid with Christ in God.*

In this verse and the next the exhortation is confirmed by two motives; the one taken from the condition of the faithful in this world, the other taken from the consideration of their estate in the revelation of the glory of Christ in the last day. The first is in this verse, the latter in the next.

There are two things in the condition of the faithful on earth which should make them little to mind earthly things, or desire to continue long in the world.

First, That in respect of distresses, they are as dead men while they live; secondly, That the happiness they have, which is the life of their lives, doth not appear, but is hid with God in Christ.

For ye are dead. The faithful are dead three ways while they live: for, first, They are dead to sin in respect of mortification; secondly, They are dead to the law by the body of Christ, Rom. vii. 4, Gal. ii. 19, in respect of justification; so as now the faithful do no longer wait upon the law for righteousness, but upon a second marriage they have it from him that was raised from the dead for them.

They are dead to the world, and that in three respects: first, In respect of their own voluntary forsaking of the world, and their mortifying of earthly desires, joined with a sense of their own mortality; so was Paul as a man crucified to the world, Gal. vi. 14. Secondly, In respect of the world's account of them. For so soon as men get any true grace, and retire themselves from the excesses of the time, they are neglected and forgotten, as dead men out of mind. Thirdly, In respect of the multitude of afflictions which do many times overwhelm and drown Christians. It is not unusual in scripture to say of men in desperate crosses, they are dead men. The prophet Isaiah calls the people in captivity dead men, when he saith, 'thy dead shall live,' Isa. xxvi. 19. The apostle Paul saith thus, 'If we be dead with him, we shall live with him,' 2 Tim. ii. 11. Which he seems to explain in the next verse thus: 'If we suffer with him, we shall also reign with him.' Thus David saith, he was 'as a broken vessel, forgotten as a dead man out of mind,' Ps. xxxi. 12. And in another place he saith, he was 'brought to the dust of the earth,' Ps. xxii. 15. And in the eighty-eighth Psalm he saith, his 'soul was full of evils, he was counted among them that go down to the pit, free among the dead, like the slain lying in the grave, yea, he was laid in the lowest pit, in the darkness, in the grave,' &c., Ps. lxxxviii. 4–6. I spare to allege other scriptures.

Uses. The use may be to teach us, as to observe hence what may befall the best man, so in the consideration of our own estate, to say within ourselves, as Job did, 'If I have done wickedly, woe unto me, and if I have done righteously, I will not lift up my head, being full of confusion, because I see mine affliction,' Job x. 15. For though the Lord hath not yet thus overwhelmed thee with distress, yet inasmuch as he may do it to thee, as well as to others, his dear servants, it should cause thee to walk humbly before God, and to learn to die to the world, before the world be dead to thee.

Again; Hath misery broken in upon thee, and prevailed over thee, so as thou seemest to be laid in darkness, as they that have been dead long ago? Let not thy spirit be in perplexity in thee; no strange thing is befallen thee; God's children are but dead men in this world. Remember the time past, and meditate of God's works of old; stretch forth thy hand unto God, and let thy soul desire after him; if he shew thee his loving-kindness, thou hast enough; hide thee with the Lord by daily and secret prayer, and he will teach thee his will, and his Spirit shall lead thee, and if he see it meet, he will bring thy soul out of adversity, and execute his righteous judgment upon all those that have oppressed thee. It is the Lord that quickeneth the dead, and calleth things that are not as if they were, Rom. iv. Lastly, Hath the Lord delivered thee out of desperate and deadly crosses? Then let 'the vows of God be upon thee, and render thou his praise, and confess his name before the sons of men,' Ps. lvi. 12, 13.

Your life is hid. Doct. The happiness and spiritual felicity of Christians is hid; and that usually from the men of the world, and many times from the faithful.

Their life is hid from the men of this world: first, Because God, who is their life, Deut. xxx. 20, is hid from them; secondly, Because the glory of their natural life is many times buried in the gulf of outward trouble, 2 Cor. vi. 9; thirdly, Because the life of grace, which is only brought to light by the gospel, 2 Tim. i. 10, is hid from the perceiving of the natural man, whom the god of this world hath blinded, 2 Cor. iv. 4; fourthly, Because the way of holy conversation is hid from them; for carnal men are all strangers from the life of God, Eph. iv. 18, it is a narrow way, and few there be that find it, Mat. vii. 14; fifthly, Because many of the privileges of a gracious life are hid from them: as, 1. The enrolling of a Christian in the book of life, Isa. iv. 3, Phil. iv. 3; 2. The seal of the Spirit of promise, 2 Cor. i. 22; 3. Pardon of sin,—wicked men perhaps know the faults of God's children, but not the forgiveness of those faults; 4. The power of the means,—the word is a savour of life, 2 Cor. ii. 14, and hath spirit and life in it, John vi., yet it is as a treasure hid in the field, or a little leaven hid in three pecks of meal, Mat. xiii.; 5. Comfort in their affliction,—wicked men know their afflictions, but not their consolations, 1 Cor. ii. 9; they seldom or never mark the glorious issue, and how God compasseth them about with joyful deliverance. And generally we may burst out with the psalmist, and say, 'How great is the goodness thou hast laid up for them that trust in thee!' Ps. xxxi. 19. It is great goodness, but yet, note that he saith, it is laid up. Lastly, In respect of the life of glory the world knows not Christians; for 'it doth not yet appear what they shall be,' 1 John iii. 1, 2.

Seeing this is so, that the life of Christians is hid

from the world, as it should infer the apostle's former exhortation, so it should further teach us, not to respect nor care for the judgment, counsel, censures, &c., of carnal men, in the whole or any part of Christian life, for it is hid from them, and they know not of what they speak.

Nay, in the second place, sometimes the life of a Christian may be hid from Christians also themselves, so as they cannot discern their own happiness, especially in some fits of temptation, and seldom or never do they fully discern in this world so much as the glory of their present estate. David thought he was cast out of God's sight, Ps. xxxi. 22, and he most mournfully makes his moan in the seventy-seventh Psalm, as if he were almost resolved that the Lord would not be merciful to him. Jacob cries out, 'My way is hid from the Lord,' Isa. xl. 27; and the people somewhat vehemently say, 'Verily thou O God hidest thyself, O God the Saviour of Israel,' Isa, xlv. 15. Which should comfort afflicted Christians, since they may here see that it hath been an usual distress of God's dear servants to have their life hid in God. And withal it may warn us, let him that now standeth in the refreshings of the comforts of God's presence, take heed lest he fall. But especially it should quicken us to a desire to be gone, and to be in heaven, that we might be past all danger.

But lest Christians should be discouraged, he addeth two comforts: first, It is with Christ; secondly, It is in God.

With Christ. The life of Christ also was hid while he lived: for, first, The glory of his divinity was covered as it were with a 'vail in his flesh; secondly, His outward glory of his life amongst men was obscured by the many crosses he sustained for our sins, Isa. liii. 7, so as the world did not own him, and he was without form, and despised among men; thirdly, His life was hid in the grave; fourthly, It was hid in respect of the horrors he felt in his soul, the Lord as it were hiding his loving countenance from him for the time; fifthly, His glory in heaven is hid from the world, and the saints on earth have but a glimpse of it. All this may comfort us, seeing nothing can befall us but what hath befallen our head; and if the world will not acknowledge our glory, and the beauty of the profession of sincerity, it matters not; it could not see the excellency of Christ when he was on earth.

In God. Our life is hid in God either in respect of object, because it principally consists in the vision of God, or causally, as God is the first cause to beget it and still to preserve it; or else with Christ in God—that is, with Christ, who incomprehensibly rests in the bosom of the Father; or, lastly, in God —that is, *apud Deum,* in the power of God, to dispose of it at his pleasure. Which should comfort us, seeing none hath power over our life but God, and teach us to commend our spirits into his hands.

Ver. 4. *When Christ, who is our life, shall appear, then shall ye also appear with him in glory.*

These words contain the second motive to persuade to the meditation of heavenly things. If men would consider of the certain and glorious appearance of the Lord Jesus Christ, when he shall come to take account of all the actions of all men, and put an end to all the earthly felicities which man hath with so many inventions sought, and withal but think how unavailable all earthly things will be at that day, either to deliver from the terror of the judgment, or the horror of the everlasting misery will certainly follow, if men be not more careful to provide for their souls beforehand, by following the study of better things; but especially if men would consider the great gain and profit that godliness at that day will bring, and the incomparable glory that all heavenly-minded Christians shall then be exalted unto; the thought of these things, daily and truly laid unto men's hearts, would much excite and stir up to a constant care of preparing ourselves against that day, and would greatly wean us from the cares and delights in these transitory and earthly things here below, that will so little avail the owners in the day of death, and will be of so little use in that immortal estate unto which after this judgment the godly shall be translated. So that these words offer two things to be intreated of: first, The glorious appearance of Christ; secondly, The glorious appearance of the Christian in the day of Christ.

But before I enter upon the particular and full discourse of those two glorious appearances, some things may be briefly and generally noted.

1. That the knowledge of those last things is not

a curious or unprofitable knowledge, but, contrariwise, ought to be searched after, as exceeding useful in the life of man.

2. That the doctrine of the glory of Christ and Christians in that last day is now but little known or discerned, and that the word 'appear' imports, so as the fulness of Christ's majesty, or of the Christian's glory, will not appear till the very judgment-day. The better sort know but in part; and the worse sort are so blinded by the devil, and besotted with sensuality and the love of earthly things, and withal are so conscious to themselves of the evils they are guilty of, that they have no desire to discern, or to be taught to know the doctrine of Christ's coming.

3. Those words, 'which is our life,' are not to be altogether passed over; they plainly affirm that Christ is our life,—and this is an honour that the Lord challengeth to himself; and therefore, as he would be acknowledged to be 'the way' and 'the truth,' so also he addeth, 'I am the life,' John xiv. 6; and to this end he came, that men in him might have life, John x. 10. And with great reason is Christ said to be our life, for he formed us at first when we were not, and quickened us when we were dead, and hath provided a better life for us, and doth preserve us unto eternal life, and daily renew life and power in the hearts of his people, and will raise our bodies at the last day. The consideration hereof may both teach us and try us. It may teach us, as to acknowledge that we have received life from Christ, so to dedicate what remaineth of our life to the honour and service of him that is the author and sole Lord of our lives, and withal to run unto him for the daily preservation and renewing of life and loveliness in us. And it may try, too; for till we can truly say out of feeling and experience, Christ is the life of our lives, we shall hardly find reason of comfortable hope in our appearance before him at the last day. And they only may truly profess that Christ is their life that first can live by the faith of Christ, accounting themselves to have enough if they may see comfort in God's promises made in Christ, and feel the joyful fruits of Christ's favour and presence, howsoever it go with them for outward things. Secondly, That do continually sacrifice and devote unto Christ their best desires and endeavours, and that with resolution to cleave to his service all the days of their life. And thirdly, That can bewail his absence or displeasure as the most bitter cross; so as they could feel, and out of affection say of such times and such a condition, that the true life of their life was absent or removed from them.

Now I come to the appearance of Christ. I have not here to do with the appearance of Christ as it is considered in the fore-ordination of God before the foundation of the world, 1 Pet. i. 20, but of the accomplishment of it; and so Christ's appearance is of divers kinds : for first, He hath appeared unto the whole world as the true light that made the world, and lighteneth every man that cometh into the world, John i. 9, 10; and thus he appeared in the light of nature. Secondly, He appears to the whole church, consisting both of good and bad, by the general light of doctrine and scripture; but many receive not his testimony, John iii. 31, 32. Thirdly, He hath appeared corporally, 'in the days of his flesh, once in the end of the world, to put away sin by the sacrifice of himself,' Heb. ix. 26; 1 John iii. 5; and to dissolve the work of the devil, 1 John iii. 8. Then was fulfilled that great mystery, God was manifested in the flesh, 1 Tim. iii. 16. Fourthly, He hath and doth daily appear in the hearts of all the faithful by the manifestation of the spirit of grace, 1 Cor. xii. 7, whereby he doth not only shine, but also dwell in them, Eph. iii. 16, 17. Fifthly, He hath and doth appear in the day of death, by the ministry of his angels, to translate the blessed souls to their place of peace, rest, and joy. And lastly, He shall appear in the end of the world in glorious majesty to judge all men and angels,—and this is the appearance here mentioned.

There is noted to be a threefold judgment : The first judgment; and that was accomplished on man and angels at their first fall. Then there is a middle judgment; and so God judgeth the wicked and the righteous every day. And there is a last judgment, and that is this judgment about which Christ is here said to appear.

The doctrine of the last judgment is in a manner only to be found in the church. They were dark and uncertain things the philosopher could see by the light of nature. And the Lord's messengers have, in all ages, from the first beginning till now, mightily urged the terror of this day, to awaken the secure world. Enoch prophesied of it, Jude 15 ; so did Moses, Deut. xxxii. ; and David, Ps. l. ; and Solomon, Eccles. xi. 9 ; and Daniel, Dan. vii. 13 ; and Joel, Joel iii. ; and Malachi, Mal. iv. ; so did Christ himself, Mat. xxiv. ; and Paul, 2 Thes. i. ; and Peter, 2 Pet. iii. ; and John, Rev. ; and Jude, Jude 6. Neither is the assurance of the judgment to come warranted by the words of God's servants only, but the Lord hath left many works of his own as pledges that he will once at length for all judge the whole world for sin. The drowning of the old world, the burning of Sodom, the destruction of Jerusalem, Mat. xxiv., were assured foretokens that the Lord would not put up with the infinite iniquities of the world, but will most severely punish for sin. The pleading of the conscience foretells a judgment to come, Rom. ii. 15, 16. The sentence of death pronounced in paradise, and renewed with such terror on Sinai, did evidently assure that God meant to call men to an account. The lesser judgments in this life are but fore-types of that last and greatest judgment to come. And lastly, The dragging of men out of the world by death is nothing else but an alarm to judgment.

Yet as there is a necessary use of the knowledge of this dreadful and glorious doctrine, so there is a restraint to be laid upon us. This is one of the things wherein we must be wise to sobriety, Rom. xii. 3. We must repress the itching of our ears, and be content to be ignorant of what is not revealed : this is a doctrine to be inquired into more for use of life than to feed the curiosity of contemplation.

Concerning the judgment to come, if any ask, Who shall judge? I answer, that in respect of authority, the whole Trinity shall judge, but in respect of the execution of that authority, Christ only shall judge, and that as man, Acts xvii. 31. It is true that the apostles and the saints are said to judge the tribes of Israel and the world ; but they only judge as assessors, that is, they shall sit as it were on the bench with our Saviour Christ when he judgeth.

And if any ask, in the second place, Whom Christ shall judge? I answer, he shall judge the evil angels ; for they are reserved in everlasting chains under darkness unto the judgment of the great day, Jude 6 ; 2 Pet. ii. 4. He shall judge also the man of sin, even the great antichrist, that hath made such havoc in the church, and seduced the nations with the wine of his fornications ; even him shall he consume with the brightness of his coming, 2 Thes. ii. 8. He shall judge also all reprobates, men, women and children, of all ages, nations and conditions; for though he shall not know them, in respect of approbation, Mat. vii. 22, xxv. 12, yet he shall judge them, and make them understand he knew their transgressions. Further, he shall judge the very elect, though it shall be with a different judgment; for ' we must all appear before the tribunal seat of Christ, that every one may receive the things which are done in his body,' 2 Cor. v. 10. Lastly, in some sense it may be said he shall judge the whole world ; for ' the heavens and the earth that now are are kept (by the word of God) and reserved unto fire against the day of condemnation, and of the destruction of ungodly men,' 2 Pet. iii. And the apostle Paul saith that the fervent desire of the creature (made subject to vanity by man) waiteth for this revelation of the sons of God at the last judgment : for they are subdued under hope, and shall at that day, by the sentence of Christ, be delivered from the bondage of corruption into the glorious liberty of the sons of God, Rom. viii. 19-21.

Thirdly, It any ask where this judgment shall be ? I answer, that seeing the Lord hath not determined it, it is curious to inquire, and more curious to assign the very place, as some have, that wrote it should be in the valley of Jehoshaphat ; or as others would have it, on Mount Zion, whence he ascended. This we know, it shall be near the earth, in the clouds of heaven, where Christ's throne shall be set, and further than this we need not inquire.

There have been also many opinions about the time when it should be. Some thought, that as the world was six days in creating, and then the sabbath of rest came ; so the world should last 6000 years, (reckoning a thousand years as one day,) and then should come the eternal sabbath. Others distribute the time thus : 2000 years before the law, 2000 years under the law, and 2000 years after the law, and then comes the judgment. Others thought the world would last after Christ so long as it was to the flood from the creation, and that was, as they say, 1656 years. Others thought it should be as long to the judgment after Christ as it was from Moses to Christ, and that should be 1582. This experience hath proved false. Others say Christ lived 33 years, and the world should continue for 33 jubilees after Christ. What can be said of all or the most of these opinions and such like, but even this, that they are the blind fancies of men? For is there not a plain restraint laid upon men in this question, when the Lord Jesus said 'It is not for you to know the times and seasons, which the Father hath put in his own power,' Acts i. 7; and 'of that day and hour knoweth no man, no not the angels of heaven, but my Father only,' Mat. xxiv. 36; Mark xiii. 32; and the evangelist St Mark addeth that the Son of man himself knoweth not the day and hour. Not that simply Christ is ignorant of the time of the last judgment, but he was said not to know, because he kept it from our knowledge. Or else he knew it not as he was man, or rather in his estate of humiliation and in his human nature he did not precisely know it. But that hinders not but that in his estate of exaltation, as he is now in heaven, and hath all power and judgment committed unto him, he may and doth fully understand it.

But letting these things pass, the principal things for us to be informed in as concerning the day of judgment, and this last appearance of our Lord and Saviour Jesus Christ, are these three: first, The signs of his coming; secondly, How, or the form of the judgment itself, when he doth come; and lastly, The use we should in the meanwhile make of the doctrine of the last judgment.

For our better remembrance, the signs of Christ's coming to judgment may be briefly reduced into this catalogue.

Some signs go before, and are fulfilled before he appear. Some signs are conjoined with his appearing. The signs going before are more remote or more near. The more remote signs are these: first, The universal preaching of the gospel to all nations, Gentiles as well as Jews. Before the end come, saith our Saviour, 'This gospel of the kingdom shall be preached throughout the whole world for a witness to all nations, Mat. xxiv. 14; secondly, Most cruel persecution, even such tribulation as was not from the beginning of the world, Mat. xxiv. 9, 10, 21, 29; thirdly, A general falling away or apostasy of the churches in antichrist, 2 Thes. ii. 2, 3; fourthly, Wars and rumours of wars, famine, pestilence and earthquakes in divers places; fifthly, False prophets and false Christs, which shall deceive many, Mat. xxiv. 11, 24. The signs more near are: first, The preaching again of the everlasting gospel, Rev. xiv. 6; secondly, The detection and fall of antichrist, and the spiritual Babel, Rev. xiv. 8; thirdly, The calling of the Jews, after the fulness of the Gentiles is come in, Rom. xi. 25, 26; fourthly, Coldness and security in the world, as in the days of Noah, Mat xxiv. 37; fifthly, The shaking of the powers of heaven, the darkening of the sun and moon, and the falling of the stars, &c., Mark xiii. 14. The signs conjoined are especially two: first, The wailing of all the kindreds of the earth; secondly, The sign of the Son of man, Mat. xxiv. 30, which what it shall be I cannot describe.

And thus we are come to the very time and execution of the judgment. And therein consider: first, The preparation; secondly, The judgment itself; thirdly, The consequents of the judgment.

The preparation is twofold: first, of the Judge; secondly, of the judged. Unto the preparation of the Judge may be referred these things: first, His commission, or that singular power given him of the Father to execute judgment upon all the world, John v. 22; Mat. xxiv. 30; and this shall be then made manifest to all men; secondly, The clothing of the human nature with a most peculiar and unsearchable majesty and glory, most lively expressing and resembling the form and brightness of the Father, Mat. xvi. 27; thirdly, The attendance of thousand thousands of holy angels, in the perfections of their splendour, Dan. vii. 10; Mat. xxv. 31; Rev. xx. 11; fourthly, The choice of a place in the clouds of heaven where he will sit; fifthly, The erecting of a most glorious white throne, which what it shall be who can utter? Yet without question, it shall visibly then appear. And thus of the preparation of the Judge.

The judged shall be prepared four ways: first, By citation; secondly, By resurrection; thirdly, By collection; fourthly, By separation. First, they shall be cited to appear. The world is three times cited: first, By the prophets and fathers before Christ; secondly, By the apostles and ministers of the gospel since Christ. And the last summons is this here meant, which shall be performed by a shout from heaven, and the voice of the last trumpet; and this shall be the voice of Christ the archangel of God, and ministered by angels. For that it shall be Christ's voice, is plain; 'The dead shall hear his voice,' as he saith in John, John v. 28. And ' the Lord himself shall descend from heaven with a shout, with the voice of the archangel, and with the trump of God,' 1 Thes. iv. 16. That the ministry of angels shall be used, is manifest by the evangelist St Matthew, who reporteth Christ's words thus, ' And he shall send his angels with a great sound of a trumpet,' Mat. xxiv. 31.

Secondly, Upon this voice shall a resurrection follow, which may be two ways considered: first, Every man in his own body, ' whether he hath done good or evil,' shall revive, and rise up out of the grave, or other places of the earth, or sea, or air, Rev. xx. 13, without any loss of any part, that so every man may in his very body receive what he hath done, whether good or evil; secondly, The living shall be all changed in a moment, in the twinkling of an eye, at the last trumpet, 1 Cor. xv. 52. And this change shall be instead of death, and a kind of resurrection. Not a change of substance, but of qualities. Our corruptible shall put on incorruption, 1 Cor. xv. 53.

Thirdly, Then shall the angels gather and collect, and bring into one place, from the four winds of heaven, that is, from all the four parts of the world, all that are quick or dead, now raised or changed, elect or reprobate, Mat. xxiv. 31, xxv. 32; and such is their power, that they will be able to drive in the mightiest, wickedest, unwillingest; yea, though they were never so many millions of them.

Lastly, When they are thus brought together, there shall be made a separation; for the sheep, God's elect, shall all be put on Christ's right hand; and the reprobate, or goats, shall be compelled to his left hand, Mat. xxv. 32. And thus of the preparation. The judgment itself followeth.

In the judgment itself, I consider three things: first, By what law man shall be tried and judged; secondly, By what evidence; thirdly, What the sentence shall be.

For the first, the Gentiles shall be judged by the law of nature. The unbelieving Christians in the visible church shall be judged by the word or law, writ or preached to them, according to that of the apostle, ' They that have sinned without the law, shall perish without the law; and they that have sinned under the law, shall be judged by the law,' Rom. ii. 12. And our Saviour saith, ' He that refuseth me, and receiveth not my words, hath one that judgeth him; the word that I have spoken, it shall judge him in the last day,' John xii. 48. And the faithful shall be judged by the gospel, even by all those comforts and promises contained in or belonging to the covenant of grace, applied to them in this life, and must fully then be confirmed and accomplished. For the sentence at the last day shall be but a more manifest declaration of that judgment the Lord in this life, most an end by his word, hath passed upon man.

For the second, The evidence shall be given in principally by the opening of three books. The one is the book of conscience, and the other the book of life, Rev. xx. 12, and the third the book of God's remembrance, Mal. iii. 16. The book of conscience, Rev. xx. 12, is that record which is kept within every man, of all sorts of actions. And that conscience may at that day give in fuller evidence, it is certain that, after the resurrection, it shall be almost infinitely extended by the power of God to express this last testimony, both in the good and in the evil. The book of life is God's sacred and eternal record of all those persons that were foreordained into life, of all ages and nations. The book of remembrance will exactly express, without all failing or mistaking, all the inclinations, thoughts, affections, words, and deeds, with all circumstances or occasions, and whatsoever else may illustrate either the goodness of good men, or the transgression of the wicked.

For the third, The sentence will be upon either the godly or the wicked. The sentence upon the godly will contain: first, The opening of God's eternal counsel, and his unsearchable love, wherein he hath resolved and begun to declare his will, to bless every one of the elect, Mat. xxv. 34. Secondly, A manifestation of all the righteousness desired, thought upon, spoken, or done by the godly, 2 Cor. v. 10, and that with such fervency of affection in Christ, that he will see and remember nothing but goodness in good men, Mat. xxv. 34-41. Thirdly, A final and general absolving and redeeming of them, from the guilt and power of all sin, from the beginning of the world, in Adam or themselves, so as there shall never be either sin in them, or accusation of sin against them, 1 Cor. i. 30. Fourthly, Ordination to glory, by appointing every one of them to inherit the kingdom prepared for them before the foundation of the world. Contrariwise, the sentence of the wicked shall contain: first, A declaration of God's eternal and just hatred of them, Mat. xxv. 41. Secondly, A full manifestation and ripping up before all men and angels, of all their sins, both of nature and action, both against God or men, or their own bodies and souls, secret and open, of what kind soever, Rom. ii. 15. Thirdly, A most terrible denunciation of God's eternal curse and horrible ordination to those eternal torments prepared for them, together with the devil and his angels, 2 Cor. v. 10.

Hitherto of the judgment itself. The consequents of the judgment follow, and they are five: first, The firing of the world, that is, the dissolution of the world by a wonderful fire that shall enclose all, so as the world shall not appear till it be renewed again, and come out of that fire as out of a furnace; for as the apostle Peter saith, 'The heavens being on fire shall pass away, and be dissolved with a noise, and the elements shall melt with heat, and the earth with the works thereof shall be burnt up,' 2 Pet. iii. 10-12. And there shall be then 'new heavens and a new earth,' that is, as it were anew refined. And the apostle John saith, the heavens and the earth shall fly away from the face of him that sitteth on the throne, Rev. xx. 11, xxi. 1.

The second consequence shall be the chasing of the wicked to hell; execution being speedily and fearfully done upon them, with all horror and haste, by the angels. The third shall be the liberty of the creatures, I mean the rest of the creatures besides men and angels, Rom. viii. 19-23. But because this is a point somewhat obscure, I will endeavour, in a few words, to resolve a doubt or two.

Quest. First, How are the creatures now in bondage, that they shall need then any liberty?

Ans. They are in bondage in divers respects. For first, They are frail and corruptible, and so in bondage to corruption. Secondly, They are subject to confusions and inconstancy, as may appear by the almost infinite mutations in the air, earth, seas, fire. Thirdly, They are now forced to serve wicked men. The sun shines upon the unjust as well as the just. The heaven makes fruitful with her showers and influence the field of the wicked as well as the just. The earth is driven to feed, and to receive into her bosom, the ungodly as well as the godly, and this is a bondage. Fourthly, The visible creatures are God's great book, to proclaim the invisible things of God. Now, they stand always ready and reading too, and men will not learn by them. And so these good masters lose all their labour; and this is a bondage, to be tied to teach such as will not learn. Fifthly, The creature is made, not only the instrument, but many times the subject of man's punishment for his sins; as the earth is made iron, and the heavens brass for man's sake, and this is a great bondage. Sixthly, The creature intends immortality, which, while it fails of in the dying or expiring of the particulars of every sort, it would supply for the preservation, at least of the kinds, by a perennial substitution of new particulars in every kind; and yet loseth all this labour, because all things must be dissolved, and must be restored by another way known to God, and not now to nature. But especially, the creatures may be said to be in bondage, because since the fall, the more illustrious instincts and vigours of the most of the creatures are darkened, decreased, dulled, and distempered in them. Oh, but might some one say, how can this bondage be ascribed unto the heavens?

Sol. The heavens are not so perfect but they may admit enlargement of their excellency. Besides, they serve now promiscuously to the use of bad as well as good; neither are the very heavens without their feebleness, and the manifest effects of fainting old age. And therefore, by a *prosopopœia*, they may be said to groan together with the rest of the creatures under the common burden and vanity unto which they are subdued. It is observed, that since the days of Ptolemy, the sun runs nearer the earth by 9976 German miles, and therefore the heavens have not kept their first perfection.

Object. But how can this vanity or bondage be in any sense ascribed to the angels?

Sol. There is no necessity to include the angels in the number of the groaning creatures; and yet it will be easy to shew that they sustain a kind of bondage; for they are now made to serve earthly things, men have their angels to attend on them. And it is thought they have a kind of regency or presidency either over nations or in moving the orbs of heaven. Besides, they are put to inflict punishments on wicked men, as on Sodom. Further, they perform service sometimes not attaining their own ends. And lastly, comparatively, at least their felicity in the creation was not so absolute as it shall be in Christ; for if his coming add not unto them a more excellent condition of nature, yet out of all question it adds a fuller measure both of knowledge and joy.

Quest. 2. But what shall the creatures have in the day of Christ they have not now?

Ans. First, They shall have freedom from all the former bondage and vanity. Secondly, They shall be delivered into the liberty of the sons of God; that is, they shall have a most excellent estate when the children of God are glorified. Wherein the Lord shews his justice, in that the creature shall have restitution for what is lost by man.

Object. But shall there be a resurrection of creatures as well as men?

Sol. No; for this restitution shall be made *in specie*, not *in individuo*. Not to every particular of every kind or sort, but to the sort or kind of all creatures; and that shall be done to the creatures then found in their several sorts.

The fourth consequent of the judgment shall be the possession of the glory of Christians appointed by the sentence of the judge. But of this afterwards in the end of this verse.

The fifth consequent of judgment shall be the delivering up of the kingdom to the Father, and so the laying down of Christ's office; for when Christ hath finally and fully subdued Satan, death, and wicked men, and hath fully reconciled the elect to God, then will there be no word of any such government in heaven as was on earth. He shall not need any longer to rule them, either by civil magistrates, or by preaching and discipline, or by any other way; which only did agree to the times of the church's warfare and pilgrimage; but he shall never cease to live and triumph with them in all perfections of happy contentment and glory. Thus of the consequents of judgment. And thus also of the doctrine of Christ's last appearance. The uses follow.

The Uses. The consideration of the doctrine of the last judgment may serve for three principal uses: first, For terror; secondly, For comfort; thirdly, For instruction.

First, This is justly a wonderful terrible doctrine to wicked men, that heap up wrath against this day of wrath, and by their wilful impenitency provoke this glorious judge. How can it but be terrible, when the Holy Ghost gives warning that the Lord Jesus will then shew himself from heaven, with his mighty angels, in flaming fire, to render vengeance on all those that know not God, and have not obeyed the gospel? How can it be but terrible, when wicked men shall be punished with everlasting perdition, from the presence of the Lord, and from the glory of his power? How can it but be terrible, when they shall feel their consciences exquisitely griping them and gnawing upon them, and when they shall see the devils to torment them, and hell to devour them? when they shall see the world burning about them, and the good angels forcing them away, and all, both men and angels, applauding their judgment, and knowing all their sins? They must not think that the judge will deal then as he doth now. Now he judgeth them secretly every day, but it is many times insensibly, or with lesser plagues; but then he will most openly pour upon them the full vials of his wrath. Here they are judged that they may be amended, but there their judgment shall be that they may be confounded; for there will be no place of repentance. Deceive not thyself; Christ will not come the second time as he came the first. He came then to be judged, but now to judge; he shall then be seen with terror, that was before looked upon with contempt; he shewed his patience in his first coming, but now he will shew his power; he appeared then in the form of a servant, but now he will appear in the form of a King, greater than all kings. Then he professed not to judge any man, but now he proclaimeth he will judge all men. It was commonly thought if any man saw God he should die; alas, alas! how then shall these woeful wretches do that must see him in the unutterable fierceness of his ireful indignation? If the powers of heaven shall be shaken at his pleasure, oh! how shall the miserable heart of the guilty sinner be rent into a thousand pieces, with unmedicinable sorrows? If Felix tremble to hear tell of judgment, what will poor Felix do when he must feel judgment, both in the sentence and execution? If the word of Christ on earth had such power, as it had in the garden, to strike stubborn-hearted men to the earth, what power, think we, will it have when he speaks as the Lord from heaven? When Ezekiel, Daniel, and the apostle John, and others, saw but one angel, in a lesser manifestation of his glory, coming as a messenger of good tidings, they fall down, and are full of singular fear. If the sight of one angel be so terrible, what will the sight of all the thousand thousands of angels be, especially when they come clothed with all their brightness of glory? And if good men, that had good consciences, were so frighted, what shall become of evil men with their evil consciences? And if the messengers of good tidings do so amaze, how shall the executioners of a most terrible sentence compass them about with confusion both of face and heart? If the drowning of the old world, the burning of Sodom, the opening of the earth to swallow up Dathan and Abiram, and such like judgments, have so much horror in them, how then can any tongue express or heart now conceive the horror of this day, when all the millions of wicked men shall be delivered up to those eternal and remediless torments? If it be such a shame to do penance for one fault in one congregation, where men will pray for the offender, what a shame will it be when all thy faults shall be discovered before all the whole world, without all hope of pity or help?

Nor is it possible for them to escape this fearful judgment; the judge will not be unconstant, nor will he take reward; he will not be overlaid with confusion of businesses, he will no way be corrupted in judgment. Not to appear is impossible, and to appear is intolerable; here will be no respect of persons, nor will the judge care how it be taken, nor will he be deceived with colours and circumstances. He hath tarried so long he cannot be charged with rashness, nor can there be a hiding of any particulars from him. Every inclination, thought, desire, word, and work, shall surely come to judgment. And lastly, there can be no impediment to hinder execution.

Quest. 1. But here a question may arise, viz., Who are they that are in danger hereof?

Ans. All impenitent sinners. But yet there are some kind of sinners that are expressly named in scripture, and therefore if thou be any of that number, prevent thine own ruin by repentance, or else thou shalt certainly perish. I undertake not to reckon all; it shall suffice to mention some of the chief sinners that Christ will be sure to remember in that day. The beast and the false prophet, and all that worship his image and renew his mark, shall be then cast alive into the lake that burns with fire and brimstone, Rev. xix. 20. False teachers, which privily bring in damnable heresies, or speak evil of the way of truth, have their condemnation long since determined and agreed upon, 2 Pet. ii. 1-3. All atheists, that make a mock of religion and the coming of Christ, shall have a principal portion of the fierce fury of Christ, 2 Pet. iii. 3, &c. All covetous worldlings and greedy rich men shall then be in a woful case; for the very rust of their cankered gold and silver shall witness against them, and shall eat their flesh as it were fire, James v. 13. All merciless men shall then have judgment without mercy, James ii. 13. All whoremongers and adulterers, and all that defile the flesh, God will be sure to judge, Heb. xiii. 4. A fearful looking for of judgment and violent fire shall devour all those apostates that sin willingly after they have received and acknowledged the truth, Heb. x. 27. How sure do ye suppose shall his punishment be that doth despite the Spirit of grace by which he was sanctified? Heb. x. 29. All those that have troubled God's servants shall bear their condemnation, whosoever they be, Gal. v. 10. 'O man, thou art inexcusable that judgest another man, wherein thou art guilty thyself; for the judgment of God must needs be in truth against such as commit such things,' Rom. ii. 1-3. Especially if men grow master-like in censuring, it will increase to 'greater condemnation,' James iii. 1. All goats, or unruly Christians, that will not be kept within God's fence, that is, will not be ruled by God's ordinances and ministers, shall be separate in that day from God's sheep, and as a people accursed to be cast into an unavoidable fellowship with the devil and his angels, Mat. xxv. All hypocrites, that say and do not, or do all their works to be seen of men, and take God's covenant into their mouths, and hate to be reformed, how shall they escape the damnation to come? Ps. l, Mat. vi. and xxiii. All wicked men, with their scant measure, and deceitful weights, and wicked balances, shall never be justified in the day of the Lord, Micah vi. 10, 11. What shall I say? it were too long to proceed to reckon all, and it is a short labour to conclude with the apostle, No wantons, nor drunkards, nor railers, nor extortioners, nor thieves, nor wrathful persons, nor gluttons, nor idolaters, nor jesters, nor filthy talkers, nor fearful persons, nor liars, nor any that love lies, shall be able to stand in the day of Christ, but shall be shut out of the kingdom of heaven, and cast into the lake that burneth with fire and brimstone. And thus of the use for terror.

Use 2. Secondly, Upon the meditation of this last judgment divers lessons for our instruction are enforced: first, It should restrain uncharitable judging and censuring one of another for less matters, especially for things indifferent: 'Who art thou that judgest another man's servant? he standeth or falleth to his own master. Christ is the Lord of quick and dead. And therefore why dost thou condemn thy brother? or why dost thou despise thy brother? for we shall all appear before the judgment-seat of Christ.' Inasmuch as the Lord Jesus Christ will judge the secrets of all hearts, and give a just trial to the actions of all men, 1 Cor. iv. 5, why should we forestall his judgment, or in doubtful matters arrogate to ourselves this honour of Christ? If we could consider that we shall then every one give account unto God for himself, Rom. xiv. 12, 13, we should find work enough to do to look to our own score: 'Let us not therefore, brethren, judge one another any more.' Secondly, Are there any matters of difference amongst us? Let the saints judge them and end them, 1 Cor. vi. 2. God will be contented to put his cause to them at the last day; 'for we know the saints shall judge the world,' and therefore why should we refuse their arbitration? Thirdly, It should order and moderate our sorrows for our dead friends. We should not sorrow as people without hope, seeing we believe that all that sleep in Jesus God will bring with him, 1 Thes. iv. 13, 14, 17, 18. We shall meet together again in that day, and afterwards live with the Lord together for ever; and therefore we should comfort one another with these words. Fourthly, This summons to judgment gives a dreadful warning and admonition to the world, even 'to all men everywhere to repent, inasmuch as God hath appointed a day wherein he will judge the world in righteousness, by the man whom he hath appointed, whereof he hath given an assurance in that he raised him from the dead,' Acts xvii. 32. Woe will be unto us if that day come upon us unawares, before we have made our peace, and humbled ourselves before God, and by unfeigned repentance turned from all our evil ways. It is an unsearchable compassion that God shews when he offers us this mercy, that 'if we will judge ourselves, we shall not be judged of the Lord' in that day, 1 Cor. xi. 34. And it will on the other side excessively incense his wrath, when having such grace offered, we neglect it, and death and judgment find our sins both unremitted on God's part and unrepented on ours. Fifthly, Seeing all these things must be dissolved, how should it fire us, and daily quicken our dead and drowsy spirits to a constant care of all possible holy conversation and godliness, 2 Pet. iii. 12, unless we would discover ourselves either to be atheists, that mock at the judgment to come, or men given to a spirit of slumber, that in soul sleep it out, and will not consider our latter end?

Seeing we are all God's stewards, let us arm ourselves as they that must then give account of our stewardship. And since we have all received some of God's talents and gifts in our several places, let us be careful to approve ourselves to be good servants and faithful, such as can return them with advantage, lest the portion of the servant that hid his master's talents in the earth fall upon us. Lastly, Since the day of judgment is the day of our full and final redemption, and since he shall come as a thief in the night, even in the hour that we think not, let us therefore watch, Mat. xxiv. 44, and be ready, always careful and diligent, sighing and groaning, longing and praying, Rev. xxii., hasting to and looking for this glorious appearance and revelation of our Lord and Saviour Jesus Christ, 2 Pet. iii.

Use 3. Thirdly, This may be a singular comfort to all mortified and penitent Christians; they may lift up their heads, and rejoice with joy unspeakable and glorious; for the Lord shall then 'come to be glorified in his saints, and made marvellous in all them that believe,' 2 Thes. i. 10.

Object. But the terror of the day may amaze a Christian.

Sol. There is no spark of terror in this doctrine to a godly mind; for what should he fear, if he either consider the favour of the Judge or the manner of the judgment? For the Judge is he that hath been all this while their advocate, to plead their suits by making intercession for them, 1 John ii. 1. And therefore when he comes to sit in judgment, he cannot go against his own pleading. He is their brother, and carries a most brotherly affection; and will he condemn his own brethren? He is their head, and hath performed all the offices of a head unto them, and can he then fail them when they have most need of him? Nay, it is he that hath been Judge for us on earth, and will he judge against us in heaven? What shall I say? He died for us to shew his undoubted love, even that he might redeem us as a peculiar people to God, and will he fail us in the last act, when he should once for all accomplish his redemption for us? Besides, he hath already promised to acquit us in that day, and it hath been often confirmed, both in the word, and the sacraments, and prayer. He hath left many pledges of his love with us, and therefore it were shameful unbelief to doubt his terror. What though he be terrible to wicked men? yet by judging in severity he hath not, nor cannot, lose the goodness of his own mercy. What should we fear him judging in his power, when we have felt salvation in his name? Besides, the manner of the judgment shall be in all righteousness and mercy. Thou shalt not be wronged by false witnesses, nor shalt thou be judged by common fame or outward appearance; the Judge will not be transported with passion or spleen, nor will he condemn thee to satisfy the people; and besides, there shall be nothing remembered but what good thou hast sought or done, and not the least goodness but it shall be found to thy honour and praise at that day. And if it were such a favour to a base subject if the king should take notice of him to love him, and should in an open parliament, before all the Lords and Commons, make a long speech in the particular praise of such a subject; what shall it be when the Lord Jesus, in a greater assembly than ever was since the world stood, shall particularly declare God's everlasting love to thee, and recite thy praises, with his own mouth, of all that hath been good in thy thoughts, affections, words, or works, throughout all thy life, or in thy death; especially if thou add the singular glory he will then adjudge thee to, by an irrevocable sentence? And so we come to the second appearance, viz., the appearance of Christians in glory.

Then shall ye also appear with him in glory. The glory that shall then be conferred upon Christians may be considered either in their bodies, or in their souls, or both. The glory of their bodies after the resurrection is threefold: for first, They shall be immortal, that is, in such a condition as they can never die again, or return to dust; for 'this mortal then shall put on immortality,' 1 Cor. xv. 53. Secondly, They shall be incorruptible, that is, not only free from putrefaction, but also from all weakness, both of infirmity, and deformity; for 'though it be sown in weakness, yet it shall be raised in power; though it be sown in dishonour and corruption, yet it shall be raised in honour and incorruption,' 1 Cor. xv. 42, 43. Thirdly, They shall be spiritual; not that our bodies shall vanish into ghosts or spirits, but because they shall be at that day so admirably glorified and perfected, that by the mighty working of God's Spirit, they shall be as able to live without sleep, meat, marriage, or the like, as now the angels in heaven are; and besides, they shall be so admirably light and agile, and swift, that they shall be able to go abroad with inconceivable speed, in the air or heavens, as now they can go surely on the earth. The glory upon the soul, shall be the wonderful perfection of God's image in all the faculties of it. Then shall we know the secrets of heaven and earth. And then shall our memories, will, and affections be after an inexpressible manner made conformable unto God. The glory upon both soul and body shall be those rivers of joys and pleasures for evermore. And thus shall the man be glorified that feareth the Lord.

The consideration of this glory may serve for divers uses. First, Let us all pray unto God upon the knees of our hearts, from day to day, that as he is the Father of glory, so he would give unto us the spirit of revelation, that the eyes of our understanding might be enlightened to know in some comfortable measure, and that we might be able with more life and affection to meditate of the exceeding riches of this glory and inheritance to come, Eph. i. 17, 18. Our hearts are naturally herein exceeding both dull and blind, marvellous unable with delight and constancy to think of these eternal felicities; and this comes to pass by the spiritual working of Satan, and the deceitfulness of sin, and too much employment and care about earthly things. But a Christian that hath so high a calling, and hopes for such a glorious end, should not allow himself that deadness of heart; but as he gaineth sense by prayer in other gifts of grace, so should he strive with importunity and constancy, wrestling with God without intermission, so as no day should pass him, but he would remember his suit unto God, till he could get some comfortable ability to meditate of this excelling estate of endless glory.

Secondly, This should make us to be patient in tribulation, Rom. v. 2–4; and without murmuring or grieving, to endure hardness, 2 Tim. ii. 3; and temptations in this world, for they are but for a season, 1 Pet. i. 6; though they be never so manifold or great; and the afflictions of this present life are not worthy of the glory to be revealed, Rom. viii. 18. Though we might be dismayed while we look upon our crosses, and reproaches, and manifold trials, yet if the Lord let us have access unto this grace, Rom. v. 2, to be able soundly to think of the glory to come, we may stand with confidence, unappalled, and with unutterable joy, look up to the glory we shall shortly enjoy, when 'the trial of our faith, being more precious than the gold that perisheth, shall be found unto honour and praise through the revelation of Jesus Christ,' 1 Pet. i. 7. Yea, what were it to lose, not some of our credits, or our goods, but even our lives, seeing we are sure to find them again with more than a hundredfold advantage, at the time when Christ 'shall come in the glory of his Father, to give unto all men according to their deeds'? Mat. xvi. 27, 28. Besides, we must know that there is no talking of sitting at Christ's hand in glory, till we have asked ourselves this question, Whether we can drink of the cup he drank of, and be baptized with the baptism he is baptized with? Mark x. 37, &c. And then if we can suffer with him, we shall reign with him, 2 Tim. ii. 12; and shall be glad and rejoice with exceeding joy when his glory shall appear. And in the meanwhile the spirit of glory and of God resteth on you, 1 Pet. iv. 13, 14.

Thirdly, Seeing Christ will receive Christians into such glory, it should teach us to receive one another into both our hearts and houses, Rom. xv. 7. Why shouldst thou be ashamed or think it much, with all love and bounty, and bowels of affection, to entertain and welcome the heirs of such eternal glory? Oh! if thou couldst but now see but for a moment, how Christ doth use the souls of the righteous in heaven, or will use both body and soul at the last day, thou wouldst for ever honour them whom Christ doth so glorify, and make them now thy only companions, whom thou shouldst see to be appointed to live in such felicity for ever.

Fourthly, The thought of this glory should win us to a care to be such as may be capable of it.

Quest. What must we do that we may have comfort that we are the men shall partake of this glory, and speed well in the day of Jesus Christ?

Ans. First, 'Every one that would have this hope, must purge himself as Christ is pure,' 1 John iii. 3; we must be much in the duties of mortification; for no unclean person can enter into the kingdom of glory. And unclean we are all, till we be washed in the blood of Christ by justification, and bathed in tears of true repentance by mortification. It hath been observed before, that if we would not have the Lord to judge us, we must judge ourselves, 1 Cor. xi. 34. And if we would not have Christ to take unto him words against our souls, we must take unto us words against our sins, to confess and bewail them in secret, Hosea xiv. 3. Secondly, We must labour for the assurance of faith. It is faith that is the evidence of the things not seen, Heb. xi. 1; It is faith that shall be found to honour and praise in the revelation of Jesus Christ, 1 Pet. i. 7; it is faith to which the promise of eternal life is made, John iii. 18. Thirdly, We should labour to get unto ourselves the benefit of a powerful preaching ministry, for thereby our hearts may be wonderfully stirred up to see the glory of sincerity on earth, and it will open a wide door to behold, as in a mirror, the glory to come with an open face, changing us into the same image from glory to glory by the Spirit of God. I say not that this is of absolute necessity, as the former are, but it is of wonderful expediency. Fourthly, We must be circumspect and watchful, in special manner attending to our own hearts, that we 'be not at any time oppressed with the cares of this life, or voluptuous living,' Luke xxi. 34, 36. If ever we would be able to stand in the day of judgment, and escape the fearful things that are to come, especially we must look to ourselves in these things, lest that day come upon us at unawares. Fifthly, Do we look for the mercy of our Lord Jesus Christ into eternal life? then we must (as the apostle Jude sheweth) 'edify ourselves in our most holy faith, praying in the Holy Ghost, and keep ourselves in the love of God,' Jude 20, 21; we must be afraid of whatsoever may estrange the Lord from us, or any way darken the sense of his love; for we may be assured, if we have his favour and walk before him in the sense of it, we shall have glory when we die. Likewise, praying in the Holy Ghost, with constancy and frequency, doth marvellously enrich a Christian, both with the first-fruits of glory, even glorious joy on earth, and with the assurance of fulness of glory in heaven. Sixthly, The apostle John seems to say, if love be perfect in us, we shall have boldness in the day of judgment, 1 John iv. 17. As if he would import that to be inwardly and affectionately acquainted with Christians on earth, is a notable means to procure us gracious entertainment with Christ in heaven; especially if we perfect our love, and grow to some Christian ripeness in the practice of the duties of love, in a profitable fellowship in the gospel. It is good discretion to grow as great as we can with Christians, that so we may win the favour of Christ. Lastly, The apostle Paul shews in the second to the Romans, that 'they that seek glory, and honour, and immortality, and everlasting life,' must be 'patient in well-doing,' for they shall be rewarded according to their works; and to every man that doth good shall be honour, and glory, and power, to the Jew first, and also to the Grecian, Rom. ii. 6, 7, 10. For all that have any tidings of salvation in the gospel, or look for that blessed hope and appearing of that glory of the mighty God, must live soberly, righteously, and godly in this present world, Titus ii. 11-13. Without holiness no man can see God, Heb. xii. 14. And therefore we should be abundant in the work of the Lord, forasmuch as we know that our labour shall not be in vain in the Lord, 1 Cor. xv. 58. And thus far of the glorious appearance both of Christ and Christians. And thus also of the first rule of life, namely, the meditation of heavenly things.

Ver. 5. *Mortify therefore your members which are on earth, fornication, uncleanness, the inordinate affection, evil concupiscence, and covetousness, which is idolatry.*

These words, with those that follow to the 10th verse, contain the second principal rule of holy life, and that is the mortification of evil. These evils to be mortified are of two sorts, for either they are vices that concern ourselves most, or else they are injuries that concern the hurt of others also. Of the mortification of vices, he entreats, ver. 5-7; of the mortification of injuries, he entreats, ver. 8, 9. In the first part, viz., the exhortation to the mortifying of vices, I consider first, the matter about which he deals, and the reasons. The matter is in ver. 5, and the reasons, ver. 6, 7.

In the 5th verse there are two things: first, The proposition of mortification, in these words, 'mortify therefore your members that are on earth;' secondly, A catalogue of vices to be mortified, or the enumeration of certain special sins a Christian should be careful to keep himself from, viz., 'fornication, uncleanness,' &c.

The general consideration of the whole exhortation to mortification should imprint this deeply in our hearts, that unless we do repent of those sins that have been in our natures and lives, and be careful to flee from the corruptions that are in the world, we shall never have comfort that we are accepted with God. We should bring to the particular opening of all the verses a mind resolved of the general. And to quicken us a little the more to the respect of this doctrine, and to enforce the care of parting with our sins, I will briefly touch by the way some few reasons why we should be willing to entertain all counsel that might show us any course to get rid of sin. First, Our vices are the fruits of our corrupted nature. They arise not from any noble or divine instinct, but are the effects of base flesh in us, Gal. v. 19. And we should carry the thoughts of it in our minds when we are inclined or tempted to vice. We should say within ourselves, this evil proceeds not from anything that might declare greatness or true spirit in a man. What is passion, or lust, or covetousness, but the base work of the filthy degenerated flesh. Secondly, Our vices are the only things that defile us and make us loathsome before God and men. It is not mean clothes, nor a deformed body, or a poor house, or homely fare, or any such thing, that makes a man truly contemptible. No, no; it is only sin can defile, Mat. xv. 19, and bring that which is true contempt. Thirdly, The bond and forfeiture of the law or covenant of works lieth upon the back of every man that lives in sin without repentance. For the law is given to the lawless and disobedient, as the apostle shows, to ungodly and sinners, to whoremongers, and liars, and to all that live in sin, contrary to wholesome doctrine, 1 Tim. i. 9, 10. Fourthly, Are not strange punishments to the workers of iniquity? Is not destruction to the wicked? Job xxxi. 2, 3. What portion can they have of God from above? and what inheritance from the Almighty from on high? The hearts of holy men that have considered the fearful terrors of God denounced in scripture against the vices of men, have even broke within them, and their bones have shaken, for the presence of the Lord, and for his holy word, Jer. xxiii. 9. Fifthly, Christ will be a swift witness, Mal. iii. 7, against all fearless and careless men, that being guilty of these vices or the like, make not speed to break them off by repentance. Lastly, 'Know ye not that the unrighteous shall not enter into the kingdom of heaven? Be not deceived, for these things the wrath of God cometh upon the children of disobedience,' 1 Cor. vi. 9, Eph. v. 6.

Now I come to the words particularly.

Therefore. This word carries this exhortation to something before. If it be referred to our rising with Christ, ver. 1, then it notes that we can never have our part in Christ's resurrection till we feel the virtue of his death killing sin in us. If it be referred to the meditation of heavenly things, then it notes that we can never set our affections on things that are above till we have mortified our members that are on earth. The corruption of our natures and lives are the cause of such disability to contemplate of or affect heavenly things. And as any are more sinful, they are more unable thereunto. If the word be referred to the appearance of Christ in the former verse, then it imports that mortification is of great necessity unto our preparation to the last judgment, and will be of great request in the day of Christ.

Mortify. To mortify is to kill, or to apply that which will make dead. The Lord works in matters of grace, in the judgment of flesh and blood, by contraries. Men must be poor if they would have a kingdom, Mat. v. 34; men must sorrow if they would be comforted; men must serve if they would be free, John viii.; and here, men must die if they would live. God's thoughts are not as man's; but his ways are higher than man's ways, as the heavens are higher than the earth, Isa. lv. 10. Which may teach us, as to live by faith, so not to trust the judgment of the world, or the flesh, in the things of God.

But the manifest doctrine from this word is this, that true repentance hath in it the mortification of sin; and so it implies divers things: first, That we must not let sin alone till it die itself, but we must kill sin while it might yet live. It is no repentance to leave sin when it leaveth us, or to give it over when we can commit it no longer. Secondly, That true repentance makes a great alteration in a man. Thirdly, That it hath in it pain and sorrow. Men use not to die ordinarily without much pain; and sure it is sin hath a strong heart, it is not soon killed. It is one thing to sleep, another thing to die. Many men with less ado get sin asleep, that it doth not so stir in them; but, alas! there must be more ado to get it dead by true mortification. Fourthly, True repentance extinguisheth the power of sin and the vigour of it: it makes it like a dead corpse, that neither it stirs itself, nor will be stirred by occasions, persuasions, commandments, or strokes. It is a wonderful testimony of sound mortification when we have gotten our old corruption to this pass. And constancy in prayer and hearing, and daily confession and sorrow for sin, will bring it to be thus with us, especially if we strive with God, and be earnest with spiritual importunity, watching the way of our own hearts, to wound sin so soon as we see it begin to stir. Yet I would not be mistaken, as if I meant that a Christian could attain such a victory over sin that it should not be in him at all, nor that he should never be stirred with the temptations, or enticements, or occasions of evil. But my meaning is, that in some measure, and in the most sins, a Christian doth find it so, and in every sin his desire and endeavour is daily to have it so. And his desire is not without some happy success, so as sin dieth, or lieth a-dying every day.

Quest. But here a question may arise: Did not the apostle grant they were dead before? and if they were dead to the world, they were without question dead to sin also. How then doth he speak to them to mortify sin? doth it not imply they had not been mortified before?

Ans. I answer, The apostle may well use this exhortation, for divers reasons: first, Many of them perhaps were dead but in appearance, they professed mortification but were not mortified; secondly, It might be some of them had begun to use some exercises of mortification, but had not finished their mortification. Sure it is, and we may see it by daily experience, that many being won by the word, and smitten with remorse, have sometimes the pangs of sorrow for their sins, but quickly are aweary of seeking sorrow in secret for sin; they give over before they have soundly and sufficiently humbled their souls.

Quest. But may some one say, How long should we continue our sorrows, or how long should we judge ourselves in secret for our sins?

Ans. I answer, Thou must not give over thy sorrows: first, Till the body of sin be destroyed, Rom. vi., that is, till that general frame of sinfulness be dissolved, till, I say, thou have set some order in thy heart and life, so as the most sins thou didst before live in be reformed; secondly, It were expedient thou shouldst still seek to humble thy soul till thou couldst get as much tenderness in bewailing thy sins as thou wert wont to have in grieving for crosses, till thou couldst mourn as freshly for piercing God's Son as for losing thine own son, Zech. xii. 10; thirdly, Thou must sorrow till thou find the power of the most beloved and rooted sins to be in some measure weakened and abated; fourthly, Thou doest not well to give thy sorrows over till thou find the testimony of Jesus in thy heart, that is, till God answer thy mournful requests of pardon with some joys in the Holy Ghost, and the dews of heavenly refreshings.

Quest. But will some one say, Must we lay all aside, and do nothing else but sorrow till we can find all those things?

Ans. I mean not that men should neglect their callings all this while, or that they should carry an outward countenance of sorrowing before others, or that they should all this while afflict their hearts with discontentment, or the like. For when the apostle wills men to pray always, he means not that they should do nothing but pray, but he would have them to keep a set course of praying every day; and besides, to watch to all the extraordinary occasions or opportunities of prayer; which being done, a Christian may be truly said to pray continually, though otherwise he follow his calling diligently. The like I say of sorrowing always. But that I may express my meaning distinctly, I think, till thou canst attain the former things, thou must observe these rules: first, Thou must lay aside thy recreations and carnal rejoicings, for this the apostle James imports, when he saith, 'Let your laughter be turned into heaviness, and your joy into mourning,' James iv. 9; secondly, Thou must beg sorrow at God's hand every day constantly in the times set apart for prayer, till the Lord give thee rest to thy soul by granting the things before mentioned; thirdly, Thou must not neglect the times of special fasting and humiliation, if the Lord call thereunto, Isa. xxii. 12; lastly, Thou must use special sobriety in the restraint of thy liberty in earthly things, and be watchful to make use of all opportunities of softening thy heart. These things being observed, thou mayest seem unto men not to sorrow, and mayest follow thy calling seriously, and yet be truly said to sorrow always. Thus of the second reason why the apostle exhorts still to mortification.

Thirdly, The dearest and humblest servants of God may be called upon to mortify their members that are on earth, though they have truly and soundly repented of sin before, by reason of the evils of every day, which daily and afresh, even after calling, break out in their hearts and lives, and for which they must still renew their repentance; for their first repentance only delivers them from sins past; they must renew their mortification, as their corruptions are renewed.

Members. It is certain by 'members on earth,' the apostle means sin, and that fitly: for, first, Actual sins in relation to original sin, are as so many members that grow from it; secondly, By a metonymy of the subject, sin may be called our members, because it is brought into action by the help and service of our members; thirdly, If the apostle had spoken to wicked men, he might well have called sin their members, because they love sin as they love their members; and therefore to take away their sin, is to pull out their eyes, or to cut off their hands or feet, as our Saviour shows, Mat. v. 29, &c.; fourthly, Sins in the Colossians, and so in all the faithful, may be here called members comparatively with the body of sin mentioned, Col. ii. 12, as if the apostle should say, the body of sin is already cast off and destroyed in you by your former repentance, but yet there remains some limbs of sin, some members of it, these resist; and in this sense we may here note a lively difference between sin in wicked men, and sin in godly men. For in wicked men there is the whole body of sins, that is, all their sins unremitted, and unrepented. But in godly men, the body of sin, even the greater number of their sins, they have abandoned, only some few members of their sins remain, which every day molest them. But before I pass from these words, two things are further to be noted: first, That he saith, 'your members;' secondly, He addeth, 'which are on earth.'

Your. The apostle saith well 'your' members; for indeed properly our sins are our own, and nothing else.

Which are on earth. They are also well said to be on earth; because they are signs of the earthly man, and because they tend only to earthly pleasures and contentments, and because men with these unrepented of, are not admitted into heaven.

Thus of the general proposition; now follows the catalogue of sins to be mortified.

Before I enter upon the particular consideration of them, something may be learned from the apostle's order: first, He teacheth men to reform their own personal vices, and then orders them for mortification of injuries to other men. Sure it is, that every filthy person will be an injurious person; and till men repent of their lusts, and other such like personal corruptions, they will never cease to be injurious to other men. And ordinarily men that are notable for malice, or blasphemy, that is, cursed speaking, and such like sins as the apostle after names, they are exceeding vicious persons otherways. Instance but in such as reproach God's servants; mark it both in city and country. Who are they that raise and vent all slanders and strange reports concerning such as preach or profess the gospel of Jesus Christ in the truth and sincerity of it? I say mark them particularly. For my own part, in my little observation I have found them always either to be papists, or superstitious persons, or drunkards, or notable whoremasters and filthy persons, or people guilty of other notable crimes. Indeed, sometimes their abominations are not so commonly and publicly discoursed of, because either they are men of greater place, or else their vices are more covered over and gilded with cunning pretences; yet seldom falls it out, but their wickedness is commonly known; and many times God's children that are unjustly touched could upon sufficient grounds detect strange abominations in their adversaries; and this was unto David usually a strong argument of comfort, that his adversaries were men whom he knew to be workers of iniquity. And thus much from the order of these catalogues.

The sins here reckoned up are sins either against the seventh commandment—viz., fornication, uncleanness, inordinate affections; or against the tenth commandment—evil concupiscence; or against the first commandment—covetousness, which is idolatry.

First. Of the sins against the seventh commandment,

I might here observe, in that they are placed in the first, that God would have Christians to be especially careful to preserve their chastity; for this is one thing principal in 'the will of God concerning our sanctification, that we should abstain from fornications,' and that every one should know how to possess his vessel in holiness and honour, 1 Thes. iv. 3, 4. And to this end hath the Lord given us so many precious promises, that we might resolve to cleanse ourselves from all filthiness both of flesh and spirit, 2 Cor. vii. 1. Now, in the handling of these sins against the seventh commandment here mentioned, I will keep this order: first, I will particularly entreat of the nature and effects of each of these three sins, and generally make use of all together, and therein shew the remedies against all sins of uncleanness.

Fornication. There is fornication in title only, as when victuallers were called by the name of harlots. Secondly, There is a metaphorical kind of fornication, or allegorical; so wicked men are said to be bastards, Heb. xii.; and the Jews were born of fornication, Hosea i. Thirdly, There is a spiritual fornication; and so idolatry is fornication, and so usually termed, both by the prophet Hosea, and the apostle in the Revelation. Lastly, There is corporal fornication; and that sometimes notes whoredom in the general; and sometimes it notes that filthiness that is committed actually by unmarried persons; and this latter kind of filthiness was exceeding common among the Gentiles in all nations, especially where it was committed with such as professed to be whores; and so it was an effect of that horrible blindness into which the nations fell upon their idolatry. But I suppose it may be here taken for all adultery and whoredom. And then I come to the reasons which may be collected against this sin out of several scriptures; and generally it is worthy the noting, that ever the more the world lessens the hatefulness of this sin, the more the Holy Ghost aggravates it; as here it is set in the forefront, that the first and greatest blows of confession and prayer might light upon it. But I come to the particular reasons against fornication.

1. It defiles a man worse than any leprosy, Mat. xv.; it is filthiness in a high degree of hatefulness.

2. It makes a man or woman unmeet and unworthy all Christian society, as the apostle shews: 'If any that is called a brother be a fornicator, with such a one eat not,' 1 Cor. v. 9.

3. It is one of the manifest works of the flesh, Gal. v.

4. It is so hateful, that it ought not once to be named among Christians, Eph. v. 4.

5. It brings with it horrible dishonour. 'If a thief steal to satisfy his soul, because he is hungry; men do not so despise him; but he that committeth adultery with a woman is destitute of understanding; he shall find a wound and dishonour, and his reproach shall never be put away,' Prov. vi. 33. It is better to be buried in a deep ditch than to live with a whore, Prov. xxiii. 27.

6. It utterly makes shipwreck of innocency and honesty. A man may as well take fire in his bosom, and his clothes not be burnt; or go upon coals, and his feet not be burnt, as go in to his neighbour's wife, and be innocent, Prov. vi. 27–29; the strange woman increaseth transgressors amongst men, Prov. xxiii. 28. It is impossible to be adulterous and honest.

7. It is a sin of which a man or woman can hardly repent; for whoredom and wine, as the prophet notes, take away their hearts, Hosea iv. 11. The guests of the strange woman are the most of them in hell, Prov. ix. 18; for the wise man further avoucheth, Surely her house tendeth to death, and her paths unto the dead, Prov. ii. 18.

8. It will bring God's curse upon a man's estate. Many a man is brought to a morsel of bread by it. Prov. vi. 26; yea, it may bring a man into almost all evil in the midst of the congregation, Prov. v. 14; for fornication is a fire that will devour to destruction, and root out all a man's increase, Job xxxi. 11, 12, and therefore to be accounted a wickedness and iniquity to be condemned.

9. By this sin a man may make his house a very stew. The Lord may justly plague his filthiness in his terrible wrath, suffering his wife, children, or servants also to defile his house with like abominations.

10. If it were not otherwise hateful, yet this is sure: it will destroy a man's soul, Prov. vi. 32.

Lastly, The apostle Paul, in the First Epistle to the Corinthians, and the sixth chapter, hath divers reasons against this sin: first, The body was made for the Lord as well as the soul; secondly, The body shall be raised at the last day to an incorruptible estate; thirdly, Our bodies are the members of Christ; fourthly, He that coupleth himself with a harlot is one body with a harlot; fifthly, This is a sin in a special sense against our own bodies; sixthly, The body is the temple of the Holy Ghost; finally, The body is bought with a price, and therefore is not our own. These reasons should effectually persuade with Christian minds to abhor and avoid this wretched sin; and those that are guilty of it should make haste by sound repentance to seek forgiveness, having their souls washed in the blood of Christ; for howsoever for the present they live securely through the methods of Satan and the deceitfulness of sin, yet may they be brought into the midst almost of all evils before they be aware, Prov. v. 14. Let them assure themselves that the end will be bitter as wormwood, and sharp as a two-edged sword, Prov. v. 4; for he that followeth a strange woman is as an ox that goeth to the slaughter, and as a fool to the stocks for correction, till a dart strike through his liver, as a bird hasteth to the snare, not knowing that he is in danger, Prov. vii. 22, 23; for if the filthy person could escape all manner of judgment from men, yet it is certain that whoremongers and adulterers God will judge, Heb. xiii. 4; but because God for a time holdeth his tongue, therefore they think God is like them; but certainly the time hasteth when the Lord will set all their filthiness in order before them; and if they consider not, he will seize upon them when no man shall deliver them, Ps. l. 21, 22; especially they are assured to lose the kingdom of heaven, and to feel the smart of God's eternal wrath in the lake that burneth with fire and brimstone, 1 Cor. vi. 9, Eph. v. 5, Rev. xxi. 8, xxii. 15; neither let them applaud themselves in their secrecy; for God can detect them, and bring upon them the terrors of the shadow of death, when they see they are known, Job xxiv. 15–17; the heavens may declare their wickedness, and the earth rise against them, Job xx. 26, and the fire not blown may devour them.

Neither let any nurse themselves in security in this sin, under pretence that they purpose to repent hereafter; for they that go to a strange woman seldom return again; neither take they hold of the way of life, Prov. ii. 19; for whoredom takes away their heart, Hosea iv. 11. If they reply, that David did commit adultery and yet did return, I answer, it is true; of many thousand adulterers, one David did return; but why mayest thou not fear thou shouldst perish with the multitude did not return? Besides, when thou canst shew once David's exquisite sorrows and tears, I will believe thy interest in the application of David's example.

Uncleanness. By uncleanness here I suppose is meant all external pollutions or filthiness, besides whoredom. As, first, With devils, and that either sleeping, by filthy dreams, or waking, as is reported of some witches; secondly, With beasts, and this is buggery; thirdly, With men, and that is sodomy; fourthly, With our own kindred, and that is incest; fifthly, With more wives than one, and that is polygamy; sixthly, With one's own wife, by the intemperate or intempestive use of the marriage-bed, as in the time of separation; seventhly, With a man's own self, as was Onan's sin, or in like filthiness, though not for the same end. These, as the Gentiles, walk in the vanity of their minds, their cogitations are darkened, they are strangers from the life of God through their ignorance and hardness of heart, being for the most part past feeling, and many of them delivered up to a reprobate sense, as a scourge of other sins and foul vices which abound in them: these are the shame of our assemblies, and many times visited with secret and horrible judgments, Eph. iv. 17, Rom. i. 24, 26, 27, 29, &c.

Inordinate affection. The original word notes internal uncleanness, especially the burning and flaming of lust though it never come to action, or the daily passions of lust which arise out of such a softness or effeminateness of mind as is carried and fired with every occasion or temptation: this is the 'lust of concupiscence,' 1 Thes. iv. 5; and howsoever the world little cares for this evil, yet let true Christians strive to keep their hearts pure and clean from it, for they were as good have a burning fire in them, 1 Cor. vii. 9. Secondly, Those lusts fight against the soul, 1 Pet. ii. 12, they wound and pierce the conscience. Thirdly, The devil begins the frame of his work in these: he desires no more liberty than to be allowed to beget these lusts in the heart; he is not called 'the father of lusts' for nothing, John viii. 44; he can by these inordinate thoughts and affections erect unto himself such strongholds, 2 Cor. x. 5, as nothing but the mighty power of God can cast down. Fourthly, The apostle saith lust is foolish and noisome, and drowns men in perdition, 1 Tim. vi. 9. Fifthly, They hinder the efficacy of the word; that is the reason why divers men and women are 'ever learning, and are never able to come to the knowledge of the truth,' even this, they are carried about with divers lusts. Sixthly, They greatly purge upon faith and hope; they hinder or weaken the trust on the grace of God brought us by Jesus Christ; and therefore the apostle Peter counsels Christians not to fashion themselves according to the lusts of their former ignorance, 1 Pet. i. 13, 14. Seventhly, Those monstrous crimes mentioned in the first to the Romans grow originally from these lusts, Rom. i. 24.

The uses of all these together now follow: And, first, we may hence see great cause of thankfulness if the Lord have delivered us and kept us from these monstrous abominations; and especially if the Lord have made us sincere to look to, and to pray against, and in some happy measure to get victory over, those base lusts of the heart and evil thoughts. If there were nothing else to break the pride of our natures, this should, to consider seriously what monstrous devilish filthiness Satan hath wrought others to, and if God should leave us, might bring the best of us to; but especially this should teach us to use all possible remedies against these or any of these uncleannesses.

The remedies are of two sorts: first, For such as have been guilty of any of the former uncleannesses; secondly, For such as would preserve themselves against them, that they might not be defiled with them. There are two principal remedies for the unclean person. The first is marriage, or the right use of it. If it be in single persons, they must remember the apostle's words, 'It is better to marry than to burn,' 1 Cor. vii. 9; and if they be married, they must know that the love of their husbands or wives is the special help to drive away these impure pollutions; for such is the counsel of the Holy Ghost in the fifth of the Proverbs to them that are infected with these vicious and predominant inclinations,

Prov. v. 15, 21; and if they find (as it is certain every unclean person doth find) want of love to their own husbands or wives, then must they beg affection of God by daily and earnest prayer. But, in the second place, unclean persons must know that marriage alone will not serve turn, but they must add repentance; for lamentable experience shows that marriage without repentance abates not the power of lust. And therefore such as would deliver their souls from the vengeance to come due unto them for uncleanness, whether inward or outward, must seek to God, and with many prayers and tears beg pardon; they must be washed from filthiness by the blood of Christ, and the tears of true repentance. Neither let men deceive themselves; a little sorrow will not serve turn for these pollutions, and therefore the apostle useth the word 'washed,' 1 Cor. vi. 9, 11, to note the repentance of the Corinthians from these and such like sins. Now there can be no washing without water, neither will a drop or two serve turn.

Secondly, That those that are not guilty may be preserved against uncleanness, these things are of great use and profit: first, The word of God, and the sound knowledge of it; for, saith the Lord, in the second of Proverbs, 'If thou wilt receive my words, and hide my commandments within thee, if thou callest after knowledge and criest for understanding, if thou seekest her as silver and searchest for her as for treasures, then shall counsel and understanding preserve thee, and deliver thee from the evil way, and from the strange woman, which flattereth with her words, and forsaketh the guide of her youth, and forgetteth the covenant of her God,' Prov. ii. 1, 3, 4, 12, 16, 17. And hereunto agreeth David: for propounding this question, 'By what means a young man might cleanse his heart?' he answereth, 'By taking heed to the word,' Ps. cxix. 9. So St John, speaking to the young men, saith, 'The word of God abideth in you, and ye have overcome the wicked one,' 1 John ii. 14.

Secondly, Meditation is another great preservative: wouldst thou remove wickedness from thy flesh, even all the vanities of youth, then thou must 'remember thy Creator in the days of thy youth,' Eccles. xi. ult. with xii. 1. Thou must much and often think of the Lord God that made thee, not that thou shouldst wallow in the mire of these swinish pollutions. Besides, it is profitable to force thy heart to the often meditation of thine own mortality, that the thoughts of thy death may be a kind of death to thy lusts. This the apostle Peter implies when he saith, 'as strangers and pilgrims, abstain from fleshly lusts,' manifestly importing that if we did seriously think that we are here but strangers and pilgrims, it would tame the violence of these hateful lusts. Also we should much ponder upon the examples of such as have sinned, and the Lord hath fearfully visited them both for and in their sin; for all those things came unto them for 'ensamples,' and were 'written to admonish us upon whom the ends of the world are come,' 1 Cor. x. 6, 8, 11.

The third preservative is daily, earnest, and constant prayer unto God against them; and if we feel the beginning to rise in us, we should labour for special sorrows, even with grief of heart, to rack and crucify them. Lust will not usually out of the soul, if it get any footing, till it be fired out with confession and godly sorrow; and therefore the apostle useth the phrase of crucifying the lusts of the flesh, Gal. v. 24. And that prayer is a remedy, the apostle's own practice shews; for, when Satan buffeted him, he prayed unto God, and that thrice, that he might get the temptation to depart from him, 2 Cor. xii. 9.

The fourth preservative is to 'walk in love,' I mean Christian love to God's children, and such a love as hath both affection and society, and spiritual employment in the furtherance of the gospel. When the apostle would charge the Ephesians to avoid fornication and all uncleanness, he doth first advise them, and that seriously, to walk in love, Eph. v. 2, 3, as knowing that the exercise of true Christian love breeds such contentment and desire of holiness that it mightily fenceth the heart against all base lusts whatsoever. For they cannot stand together; and usually such as are withdrawn by concupiscence are likewise withdrawn from all profitable fellowship with God's children.

The fifth preservative is watchfulness in the daily observing of the first motions of lust, and in carefulness in directing the heart into God's presence, devoting in our covenants and desires our thoughts and affections to God. Thus Solomon, when he would give direction against the whorish woman, adviseth, 'My son, give me thy heart, and let thine eyes delight in my ways,' Prov. xxiii. 26, 27.

The last preservative is to avoid the causes and occasions of lust and uncleanness. The first is idleness. This was one of the causes of the detested uncleanness of Sodom, as the prophet Ezekiel shews, Ezek. xvi. 49; and contrariwise, diligence in our callings is a notable help to keep out inordinate desires and vain thoughts; and commonly persons overtaken with uncleanness abound with idleness. The second is fulness of bread,—that is, by a synecdoche, excess in meats and drinks, either for the measure or daintiness of them; and contrariwise, to beat down our bodies, 1 Cor. ix. 27, either by abstinence or sobriety in the use of the creatures, is a notable means to quench and abate those flames if they be risen, and to keep them also from that special aptness to rise. The third is, the high estimation of earthly things, and the too great liking of them; for this love secretly brings in lust: thus the apostle to Timothy says that the love of money and riches breeds noisome lusts, which, in short time, 'drown man in perdition,' 1 Tim. vi. 9. The like may be said of the estimation and too much viewing of apparel, beauty, &c. The fourth is ignorance and hardness of heart; for thus it was in those the apostle mentions in the fourth to the Ephesians, that greediness to defile themselves with all sorts of uncleanness arose and increased in them by reason of the insensibleness of the heart, and the blindness and emptiness of their minds, Eph. iv. 17, 18. And on the other side, lust cannot get such a head so long as any sound measure of knowledge is stirring in the mind, or tenderness remains in the heart; lust desires both a dark house and a dark mind. The fifth is evil company; and therefore the Holy Ghost gives this rule to those that would not be ensnared with the strange woman, 'Walk thou in the way of good men, and keep the way of the righteous,' Prov. ii. 20. The last is care for the flesh. It is the liberty men take not only to feed themselves in contemplative wickedness, but also to plod and cast about how to satisfy and fulfil their lusts, that doth so much confirm them in the custom of uncleanness; and therefore the apostle's counsel is, 'Take not care to fulfil the lusts of the flesh,' Rom. xiii. 14. Thus far of the sins of the seventh commandment; the sin against the tenth commandment follows.

Evil concupiscence. This vice contains all sorts of evil thoughts, and inclinations, and desires, after any kind of pleasure, profit, honour, but especially lustful inclinations or thoughts. And it differs from inordinate affection, because inordinate affection hath in it principally the burning of lust, and a kind of effeminateness, the soul being overcome and enthralled with the power of lust. Now, I think this concupiscence notes lust as it is in inclination or evil motion, before it come to that high degree of flaming or consent. And it is well called evil concupiscence, for there is a good concupiscence, both natural, and civil, and spiritual: natural, after meat, sleep, procreation, &c.; civil, which is an ordinate desire after lawful profits and pleasures; spiritual, and that is a lust for and after heavenly things, and so the spirit lusts against the flesh.

Now, that we may know the apostle hath great reason to counsel men to mortify evil thoughts, though they never come to consent, these reasons may shew: first, Concupiscence in the very inclination and first thoughts is a breeder,—it is the mother of all sorts of wickedness, if it be not betimes killed in the conception. The apostle James shews that concupiscence will be quickly enticed; yea, it will entice and draw away a man though from without it be allured with no object, James i. 14, 15; and when it hath drawn a man aside, it will conceive and breed with very contemplative pleasures; and when it hath conceived and lain in the womb of the mind, and lain there, nourished from time to time, unless God shew the greater mercy, it will bring forth,—bring forth, 1 say, a birth of some notable external evil action; and when it hath gone so far, like an impudent beldame, it will egg on still unto the finishing of sin, by custom in the practice, and so indeed (of itself) it will never leave till it hath brought forth (as a second birth) death, and that both spiritual and eternal death, and sometimes a temporal death too. Secondly, If these lusts go no further than the inward man, yet sin may reign even in these. There may be a world of wickedness in a man though he never speak filthy words or commit filthy actions. There is a conversing with the very inward lusts of the flesh, Eph. ii. 3, which may prove a man to be merely carnal and without grace, as well as outward evil life. Thirdly, This secret concupiscence may be a notable hindrance to all holy duties. This was that the apostle so bitterly cries out against in the seventh to the Romans. This was it that rebelled so against the law of his mind; and when he would do any good, it would be present to hinder it. This is it whereby the flesh makes war and daily fights against the spirit, Gal. v. 17; it is the lust after other things that enters into man's heart, and chokes the word, and makes it unfruitful, Mark iv. 19. What is the reason why many pray, and speed not? 'Is it not by reason of their lusts that fight in their members?' James iv. 1, 3, 4.

Quest. But is there any man that is wholly freed from these?

Ans. There is not. Every man hath in him divers kinds of evil thoughts; but yet there is great difference; for then is a man's estate dangerous when these lusts and evil thoughts are obeyed, Rom. vi. 11, served, Titus iii. 3, fulfilled, Eph. ii. 3, and cared for, Rom. xiii. 13. For those are the terms by which the power of them in wicked men are expressed; but so they are not in a child of God that walks before God in uprightness. The consideration of all this may break the hearts of civil, honest men; for hence they may see that God means to take account of their inward evil thoughts; and that, if very concupiscence be not mortified, it may destroy their souls, though they be never so free from outward enormities of life. Paul, while he was carnal, was unrebukable for outward conversation; but when the law shewed him his lusts and evil thoughts, he then saw all was in vain, Rom. vii. 7.

And covetousness, which is idolatry. Now followeth the sin against the first commandment; and it is described both in itself and in relation to God. In itself it is covetousness, and in relation to God it is idolatry.

Covetousness is a spiritual disease in the heart of man, flowing from nature corrupted and ensnared by Satan and the world, inclining the soul to an immoderate and confident, yet vain, care after earthly things, for our own private good, to the singular detriment of the soul. Covetousness I call a *disease*, for it is such a privation of good as hath not only want of virtue and happiness, but a position of evil in it, to be shunned more than any disease. For, as the text saith, it is an evil sickness. And this disease is *spiritual*, and therefore it is hard to be cured; no medicine can help it but the blood of Christ; it is not felt by the most, but hated only in the name of it. The subject where this disease is, is 'the heart of man,' for there is the seat or palace of this vice; and therefore St Mark adds covetousness to those vices St Matthew had said did defile a man, Mark vii. 22. The internal efficient moving cause of this evil is 'nature corrupted.' It is a sin every man had need to look to, for man's nature is stirred with it; it is a universal *quære*, 'Who will shew us any good?' Ps. iv. 7; and yet I say corrupted nature, for nature of itself is content with a little; it is corruption that hath bred this disease. The external efficient causes are the devil snaring, and the world tempting. The form of this evil is an inclination to the immoderate and confident care of earthly things, I say 'inclining the soul' to take in the lowest degree of covetousness. For some have their hearts exercised in it, and wholly taken up with it: their eyes and their hearts and their tongues are full of it. Now others are only secretly drawn away with it, and daily infected with the inclinations to it. I add, 'immoderate and confident care,' because honest labour or some desire after earthly things are not condemned. Only two things constitute this vice: first, Want of moderation, either in the matter, when nothing will be enough to satisfy their having, or in the measure of the care, when it is a distracting, vexing, continual care, that engrosseth in a manner all the thoughts and desires of a man; secondly, Carnal confidence, when man placeth his felicity and chiefest stay and trust in the things he either possesseth or hopeth for. I add, 'yet vain,' because let the covetous person bestow never so much care, or attain to never so much success of his cares, yet as Solomon saith, 'He that loveth silver, shall not be satisfied with silver; and he that loveth riches, shall be without the fruit thereof,' Eccles. v. 10. And after all his travail, his riches may perish while he looks on; or if they were more sure to continue, yet he shall not continue with them himself; for 'as he came forth of his mother's belly, he shall return naked, to go as he came, and shall bear nothing away of his labour, which he hath caused to pass by his hand. In all points as he came, so shall he go; and then what profit hath he that he hath travailed for the wind?' ver. 14, 15. The object of this care and desire is earthly things; for if it were a covetousness or desire of the best things, or spiritual gifts, that were both commended and commanded, 1 Cor. xiv. 1. These words, 'for his own private good,' note the end of the covetous man's care; for if all this care for earthly things were for God's glory, or the good of the church, it might be allowed; and I say for his good, because that he propounds to himself, though many times when he hath gotten much together, the Lord will not let him have the use of it. Note the best thing in the description is the effect of covetousness, and that is 'the singular detriment of the soul,' which may appear diversely. For first, covetousness doth infatuate and besot the mind of man, that it cannot understand. The prophet Isaiah saith of those 'dumb and greedy dogs,' that they could not understand, and he giveth the reason; 'for,' saith he, 'they all look to their own way, every one for his advantage and for his own purpose and profit,' Isa. lvi. 11, 12. And Solomon seems to say, that if covetousness be in the heart of a prince, it will make him destitute of understanding, Prov. xxviii. 16. And it is certain, mark it, worldly-minded persons are the most dull and incapable persons in spiritual things, almost of all other sorts of men; for though they would get a little understanding while they are hearing, yet the cares of life presently chokes all. Secondly, Covetousness, 'pierceth the soul through with many a sorrow,' 1 Tim. vi. 10. The covetous person is seldom or never free from one notable vexation or other. His heart is troubled, and he will trouble his house also; as Solomon saith, 'he that is greedy of gain, troubleth his own house,' Prov. xv. 27. All is continually in a tumult of haste and hurry; what with labour, and what with passion and contention, the covetous man and his household never live at heart's ease and rest. Thirdly, Covetousness, and the desire to be rich, bring into the soul a wonderful number of temptations and noisome lusts, enough to damn him, if he had no other sins, 1 Tim. vi. 9. Fourthly, It is here added that covetousness is idolatry; it makes a man an idolater. Mammon is the idol, and the worldling is the priest that sacrificeth to mammon. Now, the covetous man serves his mammon with a twofold worship; for with inward worship he loves, desires, delights in, and trusts in his wealth; and for his outward service he spends all his time upon his idol, either in gathering, or keeping, or increasing, or honouring it. Lastly, What should I number particulars? Covetousness! why, the apostle saith, it is the root of all evils. For there is almost no kind of sin but the sap of covetousness will nourish it. If the Lord had but the ripping up of the heart and life of a covetous person, and would describe his vices before us, oh! what swarm of all sorts of evils could the Lord find out? Well, let us be assured of this general, that howsoever covetous persons may colour matters, yet indeed they are wonderful vicious persons; neither are their sins the fewer or lesser because they discern them not; for the dust of earthly profits hath put out their eyes, they cannot see nor discern, as was before shewed.

Quest. But who is covetous? For all men, while they cry out against the sin, deny that they are covetous. It is rare to find any covetous person that will confess that he is covetous; and, therefore, for answer hereunto, it will not be amiss, out of the word of God, to shew the signs of a covetous man.

The first sign of a covetous man is the desire to have the sabbath over, that he might be at his worldly affairs. A covetous man thinks all the time set apart for God's service exceeding tedious and long; and he hath a great inward boiling of desire to have such times and employments past. The sabbath is wonderful burdensome to a worldly mind, especially if he be restrained from worldly employments. The prophet Amos bringeth in the covetous men of his time, saying thus in the discontentment of their hearts, ' When will the new moon be gone that we may sell corn, and the sabbath that we may set forth wheat?'

The second sign of covetousness is oppression and fraud, Prov. xxviii. 16, 1 Thes. iv. 6. When men, to compass gain, care not how they vex and rack the poor, or such as live under them, or in buying or selling, out of greediness of gain, circumvent and pill and defraud others, by customary lying, or false weights, measures, or balances, or any other fraudulent course, this is an evil covetousness. Usury also, that is, a desire to increase riches by interest, is a palpable sign of covetousness, especially in these times, when the sin of usury is so universally condemned; for if men were not besotted with the love of riches, they would not dare to live in such a damned sin. But I think all men easily know that usurers are covetous, and therefore I need not prove it.

The third sign of covetousness is greedy and distracting care; I mean such a care as devours a man's thoughts, that every day will keep possession in a man's soul, and run in his mind continually, both sleeping and waking, plodding and carking cares. And this may be discerned by comparing these cares with our care for eternal things. When we have more care for this world than for heaven, we need go no further, but resolve upon it, covetousness hath deceived us. Neither do I mean that they only are covetous, that immoderately disquiet themselves with continual cares for getting of treasures and the superfluities of abundance; for it is sure that covetousness may be in us in a high degree, though our cares be but about things that are necessary, as about the things we must eat or put on, as the comparing of the 15th verse of Luke xii. with ver. 21, 22, will shew. Now the care for necessaries is not simply forbidden, because we are bound to use the means with diligence and carefulness; but the care that is a sign of covetousness may be discerned by the very terms the evangelist St Luke useth to describe it by; for in the 22d verse, our Saviour saith, ' Take no thought for your life,' &c.; and by taking thought he notes a perplexed inward sorrowful and fearful care about life, and the things thereof. And ver. 26, he saith, 'Why take ye thought for the raiment?' as if he would have us note that it is a property of covetous cares to be deeply drowned in perplexity, even about trifles and small matters; and surely we may observe worldly-minded people, and one would wonder to see how they vex and disquiet themselves about every mean occasion, especialy if there be the least colour of any profit or loss towards. Again, our Saviour upbraideth those that are carried with those cares, that they have but 'a little faith;' whereby he shews that then our cares are faulty, and arise from the infection of covetousness, when they are raised by unbelief and mistrustfulness of God's providence or promise. Lastly, in the 29th verse, our Saviour saith thus: 'Therefore ask not what ye shall eat, or what ye shall drink, neither stand in doubt,' or, as ye may see it rendered in the margin, 'neither make discourses in the air;' and by these last words he notes another property of a covetous person, and that is when he hath his head tossed with cares or fears, either about the compassing of his profits, or preventing of losses, &c., he is so full of words and many questions, what he shall do, and how he shall avoid such and such a loss, that he hath never done either moaning himself, or consulting to no purpose, in things that either cannot be done, or not otherwise, &c.; or it may note this endless framing of projects for the compassing of his desires. Thus of the signs. Yet notwithstanding these signs, I must needs confess that covetousness is not easily discerned, both because it is an inward distrust in the spirit of a man, and also because there comes to this vice usually feigned words, 2 Pet. ii. 3; to hide it from the view of others, or subtle thoughts and evasions to blindfold the conscience within; and besides it is the nature of this sin quickly to darken the discerning of the mind; and therefore I think covetousness in the most may be well called coloured covetousness, 1 Thes. ii. 5, it is so on both sides masked.

The use of all should be to teach us, as the author to the Hebrews saith, to 'have our conversation without covetousness,' and to be 'content with the things we have,' resting steadfastly upon the promise of God, 'I will not fail thee nor forsake thee,' Heb. xiii. 5. And to this end we should pray, as David did, that God would 'incline our hearts to his testimonies, and not to covetousness,' Ps. cxix.

Quest. But what are the best remedies or preservatives against covetousness?

Ans. There are these things, among the rest, that are of great use to preserve us from covetousness, or to weaken the power of it.

The first is that which I mentioned before, viz., prayer to God daily that he would incline our hearts to his testimonies, that so we might have our minds drawn away from the cares of covetousness. The second is meditation. And there are divers things which, being seriously thought of, may prevail against the perplexed cares of covetousness. As, first, Example, and that either of godly men and the holiest worthies of the Lord, that in all ages have willingly confessed themselves to be strangers and pilgrims, looking for a city in another country, having a foundation whose builder and maker is God, Heb. xi. 9, 10, or else of wicked men; for it is so base a vice that it should be found in none but Gentiles, Mat. vi., that know neither God's promise nor providence; and sure it is found in none but ungodly men that are 'strangers from the covenant of promise.' Secondly, The nature of man; for consider, the soul of man is a celestial thing and divine, and hath nothing from the earth. And the body of man is erected, with a face towards heaven, and the whole earth is under man's feet, and hath its name from treading upon it, to note that man should walk on it with his feet, not dote on it with his heart. Thirdly, The nature of covetousness; it will never be satisfied, and how should it? For the desire of the covetous is not natural, but against nature. Natural desires are finite, but unnatural desires find no end, and therefore cannot be filled with the finite things of the world; besides, earthly things are vain and empty. Now the vessel that is only full of wind is empty still for all that. So is the mind of the covetous. His heart will be no more filled or satisfied with gold than his body with wind. *Non plus satiabitur cor hominis auro quam corpus aura.* Hereupon it is that a covetous man is always poor, and hath not what he hath, but hath his wealth as the prisoner hath his fetters, viz., to enthral him. Fourthly, The nature, promise, and providence of God. He is a 'heavenly Father,' Luke xii. 30. Is he a Father? Why then do we doubt of his willingness to help us? And is he a heavenly Father? Why then do we question his all-sufficiency to provide what we need? Besides, hath he given us life, and will he not give us food to preserve life? Doth he daily provide for thousand thousands of fowls, that are base creatures, and will he not provide for man, whom he created after his own image, and made him lord of all creatures? Doth he clothe the grass of the field, which is to-day, and to-morrow is cut down, and will he not clothe man? Oh, the weakness of our faith! Besides, is not the Lord engaged by promise never to leave us nor forsake us? Fifthly, The condition of the covetous. All his care cannot add a cubit to his stature. And besides, the poor and the usurer meet together in many things. One God made them both, one sun lights them both, one heaven covers them both, and one grave of earth shall hold them both. Sixthly, The gain of godliness. It is better thrift to covet after godliness, for it hath the promises of this life and the life to come, 1 Tim. vi. 8. And who can count the gain of godliness, seeing God is the godly man's portion, P's. xvi., and his exceeding great reward? Gen. xv. 1.

The third preservative is the daily practice of piety. If we would seek the kingdom of God first, both in the first part of our life, and in the first part of every day of our life, as well in our houses as in God's house, these religious duties constantly performed would be a great and continual help against worldly cares, they would cleanse our hearts of them, and daily prepare our hearts against them. But how can it be otherwise with a man than it is? They must needs live and die the drudges of the world, seeing they have no more care of holy duties at home or abroad; they live like swine, without all care of anything but rooting in the earth.

The fourth preservative is the due preparation for Christ's second coming. For when our Saviour Christ had dehorted men from the cares of this life, he adjoins this exhortation: 'Let your loins be girded about, and your lights burning; and ye yourselves like unto them that wait for their master, when he will return from the wedding, that when he cometh and knocketh they may open unto him immediately: blessed are those servants whom the lord when he cometh shall find watching,' &c. One great reason why covetous men do so securely continue in the immoderate cares for this world is because they do so little think of death and judgment. Whereas, on the other side, Christians do with some ease withdraw their hearts from the world, when they have inured themselves to die daily by the constant remembrance of their latter end, and by holding fast the evidence of faith and hope, waiting when Christ will call for them.

The fifth preservative is to shun the means and occasions of covetousness. And to this end it is good not to converse much with covetous persons, or to get ourselves liberty to conceive the hope of any long prosperity and rest in the world; and generally we should labour to observe our own hearts and other men's lives, and what we find to be a means to kindle or inflame covetous desires, that we should avoid, and betimes set against it, or mortify it. And thus far of covetousness. And thus also of the catalogue of sins from which he doth dissuade; the reasons follow.

Ver. 6. *For the which things' sake, the wrath of God cometh on the children of disobedience.*

Ver. 7. *Wherein ye also walked once when ye lived in them.*

These words contain two reasons to enforce the exhortation in the former verse. The one is taken from the evil effects of the former sins, ver. 6. The other is taken from their own experience, while they lived in the estate of corruption, ver. 7. In laying down the reason from the effect, two things are to be noted. First, what sin brings, viz., the wrath of God; secondly, upon whom, viz., upon the children of disobedience.

Before I come to entreat of the wrath of God apart, I consider it as it stands in coherence with the former reason. For in these words we are assured that man living and continuing in filthiness and covetousness shall not escape God's wrath; for they incur both his hatred and his plagues, both which are signified by the word 'wrath.' And if any ask what plagues filthy persons and covetous persons shall feel, I answer briefly and distinctly, that neither of them shall escape God's wrath, as the scriptures plentifully shew. The filthy person brings upon himself God's curse, temporal, corporal, spiritual, and eternal. Temporal, for whoredom, and any kind of uncleanness, brings upon men many temporal plagues in their estate, the fire of God's judgments consuming many times their whole increase, as hath been shewed before. Corporal, for God many times meets the sins of the body with judgments upon the body; so that many filthy persons, after they have consumed their flesh and their body by loathsome diseases which follow this sin, in the end say with the foolish young man, 'O how have I hated instruction, and despised correction! Now I am brought almost into all evil in the midst of the assembly,' Prov. v. 12, 14. Spiritual, for uncleanness breeds in many a reprobate sense, Rom. i. 24, 26, &c., and final impenitency. Many also for their filthiness are pursued with secret and fearful terrors of conscience, and sometimes frenzy, and desperate perturbations. Eternal, for the adulterer destroys his own soul, and is shut out of the kingdom of heaven, as hath been also before declared. Neither let the covetous person think he shall speed any better, for God hates him wonderfully. And therefore the prophet Ezekiel saith, that the Lord smites his fists at the covetous, Ezek. xxii. 13, which is a borrowed phrase, to express most bitter and sharp threatenings. Now lest the people should object that those were but great words, the Lord would not do so, they would deal well enough with the Lord; he preventeth it, and saith, 'Can thine heart endure, or can thine hands be strong in the days that I shall have to do with thee? I, the Lord, have spoken it, and will do it,' ver. 14. Let covetous persons, without further inquiry, assure themselves that covetousness is a main cause of all the evils that are upon them or theirs, and besides, they may be assured that all the service they do to God is abhorred, and mere lost labour: 'it were to no purpose if they would bring him incense from Sheba, and sweet calamus from a far country; their burnt-offerings would not be pleasant, nor their sacrifices sweet unto him,' Jer. vi. 13, 20.

Object. But covetous persons are of most men so well furnished, that there is not that means to bring them to any great hurt.

Sol. The prophet shews that God can lay a stumbling-block before them, and father and son together may fall upon it, and neighbour and friend may perish together, Jer. vi. 21. The Lord hath means enough, when men little think of it, to bring down rebellious sinners.

Object. But we see covetous persons and wealthy worldlings escape the best and longest of many others.

Sol. The prophet Amos saith 'The Lord hath sworn by the excellency of Jacob, I will never forget any of their works,' Amos viii. 5-7. Though the Lord may defer, yet certainly he will never forget; and therefore they are not a jot the better for escaping so long. But howsoever they might escape outward judgments, they yet may be infallibly sure they have sinned against their own souls, Hab. ii. 10, and that they shall know in the day of their death; 'their riches shall not then profit them, when the Lord taketh away their soul,' Job xxvii. 8; 'he that is a great oppressor shall not prolong his days,' Prov. xviii. 16; for 'he that getteth riches, and not by right, shall leave them in the midst of his days, and at his end shall be a fool,' Jer. xvii. 11. How horrible then shall that voice be, 'Thou fool, this night shall thy soul be taken from thee.' Luke xii. 16. And thus far of the words, as they concern the coherence with the former words. Now I consider them as they are in themselves. And first of the wrath of God.

Wrath of God. It is apparent that wrath in God belongs to his justice. And justice may be considered as it flows from God four ways: first, As he is a free Lord of all, and so his decrees are just,' Rom. ix 13, 14. Secondly, as he is God of all: and so the common works of preserving both good and bad, are just, 1 Tim. iv. 14, Mat. v. 45. Thirdly, As a Father in Christ, and so his excellency, the God of believers; and thus he is just in performing his promises and infusing his grace, and in bestowing the justice of his Son. Fourthly, As judge of the world, and so his justice is not only distributive, but corrective; and unto this justice doth wrath belong.

Anger in man is a perturbation or passion in his heart; and therefore it hath troubled divines to conceive how anger should be in the most pure, happy, and bountiful nature of God, and the rather seeing affections are not properly in God. Neither is their declaration full enough that say it is given to God improperly and by anthropopathy; for I am of their opinion that think anger is properly in God: first, In such a manner as agrees to the nature of God, that is, in a manner to us inconceivable; Secondly, In such a sense as is revealed in scripture.

The wrath of God in scripture is taken sometimes for his just decree and purpose to revenge, John iii. 36; sometimes for commination or threatening to

2 o

punish. So some think it is to be taken in those words of the prophet Hosea: 'I will not do according to the fierceness of my wrath,' Hosea xi. 9, that is, according to my grievous threatenings. Sometimes it is taken for the effects or punishments themselves, as in the epistle to the Romans, 'Is God unrighteous which bringeth wrath?' Rom. iii. 5. It is well rendered 'which punisheth.'

The wrath of God is distinguished by divers degrees, and so hath divers names; for there is wrath present, and wrath to come. Present wrath is the anger of God in this present life, and is either impendent, John iii. 36, or poured out. Wrath impendent is the anger of God hanging over men's heads, ready to be manifested in his judgments; and so wrath hangs in the nature of God, and in the threatenings of his word, and in the possibilities of the creatures. Wrath poured out, is the judgment of God fallen upon men for their sins by which they provoked God, and so there was great wrath upon the people in the destruction of Jerusalem, Luke xxi. 23; and thus he revealeth his wrath from heaven upon the unrighteousness of men, Rom. i. 17. Wrath to come, Mat. iii. 7, Rom. ii. 5, is that fearful misery to be declared upon the soul of the impenitent at his death, and upon soul and body at the day of judgment, in the everlasting perdition of both.

But that we may be yet more profitably touched with the meditation of this point, I propound six things concerning God's wrath further to be considered: first, The fearfulness of it; secondly, What it is that works or brings this wrath upon us; thirdly, The signs to know God's wrath; fourthly, The means to pacify it; fifthly, The signs of wrath pacified; and lastly, The uses of all.

For the first, The fearfulness and greatness of God's wrath or anger for sin may appear three ways: first, By scripture; secondly, By similitude; thirdly, By example. That God's anger for sin is exceeding terrible and fearful, I will shew by one place of scripture only, and that is the first of Nahum the prophet; for he saith, 'God is jealous, and the Lord revengeth, the Lord revengeth,' where the repetition shews the certainty of it, that God will be as sure to revenge as ever the sinner was to sin. But this is more confirmed, when he saith, 'He is the Lord of anger;' as if he would import that his anger is his essence, as if he were all made of anger, and that he is the author of all the just anger that is in the world. And if the drops of anger in great men have such terror in it, what is the main ocean of anger which is in God himself? And to assure us yet further of the terror of his wrath, he addeth, 'The Lord will take vengeance on his adversaries;' which signifieth that the Lord will account of impenitent sinners, as a man accounts of his worst enemies, and therefore the Lord will shew his displeasure to the uttermost of his deserts and his justice. And therefore if any do object that they see it otherwise, for the plagues of wicked men are not so many nor so great as their sin, he answereth that, and saith, that the Lord 'reserveth wrath for his enemies.' He hath not inflicted upon them all they shall have, there is the greatest part behind; the full vials of his fury are not yet poured out. And if any should reply, that they have observed that wicked men have prospered long, and escaped for a great while without any punishments to speak of, the prophet answereth that, and saith, that the Lord is 'slow to anger,' that is, he is many times long before he manifests his great displeasure; but he is 'great in power,' that is, he is of singular fierceness and irresistibleness when he doth enter into judgment; he will not fail, nor be hindered. And if any would hope that God would change his mind, that also is prevented, the prophet avouching it confidently that he will not surely 'clear the wicked.' And this is the more certain, because of the dreadful means that the Lord hath to declare his anger: 'His way is in the whirlwind, and in the storm, and the clouds are the dust of his feet.' The meaning is, that God hath ways to execute his judgment—ways, I say, that are irresistible (for who can stay a whirlwind?)—and terrible like the storm, plagues falling thick and threefold, like the drops of the tempest; and in the means the Lord can run like a giant, running fiercely, and raising the dust with his feet. And to this give all the creatures witness: 'He rebuketh the sea, and it drieth. Bashan is wasted, and Carmel, and the flower of Lebanon is wasted. The mountains tremble before him, and the hills melt, and the earth is burnt at his sight; yea, the world, and all that dwell therein.' And therefore, 'who can stand before his wrath? or who can abide the fierceness of his wrath? His wrath is poured out like fire, and the rocks are broken by him.'

The wrath of God, to shew the exquisite and intolerable and remediless pain that wicked men feel when they bear it, is compared to a consuming fire; and, to note the infiniteness of it, God himself is said to be a consuming fire, Heb. xii. 29, Deut. iv. 24. Moses also saith, that the fire that is kindled in God's wrath shall burn to the bottom of hell, and it were able to consume the earth with her increase, and set on fire the foundation of the mountains, Deut. xxxii. 22.

Thirdly, Who can think the anger of God not to be infinitely terrible, that can but seriously consider these examples and precedents of it?—first, God's reprobating or fore-damning of millions of men; secondly, The sin of Adam pursued with such inconceivable judgments upon him and his name; thirdly, The drowning of the old world, the burning of Sodom, the opening of the earth to swallow up the rebellious, the sea swallowing up Pharaoh and his host; fourthly, The forlorn estate of the Gentiles, not looked after for many hundred years; fifthly, The Jews, sometimes the only people to whom the Lord drew near, now made a curse and astonishment and a hissing throughout the earth; sixthly, The torments which Christ himself endured when he was but surety for sinners; seventhly, What are wars, famines, pestilences, diseases, seditions, heresies, and the infinite molestations in the life of man, but so many evident proofs of wonderful anger in God; eighthly, The testimonies of afflicted consciences be lively in this point: when but a drop of anger lights upon the soul of man in this world, how unable is he to sustain his spirit—what floods of tears flow from his wounded heart! lastly, The burning of the world, and the flames of hell shall one day make full proof of God's anger. And thus of the first point.

For the second, Wrath is wrought or brought upon us four ways: first, The law works wrath, for being transgressed, it breeds displeasure, pleads for judgment, records sin, and presents it in God's sight; secondly, Christ in the ministry of the word applies wrath, or discovers God's indignation, and so he is said to smite and slay the wicked, Rev. xix. 15;

thirdly, The magistrate is a revenger in executing God's wrath, Isa. xi. 3; fourthly, Wrath is brought upon us by God's army: the creatures are God's warriors, they fight for the Lord against sinners, and are speedily and irresistibly armed when God is pleased to raise them.

Thirdly, Concerning the signs of God's anger, we must understand that God's eternal anger towards other men in particular cannot be known, nor his temporal anger by any ordinary way of certainty, except it be extraordinarily by revelation, as to the prophets or apostles; for by outward things we cannot know God's love or hatred to particular persons, only God's public anger to public states may be known, and so may his private anger to ourselves in special.

There are three signs to know God's public anger: First, The prediction of his ministers: as, extraordinarily, the prophets from vision or revelation did foretell the judgments to ensue. And, ordinarily, wrath may be known by the comminations of faithful preachers. For when upon observation of threatenings in the law made to such sins as then abound, they do with one consent in many places with instance and confidence give warning of plagues to ensue, it is time for the world to awaken. The Lord's secrets are with his servants, and he will make good their righteous threatenings. Secondly, The signs in heaven, or earth, or sea. Prodigious sights or signs in the sun, or moon, or comets, or strange births, or the extraordinary raging of the seas, and such like. Thirdly, Public plagues are both signs of wrath present, and withal they give warning of greater wrath to come if we do not repent. Such are famine, war, pestilence, and other raging diseases, the death of great princes, and the sudden and common death of the best men, these all foretell evil to come. As we may know fire, so may we know God's anger. We know fire either by the report of men worthy to be credited, or by the smoke, or by the flame beginning to break out; and so may discern God's wrath, either by the relation of his ambassadors that are faithful men, or by the smoke of prodigies or wonders in heaven and earth, or else by the flame of judgments already begun. And thus of the signs of God's public anger.

The signs of God's anger to a particular man are

such as these: first, If a man have not the marks of a child of God upon him; for whom God loves and is not angry with, they are marked with peculiar graces as indelibly as they were marked in Ezekiel with the letter *Tau*, Ezek. ix. Secondly, If he find himself directly under the threatenings of God's word. Thirdly, If there be no effectual working of the Spirit of grace in the use of the means. It is a plain sign of God's anger when a man hears the word powerfully preached, and reads and prays without all affection or life, and is so constantly; for if the Lord were pleased, he would shew himself in the use of the means of communion with him. Fourthly, A man may gather something by his crosses; for if he find a sting in them, that God fights against him in them, so as they pierce and vex and disquiet his soul with perplexity, but especially if he find his heart also closed with hardness, so as he do not call when the Lord bindeth him, this is in all likelihood not only a sign of wrath, but that the wrath increaseth, Job xxxvi. 13, this is the rod of indignation. Fifthly. If a man live in some sins, they are manifest signs of wrath; as persecution, 1 Thes. ii. 16; whoredom, Prov. xii. 14; hatred of the brethren, 1 John iii. 14; withholding the truth in unrighteousness, Rom. i. 18; covetousness and uncleanness, Eph. v. 3, 5; and generally all sins contained in any of the catalogues against which the Lord denounceth his judgments in several scriptures. Lastly, Sometimes God's anger is felt in the terrors and pain of the conscience, the Lord making some men to feel the edge of his axe, and fighting against them with his terrors. Now wheresoever these are felt by a soul that hath not been truly humbled for sin, they are assured pledges and beginnings of God's wrath from heaven.

Hitherto of the greatness, means, and signs of God's anger. Now of the way to pacify God's anger when it is perceived. God's public anger is pacified and stayed: first, By the prayers and fastings of the righteous. And, therefore, it is the prophet Joel's counsel, that if they would have the Lord 'repent him of the evil, and return and leave a blessing behind him,' they must 'sanctify a fast, and call a solemn assembly,' Joel ii. 13, 14, &c.; secondly, By the severe execution of justice by magistrates upon notorious offenders, and thus Phinehas stayed the plague, Num. xxv. 1; thirdly, By the general repentance of the people, and thus God's anger towards Nineveh was pacified, Jonah iii.; fourthly, and especially, By the intercession of Christ entreating for a city or nation; so was Jerusalem delivered out of captivity, as the prophet Zechariah declares, Zech. i. 12.

Concerning the pacifying of God's anger to particular persons, I will first consider what will not pacify it, and then what will pacify it. For the first, No multitude of gifts can deliver thee, and the most mighty helps cannot cause the Lord to withdraw his anger, Job xxxvi. 18. It will not avail thee to come before the Lord with burnt-offerings and with calves of a year old. The Lord will not be pleased with thousands of rams, or with ten thousand rivers of oil. Nor will the son of thy body make an atonement for the sins of thy soul, Micah vi. 6, 7. To cry, 'Lord, Lord,' at home, Mat. vii., or 'The temple of the Lord, the temple of the Lord,' Jer. vii., abroad, will not a whit abate of his fierce anger; and as little will it avail to build churches, mend highways, erect tombs for dead prophets, or the like works of labour or cost.

Now for the affirmative, if we speak properly, nothing will quench God's anger but the blood of Christ; for he is the propitiation for our sin, 1 John ii. 2, Rom. v. 9. Yet in some respects, and as means the Lord doth appoint unto us, that we might be capable of reconciliation, these things are available: first, The duties of mortification, as confession of sin, and judging of ourselves, and examining of our hearts and lives. 'If we acknowledge our sins, he is faithful and just to forgive us our sins,' 1 John i. 9; and 'if we judge ourselves, the Lord will give over judging us,' 1 Cor. xi. 34. If disobedient Israel will return and know his iniquities, the Lord will not let his wrath fall upon him, Jer. iii. 12, 13. Godly sorrow also is very available to quench wrath. If Jerusalem will wash her heart, she shall be saved, Jer. iv. 14; the Lord will hear the voice of our weeping, Ps. vi. 8. Prayer also is of great use and force, for the Lord is a God that heareth prayer, Ps. lxv. 2. And the prophet Zephaniah sheweth, that if the people can learn a language once to call upon the name of the Lord in the sincerity of their hearts, Zeph. iii. 9; he will not pour upon them that fierce wrath which shall certainly fall upon all the families that call not upon his name.

Secondly, Faith in the blood of Christ procureth reconciliation and forgiveness of the sins that are past, through the patience of God, Rom. iii. 25; especially the work of faith, whereby a Christian, perceiving God's anger, and encouraged with the support of God's covenant and promise in Christ, doth in all tenderness of heart, importune God's free mercy, and wrestle and strive with importunity, casting himself upon Christ for shelter, and seriously setting himself against every iniquity, even because there is hope.

Finally, We may discern that God is pacified divers ways: first, By induction from the practice of the former rules; for if we do what God requires, we may conclude and infer we shall receive what God promiseth. Secondly, It may be perceived by God's presence in the means. If we find our hearts unloosed, and the passages of the means again opened, that is a comfortable testimony that the Lord is returned. Thirdly, It may be perceived by the witness of the Spirit of adoption, speaking peace to our consciences, Ps. lxxxv. 8, and with unutterable joys quieting and satisfying our hearts.

Uses. The use followeth. And first, The doctrine of God's wrath may greatly humble and astonish impenitent sinners. 'Is the anger of the Lord kindled against thee? How long then wilt thou be without innocency?' Hosea viii. 5. Be not a mocker, lest thy bonds increase. Isa. xxviii. 22. Art thou an unclean person, a railer, a drunkard, an usurer, a swearer, a liar, a profaner of God's sabbaths, a voluptuous epicure, a carnal worldling, or the like? Be not deceived, nor let any deceive thee with vain words, crying peace, peace, daubing with untempered mortar; for assuredly the wrath of God for these things, cometh upon the children of disobedience, and 'who knows the power of his wrath?' Ps. xc. 11. Secondly, Seeing God's wrath is so exceeding terrible and fierce, blessed are all they that are delivered from it in Jesus Christ. We should be stirred up to constant thankfulness, because the Lord hath forgiven us the punishment of our sins, so as now there is no condemnation to us, being in Christ Jesus, 1 Thes. v. 8, 9, Heb. iii. 11, 12.

Lastly, Seeing the Lord's anger is so dreadful, we should all learn to walk before him in all uprightness, and fear, and trembling, fencing ourselves with the breastplate of faith, and the helmet of hope, being in all things sober and watchful, taking heed to ourselves that we be not hardened through the deceitfulness of sin. And thus of the wrath of God.

The second main thing in this verse to be considered of is, the persons upon whom it falls, viz., 'the children of disobedience.' And by children of disobedience, he meaneth generally wicked and unregenerate men. Now, wicked men are of two sorts. Some are clearly out of the church, and have been branded in several ages with several terms of distinction; as now the infidels, and before, all the uncircumcised Gentiles. Before the flood, they were called sons of men. Now others are in the church, and are children of God by creation, general vocation, and external profession; but indeed are wicked and profane Esaus. The former sort were disobedient men, and the latter are disobedient children. And these disobedient children in the church are of two sorts: for some will not be tied to live in their father's house, but that they may the more securely sin and wallow in all filthy abominations, they shun God's house for the most part, and live without any conscionable subjection to any ministry. Such was the prodigal son, and such are our common swearers, drunkards, and unclean persons; nay, they go further, for they speak evil of their Father's house, and slander their own mother's sons. Now, the other sort live in their Father's house, they come to hear, and receive the sacraments; they are there at bed and board, but yet they will do what they list. They will not be persuaded by the word, Spirit, or servants of God; and so they are children of unpersuadableness. They will not believe their Father's threatenings or promises, and so they are children of incredulity. They will not conform themselves to their Father's will, and so are called children of disobedience.

Now, the estate of both these sorts of disobedient children is, that the fearful wrath of God is upon them; no father can so plague and cast off a wicked son, as they are sure to be plagued and cast off of God. As they are children of disobedience by their own stubbornness, so are they children of wrath by God's justice; and if they continue thus, they may prove children of perdition.

Quest. But how may the children of disobedience be known?

Ans. We may gather signs either from the consideration of these words, or from other scriptures. From these words two ways: first, He is a child of disobedience that is led and ruled, and hath all his thoughts and affections, and his actions, as it were, framed and begotten, and nursed up by the corruption of his nature, arising from the disobedience of the first man, or by the temptations of Satan, the prince of all darkness and disobedience. It is one thing to sin by infirmity, to fall by occasion into a sin, and another thing to be led and ruled, and to frame one's life and employment, after the rules and projects that are hatched by the flesh or Satan. To be a child to sin, that is to be ruled and mastered and led by it, to be as it were at the command of lust and corruption, that is not in a child of God, standing in uprightness. Secondly. The word here rendered disobedience, imports unteachableness, such a disobedience as is wilful; when a man sins, and will sin, and will not be persuaded either by God's word, or God's Spirit, or God's people, that would advise or admonish him. To be of an incurable or unteachable disposition, is a rank sign of a child of disobedience.

Further, if we mark the coherence in the second chapter of the epistle to the Ephesians, ver. 2, compared with the first, we may easily discern that a child of disobedience is 'dead in trespasses and sins.' His soul can lie at rest, though he be guilty of never so many sins. Cast a mountain on a dead man, and he will not complain or ail anything. And sure it is a notable sign of a child of disobedience, to be guilty of a multitude of sins, and yet to be senseless under them; to be able to go from day to day, and week to week, and month to month, and never to ail anything, for any sound remorse he finds for his sin. Especially when men are at that pass, that the prophet Jeremiah complained of, that 'though God strike them, yet they are not grieved; yea, though the Lord consume them, they refuse to receive correction, and make their faces harder than a rock, refusing to return,' Jer. v. 3.

Quest. But may not the wrath of God come upon his own children? Is God never angry with his own servants?

Ans. God may be angry with his own people; for when the prophet David saith, ' his anger endureth but a moment,' Ps. xxx. 5, he implies then that God will be angry. And in the 89th psalm, though the Lord saith he will not take away his goodness and his mercy, yet if they keep not his law, he saith expressly, he will ' visit their transgression with the rod, and their iniquity with stripes,' Ps. lxxxix. 32, 33. And thus he is angry with them sometimes for their covetousness, Isa. lv. 17; sometimes for their careless worship, Isa. lxiv. 5–7; sometimes for unworthy receiving, 1 Cor. xi.; sometimes for their loss of their first love, Rev. ii.; but generally every gross sin angers God, by whomsoever it be committed. But yet there is great difference between God's anger towards his own children, and that wrath that cometh upon the children of disobedience; and that principally in three things: 1. Wrath coming upon the faithful is not eternal, but temporary, and in this life only, for they are ' delivered from the wrath to come,' 1 Thes. i. 10; for there is no condemnation to them that are in Christ Jesus, they are already passed from death to life. But so are not wicked men; for God is so angry with them in this life that his anger may continue for ever, and not be extinguished in their very death. And not only so, but God's anger with his own children, even in this life, is not for all their days, but only a very short time of their life. For as David saith, ' his anger endureth but a moment: weeping may endure for a night, but joy cometh in the morning,' Ps. xxx. 5. And in another place he saith, ' he will not always chide, neither will he keep his anger for ever.' Ps. ciii. 9. And the Lord witnesseth by the prophet Isaiah, that he forsaketh but for a small moment, he hideth his face in a little wrath, but he hath mercy with everlasting kindness, Isa. liv. 7, 8. When a child of God falleth, he is sure he shall rise, Micah vii. 8: but it is not so with the ungodly. 2. As God's wrath differs in the continuance, so it differs in the measure: it is milder towards his children than it is towards the children of disobedience; which appears to be so two ways: for, first, God's anger, as it is manifested in outward judgments upon his own people, is ever proportioned to their strength: he doth not consider what their sin deserves, but what their spirits are able to sustain. 'He will not suffer them to be tempted above that which they are able, but will give issue with the temptation, that they may be able to bear it,' 1 Cor. x. 13. And the prophet Isaiah sheweth that the Lord hath great care lest, by contending over long with his people, the spirit should fail, and the soul which he hath made, Isa. lvii. 16. And the prophet David shews, that God 'deals not with his people after their sins, nor rewards them after their iniquities; but as a father pitieth his children, so the Lord pitieth them that fear him,' Ps. ciii. 10-14. But now with the wicked it is much otherwise, for the Lord never asks what strength they have to bear it, or how they will take it, but what sin they have committed, and how they have deserved it. Besides, the affections of God's children are sweetened with many mercies; for though the Lord be angry for their sin, yet, if they will seek God and work righteousness, Isa. lxiv. 5, they may hold out to bear the cross, for the Lord will meet them in the use of the means, to the great ease and joy of their hearts. Excellently speaketh the prophet David unto the Lord, acknowledging this point, when he said, 'Thou answeredst them, O Lord our God; thou wast a God that forgavest them, though thou tookest vengeance of their inventions,' Ps. xcix. 8. And the prophet Micah seemeth to say, that while God's people sit in darkness, yet the Lord can be a light unto them, Micah vii. 7, 8, for their God will hear them. And herein also the Lord reserveth his mercies from the wicked, so as when they fall they have no assurance of rising, nor is the Lord careful to lighten their darkness: I mean, they have no promise for it. For if the Lord shew them favour, if they repent not, it will make them more inexcusable, and their judgment the heavier. 3. It differs in the end, for the end of God's wrath on his own servants is their good and salvation. They are judged, that they might not perish with the world, 1 Cor. xi. 32; and they are whipped by the Father of spirits, that they may bring forth the quiet fruit of righteousness, Heb. xii. 11. In a word, God's judgments are as medicines to heal them. But, on the other side, wicked men are vessels of wrath, and all tends to the fitting of them to destruction. The Lord comes not to them to try, but to consume; not to better them, but for their wilful impenitence to declare his justice upon them. All these their differences are notably expressed by the prophet Isaiah in his 27th and 28th chapters; for he sheweth that the Lord is a careful and wise husbandman, and the husbandman in nature hath this discretion, that he should not plough all day to sow, Isa. xxviii. 24. So is it with the Lord; he doth not continue still ploughing with long furrows upon the backs of the righteous. When he hath ploughed up the fallow ground of their hearts, he will not still go over them to break the clods that remain; but having once made himself a furrow, he will sow and not plough. And for the second, the prophet seriously expostulateth with such as should anyway incline to think that the wicked and godly were smitten alike. 'Hath he smitten him,' saith the prophet, 'as he smote those that smote him?' Isa. xxvii. 7. As if he should ask, hath the Lord plagued Israel as he plagued those that were enemies unto Israel? And then he shews this difference, that when the Lord came to visit Israel, he contended with him 'in measure,' and smote him 'in his bunches,' ver. 8; whereas when God smites at a wicked man, he smites at the root, and after many blows he will continually have him down. And for the least [1] difference, the prophet shews further, that 'by this shall the iniquity of Jacob be purged, and this is all fruit to take away his sin,' ver. 9; as if he would plainly affirm that God meant so to cast Israel into the furnace as nothing should be left but the dross; his purpose was therefore to afflict him that he might medicine him against his sin. And thus of the sixth verse.

Ver. 7. *In which ye also walked some time when ye lived in them.*

These words contain the second reason to enforce the mortification of vice, and it is taken from their own experience; as if he would say, ye have lived a long time in these corruptions and sins, and therefore it is sufficient that you have spent the time past in these lusts of the Gentiles, it is high time now to abandon them. Besides, you should remember the misery you lived in by reason of sin, and

---

[1] Qu. 'last'?—ED.

from thence learn to confirm yourselves in a constant course of resisting and striving against the occasions and beginnings of those sins.

From the coherence and the general consideration of the whole verse divers things may be briefly noted: first, That the knowledge and meditation of a man's misery by nature is a good medicine to kill lust and covetousness. The apostle, like a wise physician, useth here the counsel hereunto as a principal part of his direction. For in that he puts them in mind of it, it shows that they should mind it by themselves much more. For not only it will show that these sins did then abound, but the very thought of such a woful estate will beat down and kill by degrees the vicious inclinations of nature unto such sins. Secondly, In that the Colossians can bear it to be told of their sins past, it gives us occasion to take notice of this for a truth, that where a man hath soundly repented of any sin, he can easily bear it, to be touched with the remembrance of it, and with lowliness doth endure the needful discourse concerning it. It is a notable testimony that a man hath not truly repented of sin, when he is so impatient and unquiet in the mention or remembrance of sin. If a man have a wounded arm, while it is uncured, the least touch of it makes a man start and cry out; but when it is whole, you may grip it hard, and yet he aileth nothing at all. So it is with our consciences in matters of sin. They are but in a miserable case that rage, and fret, and revile when the sins they have lived in are by public doctrine disgraced or threatened. But may some one say, To what end doth the apostle so often put them in mind of their sinfulness and misery past? I answer, He doth it for great reasons. For the more men think of their misery by nature, the more it quickeneth to a sense and admiration of God's mercy, that hath drawn them out of such a wretched estate. Besides, it is a notable means to keep a Christian humble, and to make him watchful over a nature that by lamentable experience hath been so prone to sin, and it serves to stir up Christians to a more eager desire and diligence in using the means to advantage them in knowledge and grace. 'Tis now time to redeem the time that hath been so long lost. And it will make a child of God industrious in God's work, seeing he hath spent so much time in the service of the devil, the world, and the flesh. And further it helps a man to some measure of patience and meekness and compassion, in dealing with the sins of other men, considering that he himself hath been 'unwise, disobedient, serving the lust and divers pleasures,' &c. And lastly, (as was before noted) it serves to kill the daily lusts that may bud and sprout out after calling.

Now concerning the remembering of the sins of others, we must know the apostle had a warrant by his calling and commission to rehearse the sins of others. For God's ministers are enjoined to shew God's people their sins. But a like liberty is not lawful to every private man. Private men may remember others of their estate past, if it may stir them up to thankfulness, or if it may further them in humiliation for new offences, or they may exhort one another, lest any be deceived by sin, and so for prevention of corruption unto which they are by nature prone, or in some special cases to clear God's justice against hard-hearted sinners. Otherwise it is a vile and sinful course to be raking into the lives of others; but especially to be grating upon the faults past of penitent sinners. Where God hath pardoned, what hath man to do to impute? And thus of the coherence and general consideration of the words.

This verse contains two specialities of their misery by nature: first, Their continuance in sin, in that he saith, ' ye walked;' secondly, Their delight in sin, in that he saith, ' ye lived in them,' that is, it was the life of your life.

In which. That is, in which sins, and so it teacheth us that we should be more troubled for sin than for crosses. For he doth not say, in which miseries or judgments, but in which sins and corruptions. As any are more spiritual, sin is their greatest sorrow, and as any are more carnal, they are more troubled with crosses.

Ye. A man can never be soundly and profitably humbled till he mind his own sins. The knowledge of sin that is transient is dangerous, as we may see in the pharisee: the more he knows by the publican, the prouder he is in himself; but the knowledge that is reflected is profitable. And therefore the publican that troubled himself about his own sin, went home more justified than the other. And therefore the apostle here tells not of the misery of other men, but expressly guides them to the consideration of their own misery. This should teach us, without shifting or delay to search and try our own ways, and to grow skilful in recounting the evils of our own lives. The true knowledge of ourselves is a great step in a holy life. It is that the most of us never attain to. And yet it is of singular use; it would make us humble in ourselves, compassionate towards others, easy to be admonished, tender-hearted in God's worship, more apt to godly sorrow, and of great ripeness and dexterity of knowledge in cases of conscience.

Also. Sin is a poison that overflows all sorts of men. This *also* takes in rich men, and great men, and learned men, and old men, and the civiller sort of men. There is no estate, calling, or condition of men, nor sex, or nation, but they have been infected with this plague. It hath run over the whole earth. And therefore it should humble rich men, and learned men, and all sorts of men. Look not at thy wealth, or thy wit, or thy learning, or thy nobility, or thy fame amongst men, look at thy filthy nature; thou hast now, or thou hast had, the plague upon thy soul; and as wise, and learned, and rich, and civil, and noble as thou, have died of this sickness, and are in hell.

Walked. This word notes not only inclination to sin, but action; not only words, but practice; and in practice, not only a falling by infirmity, but continuance and progress in sin. To walk in sin is to proceed in sin from one kind to another, and from one sin to another, and to lie and dwell in sin. And this is the wretched condition and thraldom of every one by nature, thus hard is it to give over sin, and were it not for the great mercy of God, thus would all men continue.

Quest. But what should be the reason that men continue so long in sin, and are so loth to get out of this miserable path?

Ans. The soul by nature is dead in sin, Eph. ii. 1, and all flesh is covered with a veil of blindness, Isa. xxv. 8, and Satan, the prince of darkness, works effectually in the children of disobedience; besides, the course and custom of the world, that lies in wickedness, 1 John v. 18, Eph. ii. 2, much hardens and confirms the sinner, and the mind and will of the flesh is stubborn. And withal every wicked man is a great student; he deviseth and imagineth, and forecasteth how to find out ways, to set himself in a way that is not good. And many times God in his fearful judgment delivers many a man up to a spiritual lethargy and slumber and reprobate mind, 'that hearing he may hear, and not understand, and seeing he may see and not perceive, having his heart false, and his ears dull, and his eyes closed up, lest he should be converted and humbled,' Acts xxviii. 27.

The use may be to teach us to enlarge our hearts in the sense of God's goodness, that hath delivered us from an estate that was in itself so fearful. Especially it may comfort us against our infirmities, that howsoever we fail by occasion, yet by God's mercy we do not walk in sin. We proceed not from degree to degree, and from sin to sin. It is a happy time with a Christian when he getteth victory over his sins, so as at least by degrees he gets down the power of them. And on the other side, they are in a woful estate that have their corruptions growing upon them both for power and number and continuance. O woe will be unto them when the Master shall come and find them so doing! And thus of the first speciality.

The second is, 'ye lived in them,' that is, ye set the delight of your hearts upon them. Sin was the life of your lives. None many times more lively and in greater jollity than such as are in greatest danger of God's wrath; and so cursedly vile is man's evil disposition, that as many men are the more sinful, they are the more secure and full of carnal liveliness. Who more frolic than our drunkards, swaggerers, swearers, abominable filthy persons? Yea, they carry themselves as if they had found out a life of excellency and contentment above all other men, and yet are buried in the ditches of monstrous wickedness, and are descending swiftly to their own place, hasting to the vengeance to come. Many times the holiest men are most pensive, and the vilest men most lively.

Lived. There is a fourfold life of men: the life of nature, the life of corruption, the life of grace, and the life of glory. The first life Adam lived before his fall; the last, the blessed live in heaven; the third, the godly live after their conversion on earth; and the second is the life of all the unregenerate. Sin is alive; it hath a living being in the uncon-

2 P

verted sinner; it is a monster engendered in the heart of man by conjunction with Satan, seating his several limbs in the several faculties of the soul. Now, it will not be amiss to consider how we may know when this monster is alive, and when he is dead. Sin may be known to be alive: first, By the flaming desires of the heart and thoughts of the mind, inordinately bent upon things forbidden. Secondly, By the command and authority it holds over all the faculties and powers of the soul and body, using them as servants and executioners of the lusts of the flesh. Thirdly, By the contentment men place in known evils. Fourthly, By customary practice. And lastly, If this monster, by the deceitful working of Satan, should sit still for a time, (as many times it doth even in the worst men,) yet there is a way to try whether it be alive or no. For bring it to the law, and it will presently revive. If it be pricked and pierced with the terrors and reproofs of a sound application, it will shew itself by unquietness and unruly distempers. And on the other side: first, It is certain sin is dead, if thy flaming desires to evil be quenched; secondly, If the command over the faculty of the soul be ceased; thirdly, If a man seek and place his chief contentment in spiritual things; fourthly, If the customary practice of evil be broken off and dissolved; and lastly, If the heart will abide the searching and sound application of the law.

In them. So wretchedly is the unregenerate heart of man composed, that he doth not only live and sin, but he lives in sin, and with sin, and by sin too. He lives in sin, because he is drowned under the power and guilt of sin. He lives with sin, because he is not a guest only, but a sojourner also with his sin; sin keeps the house, and the sin[1] is at bed and board there. And he lives by sin too, for most sinners cannot contrive how to live without them. The letcher cannot live without his mistress, and the usurer cannot live without his gain, and so of the rest. All these are woful circumstances of evil, and do marvellously decipher out a soul that feels not the life of Jesus Christ in him, and they impart also a further misery. It is easy to commit sin, but it is not easy to be rid of sin; a man may also quickly forget his sin, but he shall not so

[1] Qu. 'sinner'?—ED.

quickly forego his sin; for howsoever by God's singular patience he lives for all his sin, yet by the singular wretchedness of his condition all his sins will live with him; they are not transient, but so long as he lives his sin will live with him; yea, it will go with him too when he dies, if it be not prevented with speedy repentance.

The use also of all this may be to teach converted Christians that are delivered from this woful misery, to 'walk as children of the light;' having their fruit in all goodness, and righteousness, and truth; having no further fellowship with the unfruitful works of darkness,' seeing all is now 'made manifest by the light,' Eph. v. 8, 9, 11, 13; yea, they should strive to express as much life of contentment in the works of new life and light, as before they ever felt in the paths of sin and darkness; and if wicked men walk on with such unwearied resolutions and endeavours in such a dangerous estate, how should Christians be stirred to all possible constancy in well-doing, seeing they are sure that all that walk uprightly walk safely? Thus of the seventh verse.

Ver. 8. But now put ye away even all these things, anger, wrath, malice, cursed speaking, filthy speaking, out of your mouth.

Hitherto of the mortification of vices, especially against a man's self; now follows the mortification of injuries. And therein I consider: first, The exhortation itself, in the 8th verse and a part of the 9th; secondly, The reasons, ver. 9, 10, 11. In the exhortation I consider, first, The charge, 'put away even all these things;' secondly, The catalogue of injuries to be put away and mortified, 'anger, wrath, malice,' &c.

From the coherence, in that the apostle fastens this branch of the exhortation upon the remembrance of their misery in the former verse, it shews that the meditation of our misery is as good to kill or beat down the power of rage, and strong passions, and distempers, as it hath been shewn to be good to kill lust and covetousness. When you see men or women of heady passions and violent affections fall into affliction of conscience, then imagine they will hurl off their natures and grow more calm and meek, but till then seldom do any mend, or not for any long time.

Now. That is in the time of grace; and so it

gives us occasion to consider that grace yields no liberty to sin. Now that thou hast received the true grace of God, there is no time left for passion, fretting, cursed speaking, or filthy speaking, or lying, or any such injurious evils. Grace enjoins us to take leave of our old affections and our own perverse courses. Many such things as before thy conversion might in some respects been more borne withal, must now be left; for the converted Christian must live circumspectly and precisely, watching in all things, and walking wisely both at home and abroad; he must part with his old humours and perverse qualities; and therefore their condemnation sleepeth not that 'turn the grace of God into wantonness,' Jude 4.

Put away. Sin is not truly repented of till it be put away. Now sin is put away two ways: first, By justification, and so God puts away our sins; for when God pardoneth iniquity, he casteth it away and never sees it or remembers it more, Micah vii. 18, 19; secondly, By sanctification, and so we must put away our sins. We must put away or pull down sin, as the rebel puts down his weapons when he seeks the service of his prince; or we must deal with our sins as God deals with the mighty, that is, we must put them down from their seats. If we cannot destroy them from living, yet we may disturb them sitting, or reigning, or resting in us; or we must put them away as the wronged husband doth his filthy wife. We must divorce our sins, that by covenant they should never be ours more. We will never love them, and let them sleep in our bosom, and dwell with us, and be familiar with our natures, as they have been. Now we put away sins three ways: first, By confessing them to God; secondly, By godly sorrow, washing the stain and filth of them from off our hearts; thirdly, By renouncing and forsaking the practice of them; all are here intended, but the last principally. And this we must know will not be done with ease, if it be truly and soundly done. The prophet Micah means something when he saith of the Lord, 'He will subdue our iniquities;' and then after saith, 'He will cast them away into the depths of the sea,' Micah vii. 19. Must God subdue if he cast away? Then man must be sure of it, that he must labour seriously the subduing of his sin before he can have any comfort or success in putting them away. Sins are like an army of rebels, that will not be vanquished without some ado.

All these things. In the original it may be read, 'all things.' It is true that God many times puts his servants to it, even to deny and put away all things; they must deny themselves, Luke ix. 24, and their credits; yea, and their lives too, Mat. x. 39, if need be; they must deny the world, and their profits and pleasures, 1 John ii. 16, 17; yea, they must deny and forsake, and, which is more, rather than leave Christ and the sincerity of the gospel, they must hate father and mother, wife and children, and brethren and sisters, or else they cannot be Christ's disciples. But I restrain the sense, as it is here, unto sins only. And so it notes that every man that will truly repent must resolve to part with all sins as well as one; he must desire and endeavour to hate and put away every sin, as well the sins have been named as the sins are to be named. As we would have God to 'receive us graciously, and take away all iniquity,' Hosea xiv. 3, as well as one, so we must resolve sincerely to put away every sin as well as one. If the Lord should leave one sin unforgiven it might be enough to condemn us, and so if we leave but one sin that we have no desire nor will to repent of, that one sin would plead against us that we had not truly repented of the rest. If we mark the true catalogue of sins which here followeth, it shews that we must forsake all sorts of sins as well as one; for we must forsake and put away inward sins as well as outward, for he saith 'put away anger and wrath;' we must put away lesser sins as well as greater, for he saith, put away filthy speaking, as well as before he had said, mortify fornication and uncleanness. Now, that we may be encouraged to this sincerity in forsaking all sin as well as one, we may consider divers motives: first, Christ suffered for all sins as well as one; and therefore we should 'arm ourselves with the same mind, in suffering in our flesh to cease from sin' indefinitely, 1 Pet. iv. 1, that is, from all sin. Secondly, We would have God grant all our requests, and not leave one out. Nay, we have a promise that we shall obtain whatsoever we ask in Christ's name, Mark xi. 24, and therefore it is reason, when God calls for the repentance of all our sins, we should do it, and not leave one out. Thirdly, Christ is all in all things, and filleth all in all things, Col. iii. 11, Eph. i. 23, and therefore it is as easy for thee, if thy heart be right, to receive and procure from Christ virtue and strength against every sin as well as against any sin. Fourthly, This is all fruit, even the taking away of every sin, Isa. xxvii. 11, what pleasure or profit soever they might bring to us. When God looks for signs and marks of truth and uprightness, this fruit of true desire to repent is all fruit; it is wonderfully liked of God, and if he may find this heart and desire in us, he accounts it instead of all other things. Fifthly, Christians are made partakers of every heavenly gift, even every spiritual blessing in heavenly things, 1 Cor. i. 7, Eph. i. 3. Men, as they would put on every grace, so they must put off every sin. Lastly, God will shew us all his good, Exod. xxxiii. 19, xxxiv. 6, 7; he will withhold from us nothing that may be good for us, Ps. xiv. 11, even till he give us proof of his glory in every divine attribute. And why, then, should not we by serious and sound confession strive even to shew him all our evil, that we might obtain pardon for them and strength against them? But if none of these reasons may persuade with us to be upright and sincere, then let us know that though we favour and hide and extenuate our sins, yet the time will come when all shall be naked and manifest before God, even all the sins that are found upon us. And therefore it were better to confess them now, that God might not charge them upon us then, and to forsake them now, that being washed from them by repentance, and justified from them by the Spirit of the Lord Jesus, we may then be accepted as if we had never committed them.

Quest. But can a Christian put away all his sins in this life?

Ans. He may, and I will shew you how by a distribution: 1. Unwilling defects, as belonging to original sins, are pardoned the first moment of conversion. 2. Sins of ignorance are removed by general repentance, and by the daily sacrifice. 3. Sins not loved nor rooted are done away by an absolute forsaking of them. He that will continue any longer in sins that bring him no profit or pleasure, and such evils as he hath power to leave if he will, if these be not given absolutely over, it is to no purpose for a man to talk of repentance. 4. Particular sins that a man hath greatly loved they are put away by serious and distinct labour in prayer, and sensible sorrow and grief of heart for them; for less than this will not suffice for particular beloved sins. Now lastly, there will remain certain remnants of some sins that have roots in our corrupted dispositions, even after the first repentance. Now these are said in God's acceptation to be put away, when a man prays against them and mourns over them, and daily judgeth himself for them; and so they may be in his nature, and yet be truly, though not perfectly, put away. And thus of the general charge. The catalogue follows. And the sins are either sins of the heart or sins of the tongue. The sins of the heart are anger, wrath, malice. The sins of the tongue are blaspheming or cursed-speaking, filthy speaking, and lying. First, of the sins of the heart.

Anger, wrath. I suppose these words express one and the same sin; it may be the two words import two degrees of anger. For there is inward fretting, without words or sign; and there is open anger, a signified passion that discovers itself by outward shows. Both are justly condemned.

Anger may be considered: 1. As indifferent; 2. As laudable; 3. As a vice. Anger is a natural passion, and so in itself neither good nor evil, as it is a sense with dislike of injury; so Adam might have conceived anger against the serpent. The reason of the stoics that condemn anger as a natural passion for evil, because it is a perturbation, is without reason; for all perturbation is not evil, but unjust perturbation only; for Christ was angry and vexed, and grievously troubled, as at the death of Lazarus, and yet he was without sin.

Now for the second: anger may be considered as laudable and good; for that there is such an anger, I will not stand upon the distinction of the schoolmen that there is anger of zeal, and anger of vice. The scripture manifestly shews there may be good anger. The apostle saith, 'Be angry and sin not,' Eph. iv. 26; and Solomon saith, 'Anger is better than laughter,' Eccles. vii. 3; and the evangelist saith, our Saviour 'looked about upon them angrily,' Mark iii. 5; and St Matthew saith, 'he that is angry with his brother without a cause,' Mat. v. 22, as if he would acknowledge a just anger, when there was a just cause of anger. Now this good anger is a godly passion of just zeal, of justice, conceived against sin in ourselves or others, that desireth just revenge to the saving of the person, appeasing of God's anger, or the promoting of the kingdom of Christ. I say, it is a godly passion. For there are two sorts of natural passions. Some are so evil they can never be good, as envy; some are so natural, as they may be either good or evil as they agree or disagree with the law of God, and such is anger. I say just zeal, for I know that every zeal hath not always either good cause or good effect. I add *against sin*, because it must not be our indignation at the person. And we may be angry and vexed at our own sins, as Paul was, Rom. vii., as well as at the sins of others. And revenge also is the end of anger; for so may a Christian be revenged on himself as a fruit of godly sorrow, 2 Cor. vii. 10, as also he may desire the just revenge of the magistrate upon others. The end must be to save the person, not to express our spleens, and to appease God's wrath, as Phinehas did, and others of God's servants. And lastly, to promote Christ's kingdom by saving a soul from sin, James v. 20. But it is vicious anger is here meant.

Vicious anger hath her degrees; for there is, 1. The offence, a grief of the heart. It may be this is that the apostle hath, Eph. iv. 31, and is translated 'bitterness.' 2. Inflamed anger, or the inward working of this bitterness, or vexation, or offence, or grief. 3. Outward rage; neither are all men of one fit in their anger; for some are quickly angry, and quickly appeased; some are slow to anger, and slow from anger; some are quickly inflamed, but slowly pacified. The best is, slowly to kindle and quickly to be satisfied; but all are naught.

Now, concerning vicious anger I propound two things principally to be considered: 1. Reasons; 2. Remedies against it. Now for the first: There are divers things might persuade a Christian to make conscience of the mortification of anger and frowardness: 1. The commandment of God, which is express, 'Be not hasty in thy spirit to be angry,' as Solomon recordeth it in the 7th of Ecclesiastes. 2. The praises the Lord gives to men that can bridle their anger, and the disgraces the Holy Ghost casts upon impatient persons, as Prov. xiv. 29, 'He that is slow to wrath is of great understanding; but he that is hasty of spirit exalteth folly;' and again, Prov. xix. 11, 'It is the discretion of a man to defer his anger; it is his glory to pass over a transgression;' and again, Prov. xii. 8, 'A man shall be commended according to his wisdom; but he that is of a perverse heart shall be despised;' and in the place of Ecclesiastes before alleged he saith, 'Anger resteth in the bosom of fools.' 3. The nature of evil anger. What is anger but the fury of the unclean spirit, the madness of the soul, the unrest of all faculties, a very beast within the heart of man? 4. The effects of anger, which may be considered either more generally or more particularly; and the particular evil effects are either internal or external. The internal effects are such as these: 1. It blinds the mind; the just anger troubles the mind, but unjust anger blinds it. 2. It looseth the bowels of pity and mercy, especially from the persons. A man hath no affections neither for duties of piety nor of mercy. 3. It grieves the Spirit of God, Eph. iv. 30, 31. 4. It lets in the devil into a man's heart, Eph. iv. 17. The external effects are these: 1. It will interrupt prayer, as the apostle Peter intimates; if there be frowardness through indiscretion or contempt in the family, that will interrupt prayer, and work a negligence in God's worship, 1 Pet. iii. 7; and therefore it is one thing the apostle Paul expressly requires we should look to concerning prayer, namely, that men pray, as without doubting, so without wrath, 1 Tim. ii. 8. 2. It is a great hindrance to the profit of hearing, and therefore it is one of the apostle James his rules, that if we would profit by the word, we should be 'slow to wrath,' James i. 19, 20. 3. It doth notably shame a man, and discover and blaze abroad his folly; for, as Solomon observeth, 'He that is of a hasty mind exalteth folly,' Prov. xiv. 29; and in the 12th chapter and 16th verse he saith, 'A fool in a day may be known by his anger.' 4. Anger disables a man for society; for it is God's commandment or advice that we should 'make no friendship with an angry man, nor go with a furious man,' and as for other reasons, 'lest we learn his ways, and receive destruction to our own souls,' Prov. xxii. 24, 25. And, in general, anger is the door or gate of vice, and therefore David, in the 37th Psalm, saith, 'Cease from anger, leave off wrath, fret not thyself also to do evil,' as if he would imply that to abound in anger is to abound in sin; and it cannot be but a man must be guilty of much sin that lives in fretting and passion and inward unrest; and Solomon saith plainly, that 'a furious man aboundeth in transgressions,' Prov. xxix. 22. Besides, anger brings God's curse upon a man, as it is in Job, 'Anger slayeth the foolish,' Job v. 2; it bringeth many times great and sudden judgments, and as Solomon observes, 'A man of great wrath shall suffer punishment, and if thou deliver him, yet thou must do it again,' Prov. xix. 19. Hence it is that our Saviour, Christ, denounceth judgment both temporal and eternal against unadvised anger in the 5th of Matthew. And thus of the reasons.

The remedies against anger are of two sorts: 1. There are remedies for anger in ourselves; 2. There are remedies for anger in others.

There are divers things good to repress and subdue and mortify anger in ourselves: 1. From the coherence of these words with the former verse, it appears that the serious and frequent meditation of our misery is a good means to cut down the power and unruliness of our passions. 2. Saving knowledge will make a man 'peaceable, gentle, easy to be entreated,' James iii. 17; and the true reason why there is so much passion many times in the heart is because there is so little knowledge in the head; for passion and folly are twins. 3. To prevent anger, or to restrain it, it is good to take heed of meddling with the strife that belongs not to us, but carefully to mind and meddle with our own business, Prov. xxvi. 7; especially we should take heed of meddling with foolish and indiscreet persons, for 'he that contendeth with the foolish, whether he rage or laugh, there is no rest,' Prov. xxix. 9. 4. We must not 'give place to wrath,' nor let it have a vent by sudden and unadvised words, or by suffering our affections to increase in swelling and desire of revenge. We should silence our passions, and resolve to suspect and restrain our words. Anger smothered will languish, but let out will flame unto further mischief. 5. We should divert the course of our anger, and spend the heat of our affections upon our own sins; and it were good to get into our heads a catalogue of some of our chiefest corruptions, that if we be suddenly tempted to anger, we might presently think of those sins, and spend our zeal upon them. 6. We should consider him that provokes us to anger, that he is the instrument of God to try our patience, and that if he do it wilfully, it is a brand of his folly. Lastly, The meditation of the passion of Christ is an excellent remedy to kill anger, and to crucify it. And thus of anger in ourselves.

Now, the remedies for anger in others are such as these: first, Silence. Unto many natures to answer again is to put fuel to the fire; for anger is fire, and words are fuel. Secondly, If thy silence will be interpreted to be sullenness or contempt, (for some think they are despised if they be not answered,) then the next remedy is a soft answer, Prov. xv. 1. And thirdly, It seems that a gift in secret is good to pacify anger, for so Solomon thinks, Prov. ii. 14. But fourthly, If this will not serve, then it is good to give place to it, Rom. xii. 19; I mean, to go away from the angry person till his anger be over. But especially take heed that thou provoke not anger, for 'the forcing of wrath bringeth out strife,' as the churning of milk bringeth forth butter, and the wringing of the nose bringeth forth blood, Prov. xxx. 33.

The use of all this may be to humble every one of us. We may lay our hands upon our mouths, and repent of our foolishness in our passions, Prov. xxx. 32. And we should for hereafter be careful in all companies, but especially in our families, to avoid the customary sins of passion. Peevishness and this daily fretting and chafing is a cause of much sin and disorder, and a notable let of piety, and an extreme affliction to others that are troubled with it: 'It is better to dwell in the corner of a house top than with a brawling woman in a wide house,' Prov. xxi. 9; for a continual dropping in a rainy day and a contentious woman are alike, Prov. xxvii. 15. Thus of anger and wrath; malice followeth.

Malice. The word κακια is diversely taken. Sometimes for evil of punishment, or grief for crosses, Mat. vi. 34; sometimes for wickedness in general, or the evil habit opposed to virtue, Acts viii. 22; sometimes for malice or hatred, and so it is taken, Rom. i. 29, 1 Cor. v. 8, and so it is to be taken here; and this malice is nothing else but anger inveterate.

Malice hath divers degrees. For it begins in the

base estimation and loathing of the heart, Lev. xix. 17; and then it proceeds to a desire, that plods and waits for every opportunity of revenge, and so it is grudge. Afterwards it becomes open, and shews itself by inflation, which is, when a man goes so as he thinks his neighbour not worthy to be looked upon. Secondly, By strife and contention, suits and brawls. Thirdly, By bitterness and gall, in censuring and judging. And lastly, By wilfulness, and a resolution not to be entreated.

Again, malice is varied by the persons in whom it is. There is public malice and private malice; public malice is in public estates, and is shewn by factions and divisions. Private malice is varied by the objects, for there is a malice in wicked men against God's servants; thus 'they have hated them that rebuke in the gate,' Amos v. 10. Thus all the members of Christ are hated of the world, 1 John iii. 15; and this hatred of goodness is exceeding ill interpreted of the Lord; he accounts it as manslaughter, 1 John iii. 11, and will accordingly judge it, Ps. cxxix. 5–7.

There is also domestical malice, between husband and wife, brethren and sisters, servants and masters, &c. This domestical grudge or malice is exceeding hateful to God, and hurtful to the family. Besides, it is desperate, for 'a brother offended is harder to win than a strong castle,' Prov. xviii. 19; and the Lord hates all that have any hand in it; for 'he that soweth discord among brethren,' Prov. vi. 19, is one of the six things the Lord hates.

There is also malice abroad, between man and man, in controversing; and that kind of malice is principally here mentioned. Now, this kind of malice is not always open and professed; for 'he that hateth,' as the wise man saith, many times 'dissembleth with his lips, and layeth up deceit within him;' there may be 'seven abominations in his heart,' though he 'speak fair,' Prov. xxvi. 24, 25. And in another place he saith, 'hatred may be hidden with lying lips,' Prov. x. 18; but of what kind soever it be, it is exceeding naught, and to be avoided. Now, concerning this sin, I further propound two things: 1. Reasons; 2. Remedies against it; and then I will touch some use of all.

And the first reason may be taken from the vile nature of it. It is a vice so transcendent, that it passeth other vices. It hath been usually said, that to be angry is human, but to persevere in anger (which is this malice) is devilish; and therefore it is reckoned in the 1st to the Romans amongst the monstrous sins which the monstrous Gentiles fell into. Besides, to 'hate and be hateful,' is a dangerous sign of unregeneracy, Titus iii. 3, even that a man was never truly converted, for 'he that saith he is in the light and hateth his brother, is in darkness until now,' 1 John ii. 9. Thirdly, It is worthy to be repented of and carefully shunned, even for the ill effects of it, for it is like leaven, 1 Cor. v. 8, it will sour and spoil whatsoever praiseworthy qualities were in a man before. And it is a great let both to the word and prayer; and thence it is that the apostle Peter exhorts, that if we would grow by the word in affection and practice, we must then 'lay aside all malice and envy,' 1 Pet. ii. 1, 2; and the apostle James shews in his fourth chapter, that many desire, and ask and have not, and he implies, that (among other things) their warring and fighting, and jangling contentions, were the cause of it. But our Saviour Christ is expressly plain, that if men's stomachs be so big they will not forgive, the Lord will not forgive them, though they be never so importunate, Mat. vi. 14; and besides, men that in their passionate grudges are so hasty to strife, are many times brought to those straits in the end, that they know not what to do when they are put to shame by their adversaries, Prov. xxv. 8. Further, Solomon observes, that men that think to hide their grudge and hatred, have their wickedness many times shewed before the whole congregation, Prov. xxvi. 26; and they that dig pits in their spite for others, by the just providence, fall into the same themselves, Prov. xxvi. 27. Few malicious persons prosper; he that by his malice is carried into contention, knows not what he doth, for he is as he that letteth out the water, Prov. xvii. 14; a whole flood of mischief may break in upon him, that he dreams not of, for 'he that hateth his brother,' as St John saith, 'walketh in darkness, and knows not whither he goeth, for the darkness (of malice) hath blinded his eyes,' 1 John ii. 11. Finally, let such as will not be reconciled, nor agree with the adversary quickly, fear that prison that is threatened by our Saviour, even the prison of hell, into the which, if they be cast, they 'shall not come out till they have paid the uttermost farthing,' Mat. v. 26. And on the other side, it is a singular praise to be ready, and forward to be reconciled, and lay aside malice and discord, and a crown of reward' shall be given to such as seek peace and agreement; yea, a double crown, one because he will be reconciled, and another because he seeks it, and asketh peace first.

The remedies against malice follow; and they are of two sorts. For malice is to be medicined in our own hearts, or avoided; or it is to be compounded, or prevented in others. Now, to take order that malice might not infect us, these rules are to be observed: first, We must take heed of the causes of malice, and they are either within us or without us. Within us there is pride, Prov. xiii. 10, and impatience, and envy, and in some natures a very lust to contend, a kind of petulancy, and a very spirit of contradiction. Now, unless we keep out or subdue these, it cannot be but grudge and malicious discords will transport us. Again, without us there is the tale-bearer and scorner, and the froward person, and the busy body, called the 'man of imaginations;' all these must be shunned and avoided, if we would live without malice or contention; for 'where no wood is, there the fire goeth out, and so where there is no tale-bearer, strife ceaseth,' Prov. xxvi. 20. And the like may be said of contentious and froward persons, for 'as coals are to burning coals, so is a contentious man to kindle strife,' Prov. xxvi. 21. If a man find himself apt to grudge or strife, it is his best way to keep out of the way of froward persons that may soon fire him. The like counsel must be given concerning the scorner; for saith the wise man, 'cast out the scorner and contention shall go out,' Prov. xxii. 10; and it is sure that he that would not be infected with hatred, his best way will be to hate the busy body. Now, if this direction will not serve the turn, then in the second place, thou must mortify thy rising malice, and confess it with grief unto God, till by prayer thou get some victory over it. Thirdly, Much malice and grudge would be avoided, if we did but observe that counsel, Lev. xix. 17, namely, that when we did conceive dislike of any thing in our brother, for which we did fear we should hate him, we should go to him, and reprove him, rebuking him plainly for his sin; many times a seasonable reproof draws out the poison of beginning grudge and malice. Fourthly, It is good to meditate upon the passion of Christ, and of his readiness to forgive, even upon the cross, great wrongs and worser enemies. We should lay a necessity upon ourselves, to be advised before we would admit contention, or the resolution to contend; for as Solomon saith, 'by pride cometh contention, but with the well-advised is wisdom,' Prov. xiii. 10, even this wisdom to forbear contention. Finally, in the 4th to the Ephesians, the apostle before he saith, 'Let all bitterness, and wrath, and malice, &c., be put away,' he said in the verse before, 'Grieve not the Holy Spirit of God, whereby ye are sealed to the day of redemption,' Eph. iv. 30, 31; as if he would import, that a man might be induced to put away malice, and the rest of the vices there named, with great ease and readiness, if he would obey the motions of the Spirit, and busy himself seriously about the assurance of his full and final redemption, daily thinking of the time when he shall be rid of all wants and sins, and wrongs too. If we could oftener think of God's judgments, and the great day of revenge and recompense, it would cause us to have less stomach to be our own judges and revengers; and if the Spirit of God might rule us, our flesh would have little heart to busy itself about the works of malice.

Now, for malice in others, it must be considered either as it is to be compounded, or as it is to be avoided. And for the compounding of it, observe these rules: first, If thou wilt not do good for evil, which yet is required, Prov. xxv. 21, yet be sure thou render none evil for evil, Rom. xii. 17. Secondly, 'If thy brother have aught against thee,' so as thou be privy to thyself that thou hast done him any wrong, or given him any cause so to conceive, then go thou and seek reconciliation, render it and ask it of him. Thirdly, If the contention be yet secret, follow Solomon's counsel, say nothing of it to others, but 'debate thy cause with thy neighbour himself, and discover not thy secret to another,' Prov. xxv. 9. Peace might soon be made with many men, if the discord were not made so public. Now for avoiding of contention and malicious discords, there are divers rules of great use: 1. Meddle not with the strife that belongs not to thee, Prov. xxvi. 17; 2. Contend not with fools: thou shalt never have done if thou meddle with foolish persons, for whether they rage or laugh, there is no rest, Prov. xxix. 9; 3. Let nothing be done through vain glory, Phil. ii. 3; 4. Speak evil of no man, Titus iii. 2; 5. Be courteous and tender-hearted, Eph. iv. 31, 32; 6. Wrong no man, but follow that which is good, both amongst yourselves and towards all men, 1 Thes. v. 15; lastly, Pray for a covering love, for hatred stirreth up strife, but love covereth all sin, Prov. x. 12.

The use of all this may be both for reproof and for instruction. For reproof of many men that are fearfully soured with this leaven, they do not only 'let the sun go down upon their wrath,' but they let the sun go his whole course, and can find no time from the one end of the year unto the other to compound and lay aside their discords. Nay, so hath malice seated itself in some dogged and spiteful natures, that it seemeth to proclaim it will never lose possession till the devil, the father of malice, hath full possession both of soul and body. But let every godly mind be persuaded to avoid this monstrous sin, yea, let us strive to avoid the very beginning of it; or if nature have such corruption, that for the present we cannot get our hearts rid of all secret poison of dislike, let us be sure we be but 'children in maliciousness.' It is a monstrous wickedness to have a head that is exercised to strife, and a heart that hath a kind of sinful dexterity in framing and plodding for malicious courses. And thus much of malice.

Cursed speaking. The word in the original is βλασφημία, blasphemy. Now blasphemy or cursed speaking, it is a sin either against piety, or against righteousness. As it is against piety, it is blasphemy; to reproach or reason against the person or nature of God, or against the providence and works of God, or against the worship of God and the means thereof; and so it is cursed speaking and a kind of blasphemy to repine at God's works, 1 Cor. x. 10; to reproach God's sabbaths, Lament. i., or messengers, 1 Cor. xvi. 16, or his word. Also there is a cursed speaking which is against righteousness in the second table, and thus it is cursed speaking when subjects curse the king, Eccles. x. *ult.*; when masters threaten their servants, Eph. vi. 9; when parents provoke their children, Eph. vi. 4; when husbands are bitter to their wives, Col. iii. 19, when wives brawl and chide with their husbands, Prov. xxv. 24; when great men lord it over the poor, Prov. xiii. 8, and the like. Cursed speaking is either before the face, and so it is strife of words; or behind the back, and so it is backbiting or whispering, 2 Cor. xii. 20. It is cursed speaking to mock and scorn; it is cursed speaking to judge and censure; it is cursed speaking to slander and disgrace; it is cursed speaking to be ever complaining in all places. Finally, it is cursed speaking when men speak evil of any man, and there is a special kind of it in speaking evil of godly men, and this properly is blasphemy in the second table, for the Lord, for the honour he bears to his people, is pleased to afford the name of blasphemy to their reproaches, as importing that he takes it as if he were reproached himself.

We should all of us take heed of cursed speaking, of what kind soever, for it ariseth of ill causes, as envy or malice; and it hath ill effects, for it is certain thou had as good pierce others with a sword as smite them with thy tongue. And, therefore, a bitter and cursed tongue is often compared in the scripture to the sting of adders, and to a sword, yea, a sharp sword, to a razor, and to arrows, and the like; besides the hurt it doth to thyself; for 'if thou bite and devour, take heed thou be not devoured,' Gal. v. 15. And it is just with God thou shouldst be judged and censured, that accustoms thyself to judge and censure, Mat. vii. 1. And though thou speak evil never so secretly, yet God doth many times wonderfully discover the shame of it before others; and if man would not judge thee for thy evil tongue, yet it is certain God will, James v. 9. And it is many times seen that men and women of distempered and spiteful tongues are made a very abomination amongst men, Prov. xxiv., so as all men are weary of them and shun them. Lastly, scornful and cursed speaking proves a notable hindrance to the success of the word, 1 Pet. ii. 1, 2, and that these kind of people might observe. When they come to hear, they receive not a blessing: and why? but because blessing is so far from their lips; as they loved cursing, so it cometh to them.

The use of all may be to exhort us to 'put away far from us a froward mouth and perverse lips,' Prov. iv. 24, and that 'nothing be done through strife,' but rather that 'all things be done without murmuring or reasonings,' or brawlings, or revilings. And herein such as fear God should strive to give good example, seeing they are as lights in the midst of crooked and perverse people.

Quest. But what are the remedies of cursed speaking?

Ans. If we have sinned through bitterness, we should observe two rules: 1. Let thy own words grieve thee, Ps. lvi. 5, that is, labour by prayer and godly sorrow to beat down the power of thy perverseness, without defending, excusing, or extenuating of thy frowardness; 2. Keep thy heart with all diligence, Prov. iv. 23, 24. Look to the first risings of thy passions. For bitterness is first in the heart before it can come into the tongue. Now for preventing of evil speaking in others, the only rule is to give them no occasion, either by words or injurious and wicked life.

Object. But they will rail and revile without a cause.

Ans. Then observe these rules: 1. Betake thyself to prayer, so did David, Ps. cix. 2–4; 2. It is good ofttimes to be as a deaf man that heareth not, Ps. xxxviii. 13, 14; 3. Be sure thou be careful thou wrong not the names of others, else though thou be innocent in the things imputed, yet thou art justly scourged with the like evil; 4. The constantest and surest medicine for railing is a holy continuance in godly conversation; for though for the present it seem not to profit the railer, yet in time to come it may, Phil. ii. 15. I add also Solomon's rule, namely, with an angry countenance to drive away a backbiting tongue; for that is many times the bellows to kindle the fire of bitterness and fierce speaking.

Filthy speaking. This is another of the wretched vices of the tongue, to be with all care and conscience avoided by a Christian. And, therefore, the apostle, in the fifth to the Ephesians also, as well as here, puts it into the catalogue of evils he would most seriously dissuade them from, and out of that chapter we may gather divers reasons against it: 1. We are dear unto God, and therefore should follow him as dear children. Now of all things we never saw any colour of this in God. Angry speaking indeed is sometimes for our capacity given to God, but never filthy speaking, or any the least glimpse of it. 2. Our love should be as Christ's was. Now his was to profit, not to infect, and it was pleasing to God, not hated, as this filth of words must need be. 3. It is a shame and uncomeliness, and dishonour to a Christian. 4. If any would object it is but a small matter, the apostle would soon answer, men ought not to be deceived with vain words, for it is sure that 'because of this and such like things cometh the wrath of God upon the children of disobedience.' 5. This is a froth of filthiness that should only be found in unregenerate men that lie in darkness, and it is a work of darkness to speak filthily as well as to do filthily. 6. If we be children of the light, we should show it by our fearfulness to speak or do anything that were unpleasing to God; and we should show it by reproving such filthiness in others; for such filth, if it be not reproved, is not regarded, but a Christian reproof will make manifest in some measure that it is not good nor agreeing to truth and righteousness and goodness. 7. Men are in some degree of a lethargy that use this sin. 8. A Christian ought to walk exactly, strictly, precisely, or circumspectly; it is no more than he is bound to do to make conscience of the least filthy word as well as of filthy actions, and therein to take notice of God's will. And thus of the second vice of the tongue.

Ver. 9. *Lie not one to another, seeing that ye have put off the old man with his works.*

Lie not one to another. This is the last vice in the catalogue. Lying is given oftentimes to the dumb creature; and so images lie, and teach lies; and so the wonders of antichrist are lying wonders, 2 Thes. ii. 11. But it is most usually and properly ascribed to man; and so he lies either in nature, or in work, or in word. In nature; and so the prophet David saith, 'Men of high degree are a lie,' Ps. lxii. 9. In work; and so men lie either through hypocrisy or deceit. Hypocrisy is lying, whether it be in worship to God, Isa. lix. 13, or carriage towards men, Rev. ii. 9. Deceit is lying, and therefore the bread of deceit is called 'bread of lying,' Prov. xx. 17. But most properly a lie is in word; and so there is a lie in doctrine when men teach falsehood, or apply truths to wrong persons or for wrong ends. The devil is a lying spirit in the mouth of many teachers. Men lie also in false witness-bearing, so do they in slandering and flattering. But most strictly lying is in the report of things untrue in conversing with men, whether at home or abroad.

There are many reasons why a Christian should take heed of lying: first, If we consider the cause of lying; it is the devil, he is the father of lies, John viii. 44. Secondly, If we consider the nature of a lie; it is most shameful and hateful; and therefore the liar denies his lie, because he is ashamed to be taken with it; and our swaggerers hold the lie so disgraceful that they will revenge it many times with blood. Riches cannot add so much grace to a man as lying will bring him disgrace; and therefore Solomon saith, 'A poor man walking in his integrity is better than a rich man which is a liar.' And the Lord useth to reckon lying with the most monstrous sins, to make us the more to hate it, as we may see in the catalogues of the Revelation and in other places of scripture, Rev. xxi. 8, xxii. 15. Thirdly, On the contrary, to speak the truth is to shew righteousness, Prov. xii. 17. A mouth without guile is a mark of God's redeemed, Rev. xiv. 5; and the remnant of Israel, as in general they will do no iniquity, so in special they will not speak lies, Zeph. iii. 13. Fourthly, In the epistle to the Ephesians, the apostle reasons thus: 'Put away lying, speak every man truth to his neighbour; for we are members one of another,' Eph. iv. 25. It were most unnatural for the head to belie the hand, or one member to be false to another; so unnatural is it for Christians to lie one to another; for they are, or profess to be, members one of another. Fifthly, If we consider the effects or consequences of lying; for it makes us abominable to God; as 'they that do truly are God's delight, so lying lips are abomination to the Lord,' Prov. xii. 22; and a liar's tongue is one of the seven abominable things which Solomon reckoneth up, Prov. vi. 17. The law also is given to liars among the rest, as the apostle to Timothy affirms, 1 Tim. i. 10. It is one of the sins that brings upon a man's soul and body the forfeiture of the law. If lying be not restrained in time, thou mayest get such a habit of lying that thou canst hardly tell anything but thou wilt mix some falsehood with it, and that will both increase thy sin and the guilt of it. Besides, thou wilt lose thy credit, so that thou wilt hardly be believed if thou speak the truth. Sixthly, Know that God will enter into judgment with all liars, Hosea iv. 2; sometimes by ordinary judgments, sometimes by extraordinary, as he did with Ananias and Sapphira, Acts v. Now the Holy Ghost saith, 'He that speaketh lies shall not escape,' Prov. xix. 5; but 'God will destroy them that speak leasings,' Ps. v. 6; or if we could escape in this world, yet the lake that burneth with fire and brimstone is prepared for them that speak or love lies, Rev. xxii. 15.

Use. The use may be for reproof and humiliation to such as find themselves overtaken with this sin, especial if it reign in them: but more especially they are in a cursed condition that seek lies, Ps. iv. 4, and teach their tongues to lie, Jer. ix. 5. Neither let men please themselves that they can do it covertly; for liars are for the most part easily found out. There is, amongst the rest, three signs of a liar, and in one of the three he usually discovers himself: 1. To vary incontinently, Prov. xii. 19; 2. To hearken to a false tongue, Prov. xvii. 4; 3. To love lies, Rev. xii. 18. But let every one that feareth God obey this counsel of the apostle, to put lying in the catalogue of sins he would daily watch against. And because by nature we are all prone unto this sin, we should remember it, even in our prayers to God, that he would 'remove far from us vanity and lies,' Prov. xxx. 8.

Quest. Before I pass from this vice, there are certain questions to be answered, as first, whether all lying be sin or no?

Ans. That this may be understood, men use to divide lies into three sorts. There is an officious, and a pernicious, and a jesting lie. All men condemn the pernicious lie, many excuse the lie in jest, and some commend the officious lie; but the truth is, all are naught; and therefore the apostle saith, Lie not at all; for he speaketh indefinitely. But it will be objected that the midwives, and Rahab, and Michal did lie; but it must be answered, that their zeal and piety was to be praised; but the means they used was not to be imitated. If any object, that the patriarchs used lying, they must know that divers speeches of theirs, which to some seem to be lies, indeed were not; for Sarah was Abraham's sister, and Jacob was Isaac's first-born by divine dispensation and prophetically; and so Paul's speech about the high priest may be excused when he saith he knew not that he was the high priest; for from the death of Christ the right of the priesthood ceased. If it be further objected, that of two evils the less is to be chosen, I answer, that that rule is to be understood of evils of inconvenience, not of evils of sin. Now that it may further appear that it is not lawful to lie, no though it were to save others from great danger, these reasons may be weighed: 1. We may not do evil that good may come of it, Rom. iii. 2. Peter was rebuked for dissembling, though it were, as he conceived, to a good end, even to avoid offence and scandal, Gal. ii. 3. Nay, it is not lawful to him, though it were to defend God's cause, or to prevent his dishonour; therefore Job saith earnestly and in great heat, 'Will ye speak wickedly for God, and talk deceitfully for him? will ye accept his person?' &c. Job xiii. 7-9. 4. If we might lie to save others out of danger, then we might lie to save ourselves also; for we are not more bound to care for the safety of others than our own. But we may not lie to save ourselves; for then Peter had not sinned by denying his Master, keeping his faith and his heart, seeing it was to save his own life. Lastly, We might as well commit fornication with the Moabites to draw them to our religion, or steal from rich men to give to the poor, as to lie to profit.

Quest. But is it not lawful to suppress the truth sometimes?

Ans. Truth is either religious or political. For religious truth, being asked of our faith, we are ingenuously to profess it. Now political truth is to be considered either as it is required in judgment, or as it is to be used in cases out of judgment. As for the truth before a judge, it may not be concealed when thou art called to answer the truth; but in private conversing, we are not always bound to reveal all the truth; for the precept, 'Speak every man the truth,' is an affirmative precept, Eph. iv. 15, and so doth not bind always, and at all times, and in all places. Besides, charity binds us to conceal and cover many infirmities, and a wise man keeps in some part till afterwards; and besides, it is apparent men are not bound to discover their secret sins to all men. Samuel also is taught to conceal a part of the truth when he went to anoint David. And thus of the catalogue of injuries.

Seeing you have put off the old man with his works. In these words, with the verses that follow to the 12th, is contained three reasons to enforce the mortification of injuries:

1. They are the works of the old man; and they have by profession put off the old man, and so they should do his works.

2. They are now in the state of grace; they are new men, and therefore have new manners; they are by the means renewed in knowledge, and therefore ought to grow in practice, even in the mortification of what remains of corruption; they are renewed after the image of Christ, and Christ's image is the pattern of all holiness, and they must therefore leave those sins, because how like soever they be to the humours and dispositions of the most men, yet they are not found in the image of Christ.

3. God is impartially righteous and just; if men mind not mortification, he cares not for them, though they were Jews, circumcised, freemen. And contrariwise, if they do conscionably strive after the holiness of Christ, and the mortification of sins, he will accept them, though they were Grecians, Scythians, bond, &c.

In these words is heedfully to be noted: 1. The matter to be avoided, both the old man and his works; 2. The manner employed in the metaphor, 'put off,' with the time, 'have,' and the persons, 'ye.'

1. The old man is by some taken to be their old condition of life in the time of idolatry, by others, to be their custom and habit in sin; but it is generally by the most taken to be the corruption of nature, and inborn pravity, that vicious humour and ill disposition that naturally is in every one of us; it is the image of the first Adam in our hearts.

This corruption is here said to be 'the man;' because it is seated in every part of man, and because it rules and frames a man, and because it lives in man, so as sin only seems to be alive and the man dead, and because God will take notice of nothing in the sinner, but his sin.

2. The 'old man,' partly in respect of the first Adam, whose sin is ours by propagation, and who is called old, to distinguish him from the second Adam, 1 Cor. xv. 4, 5, and partly in respect of our state of corruption, which in the renewed estate we change so, that our condition after calling is said to be new, and our disposition before calling said to be old. This corruption may be said to be old also by the effects, for in godly men it waxeth old and withereth more and more daily by the power of Christ in them; and in wicked men, it spends the strength, and vigour, and power of the faculties of the soul, and makes him more and more withered and deformed in God's sight, and withal it hastens old age and death upon their bodies. Also in some men sin may be said to be old in respect of continuance. This is most fearful; age in any corruption is a most grievous circumstance of aggravation. It is best not to sin at all, and the next, to get quickly out of it.

Thus of his nature; now of his works.

The works of the old man are in general, works of darkness, of iniquity, of the flesh, vain, unfruitful, corrupt, abominable, deceiveable, shameful, and tend to death. And now particularly, if we would know what he doth, and how he is employed, we must understand that he gives laws to the members against the law of God and the mind; that he frames objections and lets against all holy duties; that he strives to bring the soul into bondage and captivity under imperious lusts; that he inflames the desires of the heart against the Spirit; that he infects our vain generation, and works both sin and wrath for our posterity. But more especially, his works are either inward or outward; inwardly he works atheism, impatience, contempt, carnal confidence, hypocrisy; he forges and frames continually, and multiplies evil thoughts; he works lusts of all sorts, he works anger, rage, malice, grief, evil suspicions, and the like. Outwardly he works all sorts of disorders, impieties, unrighteousness, and intemperance. A catalogue of his outward works are set down in the epistle to the Galatians, chap. v. 22, 23. He is here, in the coherence, described to be covetous, filthy, wrathful, cursed, and lying; and all these are well called his works, because he rests not in evil dispositions, but will burst out into action; besides, it is his trade to sin, and they are well called his works, because they are properly a man's own; for till a man repent he hath nothing his own but his sin, and it is to be observed that his works indefinitely must be put away; as if the Holy Ghost would imply, that all his works were naught; for his best works are infected with the viciousness of his person, or else they are not warranted in the word, or they are not finished, or the end was not good, or the manner not good, or they were wrought too late, or being out of Christ, they were not presented by Christ unto God, in whom only they can be accepted.

Thus of the matter to be reformed; the manner follows.

Put off. The faithful are said to put off the old man six ways: 1. In signification, or sacramentally, and so in baptism; 2. In profession, or outward acknowledgment, and so we profess to leave off the practice of sin; 3. By justification, and so the guilt of sin is put off; 4. By relation, and so in our head Christ Jesus, he is every way already perfectly put off; 5. By hope, and so we believe he shall be wholly removed at the last day; 6. By sanctification, and so he is put off, but in part, and inchoatively; the last way is here principally meant.

Now, in respect of sanctification, the old man and his works are put away: first, In the word, for so Christians are said to be clean by the word, John xv. 3, and to be sanctified by the word, John xvii. 17. The word first begins the work of reformation; it informs, renews, chaseth away the affections and lusts of sin, &c.; and then, secondly, the Christian at home puts him away by confession, and godly sorrow, and the divorce[1] of daily practice of reformation. This is in effect that which is signified in the other metaphor of crucifying the old man, Rom. vi. 6; for to crucify him is to lift him up on the cross of Christ, and to nail him with the application of God's threatenings, which causeth the pains of godly sorrow.

Have. *Quest.* Can men put off the old man in this life?

Ans. They may by inchoation, not perfectly.

Quest. But when may we have the comfort of it, that the old man is put off and crucified in us?

[1] Query?—ED.

Ans. When he is so subdued that he reigns not, for, to take the benefit of the word *crucified*, to crucify is not absolutely and outright to kill; and therefore it is said in the creed, Christ was dead, after he had said he was crucified, to note a further degree. Now then, as I conceive of it, sin is crucified when we make our natures smart for it, so repenting of our sin as we allow no sin; for to crucify a man is to leave no member free, provided that we be sure that the old man be so pierced, that he will die of it, though he be not presently dead.

Ye. The persons are indefinitely set down, to note that it is a duty required of all sorts of men, to put off the old man, and this work it is required of great men, of learned men, of wise men, of young men, in a word, of all men without exception. The uses follow.

Use. And first, We may here inform ourselves concerning the necessity of mortification, there is in us such corruption of nature, and such works of corruption, as, if they be not mortified, they will certainly mortify us; secondly, Here may be collected matter of confutation, and that of popish antiquity; for every man carries that about with him, that may prove that a thing may be ancient and yet vile; thirdly, How can the most of us escape, but the reproofs of God must needs fall upon us; for every man looks to the mending of his house, and his lands, and his apparel, &c., but who looks to the mending of his nature? Every man hath courage to put away an evil servant, and an adulterous wife, but where are the people that will resolutely set upon the divorce of sin? Men may be deceived, but the truth of God will remain unchangeable. If we have not put off the old man with his deceiveable affections and works, we have not, after all this hearing, learned Christ, as the truth is in him, Eph. iv. 22, 23. But when I speak of putting off, I mean not that sin should be put off as men put off their garments, with a purpose to put them on again after a certain time.

Ver. 10. *And have put on the new man, which is renewed in knowledge after the image of him that created him.*

In this verse is contained the second reason to enforce mortification, taken from their new estate in grace. The reason in itself intreats of the new birth, and describes it by showing what it is: 1. In general, it is the putting on of the new man; 2. In particular, it is the renewing of the mind with knowledge, and of the whole man, after the image of God and Christ.

The main general doctrine of the verse is, that all that are accepted of God in Jesus Christ have put on the new man, or are made new creatures. And for the further opening of this great point, I consider three things: 1. The necessity of the new birth; 2. What it hath in it; 3. The manner by which it is effected; and then I come to the use:

For the first, Those places of scripture most evidently prove it is of absolute necessity. The apostle to the Galatians saith, 'Neither circumcision nor uncircumcision availeth anything, but a new creature,' Gal. vi. 15; and to the Ephesians, he showeth, that if we be 'taught as the truth is in Christ Jesus,' then to 'put off the old man and to put on the new' are as the main principles of all saving doctrine, Eph. iv. 21, 24. And to the Corinthians he saith, 'If any man be in Christ Jesus, let him be a new creature,' 2 Cor. v. 17. And our Saviour Christ, in the third of John, is peremptory, 'Except a man be born again, he can never enter into the kingdom of heaven,' John iii. 5.

Now for the second: Whosoever is a new creature, or hath put on the new man, it is certain he is new: 1. In his nature; 2. In his obedience. He is new in his nature, and that will appear after sound trial in four things: for first, He hath new gifts, as the gifts of knowledge or discerning, Mat. xiii. 11; the gift of prayer, or as the prophet calls it, of supplications, Zech. xii. 12; the gift of uprightness, or a spirit without guile, Ps. xxxii. 2; yea, the apostle saith they were not destitute of any heavenly gift, 1 Cor. i. 6. 2. He hath new delights, for he feels the joys of the Holy Ghost, Rom. xiv. 17; and that in new things, in which he was never wont to delight before, as in the law of God, Ps. i. 12, in prayer, in the sacraments, &c.; and also in new persons, for now all his delight is in the excellent ones, Ps. xvi. 3, that truly fear God, and no more in carnal persons; yea, and in new times too, for he was never wont to rejoice in the time of affliction, but now he finds marvellous joy 'even in tribulation,' Rom. v. 3, 4. 3. He hath new sorrows also; they are not now so much for losses, shame, sickness, or the like, as for sin, or God's spiritual judgments, or the afflictions of God's children. 4. He hath new desires also, as after purity of nature, Ps. li. 2, pardon of sin, Mat. v. 6, softness of heart, Isa. lxiii. 17, the presence of God, Ps. xlii., success of the means, audience in prayer, and the coming of Christ, 1 Tim. iv. 8, and the salvation of Israel, Rom. ix., and the like.

And as he is new in his nature, so is he new in his obedience also, and that if we respect either the manner, or the matter, or the end. If we respect the manner of his doing God's work, it is: 1. With consecration of his soul and body to God's service, Rom. xii. 1; 2. It is with delight, he loves to be God's servant, Isa. lvi.; 3. It is in Christian simplicity, harmlessness, and godly pureness, and strictness, 2 Cor. i. 12, xi. 3, Eph. v. 15. Now, secondly, If we respect the matter of his obedience, he is exceedingly changed and renewed, for now he hath respect not to one or two commandments, but to all God's commandments, Ps. cxix.; he would be sanctified throughout, 1 Thes. v. 23; he labours for inward holiness as well as outward, 2 Cor. vii. 1, Ps. xxiv. 4, 5. And as he is altered in his service of God, so is he in his calling too; for he walks more conscionably towards all men, and hath learned to practise his general calling in his particular. And thirdly, For the ends of his obedience, his praise is not now of men but of God, Rom. ii. 16; his desire is to approve himself to God, without respect of the world, how men will take it, and he will constantly profess and practise, though it be against his case, credit, pleasure, or profit.

The third thing propounded was the means of the new birth; and howsoever the most men stand affected, yet the truth of God is certain and unchangeable, the ordinary outward means to convert a soul to God, or make us new creatures, is the word preached; we are born again by this immortal seed of the word, as the apostle Peter saith, 1 Pet. i. 23; and the apostle Paul is peremptory in the Epistle to the Romans, 'How can a man believe except it be by hearing of the word preached,' Rom. x. 14, 17. The inward means is the Spirit of Christ, which in respect of his working herein is called the Spirit of revelation, Eph. i. 18, of glory, 1 Pet. iv. 14, of love, of power, and of a sound mind, 2 Tim. i. 7.

The uses follow: and first, All God's servants that have felt the power of the word renewing them may greatly rejoice in the mercies of God to them, and the rather if they further consider the privilege of their new estate; for art thou a new creature? then thou hast the benefit of a new covenant, Jer. xxxi. 33, thou hast a new name upon thee, Isa. lxii. 2, Rev. iii. 5, and a new spirit within thee, Ezek. xxxvi. 27, to comfort thee, John xiv., to direct thee, to confirm thee, and to make intercession for thee; thou hast new alliance, a new Father, even God the Father; and new kindred with all the saints, both Jews and Gentiles, Eph. ii. 14; a new prince and minister, even Jesus Christ, Isa. lv. 6; new attendants, the very angels of God, Heb. i. 14; new wages and new work, Isa. lxii. 11; a new commandment, the rigour and curse of the law being taken away; new food, even manna from heaven, the word of life; new signs and helps to guide thee in the way, Jer. xxxi. 21; and when thou shalt die, a new death, not die as other men, and a new grave or tomb, wherein no carnal man lay, thy grave being perfumed by the body of Christ; a new way to heaven, Heb. x., and a new mansion in heaven, 2 Cor. v. 8. What shall I say? but conclude with the apostle, if thou be a new creature thou shalt have all things new, 2 Cor. v. 17. And therefore let all the holy seed, the blessed of the Lord, sing new songs of praise to God.

Secondly, The consideration of the doctrine of the new birth may serve greatly for reproof of the fearful security of multitudes of people that are sunk so deep in rebellion that they cannot consider nor seriously mind their own conversion. They look not upwards to behold the angry countenance of God, nor to the times past to consider the millions of men that have perished for want of the new birth, nor within them to see the image of God defaced, and the devil entrenched in strongholds for tentations, and the conscience either awake, and then the fire of hell is within them, or asleep, and then they are in danger every moment when it will awake; nor do they consider the time to come, or think of those last things, death, judgment, and hell. Oh! the spirit of fornication, that doth enchant men that they cannot so much as mind to return. Now, if any profane spirit should ask me, Where are any such men as I have before described to be new creatures? I would answer him, They are not to be found in taverns, ale-houses, play-houses, cock-pits, bear-baits, or such like; but blessed be God there is a remnant, a tenth, one of a city and two of a tribe, that are such as the Lord doth describe, and will be accepted of in Jesus Christ.

Renewed in knowledge. Knowledge is a chief part of the new grace of a Christian, without it the mind cannot be good, Prov. xix. 2 : it is a singular gift of God to the elect, to reveal unto them the mysteries of the kingdom, Mat. xiii. 11 : it is the beginning of eternal life on earth, John xvii. 3. But we must understand that this knowledge here meant is neither natural, nor sensual, nor civil, nor moral, nor historical, nor a general theological knowledge, but a religious, saving knowledge; it is a knowledge by which a Christian sees in a mirror—he stands and wonders; it is a knowledge that will transform a man, 2 Cor. iii. 18; it is the experimental knowledge of the virtue of Christ's death and resurrection, Phil. iii. 10; it is a knowledge will keep a man from the evil way, Prov. ii.; it is a knowledge will encounter every thought and affection that exalts itself against the obedience of Christ, 2 Cor. x. 5; it is a knowledge that is 'first pure, then peaceable, gentle, easy to be entreated, full of mercy and good fruits, without judging and without hypocrisy,' James iii. 17.

The use is, to teach us, that as we would be assured we are new creatures, so we should labour to be possessed of sound knowledge; and to this end : 1. We must stand up from the dead, and withdraw from wicked society, else Christ will never give us light, Eph. v. 14; 2. We must consecrate ourselves to holy life, and seek the fear of God, for that is the beginning of this wisdom, Rom. xii. 2, Prov. i.; 3. We must deny our carnal wisdom, and become fools that we may be wise, 2 Cor. iii. 18; 4. We must walk with the wise, Prov. xiii. 20; 5. We must beg of God a lowly and a humble heart, for 'with the lowly is knowledge,' Prov. xi. 2; lastly, We must study the scripture, and attend upon daily hearing and reading, for they are the only fountains of true knowledge and wisdom, 2 Tim. iii. 16.

Renewed. The knowledge of the faithful in this life, even after calling, needs to be daily renewed; for sin makes a breach both in the heart and mind; and Satan plants daily temptations and objects against the doctrine of God, against which the mind needs new store of provision out of the word for defence; and our affections are wonderful apt to lose sense and feeling, and then there is no other way to recover sense but by renewing contemplation. And besides, inasmuch as faith and repentance must be daily renewed, therefore also must examination of life and meditation of God's promise and grace, be renewed also. Finally, we know but in part and successively, and therefore ought continually to be growing and adding to the measure of the knowledge received.

Use. This may serve : 1. For information, for here we may know the necessity of daily teaching, since we need daily to be renewed in knowledge. 2. For great reproof of that negligence is everywhere to be found, in omission of hearing or reading the scripture, or using of other private helps for knowledge. 3. For instruction; for it should teach us to be constant in the use of all the helps God hath commanded or afforded us; and we should bear infirmities in others, since our own knowledge is imperfect; and we should learn to be 'wise to sobriety,' and not think ourselves able to judge of every doctrine or work of God. The Lord hath laid a restraint upon us, and in this life we cannot attain a full knowledge, and therefore we should repress the itching curiosity of our natures, thirsting after forbidden knowledge. Lastly, We should resolve of the need we have to be admonished, instructed, directed, or rebuked, and therefore rejoice in it, if any will shew us that mercy to smite us with rebukes, or guide us in the way.

After the image of him that created him. God's image is in Christ, in the angels, and in man. Christ is the image of God in two respects : 1. Because he is the eternal Son, begotten of his substance, and therefore called the 'character of his person' or substance, Heb. i. 3; 'the image of the invisible God,' Col. i. 16, and so he hath most perfectly the nature of the Father in him. 2. Because he was manifested in the flesh, for in Christ, made visible by the flesh, the perfection, and, as it were, the face of the Father is now seen. And therefore our Saviour saith, 'He that seeth me hath seen the Father,' John xiv. 9, for the fulness of the Godhead which was in the Son being united, and, as it were, imprinted on the flesh bodily, Col. ii. 9, he did resemble, and, as it were, express his own and his Father's nature after divers manners and by divers works or actions.

The angels are God's image, and therefore called the sons of God, because they resemble him, as they are spiritual, and incorporeal, and immortal substances; and, secondly, as they are created holy, just, and full of all wisdom and divine perfections in their kind.

Amongst the visible creatures, man only bears the image of God; and so he doth: 1. By creation, Gen. i. 26; 2. By regeneration, Eph. iv. 24. He was created in it; and then falling from God by sin, he recovers the renewing of the image of God by grace and effectual calling in Jesus Christ. That this may be more fully understood, we must know that man is the image of God, either considered more strictly as a superior, or more generally as man. As a superior, man is said to be God's image in scripture two ways chiefly: 1. As a husband, and so in the family the apostle calls him the image and glory of God, 1 Cor. xi. 7; 2. As a magistrate, and so princes and rulers are called gods on earth, Ps. lxxxii. But neither of these are meant here; for this image of God here mentioned is that likeness of God which, by the Spirit of grace, is wrought in every one of the faithful after their calling.

Howsoever the perfect understanding of God's image belongs to God himself, and to the vision of heaven, yet in some measure we may conceive of it as it is revealed in the word, and imprinted in the nature and obedience of man. Two things I principally propound to be here considered more distinctly: 1. Wherein man is the image of God; 2. The differences of the image of God in man, either from that which is in Christ and the angels, or as it is to be considered in the several estates of man; and then I come to the use of all.

For the first, man is said to bear the similitude of God, or to have in or upon him the image of God, in five respects: first, In that in conceiving of God man begets a kind of image in his mind; for whatsoever we think of, there ariseth in the mind some likeness of it. Now, if we conceive of God amiss, then we commit horrible idolatry; and whatsoever service is done to the likeness we so conceive of, is done to an idol. But now when Christians taught out of the word conceive of God according to the descriptions of the word, that is not after the likeness of any creature, but in a way of apprehending of God in the human nature of Christ; or otherwise according to his nature or properties, in some true measure, this idea or form of God, as I may so call it, in the mind of the faithful, is a kind of the image of God; for to conceive a likeness of God is not unlawful, but to conceive him to be like any creature in heaven and earth, that is prohibited and unlawful. Secondly, Man is after the image of God in his substance, and therefore we are well enough said to be 'God's offspring,' Acts xvii. 28. Now man is God's image both in his soul and in his body. The soul is the image of God, as it is spiritual and simple, and as it is invisible, and as it is immortal, and as it is an understanding essence, having power to know all sort of things, and to will freely. And some think it is God's image, as there is in it a portraiture, as it were, of the Trinity; for as there is in God distinct persons, and yet every person hath the whole essence, so there is in the soul distinct faculties, and yet every faculty hath in it the whole soul, yea, is the whole soul. Now that the body also is God's image, these reasons may prove: 1. Man is said to be made after God's image in the first creation: man, I say; not the soul of man only. 2. God's image was in Christ's body, for he saith, 'He that seeth me, seeth the Father:' he saith not he that seeth my soul, nor indeed could the soul be seen. 3. When the Lord prohibiteth the shedding of man's blood, he yieldeth this reason, 'for in the image of God made he man.' Now it is manifest the soul cannot be killed, therefore man's body is after God's image. Not that God hath any body, but in three respects: 1. As man's body is a little world, and so the example of the world which was in God from all eternity is, as it were, briefly and summarily expressed by God in man's body; 2. There is none of our members almost but they are attributed to

2 R

God in scripture, and so there is a double use of our members, the one that they might serve the offices of the soul, and the other that they might be, as it were, certain types or resemblances of some of the perfections of God; 3. Because the gifts of the mind do cause the body to shine, as the candle doth the horn in the lanthorn. Thirdly, Man is after God's image in the qualities of the soul, such as are wisdom, love, zeal, patience, meekness, and the rest; for in these he resembleth in some manner those glorious and blessed attributes of God. Fourthly, Man is after God's image in respect of sanctity of actions, in that he is holy as he is holy, and in that he resembleth God in his works, as in loving and hating where God loves and hates, and in knowing and approving of things as God approves or knows of them. It is plain man resembles God in loving and shewing kindness to his enemies, Mat. v., but generally by holiness of carriage man doth resemble God, I mean in the creation did so, and by grace the faithful begin to do so. Lastly, Man bears the image of God in his sovereignty of dominion, and that both over himself and as he is God's vicegerent over the living creatures and the earth; and thus of the first point.

Now for the differences of God's image: first, That the image of God in man and the image of God in Christ differs in two things: 1. Christ was the substantial image of the Father as he was God, and we are his image but by similitude; 2. Christ as man, by reason of the personal union, is filled with almost infinite perfections above measure, which are in no man else besides.

Again, it differs from the image of God in angels, in three respects: 1. Because they excel in nature, for they are wholly spiritual, and in action they perform God's will with greater glory and power; 2. They are free from all human necessities ever since their creation; 3. They enjoy the vision of glory in the presence of glory in heaven, in a manner peculiar to their place and natures.

Now for the differences of the image of God in man according to the different estates of man, we must know the image of God according to the threefold estate of man is likewise threefold: 1. There is the image of nature, which Adam had; 2. The image of grace, which the saints now have; and 3.

The image of glory, which the blessed have in heaven.

The image of God in Adam had distinct specialties. 1. Adam was a perfect divine and a perfect philosopher, even in an instant; he knew the nature of all things in the instant of his creation, which now is attained unto with extreme labour and singular weakness. 2. He had an immortal nature free from infirmities, diseases, death. 3. He should have propagated an immortal seed after the image of God, whereas now grace will not be propagated. 4. His obedience was charged with the observation of the tree of life and of good and evil.

Uses. The image of grace hath these specialties: 1. Faith; 2. Godly sorrow; 3. The cohabitation of the flesh; 4. A feebleness and defect in the measure of grace; 5. A peculiar kind of inhabitation of the Spirit of Christ.

Lastly, The image of glory hath these differences: 1. A freedom like the angels from all terrene necessities; 2. An utter abolishing of the sinful flesh, and of the very natural disposition to die; 3. A full perfection of all graces; 4. A loss of faith and sorrow and all the works of repentance; 5. A special unutterable communion with God and good angels in glory.

The consideration of this doctrine of God's image should serve to teach us to love and admire all that fear God, since the Lord hath graced them with this honour to be like God; it is a greater favour than if they had resembled the noblest princes that ever were on earth; no, all the carnal men on earth in all their glory cannot reach to that absoluteness of excellency that is in one of the poorest of God's servants. 2. Since the seat of this glorious resemblance of God is in the heart, it should teach us especially to look to our hearts and keep them with all diligence, Prov. iv. 23, even to be conscionably careful to see to it what thoughts and affections are lodged there. The devil desires no more advantage than to have liberty to erect in the heart holds for evil thoughts and sensual desires. 3. If it should be our glory to be fashioned after the image of God, then it condemns the abominable security of the most men, that are so mindless of the repair of the loss of this divine gift, and instead thereof, with so much care fashion themselves after this world, Rom. xii. 2, or after the lusts of their own and old ignorance, 1 Pet. i. 14, or after the wills and humours of men, 1 Pet. iv. 2. 4. How are we bound unto God for this unsearchable love, that is pleased to restore unto us this divine gift through the gospel of Jesus Christ! Thus in general of God's image.

But before I pass from these words, there is further to be considered: 1. The form of speech, in that he saith not, 'his image,' but 'after his image;' 2. The efficient cause, noted in those words, 'of him that created him.' For the first, we must understand that to say, 'man is the image of God,' and 'man is after the image of God,' is not all one; for man is said to be the image of God because he is truly so, and he is said to be after his image because he is not perfectly so; Christ only resembles God in full perfection.

Now for the efficient cause of God's image; he is described here by a periphrasis, 'he that created him.' Man was two ways created: 1. In respect of being, and so God created him; 2. In respect of new being, and so Christ created him, Eph. ii. 12, 1 Cor. viii. 6; neither of these senses can be well excluded. And if the words be understood of the first creation, then these things may be observed: 1. That Adam was not to be considered as a singular man, but as he sustained the person of all mankind, else how could we be said to be created after God's image? and as in him we received this image, so by him we lost it. 2. That the interest we have now to creation is not sufficient to salvation; and therefore they are grossly deceived that think God must needs save them because he made them. 3. That the Lord would have the doctrine of the work of creation to be remembered and much thought upon by converted Christians; and the rather because it serves for great use in our regeneration; for it furthers both repentance and faith, and therefore in divers places of scripture, where the Holy Ghost entreats of doctrine of repentance and faith, the word 'create' is metaphorically used, to assure us that God will perform his promise, though it were as hard a work as to create all things at first. Thus he hath promised to 'create a clean heart,' Ps. li., and to 'create the fruit of the lips to be peace,' Isa. lvii. 19, and to 'create upon every place of Mount Sion, and upon the assemblies thereof, a cloud and smoke by day, and the shining of a flaming fire by night, that upon all the glory may be a defence,' Isa. iv. 5, and to create light, Isa. xlv. 7, and deliverance out of afflictions. Besides, the doctrine of the creation teacheth us the fear of that dreadful majesty that was able to work so wonderfully, Ps. xxxiii. 7-9; and it enforceth humility, by shewing that we are made of the dust in respect of our bodies, and that our souls were given us of God with all the gifts we have in our minds; as also by giving us occasion to consider the image of God that we have lost. And thus of creation as it is referred to God.

Secondly, It may be referred to Christ, and so be understood of our regeneration, which is, as it were, a re-creation or a new creation; and in this sense it shews that we should conform ourselves to the likeness of him that doth regenerate us by his word and Spirit. But may some one say, Is there any difference betwixt the image of God in us, and the image of Christ in us? I answer, That to be fashioned after the image of Christ hath two things in it more than is properly in conformity to God's image; for first, We must be like him in sufferings, Rom. viii. 19; and secondly, In the impressions of the virtue of his death and resurrection. Rom. vi., Phil. iii. And thus of the tenth verse.

Ver. 11. *Where is neither Grecian nor Jew, circumcision nor uncircumcision, Barbarian, Scythian, bond nor free: but Christ is all in all things.*

This verse may contain another reason to persuade to mortification and holy life. And the reason may be taken from the great respect God hath of true grace in Christ, and the little love or care he hath for anything else. A Barbarian, a Scythian, a bondman, if he have grace, shall be accepted; whereas a Grecian, a Jew, a free-man, without grace, is without respect with God: Christ is all. It may be the apostle here meets with the false apostles, that so much urged the observation of Jewish rites, and stood so much upon it, to divert the people from the sound care of reformation of life, by filling their heads with questions and vain wranglings about the law; whereas the apostle shews men may be absolute and complete in these outward observances, and yet their circumcision avails them nothing before God. Here are then evidently two things in this verse: first, What it is God stands not upon; secondly, What it is. is all in all with him.

Where there is neither Grecian nor Jew, circumcision nor uncircumcision, Barbarian, Scythian, bond nor free. Out of these words these two things may be observed:

1. That nothing without Christ can make us truly happy. The image of God or felicity of man stands not in birth, freedom. natural parts, or outward observances, for 'he is not a Jew that is one outwardly,' nor is that liberty that is only in the flesh, nor is that wisdom that is only in learned men, such as were the Grecians. Dives was a rich man, Goliath was a strong man, Ahithophel was a wise man, Absalom was a fair man, Esau was circumcised, and Cain was well born, and yet all these are in hell.

2. That in Christ there is no difference, all is one, whether thou be poor or rich, Jew or Gentile, bond or free, male or female, Gal. iii. 28; with God there is no respect of persons. In the power of his ordinances, as by name, in the preaching of the gospel, he extends his mercy both to Jews and Gentiles, Rom. i. 16; so in the disposing of his gifts, 1 Cor. xii. 13, he bestows knowledge and other graces upon people of all sorts; and for acceptation, whosoever feareth him and doth righteousness, he is accepted, of what nation or state soever he be, Acts x. 34; and all this will more fully appear, when he shall judge every man, without respect of persons, according to his works, at the last day, Rom. ii. 10.

Uses. The consideration hereof may teach us divers things: first, To fear God and forsake our sins, since he is a God so terrible that will not be swayed with outward respects, Deut. x. 16, 17, Acts x. 34, 1 Pet. i. 17; secondly, Not to stand upon outward birth or greatness in the world, nor to pride ourselves in our wits, or rest ourselves upon our outward serving of God, for 'the Lord accepts not the persons of princes, nor regardeth the rich more than the poor,' or the learned more than the unlearned, 'for they are all the work of his hands,' Job xxxiv. 19; thirdly, To be industrious in well-doing, seeing he that doth good shall be accepted, whether he be bond or free, Grecian, Barbarian, one or other, Rom. ii. 8-10, for the same God is Lord over all, and rich unto all that call upon him, Rom. x. 11, and endeavour by well-doing to approve themselves in his sight; fourthly, Not to despise poor Christians, seeing God accepts of them, and hath made them rich in faith and heirs of a kingdom, James ii. 1, 5; fifthly, Not to give titles to men, Job xxxii. 21, 22, and by servile flattery or fears to be so much taken up with their more outward places; lastly, Magistrates in the administration of justice should resemble this absoluteness of God, so as no respect of persons, poor or rich, friends or foes, strangers or home-born, should carry them besides the just regard of the cause, Deut. i. 17, 2 Chron. xix. 6.

But Christ is all in all. And so he is: 1. In respect of the union of the mystical body, as it is he in whom every one that is a new creature is considered to be and consist; every convert is 'created in Christ Jesus,' Eph. ii. 10. 2. In respect of sufficiency, a man needs no more than Christ, he only may suffice; the whole completeness of salvation is in Christ. 3. In respect of efficiency, if we look upon the benefits conferred upon all Christians by Christ, he makes amends for all wants; he is instead of liberty to the servant, and instead of birth and honour to the Scythian and Barbarian; he is the substance of all shadows to the uncircumcised. What shall I say? He is righteousness, Dan. ix. 24, and riches, Col. i. 27, and wisdom, 1 Cor. i. 30, sanctification and freedom, 2 Cor. iii. 17, and a recompense to Christians, Isa. xl. 10; yea, in him all things are theirs, 1 Cor. iii. 12, and, as the pledge of all, they have received the Spirit of the Son into their hearts, Gal. iv. 6.

Uses. The use of all this may be divers: 1. Unto us, therefore, there should be one Lord, even the Lord Jesus Christ, 1 Cor. viii. 6. 2. All sorts of men should strive by all means to set out and shew Christ only. Ministers should teach Christ only. Magistrates should chiefly intend the glory of Christ. Nay, all sorts of men should seek Christ in choosing callings, wives, servants, places of abode, &c. Christ should be all in all with us; yea, in those we have to deal withal, we should bear with many wants and weaknesses, so they have Christ, for that is all in all. 3. We should learn to be satisfied with Christ. Though we want health, or liberty, or wealth, or worldly friends, or great wits, or strong memories, &c., Christ makes amends for all; he is enough. If the Lord have given us Christ, he hath done enough for us, though it be sure that with him he will give us all things also. 4. This may greatly reprove the wonderful stupidity of men, that are so taken up with admiration of these outward privileges, whenas we see how all is vain without Christ, what shall it profit a man if he had all honour and riches, and countenance of friends, and the pleasures of life, if when he came into God's sight he might have no acceptance for his soul? If Christ be all things, then without Christ all things else are nothing. But especially this doctrine serves for singular comfort to God's children in all their distresses, and that will better appear if we consider the particulars.

For first, Are they afflicted in conscience under the sense of God's anger and their own sins? Why, he is the propitiation for their sins, Rom. iii. 25; he is the end of the law for them, Rom. x. 4; yea, all that the law can require of them; he will be their witness and their testimony, Isa. lv. 6, 1 Cor. i. 6; he gives them promises, and faith to believe them, Gal. iii. 22; and it is his blood that perfectly cures and cleanseth them from all their wounds and sins, 1 John i. 7. Secondly, Are they distressed under the power of Satan's temptations or accusations? Why, he sitteth at the right hand of God, to see that nothing be laid to their charge—he maketh intercession for them, Zech. iii. 1-3, Rom. viii. 33. And for the stings of this old serpent, he is a continual brazen serpent, John iii.; they may but look upon him and be healed; yea, he was tempted himself that he might succour them that are tempted, Heb. ii. 18; and his power dwelleth in them, to be manifested in their weakness, 2 Cor. xii. 9; and he came into the world on purpose to dissolve the work of the devil, 1 John iii. 7. Thirdly, Are they dismayed with the sense of their own weaknesses and ignorances? Why, they have such a High Priest as is touched with their infirmities, Heb. iv. 15, and knows how to have compassion on the ignorant, Heb. v. 1. He will not break the bruised reed, nor quench the smoking flax, Isa. xlii. 2, 3. Fourthly, Are they pressed with outward troubles? Why, Christ is the merit of their deliverance from this present evil world, Gal. i. 4. He is the sanctification of their crosses, so as 'all shall work together for the best to them that love God,' Rom. viii. 28; yea, he will be their consolation, so that as their sufferings abound, his comfort shall abound also,

2 Cor. i. 5; or if he do not deliver, then he makes a supply, by giving them better things out of the riches of his glory. He is a husband to the widow, and a father to the fatherless, and as the shadow of the rock in a weary land to them that are persecuted and driven to and fro by the hot rage of evil men, Isa. xxxiii. 2. Lastly, Are they in the fear or in the danger of death? Why, Christ is all in all here also, for he hath overcome death for them, Hosea xiii. 14; he hath opened the way to heaven, Heb. x. 19; he hath destroyed him that had power over death, Heb. ii. 14; he hath freed them from the wrath to come, 1 Thes. i. 10; he hath begotten in them a lively hope of a happy issue from the passage of death, 1 Pet. i. 3; he is the first-born of the dead, Col. i. 17; and he will be the resurrection and the life unto them, John xi. What shall I say, but conclude with the apostle, 'Christ is in life and death advantage,' Phil. i. ; only that Christ may be all in all to us, we must hear him, we must believe in him, we must deny ourselves and take up our cross and follow him; and, finally, we must live to him, and die in him.

And thus of this eleventh verse, and so of the second part of the general exhortation.

Ver. 12. *Therefore, as the elect of God, holy and beloved, put on bowels of mercy, kindness, humbleness of mind, meekness, long-suffering;*

Ver. 13. *Forbearing one another and forgiving one another, if any have a quarrel against another: even as Christ forgave you, so also do you.*

There are three things requisite to holy life: first, The meditation of heavenly things; secondly, The mortification of vice; thirdly, The exercise of holy graces and duties. Of the first, the apostle hath entreated from ver. 1 to ver. 5. Of the second, from ver. 5 hitherto. Now, in these words, and those that follow to the 18th verse, he entreats of the third, for he gives rules for the obedience of the new man, and those rules are more special or more general. The more special rules are from the 11th verse to the 16th: the more general rules are in the 16th and 17th verses; the one concerning the means of holy life, ver. 16, and the other concerning the end of holy life, ver. 17.

The special rules give in charge the exercise of

nine graces; and in the setting down of these rules I observe: 1. The motives to persuade to the observation of them, and they are three: the one taken from their election, the other from their sanctification, the third from the love of God to them; and these are briefly thrust together in a parenthesis in the beginning of the 12th verse. 2. The manner how they be charged with these graces, and that is noted in the metaphor 'put on.' 3. The graces themselves, and they are in number nine. Some of them have their greatest praise in prosperity principally, as 'mercy, kindness, meekness, humbleness of mind;' some of them concern the times of adversity principally, as 'long-suffering' and 'clemency' in 'forbearing and forgiving;' some indifferently belong to all times, as love, peace, thankfulness, or amiableness. ver. 14, 15.

Now, from the coherence imported in the word 'therefore,' divers things may be noted:

1. In that he prescribes the mortification of vices before the exercise of graces, it shews that till vice be mortified, grace will not grow nor prosper. The true reason why many men thrive no better in the gift of God's Spirit is because they are so little and so slightly in confessing and bewailing of their corruptions of heart and life.

2. In that he rests not in the reformation of vices, but prescribes also rules of new obedience, it shews that it is not enough to leave sin, but we must be exercised in doing good. It will not serve the turn of the husbandman that his fruit-trees bear no evil fruit, but he will cut them down if they bring not forth good fruit; barrenness is cause great enough of hewing down.

3. Men that are truly renewed after the image of Christ are willing to be appointed and prescribed for the attaining and exercise of every holy needful grace and duty. He that hath true experience of the beginning of any true grace hath a true desire, and a willing endeavour, and a just estimation of all grace; for as he that repents of one sin loves no sin, so he that travails in the birth of any grace desires all grace, so far as in conscience he knows them to be required of God; and in some degree, except it be in the time of violent temptations, or that the loss of the means occasion any deadness or faintness in the desires of the heart, or that there be a relapse into some presumptuous sin after calling.

4. If this 'therefore' carry us to the former verse, then we are informed that our endeavour after mercy, meekness, patience, love, peace, or the rest, will never want acceptation with God. And, withal, we may take comfort if we would seriously set about the practice of these, though we found many lets, and doubts, and difficulties, yet Christ will be all in all to help us and give good success.

Thus of the coherence; the motives follow, and first of election.

Elect. God's servants are God's elect, and that both in respect of election before time, and also in respect of election in time; for the Lord hath in his eternal counsel chose them in Christ, to the obtaining of salvation to the praise of his grace. Eph. i. 4, 5, Rom. viii. 19. And besides, at some time in their life the Lord doth select and separate them from out of the world and worldly courses to the profession of sincerity, having sanctified them by the Spirit.

Use. The doctrine of election hath both consolation and instruction in it: it is full of comfort if we consider the privileges of God's chosen, even those great favours he shews them; when he begins once to discover his everlasting choice of them, the Lord doth ever after avouch them for his peculiar people, to make them high in praise and in honour, Deut. xxvi. 15, 16. 'The men of their strife shall surely perish and come to nothing,' Isa. xli. 8, 11, 12. The Lord will help them and comfort them in all strife, he will be a wall of fire round about them, and the glory in the midst of them; the Lord will own them as his portion, that he hath taken to himself out of the whole earth, Zech. i. 5, 12. He will use them as his friends, he will hear their prayers, and communicate his secrets unto them, John xv. 19. But who can count their privileges? No tongue of men or angels are able to do it; which, since it is so, we should take unto us continually the words of the psalmist, and say every one of us, 'Remember me, O Lord, with the favour of thy people, and visit me with thy salvation, that I may see the felicity of thy chosen, and rejoice in the joy of thy people, and glory with thine inheritance,' Ps. cvi. 4, 5. Especially we should labour to make our calling and election sure, 2 Pet. i. 10; for then we shall be safe, inasmuch as thereby an entrance is ministered unto us into the kingdom of Jesus Christ.

Now, if any shall ask, Who they are that may be sure of their election? I answer, first, with the apostle Paul, they that receive the gospel in power and much assurance, with joy in the Holy Ghost, though it should be with much affliction, 1 Thes. i. 5, 6; and with the apostle Peter, such as to whom God hath given precious promises, and such as fly the corruptions of the world through lust, that join virtue with their faith, and knowledge, and temperance, and patience, and godliness, and brotherly kindness, and love, 2 Pet. i. 4-7, 10; lastly, If we be comforted in our election, we should then labour to inflame our hearts out of the sense of this everlasting goodness of God, even to set up the Lord, and to fear him, and walk in his ways, and particularly by the apostle's direction, to be very careful of these holy graces that follow.

Thus of the first motive.

Holy. They are holy divers ways; for they are holy: 1. In the head; 2. In their laws; 3. In their sacraments, in respect of which they are sacramentally holy; 4. By imputation; 5. By hope, Gal. v. 6, of that consummate holiness in heaven; 6. In their calling, so they are saints by calling, 2. Cor. i. 1; 7. As they are temples of the Holy Ghost. But the holiness of sanctification is here meant, and so they are holy by inchoation.

Holiness is essential to a child of God; God's elect are holy; this is everywhere proved in scripture, Deut. vii. 6, Isa. iv. 4. I will not stand upon it, only for instruction let us from hence observe, that if ever we would have comfort of our election, we must labour to be holy, and that both in body and in spirit, 2 Cor. vii. 1, Eph. v. 3; we see they are here joined, and we must not separate them.

Quest. But may some one say, Seeing no man is without his thousands of sins and infirmities, what must we do that we may have comfort that we are holy in God's account, being so many ways faulty in our natures and actions?

Ans. For answer hereunto, we must know that there be four things which, if a man do attain unto, though he hath otherwise many infirmities, yet he is holy in God's account, yea, in the holiness of sanctification. The first is this: If a man can so far forth subdue his corruptions that sin reigns not in him, so long as it is in him but as a rebel, it doth not frustrate his comfort in his sanctification. 2. If a man's prayers, desires, and endeavours be to 'respect all God's commandments' as well as one, justice as well as piety, holy times as well as holy things, inward obedience as well as outward, secret obedience as well as open, avoiding lesser sins as well as greater. 3. If a man be sincere in the use of the means that make a man holy, preparing his heart to seek God in them, esteem them as his appointed food, mourning for want of success desired, endeavouring to profit by every ordinance of God, and that at all times as well as some times, at home as well as at church. Lastly, If a man can find comfort in the pardon of his sins, he needs not doubt of his acceptation to be holy.

Beloved. In this word is lodged the third motive, which is taken from God's love, as if the apostle would affirm that if Christians did seriously consider what it is to be loved of God, they would find full encouragement to all grace and duty. Now this may be better opened, if we consider but the properties of God's love, wherein it wonderfully excels; as first, If God love thee, it is with a free love, Hosea xiv. 4; he stands not upon thy desert or worthiness. Again, he loves first; he loves before he be loved; he loved us when we hated him; he chose us when we did not choose him. 3. God's love is wonderful tender; which will appear if we consider that he is not only gracious, but 'merciful, slow to anger, of much kindness, and repenteth him of the evil,' Joel ii. 13. 4. God's love is natural, not forced, and therefore he is said to 'quiet himself in his love,' Zeph. iii. 17, and himself loveth mercy, Micah vii. 18. Lastly, His love is an everlasting love, Jer. xxxi. 3; where he loveth, he loveth to the end, John xiii. 1. And therefore we should labour to know the love of God to ourselves, even to be particularly assured that we are God's beloved, or else this could not be a motive to holiness, as here it is; and besides, the meditation of God's love to us should encourage us against all crosses, for God will give his beloved rest, Ps. cxxvii. 2; they shall be blessed, and it shall be well with them; they shall be delivered, for he will help with his right hand, Ps. lx. 5. But especially it should hearten us against the scorns of the world, and the hate of wicked men. If God love us, it mattereth not greatly who hate us. And in special, the meditation of this love of God should teach us to tire ourselves with these worthy graces as so many ornaments; for thus should the beloved of God be decked. And doth the Lord love us, and shall not we strive to shew our love to him again, even by loving his word, glory, children, presence, and commandments? Lastly, We may here learn how to love, for God loves: first, Those that are holy; secondly, Those whom he had chosen. So it should be with us: first, We should choose for holiness, and then love for our choice. This may teach the people how to love their magistrates and ministers, and so wives and servants, and contrariwise.

Thus of the motives; the manner follows.

Put on, viz., as men do their garments. It is true that these graces for the worth of them are royal, and so must be put on as the king doth his crown, or the prince elected his robes. It is also true that for safety these graces are as armour to defend us against the allurements of the world, or the reproaches of evil men, and so may be put on as the soldier doth his armour. Besides, these graces are required in us as the ornaments of a renewed estate, and so are to be put on, as the new baptized was said to put on his new garments. But I think the metaphor is taken generally from the putting on of raiment.

Divers things may be here noted: 1. It is apparent that these graces are not natural; the shadows and pictures of them may be in natural men; and what wicked men can get is but by the restraining spirit, or by reason of natural defect, or for ill ends. It is certain a man may be said to be born as well with clothes on his back as with grace in his heart.

2. How should the hearts of many smite them to think of it, how they neglect this clothing of their souls with graces. They every day remember to put on apparel on their backs, but scarce any day think of putting on virtue for their hearts. Oh, when thou seest thy naked body clothed, shouldst thou not remember that thy soul, in itself more naked than thy body, had need of clothing also? Oh, the judgment that abides many a man and woman! how excessively careful are they to trim the body, and yet are excessively careless of trimming their souls; that have so many gowns for their backs that they have never a grace for their hearts. Yea, the better sort may be humbled if they search their hearts seriously; for either they want divers parcels of this holy raiment, or else they are not well-fitted on them; they hang so loose many times there is little comeliness or warmth by their wearing of these graces. But let us all be instructed to remember these graces, and by prayer and practice to exercise ourselves in them, and daily to be essaying how we can put them on, till by constant use of all good means we can grow spiritually skilful in wearing of them, and expressing the power of them in conversation, as plainly as we shew the garments on our backs, resolving that these virtues will be our best ornaments, and that they are best clad that are clothed with these godly graces in their hearts.

Thus of the manner; the enumeration of the graces follow.

Bowels of mercy. From the coherence I note two things concerning mercy: first, That it is not natural; we are exhorted to put it on; naturally we are hateful and hate one another, Isa. xi.; which should teach us to observe and discern the defects of our hearts herein, and by prayer, James iii. 17, 19, Titus iii. 3, to strive with God for the repair of our natures; and in all wrongs from wicked men to be less moved, as resolving it is natural with them.

2. We may note here that mercy is as it were the door of virtue. It stands here in the forefront, and leads in and out all the rest; it lets in humility, meekness, patience, &c.

Now in these words themselves I observe three things:

1. That mercy is of more sorts than one, therefore he saith *mercies*; one mercy will not serve the turn; he that hath true mercy hath many mercies, or ways to shew mercy; many miseries in man's life needs many sorts of mercy, Luke vi., Mat. xxv.

There is mercy corporal, and mercy spiritual; it is corporal mercy to lend, to give, to visit, to clothe, to feed, to protect from violence; hospitality to strangers, and the burial of the dead, are also corporal mercies. Spiritual mercies are not all of a sort, for we may shew mercy sometimes in things wherein no man can help, as by praying unto God for help. Now in things wherein man can help, the mercy to be shewed respects either the ignorance or other distresses of other men. The mercy to the ignorant is either instruction in the things they should know, or counsel in the things they should do. Now his other distresses arise either from his actions or from his passions; his actions are either against thee, and so thy mercy is to forgive; or against others, and so thy mercy is to admonish or correct. Thy mercy towards him, in respect of his passions or sufferings, is either in words, and so it is consolation, or in deeds, and so it is confirmation. What shall I say? There is the mercy of the minister, and the mercy of the magistrate, and also the mercy of the private man.

2. *Mercies* notes that it is not enough to be merciful once or seldom, but we must be much in the works of mercy; seldom mercy will be no better accepted with God than seldom prayer; we are bound to watch to the opportunity of mercy, and we shall reap not only according to the matter, but according to the measure of mercy, Hosea x. 12.

3. It is not enough to be merciful, but we must put on the bowels of mercies, and this hath in it divers things. For it imports:

1. That our mercies must be from the heart, not in hypocrisy or for a show, it must be true and unfeigned mercy.

2. That there should be in us the affections of mercy; we should love mercy, and shew it with all cheerfulness and zeal, Micah vi. 8, Rom. xii. 8, 2 Cor. ix. 7-15.

3. That there should be a sympathy and fellow-feeling in the distresses of others. These bowels were in Christ, in Moses, and Paul.

4. That our mercy should be extended to the highest degree we can get our hearts to; that was imported by the phrase of pouring out our souls to the needy, Isa. lviii. 10.

Use. The use of this doctrine of mercy may be: first, For instruction, to teach us to make conscience of this holy grace, and to be sure we be always clad with it, according to the occasions and opportunities of mercy. And to this end we should labour to stir up ourselves by the meditation of the motives unto mercy such as these: God hath commanded it, Zech. vii. 6, Hosea xii. 10. They are our own flesh that need our mercy, Isa. lviii. Our heavenly Father is merciful, yea, his mercy is above all his works, Luke vi. 33, Ps. lxxxvi.; yea, he is Father of all mercies, 2 Cor. i. 3. Mercy will prove that we are righteous, Ps. xxxvii. 21, and blessed, Micah v. 7, and that the love of God is in us, 1 John iii. 17, and that our profession of religion is sincere, James i. 27, and that our knowledge is from above, James iii. 17, and that we are true neighbours and right Samaritans. God wonderfully accepts of mercy above many other things, Micah vi. 8, Hosea vi. 6, and accounts what is that way done to be done as it were to himself, Prov. xiv. 31, xix. 17. Besides, what is mercifully bestowed is safest kept; the surest chest to keep our goods in is the bosom of the poor, the house of the widow, and the mouths of the orphans. What shall I say? Mercy rewards our own souls, Prov. xi. 17, assures us of forgiveness of sins, Prov. xvi. 6, makes the heart cheerful and steadfast, 1 Cor. xv. 58. It shews us life, righteousness, and glory, Prov. xxi. 21; and we shall reap after the measure of mercies, both in this life, and at the last day, Hosea x. 12.

Only in shewing mercy we must look to divers rules: 1. It must be holy mercy, not foolish pity; as magistrates must not spare where God will punish; for this is everywhere a monstrous wickedness in careless magistrates, under the pretence of mercy they spare the punishment of drunkenness, whoredom, but especially blood, and the profanation of the sabbath. It is a wonder that many magistrates should ever go to heaven, they are guilty of so much blood and wickedness, by not executing the judgment of God and the king upon such villanies. And it is not mercy, under pretence of housekeeping, to entertain disordered persons, swaggerers, drunkards, swearers, gamesters, and the like. He that will shew mercy must have a good eye, Prov. xxii. 9, to consider where, and to whom, and how, he shews mercy; the true merciful man doth measure his affairs by judgment, Ps. cxii. 5. 2. Thy mercy must be speedy mercy; thou must not say Go, and come again to-morrow, if thou canst do it now, Prov. iii. 28. 3. It must be of goods well-gotten; God hates robbery for burnt-offering, Isa.

2 S

lxii. 8. 4. We must look to our ends, for that mercy is lost that is shewn to win the praise of men, or for any other carnal respect.

Secondly, The consideration of the doctrine of mercy may serve for the great reproof of the want of mercy in men, and that monstrous unmercifulness that everywhere abounds amongst men. We may complain that merciful men are perished; or if mercy get into the hearts of some, it is like the morning dew, it is quickly dried up. But the world is full of usury and cruelty and oppression; the world hath almost as many wild beasts and monsters as it hath landlords in divers places. And shall nothing be said, think we, in the day of Christ, to unmerciful ministers and church governors also? Oh, the blood-guiltiness of many monsters rather than ministers, that feed not, or not with wholesome food, the souls of the people! And is there not 'tithing of mint, and cummin, and annis,' while 'the weightier things of the law are let alone'? It is no mercy to spare idle and scandalous and idol-shepherds. What should I speak of particulars? There is unmercifulness even in the lender; there is no borrowing unless thou wilt be 'a servant to him that lendeth,' Prov. xxii. 7. Oh, what sums of money are spent upon hawks, hounds, cocks, bears, players, whores—for I may well join them together —gaming, drinking, apparel, feasting, &c., which should be profitably spent upon the necessities of the poor! But let men repent of their unmercifulness; for the curse of God is upon them, Prov. xiv. 21, xx. 21; and the Lord takes the wrong as done unto himself, Prov. xiv. 31; their cry shall not be heard, Prov. xxi. 13, nor their fasting nor sacrifice accepted, Isa. lviii., Hosea vi. 5; and God will spoil their souls, Prov. xxii. 23; and judgment merciless shall be to them that shew no mercy, James ii. 13.

Thirdly, This doctrine is exceeding comfortable, too; for here is implied great comfort to all God's children; for if God require such tender mercy in me, he will certainly shew mercy himself. And again, poor men may be much encouraged to consider how careful God is of them, and how much mercy he requires to be shewed them; yea, it is a comfort to them, if they be godly poor, that there being so many kinds of mercy, they may shew mercy themselves, even to their richest benefactors, by spiritual mercy. And this also must needs be comfortable to merciful men; for as God requires mercy, so it is sure he will reward mercy, Ps. cxii. 4, Isa. lviii. 7, &c.

Thus of mercy.

Kindness. The word is courtesy or goodness, *comitas.* It is sure the Lord requires this Christian courtesy or goodness of disposition and carriage in every convert, Eph. iv. 32, Gal. v. 22; and kindness is one of the things we should approve ourselves by, 2 Cor. vi. 6. Now Christian courtesy or goodness hath in it these things: 1. It salutes willingly, 1 Pet. v. 14, Ruth ii. 4, Judges vi. 12, Mat. xi. 14. 2. It is fair and amiable in conversing, not harsh, sullen, crabbed, untractable, clownish, desperate, scornful, hard to please, churlish, or stately. 3. In matters of offence, it is easy to be entreated, kind to enemies; it qualifies the speeches of the angry with good interpretations, and sometimes it yields to their affections; it will sometimes part with right for peace sake; it will forgive, James iii. 17, Luke vi. 33, Eph. iv. 32. 4. In the praise or happiness of others, it is without envy. 5. It is easy to liberality and prevents, 1 Pet. ii. 5, Rom. ii. 4. 6. It loves brotherly fellowship.

Use. The use may be both to humble and to teach. Certainly the failings of the best of us may much abase us; and the knowledge of it that God requires it should teach us to make conscience of it, by prayer and holy striving with our natures, to endeavour to express this fairness and kind conversing. Since religion requires courtesy as well as piety, we should labour to be unrebukable therein also; especially we should put on this virtue in using means to win others to the truth.

Here also we may see the vanity of their aspersion that say religion will make men stoical and uncivil.

Yet lest any should mistake, we must know that courtesy hath not in it the honouring of evil men, or the rejoicing at the evils of any man, or a promiscuous respect of all, both good and bad alike; no, nor of all good alike in the measure of manifestation; nor hath it an openness in unadvised communicating of secrets to all; nor a lightness of familiarity in contracting an inward friendship without due respect of the disposition and conversation of the parties.

Thus of kindness.

Humbleness of mind. I shall not need to shew that humility or this humbleness of mind is required; for it is plain in the text; but rather I would consider what it is, and then make use of it. And first, I consider of it negatively, by shewing what it is not. It is not silliness, arising out of the ignorance of a man's place or gifts, nor is it any careless disregard of a man's self, nor every abasing of a man's self; for wicked men, to compass their ends, can humble themselves to hell, Isa. lvii. 9. Nor is it a will-worship, when a man, by voluntary religion, layeth hard things upon his body; thus it was no humility to forbear touching, tasting, handling, or, upon pretence of unworthiness to employ the King's Son, to bring in mediation of angels or saints, as inferiors in the court. Nor is it complimental courtesy, for we see that may be in greater exactness in men, and yet monstrous pride and malice be lodged in men's hearts. Nor is it any counterfeit submissiveness, as when some men scorn to refuse offices, and yet fret afterwards when they go without them, or else refuse of purpose to be the more importuned. Nor is it humbleness of mind to be (with fretting) complaining of our wants out of emulation of others; nor is it only to be humbled, for humiliation and humility differ.

Now, that the nature of this grace may be found out, we must consider, that usually it is begotten in a man by the power of the word, and follows the breaking of the heart by mortification, and declares itself both inwardly and outwardly. Inwardly humbleness of mind hath in it a sight and sense, and digested opinion of our own great unworthiness, and is not easily stirred to great thoughts with vain applauses. It hath in it a tender sense of temptations, a hatred of hypocrisy, and a willingness to suffer afflictions, and a contentation in some measure, in what estate soever it pleaseth God to bring a man to. Outwardly it expresseth itself both towards God and men; towards God it keeps a man lowly in the use of the means, and hath a continued fear and awful sense of God's presence, Micah vi. 8, and stands not at it to be accounted vile for the service of God, 2 Sam. vi. 22. In carriage towards men, it is not affected in words or gestures, it is not censorious, nor arrogant, Ps. cxxxi. 1–3, nor contentious, Phil. ii. 3. It desires not open and public places; it is not swelled with praises, nor it affects not the vain praises of itself; but contrariwise, it makes a man go before in giving honour, and not to think much to equal himself with them of the lower sort, Rom. xii., rejoicing in the love of a poor Christian, as well as of a great man. It will make a man subject to and thankful for admonitions, and willing to embrace the truth, though it be found in the possession of others. Finally, it is joyful upon the doing of any good, and thankful for lesser favours.

Use. The use is, as for humiliation under the sense of our wants in expressing the practice of this grace, so for instruction, to teach us to labour after it, as a most praiseworthy virtue; we should seek lowliness, as the prophet speaks, Zeph. ii. 3; and to this end we should contemplate of the motives hereunto. For humility is one of the graces we are especially charged to imitate in Christ, Mat. xi. 29. It is a grace that God highly accounts of; he holds us worthy of our vocation if he may see this in us, Eph. iv. 1, 2. The Lord himself will, in his special reviving presence, dwell in the contrite and humble soul, Isa. lvii. 15, Ps. xxxiv. 18. He will not despise their prayers, Ps. cii. 17. Wisdom is with the lowly, Prov. xi. 2. The Lord will heal them, and create the fruit of the lips to be peace, Isa. lvii. 15, 19. Howsoever it may go with the humble otherwise, yet the Lord will he sure to give grace to the humble, 1 Pet. v. 5, 6. Lastly, Humility goeth before honour, the Lord will exalt us if we abase ourselves, and we are most precious in his eyes when we are most vile in our own eyes. And contrariwise, this may shew us the hatefulness of pride, &c.; the more the Lord stands upon humbleness of mind, the more it imports he abhors pride. And that the nature and praise of true humility may the better appear, it will not be amiss to set out the sorts of pride.

Generally, pride is expressed either in things that concern God, or in things that concern man. In the things that concern God, there is the pride of the atheist, whereby he strives to remove the sense of the being of God; and the pride of the heretic, when he assaults the attributes of God, or his persons; and the pride of the papist, who will claim by his merits; and the pride of the curious, who will search into things not revealed; and the pride of the persecutor, who will pursue, by slanders or violence, the power of God's ordinances; and the pride of the impenitent, that dare live and die in his sins without care of God's threatenings. And towards men pride is discovered divers ways, as by impugning the fame of the best men, by the singularity of conceit of worth above others, either for place or gifts, by bragging and boasting, by vain joys, either for place or gifts, by striving for offices and highest places; yea, there is a spiritual pride in every grace and holiness. Now, contrary hereunto is that humility God requires in this place.

And thus of humbleness of mind.

Meekness. Christian meekness hath in it, as I conceive, these things: first, A quietness of heart in the freedom from passion, by which one is slow to anger, and not easily provoked. Secondly, A teachableness and tractableness, or being easy to be persuaded, Isa. xi., James iii. 17. Thirdly, A childlike confidence in God's care and providence, becoming in that respect as a little child, Mat. xviii. Fourthly, It is not swelled with prosperity. Fifthly, It thinks not much of the yoke of Christ, Mat. xi. 30: in what measure a man is truly meek, in the same measure he accounts God's service a reasonable and easy service. Sixthly, In conversing it hath two principal properties: the first is fear, 1 Pet. iii. 2, 3, as it is opposed unto boldness, conceitedness, rough-heartedness; the second is an evangelical harmlessness or simplicity, 2 Cor. xi. 3.

Use. The consideration may much humble the best of us, if we consider how passion doth overmaster us, and how success doth swell us, and how still our hearts are after an inconceivable manner against the power of the means, and how unquiet we are for want of confidence in God. Oh, where is this conversation with fear to be found? And for the simplicity that is in Christ Jesus, how is it mixed in some, and wanted in others, and lost in many who are beguiled of the serpent? Yet inasmuch as this grace is indispensably required that it should be put on, let us stir up our hearts, as to seek righteousness, so to seek meekness with it.

And to this end we should avoid what doth encounter it: as, namely, we should take heed of lust, and malice, and covetousness, and contention; for these things will wonderfully disturb the heart, and fill it marvellously with perturbations: and also we should meditate of the encouragements to this grace; for meekness would much avail us in the profit and power of the word, James i. 21, 22, Isa. xxix. 19; and God hath promised to water this grace with secret joys and careful refreshings, Mat. xi. 29. Besides, God doth in special manner undertake their protection, as the places in the margin will shew, Ps. lxxvi. 1–9, cxlvii. 5, 6, and cxlix. 4. For meekness in the hid-man of the heart is a thing much set by, 1 Pet. iii. 4; he will guide them in judgment and teach them his way, Ps. xxv. 9.

Long-suffering. By long-suffering is meant, as I take it: first, An unwearied firmness of heart, holding out under all crosses, temptations, oppositions, &c., the mind not being easily broken, put out, confounded, discouraged, distempered, or unquieted with any kind of passion: and so, indeed, it is nothing else but the perseverance of patience; secondly, There is a long-suffering which is a spiritual perseverance of hope under the promise, with an expectation of the performance of it, Heb. vi. 12, 15. There is a long-suffering in our carriage towards others in regard of their reformation, and so we should suffer long in hope of the conversion of the wicked, 2 Tim. iv. 2, 5, and in expecting the reformation of infirmities in God's children, whom we love and admonish, 1 Thes. v. 14. And this is the praise of Christian love, that it doth suffer long, 1 Cor. xiii.

The long-suffering is an excellent grace and a worthy ornament, meet to be put on as well as any of the rest, and would wonderfully grace the lives of Christians. And the rather should we love it, and long after it, because it is so eminent a praise in God himself, Rom. ix. 22, Luke xviii. 7, and in Christ; yea, as any have excelled in the church, so have they been approved in the trial of this grace, as were the apostles. But it is enough to commend it, it is an excellent fruit of the sanctifying spirit, Gal. v. 22. Only we must know there is great difference between enduring long and long-suffering; for true Christian long suffering is accompanied not only with patience, but with diligence, Heb. vi. 12, Col. i. 11, 1 Tim. iv. 5, and joyfulness, and watching in all things, but especially with the renewing of faith in God's promise and providence.

Ver. 13. *Forbearing one another, and forgiving one another, if any man have a quarrel to another: even as Christ forgave you, even so do ye.*

There are two virtues in conversing that concern adversity: first, Long-suffering under crosses; and secondly, Clemency under injuries.

Of long-suffering before: first, Of clemency in this verse, where two things may be noted: 1. The duty required; 2. The reason rendered for the urging of the duty. The duty is propounded in the two principal parts of it, viz., to forbear and to forgive; and amplified by the supposition of a case, 'if any man have a quarrel to another.' The reason is from the example of Christ forgiving us.

Forbearing. The original word is rendered sometimes to maintain, Acts xviii. 14, sometimes to suffer, to endure, 1 Cor. iv. 12, 2 Thes. i. 4, 2 Tim. iv. 4, Heb. xiii. 22, sometimes not only to endure, but forbear also, 2 Cor. xi. 1, sometimes to support, Eph. iv. 1. In the two last senses it may be well taken here.

Now if we would distinctly know what it is to forbear one another, as it here imports a main part of Christian clemency, we must understand that it is not an omission of holy duties to others, nor a refusing to satisfy others in their griefs or offences, nor a shunning of their company, nor yet a swallowing down of all sorts of injuries, committed with a high hand, without acknowledgment or satisfaction. But out of clemency to forbear others, hath in it such things as these: first, A freedom from the thirst of revenge; secondly, A bearing with the infirmities of others, which may be performed two ways: 1. By covering them, and not blazing them abroad if they be secret; and, 2. By silence, in not reproving them when they fail merely in frailty; thirdly, It hath in it not only a bearing with them, but a bearing of them, Gal. vi. 2; and that I think may be two ways also: 1. In not stirring or provoking their infirmities; 2. By pleasing our neighbours' humour in that which is good to edification,

Rom. xv. 1, 2; fourthly, There is a forbearance in matters of wrong to us; and thus to forbear is not to prosecute every wrong, either by answers or by suits. And this forbearance is to be practised when we are able to revenge, else it is no thanks to us to forbear when we want either power or opportunity to do it. Secondly, It is forbearance not to meet wrong with wrong.

Or thus, there is a threefold forbearance: first, In judgment, when in doubtful cases we suspend our opinions or censures; secondly, In words, which consist either in not answering or in giving soft answers; thirdly, In deeds, when we render not evil for evil.

Again, forbearance is varied from the consideration of time, for in some things we must forbear ever, never taking notice of the infirmities or wrongs, as in some weaknesses that are by mere oversight or ignorance, and in some things we must forbear for a time, that is, till there be a fit opportunity to admonish or correct, &c.

Uses. The consideration thereof serves greatly for the reproof of that wretched distemper in many that profess the same faith and hope, provoking one another, and consuming one another, and by frowardness disquieting the rest and content of others. Is not here an express charge that we should forbear one another? Have we not here the example of Christ who did so, who might have a thousandfold more just reason to upbraid, censure, or find fault than we have, or can have? Besides, this distempered peevishness and froward misconceiving and censuring, it is bred of ill causes, for it comes either of malice or ignorance. Of malice, for love covereth a multitude of sins, especially it suspendeth doubtful actions; of ignorance, for it is certain a wise man will keep in till afterwards, or hold it his glory to be able to pass by an offence. Further, this sin may be aggravated by the relations that are mutually between Christians. Are they not fellow-members, co-heirs, fellow-citizens, partakers of the same afflictions? are they not brethren? &c. Besides, is not this also a constant justice, that they that judge are judged, they that censure are censured? and doth not this envying and jangling give occasion of rejoicing to adversaries? Doth it not many times so transform Christians that it makes them very like wicked men, when they grow so distempered that they revile their own mothers' sons? Ps. l. 20. In the fifth to the Galatians the apostle urgeth this reproof by divers reasons, such as this: A little of the leaven of these distempers will sour the whole lump; and those courses tend not to any good, but to the disquieting of God's people, and it is not a small matter to trouble and vex them. Besides, inasmuch as Christians have trouble enough other ways, it doth not become them to trouble their brethren; and we should be so far from troubling our brethren, as we should rather serve them by love; and if men will needs bite one another, let them take heed lest they be devoured one of another. Lastly, If men will not be warned, then let them know the Judge standeth at the door, James v. 9.

Now that we may attain this forbearing, even to be rightly ordered towards the infirmities or wrongs of others, we must labour to get more Christian love of others; for that will endure all things, and believe all things, and make us able to bear; and it will drive out suspicion, which like a wretched beldame is the mother and nurse of all murmurings and vain jangling: and besides, we must get a greater knowledge of our own selves, and our own ignorance and corruptions; for when we seem to ourselves to be something, deceiving ourselves, we are ready with intemperance to apprehend supposed indignities when none are offered, Gal. vi. 1–3. Or if thou must needs speak, then speak the words of admonition, even God's words, if thou be sure they have sinned, instead of thine own vain and passionate upbraidings, or reproaches, or censures.

One another. Observe that usually where there is any contention or quarrelling, both sides are guilty; though one principally do the wrong, yet few men are so temperate but they do wrong again, either in words, or deeds, or affections; and therefore thou shouldst forbear, seeing thou art privy to thyself, that in this business thou hast not been such as thou shouldst be.

Forgiving. The word signifies sometimes to give, 1 Cor. ii. 12, Phil. i. 29; sometimes to give freely, Luke vii. 21, Acts xxvii. 24, Rom. viii. 32, Gal. iii. 8, Philem. 22; sometimes to remit freely the punishment, Acts iii. 14; sometimes to deliver up for favour, or to pleasure others; sometimes to forgive; and so here.

Quest. But can any man forgive sin to another?

Ans. 1. Man may forgive the trespass, though not the sin. 2. Man may forgive the punishment that by man might be inflicted, so as not to require it. 3. Man may pray to God to forgive it.

Object. But it is said no man can forgive sin but God.

Sol. True; no man can remit the eternal punishment, or the curse of the law, or take away the guilt of sin before God. But man may forgive it as far as concerns himself.

Object. Now others may object contrariwise, that 2 Cor. ii. 7, they are willed to forgive, and yet the sin of the incestuous person was not so much a trespass that concerned them, as a sin against God.

Sol. This sin also was a trespass against them: 1. As it was a scandal; 2. As it might cause them and their profession to be evil spoken of for his sake. Again, to forgive in that place, may be taken in a large sense for to be reconciled to him.

Quest. Is reconciliation necessarily comprehended under forgiveness?

Ans. We are tied to seek it and desire it, and to use all humble and just and discreet courses to attain it. But if it will not be had, we are discharged if we forgive. Neither unto obstinate offenders, that will not acknowledge their sin, are we bound to remit the punishment, or sometimes to notify the pardon of the fault.

If any man have a quarrel to another. When he saith here 'if any man,' it imports that such Christians might be, as there should be no jars amongst them. Discords might wonderfully be prevented if there were care and discretion in men.

The word rendered 'quarrel' signifies a complaint. Certainly it is a great weakness to be upon every occasion complaining of the wrongs are done us, and making report of them to others. And it shews, too, that we should forbear and forgive even in such things as these.

And where he saith 'any man,' it shews no men are exempted from the practice of clemency. That which is here required of one is required of all, no greatness of gifts or place can privilege any.

As Christ forgave you, so do you. 1. Examples in all rules of practice move much.

2. As here the head of the church is an example to all his members, so should those that are heads of the commonwealth or family carry themselves so as by their examples to direct as well as by their precept, not only shew what to do by commanding, but how to do it also by example.

3. Especially in forbearing and forgiving. Example in great persons doth wonderfully affect the common people; and, therefore, because there are so few on earth, here is one from heaven.

Quest. But why is there added reason to this virtue, and not so to each of the former?

Ans. 1. Because the conscience is soon persuaded in the general that the rest are good, as humility, meekness, &c. But now we are wonderfully hardly persuaded to forgive. 2. The Lord may well add reasons to persuade to forgive, because of the special danger of not forgiving; for if a man do not forgive, there is express threatenings that he shall not be forgiven, Mat. vi. 14, xviii. 25.

Quest. But how is Christ said to forgive?

Ans. Remission of sins is attributed to Christ: 1. As the meritorious cause of forgiveness; 2. Because he applies it; 3. Because the Christian in his name sues out the pardon of his sins, and by him procures forgiveness. Certainly it may be a singular comfort to all distressed souls if they consider that he is their brother, head, Saviour; even he that shed his blood for them is he that disposeth of all pardons and applies remission of sins. Sure it is no hard matter to get a pardon from him: that is so engaged in his love to us.

Here also we see that the action of Christ is the instruction of the Christian. Christ forgave, so must he. We must remember the distinctions of Christ's actions. Some were miraculous, as fasting forty days, raising the dead, &c.; these are not to be imitated, because they cannot. Some are peculiar actions belonging to his office, as to redeem, or make intercession, &c.; these also are proper to him only. Now some are moral; these last are only imitable. Or thus: Some actions of Christ he did as God, some as mediator, some as man. The last only bind us to follow.

Again, in that we are bound to forgive, as he forgave, it not only teacheth that we must do it as well as he; but for the manner of it as he did. And how was that? First, Christ forgave his inferiors; secondly, Christ forgave great faults as well as less, yea, all sorts of faults, yea, though they were often fallen into; thirdly, Nothing was too dear to Christ to merit or confirm his forgiveness, therefore he shed his own blood, he stood not upon his profit or his case; fourthly, Christ uses all means to prevent offending; fifthly, Where Christ forgives he forgets; sixthly, Christ forgives two ways: 1. Upon the cross before men did repent; 2. By the gospel publishing his pardon upon man's repentance; he did not carry them grudge till they repented; and all these ways should we imitate Christ.

Lastly, Observe here the certainty of assurance; for if a man did not certainly and infallibly know that Christ did forgive him, how could that be made a reason if he did not know it to be?

And thus of clemency, and so of the two first sorts of graces.

Ver. 14. *And above all these put on love, which is the bond of perfectness.*

The virtues that ought to reign at all times are love, peace, and thankfulness. Of love in this verse, which the apostle sets out as the most noble, ample, and profitable of all the virtues, two things are here to be considered: first, The dignity of love, where he saith, 'Above all put on love,' &c.; secondly, The use of it, it is 'the bond of perfectness.'

Above all these. Some read, 'with all these;' some read, 'for all these,' meaning that all the former do flow from this, and therefore we should get love that we might be merciful, humble, &c. And so it would import that we should get love, that we might approve ourselves that these are not mere compliments, or dissembled offices, or things taken up for wrong ends.

But most properly and commonly it is read as here, 'above all these.' And so notes the dignity of love above all other virtues; for it is indeed more excellent both in respect of causation, as they say in schools, because it begets the rest as the efficient cause, and for the preservation of it other virtues are practised, or the final cause of them; as also, it is above the rest in acceptation, whether we respect God or man. And thirdly, It is above the rest in respect of continuance, 1 Cor. xiii. 8. And this may serve to reprove our great neglect of so noble a grace; and it may teach us in our prayers to remember to pray for this, and in our practice to provoke unto love, Heb. x. 24.

Object. A cavil of the papists must be avoided here, for they absurdly reason thus: If love be above all virtues, then it is love that makes us just in God's sight.

Sol. But for answer we may easily satisfy ourselves with this, that before men, and in conversing with men, love is above all. But before God faith is above all; love is above faith only in some respects, as in continuance, but faith is above love in justification.

Put on. Love is not natural; it is a virtue that in the truth of it is wonderful rare in the world, for man is unto man naturally a wolf, a fox, a bear, a tiger, a lion, yea, a very devil; and that is the reason why men are so constant in malice, it is natural with them; and this is the reason why unity and loving concord is found in no calling amongst men.

Love. Love is of divers kinds: there is natural, civil, moral, and religious love. It is natural love for a man to love himself, his parents, kindred, &c. It is civil love that is framed in us by the laws of men, by authority from God, whereby we are brought not to violate the rules of justice or society. In moral love, that love of friends is of eminent respect; but it is religious or Christian love is meant here.

Christian love is carried both towards God and towards men, and both may be here meant; for the very love of God may be required as needful in our conversing with men, because we can never love men aright till we first love God; and besides, we are bound in our carriage to shew our love to God, by zeal for his glory, and avoiding sin in our callings for the love we bear to him.

Sure it is that the true love of God is exceeding needful to be put on as a most royal robe; I say, the true love of God, and therefore I advise all sorts of men, as to labour for it, so to try themselves whether this love of God be right in them. If we love God, we receive them that come in his name, John v. 43, and the love of the world doth not reign in us, 1 John ii. 15, 17; and we are much in thinking of God and godliness, for we often think of what we love, and we love the word of God, John xiv. 27; and in adversity we run first to God for help, denying ourselves to bring glory to God, subjecting our wills to his will, glorying in the hope of his mercy; and it is certain also if we love God aright, we desire his presence, both of grace and glory. And this love will compel us to holiness, 2 Cor. v. 14, causing us to hate what he hates, and to obey his commandments; and besides, kindness from God will wonderfully inflame us and content us.

The love to men is love of enemies, or brotherly love of God's children. Christians are bound to love their very enemies; and this kind of love must be put on as well as the other, only let us advisedly consider what the love of enemies hath in it. When God requires us to love our enemies, he doth not require us to love their vices, or to hold needless society with their persons, or to further them in such kindnesses as might make them more wicked, or to relinquish the defence of our just cause; but to love is not to return evil for evil, Rom. xii., neither in words nor deeds, 1 Pet. iii. 8, 9, and to pray for them, Mat. v., and to supply their necessities as we have occasion, Rom. xii. 19, Exod. xxiii. 4, 2 Chron. xxviii. 8, 9, 13, 15, 2 Kings vi. 22, overcoming their evil with goodness, and in some cases to be extraordinarily humbled for them, Ps. xxxviii. 13.

But I think the love of brethren is principally here meant. This is a fire kindled by the sanctifying Spirit of God, 2 Tim. i. 7; this was intended in our election, Eph. i. 14; this proves our faith, Gal. v. 6; this nourisheth the mystical body of Christ, Eph. iv. 17; this love is without dissimulation, Rom. xii. 9, 2 Cor. vi. 6; it is diligent and labouring love, 1 Thes. i. 3, Heb. vi. 10; it is harmless and inoffensive, Rom. xiii. 10; it woundeth not by suspicious provocations or scandals, Rom. xiv. 15; it is not mercenary, for as God is not to be loved for reward, though he be not loved without reward, so we must love men, not for their good turns they do us, but for the good graces God hath given them. And we should shew our love in using our gifts for the best good of the body, Rom. xii. 6, 7; and manifest our compassion and fellow-feeling by counsel and admonitions, 2 Cor. ii. 4, and consolations, Phil. i. 7; and all ways of edification, 1 Cor. viii. 1; and by the works of mercy, 2 Cor. viii. 24; avoiding contention, Phil. ii. 3; and covering the infirmities one of another, 1 Pet. iv. 8.

Thus of the dignity and nature of love; the use of it follows, which is—

The bond of perfection. Love is said to be the bond of perfection three ways: first. Because it is a most perfect bond, and so it is a Hebraism; for all virtues are, as it were, collected in love; all other virtues will soon be unloosed, unless they be fastened in love; neither doth it only tie virtues together, but it gives them their perfection, moving them, perfecting them, and making them accepted. And it is most perfect, because it is most principal among virtues, nothing is in this life well composed that is not directed hither.

But let none mistake: he doth not shew here how we may be made perfect before God, but how we might converse perfectly amongst men. And so the sum of this sense is, that all should be well with us, in living one with another, if love flourish amongst us; perfection consisteth in love by way of bond.

Secondly, It is a bond of perfection, because it is the bond that ties together the church, which is the beauty and perfection of the whole world.

Thirdly, It is a bond of perfection, as it leads us to God, who is perfection itself; yea, by love God is joined to man, and dwells in him.

Use. The use of all is, seeing love is of this nature, use, dignity, and perfection, therefore we should labour to be rooted in love, even every way firmly settled in it. And to this end we should labour more to mortify our own self-love, and the care for our own ease, profit, credit, &c.

And this may wonderfully also shame us for those defects are found in us. It may greatly reprove in us that coldness of affection that is even in the better sort, and those frequent janglings and discords, and that fearful neglect of fellowship in the gospel in many places, and all those evil fruits that arise from want of the exercise of this grace, such as are suspicions, blind censures, &c. And thus of love.

Ver. 15. *And let the peace of God rule in your hearts, to the which also ye are called in one body; and be thankful.*

In this verse he exhorts unto the two last virtues, peace and thankfulness. In the exhortation to peace, there is the duty and the reason. The duty in these words, 'Let the peace of God rule in your hearts,' where I consider the nature of the virtue—'peace;' the author of it—'God;' the power of it—'let it rule;' the seat or subject of it—'in your hearts.' The reason of it is double: first, From their vocation—'to the which ye are called;' secondly, From their mutual relation, as 'members of one body.'

Peace. Peace is threefold, internal, external, and eternal. Internal peace is the tranquillity of the mind and conscience in God, satisfied in the sense of his goodness, Rom. xiv. 17. External peace is the quiet and concord in our outward estate and carriage, Eph. iv. 3. Eternal peace is the blessed rest of the saints in heaven, Isa. lvii. 2. The last is not here meant.

Of God. Peace is said to be of God in divers respects: 1. Because our peace should be such as may stand with the glory of God, so we should seek the truth and peace, Zech. viii. 19. 2. It may be said to be of God, because he commandeth it, 1 Cor. xiv. 31. 3. Because he giveth it, he is the author of it; hence peace is said to be a fruit of the Spirit, Gal. v. 22; and God is said to be the God of peace, 2 Cor. xiii. 11, 1 Thes. v. 23, Heb. xiii. 20. In this last sense I think it is meant here.

Let it rule. The original word is a term borrowed from running a race; and it imports, let peace be the judge, let it sit and oversee, and moderate all the affections of the heart, seeing we are in a continual strife, whereas our affections would carry us to contentions, discords, brawlings, grudges, and divisions, &c. Let the victory be in the power of peace; let peace give the applause, and finally determine the matter.

Thus of the explication of the sense of the words,

Now all these words may be first understood of internal peace with God, and then God may be said to be the author of it in divers respects:

First, It may be said to be of God, because he sent his Son to merit it. Hence Christ is said to be our peace, Eph. ii. 14, 17; Prince of peace, Isa. ix. 6; Lord of peace, 2 Thes. iii. 16. Secondly, Because he sends his messengers to proclaim it and invite men to it, Isa. lii. 7. Thirdly, Because he sends his Spirit to work it, Gal. v. 22.

Now this peace of God is said to rule:

First, When it oversways doubts and tentations, establishing the heart in the confidence of the assurance of God's love in Christ, which is when a man can say, as the apostle did, 'I am persuaded neither principalities nor powers, neither heights nor depths, things present nor things to come, shall ever be able to separate us from the love of God which is in Christ Jesus.' Catharinus, a very papist, could gather certainty out of this place.

Secondly, When in our carriage we continually fear to offend God, or do anything that might disturb the peace of our consciences.

Thirdly, When in adversity we can deny ourselves, and rather choose to suffer affliction than forego the peace of Christ in our hearts, John xvi. 33.

Now when the Holy Ghost adds 'in your hearts,' it implies that true peace with God will encounter both presumption and hypocrisy and diffidence. Presumption, for it will rule in our hearts; it will not abide hardness of heart and the spiritual slumber; it will not rest till there be affections of godliness, as well as common profession of it. Hypocrisy, for it notes that it will not rule only by keeping justice in a man's life, but it will rule within a man's thoughts and affections. Diffidence, and so these words excellently encounter a fear in weak Christians, Oh, I shall lose my peace and that rest I have! Now, this is answered here,—thy peace is in thine heart, and therefore who can take it from thee? It is not like thy money and credit, &c., for these may be taken away. But peace can no man nor devil take away without thine own consent; it is in a chest where no hands can come but God's and thine own.

Uses. First, The use of this may serve for reproof of that lamentable security that is in most men about their inward peace with God, not only that most men wretchedly procrastinate through the hardness of their hearts, refuse peace in the season when God offers peace and beseecheth them to be reconciled, but also for that the most men confirm themselves in this presumption that they are in God's favour when indeed they are not. It was the fault of some prophets, Jer. xxiii. 17, 18, and is too common a fault of many ministers, to cry, 'Peace, peace, when there is no peace,' by reason of the sins men live in without repentance. The Holy Ghost in many places complains that such is the state of the most men, that they have not known the ways of peace, Ps. xiv., Rom. iii. 17. And the day of judgment shall find many that cry peace and safety, while they are ready suddenly to perish, 1 Thes. v. 3. Jehu could say, What peace so long as the whoredoms and witchcrafts of their mother Jezebel remain? So may not we say, What peace can there be unto men, though the world struggle and gainsay, so long as lip-service, swearing, profanation of the sabbath, blood, drunkenness, whoredom, contempt of the word, &c., do so much abound without amendment?

Secondly, Hence we may learn by all means to seek the peace of God into our heart; and to this end we must be God's people, Ps. lxxxv. 8, and get a humble and contrite heart, Isa. lvii. 15, 19, Ps. xxxvii. 11, and soundly labour our justification by faith, Rom. v. 1; we must be good and true in our hearts, Ps. cxxv. 5, and work righteousness, Isa. xxxii. 17, Rom. ii. 10, Gal. vi. 16, and study the scriptures, waiting upon the word preached, Isa. lvii. 19, Luke x. 6.

Thirdly, It may serve for comfort to all God's servants that seek true peace. The Lord would have them to have peace, and to have plenty of it that it may rule in them.

Object. Oh, but I have many and great afflictions in the world.

Sol. What though? In Christ thou mayest have peace, John xvi. 33.

Object. Oh, but I cannot see which way I should have any peace.

Sol. He will 'create peace,' Isa. lvii. 19.

Object. Oh! but the devil is very violent in tempting.

Sol. The God of peace will tread the devil down shortly, Rom. xvi. 20.

Object. Oh! but the peace we have, neither is, nor here will be perfect.

Sol. Peace shall come, Isa. lvii. 2.

Object. Oh! but I am afraid lest my peace with God break, and so hold not.

Sol. 'The mountains may fall, but God's covenant of peace shall not fall,' Isa. liv. 10.

Thus of internal peace; external peace follows, and it is either domestical, or ecclesiastical, or political. Peace should rule our houses, and shew itself by freedom from bitterness, and chiding, and brawling, and absurd peevish passions.

And for church peace, to write a word or two of that, it is not only a rest from persecution, but also from discords within; this is a marvellous blessing. This peace hath not in it a confusion of all sorts of men, joined together in one universal amity, though they be never so wicked; for Christ came not to send such peace, and the word is a fan that will make a division. The world will hate, and darkness will not mix with light; the children of the prophets will be as signs and wonders even in Israel. But this peace is a holy amity and heavenly concord, in the true members of the mystical body, both in consent and doctrine. This peace in the church is of singular worth, and occasions unspeakable joy and growth in the church; this is to be sought and prayed for of every Christian, but especially it should be the care of church-governors; and certainly there would be more peace if they would more and more love goodness, and honour good men, and more carefully prevent and severely purge out the leaven of corrupt doctrine, and wicked life, and so tithe mint and cummin as not to neglect the weightier things of the law, especially if they would more disgrace flatterers and slanderers, that employ their whole might to make the breach worse.

Political peace is either private, and so it is a rest from suits and quarrels; or public, and so it is a rest from wars, and rebellions, and tumults.

But I think by external peace here is meant, in general, concord, and a quiet, harmless, peaceable course of conversing with men in all our carriage. Now, God is said to be the author of it, in that it is his gift, and special providence to work it amongst men; and it is said to rule, when we can prefer public peace before our private respects, and when we can seek it, and not stay till it be sought of us; and when we can forbear and forgive, notwithstanding any inequality. Now this peace may be said to rule in the heart, though it be external, because if corrupt passions be killed in thee, as envy, rage, malice, desire of revenge, &c., men would easily agree in life; bind the heart to the good abearing, and the hands will bind themselves.

The use may be both for reproof of the perverse dispositions of the most men that will not live in peace, but with all falsehood and sin, nourish debate and vain contentions; as also it may inform and inflame men to desire peace, to seek it, yea, to follow after it, Ps. xxxiv. 13, 14, Rom. xiv. 18, Heb. xii. 14. But that men might attain peace they must have salt in themselves, Mark ix. 50, that is, by mortification season, tame, and purge their own heart; yea, they must use the salt of discretion, and to that end pray God to make them wise in their conversation; yet men must ever remember so to seek peace as to retain truth too, Zech. viii. 19, Heb. xii. 14, James iii. 18; peace without holiness is but profane rest.

Thus of the duties; the reasons follow:

To the which ye are called. We are called to peace not only by men, who by their laws require peace, but chiefly by God, and that two ways: first, In the general precepts of the word, which are set down in divers places; secondly, In special manner, in the word of reconciliation; that word that converts us and reconciles us, doth at the very first show us the very necessity and worth of peace; as the sense of our need of God's mercy makes us merciful to men, so the sense of our need of peace with God makes us peaceable with men.

This confutes their folly that say forwardness in religion makes men turbulent. Most wretchedly doth profane men sin against God's people in that aspersion, for they are called to peace, and are the most peaceable people in the world. But let all that fear God even show the fruit of their holy calling by approving themselves to be lovers of peace.

In one body. The second reason is taken from their mutual relation amongst themselves, they are members of one body, and as it is unnatural and unseemly to see a man tear his own flesh, so it is most unnatural and unseemly for Christians to bite and devour one another, by jarring and complaining, and wrangling one with another; and we should hence learn to speak all one thing, and have all one faith, and one heart, and so live in peace that the God of love and peace may be with us. But of this mystical union in the former chapter.

Thus of peace; thankfulness follows.

And be ye thankful. Thankfulness is either to God or men. It is the latter here is meant: thankfulness to men must be considered in itself, and in the amiable performance of it, for the word is by some rendered *amiable*. And it may be it notes but the right manner of affecting in giving or receiving thanks.

This thankfulness hath in it principally gratitude, that is, thanks in words, yet it may contain also gratuities, that is, tokens of goodwill whereby we endeavour indeed to recompense good for good.

Thankfulness is sometimes in desire, sometimes in deed. It is true thankfulness unfeignedly to desire opportunity to shew it.

Thankfulness may be due not only to godly men, but also to wicked men; yea, such as turn to be our enemies, we should watch to the opportunities of doing them good though they be evil.

Now, the amiableness required is either in him that must perform thankfulness, or in him that must receive it.

In performing thankfulness we must observe these rules: first, It must be wholly; secondly, It must be in all places; thirdly, It must be without flattery, or insinuation to beg new favours; fourthly, It must be without the favouring of the vices of others.

In receiving thanks there are these three rules:

1. That he intend not to bring into bondage by shewing of kindness, for so to receive kindness were to lose a man's liberty.

2. That out of pride he wax not conceited by complaining of unthankfulness, for the mere want of manner or measure he expects, where he might see it comes not of ingratitude, or a will not to give thanks, but merely out of natural defect, or want of skill or will to compliment it.

3. That he water what he hath sowed, that is, labour to keep kindness afoot by nourishing it at fit occasions and opportunities of doing good.

Ver. 16. *Let the word of Christ dwell in you richly in all wisdom, teaching and admonishing one another in psalms and hymns and spiritual songs, singing with grace in your hearts to the Lord.*

Hitherto of the special rules of holy conversing with men: The general rules follow, ver. 16, 17, and they concern:

1. The means of holy life, ver. 16, viz., the word.
2. The end of holy life, ver. 17., viz., the glory of Christ.

The 16th verse contains an exhortation to the careful, and plentiful, and frequent use of the word.

Doctrine from coherence.

The word is the principal means not only to make us religious and holy in our behaviour towards God, but also to make us righteous, just, and amiable in our carriage towards men. It is the word that makes us: 1. New creatures, 1 Pet. i. 23, James i. 18; 2. Humble, Isa. lxvi. 2; 3 Meek, Ps. xlv. 4, where it is called, 'the word of meekness,' not because it requires it, and containeth discourse of the praises of it, but by effect, because it makes men so; 4. Patient and long-suffering, Rev. iii. 10, 'The word of my patience.' It begets patience, yea, such patience as Christ will own, yea, such as by influence comes from Christ by means of the word; 5. Clement, able to forbear and forgive, James iii. 17; 6. Loving, able to express in carriage the affections and duties of love, Phil. i. 9, ii. 14, 16; 7. Peaceable, Isa. ii. 2, 4. The word shall judge all strife, so as men shall not only lay aside the effects and means of contention and hostility, but become by the power of the word willing to 'serve one another in love,' yea, to abide the 'labour of love,' noted by mattocks and scythes. No work so base or laborious but godly men, persuaded by the word, will undertake them for the good and peace of the church and their brethren. I might instance in the rest of the virtues, but these shall suffice.

Use. This should inform us concerning the causes of the viciousness of the lives of the most. It is because they so stubbornly rebel against the word, either refusing to hear it, or hardening their heart against the working of it. And secondly, If we find our corruptions in ourselves to get head, and make us not only a burden to ourselves, but an offence to our brethren, we should come to the word and to Christ's ministers, for there we may find help if we will be advised ; and if our servants and children in their carriage be disordered, we should bring them to God's house, that there they may be framed to a greater care of their behaviour in our house.

Thus of the coherence.

This verse in itself contains an exhortation concerning the word of God ; and thus he exhorts to the right use : first, Of the word in general ; secondly, Of one part of the word, which is the Psalms. Concerning the word in general, here is to be considered : first, The author of it, ' word of Christ ;' secondly, The manner of entertainment of the word, let it ' dwell in you plenteously in all wisdom ;' thirdly, The end or use it should be put to : 1. To 'teach' in what we know not ; 2. To 'admonish' in what we do not.

Word of Christ. Λογος, the *word*, is taken sometimes for Christ himself, John i. 1. And so it is true that we should labour that the Word Christ should dwell in us. Sometimes for preaching, Acts xx. 7, and so it is true that we should grow so careful and skilful in remembering the sermons we hear, that our hearts should be stored with riches of that kind. Sometimes for memorable sayings, Acts ii. 22, xx. 35, 1 Tim. iv. 9, 2 Tim. ii. 11, Tit. i. 3, 6, Heb. vii. 28, Rom. xiii. 9. And so it is true that a Christian should be so familiarly acquainted with scriptures, that all the memorable sayings in them should be ready in their memories.

But to come nearer : By 'the word of Christ' some understand the counsels and exhortations of Christ concerning the contemning of the world, to the intent to devote ourselves to the contemplation of heavenly things. Some understand the promises in scripture concerning Christ, or to be had in him. Some understand that part of the scripture which Christ by his own mouth uttered. It is true that in every of these a Christian should be exceeding rich.

But I take it that all these senses are too strait and narrow for this place. By 'the word of Christ,' therefore, I understand, the whole word of God contained in both the Old and New Testaments. And this is said to be the word of Christ four ways :

First, As Christ is the subject of it ; the sum of the word is Christ ; secondly, As it is the proper inheritance and riches of the body of Christ, the dowry he hath bestowed upon his church ; thirdly, As he is the conserving cause of it ; fourthly, As he is the author of it ; and so I take it here principally to be meant.

Christ is the author of the word : first, In respect of inspiration, 2 Pet. i. 21. Secondly, In respect of commission to his ambassadors, Titus i. 3 ; he doth not only indite the embassage, but gives commission to the ambassadors. Thirdly, In respect of confirmation, externally, Mark xvi. 20, by the signs that follow it ; and internally, by the seal of the Spirit, Eph. i. 13. Fourthly, In respect of personal promulgation of it, in that, in the Old Testament, in human shape he appeared to declare it to Adam, Abraham, Jacob, and the patriarchs, and also by visions to the prophets ; and in the New Testament by incarnation, taking truly our nature, did, by lively voice, in his own person preach the gospel to men. Fifthly, In respect of energy, or the power and efficacy of the word, which wholly depends upon Christ, and is shewn by the growing of the word notwithstanding all oppositions, and that it cannot be bound, though the ministers of it suffer, 2 Tim. ii. 9 ; and in the difference of power between Christ's ministers and hirelings ; yea, hence it is so lively and mighty in operation, that it discerns and discovers the very secrets of men, and tells tales of the hearers, Heb. iv. 12, 13.

Use. The use is either more general or more special ; more general, either for information, to satisfy us concerning the hard sayings in scripture, and the experience of the truth of that, John viii. 43, viz., that wicked men 'cannot hear the words of Christ.' It comes from the sovereign majesty and secret excellency of the word, and the spiritual nature of it, as the word of Christ, removed from the sense of the carnal reason and fleshly affections of unregenerate men. And also this serves for instruction, and that either negatively or affirmatively.

Negatively, the use is, therefore, take heed of sinning against the word of Christ ; and as men sin against the word many ways, so principally six ways :

First, By contemning of it, John xii. 48, Heb. ii. 2 ;

secondly, By betraying it to Satan, letting him steal it out of our hearts, Mat. xiii. 20; thirdly, By choking it with cares and lusts, Mat. xiii. 21; fourthly, By making it of none effect (ἀκυρουντες) by traditions; fifthly, By a proud challenging of the knowledge of it to ourselves, 1 Cor. xiv. 36; sixthly, By being ashamed of our obedience or profession of the words of Christ when we are amongst sinful and wicked men, Mat. viii. 38.

Affirmatively, it may teach us four things:

1. To receive the word of God with all humility and meekness, James i. 21.

2. To receive it with faith, Heb. iv. 2.

3. To glorify the word of God, Acts xiii. 48; which we do, first, When we ascribe the praise, not to men, but to Christ; secondly, When we esteem it more than the words of the greatest men.

4. To be careful of our carriage and practice, that so the word of Christ which we profess be not evil spoken of, Titus ii. 5: for the blame of our evil life will be laid upon the word; they will say, This is their gadding to sermons!

In special, seeing the word is the word of Christ, it should teach,

First, Ministers four things:

1. To teach it with boldness, ἐν παρρησιᾳ, not fearing the face of any man, Acts v. 31.

2. To attend upon the word only, and not meddle with civil businesses. Is it meet to leave the word of Christ to serve tables? Acts vi. 2.

3. To humble themselves to walk with God in so good a function. 'Who is sufficient for these things?' We speak not our own words, or the words of men; for then wit, reading, learning, and direction might perfect us; but we speak the words of Christ, and therefore our fitness and sufficiency to speak to men's consciences comes of the immediate blessing and assistance of Christ.

4. To deliver the word with all faithfulness, studying to approve themselves as the workmen of God, seeing they deliver the word of God, dividing the word aright, 2 Tim. ii. 15, holding fast the faithful word of doctrine, Titus i. 9; not making merchandise of the word, but as of sincerity, and as of God, in the sight of God, speaking in Christ, 2 Cor. ii. 17; casting from them the cloak of shame, not walking in craftiness, nor handling the word deceitfully, but in declaring the truth; approving themselves to every man's conscience in the sight of God, 2 Cor. iv. 2.

Secondly, The people, to embrace the word, press to it, never be ashamed of it nor give it over, but receive it constantly with joy, though it cost them much pains and many crosses and disgraces, 2 Thes. i. 5: for this constant receiving of and cleaving to the word makes them exceeding dear to Christ—as dear as his mother and his brethren. This is the choosing of the best part, Luke x. 42; this is a sign that they are the disciples of Christ, John viii. 31, that they love Christ indeed, John xiv. 23, 34, that they be in Christ, 1 John ii. 5. She said well that said of Christ, 'Blessed was the womb that bare thee, and the breasts that gave thee suck;' but Christ adds, that 'they are more blessed that hear the word of Christ and keep it,' Luke xi. 28. The blessed Virgin was more happy in that she conceived Christ in her heart than that she bare him in her womb.

Thus of the author of the word.

The entertainment of the word follows; and here the apostle designs, first, The subject persons, 'you;' secondly, The measure, 'dwell plenteously;' thirdly, The manner, 'in all wisdom.'

First, I consider of the expositions of all the words, which are very full of senses, and then make use of all together.

In you. These words note unto us two things: first, The persons who must entertain; secondly, The place where, 'in you,' that is, in your hearts.

First, For the persons. The apostle would have us know, that not only clergymen, (Epaphras and Archippus,) but laymen of all sorts, are tied to the study of scriptures.

I distribute the sorts:

First, Young men as well as the gray hairs, 1 John ii. 12; for the word helps them to overcome the devil, even all temptations to lust and ungodliness whatsoever; yea, by the blessing of God, many times it makes them wiser than the ancient, Ps. cxix. 100.

Secondly, Distressed men as well as such as live at ease and prosperity, and abound in leisure; I say, such as have many cares and troubles, distressed either by crosses, Ps. cxix. 92, or by persecutions, Ps. cxix. 87, or by contempt, Ps. cxix. 141.

Thirdly, Ignorant men as well as learned men; such as are simple in respect of natural parts, or untaught in respect of education, are tied as well as others; they may not say they were not brought up to learning; for many times simple and unlearned people, in the very entrance into the word, Ps. cxix. 129, 130, when they bring good and holy desires with them, get more light of the wonders of God's law in few weeks, than many great, learned men do in all their days, for sound saving knowledge.

Fourthly, Women as well as men are bound hereunto, Prov. xxxi. 26, i. 8; yea, such women as are full of business and cares; not good women or wives, but good housewives also are tied; yea, not only to learn the word, but to teach it, as the places shew.

Thus of the persons.

Secondly, 'In you,' notes the place that the word must be entertained in; in you, that is, in your minds, for contemplation; in your hearts, for holy desires and affections; in your consciences, to guide them to a holy manner of giving sentence, &c. This is that which is promised to the faithful in the covenant of grace, Jer. xxxi. 33, and noted as the sign of the righteous, Ps. xxxvii. 21.

Dwell. A metaphor borrowed from household entertainment, and notes three things unto us:

1. That the word should be familiar to us, and known of us readily, and we so acquainted with it as with our brethren or sisters: 'Say unto wisdom, Thou art my sister,' &c., Prov. vii. 4. To note, that as in nature he is accounted a singular idiot that knows not his own brothers or sisters, so in religion, in God's account it is extreme simplicity and blindness not to be familiarly acquainted with the grounds of behaviour and comfort as they are contained in the word.

2. That it should be domestical; we must get it into our houses, as well as our churches, and that three ways: first, When we come home from God's house we should keep the word taught afoot by repetition of it, and by talking of it upon all occasions, that the life of doctrine be not lost. Secondly, There is required a familiar teaching, and plain and familiar instructing of servants, distilling of the principles and profitable precepts of the law as they are able. God gave his testimonies to Israel, not that the clergymen should have them in the temple and synagogue, but that parents should have them in their several dwellings to instruct their children and their children's children, Ps. lxxviii. 5, 6, Deut. vi. Thirdly, The admonitions, rebukes, counsels, and encouragements used in the family should be grounded on the word; for conscience only is the fountain of all right subjection and obedience. The bonds of nature, because he came out of thy loins, or the bonds of policy, because he is thy hired servant, are too weak to enforce, of themselves, a constant, and cheerful, and just subjection. The true reason why men speed so ill in their servants and children is because they nurture them with their own words, but distil not into their consciences the words of Christ.

Quest. But to what end should there need all this ado about the scriptures in our houses? what good comes of it?

Ans. If it be not intimated sufficiently before, yet plainly understand that the word is to be exercised in our houses: first, As a refuge against affliction and domestical crosses, both to direct and comfort us, Ps. cxix. 143, 147, 165; secondly, As a means of instruction to our ignorant children and servants; thirdly, As a means of the sanctification of the creatures, and our callings, 1 Tim. iv. 4; lastly, Seeing Satan will tempt us, and our natures will be vicious not only in God's house, but in our own houses, we have reason to carry the medicine to the fore, and to bring the sword of the Spirit, which is the word of God, home with us, and draw it there, seeing the devil will cast his fiery darts there. He that is in danger of a subtle and furious enemy always must look unto two things: first, That he hath on all his armour; secondly, That he be ready at all times, in all places, when his adversary will encounter with him. A malicious and skilful adversary desires but to find his enemy unarmed in one part of his body, or in one place; so is it with us, for because men have no sword of the Spirit at home, therefore it comes to pass that men that have good affections in God's house have base and vile affections in their own houses. Thirdly, It notes that the word must be constantly entertained and exercised in our houses, Ps. cxix. 112; for they are not said to dwell with men that lodge there only for a night or a day or two, so the sudden and passionate use of the word now and then will not serve it.

Plenteously. The original word, πλουσιως, notes two things: 1. The measure, and so it is well rendered 'plenteously;' 2. The worth of the knowledge of the word, and so it is by some rendered 'richly.' In the first sense, it teacheth us that we should labour by all means to abound in the knowledge and use of the word. It should be not in a scant and sparing measure, or in some parts of it, but we should grow from measure to measure, and from knowledge to knowledge. In the second sense, it teacheth us that the knowledge of the word is the Christian's riches; so he saith, 1 Cor. i. 5, 'rich in all speech and knowledge.' Christians should account their utterance in holy and profitable speeches and conferences, and the inward notions of saving knowledge, as their best wealth, so as they should never think themselves poor so long as they may have plenty of knowledge in the use of the means. Thus David reckons of his wealth: 'God's statutes more dear to him than thousands of gold and silver,' Ps. cxix. 72; and that knowledge he can get from the word out of God's treasury, maugre the malice and power of the devil or evil men, he accounts more worth than rich spoils, Ps. cxix. 162; this may appear in the contrary in the case of the Laodiceans, Rev. iii. 18, 19.

In all wisdom. Wisdom is sometimes taken for virtue, as folly is for sin; but here I take it for knowledge, and that not as the gaining of heavenly wisdom is the end of the entertainment of the word, but as it notes the manner how we should entertain the word. This wise manner of entertaining the word I consider both negatively and affirmatively.

Negatively: to handle the word wisely is not to handle or use it: first, Coldly, fruitlessly, or unaptly; secondly, Perversely, in wresting the word to ill ends, to nourish curiosity, ambition, or sin; thirdly, Carnally, as the Capernaites, that know no flesh of Christ but the flesh of his body, nor any eating but carnal; fourthly, Not indiscreetly; when we come abroad into company, we should so profess and use the word as that we dishonour it not by indiscretion, by not heeding places, times, occasions, &c.

Affirmatively: to use the word wisely is, in the general, especially to teach ourselves, and to this end: first, To understand it. Secondly, To seek profitable things, not curious and pleasing things only. Thirdly, So to try all things as to keep that which is good: good, I say, particularly, and for our own use; there be some things in hearing, reading, &c., that do exceedingly not only affect us, but are in special manner fitting us; now it is a special wisdom to keep these things whatsoever else we lose. Fourthly, To wait upon all the opportunities of getting profit by the word, to know our seasons, Jer. viii. 7. Fifthly, In carriage abroad, not to be so indiscreetly open in the discovery of our minds, and knowledge, and opinions, as to be catched by the fraud of any, and to this end not to trust all that feign themselves to be just men, Luke xx. 20.

In all wisdom. 'All' for measure, 'all' for diversity of the things known, 'all' for sincerity of the observation of the rules of wisdom; in the manner of entertaining the word; 'all wisdom,' that is, all necessary to salvation.

Thus of the explication.

The uses follow, and those are either general from all the words, or special from each of them. The general uses are for reproof, information, instruction, or consolation.

1. For reproof: if it must be thus of all entertained, how great a sin is it to neglect or contemn the word! and inasmuch as this is a great and common sin, it is required and requited by God with four singular curses. The first judgment upon the contemners of the word is, that all the comforts of the word are unto them as a sealed book, Isa. xxix. 11; so as that word which is to the faithful a wellhead of all true and sound joy, unto them is of no taste or power; they can find some savour in any pursuits and sports, &c., but none in the word. The second judgment is, that when they do, for fashion, or for fear, and other ill ends, come to hear the preaching of the word, they are many times slain by the word of God's mouth, and the prophets even mow down scores, hundreds, and thousands of them, so as they are pierced and galled, smitten and buffeted with the terrors of the word, (which is only open to rebuke them,) and they see that threatening many times comprehends under it multitudes of men.

Object. But this comes only of the severity of the teachers, that set themselves to preach damnation, and to utter terrible things.

Ans. This was the objection in the prophet Micah his time, Micah ii. 7, and uttered by such as bare the name of Jacob, to whom all the promises did belong; and they were answered by the prophet, that for resolving of their doubt, they should ask two questions of their own consciences. The first was, Whether they thought their works were like the works of Jacob and the rest of the ancient saints, to whom such comforts did belong? or whether such vile profaneness and wickedness were found in Jacob as was apparently found in them? The second question was, Whether they did not see that the words of God were always good to such as walk uprightly? In all which he shews that it is not the uncharitable severity of God's servants, (for the doctrine is good to good men,) but the vile profaneness and contempt of the word in the people, that made them liable to such terrors in the word.

The third judgment is, that all civil praises in men that contemn the wisdom of God in the word are singularly vile in God's sight, Jer. viii. 8, 9, and he instructeth in wisdom.

Lastly, 'Salvation is far from the wicked,' Ps. cxix. 155; because they seek not God's statutes, the evidence of the hope of a better life is removed from them, so as, speaking from their own sense, they avouch it that no man can be sure of eternal life to himself. And if in the general profane neglect of the word be thus sought out and judged of God, then surely those persons must needs be in great danger that never opened their doors to the word, never taught their children and servants, scarce ever had a bible in their houses; but especially such as shun the word as a true rock of offence. Yea, many of God's children may be justly rebuked in this, that they are so far from shewing that the word hath dwelt plenteously in them, that whereas for time and the plenty and power of the means, they might have been teachers, they have need again to be taught the very principles, Heb. v. 12, 13; and they shew it that they are so inexpert and unskilful in the word of righteousness.

2. The second general use is for information. See the admirable largeness of the word and the perfectness above all other things under the sun, Ps. cxix. 96. It is good for worship in the temple, it is good for our affairs in the family, it is of use in prosperity and in adversity, it fits for the profit of all sorts of men, at all times, and in all places, and so doth nothing else in the world.

3. The third general use is for instruction. The meditation of the entertainment of the word in all these words required should teach us to open our churches, open our houses, yea, our hearts and all, for the word. And to this end to consecrate ourselves to the study of the word in all the means, both public and private.

Object. But if I should, it will be in vain, I have such an ill memory, &c.

Ans. 'The beginning of the word is truth,' Ps. cxix. 160; and men should find by experience the contrary to their fears, if they in sincerity sought unto God in the word. And as for ill memory, we must know that a good memory is the gift of God, as well as a good heart, and no man hath it naturally. Wicked men may have large memories, but not sanctified to contain holy things; and therefore if men would seek to God in uprightness of desire, whatsoever they lost, yet the judgment or answer of God in the word preached, or by reading or conference, (which resolveth their doubts, pointeth at the means to redress their corruptions, &c.,) should not be wholly forgotten. 'The judgments of his righteousness endure for ever.' That part of knowledge that particularly answers their desires, or the experience of their want in themselves, this shall be deeply imprinted in them by God, so as the virtue thereof shall never be lost. To conclude, seeing the Holy Ghost requires all careful entertainment of the word, we should do that unto it that we would do for the entertaining of some great man into our houses. 1. Make clean the room of our hearts, purge out hypocrisy, malice, &c. 2. When the word is come in, molest it not, take heed of strange affections, passions, and lusts. 3. Receive it with joy, and express all the signs of joy.

4. The last general use is for consolation unto all such as love the word. They should encourage themselves, and say with David, 'Thy statutes shall be my song so long as I continue in the house of my pilgrimage.'

Object. But our inward desires and delights in the word are mixed with outward disgraces and scorns of men: we are reproached, slandered, rebuked, &c.

Ans. 'Hearken unto me, ye that know righteousness,' (not ye that talk of it, or hear them that teach it, but ye that know indeed what sincerity means,) and ye of the people 'in whose hearts are my laws,' Isa. li. 7; as if God would wish them to look up and see the great reward of their well-doing.

Object. But they might say, we are taunted, and threatened, and disgraced.

Ans. 'Fear not the reproach of men, nor be afraid of their rebukes.'

Object. But we see that wicked scorners escape unpunished, and are in better credit doing ill than we doing well.

Ans. Though God do not by sudden judgments destroy them all at once, yet he promiseth that his curse shall secretly and insensibly eat them as the moth. God doth daily judge them, though we see it not; and for the faithful, their righteousness shall never be taken away by the reproaches of men, but it will endure for ever, &c., Isa. li. 7, 8.

Thus of the uses in general.

From the particular consideration of each of the words, divers special uses may be made.

Dwell. First, If the word must dwell with us, it should teach us to practise what we are here exhorted,—get the word into our houses, let it so dwell with us that nothing found more in a Christian house than the word; that is to live comfortably. This is to live in the shadow of the Almighty, Ps. xci. 1, in the very light of God's countenance, Ps. cxl. A house without the word is a very dungeon of darkness. To exercise ourselves in the law, it will give our hearts rest in the days of evil, Ps. xciv. 12. The father's commandment and the mother's instruction would lead our children and servants when they walk; it would watch for them when they sleep; and when they wake, it would talk with them; it would be a lantern, and the very way of life to them. It would keep them from the strange woman, Prov. vi. 20-25; there would not be such filthiness in many houses as now commonly appears to be. What can better preserve Jacob from confusion, or his face from being pale, than if he might see his children, the work of God's hand, framed and fitted by the word in regeneration and the duties of new obedience? This would make religious parents to sanctify God's name, even to sanctify the holy one, and with singular encouragement from the God of Israel, Isa. xxix. 22, 23.

In you. Secondly, In that the people are made the subject persons to be exhorted hereunto, it plainly confutes the opinion and practice of the papists, that either hide the word in a strange tongue, or prohibit private men from the domestical and daily use of it. But the apostle doth not envy it in the Lord's people, that the word should dwell plenteously in them as well as in clergymen.

Plenteously. Thirdly, In that he requires the word should not only dwell with us, but for measure be plenteously there, it should teach us in practice to endeavour it. But for explication of this use, I consider of two questions to answer them:

Quest. 1. What must we do that the word might be in us plenteously, and the knowledge of it abound?

Ans. Six things are to be practised: 1. We must walk at liberty, freeing our heads from worldly cares, lusts, and delights, Ps. cxix. 45. 2. We must avoid evil company, and say with David, 'Away from me all ye wicked, for I seek God's statutes,' Ps. cxix. 115. 3. We must strive to take away the lets of the practice of what we do know: this David calls the lifting up of his hands to God's law, Ps. cxix. 48. 4. We must exercise ourselves in the word day and night, in reading, hearing, meditating, conference, propounding of doubts, and comparing of places; and all times, by all ways, turning ourselves into all forms to gain knowledge. 5. We should by prayer beseech God to do two things for us: first, To give us the spirit of revelation, Eph. i. 18; secondly, To give us larger hearts, Ps. cxix. 32. 6. We must be thankful for what knowledge we do get by the means, Ps. cxix. 171.

Quest. 2. But how may we know whether the word do dwell plenteously in us?

Ans. It may be tried and discovered seven ways: 1. By our growth in true humility and meekness, Ps. xv. 3. 2. By the confirmation of the testimony of Jesus in our hearts, 1 Cor. i. 5, 6. 3. By the measure of our growth in the love of God and his people; yea, and thus we may try our declining in the vigour of knowledge, (for knowledge had in abundance may be blasted, and grow singularly dull and feeble,) for as our affections to the means, and to God's children is, so is the vigour of our knowledge. He must not say he knows God that hates his brother; yea, and so will it serve for trial to every one in the degrees of ascending or declination even in God's children. 4. By the desires and secret muses of our hearts, for then we grow in knowledge and have store of it when we can say as David doth, 'I have remembered thy name, O Lord, in the night,' Ps. cxix. 35; and as the church saith, 'The desires of our souls is to thy name, and to the remembrance of thee, and our spirits within us seek after thee,' Isa. xxvi. 9. 5. By our confidence in it. A man that hath gotten a great deal of wealth, money or lands, enlargeth his heart to a great confidence in it; so a Christian hath gotten a great deal of saving knowledge when he is able to make it his portion in all estates, whatsoever befalls him, Ps. cxix. 57; it shews men have but a little of the word in them when every cross can dissolve their rest and confidence. By our measure of liberty from the power and bondage of special corruptions, John viii. 31, 32. 7. By our ability in admonishing. They are full of goodness and knowledge that are able to admonish, Rom. xv. 14.

Richly. Fourthly, In that the word must dwell in us richly, it may serve: 1. For reproof, and that two ways: (1.) Of men's worldliness, that think any other riches would serve the turn, but to be rich in God they never desire it, but all in vain, as the parable shews, Luke xii.; (2.) Of men's hypocrisy, they say they are rich when they are not, Rev. iii. 18. 2. For instruction, therefore let heaven suffer violence: a Christian should be no more aweary of his pains in seeking this riches of the word than carnal men are of their worldly profits; yea, we should pray God so to quicken us that we may keep his testimonies as we would keep treasure, Ps. cxix. 11, lxxxviii. 72.

Lastly, In that he adds, 'in all wisdom,' it should teach us, first, To pray to God with David, that he would 'teach us good judgment and knowledge,' Ps. cxix. 66; and secondly, To make conscience, as to get understanding of the word, so to use wisdom and discretion, both in the bettering of our knowledge, and in practising the same. The same scripture that binds us to a plentiful use of the word binds us to a wise use of it.

Thus of the second thing, viz., the entertainment we must give to the word; the end or use the word should be put to follows.

Teaching and admonishing yourselves or *one another,* viz., your fellow-members and partakers with you of the same promises and hope.

These words may be referred either to the general exhortation before, or to the particular charge concerning psalms or hymns afterwards. I principally consider them as referred to the general exhortation before; and so I note, that though there be many good effects of the word, or many uses it should be put to, yet teaching about things not known, and admonishing about things known and not practised, are chief.

Object. It seems this place favours the opinion of such as hold that Christian neighbours met together upon the Lord's day, or at other times when there is no public exercise, may labour to edify themselves, by instructing one another out of the word privately.

Ans. It is not unlawful so to do; and this place doth approve of it, so as they keep themselves within their bounds, viz., that the matter taught be not against piety, the true peace of Zion; and that the manner be plain and familiar, as family instruction should be, by keeping afoot public doctrine, by conference, propounding of doubts, or instructing of the ignorant out of such places as they do undoubtedly understand.

Concerning teaching, we must know that God doth teach by his Spirit, Neh. ix. 20, by his rod, Isa. xxvi. 9, and by his word, so here; but that which we are here to note is, that the word is to be used by every Christian, even for instruction; this is the end why the law was given, Exod. xxiv. 12; a wise man having gotten knowledge into his head, must by his lips spread it abroad, Prov. xv. 7.

Quest. But whom must we teach?

Ans. Principally ourselves, so as we consider our own ways to turn our feet into God's testimonies, Ps. cxix. 59; yet also we are to teach one another, when we spy our brethren to be ignorant; so should not only ministers do, but masters of families, and every Christian in conversing with others.

Admonishing. Man is admonished: 1. By the rebukes of the law, James ii. 9; 2. By the example of scripture, 1 Cor. x. 11; 3. By the Spirit of God, Isa. xxx. 21; 4. By the conscience in wicked men many times; 5. Men are rebuked by their own words, Job xv. 6; 6. By the words of other men, especially as admonition is grounded on the words of God; so here.

Concerning admonition I propound four things: 1. Who may admonish? 2. Who are to be admonished? 3. How? 4. The uses.

Quest. 1. Who may admonish?

Ans. Ministers may, 2 Tim. iv. 12; parents may, Eph. vi. 4; yea, men ought not to reject the admonitions of their wives, Gen. xxi. 12; nay, which is more, they may not despise the judgment of their servants, Job xxxi. 13.

Quest. 2. Who are to be admonished?

Ans. I consider it, 1: Negatively: not:—

(1.) They that sin against the Holy Ghost.

(2.) Heretical men after once or twice warning, Titus iii. 10.

(3.) Not stubborn, wilful, scornful, profane persons; not dogs and swine, Mat. vii.; not the scorner, Prov. ix. 8.

(4.) If it be about wrongs and abuses offered to us, either by hypocritical friends or open enemies, it is a godly man's part, at some times and in some places, to be 'deaf and dumb, as if they understood not, or as men in whose mouths are no reproof,' Ps. xxxviii. 14.

2. Affirmatively: in general every man, Acts xx. 31. In particular, I instance only in some sorts of men. We must admonish unruly professors, 1 Thes. v. 14; besides, ordinary wicked men that appear not to be scorners, not only may but ought to be admonished, that the light may manifest their works, Eph. v. 11, that they may become sounder in the faith, Titus i. 13; and though this be not amongst men for the time any whit pleasing, yet the blessing of goodness shall come upon them; whilst they that flatter men in their sins, and say to the wicked, Thou art righteous, shall be cursed and hated of the multitude, Prov. xxiv. 24; yea, none are so wise and godly but they may be admonished, Prov. ix. 9; such as are full of goodness and knowledge, able to admonish others, Rom. xv. 14; but it should be our most usual and principal labour to admonish our own souls, and reprove our ways in God's sight, Job xxiii. 15; for it is a special way by which a wise man may be profitable to himself, Job xxii. 2.

Quest. 3. What rules are to be observed in admonition?

Ans. In admonition we must consider, first, How to perform it; secondly, How to receive it. In performing admonition, we must especially look to two things: first, That the ground of admonition be out of the word of God, being the words of Christ, not our own words. To this end we should store ourselves, and hold fast the faithful word according to doctrine. First, We should be constantly stored with grounds out of the word, both for matters of opinion, and against the corruptions of man's life, and for performance of holy duties, that as we have occasion we may rebuke, &c., Titus i. 6; secondly, We must see that the manner of admonition be right. Admonition is to be performed: first, With innocency; we must not be faulty ourselves, or if we have been, we must plainly acknowledge it before we admonish; secondly, With discretion, which must be shewn in three things: first, That we be sure that they have offended, not led to it by suspicion of our own hearts, or by hearsay, or by outward appearance, not judge by the hearing of our ears, and sight of our eyes, Isa. xi. 3; secondly, That if we know it to be an offence, we must consider whether it be not of the number of those offences a wise man must hold his glory to pass by, Prov. xix. 11; thirdly, That it be done seasonably, with love, admonishing as a brother, 2 Thes. iii. 15; fourthly, With meekness, Gal. vi. 1; fifthly, With secrecy, Mat. xviii. 15, Prov. xxv. 9; sixthly, With plainness, spare no words to satisfy them, Lev. xix. 17; seventhly, With compassion and tenderness, 2 Cor. ii. 4; eighthly, With perseverance, Prov. xiii. 19, we must not be weary and discouraged, but accomplish it; ninthly, With all authority, Titus ii. 15, that neither ourselves nor God's ordinances be despised.

In receiving admonition, we must look to four things. We must receive admonition: first, With love and holy estimation, 1 Thes. v. 12, Ps. cxli. 7; secondly, With all humility, readily inclined to suspect ourselves, knowing that we have cause to say and think of ourselves as that worthy man did, 'I am more foolish than any man, and have not the understanding of a man in me,' &c., Prov. xxx. 2, 3; thirdly, With subjection and direct acknowledgment, giving glory to God; fourthly, With reformation, else all is in vain.

The uses are: first, To teach us therefore to stir up ourselves to perform this mercy in admonishing, for a wise man, even Solomon's wise man, that is, a religious wise man, may learn wisdom by it, Prov. ix. 9. Yea, it is as a golden ear-ring to the wise and obedient ear, Prov. xxv. 12. And he that rebuketh, shall find more favour at the length, than he that flattereth with his tongue, Prov. xxviii. 23. Men are said to be pulled out of the fire by admonition, Jude 22, 23. Secondly, We must take heed of sinning against admonition. Now, men sin against admonition three ways: first, In not performing it. This hath very ill effects, such as these: not admonishing breeds dwelling suspicions; suspicions breed a very habit of misinterpretation; misinterpretation begets a lothness to come unto the light, to shew the reasons of dislike; this lothness begets a very separation in heart; separation begets a decay of love to the means; decay of respect to the means begets a decay of zeal and gifts, and from hence there is a highway to internal or external apostasy, or some great judgments of God. Secondly, In not performing it aright, as when men make their wrath to fall upon the fatherless, or dig pits for their friends, Job vi. 27; or when men respect God's person, Job xiii. 8, 9, and make the pretence of God's cause, glory, name, &c., to be the colour for the venting of their own particular envy and dislike; or when men never have done, but grow impudent, and reproach men ten times, and are not ashamed, Job xix. 3. To conclude, when men fail in the manner before described, want innocency, discretion, meekness, love, &c. Thirdly, In not receiving admonition; and thus men fail diversely, when men shift, excuse, deny, extenuate, &c., and yet in heart be convinced; or when men fall into passion, or grudging, or traducing afterwards; or when men would fain make the admonisher to sin in the word, and lay snares for him that rebukes, Isa. xxix. 21. But there are some are worse than any of these, for they are such as none dares declare their way unto their face. Men dare not, they are so passionate and haughty; but God will lay them in the slimy valley where are many already like them, and innumerable more shall come after them, Job xxi. 31, 32. Many are the ill effects of resisting admonition. It is a sign of a scorner, Prov. xiii. 1, xv. 12, and that men are out of the way, Prov. xv. 10, it brings temporal judgments and shame upon them, Prov. xiii. 18, Hosea iv. 4, 5; men may also come to that horrible condition, by resisting admonition, that they being perverted, shall go about damned of their own souls, Titus iii. 10, 11.

Thus of the general exhortation.

The special exhortation concerns one part of the word, and that is the psalms, which are here to be considered.

1. In respect of matter, 'psalms, hymns, and spiritual songs.'

2. In respect of the manner, 'singing with grace in your hearts to the Lord.'

The matter is here three ways to be considered: first, In the ground, foundation, or authority of the psalms we use, viz., they must be the word of Christ, that is, contained in the scriptures. Secondly, In the kinds of psalms. There are many sorts of psalms in scripture, the psalms of Moses, David, Solomon, and other prophets; but all are here referred to three heads; they are either psalms, specially so called, or hymns or songs. Great ado there is among interpreters to find a difference in these. Some would have psalms to be the songs of men, and hymns of angels; some think they differ especially in the manner of music; some are sung by voice, some played upon instruments. But the plausiblest opinion is, not to distinguish them by the persons that use them, or by the kind of music, but by the matter. And so they say psalms contain exhortation to manners or holy life; hymns contain praises to God, in the commemoration of his benefits; songs contain doctrine of the chief good, or man's eternal felicity. But I think there needs not any curious distinction. It may suffice us, that there is variety of psalms in scripture, and God allows us the use of every kind. Thirdly, The property of the psalms: they are 'spiritual,' both because they are indited by the Spirit, and because they make us more spiritual in the due use of them.

From hence, then, we may learn these things:

1. That singing of psalms is God's ordinance, binding all sorts of men, Eph. vi. 19, James v. 13. Ps. lxvi. 1, 2, xcii. 1. cxxxv. 3; a part of our goodness, and a most comely thing.

2. That a Christian should chiefly recreate himself in singing of psalms, James v. 13. God doth not allow us other recreations to shoulder out this, as the most do.

3. That we should sing psalms in our houses as well as our churches, both for daily exercise, Ps. ci. 1, 2, and when Christians meet together, 1 Cor. xiv. 26, Eph. v. 19.

The manner follows. There are four things required of us in singing of psalms: first, We should teach and admonish in the use of them, and that either ourselves, by considering the matter, or others, as the ministers in appointing of psalms for the congregation, or the master of the family, or when Christians meet, there should be choice of such psalms as may instruct, or comfort, or rebuke, according to the occasion. There is edifying even in appointing of psalms, 1 Cor. xiv. 26. Secondly, We must sing with grace. This is diversely interpreted. Some understand it of the dexterity that should be used in singing, to affect ourselves or others; some take it to be that inward comeliness, right order, reverence, or delight of the heart in singing; some would have it signify thanksgiving. But I think, to sing with grace, is to exercise the graces of the heart in singing. We must sing with holy joy, Ps. ix. 2, with trust in God's mercies, Ps. xiii. 5, with a holy commemoration of God's benefits, Ps. xlvii. 6; yea, with the prayer and desires of our hearts, that our words in singing may be acceptable, Ps. civ. 33, 34. Thirdly, We must sing with our hearts, not with our tongues only, outwardly for ostentation. To sing with our hearts is to sing with understanding, Ps. xlvii. 7, 1 Cor. xiv. 14, with sense and feeling. Hence we are said to prepare our hearts before we sing, Ps. lvii. 7; and it is to be observed, that David bids his tongue awake, Ps. lvii. 8; noting that he observed in men a lethargy, not a hoarseness of voice, but a slumber in heart, when they used the voice. Fourthly, We must sing to the Lord, Eph. v. 19, that is, both to God's glory, and in sense of God's presence, and upon a holy remembrance of God's blessings. This is to sing to his name.

The use is: first, For instruction; when we are merry to sing psalms, James v. 13; yea, to account this as heavenly melody, Eph. v. 19, a precious perfume for our chambers, a holy homage to God, 'the calves of our lips,' yea, we should resolve against all the profane contempt of the world to praise God thus while we live, Ps. cxlvi. 2, civ. 33, and to this end we should strive against the objections and backwardness of our own natures; for the flesh will object against singing of psalms, as well as against praying, reading, &c. Secondly, For reproof of such as set their delight in fleshly lusts and sports, in dancing, gaming, &c., in singing of carols, ballads, filthy rhymes, &c., all which delights are so far from being spiritual, that they make our hearts far more fleshly and carnal; yea, it reproves the best of us, for want of the right manner in the use of singing, in all the four things before, which we should be humbled for as for any other our sins.

Thus of the sixteenth verse.

Ver. 17. *And whatsoever ye shall do in word or deed, do all in the name of the Lord Jesus; giving thanks to God, even the Father, by him.*

This verse contains the second general rule to be observed in our conversation, and it is an exhortation to the minding of the right end in all our actions. In the former verse he took order for the means of holy life, here he takes order for the end of it.

Doct. In general, unto the goodness of the action a good end is essentially required; for though a good intention make not the action good, yet without a good intention the action cannot be accepted as good in God's sight. It is a good thing to hear and follow Christ, but not good in the Capernaites, that follow for the loaves, or in the pharisees, that hear to carp or carry tales, and inform against him. It is a good action to use our knowledge, but ceaseth to be good in us when it puffeth up and is done for vain ostentation. It is good to receive the sacraments; but yet circumcision was not good either as the sons of Jacob required it, nor as the king and his sons received it. Works of holy and religious services are good; but when men come to church on the sabbaths to make amends for their sin on the week-days, it ceaseth to be good to them. It is good to honour God's ministers; but where men honour them either to keep their own credit with the people, as Saul honoured Samuel, or that they may excuse them, as in the parable, Luke xiv. 19, such honour is not good. Works of mercy are good; but being done for praise of men, or to merit by them, they come under a negative precept, 'Give not your alms,' Mat. vi. It is good to forbear one another; but not good in such men as forbear only for want of power or opportunity to revenge; and therefore we should inform ourselves better, and as we would have God to accept or bless us, to get good ends to our actions.

Thus of the general.

In this verse the end of well-doing is two ways considered: first, As it is the end of intention, that is, that we should propound and aim at, as the motive and mark of our endeavours, and that is ordered and required in these words, 'Whatsoever ye do in word or deed, do all in the name of the Lord Jesus.' Secondly, It is the end of consummation, that is, that by which we finish our works, and that is required in these words, 'giving thanks to God, even the Father, by him.' In short, the end of intention is the glory of God in Christ, the end of consummation is the giving of thanks when we have done our endeavours.

In the first part I consider:

1. What should be the main end of our actions—'Do all in the name of Christ.'

2. How we are tied to it: first, For persons—'ye;' secondly, For kinds of employment—'in word and deed;' thirdly, For extent—'whatsoever ye do, do all.'

Do all in the name of the Lord Jesus. Here four things are required of us:

First, That all be done in the assurance of the love of Christ; that we be sure that we know Christ, as we know a man by his name; that when we go to do God's work, we be first sure of Christ's reward. This is to be shod with the preparation of the gospel of peace, Eph. vi.

Secondly, That all be done in the name, that is, by the authority, of Christ, and his warrant in his word; not in the name of Moses for ceremony, or in the name of angels or saints for intercession; nay, in all we do our conscience should be tied only properly by the command of Christ, not because such great men would have it so, or I did it to please my parents or kindred, &c., for then thou doest it in the name of men, and not of Christ.

Thirdly, That all be done with invocation or calling upon God in the name of Christ, all should be consecrate and begun with prayer.

Fourthly, and principally, That all be done to the glory of God in Christ, this should be the scope of all our actions, 1 Cor. x. 31; all should breathe and savour of Christ.

In word. Doct. God requires to be glorified by the very words of Christians, and contrariwise holds himself many times dishonoured by their words. He that keepeth his tongue, keepeth his life, Prov. xiii. 3. The honour and dishonour of the tongue is largely explicated, James iii. But the use is for instruction, to teach us: first, To take heed of dishonouring Christ by our words; but in special we should take heed of words of disgrace and slander to the members of Christ, of vain words, Eph. v. 6, that bolster men up in presumption against repentance and faith in Christ, of passionate and bitter words, Job vi. 3, of words of deceit, Ps. xxxvi. 3, of the words that come from or tend to the strange woman, filthy words, Col. iii. 8; yea, take heed of high words, for high talk or the lips of excellency becomes not a fool, Prov. xvii. 7; for evil words greatly provoke God, and call for stripes, bring many a cross upon a man, and are snares to men's souls, Prov. xviii. 6, 7. Secondly, It should teach us to endeavour to bring glory to God by our words. To this end we should for matter learn to speak the words of clemency, 2 Chron. x. 7; words of wisdom; words of sobriety and truth, Acts xxvi.; words of righteousness, John vi. 25; wholesome words, 2 Tim. i. 13; words of eternal life, John vi. And to this end we should observe divers rules:

1. That our words be not many, for in a multitude of words cannot but be sin; we are not able to wield aright many words.

2. That we know and not forget God's 'ten

words.' The ignorance of God's ten laws causeth that men know not how they offend in their tongues, but in the ten words of God is an absolute pattern of all uprightness both of heart, speech, and life.

3. That we be much and often in taking unto us the words of confession and prayer, Hosea xiv. 3, Zeph. iii. 9. Our speech is purified and God much glorified by often confession and prayer; this is to speak a pure language.

4. Our ear must seek learning, Prov. xviii. 11; we must be swift to hear and slow to speak, James i., and be contented to be taught as well how to speak as how to live.

Lastly, We must tame our tongues, make conscience of mortification for our sins in word, as well as for evil deed; set a watch before the door of our lips, and pray God to open them.

Or deeds. *Doct.* God will have deeds as well as words; our hands must be bound to good behaviour; and that our labours and works may be done to God's glory, they must be done: 1. With prayer, Ps. ix. 20; 2. With warrant from the word; 3. With faith in God's promise for the success; for 'whatsoever is not of faith is sin;' 4. With perseverance; they are not good works till they be finished and accomplished.

Whatsoever. This word is a note either of universality or perfection. Of perfection, I say, in this sense. Whatsoever ye do or settle about, do it all, that is, let it be complete and perfectly done; but I take it here as a note of universality.

Doct. We are bound to glorify God not only in word and deed, but in all our words and all our deeds; we are tied to every good work, to respect all God's commandments; we are bound to glorify God, not only in actions of worship, but of righteousness too. Not only in religious businesses, but in civil offices; not only in our general calling, but in our particular. Not only abroad, but at home; making conscience not only of filthy deeds, but of filthy speaking; not only of great and crying sins, but of lesser sins; not only of our open deeds, but of our carriage in secret. Use is for reproof; men discover their unsoundness of heart in this respect exceedingly. Many will not forswear that will swear at every word, at least by less oaths, as by the mass, faith, troth, &c.; many shopkeepers will not bear false witness in a court, that will lie daily in selling their wares; many will look to their carriage abroad, that care not how to order themselves at home; many will not do their own work by keeping shop, or travelling on the sabbath, that never stick at it to speak their own words on the sabbath. But if the case of such like men as these be to be suspected, how fearfully bad is their case that are so far from making conscience of every word and deed, as they are to every good work reprobate! that are neither good at home nor abroad, neither in worship nor life, neither to others nor to themselves! Titus i. 16.

Ye. *Doct.* They that have comfort in their election and God's love, they that have begun to make conscience of their ways, and to love the word, they that make a profession of the name of Christ, above all others are exactly to look to themselves, to every word, and every deed: 1. Because they are nearer the courts of the great King, they live always in the presence-chamber. 2. Because God hath bestowed upon them more blessings, and therefore as he gives more wages, requires more work. 3. Because they are more observed than any other. A loose word is more noted in them than execrable blasphemy in others; they are more talked of for seeing a vain sight than others for haunting of lewd plays. 4. Because their hearts are made pure by the blood of Christ; and fine white linen is sooner and deeper stained than coarse rags. 5. They are trusted with more glorious riches. A little sin in them much grieves God's Spirit, whereas a great sin troubles not a wicked man that hath no Spirit of God in him. 6. They are sure to have a recompense of reward for every good word and work, and therefore, to further their own reckoning and glory, should be abundant in the work of the Lord.

Use therefore to quicken us to a desire to walk precisely, circumspectly, exactly, Eph. v. 15, striving to redeem the time that hath been lost in the service of sin and the world.

Giving thanks to God, even the Father, by him. These words are diversely considered.

Some think the former words are an explication of these, as if he should say, be careful in all things to glorify God, for this is right thanking of God;

when men do not only praise God in words, but in obedience.

Some think in these words is lodged a reason of the former, as if he should say, Glorify God in all your actions, and seek to God by prayer in the name of Christ, and ye shall be sure of singular blessings and grace and comforts from God; and in the assurance thereof, when ye provide to pray or practise, provide thanks ready also, for God will not fail in the success.

Some think these words to be an enlarging of the former rule, by wishing them, whatsoever falls out, to be thankful, so as neither prosperity puff them up, nor adversity deject them; but I take it to be a distinct rule from the former, and so here is to be noted:

1. The duty required, viz., 'give thanks.'
2. The explication of it: 1. By the object, 'to God, even the Father;' 2. By the efficient cause, 'by him.'

Giving thanks. Concerning our thankfulness to God, I consider: first, the necessity of it. God will not dispense with it; therefore in Eph. v. 20, the former rule being omitted, this is specially urged; and 1 Thes. v. 18, this is charged upon us as the will of God in Christ Jesus. Secondly, For what we must give thanks, viz., for Christ as the fountain of all favour; hence the sacrament ordained to that end; for all the comforts of God's election and love, for all graces and means of grace cohere; for our liberty in Christ, even unto outward things, 1 Cor. x. 30; for any success or victory over our corruptions of nature, Rom. vii. 25; in short, for all things whatsoever, 2 Cor. iv. 15, 1 Thes. v. 18.

3. How? viz., Not like the pharisee, with pride of heart, and self-liking, with opinion of merit, or with ostentation, but with observation of four rules: 1. If we bless, we must 'bless in the spirit,' 1 Cor. xiv. 16, that is, with understanding and feeling in our hearts. 2. When we give thanks, we should do it with such tenderness, that our praises should awake the graces of God's Spirit, to make them get life and grow. Our praises should stir up faith in God's promise, love to God's glory, fear of God's presence, hatred of our sins, joy in the Holy Ghost, 2 Cor. iv. 15. 3. With a deep sense of our own unworthiness; and thus the four and twenty elders are said to cast down their crowns and fall on their face, when they praised God, Rev. iv. 9, 10, vii. 12, Luke xvii. 4. By all means. We must praise God by psalms, prayer, celebration of the sacrament, works of mercy and obedience.

4. How long? That is answered, Eph. v. 20, Rev. vii. 12,—always. If we must pray always, then we must praise always; we may no more neglect thanksgiving than prayer. Nay, when prayer shall cease, because all mortal infirmities and wants shall cease, yet thanksgiving must go with us within the vail, and live with us for ever in heaven.

Use 1. To inflame us to the holy practice of thankfulness daily, and always watching hereunto, preserving sense, not forgetting God's mercies, even making it our daily sacrifice. To humble us under our unthankfulness for grace, knowledge, the word, fellowship in the gospel, and all kinds of blessings; yea, we sin greatly in not giving thanks for our success in our callings; yea, many are not yet instructed to give thanks for their food. Let those remember that men are said then to eat to God when they give thanks, Rom. xiv. 6. To whom then do they eat that give not thanks? Certainly not to the Lord. Finally, If the poor Gentiles were so punished for unthankfulness, Rom. i. 21, that had but the glimmering light of nature to guide them, and read their lessons only in the book of God's works, what shall become of us in the day of the Lord, that have the light of scripture, of the gospel, of the Spirit, of the sacraments, and so many incomparable favours bestowed upon us? Unless we repent of our unthankfulness, we shall perish with a worse destruction than Tyrus and Sidon, or Sodom and Gomorrah.

To God, even the Father. These words are to be understood, not dividendly, but conjoinedly, and so declare who is our God, even he that hath proved himself a Father in Christ, loving us in him, and accepting of us, and heaping many blessings upon us,—two sweet words. He is a God, there is his majesty; he is a Father, there is his love, and therefore great encouragement to go to him with all suits and praises. With all suits: he is God, and therefore able to help; and Father, and therefore willing to help. With all praises: he is God, and therefore meet to be worshipped; he is Father, and therefore

2 x

will accept the calves of our lips, not according to what we bring, but according to what we desire to bring; and all this should make us both to hate it to praise men or angels, or sacrifice to our nets, and also to honour him with the affection of children, and with the fear of creatures.

By him. These words may be referred:

1. To singing of psalms in the former verse; and so they note that all joy is vain without Christ, yea, these spiritual and better sorts of delight are vain unless Christ be ours. How miserable art thou when thy tongue sings psalms, and Christ dwells not in thine heart! Many men sing the word of Christ that have no part in the Word Christ.

2. To the word 'Father' next before, to note that God hath shewed himself a Father in bestowing many mercies upon us by Christ, and so the consideration of God's mercies by Christ should breed thankfulness.

3. To the word 'thanksgiving,' and so they note the efficient helping cause, and teach us, that as Christ brings down God's graces and blessings to us, so he carrieth up our praises to God; and as we must pray in his name, so our praises will not be accepted unless they be made in his name, and presented in his intercession.

Thus of the general rule.

Hitherto also of the first main part of the information of holy life, viz., the information of our life in general. Hitherto the apostle hath taught us what to do in our general calling as Christians. Now, from ver. 18 to ver. 2 of the next chapter, he shews us what we must be in our particular standings. Or thus: Hitherto he hath given moral precepts, now he gives economical. Or rather thus: Hitherto he hath set down the duties belonging to all Christians, now he informeth us in the duties special, as they are wives, husbands, parents, &c.

Ver. 18. *Wives, submit yourselves to your husbands, as it is comely in the Lord.*

Ver. 19. *Husbands, love your wives, and be not bitter unto them.*

Before I come to the particular consideration of these words, I must observe something from the coherence and general consideration of all the verses together.

Doct. 1. It is plain that men are to be taught how to govern themselves in their houses, as well as in the duties of their general calling. This is meet to be noted; because some men's either ignorance or wilfulness and profaneness is such, that they think ministers should not meddle to tell them how to live at home, or how to carry themselves in their shops.

Doct. 2. From coherence. That we may live comfortably and blessedly in our families and particular callings, we must labour in the daily and constant use of the means to be sincere in the general. The study of the word to frame men to be good men and women in God's sight, would make men good husbands, servants, children, wives, &c.: first get to be a good man, and then thou wilt the easier prove a good husband, &c.

Use. First, For reproof of such as cannot abide to see their children or servants to hear sermons, study the scriptures, labour for grace, &c.; whereas nothing would more fit them to all pleasing in their carriage at home. Secondly, For trial: if religion and the profession of it make thee not a better wife, husband, or servant, suspect thyself that all is not right, but that thou art a hypocrite; repent and amend. Thirdly, For instruction: if men find such stubbornness in their wives, or children, or servants, the best way is to give them more liberty to the means, and to drive them into God's house to hear the word; to call upon them to read the scriptures, and to use such like holy exercises; for if this will not mend them, nothing in the world will.

3. Before I consider the particular members of a family, I must entreat generally of the whole; and concerning the government of a family by the rules of God's word, I consider four things:

1. The authority of it. There is a way how to walk in uprightness, even in our houses, so as God will come to us if our families be rightly ordered, Ps. ci. 2. There is a wisdom or saving knowledge how to erect and found a holy family, and how to order and establish it, Prov. xxiv. 3. There are many administrations, as the administration of a church, of a city, or commonwealth; so likewise the administration of a family, yet but one Lord, 1 Cor. xii.; yea, the governing of a house honestly or in holy comeliness is manifestly expressed, 1 Tim. iii. 5.

2. The antiquity of it. It is the most ancient

of all governments, yea, out of which all the rest sprang. The church was bred and cherished by this government in families for many hundreds of years in the beginning of the world, even till the people came out of Egypt.

3. The utility of it. It is called 'a perfect way,' Ps. ci. 2, and that in three respects: first, As opposed to hypocrisy: it shews a man's way is not hypocritical when a man will not only look to his feet when he goes into God's house, but is careful how to walk uprightly in his own house. Secondly, As it is the ground and field of practice: knowledge is never perfect till it be practised, and the most ordinary way of practice is at home. Thirdly, As it perfects us in blessedness, in that it brings God's promise into execution; besides, the family is the seminary both of church and commonwealth, Gen. xviii. 19, for it brings forth and brings up a seed; it preserves the commonwealth; and as it frames by education a holy seed, it preserves the charge.

4. *Quest.* What things are necessary and requisite unto the blessed being of a family?

Ans. For the erecting and establishing of a blessed family, three things are principally necessary: first, A holy coming together; secondly, A holy living together; thirdly, A special fitness in the head of the family. For the first, it is greatly material to the perpetual well-being of a family that all heedfulness be observed in the first erecting of it; for, as many order the matter, they so provoke God by the first entering upon the family, that the family travels ever after under the burden of God's anger, or great inconvenience, and cannot prosper. And thus men fault—

Either by venturing without a calling or means to live, or by overleaping God's ordinance of contract, or by venturing upon marriage with persons that have foul diseases, as the leprosy, French pox, &c. ; but especially when—

First, More wives than one are brought in; secondly, There is not sufficient distance in blood, but the marriage is incestuous; thirdly, Another man's wife is brought in, either the betrothed wife, or the unjustly divorced wife, of another man; fourthly, There is not consent of parties, but the marriage is forced; fifthly, There is not consent of parents; sixthly, An infamous or scandalous person is chosen to be a yoke-fellow; seventhly, There is not equality either for religion, but a believer is matched with an unbeliever,—or age, or estate, or disposition.

And a like dangerous disorder there is in taking into the family of disordered servants—such as are swearers, filthy and scandalous persons—against which sins there lie known threatenings of God; and so with their sins they bring in God's curse.

The second thing that makes a family blessed is a holy living together; and there are four things that are requisite especially to the good estate of the house: first, The constant practice of piety and private worship; secondly, the right order of employment in the mutual labours of the family; thirdly, Household discipline or reformation; fourthly, Hospitality, or a right respect of strangers. For the first, the piety that is to be practised stands of six parts: first, Prayer and thanksgiving to God. Men must pray everywhere, 1 Tim. ii. 8; our meats and callings must be sanctified by the word and by prayer, 1 Tim. iv. 4. Thus David prayed morning and evening and at noon, Ps. lv. 17; so Daniel; yea, it is a brand of profane and abominable persons, they call not upon God, Ps. xiv. 4; yea, those families are in great danger of his wrath that call not upon his name, Jer. xx. Secondly, Holy conference betwixt the members of the family, as between husband and wife, 1 Pet. iii. 7, and between father and children, Deut. vi. 21, 22. Thirdly, Singing of psalms, Col. iii. 16, Eph. v. 20. Fourthly, Repetition of doctrine publicly taught, examining it by the scriptures alleged, as did the Bereans, Acts xvii. Fifthly, Fasting upon extraordinary occasions is very plain, Zech. xii. 16. Lastly, The parents' instruction, Ps. lxxviii. 2-4, Deut. vi. 6.

Quest. But what things may be taught in the family?

Ans. First, The common grounds of God's service and worship; this is to teach them to fear God. Secondly, The meaning of the sacraments, Exod. xii. 25, 26, xiii. 14. Thirdly, The law, Deut. vi. 6; that is, the common grounds of honesty and vice; teaching to love such and such virtues, and hate such and such vices. Fourthly, The use and consideration of God's great judgments: therefore God will tell Abraham of the destruction of Sodom, because he will make use of it in his family. Fifthly, The report of God's great works of old, Ps. lxxviii. 2, 3. Sixthly. To hope in God, acquainting them with their natural miseries, and training them up by warning them to take heed of the common presumptions of the wicked, and by distilling unto them the grounds of practice and promise concerning God's mercy to their souls and their last salvation. Seventhly, We should acquaint our households with the general course of the scriptures; thus Timothy knew the scriptures of a child, 2 Tim. iii. 15; for an exact knowledge of all scriptures was impossible for a child to attain. Lastly, The things received by public doctrine should be enforced and kept afoot in the family; if any pass these bonds, they intrude upon the minister's office, and ought to fear Uzzah's curse, and therefore as men should instruct, and so avoid the common profaneness of the world in neglecting God's ordinance, so they should be wise to sobriety, and keep themselves in all fear and humility within their own line and measure.

Thus of piety.

The second thing required is a holy order of employment in all the members of the family, in their mutual labours for the good of the outward estate of it, Gen. iii. 19, 1 Cor. vii. 20. Unto the orderly performance of the labours of a family five things are required:

First, Diligence. Secondly, Peace, else all sacrifice is in vain, Prov. xvii. 1. Thirdly, Providence. It is not the hand of the diligent, but his thoughts that bring abundance; care is required, not the care for success, for that is condemned, Mat. vi., but the care for the duty, Prov. xxi. 5. Fourthly, Retiredness; they must keep at home. Servants must not be stealing out of the family without leave; nor masters leave their staudings. Keep thy foot from thy neighbour's house, Prov. xxv. 17. If a man cannot be found in the place of his labour, he is like 'a bird that wandereth from his nest,' Prov. xxvii. 19. Fifthly, Frugality, in living within their compass, and not spending above their means; they must make their lambs serve for clothing, and the goats for rent or hire of the field, and the milk of the goats must be sufficient for them and their families and for the sustenance of the maids, Prov. xxvii.

27. It is not a good rule to make reason judge of their needs, or to propound unto themselves, I will spend no more but what I need; but they must look to their means, to spend according to that; for ordinarily there is not so little coming in but God can make it suffice, or will himself send them supply.

The third thing required is domestical discipline. Thus Jacob searcheth his house, purgeth it of all idols and superstitious monuments, admonisheth his people of the fear of God, Gen. xxxv. 2, 3. Thus Job sacrificeth for his children, Job i. 5. Thus David will rid his house of slanderers, liars, apostates, &c. And so should we see to the reformation of abuses by admonition, rebukes, correction, or complaints to the magistrate, or elders of the church. The father in his house is the keeper of both tables.

The fourth thing is the right order of hospitality and respect of strangers, and it stands in two things: first, In seeking, by all means, to bring God's ministers or servants into our house, Heb. xiii. 2, 1 Pet. i. 1, that they might help us, and as it were bless and perfume our houses by their prayers, counsel, comforts, admonitions, &c., Rom. i. 11; secondly, In providing that no strangers be admitted or permitted that will hinder God's worship or any way the good of the family; they must not be within our gates that will not join with us to sanctify the sabbath in our dwellings, Ex. xx; yea, if they be disordered persons we should use them as the false prophet, that they may say, 'Thus was I wounded in the house of my friend,' Zech. xiii.

The use is: first, Against the papists, and that principally two ways: 1. In that they forbid marriage, and so hinder the erecting of families to God; 2. In that they forbid knowledge to lay-people, and so hinder the good government of the family.

Secondly, Against great abuses even amongst us. There is that open profaneness in the most houses, that if they searched with lights there would no prayer, reading of scripture, holy conference, singing of psalms, or instruction be found there; but without light men may find their houses full of swearing, deceit, lying, false measures, and weights, and all kind of filthiness, to the singular detriment of the family; for hence it is that many families do in vain rise early, and go to bed late, and eat the bread of painfulness and sorrow, for God for these sins will not build the house. Sometimes this is plagued by open judgments; sometimes God's curse secretly, like a moth, eats down the prosperity of the house. But always all such families are very hateful to God, even like the dens or cages of wild beasts. 2. It may humble the best of us, if we search into our neglects, ignorances, and omissions of the many duties we should perform in our houses.

Thirdly, For instruction, to teach us by prayer to seek a way of God for us and our houses, and to beseech God to build us an house, 2 Sam. ii. 7, 11, 25, 27, 29, and by all means to labour to live godly at home in the practice of piety; this is to bring salvation to our houses. Thus our families would become as little churches, Rom. xvi, 1 Cor. xvi. Yea, wonderful hath been the success of this holy order in some families. Thus the house of David hath become as the house of God, Zech. xii. 8. Yea, if we were thus careful, God would hedge us and our families round about, and all that we have, that Satan could not touch us; he cannot break God's fence without God's leave, Job i. 10. Our tabernacles would then flourish and stand long, Prov. xii. 7, xiv. 11.

Thus in general of household government, or the order generally belonging to the good estate of all the members.

Now I come to consider each member in the family; and the apostle divides them into three couples: the wife and the husband, the child and parents, the servant and master.

Doct. There are two reasons why the husbands and wives are charged in the first place, viz., first, Because that in this order they were thus instituted of God; he first made man and wife, and in the order of nature these first found the family; and so the apostle keeps the order of nature and the first institution. Secondly, Because the good behaviour of the inferiors in the families lieth much in the good example of the husband and wife; if they be filthy, wasteful, or blasphemers, usually their children and servants are so; and many times it holds in the contrary, for their good example either makes the family in imitation grow like them, or at least it restrains much evil.

Quest. But why is the wife first appointed to her duty before the husband?

Ans. Because in the order of the family she must first mend before the husband (howsoever, before God's judgment-seat they shall be tried equally) in domestical behaviour; if she would have her husband reformed of wickedness or ill dealing, she must first mend herself.

Thus of the general consideration.

Wives be subject to your husbands, as is comely in the Lord. In these words the wife's duty is first laid down: 'Wives submit to your husbands;' secondly, It is enlarged or confirmed: 1. By a reason, 'it is comely;' 2. By a limitation, 'in the Lord.'

In laying down the duty I consider: first, Who are charged, 'wives;' secondly, With what, 'be subject;' thirdly, To whom, 'to your husbands.'

Wives. *Doct.* All wives generally and indefinitely are tied to a holy order of subjection to their husbands, without distinction of years, the elder women and the younger, Titus ii. 8, and without distinction of estate; poor men's wives must be subject as well as citizens' wives, or Gentiles,[1] a great fault in the baser sort. Their houses, in respect of rudeness, are as void of righteousness as they are of riches. Great men's wives also must be subject; Pharaoh's daughter, and Vashti the empress, yea, though there be inequality of means, as if the wife were a lady and the husband but a meaner man, yet she must be subject, and he not wait upon her.

Use. 1. For comfort of wives; nothing is required of one but what is required of all. 2. Of husbands, in respect no means of estate or alteration in their condition can lose them their honour in the subjection of their wives. And 3. Every woman should learn to do her duty, seeing all are bound to it.

Be subject. Here I consider: 1. What is required, viz., 'be subject;' 2. In what manner it is required, that is, in the indefinite propounding of it, without exception of time or place, &c.

In the first I consider: first, That it is; secondly, I answer a question; thirdly, What it is.

First, That subjection in women is required without dispensation by God, as his ordinance is plain by

[1] Qu. 'gentles'?—ED.

these scriptures, Gen. iii. 19, Eph. v. 24, Titus ii 5, 1 Pet. iii. 1.

Secondly, The question is, why the apostle only propounds here the wife's subjection, without mentioning any other duty?

Ans. 1. I might say it is the wisdom of God to scatter directions and comforts, that we may not find them all in one place, to stir us up to the more diligence in study of the scriptures, and with great good success many times; for while they are seeking to learn to be good wives, they meet also with those directions that make them good women too. God many times when we seek one blessing causeth us to find many.

2. I may say that it is the wisdom of God to epitomise and draw things into a short sum, that we may be more familiarly acquainted with his will. Thus when he would propound his eternal rules of all righteousness in the law, he chooseth to give them in ten words, that men might grow to be as familiarly acquainted with them as with any ordinary matter, that they might always have them before their eyes, and bind them to the fringe of their garments; so God gives women their duties in one word, that it might be engraven in their hearts, and sewed down before their eyes in capital letters upon their cushions: BE SUBJECT should never be out of their minds.

3. Because of the necessity of it; if God may not have this duty, he will not accept of the rest; though they be fair, rich, wise, provident, diligent, &c., yet if they be not subject, they are not regarded of God.

4. Because women most fail in this. The special duty of the husband is love, and of the wife subjection; the man most fails in love, and the woman in subjection.

Thirdly, I consider what this subjection is; and here, first, What it is; secondly, What it is not; thirdly, The means that women are to use that they may be subject.

For the first, in the right discharge of their subjection, wives are tied to five things: first, Honour; secondly, Faithfulness; thirdly, Fear; fourthly, Labour; fifthly, Submission.

To be subject, is first to honour them; to be faithful, to fear them, to be diligent in labour for them and their family, and to submit to them.

1. They must honour their husbands as their superiors and heads, 1 Cor. xi. 3; and this they must do: first, By giving reverent titles to them, 1 Pet. iii. 6.

2. Secondly, By striving to resemble the very properties and praiseworthy qualities of the husband,— she should be his image or his glory. And thus also in his absence she should resemble his authority over the family. Women should choose such husbands as they would not only live with and love, but such as they would live by, even such as they would set before them as patterns of their natures and lives.

3. By living without suspicion, making the best interpretation of their doubtful actions. Michal is made a precedent of contempt and suspicion, when she so sinfully taunts and misinterprets David's dancing before the ark in presence of the maids of Israel.

4. By leaving to him the secrets of his public employment, and keeping her to her own measure in caring for domestical matters; she may not be of an inquisitive humour, to lay a necessity upon the husband to reveal to her all occurrents, especially when the husband is either magistrate or minister.

5. By yielding him due benevolence, 1 Cor. vii. 3; she may not without calling or consent refuse her husband's bed.

6. By striving to advance her husband's credit; she must not shame her husband, Prov. xii. 4. Wives shame their husbands: 1. When their feet will not keep in their own house, Prov. vii. 11; 2. When they blaze abroad his infirmities; 3. When they neglect the care of his children, either for manners, apparel, or employment, Titus iii. 5; 4. By living in any scandalous sin, as when they be false accusers, given to much wine, intemperate, &c., Titus ii. 3, or busybodies, 1 Tim. v. 13, 14.

The second part of subjection is faithfulness. They must shew all faithfulness: 1. In respect of the marriage-bed, Prov. ii. 17. 2. In respect of expense, she must not be wasteful, for this is to pull down the house with her own hands, and ever the more secretly, the more sinfully, Prov. xiv. 1; she should save and not spend without consent. 3. In respect of the business of the family, she should be such as her husband's heart may trust in her. It is a great sin in wives when they must be told not only what to do, but when they are charged with the care of such and such things, they must need to be continually told, and yet be careless still. 4. In the secrets of the family; not disclosing them to strangers, but so taking notice of them as not to discover them without the consent of the husband, as the faults of Zion must not be told at Gath. 5. In entertainment, that none be admitted that are suspected or disliked by the husband.

The third thing is fear, Eph. v. 33, 1 Pet. iii. 1, 2. They should shew the fear of their husbands: 1. By reverent behaviour to him, not rude, audacious, bold; 2. By striving to be inoffensive, avoiding or preventing what might stir him to anger or dislike or grief; 3. By giving soft answers when he is angry, Prov. xv.; 4. By forbearing passion or frowardness, even with others in his sight; 5. Making him her covering when they are abroad,—but many women are so intemperate and wilful, that a man might as soon hide the wind with his fist or oil in his hand as cover the infirmities of his wife, Prov. xxvii. 15, 16; 6. By living quietly without contention,—she must not disquiet him.

Fourthly, Her labour. Her labour is of two sorts: first, To appoint unto the family, and oversee their ways, Prov. xxxi. 27; secondly, She must labour with her own hands, Prov. xiii. 27, 19, and this labour of her hands is prescribed with six rules:

1. She must not spend months or years in staying for some employment she could like to make a calling, but she must presently seek by all means to find out labour: 'she seeketh wool and flax.'

2. She must not stand upon finer works, as scorning baser employment, but be content to 'set her hands to any labour' that is meet; thus she 'spinneth and seeketh wool and flax,' Prov. xxxi. 13, 19.

3. She must not spend her time in working of toys or curious things, good for nothing but to shew skill and wear out time, but about profitable things for the family, as carpets, ver. 22; sheets, ver. 24; the clothing of her family, her husband, and her children, ver. 21, 23.

4. She must not lie abed till nine or ten o'clock, but she must 'rise while it is yet night,' ver. 15, and 'her candle is not to be put out by night,' ver. 18.

5. She must not be fickle and unconstant, to change from work to work, to no profit, beginning many things, and finishing little or nothing, but against all weariness or other impediments she must gird her loins with strength, and strengthen her arms.

6. Lastly, All must be done cheerfully, not grudgingly, ver. 13.

The fifth thing is submission, Eph. v. 22, and she must submit herself:

1. To her husband's directions, and live by the laws prescribed her by her husband, Eph. v. 23, as the church doth teach and live by the word of Christ, else no true church. Thus the woman asketh leave to go to the prophet, 2 Kings iv. 22. And the wife is charged not to fast without consent, 1 Cor. vii. 4. And thus also she must receive directions for the affairs of the family.

2. To his restraints, so as she be contented to be restrained of her ease, will, desires, delights, &c. 'Thy desires shall be subject to thy husband,' Gen. iii. 19. Thus the church must deny her own reason, profit, pleasure, &c., and submit herself to Christ, Eph. v. 23. Thus must the wife cast about 'how to please her husband,' 1 Cor. vii. 34.

Thus of what it is.

Secondly, I consider what it is not, or what the wife is not bound to, though she must be subject. In general, their subjection doth not lead them into bondage, and make them slaves and vassals to them, they remain still their companions and yokefellows.

In particular, there are some things spiritual, some things domestical, some things in her civil carriage, from which she is not restrained by her subjection.

In matters of religion, she cannot be forced to neglect the means to save her soul; the unbelieving husband cannot compel the wife to forsake her faith and religion, and the means thereof, to please him. Again, though her sex bar her from instruction in the church, and her husband's authority bar her from sole instruction in the family, yet notwithstanding, under her husband, she may instruct her children, Prov. vi. 20, and family, Prov. xxxi. 26. Besides, though her husband were never so great, wise, lordly, &c., yet she may admonish him, and he ought to be crossed of his own course and will by her, as Abraham by Sarah, at God's appointment, who charged him to hear her in what she said, and to do it, Gen. xxi. 12.

In domestical matters, she is not subjected to his tyranny and blows, nor is she bound to bear with or consent to, or conceal his whoredoms; she is not bound to imitate his example, or obey his will, to do that that is ill. And lastly, her subjection doth not bind her to deliver her body when she is apart for her disease, Lev. xviii. 19, Ezek. viii. 6.

In civil matters I instance in one. She is not utterly barred out from works of mercy, for though she may not take of his substance to spend it, no, not in works of piety and mercy, yet of her own labours she may take to give to the poor, or for pious uses, Prov. xxxi. 20.

Thus of what not.

Thirdly, That women may perform this subjection. 1. They must keep home. 2. They must seek this ability of God, for he gives the graces of the wife. Nature makes her a woman, election a wife, but to be prudent and subject is of the Lord, Prov. xix. 14, and there she must seek it of God. 3. They must preserve and keep warm in their hearts the love of their husbands, for all disobedience ariseth of want of love. Lastly, They must consider the reasons and encouragements to subjection.

First, He is thy head, and therefore be subject, 1 Cor. xi. 3; secondly, If the shame of men will not move thee to be subject, yet have power on thine head, because of the angels, 1 Cor. xi. 10; but especially consider the encouragements.

1. It should weigh much with them that God hath imposed such a free and ingenuous subjection. It is not boundless, when they may be still companions. 2. That God, that requires them to be subject, chargeth husbands to use them well and kindly, to accept their obedience. 3. God hath valued the price of a good wife, and set the rate to be above pearls, Prov. xxxi. 10. Finally, Their labour in the Lord shall not be lost, for they are much set by of God, 1 Pet. iii. 4; he will bless them with the fruit of their womb, Ps. cxiii. 9, cxxvii. 3; yea, the salvation of their souls may be furthered by the right performance of family duties.

Thus of the things required, viz., 'be subject.'

The manner how it is required follows. 'Be subject' indefinitely, and so sheweth that they must be subject : 1. Not outwardly, but in spirit, Mal. ii. 15; 2. Not abroad only, but at home; 3. Not sometimes, but constantly always; 4. Not in some things, but in everything, Eph. v. 24; 5. Not for fear or shame, but for conscience sake, and voluntarily. Here I may take in the distinction; subjection is twofold : 1. By God's institution, and so wives are subject in that they are commanded to be so, and God hath taken pre-eminence from them; 2. By will, or the conscience cheerfully yielding obedience to God's will, and thus only good wives are subject.

Thus of the duty charged upon them.

3. The persons to whom it is due follows.

To your husbands. These words may be considered exclusively and inclusively. They exclude all others; she is not to be subject to her servants or children, or the strange woman brought in by the husband. And so also they include all husbands; they must be subject to their husbands; not the wise only, but the foolish; not the courteous only, but the froward; not the rich only, but the poor also.

Thus of the laying down of the duty.

It is amplified : first, By a reason, 'it is comely;' secondly, By a limitation, 'in the Lord.'

As is comely. ὡς ἀνῆκεν. The original word is rendered three ways :

1. As ye ought, *ut oportet;* and so it is a reason from God's institution; ye must do it, God indispensably requires it.

2. As is meet, *ut convenit.* It is meet especially two ways : 1. God hath given power over all in the family but one, and therefore great reason and equity ye be appointed subject unto him, and it is not meet ye should rule so many if you will not obey one. Again, ye are professors, and have given your names to Christ, and therefore it is meet that you especially strive to be good wives, and better than any others, lest the word be evil spoken of.

3. As is comely, *ut decet;* so it is here translated. The wife's comeliness is not in beauty, Prov. xi. 22, xxxi. 30, nor in the gorgeousness of apparel, 1 Pet. iii. 3; but a wife's comeliness is especially:

1. In her wisdom, Prov. xiv. 1, and that to be shewed in two things : first, In her skill to please her husband, neither offending him with chiding

words nor sullenness, puling, or crying, which is found to vex some men more than words; secondly, In her skill to manage the business of the house, both seasonably, discreetly, and with providence.

2. In her meekness, it is exceeding comely, where the hid man of the heart is incorrupt with a meek and quiet spirit; this is better than all apparel, 1 Pet. iii. 3, 4.

Thirdly, Here it is in her subjection; for as it is an uncomely thing to see the body above the head, so it is to see a wife that will rule and not be subject to her husband.

And if the wife labour to adorn herself thus, she shall appear comely to God, 1 Pet. iii. 4, to men in the gate, Prov. xxxi. 23, 31, to her husband and children, Prov. xxxi. 28; yea, she is an ornament to sincerity and holiness itself, Titus. ii. 3.

In the Lord. 1. These words are expounded diversely.

First, 'In the Lord,' that is, in the fear of God, as unto the Lord in obedience to his ordinance, for God's sake, because God requires this at your hands.

In this sense it may serve for two uses: first, For terror to wicked wives. They must answer it before God; he will avenge their not subjecting of themselves; he will certainly account with them if they be whorish, contentious, idle, careless, or wasteful, &c.

2. It is a great comfort unto a godly woman; her subjection is in the Lord. It is in God's account even as a sacrifice to him; he takes it as done to himself. God honours her obedience in the family, as if it were piety in the temple; and this may the more support them if their husbands be unkind.

Secondly, 'In the Lord,' that is, so far as they command in the Lord. They must so love their husbands, as they cease not to love God; and so be subject to them, as they leave not their subjection to God. Their covenant with their husbands no way infers the breach of this covenant with God, and thus it is principally here meant.

Thus of the wife's duty.

The husband's duty follows in the 19th verse.

Husbands, love your wives, and be not bitter unto them. Doct. In general, husbands must be told their duties as well as wives. As they would have them mend, so they must mend themselves; and as they would have comfort by living with them, so they must make conscience to practise their duty to them. It is not the having of wives or husbands that breeds contentment, but the holy performance of duties mutually.

The duty of the husband is propounded here: first, By exhortation, 'Husbands, love your wives;' secondly, By dehortation, 'Be not bitter unto them.'

In the exhortation there is the person exhorted, 'husbands;' the duty, 'love;' the persons to whom they owe it, 'your wives.'

Husbands. This indefinite propounding of it shews that all sorts of husbands are bound to shew this duty, poor and rich, learned and unlearned, young and old.

Love. Concerning the husband's duty as it is here expressed, I consider six things: first, That it is indispensably required; secondly, Why this duty only is named; thirdly, How he must shew his love; fourthly, Reasons why; fifthly, I answer certain objections; sixthly, The lets of the performance of love.

First, It is required, Gen. ii. 24, Eph. v. 25, Titus ii. 2.

Secondly, The apostle names this duty in this one word, either because the Lord of purpose would have them study the whole scriptures, that while they seek for directions to make them good husbands, they may find also counsel to make them good men; or else in this word is comprehended their duty, that so this being their word, they might write it in their hearts and have it ever in their eyes to do it; or else it is because this is most necessary, and as women fail in subjection, so do men in love.

For the third, viz., how he must shew his love, we must understand that the husband owes the wife: first, Natural or civil love, as a married man; secondly, Spiritual love, as a Christian married man.

For the *first*, The love of the husband is to be shewed four ways:

1. By cohabitation, 1 Pet. iii. 7. He must dwell with her, not wander from his wife, nor depart without calling and consent, nor dwell with drunkards, whores, or gamesters; dwell, I say, in his own house, not in the ale-house, &c.

2. By chastity; and that, first, by avoiding unfaithfulness to her bed, not following the strange woman. This sin of whoredom, it consumes men's

strength, wastes men's substance, compasseth men with evil in the midst of the congregation; is worse than theft; exceedingly hateful in God's sight, and disgraceful amongst men; destroys the soul, both by making men without understanding, and sending them to hell, Prov. v. 19, vi. 25, and ix. 16; Job xxxi. 7, 8, &c. Secondly, By yielding her due benevolence, nor departing from her bed without consent.

3. By honouring her, 1 Pet. iii. 7. The husband must shew that he honoureth her:

First, By suffering himself to be admonished by her, Gen. xxi. 12.

Secondly, By using her as his companion, not lording over her as his slave.

Thirdly, By trusting her with disposing of such things in the family as she is fit for and faithful in, by giving her employment according to her gifts.

Fourthly, By not disgracing her before others, but choosing a fit time in secret to find fault with her.

Fifthly, By not speaking when she is in passion, but forcing both her and himself in all matters of difference to speak when they are both out of passion.

Sixthly, By yielding a free and just testimony of her praises, Prov. xxxi. 28.

4. By cherishing her, Eph. v. 28. And this he performs:

First, By providing her maintenance according to his ability, and that in labouring so in his calling as he may provide for her while he lives, and leave her some means when he dies. And for manner, doing it cheerfully, not stay till it be wrung from him, as from churlish Nabal. Thus do not they that spend at ale-house, upon whores, or sports, bear-baits, plays, gaming, or apparel, that should serve for maintenance of wives and children at home.

Secondly, By protecting and rescuing her from wrongs and dangers, 1 Sam. xxx. 5.

Thirdly, By delighting in her love; yea, not erring or wandering in his love continually, Prov. v. 19.

Secondly, He owes her spiritual love as well as natural. So Christ loved his church, not only to enrich it, but to sanctify it, Eph. v. 25, 26. They must dwell with them as men of knowledge to help them, not only by labour, but by knowledge also, 1 Pet. iii. 7.

The religious love he must shew:

1. By forgiving her offences upon her repentance. This is one way whereby Christ makes his church holy.

2. By edifying her by counsel, exhortation, admonition, consolation, &c.

Fourthly, The reasons why he must love her are:

1. Because God requires it.

2. God so requires it as a man must leave his father and mother to cleave unto his wife, Gen. ii. 24.

3. The example of Christ should enforce it, Eph. v. 25.

4. She is his own flesh, and no man ever hated his own flesh, Eph. v. 29.

5. Lest prayer be interrupted, 1 Pet. iii. 17.

6. Thus he shall shew himself a member of Christ, and to be like his head, Eph. i. 30.

7. It will preserve a man from the temptations and enticements of the strange woman, Prov. v. 19, 20; yea, and from all evil company and unthriftiness.

Fifthly, The objections follow:

Object. 1. She was of mean birth, condition, or portion, when I married her.

Ans. So, and much worse, was the church before Christ married her, and yet Christ loves her.

Object. 2. But, since marriage, she is idle, froward, wasteful, &c.

Ans. This is a reason to move thee to pray for her and to watch over her ways, to admonish and instruct her, but this is no reason to move thee not to love her: for the church sinneth after calling, and yet Christ loves her, and shews it by his intercession for her in heaven, and by labouring to cleanse her by his Spirit and word in earth.

Object. 3. But she is a carnal and unregenerate woman, a mere wicked woman, that neither doth nor will fear God, and Christ doth not love heretics, or hypocrites, or profane persons and pagans.

Ans. Though this reason from Christ's example doth not hold, yet the reason from God's institution binds thee; thou must love her not because she deserves it, but because God requires it.

Quest. Is a man bound to esteem his wife above all women?

Ans. In respect of the affection and practice of the things essentially necessary to conjugal duty he is, but not in opinion of his praises, for that is the commendation of the good wife, not of every wife, Prov. xxxi. 30.

Thus of the objections.

Sixthly, The lets follow.

Quest. How comes it to pass that men do not perform this duty?

Ans. 1. It is in some by reason of their sinful coming together, as in sudden marriages, when they are done before there be a calling or affection in the heart. So when men have ill ends, as those men that marry their wives not for grace or favour, but for wealth; when they are possessed of both, they will love their wealth and hate their wives.

2. Corruption of nature is the cause of want of love; they are wicked men, therefore wicked husbands.

3. It comes to pass because men do not by prayer seek love of God; neglect of prayer and mortification is the cause.

4. Men love the strange woman, and therefore love not their wives, or they love other men's wives.

5. It comes to pass by the untowardness of the wife; for though that be no just reason to the husband, because he should love her because God commands him, yet it is a just judgment of God upon her.

Thus of what is required.

Love—viz. indefinitely—first, In heart as well as in word, Mal. ii. 15; secondly, Not before others only, but privately; thirdly, Not sometimes, or the first week, month, or year, but for ever, constantly; fourthly, For conscience sake, and not for shame or respect of her friends, or while her means do last.

Your wives. This is added: first, To exclude all others,—all others, I say, not from Christian love in the general, but from conjugal love; secondly. To include all wives, though poor, less wise, or frugal, froward, &c.

Thus of the exhortation; the dehortation follows:

Be not bitter unto them. In these words the apostle doth mollify the authority of the husband, and provides that it pass not into tyranny. Here I consider four things: first, What it hath not in it; secondly, How men shew themselves bitter to their wives; thirdly, The means to cure this bitterness; fourthly, The reasons to move thereunto.

For the first, this exhortation to love and dehortation from bitterness doth not bind them:

1. To love their vices; they may know them to be the weaker vessel, yea, take notice of the weakness of the vessel.

2. To lose his own authority by lightness and vain behaviour.

3. To omit the performance of holy duties to please her humour.

4. To give her a licence to do what she list, and live how she will.

5. From finding fault and reproving, so as they use not their own words, but God's.

Lastly, distinguish their natures: wives of soft and gentle natures must be used with all gentleness, but that lets not but that wilful and stubborn wives may be held down to a meet subjection.

Men shew their bitterness: first, By words, and that diversely, when they reproach them for their infirmities or deformities, or when they grow quarrellous, finding fault with everything, or grow into passion upon every occasion; secondly, In deeds, by using them discourteously, or by unjust restraint; or lastly, By blows. Many men have little growing in their furrows but wormwood; they have a true gall of bitterness in them; they may be compared to the star in Rev. viii. 11, for as that made the third part of the waters bitter, so are more than three parts of the words of many husbands bitter words; yea, as if their natural frowardness were not enough, some men will sharpen and whet their tongues to sound out cursed words like swords or arrows; yea, some are so unappeasable, their anger is like the fool's wrath, Prov. xxvii. 3; these are a brood of Chaldeans, a bitter, a furious nation.

For the cure of this bitterness, four rules are to be observed:

1. Men must pray God to cast something into their fountain to sweeten it.

2. They must turn the course of this humour, and spend it upon their sins, in the practice of the duties of mortification.

3. Eat God's book, for that will enable men to godly sorrow, by being bitter in their bellies, and will sweeten their mouths.

4. Look to the roots of bitterness, stay the spring of it in the beginning, take heed of a custom in frowardness, for then only custom in the use of the means will cure thee; again, it will cost them daily sorrows before they can get their natures thoroughly healed.

Lastly, The reasons follow why they must mortify bitterness.

1. It is a wise man's glory and discretion to pass by infirmities, Prov. xix. 11.

2. She is not his footstool, but his helper.

3. Seeing we are heirs of blessing, let us bless and not curse; if God hath sweetened our hearts with grace, let not our fountains send forth bitter waters and sweet.

4. The apostle requires that all bitterness be put away, *all* for degrees,—it is not enough we are not so bad as some be,—and in *all* persons.

5. Lastly, it is a part of our good works and holy conversation to mortify bitterness and envy and strife. Hereby we must shew that we have the wisdom that is from above, for if our knowledge be right, it will make us peaceable, gentle, and easy to be entreated. On the other side, if men sharpen their tongues to cursed and bitter speaking, they may not boast of their knowledge, for such wisdom is carnal, sensual, and devilish, and they are liars against the word, James iii. 13, 17.

Use is for instruction to all husbands that fear God, to approve themselves unto God, in their sincere and loving behaviour towards their wives, especially they should take notice of this vice of bitterness; or if they have failed this way, they should recover themselves, repent and amend, and not be like those wretched persons that draw iniquity with cords of vanity, and call bitter sweet: it is ill to fault this way, but worse to excuse, defend, or deny it.

Thus of the husband's duty.

The next couple in the family is parents and children.

The duties of children is set down first, because the inferiors are charged first, and chiefly to mend and perform their duties.

Ver. 20. *Children obey your parents in all things, for this is well-pleasing to the Lord.*

The exhortation hath in it two things: first, Their duty; secondly, The reasons of it. Their duty hath in it four things: first, Who are charged, 'children;' secondly, What is charged upon them, 'obey;' thirdly, To whom they owe it, 'your parents;' fourthly, The extent, how far forth, 'in all things.' The reason is, because though it were not grateful and pleasing to the parents by reason of their waywardness, yet it is well-pleasing to God.

Children, viz., All children, without difference of sex, both sons and daughters; or of age, not only infants, but children grown and of riper and full years of condition; the children both of poor and rich.

Obey. The obedience of children must be considered:

More specially at some times, and so they must obey—

1. In the choice of their callings.

2. In the election and disposing of their marriages; it must be with consent of parents. Thus did Isaac, Gen. xxiv. Thus even Ishmael, Gen. xxi. 21. Thus Jacob, Gen. xxvii. 46, xxviii. 9. Thus Samson, Judges xiv. 2. And this power hath every father over his virgin, 1 Cor. vii. 36, 37.

More generally. Here I consider: first, That they must obey not in some things at some times, but always throughout the course of our lives; this is plain here, and likewise charged, Eph. vi. 2.

Secondly, How they must obey. Children must perform obedience:

1. With reverence internal and external; internally they must conceive a holy estimation and tenderness of respect, and honour and observance of their parents; and externally they must shew it by all reverent behaviour, as by rising up before them, by giving them the honour to speak first.

2. With readiness to receive and hear instruction, Prov. i. 8.

3. With endeavour to fulfil their desires, by their labours or otherwise.

4. With submission: first, To their rebukes, Prov. xiii. 1; secondly, To their restraints in diet, apparel, recreations, &c.; thirdly, To their corrections.

5. With piety, praying for them; for if they

must do it for all men, much more for them; and if for all in authority, then for parents, 1 Tim. ii. 1.

6. With all meekness of love, shewed three ways:

(1.) By obeying, without inquiring, discoursing, murmuring, or contending.

(2.) By bearing their infirmities, either of body, age, or mind; obey, though aged, diseased, crabbed, &c.

(3.) Obeying without respect of profit. Some children are obsequious so long as anything is to be had from their parents; but when they have all they must have, then their forwardness to please is neglected: this is a base and mercenary obedience.

7. With all thankfulness and gratitude, a great part of which is to recompense their parents' kindness by relieving their wants, if they fall into wants, 1 Tim. v. 4.

Your parents. Viz., Both your parents: not your father only, but your mother also, Lev. xix. 3, Prov. xv. 20.

In all things. *Quest.* But must they be obeyed in sin?

Ans. No; you must so obey your earthly father as you disobey not your heavenly Father; therefore 'in the Lord' is added, Eph. vi. 1. But else we must obey in all things that are not apparent to be sinful, though against our ease, profit, credit, &c.

Or more plainly thus: All things are of three sorts: first, Some things are simply good; this must be done though the parents forbid, because God commands. Secondly, Some things are simply evil; these things must not be done though parents command, because God forbids. Thirdly, Some things are indifferent; in these children must obey, though their parents require things never so unmeet, for things may be unmeet that are not unlawful.

Thus of the doctrine of their obedience.

Against this doctrine children object many things.

Object. I am now in better estate, in higher place, of better gifts, or such like, than my parents.

Ans. This is no reason to withhold obedience and reverence; for Joseph was a prince in Egypt, and Jacob in great want. Solomon sits in his throne of majesty, and yet, when his mother comes to him, he yielded all reverence; the throne did not make her cease to be a mother: yea, our Saviour Christ infinitely excelled his parents, and yet he was subject unto them, Luke i. 51.

Object. But our Saviour saith, 'Call not men father on earth,' Mat. xxiii. 9.

Ans. The words are not to be understood simply but comparatively, and that either to God or to the pharisees: call no man father as thou callest God Father, but so give titles to men as all honour and sacred estimation of God's fatherly care be preserved; and call no man father as the pharisees ambitiously desire to be called. Give not trust and child-like honour to men of what profession soever, that you should only trust in them; and by performing honour, or obedience, or recompense to them, grow careless of the duties you owe to your own parents, as the pharisees taught, Mat. xv. 5.

Object. But my parents require base things, and such as cast a kind of discredit upon me in the world.

Ans. Consider not the things required, but God's ordination. Besides, God the Father required of Christ to bear the cross, spitting in' the face, &c., yet he willingly obeyed.

Object. But my parents are disordered persons, and foolish, &c.

Ans. Pray for them, but despise them not. Besides, God knows what is good for thee, and therefore hath caused thee to come out of the loins of such parents, and required subjection of thee.

Object. They are not my natural parents, but my stepfather or stepmother.

Ans. Yet they must be obeyed; so Ruth obeyed Naomi, and Moses Jethro, Exod. xviii. 19.

Object. They are not parents at all, but my kindred only, as my uncle, aunt, &c., with whom I am left in trust.

Ans. Thou must be ruled by them; so was Esther by Mordecai.

Use 1. This condemns the doctrine and practice of papists, that defend the vows of solitary and single life of children without consent of parents; and it meets with the doctrine of the pharisees, that would dispense with children's relieving of their parents, so they would bestow it upon them, Mat. xv.

Use 2. This may serve for reproof of stubborn and ungracious children that forsake their parents' instruction, Prov. i. 8; but especially such monsters as despise their parents when they are old, or mock them, or curse them, or chafe them, or rob them, &c., the cursed estate of such children is set down in these scriptures, Prov. xv. 20, xix. 26, xxiii. 22, xx. 20, xxviii. 24, and xxx. 11, 17.

Thus of the duty; the reason follows.

There are many reasons why they should obey:

1. Children have their substance from them, even their life and their education; their parents then took care of them when they had no rag to cover their nakedness, nor morsel to put into their mouths, and what can children render equivalent hereunto?

2. Christ himself was obedient to his parents, Luke ii. 51.

3. This is the purity and uprightness of children, and hereby they must be tried, and tried whether their work be pure, Prov. xx. 11.

4. The consideration of God's judgments upon wicked children should much move, such as were Ham, Esau, Absalom, Abimelech, &c.

5. If thou obey not thy parents, thou mayest live to be requited by thy children.

6. In the 6th of Eph. 1–4, there are many reasons why children should obey.

First, It is in the Lord,—that is, their obedience is both commanded by God, and it is for God; and besides, it is no further urged than as may stand with faith and piety to the Lord.

Secondly, This is right; it is children's justice.

Thirdly, This commandment that requires this is the first commandment with promise, for this had a promise in the very first promulgation of it in the table, written by the finger of God; whereas all the rest had their promises annexed afterwards by the ministry of Moses.

Object. But the second commandment had promise in the first promulgation of the law.

Ans. Some answer the words of the second commandment are a proposition, not a promise; but this answer satisfieth not. Some say the promises mentioned in that commandment belong to the whole law, and not to that commandment alone; but I think the plainest answer is: The fifth commandment is the first commandment with promise, viz., in the second table.

A fourth reason is, Children must obey, for so it shall go well with them; they shall get good and contentment, and God's grace and blessing by so doing. Fifthly, They shall live long on earth to enjoy the blessing of God.

Object. Wicked children live long.

Ans. Their life is a death, and it is not well with them, Isa. lxv. 20.

Object. God's children do not live long.

Ans. For the most part they do. 2. I say, if God perform not this promise absolutely in the letter, yet he performs this blessing by commutation into a better, as when he gives them eternal life for long life.

But the reason why children should obey is here mentioned in the text:

It is well pleasing to the Lord. Some leave out ' to the Lord,' and so the argument is more general, for obedience is exceeding pleasing to their parents, Prov. x. i., xv. 20, xix. 13, xxiii. 16; and besides, it is pleasing to God; but I see no reason to leave out the words.

Some render ἐν κυρίῳ, ' in the Lord,' and so here is: first, A limitation; they must obey, but in the Lord. Secondly, They must obey,—not because nature and civility requires it, but for conscience sake, as God's institution.

But I take it as it is here rendered, ' to the Lord.'

Well-pleasing to the Lord. From the consideration of these words, I observe four things:

First, That it is not enough to serve God, but we must so serve as we please him, Heb. xii. 28.

Secondly, That there is a way how to please God even in family duties, and these external and ordinary things at home; and this serves: first, To shew God's great love to man in that he frames himself to men's condition, and likes what may like them, will be pleased himself with what pleaseth them: obedience and service to men he accounts a service to himself. Secondly, It is a great encouragement to diligence and conscience in these family duties, inasmuch as they will not only please man, but God. Thirdly, It reproves hypocrites that care to be good nowhere but in God's house, but God will have obedience and not sacrifice; yea, here he will be served with obedience to men.

Thirdly, That even children are bound to make conscience of their ways, and to learn to please God in their youth: first, God requires it, Eccles. xii. 1, Ps. cxlviii. 12. There is scripture for babes and young men as well as old men. Secondly, There are worthy examples to excite them recorded in scripture, as the examples of Joseph, Samuel, David, Josiah, Jeremiah, Daniel, and Timothy; yea, this was a great praise in Jeroboam's young and dying son, 1 Kings xiv. 3. Thirdly, A conscionable care in children to please God is much praised in scripture; they are blessed that bear the yoke in their youth, and the workmanship of grace and obedience in the hearts and lives of children is like the graving of a king's palace, Ps. cxliv. 12. A happy thing when the young men see visions, as well as old men dream dreams, Joel ii. Then doth the church flourish when the son marrieth the mother, Isa. lxii. 5.

Use 1. This should teach parents to begin betimes to teach their children the trade of their way, Prov. xxii. 6, and to bring them up in the instruction and admonition of the Lord, Eph. vi. 4.

Use 2. Parents should learn also to be content that their children serve and please God as well as them. Some parents are so bad that they neither will instruct their children themselves, nor abide it, that they should hear sermons, read the Scripture, seek the company of such as fear God or sanctify God's Sabbaths.

Use 3. This should teach all to repent even for the sins of their youth, Ps. xxv., for they were then tied to please God as well as afterwards.

Use 4. That God will be pleased and will accept the endeavours and conscionable cares and obedience, even of children. This is a comfort to children, that though they cannot please wayward parents, yet they shall please God; and again, it reproves froward parents. Is God pleased, and art thou displeased? Doth God love and like the desires and endeavours of his child, and dost thou dislike?

Thus of children's duty; the parents' duty follows.

Fathers, provoke not your children to anger, lest they be discouraged. Doct. From the coherence, parents must perform their duty to their children. It is not an easy thing to be a father and mother in performance of fatherly and motherly duties.

Provoke not. Doct. Men are in general here to learn that it is not enough to abstain from sin, but they must abstain from all provocations to sin. It is not enough to abstain from whoredom, but men must abstain from wanton attire, from suspected places, from filthy speeches, from chambering and wantonness; not enough to abstain from murder, but men must abstain from bitter and provoking words. It is not enough to abstain from idolatry, but men must abstain from all the monuments and occasions of idolatry, and therefore men must abstain from all marriage with papists, and from making of images of the Trinity, &c. If men would avoid perjury, they must take heed of common swearing; so ministers must not only call for peace and unity, but they must take heed of provocations to discords when all is at peace.

Thus of the general.

The words of this verse are a dehortation, and therein is: first, The duty of parents; secondly, The reason of it.

Parents. All parents are tied to perform their duties to their children; none are too good to do it. Use for reproof of such women as think themselves too good to nurse their own children, and of such fathers as turn the care of their children wholly to others.

Provoke to wrath. Here I note the manner of setting down their duty, and the matter.

The duty of parents is negatively set down, to teach that parents must not think only of their sins against God and abroad to others, but they may be guilty of much sin in trespassing against their own children. If parents were otherwise never so honest or religious, yet the careless discharge of their duty to their children may much provoke God, and will certainly be found on their score if they repent not.

Quest. But why is the duty of parents in this place so sparingly set down but in one branch of it, and that negatively?

Ans. It is not to allow parents to be less careful, but it may be the apostle spares them here, because in respect of other relations they are charged before and after, as husbands and masters. Again, it may be the apostle would have children to know they have not that liberty to inquire into their parents' faults, or to reckon it as a part of their skill to find them out. Parents shall account to God, but not to their children. Thus of the manner of setting their duty down; the matter follows.

Provoke not. Parents fault two ways, either by too much severity, or by too much indulgence; the former is here restrained. Again, the provocation is twofold, either to sin or to passion. It is a most cursed thing for parents to provoke their children to sin by counselling them to evil ways, or encouraging them to lewd courses. This the apostle holds too horribly vile for any professing religion, or the fear of God, and therefore mentions provocation to anger.

Concerning this provocation to anger, I consider three things: first, How parents provoke their children; secondly, What they must do that they be not provoked; thirdly, What is not forbidden in these words.

Parents provoke their children: first, By word; secondly, By deed.

1. By word three ways: first, By burthening them with unjust and unmeet precepts; secondly, By pursuing them with contumelious words, especially when they be always chiding and rating of them; thirdly, By disgracing of them to others before their face, or behind their backs.

2. By deeds five ways: first, By careless education; for though children find not fault with this at first, yet when they come to be of years, and find their own unfitness for calling or society, &c., then they fret against their parents' neglect. Secondly, By discourtesies and unkind usage of them when they be grown to be of years. Thirdly, By unjust dealing about their marriages, when either they restrain them of marriage, when they have a calling to it, and a liking of meet person, and thus they provoke them to incontinency; or when they compel them to marry when they have no calling nor liking, and thus they provoke them to discontent. Fourthly, By indiscreet and immoderate passion and severity in correcting them. Fifthly, By unjust restraints, either of present necessaries of food and raiment, Mat. vii. 9, 10. 1 Tim. v. 8, Prov. xiii. 22, or in not laying up for them, 2 Cor. xii. 14.

Secondly, That parents may not provoke their children: 1. They must begin betimes to teach them their duties, for ignorance is wayward. 2. They must sow the seeds of piety and godliness in their hearts; as they draw out reason by degrees, so there is a conscience even in children as well as reason if it were informed, and conscience would make them not only religious to God but dutiful to parents. 3. They must not give their children too much liberty at the first; for if they do, then will just restraint afterwards be provocation. 4. They must pray for them to God; many pray for children, and so for their being, that afterwards never pray to God to guide their hearts, and so for their well-being. 5. They must in general strive to teach or guide them by encouragements and allurements. Correction is not as diet, but as physic; and thus recreation is not to be denied them, Zech. viii. 5. 6. If nothing else will restrain passion in children, they must impose silence upon them. He that imposeth silence on a fool mitigateth anger, Prov. v. 26.

3. This dehortation hindereth not but that parents may: (1.) Rebuke their children; (2.) Correct them. Prov. xiii. 24, xxii. 15, 17, xxix. 15, 17, xxiii. 13, xxv. 14, xix. 18, 19.

Thus of the duty.

Children. Viz., All children, sons and daughters-in-law, as well as natural children; and these are provoked:

1. By groundless jealousies and suspicions testified by secret listening, questioning, and inquiring enviously after everything they do or say.

2. By suffering servants to vex or molest them.

3. By evil reports of them.

4. By giving evil counsel, or reporting of faults to the son against his wife, or to the daughter against her husband. To make debate is ill in any, but much worse in parents.

This of the parties to whom they owe this duty.

Lest they be discouraged. The reasons follow.

There are many reasons why parents should be careful by all means to keep anger out of their children: 1. Wise men and godly men can scarce govern this affection without sinning, Ps. iv., much less children. 2. Anger is a great provoker of God's anger. It breeds a guiltiness of God's anger, Mat. vi. 3. It lets in the devils, Eph. iv. 26; and usually Satan, in the times of these passions, sows the most hellish seeds, and stirs most impious thoughts in them. 4. It may bring them into great mischief in time, Prov. xxviii. 18. 5. It is a great let to sound instruction and knowledge, Eccles. vii. 11, Prov. xiv. 29. 6. The angry person is usually suspicious, and so unfit for society with men, Prov. i. 22, 24; yea, it is a great hindrance, both to the profit of the word, James i. 21, and the power and success of prayer, 1 Tim. ii. 8. 7. Sometimes this rage in young persons is not to be cooled but with blood, as in Cain.

But to omit the reasons, here parents must not provoke their children lest they be discouraged.

Concerning discouragement in general we must know that it is a great sin to discourage others, and a great hurt to be discouraged; the people must not discourage their teachers, Heb. xiii. 17; those that are in authority must not discourage such as are faithful and desirous to approve their fear of God, and to discharge their duties. Governors in the family must not discourage servants or children in their good beginnings and desires after good things. Again, this is a Christian mercy and compassion to comfort and encourage the feeble, 1 Thes. v. 14; and lastly, God's fainting children should be admonished to be of good comfort, and to strengthen their knees, 2 Cor. xiii. 11, Isa. xxxvi. 3, 4.

Concerning the discouragement of children, Christian parents should be careful, for they may be discouraged:—

1. From the service of God, when they shall see carnal men use their children better than they that make such a profession of piety.

2. From the capacity and desire after the undertaking of the knowledge or exercise of great things; discouragement breaks their spirits and makes them pusillanimous.

3. From the hope to please, and so from the confidence of the parents' love, and then at length from the very means of pleasing either by honour or obedience. This of the duty of parents and children.

The third couple in the family are servants and masters.

The duty of servants is set down, ver. 22-25.

Ver. 22. *Servants, be obedient to them that are your masters according to the flesh in all things.*

In all the words that concern the duty of servants, I observe:

1. An exhortation, ver. 22, 23.
2. Reasons, ver. 24, 25.

The exhortation is two ways to be considered:

First, As it is briefly set down. Here is: 1. The parties exhorted, 'servants;' 2. The duty wherewith they are charged, 'be obedient;' 3. The persons to whom, 'to your masters.'

Secondly, As it is explicated. In the explication, I consider:

1. The provisos about their obedience.
2. The form or manner how they must obey.

The provisos are either for limitation, to curb masters; they are to obey according to the flesh; the souls and consciences are not in bondage to men; or for extent, to servants; they must obey in all things.

The manner how they must obey is set down:

Negatively,—1. not with the eye-service; 2. Not as men-pleasers.

Affirmatively,—1. with singleness of heart; 2. With fear of God; 3. Heartily, as to the Lord. The reasons are: 1. From hope of reward and wages from God, ver. 24; 2. From the certain vengeance of God upon them that do wrong, ver. 25.

This is the order of the words.

From the general consideration of all the words, I observe five things:

1. That servants are to be instructed out of the word; which reproves masters that restrain servants from hearing the word in God's house, and open not the book of God to them in their own houses.

2. A 'question' may here be moved, Why should the duty of servants be thus largely in so many words set down?

Ans. 1. Because usually men shew less compassion to servants; therefore God takes the more care of them. Many men will have some care of their children to see them taught in some manner, but their servants they wholly neglect. Therefore God, who is as a Father to servants as well as children, provides large instruction and comforts for servants, if they will come to his book to be taught.

2. The careful apostle saw that in the first conversion of men from Gentilism to Christianity, there was greatest danger of disorder and scandal in servants, partly out of weariness of their bondage and servile condition, partly because men would less spare to tell of their faults; therefore the apostle, as most fearful of them, spends many words in the teaching and encouraging of them.

3. We may note here the candour of the apostle. He doth freely deliver his mind in the behalf of servants with a full vent of words, with great care, with-

out holding back anything that belongs unto them. He was not of the mind of most preachers now-a-days, that hold the discourse of family duties, especially of servants, too base a subject for their wits and learning to be employed in; neither was the apostle of the humour of lawyers, that seldom speak much but for great men, or when they may have great gifts: the apostle speaks as much for a servant that could do nothing for him as for the masters.

4. In laying down his speech to servants he both teacheth and comforteth them; but for order he first teacheth them; and as any is more ignorant, this course is more needful to be held. The common people should be in this manner dealt withal; they must first be rebuked, convinced, exhorted, taught, and then meet comforts to be applied, and not before.

Lastly, The scope and drift of the apostle in all these words is to keep servants in order, and that first, To hold servants in obedience, that none under colour of liberty in Christ should break up their subjection to their masters. He was no Anabaptist. Secondly, To meet with the faulty obedience of such servants as were resolved to stay in service. He meeteth here with five faults in servants:

1. The first fault in servants is half service, or to obey in what they list; this he correcteth when he saith, 'in all things.'

2. The second fault is eye-service.

3. The third fault is profaneness. Most servants never respect piety and God's fear, but only to please their masters; this he meeteth with when he saith, 'not as men-pleasers, but fearing God.'

4. The fourth fault is hypocritical service; this he meeteth when he addeth, ' in singleness of heart.'

5. The fifth fault is baseness of mind and discouragement; this he would prevent in the two last verses.

Thus of the general.

Servants. The servants in the apostle's time were for the most part bond-slaves, bought and sold as beasts, and their masters were infidels and cruel to them; and yet, many of these servants were converted to the faith of Christ. Where we may learn that men's slaves may be God's servants, he hath his elect among these; the dear children of God in this world may be abased to the most vile misery, and a most servile condition.

The uses are: first, To shew that felicity is not in outward things; for God's servants that had attained the chief good, yet were in most base condition in respect of the things of this life.

Secondly, To teach us patience in lesser crosses; whatsoever thou art, yet thou art not a bond-slave, therefore be patient; such as have been dear in God's sight have been worse used than thou art.

Thirdly, To teach us compassion to the baser sort of men, for God's elect may be among these.

Lastly, This is a great comfort to the abject.

But howsoever bought servants were most usual in the apostle's time, yet hired servants were used then too, and are here meant as well as the other; yea, all servants, though they were nobles serving in princes' court, are tied to the duties generally here required.

And as any servants have more knowledge, and do profess sincerity in religion, they are the more tied to be careful servants to men; they should not only be better men and women, but better servants also.

Thus of the parties exhorted.

Be obedient. Here I consider two things:

1. That they must obey; they must approve themselves to their masters, not by wearing their cloth, or cognisance, or by words and compliments, but by painful and careful obedience.

2. How they must obey; and that may be opened thus:

First, With reverence, with all honour, 1 Tim. vi. 1, both internal; with high account and estimation of their masters; and external, with reverent words and behaviour.

Secondly, With all fear, 1 Pet. ii. 18, Eph. vi. 5; and this they should shew: first, By avoiding what might offend; secondly, By not answering again; thirdly, By a holy endeavour to please them.

Thirdly, With subjection to rebukes, 2 Pet. ii. 11; secondly, To correction, 1 Pet. ii. 19, 20; thirdly, To their restraints: first, In respect of diet; they must not be their own carvers. Secondly, In respect of place; they must keep the bounds of the family, and not at their pleasure be gadding out either by night or day upon any pretence without leave. Thirdly, In respect of company; they must bring none into the family that are lewd persons, or of what sort soever, against the liking of the master; nor may they keep company abroad to the just offence of their masters. Fourthly, In respect of apparel; though they have never so good means, yet they must be attired as becometh servants.

And this subjection also they should shew in a ready acknowledgment of their fault when they understand it. It is a great fault in servants that though they understand, yet they will not answer. First, acknowledge and give glory to God, and submit themselves to their masters, Prov. xxix. 19.

4. With all good faithfulness, Titus ii. 10. This faithfulness is required :

1. In respect of the goods of the family; and thus: 1. They must shew their faithfulness in not daring to purloin the least penny from their masters; no pickers, Titus ii. 10. 2. It is not enough that they are true, but they must be thriftily careful to see that nothing be spoiled or lost, or miscarry any way by their default and negligence. This was the great testimony of Jacob's faithfulness, Gen. xxxi. 36.

2. In respect of secrets. They must keep the secrets of the master, and of the family; yea, and of the trade and calling too.

3. In respect of the business of the family; and here their faithfulness standeth in two things :

1. In diligence of labour. He is not a faithful servant that eats the bread of idleness, as many serving-men do that can tell of no calling but attendance.

2. In trustiness; and in this servants must be faithful two ways : first, In their care to their masters' directions executed in the family, as if they had been present; secondly, In their speedy despatch of business abroad. A slothful messenger is an exceeding provocation to them that send him; and it is a wretched fault in servants when they are sent forth of the family about business they cannot find the way in again in any due time.

Thus of the duty to which they are exhorted.

To them that are your masters. They must be subject and obedient to all masters, indefinitely, without difference of sex, (and so to the wife or widow, 1 Tim. v. 14, Prov. xxxi.,) or of condition : they must be obedient to the poorest, as well as the rich.

Thus of the laying down of the exhortation; the explication follows; and first of the provisos :

According to the flesh. These words may be referred to masters, and then the sense is this, that servants must be obedient even to such masters as are fleshly and carnal men; they must obey though their masters be ethnics or profane persons. It is a great praise for a servant to men to be God's servant also; but it is a greater praise to be a religious servant of an irreligious master, to fear God in a profane house.

2. To servants; and so they are a limitation. They are subject only in respect of their flesh and bodies; and so here is two things to be observed :

The one expressed. The bodies of servants are in the power and at the disposing of the masters; and therefore servants must learn to subject their flesh to their masters' both commands, restraints, and corrections.

The other implied. The souls of servants are not in the power and at the disposing of masters; their spirits are free, nor master nor king can command the conscience.

Use is, first, For reproof of such servants as give more to their masters than is due. Thou oughtest to be of the same calling, trade, labour, &c., that thy master is of; but thou art not bound to be of the same religion or humour with thy master. It is a great fault not to give the body to thy master, but a great fault also to give both body and soul to be at his disposing; both are extremes.

Secondly, Should servants fear their masters because they have power over the flesh? How much more should we fear God, that hath power to destroy both soul and flesh in hell? Mat. x.

Thirdly, This may be a great comfort to a servant. Thy soul is as free as the soul of him that sits on a throne; thy service in the flesh derogates nothing from the liberty of Christ in thy heart; thy best part is free.

In all things. Servants must obey in all things, even in things that be against their credit, profit, liking, ease, &c. There is a great sturdiness in many servants; either they will not do some things required, or not at the time when they are bidden, or not in the manner, but as they list. These courses are vile, and here condemned.

Object. But unlawful and unmeet things are required.

Sol. I answer that in cases of this nature, three rules are to be observed by inferiors:

First, If the matter required be only inexpedient and unmeet, thou must obey. Neither doth this rule let, but that servants or inferiors may use all humble and lawful means to prevent unmeet things.

Secondly, Thou must be sure it be sin that thou refusest. Thou must not disobey upon conceit, or conjecture, nor upon thine own humour and opinion; but it must appear by the word of God to be a sin, or else thy conjectures are no ground of disobedience. If thou must needs doubt on both sides, it is better doubt and obey than doubt and disobey.

Thirdly, When it is apparent to be impious and sinful that is required, yet thou must look to the manner of disobedience. Thou must yield thyself to obey by suffering; yea, it is a wretched fault in servants or inferiors, that are urged to unlawful things, to refuse with sturdy, and insolent, and provoking words, or behaviour. God frees thee from disobedience in act, but he frees thee not from reverence, and from an holy estimation and humble demeanour.

The use is for great reproof of servants' both indiscretion and stubbornness; and withal it chargeth masters; they must not require their servants to lie and swear in their shops only to please and profit them, nor may they make their servants break God's Sabbaths to satisfy their wills.

Object. But are they not required to obey in all things?

Ans. They are; but before he saith according to the flesh, in labour, not in sin, and after he saith they must so please men as they fear God too.

Thus of the provisos.

The form of their obedience is set down: first, Negatively—'not with eye-service,' 'not as men-pleasers.' Secondly, Affirmatively: 1. 'With singleness of heart;' 2. 'Fearing God;' 3. 'Heartily.'

Eye-service. Some take it thus, Not with outward service, not only do the labour of the body, but bring the care, providence, affection of the heart; or thus, Be obedient to your masters, and let not your eye be only upon your masters, but upon God, the great Master of all masters and men.

But I think the proper meaning of the word is, Not with eye-service,—that is, not only in the presence of your masters, not only when their eye is upon them; so that he meets with the wretched faultiness of such servants as, when their masters' backs are turned, neglect their labour, fall to loitering, or get them out of the doors; or, which is worse, fall to wantonness, drunkenness, filching, smiting of their fellows, and quarrelling: these servants shall have their portion at the day of Christ, Mat. xiv. 48. And if eye-service be condemned, what shall become of such servants as are not good, no, not so long as their masters are by them?

Not as men-pleasers. Object. Is it a fault for servants to please their masters?

Ans. No, it is not, for they are commanded to please in all things, Titus ii. 9; but two things are here condemned: first, So to please men as never to care for pleasing God; so to attend a corporal service as not to care for the saving health of their souls: this is profaneness. Secondly, Such servants are here taxed as seek by all means to please their masters, but not to profit them. Such are they that are flattering, soothing persons, that serve their masters only with fair words, but else are empty persons. Such, or rather worse, are they that apply themselves to their masters' humours, to feed them with tales, or praising their ill courses and counsels, or executing their sinful minds. These servants are many times the firebrands of contention, alienate parents from their children, friend from friend, and keep malice on perpetual foot. These are here rebuked. But let us consider farther, Is this such a fault in poor servants, that can pretend many things, to be men-pleasers,—how foul a vice is it in free men that are in no wants or restraint,—how hurtful is it to be a man-pleaser in the courts of princes and in the houses of nobles! How detested a vice is it in such as are magistrates and public states! And is it naught in the court and country? certainly it is much more vile in the pulpit and in churchmen; and even the greater they are, the worse and more abominable is their soothing and daubing.

Thus of the negative.

In the affirmative are three things; and the first is singleness of heart.

In singleness of heart. Concerning singleness of heart, I consider it two ways:

First, In the general, as it is in God's servants.

Secondly, In special, as it is in men's servants.

Singleness or sincerity of heart, as it is in God's servants, I consider of in two things:

First, In the nature of it.

Secondly, In the signs of it.

Singleness of heart may be discerned by the contrary to which it is opposed:

1. As it is opposed to hypocrisy; a sincere-hearted man is no hypocrite, and shews it three ways:

First, He had rather be good than seem so, as in case of alms, Rom. xii. 8, compared with Mat. vi. 2; so in the case of piety, he had rather have grace and sound knowledge than an empty show of it.

Secondly, He will serve God at all times as well as at one time. It is a note of a hypocrite that he will not pray at all times; he will serve God when he is sick, but not when he is well, Job xxvii. 7–9. So it is vile hypocrisy to come to church in Lent to hear sermons, but never come there, or but seldom, all the year after.

Thirdly, He minds inward secret domestic holiness and piety, as well as outward open and church holiness. He is a hypocrite that kneels down when he comes into the church, and never prayeth in his family at home. It is vile hypocrisy and palpable in such men as have knees of prayer when they first come up into the pulpit, and no words of prayer when they are risen up to speak for or to God's people.

2. As it is opposed to fleshly wisdom, 1 Cor. i. 12. There is a threefold wisdom of the flesh that batters and keeps out singleness and sincerity of heart:

1. The first is a reaching after private ends in public employments, as preaching for gain, 2 Cor. ii. 17.

2. The second is a cunningness in committing or hiding sin. It is sincerity to be wise to do good, and simple concerning evil; to be a bungler in acting it, and to have nothing to say in defence of it when it is done, Rom. xvi. 19.

3. The third is fraud, shifting, subtlety, and guileful and deceitful dealing in men's course for the things of this life. Thus Esau is a wild and cunning man, able by reason of his craft and subtlety to live in a wilderness; but Jacob is a plain man, a single-hearted man; he can make no shift to help himself in earthly things by fraud or craft, but is open and plain in all his dealings for the world, but a man of great reach for matters of his soul. This is a pattern of true singleness, simplicity, and sincerity.

3. As it is opposed to a double heart,—opposed, I say, to a heart and a heart, and a double heart is either a wavering heart or a divided heart. Men have a double heart that waver and are tossed with uncertainties,—such as are now for God and godliness, and shortly after for sin and the flesh; now are resolved to leave such a fault, as persuaded it is a fault; and by and by they will to it again, as persuaded it is not a fault. Here is no singleness of heart. And thus the heart is double in respect of times; it is double also as divided in respect of objects. I instance in two things: first, In matter of worship. The people that came to inhabit Samaria had a divided heart; for they feared the God of the country because of the lions, and they feared the gods of the nations also, 2 Kings xvii. 33. Such are they that fear God's threatenings in his word, and fear the signs of heaven too. Secondly, Our Saviour instances in matters of the world. The mind, which is the eye of the soul, cannot be said to be single when it is distracted; men cannot serve God and Mammon, Mat. vi. 21–24.

4. As it is opposed to spiritual pride; a single heart is a humble heart, as Job sheweth, Job xi. 15, 16; and sheweth itself in two things: first, That if God send crosses, it will not answer or justify itself, but make supplication, and so acknowledge God's love, as withal it will confess that God doth judge them for their corruptions. Secondly, If the sincere-hearted man pray to God, and the Lord be pleased to answer him by unutterable feelings, even by the witness of the spirit of adoption, yet he will be so far from spiritual pride and conceitedness, that, fearing before God's mercies, he will be as if he believed not that God had heard his voice.

5. As opposed to perturbation and disquietness of the heart, arising either from the cloudiness and muddiness of the judgment, not able to discern things that differ, Phil. i. 10; or from the unrest of the conscience, shewed by hourly or frequent checkings, 2 Cor. i. 12; or from the infidelity or grudging or distrustfulness of the heart, Acts ii. 46.

6. As opposed to offensiveness; and so the single-hearted man is neither offensive by wrongs nor by scandals. In respect of wrongs, he is innocent as the dove: he is no horned beast to pelt and gore others, Mat. x. 16; and in respect of scandals, he is desirous to live without blame from those that are without, or grief to the faithful, Phil. ii. 15, i. 10.

Out of this may be gathered the signs or properties of a single or sincere-hearted man: 1. He had rather be good than seem to be so. 2. He strives to be good in secret at home; in heart as well as openly and abroad. 3. He serves not God by flashes or fits, but is constant, and will pray and serve God at all times. 4. He is a plain man, without fraud and guile in matters of the world; he loves plainness and open dealing, yet he is not simple, for in matters of his soul he is of great reach, and forecast, and discretion, &c. 5. He is a bungler in sin; he knows not the method of Satan. 6. He doats not upon the world; he can use it as though he used it not; he is not tossed with distracting cares. 7. He cannot abide mixtures in the worship of his God; he is neither idolatrous, nor superstitious, nor humorous. 8. Good success in grace and innocency makes him more humble, and fit to grieve for sin, and feel the weight of it; he struggles as much against spiritual pride as against other sins. 9. He doth not allow himself to murmur nor repine, either through infidelity at God, or through grudging envy at men, or distress himself with vain fear about how he shall do hereafter. 10. He is harmless; desirous so to live as he may wrong none in worldly matters, nor offend any in matters of religion. 11. He makes conscience of lesser sins as well as greater; this is his godly pureness. 12. He is blessed of God after some progress in piety with two singular favours: first, He discerneth things that differ; secondly, He hath the power, quietness, and joy of a good conscience.

Here also may be gathered negative signs; they are not single-hearted: first, That are hypocrites taken up about the gilding of the outside; secondly, That will serve God but at some times; thirdly, That are skilful in sin to commend it, or impudent to defend, deny, or extenuate it; fourthly, That are of a guileful and fraudulent disposition; fifthly, That are eaten up with worldly cares; sixthly, That are scandalous: yea, some of God's children may hang down their heads under the fear that their hearts are not so single as were meet, by reason of their spiritual pride, the raging muddiness of judgment, and the unrest of the heart and conscience.

Thus of singleness of heart in God's servants.

Men's servants shall approve themselves to be single-hearted:

1. If they can honour and obey poor masters as well as rich.

2. If they can be careful to serve and profit with all heedfulness, and love froward masters as well as the courteous.

3. If they can obey for conscience of God's command, though they have no hope of reward from men, or conceit, nor fear of shame or punishment.

4. If they be as good within as without; serve with pure intention.

5. If they will be diligent in the master's absence as well as in his presence.

6. If they will be true in the least penny; not touch their master's goods to purloin it, though they might secretly help themselves.

7. If they will labour when they might be at rest.

8. If they will restore what they have ill gotten; or if they be not able, will humble themselves by acknowledgment, though none were able to accuse them.

Use is for encouragement to all servants and journeymen to get and express this uprightness and singleness of heart; for better is the poor that walketh in his singleness of heart, than he that abuseth his lips and is a fool, Prov. xix. 1; yea, we should all take heed that Satan beguile us not from the simplicity that is in Christ Jesus.

Thus of singleness of heart.

Fearing God. The second thing required in the manner of their obedience is the fear of God.

The fear of God in a servant must have four things in it:

First, A not guiltiness of the common vices of servants, as swearing, whoring, stealing, gaming, &c.

Secondly, They must fear God's presence, even do their business faithfully, not because the eye of their master, but of God, is upon them. This is one part of their fear of God.

Thirdly, They must pray daily to God for their masters, and the family, and for good success upon their own labours. This proved that Abraham's servant feared God, Gen. xxiv.

Fourthly, They must be religious in the general duties of piety to God, as well as in the particular duties of service to their masters; they must so serve men as they fear God also.

Uses. First for servants, and then for masters. Servants must learn to do all their labour fearing God, even that God (1.) that set them in that calling; (2.) Whose eyes always behold how they discharge their duty in their calling. And inasmuch as the fear of God is made the ground here of other duties, they should learn to be the better servants to men because the fear of God. Masters also must learn, first, what servants to choose,—not such only as will do their work, but such as fear God also; and if they have failed in that, they should labour now to beget and nurse the fear of God in the servants they have, for God's fear would make their servants more dutiful to them; besides, the reason why their servants fall to whoring, stealing, unthriftiness, &c., is because the fear of God is not in them.

Quest. But what should masters do that their servants might fear God?

Ans. Four things: first, They should pray and read the scriptures in their houses, and catechise their servants; secondly, They should bring them to the public preaching of the word; thirdly, They should give them good example themselves; fourthly, They should restrain them from profane company, and encourage them, and allow them liberty at convenient times to converse with such as fear God.

Thus of the fear of God.

Ver. 23. *And whatsoever ye do, do it heartily, as to the Lord, and not unto men.*

The third thing required in their obedience is that they do it heartily. In this verse is the manner of the duty, and the inducement thereunto.

Heartily, ex animo. The obedience of servants should be a hearty obedience. The apostle will not have only fear of God, but love of the master. Their obedience must begin at heart, not at hand or foot; if the heart be not with their obedience, the master may have their labour; and that he hath of the ox, but such servants lose their labour.

Quest. What is it to obey *ex animo?*

Ans. It is to obey voluntarily, and out of a heart and affection rightly ordered; but especially it is to obey out of a judgment well informed.

The use is, therefore, to urge them to do it; and here I would consider of the objections of servants why they cannot obey *ex animo.*

Object. 1. Bondage is against nature.

Sol. It is against nature as it was before the fall, but not as it is now since the fall.

Object. 2. But Christ hath made us free.

Sol. Free in soul in this life; not in body till your bodies be dissolved, or till death.

Object. 3. But my master is froward.

Sol. Yet thou must be subject, 1 Pet. ii. 18.

Object. 4. But he doth not only give ill words but blows.

Sol. Perhaps it is needful, for a servant will not be corrected by words, Prov. xxix. 19.

Object. 5. But he correcteth me unjustly.

Sol. First, Who shall judge this? Shall servants themselves? Secondly, It is acceptable if, for well-doing and for conscience, thou endure to be buffeted, &c., 1 Pet. ii. 19, 20.

Object. 6. But my master is not only a froward man, but a wicked man, and an enemy of Christ.

Sol. Yet thou must honour and obey him willingly, 1 Tim. vi. 1, 2.

Object. 7. But I am a hired servant, not a bought servant.

Sol. Indeed, masters have not that power over them they have over bond-slaves, but yet all servants are here bound to obey heartily.

Object. 8. But unmeet things are required.

Sol. Discern things that differ, but yet obey in all things. All this reproves grudging, and slow and stubborn servants.

Whatsoever ye do. Not only fair, easy, cleanly, and best sort of works are to be done willingly, but all, or any kind of labour whatsoever, though never so base or vile.

As to the Lord and not to men. Doct. Servants, in obeying their masters, serve the Lord.

The use is both for instruction of servants and for comfort. For instruction, they must serve their masters as they would serve the Lord, with all faithfulness, diligence, willingness, providence, conscience, &c.

For comfort and encouragement also is this doctrine, and that three ways:

First, Here is a limitation; they must do no service to men that is against the Lord.

Secondly, Art thou a servant? Care not for it, thou art Christ's freeman.

Thirdly, Let not the baseness of thy work discourage thee, for in serving thy master thou servest God as well as if thou wert preaching or praying, &c. When the apostle saith, 'not unto men,' we must understand, not principally or only. Thus of the exhortations; the reasons follow.

Ver. 24. *Knowing that of the Lord ye shall receive the reward of the inheritance: for ye serve the Lord Christ.*

In this verse servants are persuaded to obedience, by a reason taken from the retribution or reward of their service; and the matter of the verse is comprehended in this syllogism. What faithful men soever serve Christ, and do their duty to him faithfully and cheerfully, shall receive of Christ the reward of inheritance. But you Christian servants, when you perform your obsequious obedience to your masters, serve the Lord Christ; *ergo*, you shall have the reward of the inheritance.

Knowing. Doct. Servants may and ought to know, and be assured of their own salvation.

Use is for confutation of papists, and unsound men, that deny certainty of salvation; for if servants, that have not the greatest wits or knowledge, that are employed about small businesses, that have not so much liberty nor learning as other men, &c., yet may be assured not by conjecture or hope, but by certain knowledge, by most undoubted faith; then what colour of reason can there be why other Christians, the Lord's people, should be denied this knowledge? And therefore, in the second place, it should teach us to make our calling and election sure.

Reward. Doct. The works even of servants shall be rewarded.

Use is for the comfort of servants, and for reproof of the unbelief that is many times in God's children, doubting of God's acceptation of their prayer and holy endeavours. Shall the base and secular works of men's servants be rewarded, and the great works of piety in God's service not be regarded?

Of the Lord. God will be paymaster unto servants; and in that they are turned over to God for payment, it implies that most masters are careless and unmerciful; and this they are not only in with-holding convenient food and raiment, but in sending their servants after long time of weary labour out of their families empty, and without means to live in the world.

Reward of inheritance. Two things are here affirmed of heaven: first, It is a reward, and so free; secondly, It is an inheritance, and so sure.

There are four uses may be made of this doctrine: 1. We should much love, esteem, and desire heaven; it is the reward of God. Princes give great gifts, but God's least gift must needs be glorious. 2. We should learn to be liberal as God is liberal,—give freely, give largely. 3. Here is a plain confutation of the merit of heaven, for heaven is an inheritance. Now, the son doth not inherit[1] the father's lands; he hath not his lands in measure according to his deserts, for most an end the land is purchased before the son be born; much less can we merit heaven, and the rather because we cannot allege so much as this, we came out of the loins of the father, seeing we are children but by adoption.

For ye serve the Lord Christ. Doct. Christ is the chief Lord, and therefore masters should be well advised how they use their servants, for they are Christ's servants; and servants should be careful how they obey their masters, for they must account to this Steward.

Thus of the first main reason.

Ver. 25. *But he that doeth wrong shall receive for the wrong that he hath done; and there is no respect of persons.*

Some take this twenty-fifth verse to be a conclusion of the whole doctrine before concerning family duties; as if he would signify that he would not have this doctrine of household government more contemned than the doctrine of piety or righteousness; for whatsoever wife, husband, child, father, or servant shall do wrong in the neglect or breach of these commandments for the family, shall be sure

[1] Qu. 'merit'?—ED.

to receive for the wrong he doth at God's hand, without respect of persons.

Some understand the verse as a threatening to servants, if they do any way wrong their masters.

But the commonest interpretation is meetest, viz., to understand it as a reason taken from the certain vengeance of God against all masters that wrong their servants, and so is the second main reason to urge their obedience.

In the verse I likewise observe seven doctrines:

1. Masters must account to God for all the wrong they do to their servants in word or deed.

2. All masters shall be punished of God that do wrong, if they repent not, though they were otherwise never so great; yea, though they were never so good or righteous men; for if good men wrong their servants, God will requite it, and chasten them for that as well as for other sins.

3. The sovereignty of disposing an exact, full, and final vengeance belongs to God only; men administer only a part or drop of it.

4. God will rise up in the defence of the poorest and meanest Christians, to right their wrongs.

5. Servants may not right their own wrongs, and return words for words, or blows for blows, but commit that to God.

6. Servants must be subject not only to the courteous and just, but to the froward and injurious masters.

Lastly, God is no respecter of persons or faces. He cares no more for the master than for the man; all are one in Christ Jesus; there is neither bond nor free, Jew nor Grecian, rich nor poor, but Christ is all in all things, as is before declared, ver. 11.

Thus of the duties of servants.

Thus also of the doctrine of the third chapter.

THE LOGICAL ANALYSIS OF THE FOURTH CHAPTER.

THE first verse of this chapter belongs unto the special rules of the former chapter, and contains the duty of masters, and the reason of it. Their duty in these words, 'Ye masters, do that which is just and equal to your servants.' The reason in these words, 'knowing that ye also have a master in heaven.'

In the second verse, and so to the end of the chapter, is contained the conclusion of the whole epistle.

This conclusion contains: first, Matter of exhortation, to ver. 7; secondly, Matter of salutation, from ver. 7 to the end.

The exhortation may be three ways considered: first, As it concerns prayer, ver. 2–4; secondly, As it concerns wise conversation, ver. 5; thirdly, As it concerns godly communication, ver. 6.

Concerning prayer two things are to be observed: first, The manner; secondly, The matter. In the manner, three things are required: first, Perseverance; secondly, Watchfulness; thirdly, Thankfulness, ver. 2.

In the matter, consider: first, The persons for whom, 'praying also for us;' secondly, The things for which, 'that God may open,' &c. These things are first briefly laid down, 'that God would open to us a door of utterance;' or secondly, more fully explicated: first, By the subject, 'to speak the mystery of Christ;' secondly, By a reason, 'for which I am in bands;' thirdly, By the end, 'that I may utter it as becometh me to speak,' ver. 3, 4.

Wisdom of conversation is propounded with limitation to the respect of some person, viz., 'them that are without,' ver. 6.

In that part that concerns gracious communication there are two things: first, The precept, 'let your speech,' &c.; secondly, The end of the precept, 'that ye may know how,' &c. In the precept, note first the properties of speech: first, 'Gracious;' secondly, 'Powdered with salt;' thirdly, The continuance, viz., 'always.'

Thus of the exhortation.

The salutation follows, from ver. 7 to the end. Where observe: first, A narration as an entrance; secondly, The salutations themselves.

The narration is in ver. 7–9, and it concerns, first, Tychicus, ver. 7, 8, and Onesimus, ver. 9.

Concerning Tychicus there are two things: first, His praises with relation to all Christians, 'a beloved brother;' or to Christ, 'a faithful minister;' or to Paul, 'a fellow-servant.' Secondly, The end of his mission, which is threefold: first, To 'declare Paul's estate;' secondly, To 'know their estate;' thirdly, To 'comfort their hearts.'

Concerning Onesimus, there is likewise: first, His praises in relation to all, so he is 'a brother, faithful, beloved;' relation to them, he is 'one of them.' Secondly, The end of his mission is to 'make known,' &c., ver. 9.

The salutations follow; and they are: first, Signified; secondly, Required. The signified salutations are from ver. 10 to 15; the other from ver. 15 to the end.

The salutations signified are from six men, three of them Jews, viz., Aristarchus, Marcus, and Jesus, ver. 10, 11; and three Gentiles, Epaphras, Lucas, Demas, ver. 12–14.

The Jews are described: first, By their names;

secondly, By their country—they were of the circumcision; thirdly, By their praises, and so for what they were to the whole church, labourers, fellow-workers to the kingdom of God, or to Paul, and so they were to his consolation, ver. 11.

The salutations of the Gentiles follow, whereof the first is of Epaphras, who is described: first, By his office, a servant of Christ; secondly, By his relation to them, ' he is one of you ;' thirdly, By his love to them, shewed by his striving in prayer for them; fourthly, By his zeal not only for them, but the neighbour churches, ver. 13.

Thus of the salutations signified.

The salutations required follow; and those are either particular, ver. 15–17, or general, ver. 18.

The particular salutations concern either the Laodiceans, ver. 15, 16, or the Colossian preacher, who is not only saluted, but exhorted, ver. 17.

The general salutation hath in it: first, A sign, ' the salutation by the hand of me, Paul ;' secondly, A request, ' remember my bonds ;' thirdly, A love, ' grace be with you, Amen,' ver. 18.

THE METAPHRASE UPON THE FOURTH CHAPTER.

VER. 1. Masters also must do that which is just unto their servants, both for their souls and for their bodies also, in diet, wages, or correction; and that which is equal, both while they stay with them, in allowance of recreation, and respect of their weakness and sickness; and when they go from them, not to let them go away empty; knowing that they themselves are servants unto God who is in heaven, and will call them to accounts.

Ver. 2. To conclude. I return again to all sorts of Christians, and exhort them to three things principally: the first is about prayer; the second is about their carriage; the third about their speeches. For their prayers there are three things exceeding necessary: perseverance, and Christian watchfulness, and thanksgiving for the graces and blessings they do receive.

Ver. 3. Remembering us also in their prayers, that God would open unto us a door of utterance, with liberty, courage, power, and good success to break open the mystery of the gospel of Christ, for which I am now in prison.

Ver. 4. That I may so speak of those dreadful secrets, that I no way derogate from the majesty of them, or that trust that is committed to me, or expected from me. Thus of what I would specially commend to you about prayer.

Ver. 5. Now for your carriage. I would have you especially look to yourselves in respect of your behaviour before or amongst the wicked, who are not of God's family, and strangers from the life of God: it were an admirable thing to carry yourselves in a wise and discreet manner towards them. Hence, and by all other ways, shewing yourselves to be skilful merchants in redeeming the time which hath been lost.

Ver. 6. And for your communication, let it be of good and holy things; not offensive, or slanderous, or filthy; and powdered with the salt of discretion and mortification: and thus let it be always, and in all companies, that ye may speak fitly unto every man, and to his place and the occasion.

Ver. 7. I have sent over Tychicus to declare unto you my whole estate, who is both a godly man, well respected, and a painful minister, that joins with us in God's works.

Ver. 8. And withal, I send him to know how you do, and to comfort you by all means with hearty consolations.

Ver. 9. And with him I have sent Onesimus, who is now a godly man, truly sincere and well respected, even he that was born or brought up amongst you. These two will relate all things to you.

Ver. 10. I have also divers commendations to deliver to you, some from some Jews, others from Gentiles. Of the first sort are Aristarchus, and Marcus, and Jesus. Aristarchus is my prison-fellow. Marcus is Barnabas' sister's son, and it is he concerning whom heretofore you received some advertisements not to admit him; but now, if he come unto you, receive him.

Ver. 11. Jesus, by his good carriage, hath gotten himself the surname of Just. These three are Jews, and indeed the only men that constantly hold out to help forward the kingdom of God. They are men in whom I am much comforted.

Ver. 12. Those of the Gentiles that desire to be remembered to you are Epaphras, Luke, and Demas.

Epaphras is a worthy servant of Christ, and the dearer ought he to be to you, because he is one of you. He striveth mightily for you in all sorts of prayers, being importunate with God, that you might hold out without declining, and be more and more complete and full in the knowledge and practice of the whole will of God.

Ver. 13. For I bare him witness that he is inflamed with great affection both for you and them of Laodicea and Hierapolis.

Ver. 14. Luke also, a physician, both godly and greatly respected, saluteth you, and Demas.

Ver. 15. I pray you also to remember my salutations to the brethren of Laodicea, especially to Nymphas and that religious family who, for their piety and good order, are, as it were, a little church.

Ver. 16. And when this epistle hath been publicly read of you, send it to the church of Laodicea to be read there also, together with the letter which was sent to me from Laodicea.

Ver. 17. Commend me also to Archippus your preacher, and charge him to take heed he do not his work by halves; but, as he hath received his commission from the Lord, so let him fulfil it, both by constancy and painfulness, and powerfulness of preaching.

Ver. 18. I join also mine own salutation, which is written with mine own hand, and not by my scribe. I pray forget me not in this restraint. The grace of God, as the only fair portion, be now and always with you. And my confident hope is, so it will.

CHAPTER IV.

VER. 1. *Ye masters, do that which is just and equal unto your servants ; knowing that ye have also a Master in heaven.*

This verse belongs unto the doctrine of household government, and contains : first, The duty of masters ; secondly, The reason, 'knowing,' &c.

In the duty : first, The parties charged, 'ye masters ;' secondly, The duty required, 'do that which is just and equal;' thirdly, The persons to whom it is to be performed, 'unto your servants.'

Masters. All masters are charged without difference ; yea, the wife as well as the husband, by a synecdoche ; the greatest as well as the meanest, and the poorest must deal justly, as well as they that have more means, &c.

Do that which is just and equal. Doctrine from the coherence. That God that promiseth eternal things will provide temporal things also. In the former chapter, God promised the reward of inheritance for servants. Here he takes order for their well-being in the world, charging masters to see that they be used justly and equally.

Just. Masters must do justly, and shew it. 1. Generally, by not requiring unjust things of them, and by choosing such servants as are just into the family, Ps. ci. 6, lest by bringing in lewd servants, the rest be infected. For if it be a great injustice to bring in an infectious servant that hath the plague upon his body, and to appoint him to work among the rest of his servants that are free from the disease, then it is much more unjust to bring in lewd servants that have the plague-sore of sin running upon them ; for the presence, and counsel, and example of lewd sinners is of more power to infect a sound soul, than is a plaguy man to poison the sound body of others. 2. More particularly, masters must do that which is just : 1. To the souls ; 2. To the bodies of their servants. They must deal justly with their souls, by helping them to grace, if it be possible; but at least, by bringing them to the public means of grace, and by private training of them up in God's fear, by prayer and instruction. The justice they owe unto their body may be referred unto three heads ; for either it concerns their maintenance, and so they must give them their portion of food convenient for them, Prov. xxxi. 15 ; or it concerns their wages, and so they must give the wages proportionable to their work, and that in due time, and without defrauding them of any part of it ; or it concerns their punishment, and so the justice of the master must be shewed both in this, that he will punish their open disorders ; as also that he will do it with instruction, moderation, and to profit them and the whole family.

Equal. Masters must not only deal justly, but they must deal equally with their servants. And masters deal unequally many ways.

1. When they require inconvenient things ; for though the servant must obey, yet the master sins in requiring unequal things.

2. When they impose more work than they have strength to do.

3. When they turn them away when they are sick ; for it is equal that as thou hast had their labour when they were well, so thou shouldst keep them when they are sick.

4. When they restrain them of liberty for their

souls. If thou have the work of their bodies, it is equal that thou take care for their souls; and if they serve thee six days, it is very equal thou shouldst proclaim liberty to them to do God's work on the Sabbath-day.

5. When they restrain and withhold their meat and wages.

6. When they send them out of their service empty, after many years' bondage, and not provide that they may have some means to live afterwards.

To conclude. It is not equal for the master to hear every word that men say of his servants, Eccles. vii. 23; nor is it meet they should bring up their servants delicately, Prov. xxix. 21; nor yet that they should leave their callings and the whole care of their business to their servants; but they ought diligently to know the state of the herds themselves, Prov. xxvii. 23.

Thus of the duty; the reason follows.

Knowing that ye have also a Master in heaven. Here are four doctrines to be observed:

1. That there is no master, but he is a servant; and therefore as he would require his work to be done by his servant, so he should be careful himself to do God's work, to whom he is a servant.

2. That God's majesty and man's authority may well stand together. Christ and Cæsar can well agree. Man's government in a family, and God's government in the world, are not opposite one to the other.

3. Ignorance of God, and the accounts must be made to God, is the cause of that security, insolency, and cruelty that is in men.

4. That it is ill to use servants ill, it will be required if they be wronged. Thus of the reason.

Ver. 2. *Continue in prayer, and watch in the same with thanksgiving.*

In this verse, with those that follow to the end of the chapter, is contained the conclusion of the whole epistle.

This conclusion contains matter of exhortation to ver. 7, and matter of salutation, ver. 7 to the end.

The exhortation may be three ways considered:

1. As it concerns prayer, ver. 2-4.
2. As it concerns wise conversation, ver. 5.
3. And as it concerns godly communication, ver. 6.

Concerning prayer, two things are to be observed:
1. How we must pray, or the manner.
2. For what, or the matter.

In the manner three things are required: first, Perseverance; secondly, Watchfulness; thirdly, Thankfulness, ver. 2.

In the matter is further added: first. The persons for whom, 'praying also for us;' secondly, The things for which, 'that God may open,' &c., ver. 3, 4.

Continue in prayer. The doctrines implied in these words are four:

1. That our mortal condition is a condition of singular vanity, in that the best of God's servants are ever wanting something.

2. That long prayer of itself is not blameworthy. Christ continued all night in prayer.

3. That prayer is of perpetual use in the life of a Christian.

4. That to pray by fits is not God's ordinance; neither that he requires, nor that he will accept.

The doctrine expressed in these words is threefold:

1. That we must hold out and pray still, and never give over prayer till we give up our souls into God's hands.

2. That we must pray upon all occasions for health, wealth, success in our callings, preservation of our estates, the blessing of God upon the word, sacraments, reading, &c., for pardon of sin, salvation of our souls, ever stretching out our desires to all the opportunities and callings to prayer.

3. We must be instant in prayer, set all aside for prayer, wait upon it, for so the word is rendered, 'to wait,' Acts x. 7.

Use is: first, For reproof of such wretched men as pray not at all, Job xxi. 14. Secondly, For reproof of such as make apostasy from the affections and practice of prayer; and this is a fault in carnal men that fall from temporary faith, or in God's children, that by the deceitfulness of sin and Satan give over their affections and careful diligence in prayer. For the first sort, we must know, that when such men lose their joy and delight in the word, they lose also their care in prayer; but they must know they do it not without singular danger; for now that hearing and prayer are laid aside, seven devils worse than that one cast out by acknowledgment, may enter in; yea, that they may fall from these affections into a reprobate sense; yea, which is worse, they are in danger of the sin against the Holy Ghost, and the more if they grow to hate prayer and despite God's grace in his children; and therefore they should be advised with all speed to repent with sound sorrow, and beseech God to forgive them, if it be possible, the thoughts of their hearts. And as for such of God's children as are decayed and fallen away from the power and practice of prayer, they should be wakened and remember themselves, both by considering the hurt they bring upon themselves, and the remedies for their recovery. The hurts befallen them by this apostasy are such as these: 1. The loss of the comforts of the sweet presence of God. 2. They put on a kind of image of the old Adam again; they look as if they were no better than carnal people; they return in many things to the filthiness they had forsaken; they form themselves to the courses of carnal wisdom, and too much like the world and the sinful profits and pleasures of it. 3. Faith and love are more and more enfeebled, less sense of God's presence, and less love to God's children. 4. They bring upon themselves a tedious dislike of the means of salvation, besides the danger of many temporal judgments.

For remedy of this great inconvenience they must do three things:

1. They must purge by godly sorrow and fasting; 2. They must labour to reduce themselves unto a holy order of living, both by a daily course of examination by the law, and also by the consecration of themselves to the constant and orderly practice of all Christian duties; 3. They must by daily importunity beseech God to give them again the words and affections of prayer; and all this they should do the more speedily, because if by long dwelling in apostasy they provoke God, though by repentance they recover themselves again, yet the joys of God's Spirit, or the great measure of them, may be lost, so as they shall never recover the joy of their salvation all their days.

Thirdly, This doctrine may serve for encouragement to many of God's poor servants against all the doubts and fears of their own hearts. These need only better information; for their discouragements arise from mistakings, as may appear by their objections.

Object. I have much hardness of heart before I go to prayer.

Sol. 1. So had David, in the entrance into many of his psalms; yet he recovereth, and exulteth exceedingly before the end.

2. Hardness of heart that is felt and mourned for is no hindrance to the success of prayer.

3. Therefore thou hast more need to pray: for prayer is a fire that melts the leaden hearts of men.

Object. I want words when I come to pray.

Sol. 1. Go to Christ, and beseech him to teach thee to pray; and pray God to give thee words, that hath commanded thee to take unto thee words, Luke xi., Hosea xiv. 3.

2. Be more in examination of thy heart and life by the law.

3. The Spirit helps our infirmities, when, for words, we know not how to pray as we ought, Rom. viii. 26.

4. The foundation of God remaineth sure, and is sealed. If thou but name the name of the Lord with uprightness, 2 Tim. ii. 20, desiring and resolving to depart from iniquity, he may have an infallible seal of salvation that but nameth the name of God in prayer, as the word is in the original.

Object. But I doubt of audience.

Sol. Consider God's nature, commandment, promise. His nature: he is a God that heareth prayer, Ps. xcv. 2. His commandment; for he as peremptorily gives his commandments to pray as he doth any of the ten commandments, and therefore will certainly accept of what he so earnestly commands. His promises also are to be collected and considered as they lie scattered in several scriptures: 'He will be near unto all that call upon him in truth;' and 'his ears are open to the prayers of the righteous,' &c.; only be thou careful that thou lie not in any presumptuous sin, and that thou turn not away thine ear from hearing the law, and that thou allow not thine own heart in wrath or doubting; for these and such like are great lets of audience.

Object. I have prayed long and often, and yet am not heard.

3 B

Sol. 1. God sometimes doth of purpose defer to grant, that so he might compel them to continue to pray.

2. Consider the things thou prayest for, whether they be such things as God will ever grant; for if we ask amiss, or only for fleshly things, or to spend upon our lusts, God will never hear, James iv. 1-3.

3. God hears divers ways; for sometimes he granteth not what is asked, but giveth what is answerable to it, or better; so he heard Christ, Heb. v. 7.

Thus of continuance in prayer.

Watching in the same. Doct. Watching is needful unto prayer, Mat. xxvi., Luke xxi. 36, 1 Pet. iv. 7. For explication whereof, we must know that watching is taken two ways, either literally or metaphorically. Literally; and so is either a judgment or a duty. Watching as a judgment is when God brings upon wicked men the terrors of the night, or, for chastisement of his servants, holds their eyes waking. As a duty, watching is a voluntary restraining of our eyes from sleep, and spending of the whole or part of the night in holy employments. Thus the church kept the night of the passover holy, Exod. xii. 42; thus Christ watched, Mat. xiv. 23-25; thus Paul, 2 Cor. xi. 23; thus David, Ps. cxxxix. 18. And this watching used by God's children was either ordinary or extraordinary. Ordinary watching is nothing but a sober use of sleep, in which we ought to be moderate as well as in eating and drinking. Extraordinarily, God's children have been used to watch either upon occasion of great judgments, Lam. ii. 19, Isa. xxvi. 9, Ps. cii. 7, Mark xiv. 38, or for preparation to some great business. Thus Christ would spend whole nights in prayer; thus he watched before his passion; or when they have lost the benefit of Christ's presence, Cant. iii. 1; and all this they have done with great success; for their reins have taught them in the night, Ps. xvi. 7, and their souls have been full as with marrow, Ps. lxiii. 5, 6. But we may justly complain, and take up the words in Job xxxv. 10, 'But none saith, where is God that made me, even the God that giveth songs in the night?'

But it is spiritual watchfulness that is here specially required; and it is nothing else but a Christian heedfulness, observation, and consideration, both for prevention of evil, and embracing of the means, ways, and opportunities of good. And thus we must watch: first, Our own hearts, to spy out where any spot of spiritual leprosy in thoughts or affections breaks out, to heal it in time. Secondly, The practices of Satan, that we be not ensnared with his spiritual baits and methods. Thirdly, The ways of God: if any mercy appear, or fountain of grace open, to snatch up our incense, and run presently to God's altar, and offer with our sacrifice the calves of our lips: or if any threatening arrest us, or judgment befall us, to make our peace speedily, and fly from the anger to come. Fourthly, The coming of Christ, either by death or judgment: specially we should 'watch, upon whom the ends of the world are come,' Luke xxi. 36. But that which is here principally meant is watching unto prayer; and thus we had need to watch: 1. To the means to get ability to pray; 2. To the opportunity and occasions of prayer; 3. To the success of it—to take notice of God's answer, and our speeding, waiting upon God till he give a blessing, or, if God hide himself, to sue out an atonement in Christ.

Thus of watching.

With thanksgiving. Doct. 1. When we have any suits to God for what we want, we must carefully remember to give thanks for mercies received, and particularly for all God's mercies in prayer, Phil. iv. 6, 1 Thes. v. 16, 17.

2. In that the apostle so often urgeth the duty of thanksgiving, it shews that naturally we are exceeding unthankful for the mercies of God, and that few of us are careful to yield God constantly this sacrifice.

3. There are divers kinds of thanksgiving, or divers ways of thanking God. For men give thanks:

1. By receiving the eucharist, which is called 'the cup of blessing,' 1 Cor. x. 16.

2. By obedience of life; for he that will truly offer praise unto God must order his ways aright, Ps. l. 23.

3. By opening our lips to sound forth his praise; and thus God's name is honoured both by the thanks or praise:

1. Of celebration, when we tell of God's mercies to others.

2. Of invocation, when we speak of God's praises to God himself in prayer. This is here specially meant; and of this I have entreated before at several times out of other places of this epistle.

Thus much of the manner how we must pray. The matter follows; and first of the persons for whom we must pray.

Praying also for us. In general, I observe three things: 1. That we ought to pray one for another; 2. That one great means to get a large heart in prayer, and the perseverance in the practice of it, is to endeavour after tender and affectionate desires to help others by prayer; 3. That Christians should desire the prayers of others; as carnal men make use of their friends to get their help for wealth, offices, &c., so should Christians improve their interest in the affections of their friends by seeking prayer of them.

Also. It is ἅμα, 'together,' and so notes that it is not enough to pray for others, but we must pray with others, and mutually help one another by faith, knowledge, and prayer.

For us. Here I observe four things:

1. That the greatest in the church need the prayers of the meanest.

2. That in hearing prayer God is no accepter of persons: he is as well willing to hear the Colossians' prayers for Paul, as hear Paul pray for the Colossians.

3. It is the duty of the people to pray for their ministers.

4. It is to be observed, that he wisheth them to pray for other preachers as well as for himself. There may be a spiritual pride in desiring the prayers of others. He did not envy that others should have room in the hearts of others as well as he.

Thus of the persons for whom.

The things for which are two ways to be considered: 1. As it is briefly laid down; 2. As it is more largely explicated.

It is laid down or propounded in these words: 'That God would open to us a door of utterance;' and is explicated in these words that follow, by the subject, reason, and end.

A door of utterance. There are divers doors in scripture, in the metaphorical acceptation of the word. There is the door:

1. Of admission into the functions of the church, John x. 1.

2. Of life; and the door of life is the womb of the mother, Job iii. 10.

3. Of protection; and so to be without doors and bars is to be without defence and protection, Jer. xlix. 31.

4. Of grace and regeneration, John x. 7-9, Rev. iii. 8.

5. Of death and judgment, Job xxxviii. 17, Acts v. 9, James v. 9.

6. Of glory, Rev. xxi. 12.

Lastly, There is a door of gifts;—as of knowledge, Rev. iv. 1, Prov. viii. 33; of faith, Acts xiv. 27; of utterance, 1 Cor. xvi. 9; so here. The door of utterance comprehends five things: first, Liberty and free passage to preach the gospel; secondly, Opportunity; thirdly, Power of preaching; fourthly, Courage and boldness, with full vent to rebuke men's sins and reveal all God's counsels, without fear of any man's face; fifthly, Success—even such utterance as will open a door into the hearts; so that to pray for the opening of the door of utterance is to pray for liberty, opportunity, power, courage, and success.

Use is, first, for ministers, and then for the people. Ministers may see here what it is that specially makes a happy pastor; not living, countenance of great men, &c., but liberty, courage, power, &c. And it greatly taxeth four sorts of ministers: 1. Dumb ministers, that utter nothing; 2. Fantastical ministers, that utter the falsehood of their own brains, that speak their own dreams, and from the vanity of their own hearts, and seek out for the people only pleasing things, daubing with untempered mortar; 3. Idle ministers, that utter not all God's counsel, for matter or for time, speak but seldom to the people, preach not in season and out of season; 4. Cold ministers, that seek not the power of preaching, strive not to approve themselves in the sight of God, and to the conscience of men.

The people also should make conscience of their duty. They may learn from hence what to pray for, and should daily with importunity beseech God to give this wide door of utterance to their teachers.

Before I pass from the matter he prays for, I must note a doctrine lies secretly lodged within the same.

We may find in the end of this verse that the apostle was in prison, and yet he doth not desire to have the door of the prison open, but the door of his heart open to utter the mystery of Christ, noting that it is a greater want to want the liberty of his ministry in respect of utterance, than it is to want the liberty of his body in respect of the prison. We should take notice of this for divers uses: 1. For thankfulness if there be a door of utterance opened in God's house; 2. For prevention of all things, as much as lieth in us, that might stop the mouths of God's faithful ministers. There are five things that stop the mouths of ministers in general: 1. Ignorance and presumptuous sins in the ministers themselves; for polluted lips are no lips of utterance; the lips of the ministers should be touched with the coals of knowledge, zeal, and mortification. 2. The sins of the people many times put the teachers to silence; the rebellion of the house of Israel made Ezekiel dumb, that he could not preach, Ezek. iii. 26, xxiv. 27. 3. The violence of persecutors prevails often to shut the wide and effectual doors of powerful preaching, 1 Cor. xvi. 9, and therefore we should pray that God would deliver his faithful ministers from unreasonable and absurd men, 1 Thes. iii. 2. 4. Discouragement and fear silence many a minister in respect of the life and power of preaching, 1 Cor. xvi. 9, 12, Heb. xiii. 17. Lastly, Human wisdom not only lets the people from the profit of hearing, but likewise it lets the minister from the power of preaching.

God would. Doct. 1. The hearts of ministers, yea, of the best ministers, are naturally shut; they have no gift to profit withal, but they have received it; and who is sufficient of himself for these things?

Doct. 2. It is God only that opens unto men the door of utterance; it is he that makes the heart of the priest fat, and creates the fruit of the lips to be peace; he openeth and no man shutteth, and shutteth and no man openeth: and it should teach them less to fear men and their rebukes, and the less to care for the rage of the oppressor; for if he will give liberty, who can restrain it? and if he will silence, who can enlarge?

Even unto us. This manner of speech notes either his humility, or his restraint in prison, or the difficulty of utterance. His humility it may note in this sense, that howsoever he hath been a blasphemer, or a persecutor, &c., yet that God would be pleased to honour him and his work so much as give utterance even to him and such as he is. His restraint in prison it may import also, and so his desire is they should not pray only for ministers that were at large, and enjoyed peace, but also even for him and such others as were in prison; for a godly preacher will not be idle, no, not if he come into prison. And thus also it notes, that the wisest men of themselves are not able to teach with power and profit the simplest and meanest men; an apostle cannot teach a prisoner without God's special aid and blessing. These words may note also the difficulty of utterance, as if he should say, You had need to pray not only for ordinary but extraordinary ministers.

Thus of the thing prayed for, as it is briefly propounded. Secondly, It is enlarged: first, By the subject; secondly, By a reason; thirdly, By the end.

The subject of the utterance is the mystery of Christ.

To speak the mystery of Christ. Christ is a mystery to the Gentiles, to the Jews, to heretics, to papists, to carnal men, yea, to godly men. It is a mystery to the Gentiles that there should be a Saviour; to the Jews, that salvation should be in the carpenter's son; to the papists, that he should be the Saviour alone; to the heretics, that he should be a Saviour in both natures; to the carnal man, that he should be a Saviour in particular to him; and to the godly man, that he should be such a Saviour.

But to express this more particularly, Christ is a mystery five ways; for there are mysteries:

1. In the person of Christ. For what tongue can describe the super-celestial union of his natures, or the treasures of wisdom and knowledge, or the fulness of the Godhead that dwells in him bodily?

2. In his life and death. The world could not comprehend the books that might be made of the wonders of his birth, life, and death. We may see in that that is written what to adore, for in this world a perfect knowledge we shall never attain.

3. In his body, which is the church. For who can declare his generation?—or express the secrets of his power and presence, in filling her, who himself is her fulness, and filleth all in all things?—or describe

the manner of the union between Christ and his members? Is not this a great mystery?

4. In the sacraments of Christ. The holy invisible presence of God is a mystery; the communion of the body and the blood of Christ, not locally or by contact, and yet truly, is a mystery; the seal of the Holy Spirit of promise upon the hearts of believers, in the due use of the sacraments, is a mystery; the spiritual nourishment that comes to the soul by such secret and hidden passages invisibly, is a great mystery.

5. In the gospel of Christ. And by the mystery of Christ in this place I think is meant the gospel of Christ: and it is called a mystery because of the hiding of it. If you ask me where the gospel hath been hidden, I must answer, it hath been hidden: 1. In the breast of God from all eternity; 2. In the shadows and types of the ceremonial law, which was the Jews' gospel; 3. In the treasury of holy scriptures; 4. In the person, obedience, and passion of Christ, who was the substance of the Mosaical ceremonies, and the quintessence of all evangelical doctrine; 5. In the hearts of Christians.

If you ask me from whom it was hidden? I answer, not from the elect—for God by preaching revealed it unto them in due time—but from wicked men, but with great difference; for to some there is no gospel at all given, as to the Gentile; to some not given plainly, as in those congregations of Israel, to whom this evangelical loaf is not divided, though in the whole lump it be given; to some not given in the power of it—for though they hear the preaching, yet by reason of mixtures, carnal wisdom, or ignorance, and confusedness in the teachers, there is little power in it; to some not given internally, though externally they have means in the plenty and power of it. If you yet ask me what causeth this hiding of the gospel from such as live even in the light of it, I answer, It is either:

1. The veil of their own ignorance.
2. The powerful working of the god of this world to blind them, 2 Cor. iv. 4.
3. The custom in sin, and customary abuse of pleasures and profits.
4. The secret judgment of God, either because he will have mercy on whom he will have mercy; or because men have been touched, and reject God's call in the day of salvation; or because they have presumptuously abused God's promises, to make them bawds for sin.

The uses follow. Is the gospel a mystery? It should teach us:

1. To esteem God's ministers, seeing they are dispensers of God's mysteries, 1 Cor. iv. 2.
2. To strive by all means to see into this secret, accounting it our wisdom and understanding to gain the open knowledge of this secret doctrine, Eph. i. 8, 9; but because every vessel is not meet to bear this treasure, we should get a pure conscience to carry this mystery of faith in, 1 Tim. iii. 9.
3. To account our ears blessed if they hear, and our eyes blessed if they see; it is a great gift of God to know the mystery or secrets of this kingdom, Mat. xiii. 11, &c.
4. In compassion to the souls of many thousands in Israel, to pray for utterance to publish more powerfully, not the common things, but the secrets of the gospel, Eph. vi. 19, there is need not of more preaching, but of more powerful preaching.

For which even I am in bonds. Either at Ephesus, as Dionysius thinks, or at Rome, as Cajetan and others think. Here are five things to be observed:

1. That the truth of the gospel ought to be so dear unto us that we should be content to suffer for it.
2. We should be willing to suffer the extremest and basest things, as here even bonds, and therefore much more the speaking against of sinners.
3. As any ministers are more faithful, they are in more danger to be troubled and molested.
4. Crosses should inflame us so much the more to sincerity. He is more eager after utterance now that he is in bonds.
5. The cause, not the suffering, makes the martyr. Not every one in bonds is a martyr, but when it is for the gospel. Men may suffer for their indiscretion and sin.

Ver. 4. *That I may utter it as it becometh me to speak.*

That I may utter it. ἵνα φανερώσω, 'that I may manifest it.'

Doct. Sound preaching is the manifesting of the mystery of Christ. This doctrine, as it shews the profit we may get by preaching, so it maintains plain teaching, and reproves such as would be doctors of the law, and yet understand not of what they speak; they darken the texts they speak of.

It, αυτὰ. Doct. As good not preach as not preach the gospel of Christ. We do nothing, if our people understand not the mystery of Christ, but remain still ignorant of the favour of God in Christ.

As it becometh me to speak. Doct. It is not enough to preach, but we must so preach as becometh the mystery of Christ, and to preach so is to preach with power, 1 Thes. i. 5; with instance and all watchfulness, 2 Tim. iv. 2, 3, 5; with patience and all constancy, with fear and fasting, 1 Cor. iv. 9, 2 Cor. vi. 4, 2 Cor. iv. 8; with assurance of doctrine, 2 Cor. iv. 13; with all willingness, 1 Cor. ix. 16, 17; with all faithfulness, 1 Cor. iv. 2; with all zeal, knowing the terror of the Lord, persuading, exhorting, beseeching, 2 Cor. v. 11, 1 Thes. ii. 12; approving themselves in the sight of God to the conscience of the hearers, 2 Cor. ii. 17, iv. 1, 2; with all holy, just, and unblamable behaviour, 1 Thes. ii. 11.

Thus do not they preach that are neophytes, young scholars, rash, scandalous, or dote about questions and logomachies, or fables and vain disputations, which breed strife and questions rather than 'godly edifying,' nor they that come 'with wisdom of words,' and the 'enticing speech of man's eloquence,' 1 Cor. i. 11, ii. 1, 4.

All this may teach ministers, by reading, prayer, and preparation, to be with their God before they come to speak to God's people. It may terrify careless ministers—Woe unto thee if either thou preach not, or not as becometh the mystery of Christ, 1 Cor. ix. 16. It may comfort good ministers; for if God stand upon it to have his work thus done, he will certainly pay them their wages; yea, if 'Israel should not be gathered,' yet 'their wages should be with God, and their work before him.'

Lastly, if ministers must preach as becometh the mystery of Christ, the people must hear as becometh the mystery of Christ, with attention, constancy, patience, reverence, in much affliction, as the word of God, with sincerity, hungering appetite, and fruitfulness.

Thus of the first branch of the exhortation.

Ver. 5. *Walk wisely towards them that are without, and redeem the time.*

These words are the second part of the exhortation, and concern wise conversation.

Walk. This is a metaphor borrowed from travellers, and notes both action and progress; hearing and talking and commending of God's servants, will not serve our turn, but we must both practise and proceed.

There is a double race in the life of a man, one natural, the other voluntary; the one is the race of life, the other is the race of holy life. In the first, men must run whether they will or no, and come to the end of it; but the other will not be despatched without great endeavour and constancy. As the most of us order the matter, the natural race of life is almost run out before we once enter the lists of walking in the race of holy life; yea, God's children are so apt to sleep and sit still and tire, that they need to be excited and called upon and encouraged in their race.

Walk, σιγκατατι. A Christian is a peripatetic; so is Christ, so is the devil, so are heretics, so are apostates, so are worldly men. Christ walks in the midst, Rev. ii. 1; the devil walks in the circumference round about, Job i.; his motion is circular, and therefore fraudulent and dangerous; the apostate walks backward; the heretic walks out on the right hand; the worldly man walks on the left hand, enticed out of the way by worldly profits, pleasures, and lusts; only the true Christian walks forward.

Wisely. Wisdom of conversation must be considered two ways: 1. Generally; 2. With limitation to the respect of them that are without.

In general, to walk wisely hath in it four things:

1. To walk wisely is to walk orderly, and the order of conversation hath in it two things: (1.) A due respect of the precedency of things, so as we must first provide for heaven, and then for the earth; first learn to die, and then to live; first serve God, and then ourselves and other men; first care for the soul, and then for the body; first seek the kingdom of God and the righteousness thereof, and then outward things. (2.) It hath in it a careful attendance to our calling with diligence and constancy and patience, 1 Cor. vii. 17, 1 Thes. iv. 11, 12, 2 Thes. iii. 6, 11. To walk inordinately (ἀτακτως) is to walk unwisely.

2. To walk wisely is to walk speedily. Walk in the light while you have the light, lose no opportunity, delay no work in harvest, John xii. 35.

3. To walk wisely is to walk uprightly, and that for matter in the newness of life, Rom. vi. 4; and for manner, exactly, precisely, circumspectly, Eph. v. 15, 16.

4. To walk wisely is to walk surely; and he walks surely:

(1.) That will live where he may have means for his soul as well as his body; he will not live in darkness, but desires to be where he may have the greatest light.

(2.) That makes the word the rule of his actions, and is sure of warrant from the scripture for what he doth, Deut. iv. 5, 6. This is to walk in the law, Ps. cxix. 1, according to the rule, Gal. vi. 16.

(3.) That will not live under any known threatening; will not venture to go on with wrath hanging over his head. He is none of those fools that will not understand though the foundations of the earth be moved, Ps. lxxxii. 5.

(4.) That walks by faith, and not by sight, 2 Cor. v. 7; trusts not in things that may be seen, which are mutable, but labours to be clothed with the garments of Christ's righteousness. He walks not wisely that walks nakedly, Rev. xvi. 15. And for manner of assurance, he that is a wise man, when he sees how careful the men of the world are to make everything sure, and what stirs there are for certainties in the things of the earth, he will not rest in probabilities for his soul, or in common hopes or presumptions, but will strive by all means to make his calling and election sure; he will not be led in a fool's paradise, and stand to the venture of his soul upon carnal conjectures, Prov. xxiv. 5.

(5.) That walks in the way of the least, and not of the most. He will not be led by the example of the multitude, or frame his life according to the commonest opinions, &c., 2 Cor. xii. 15, Phil. iii. 16.

Thus of wisdom of conversation in the general; here it is limited to conversing with one sort of men, viz., 'those that are without.'

Towards them that are without. Without are: first, All infidels, that live without the church of Christ; secondly, All hypocrites, that mind nothing but the gilding of the outside; thirdly, All wicked men in general, that live without God, without Christ, without hope in the world, 1 Cor. v. 12, 13, Luke xiii. 25, Rev. xxii. 15.

Here are two things I will but briefly touch: 1 That a Christian should be more careful how he behaves himself before wicked men than before godly men; 2. It is to be noted that he saith not *with* them but *towards* them. It is one thing to walk with them, and another thing to walk towards them; the one notes a voluntary consorting with them—this the apostle allows not; the other notes a behaviour that is well framed when, through necessity and calling, we must have to do with them.

But the main thing is, what we must do that we may carry ourselves justly towards wicked men. That this may be distinctly understood, wicked men may be two ways considered: first, As spectators of our conversation; secondly, As parties in conversing.

As they are spectators and observers, there are four things which in godly discretion we should make to shine before them:

1. All good faithfulness in our calling, 1 Thes. iv. 11, 12, 1 Tim. vi. 1.

2. All humble subjection to those in authority, shewing all meekness to all men, Titus iii. 1, 2.

3. A mortified course of living. The Gentiles will say of such, 'They are the seed of the blessed of the Lord,' Isa. lxi. 9.

4. Concord and holy love amongst ourselves, doing all things without reasonings and murmurings, Phil. ii. 15, 19.

As they are parties in conversing, they are two ways to be considered:

1. As they are evil men, but not injurious and evil to us.

2. As they are both evil men and injurious to us.

Towards the first sort our wisdom of conversation must be showed:

1. In the due observation of the circumstances of lawful things; for all lawful things are not to be done at all times, and in all companies, and in all manners: indiscretion herein doth much harm everywhere.

2 In the skilful applying of ourselves to win

them, making use of all opportunities, and speaking to them with all reverence, deliberation, compassion, instances, &c., as may become the majesty of God's truth and ordinances.

3. In the shunning of conceitedness, perverseness, frowardness, and such like things, as do marvellously provoke a carnal mind, but approve ourselves in all meekness of wisdom. It is a great wisdom in the use of our knowledge to express a constant meekness, James iii. 13.

4. In avoiding evil: 1. To them; 2. To ourselves. To walk wisely in avoiding evils to them, is to be careful that we put no stumbling-block before the blind, but cut off all occasions of reproaching or blaspheming. In avoiding evil to ourselves by them, we must look to three things: 1. That we be not infected or defiled by their company, either by needless presence, or by any kind of consent to, or approbation of, their evils; 2. That we be not beguiled by committing ourselves to them, and trusting fair pretences, John ii. 24; 3. That we yield not to them to satisfy them in the least sin; for it is not yielding will draw them, but a pure conversation with fear, 1 Pet. iii. 12.

Towards the second sort of wicked men, viz., those that are evil, and are, or are like to be injurious to us, our wisdom of conversation lieth in two things:

1. In a wise demeaning of ourselves when they do wrong or persecute us, shewing all firmness, and undaunted constancy, patience, reverence, meekness, clemency, and good conscience, 1 Pet. iii. 13–16.

2. In a discreet prevention of our own trouble as near as we can. This wisdom Jacob shewed in his dealing with his brother Esau, when he came out against him with four hundred men, Gen. xxxii. And Samuel, when he went to anoint David, 1 Sam. xvi. And Hushai when he saluted Absalom, 2 Sam. xxvi. 15. And our Saviour Christ, when he answered the tempting dilemmas of the malicious Jews. And Paul in his answer to the people about the high priest, Acts xxiii. 4. And when in the mutiny he cried out he was a pharisee, Acts xxiii. 6. It is noted as a wisdom in the prudent in evil times to be silent, Amos v. 13. It is not good provoking evil men, nor safe to pull a bear or a mad dog by the ears. It is the true ambition of a Christian to meddle with his own businesses, 1 Thes. iv. 11.

For conclusion. As we have seen what it is to walk wisely in the affirmative, so we must be informed what this wisdom hath not in it. It hath not in it a relinquishing of piety or holiness in the whole, or any part, to keep peace with wicked men, Heb. xii. 14. It hath not in it a forsaking of fidelity in the discharge of our duties. Amos must not leave the court, though Amaziah tell him it is his wisest way. Michaiah must not flatter Ahab because the four hundred prophets did. Lastly, to walk wisely is not to walk craftily and deceitfully; for such wisdom of serpents is required as may stand with the innocency of doves.

Redeem the time. To 'redeem' signifies either to recover what is lost, or to buy what is wanting. It is usually a metaphor borrowed from merchants buying and selling of commodities. 'Time' signifies either space of time or the opportunity of time; both may be here retained.

In general, as time is taken for space of time, there are divers things may be observed: 1. That time is a commodity; 2. That a Christian is a merchant by calling; 3. That as any are more wise, the more they know the worth of time, Eph. v. 15, 16; 4. That a Christian finds the want of time; 5. That if he were provident, time for holy duties might be bought; 6. Not to trade for time is a great fault, and yet a usual fault, and comes to pass because men have no stock of grace to employ, or they have never served a 'prenticeship to learn how to use time, or else they have had such extraordinary losses they cannot set up again; they have so often made shipwreck of time by misspending it, that they cannot now well set themselves in a course to use it well.

Again, if time be taken for opportunity, we may observe:

1. That there is a season, an opportunity, a due time. God hath his harvest for judgment, Mat. xiii. 30; his season for temporal blessings, as for the dew of heaven, and the fruits of the earth, Acts xiv. 17; so he hath for the manifesting of his will by preaching, Titus i. 3, for justification, Rom. iii. 26, for the testification of our justification, 1 Tim. ii. 6,

for mercy and deliverance, and the help of Sion, Ps. cii. 13, and for salvation, spiritual and eternal, 2 Cor. vi. 2. Finally, there is a season both for man to do good, Ps. i. 3, and to receive good, Isa. lv. 8.

2. That this opportunity is not obvious, not ordinary, nor easy, and everywhere to be had. Every day in the year is not the fair-day, nor every day in the week the market-day.

3. When opportunity is offered, we must not neglect it, or lose it. Ministers must preach while the door is open; the people must walk while they have the light; so we must all pray in every opportunity, ἐν παντὶ καιρῷ, Eph. vi. 18, Luke xxi. 36.

4. We must advantage ourselves by spiritual opportunities, though it be with our loss and pains. We should not think much to be at some loss for God's wares, as well as men's; and we must be content to travel as well to the market of our souls, as of our bodies, Rom. xii. 11.

In particular, concerning redeeming of time, consider: 1. What time is lost; 2. How time is to be redeemed; 3. How it must be used when it is redeemed; 4. The uses.

For the first, All time is lost that is spent idly, or in the superfluous feeding of nature, either by food, or sleep, or in ill company, or in the service of sin and the lusts of the flesh, or in the service of the world, or superfluous cares about profits, or joys about pleasures; yea, the time is lost that is spent in God's worship, where it is done idolatrously, superstitiously, ignorantly, carelessly, hypocritically, &c.

For the second, We must distinguish of times, and the persons that have time to sell, and the kinds of redeeming. There is time past; this cannot be brought back again by any price, but yet we may contract with time present for some allowance towards the loss of time past. There is also time to come. And here is first a time of glory to come, and a great bargain to be made, and for the buying of this heaven must suffer violence, and we should throng and crowd into the market to procure it by prayer, hearing, faith, alms deeds, &c. For though it be only Christ's merits that deserve it, yet these things we must do for the assurance of it. Besides, there is a time of sorrows to come. As sure as we have had our days of sin, we shall have days of sorrow and torment. This time is to be bought out with repentance, watching, fasting, prayer, strong cries; by all means endeavouring to make our peace, and fly from the anger to come.

But time present is the commodity we are with all carefulness to redeem. The devil and the world have time, our callings have time, and God is a great Lord of time. Time out of the devil's hands and the world's must be redeemed by violent oblation: time from our callings we must redeem by permutation only, making an exchange, and allowing time for godliness. In the first and chief place, time of God we must buy, both the space of time to repent in, and the opportunity of time, both for the giving and the efficacy of the means; and for this we must both offer and tender the sacrifice of Christ to pacify for time lost, and procure acceptation, and also we must offer up ourselves, souls and bodies, upon the service of opportunities, humbling ourselves to walk with our God.

Thirdly, When we have bought time we must be careful to use it well; and herein a principal respect is to be had unto the soul, for all this merchandise is for the use of the soul especially, and for religious ends. And thus we must spend some time in mortification, 1 Pet. iv. 1, 2, and some part in searching the scriptures, lest that be said of us which was said of the Jews, that whereas concerning the time they might have been teachers, they did need again to be taught the very principles, they were so inexpert in the word of righteousness, Heb. v. 12. Much time should be spent in the works of piety, abounding in the work of the Lord as we abound in time. Some time should be spent in works of mercy, both spiritual, instructing, comforting, exhorting, admonishing, &c.; and corporal, in feeding, clothing, visiting, &c. Generally, our time should be spent in well doing, Gal. vi. 9. And as for time for worldly business, we should observe the apostle's rule: 'They that have wives should be as they that have none, and they that weep as though they weep not, and they that rejoice as though they rejoiced not, and they that buy as though they possessed not, and they that use the world as though they used it not, for the fashion of the world goeth away,' 1 Cor. vii. 29, 30.

The *use* of all is for reproof of the most of us;

for some of us sin against the seasons and opportunities of God's grace, some against the very space of time. Men transgress against opportunity two ways: first, By ignorance of the signs of the seasons, Mat. xvi. 3; secondly, By a wilful neglect of the opportunities of grace when we have them. There are many things might move us to redeem the time in this respect: 1. We have our times appointed, and the bounds of our habitation assigned, Acts xvii. 26. 2. The times will not be always fair; there are perilous times, times of sorrow, anguish, sickness, tentation, want, loss, fear, perplexity, yea, we may purpose, promise, expect time of healing and curing, when we shall be deceived, and find a time of trouble, Jer. xiv. 19. Besides, Christ in the opportunities of grace is but a little while with men. There is a prime of man's life, yea, a prime of every man's ministry, John vii. 33. Further, the kingdom of God in the mercies of it may be wholly taken away if we bring not fruit in the time of fruit, Mat. xxi. 34, 41. Lastly, this is a very provoking sin; for if God give a space to repent, and men will not know the day of their visitation, must an end God casts such into a bed of affliction, after they have stretched themselves upon the bed of security, Rev. ii. 21, 22, Luke xix. 43, 44. Yea, many of God's children are greatly to blame in neglecting the opportunities of assurance of grace; and, therefore, because they are so careless in making their calling and election sure, this forsaking of the promise of God is scourged afterwards with comfortless sorrows, arising from such a sense of their corruptions, as makes them for a long time seem to be deprived of all grace and mercy, Heb. iv. 1.

Again, many men sin egregiously against the very space of time, in that they have much leisure and time, and fill it up with little or no good employment. Their estate, that have means to live without labour, is usually accounted an estate of great ease and happiness. But indeed it is an estate of much danger, for the men that abound in time without employment are liable to many temptations and lusts; besides, they are subject to almost continual hardness of heart and deadness of spirit; for it is the labouring servant that enters into his master's joy. Add that men that abound with leisure are easily drawn by the enticements of ill company, and much entangled with the sports and pleasures of the world. Sometimes such persons grow into great habit of suspiciousness, waywardness, filled with worldly passions and discontentments; sometimes they prove great meddlers in other folk's business.

The remedy for these persons, whether men or women, is to exercise themselves in some kind of profitable employment, and to labour so as some way to see the fruit of it, to eat their own bread; but especially they should be abundant in the work of the Lord, they should double their employment in reading, hearing, conference, mortification, mercy, &c.

Thus of wise conversation.

Ver. 6. *Let your speech be gracious always, and powdered with salt, that ye may,* &c.

Godly communication is here exhorted unto; and for order here is a precept, 'Let your speech,' &c.; secondly, The end of the precept, 'that ye may know,' &c. In the precept concerning our speech observe: first, The properties of speech, which are two: 1. They must be gracious; 2. Powdered with salt. And then note the continuance how long the precept is in force, and that is always.

In general we so hear that we must look to our words as well as our works, and therefore they are far wide that say, 'Their tongues are their own, who shall control them,' Ps. xii. 4.

From coherence I observe, that he walks not wisely that talks not wisely, for evil words corrupt good manners; neither may he be accounted an honest man of life that is an evil man in tongue.

The use is for trial; for if God makes us new creatures, he gives us new tongues; and if he turns the people to him by true repentance, he doth 'return unto them a pure language,' Zeph. iii. 9; and therefore, 'if any man seemeth to be religious, and refraineth not his tongue, this man's religion is in vain,' James i. 26.

Let. It is not arbitrary, (we may look to our words if we will;) but it is a flat precept, and so a matter indispensable.

Your. God is no respecter of persons; he forbids ungracious, wanton, and idle words in gentlemen and gentlewomen, as well as in poor men and labourers; he dislikes it in masters and parents, as well as in children and servants; it is as ill for the master to spend his time in idle talk, &c., as for the servant.

Gracious. Our words may be said to be gracious three ways: 1. If we respect the cause; 2. If we respect the subject; 3. If we respect the effect. In respect of the cause, good words are well said to be gracious: first, Because they flow from the free grace of God without our merit; for we do not deserve so much as to be trusted with one good word. Reason yields us conceits, and nature an instrument to speak by; but it is the God of nature that of his free grace gives us good words. Secondly, Our words ought to proceed from some grace of God in the heart, as from knowledge, faith, joy, sorrow, love, fear, desire, &c.; and in this sense, when they are in the tongue, carry still the name of the fountain whence they flow. Again, our words must be gracious in respect of the subject, the matter we must talk of must be of good things or religious matters, words of instruction, comfort, faith, hope, &c.; but especially our words should be seasoned with the daily memory and mention of God's grace to us in Christ, Ps. xl. 10. Thirdly, Our words ought to be gracious in respect of the effect, such as tend to build up and minister grace to the hearers, Eph. iv. 29; yea, gracious words are fair words, and fair words are: 1. Graceful words, words of thankfulness; 2. Inoffensive words, not railing, bitter, slandering, blasphemous, or filthy words, nay, not jesting words that are intended to provoke, irritate, disgrace, and bite; 3. Seasonable words, Prov. xv. 23; 4. Wholesome words, not filthy, rotten communication, Eph. iv. 29.

Use is: 1. For reproof; and men sin against this exhortation: first, By omission of gracious words. But, secondly, They do worse that use evil words. And, thirdly, They are worse than the former two that use their words to speak against grace and gracious courses, Eph. v. 6. But they are worst of all that love evil words, even the words that may destroy either their own souls or the souls of others. 2. Here is instruction; we must labour by all means to get ability for a gracious speech, either to God by prayer, or to men in conversing with them. And to this end: first, We must pray constantly and conscionably to God to give us gracious words. Secondly, We must get the law of grace into our hearts, Ps. xxxvii. 30, 31; yea, we should strive to be examples one to another, not only in faith and conversation, but in words also, 1 Tim. iv.; and if all Christians are charged to use gracious speeches, much more ministers: they should speak the words of God; they should keep the pattern of wholesome words, and stay all vain babblings which increase to more ungodliness, and all words that fret as a canker. Thus of the first property.

Powdered with salt. These are terms borrowed either from the use of the temple, or from common and civil use. In the temple every sacrifice was salted with salt; so must every Christian (who is God's sacrifice) be seasoned, Mark ix. 50. In the common life of man, meats that are to be kept long must be powdered with salt, to drink up or dry out corruption, and to preserve savour; so must a Christian be seasoned that will be kept to eternal life.

But, first, Here is implied that the words of men are naturally corrupt, rotten, unsavoury, and have great need of seasoning. The carnal man's words are much after the humour and infection of his mind. The talk of the covetous is usually of his mammon, farm, oxen, bargains, wares, &c. The epicure's talk is usually of his sports, dogs, cocks, horses, games, companions, or of his lusts. The superstitious man talks of his Dagon, or the signs of heaven. The wrathful man of his adversary and wrong. The ambitious man of his livings, honours, offices, offers, hopes, or his own parts and praises. To conclude, the talk of all natural men is but of natural things; and as they are of the flesh, so their talk savours nothing but fleshly things.

Salt. 1. There is the salt of doctrine, and thus ministers are the salt of the earth; 2. There is the salt of mortification, and so every Christian must have salt in himself, Mark ix. 50; 3. There is the salt of discretion, and this is the praise of the wise. None of these three may be here excluded from our word. For, first, We must receive laws for our lips, even from God's ministers; we must learn of them not only how to order our affections and life, but also how to speak, especially in matters of God and godliness. Secondly, We must mourn for the sins of the tongue as well as for other sins: we must drive out the corruption that cleaves to our words with the salt of mortification. Thirdly, We must make conscience of discretion in our words: he is a perfect man that is discreet in his words, James iii. 2; 'The tongue of the wise is as fine silver,' Prov. x. 20; and 'his heart guideth his tongue wisely, and addeth doctrine to his lips,' Prov. xvi. 23.

The use is both for instruction and reproof. For instruction, both to all Christians to season not only their words of prayer to God, but also their speech in conversing with men; and especially ministers must have salt in their tongues, with all discretion and heedfulness looking to their words, and with all authority and meet severity of rebukes drive out corruption out of the hearers; they may, they must cry aloud and spare not; they must powder them. Here likewise are those men to be reproved that have been often warned of their evil words, and mend not.

Quest. But what should be the cause why some men that have good affections and desires, yet cannot get the victory over evil words?

Ans. It comes to pass: 1. By reason of their ignorance of better words. 2. By custom in evil speech. 3. For want of constant taking of words of prayer and confession to God. 4. By defect of mortification in the heart; their hearts are not sufficiently humbled; they are too slight in godly sorrow; out of the abundance of the heart the mouth speaketh, and therefore their words are drossy and naught, because their hearts are little worth, Prov. x. 20. That these men may get victory over their evil words (which usually are against the third or the seventh or the ninth commandment) they must do three things: 1. They must go to God constantly by prayer, beseeching him to open their lips, and set a watch before the door of their mouth. 2. They must not fail to mourn over their offences in speech in secret till they have subdued them, afflicting themselves with voluntary sorrows for them. 3. They must strive by all means to accustom themselves in good speech and gracious words. Yet many professors are to be reproved for their words, for many times they are either too many, or too vain and idle, or too false, or too rash, &c. Their words want much seasoning, and it is a great fault to have a heedless tongue. Thus of the properties of speech.

Always. A Christian is bound to perseverance in good words as well as in good works: he must talk graciously, not only at some times for a passion, as when he comes newly from the sermon or on the Sabbath-day, not only in some companies, or in some arguments, but at all times and in all places, watching to all the opportunities to glorify God, or profit others by his words. Thus of the precept.

The end follows, 'that ye may know how to answer every one.' In general, I observe here two things: first, That by speaking well, we learn to speak well; secondly, That the soundest knowledge is experimental; he doth not indeed know how to answer that doth not in practice exercise himself in gracious words, though he had all places of answer and arguments in his head.

To answer. To answer doth not always import a question or demand going before, but is sometimes taken for continuing to speak, as Mat. xi. 25; it is said our Saviour answered, and yet no demand went before. Some think it is a part for the whole, and one use of words put for all uses; but I take it in the ordinary sense, as the word usually imports, and so we answer either unbelievers or believers. Concerning our Christian answer before unbelievers, there are six things may be here observed:

1. That true grace is sure to be opposed, and such as truly fear God are sure of adversaries.

2. That mortified men are the fittest to answer adversaries, especially in causes of religion, such whose tongues and pens are seasoned with salt. (Coherence.)

3. That every Christian shall find opposition, ('ye.')

4. That every Christian ought to answer for the truth; apology is the fruit, not of learning or wit only, but of godly sorrow, 2 Cor. vii. 10, ('ye.')

5. That the truth hath all sorts of adversaries, open and secret, at home and abroad, learned and unlearned, ministers and magistrates, rich and poor, every one that is carnal hath a bolt to shoot at sincerity.

6. That it is not an easy or ordinary skill to know how to answer well, for thereunto is required: first, Deliberation; he that answers a matter before he hear it, it is folly and shame to him. Secondly, Prayer, Prov. xvi. 1, Hab. ii. 1. Thirdly, Faith in God's favour and promise, Mat. x. 19, Ps. cxix. 41,

42. Fourthly, Discretion, considering persons, time, place, occasions; one kind of answer will not serve every sort of men. We answer in one manner to great men, in another manner to learned men, in another to ordinary men, Prov. xxv. 11, xxvi. 4–6. Fifthly, Patience. Sixthly, Humility. Seventhly, A good conscience, 1 Pet. iii. 15, 16.

Thus of answering unbelievers. Concerning the answering of believers, here are these things to be observed:

1. That Christians should propound their doubts one to another.

2. That strong Christians should support the weak, and help them, and resolve them from time to time, Rom. ii. 19.

3. It is not an easy matter to give a gracious, seasonable, and profitable answer.

4. That custom in gracious speech breeds, by God's blessing, an ability to give wise and sound judgment, advice, and resolution; it is not wit, learning, authority, &c., that breeds this skill.

Thus of the exhortation.

Ver. 7. *All my estate shall Tychicus declare unto you, who is a beloved brother and a faithful minister, and fellow-servant in the Lord:*

Ver. 8. *Whom I have sent unto you for the same purpose, that he might know your estate, and comfort your hearts;*

Ver. 9. *With Onesimus, a faithful and beloved brother, who is one of you: they shall make known unto you all things which are done here.*

In these words and those that follow is contained the second part of the conclusion. Before, he hath handled the common doctrine both of faith and life; now he lets loose his affection to express in particular his love to special Christians. In all the words there is to be observed: first, A narration as an entrance; secondly, The salutations themselves.

The narration is in these three verses, and the sum of it is, that Paul, being prisoner at Rome, to express his care for and love to the church, and in particular to the Colossians, sends Timothy[1] and Onesimus, the one a minister, the other a private man, both faithful, to shew them of Paul's affairs, and to visit the churches and comfort them.

Before I come to the particulars, from the general consideration of all the verses to the end of the chapter, these four things may be observed:

1. That religion extends itself to the behaviour of men, even in these more ordinary matters of life, so as men may sin or obey even in them.

2. That the love even of the best Christians, needs (for the preserving and continuing of it) even these lighter helps and observances.

3. That piety is no enemy to courtesy; it doth not remove, but rectify it. Piety doth prescribe to courtesy four ways: 1. By forbidding and restraining the art of dissimulation, and the politic serving of men's humours, and all the base courses of flattery. 2. By moderating the excess of compliments. 3. By preserving the purity of them, that they be not made the instruments of profaneness, and pollution, and wantonness. 4. By adding to them the seeds of grace and religion, Paul will salute as well as the Gentiles, but yet his matter shall tend unto grace and some good of the soul, as Col. i. 2, and in the rest of the epistles.

4. Amongst Christians there may be a pre-eminence of affection; some may be loved more than others. The apostle is desirous his doctrine may be a testimony of his love to all, but yet he cannot forbear the mention of his special respect of some.

The first thing in this part of the conclusion is the narration, and out of the whole narration these things may be noted:

1. The general care ministers should have of the churches. Paul cares for the churches far removed; yea, when himself is in great trouble, and so it might be thought he had cause enough of care for himself.

2. That the affections between faithful ministers and the people should not only be conceived, but expressed.

3. That church-governors should be careful whom they employ in the business of the church. Paul will not send a letter, but make choice of discreet and faithful men, much less would he have employed about the worship of God or the censures of the church suspicious persons, men of ill fame, drunkards, or of scandalous behaviour. How can it be otherwise, but that the grave censures of the church should be loathed and scorned, when such numbers of disordered and profane persons are admitted

[1] Qu. 'Tychicus'?—Ed.

to the denouncing, pleading, and executing of them?

4. Men should be careful how and whom they commend by word or writing. To commend evil men is to bear false witness, many times to the great hurt both of church and commonwealth.

The first particular thing in the narration concerning Tychicus is his praises. Here I observe:

1. Who commends him, viz., Paul. And this shews that ministers should be careful to preserve and enlarge the credits of their brethren; especially this is a care should be in such as excel others in place or gifts. They are far from this that detract from the just praises of their brethren, hold them down with all disgrace, labour to destroy what they build up, and pluck away the affections of the people from them; and when they have occasion to speak to them, use them contemptibly, and rate them as if they were rather their scullions than their brethren. And the sin is the worse when the same persons can countenance idle, evil, and scandalous persons.

2. To what end, viz., that this embassage might be so much the more respected; for the credit of the person wins much respect to the doctrine itself.

3. In what manner; and here observe two things: 1. That he gives him his full praise; for a man may slander by speaking sparingly in the praises of the well-deserving. 2. That he praiseth him without any 'but,' to teach us that we should not be easy in word or letter in discovering the infirmities of faithful ministers.

4. The particular of his praises; and they may be divided thus: Either they are common to all true Christians, 'beloved brother;' or proper to church-officers, and that either in relation to Christ, 'a faithful minister,' or in relation to Paul, 'a fellow-servant.'

There are four things ought to be in every good minister:

1. He must be a good man, 'a brother.'

2. He should be beloved of his people, 'beloved brother.'

3. He must be faithful; and his faithfulness stands in two things: (1.) Diligence in labour; (2.) Sincerity in giving every one their portion of rebukes, comforts, directions, &c., in due season.

4. He must be a 'fellow-servant,' one that will draw in the yoke with his brethren.

This may smite the conscience of many sorts of ministers.

Some because they are of wicked and scandalous life.

Some because they have made themselves hateful to their people by their indiscretion, covetousness, contention, &c.

Some because they are not faithful, either not true to the bed of the congregation to which they consecrated themselves, or not sincere in the use of their gifts, being idle loiterers, indiscreet feeders, men-pleasers, or the like.

Some because they are proud, humorous, self-conceited, singular, and love to go alone.

Thus of his praises. The ends of his mission follow, and they are three:

1. That he might declare unto them Paul's estate;
2. That he might know their estate; 3. That he might comfort their hearts.

For the first: If you ask what he should declare, I may answer, such things as these: the success of the gospel in Rome, the order of Paul's life and his afflictions.

If you ask to what end, I answer: 1. For approbation; the greatest men need the approbation of other ministers, yea, of other Christians. 2. For thanksgiving, that so many praises might be given to God. 3. For prayer for what was wanting, or hurtful to him or the church. 4. For consolation to them, who questionless would rejoice to hear from Paul.

Again, it is to be noted that he saith, his whole estate; for a godly man carrieth himself so as he cares not though all men see into all his courses.

Ver. 8. *Whom I have sent for the same purpose, that he might know your estate.*

Doct. The state of the people ought to be known to the minister; not their worldly estate, but the estate of their souls and consciences, and the working of the means upon them, not only for the satisfaction of the minister's affection, but for the guiding of his private preparations and prayers, and for his public doctrine. Which reproves the careless ministers that heed not the state of the people. We are watchmen for observation, as well as labourers in respect of preaching; neither can he be a good preacher that is not a careful watchman.

Again, it is a great defect in the people when the minister wants intelligence. For though it be a base humour of any to bring false reports, and a weak part in any minister to make the pulpit a place to vent their private and personal businesses, yet in the general he cannot be a good physician to the state of any congregation that is not acquainted with their diseases.

Quest. But why doth the apostle send to know their estate?

Ans. Because he would not credit reports concerning them; for he knew that wicked men out of their malice would raise monstrous slanders many times of the best-deserving people; and besides, the better sort of men are not careful of their words in reports; matters grow with telling, and every man according to his several affection sets a several emphasis upon the matter he tells, so that after a while the tale will not be worth receiving. This carefulness should teach us how to hear; especially we should be wary, and well-advised, and thoroughly informed, before, by prayer and fasting, we take up the name of God concerning the absent.

The third end is, 'that their hearts might be comforted.'

Here in general, from the apostle's care to have them comforted, observe:

Doct. 1. That Christians need comfort and encouragement.

Doct. 2. That comfort is the peculiar portion of true Christians; and contrariwise nothing but sorrow and the curse is the portion of wicked men; and if any dram of comfort be applied to wicked men, the truth of God is falsified.

Object. But this is the way to make them despair.

Ans. The blind and dreaming world is mistaken. Give me an instance of one man in this place, nay, in this age, nay, in any age, (that I can remember;) shew me any example in scripture, or any instance in experience, of one soul driven into despair by the sincere preaching of the word. It is no great thing I desire. That men have despaired I know and find, as Cain and Judas did; but that it was severe preaching that wrought it I nowhere find; and yet, for one bitter word given by us, the prophets gave ten, and yet this event never followed. Not but there is enough said many times to make despair, but that there is this providence of God that it comes not upon men by this means, but either of the melancholy of the body, or the special curse that God privately poured upon them, or by the special working of Satan by God's just permission. And yet I allow not indiscreet rashness, or rude indiscretion in applying threatenings.

Doct. 3. That it is the duty of every minister to labour to build up God's children in comfort, as the apostle doth herein express his care; but yet consider whom the apostle comforts.

1. Such as had the faith of Jesus, Col. i. 4; 2. Such as loved all the saints, Col. iv. 1; 3. Such as were fruitful hearers of the gospel, Col. i. 6; 4. Such as were constant, and laboured to be grounded in faith and hope, Col. i. 23; 5. Such as accounted Christ their greatest riches, and the gospel a glorious mystery, Col. i. 27; 6. Such as were circumcised with circumcision made without hands, and have put away the body of sins, and had with painful sorrows put away fornication, uncleanness, the inordinate affection, wrath, anger, malice, cursed speaking, filthy speaking, and lying out of their mouths, Col. ii. 10, iii. 5-8.

4. A 'question' may be here asked, whether consolations do bar out rebukes and directions?

Ans. They do not; for Paul doth comfort, and yet he rebuked in the second chapter and directed in the third; nay, many times rebukes and directions are the great doors of consolation.

Thus of Paul's care to have them comforted.

Tychicus did comfort their hearts: 1. By his presence; 2. By bringing letters to the church from Paul; 3. By his words, not of report only, relating Paul's estate to them, but of doctrine, persuading them to patience under their crosses, remembering them of the joys to come, strengthening them against the gainsayings of adversaries, the temptations of Satan, the rebellion of their own flesh, and the inconvenience of Paul's imprisonment, and lastly, instructing them how to go on in holy life.

Thus of the first part of the narration.

In the narration concerning Onesimus I observe two things: his praises, and the end of his mission.

His praises are as they stand in relation to all Christians, or in particular to them; to all he is a brother, faithful, beloved to them, and so he is one of them; the end of his mission is in the end of the verse.

Onesimus. This Onesimus was the thievish and fugitive servant of Philemon, who, coming to Rome, was converted by Paul in prison, and is now for honour's sake sent with Tychicus. From hence divers things may be noted.

1. That hateful and unfaithful persons may be converted, and made worthy, faithful, and beloved.

2. That religion and the word doth not mar, but make good servants. The word will do that which rating and stripes will not do.

3. That no man's sins, of which they have repented before God and the church, ought to be charged upon them as any disparagement in subsequent times. Where God forgives, men should not impute.

4. It is a good work to grace and credit such as by repentance return from their former evil ways.

5. Repentance and true grace is the surest way to credit; the best way to lift reproach from a man's name is to get sin off his soul.

Now in the particular praise of Onesimus I observe: first, That Christian love respects not persons. Paul is not ashamed of a poor servant, and he would have the church love whom God loves. Secondly, That there is faithfulness required of private men as well as ministers, and that faithfulness stands in three things: soundness in religion without error or hypocrisy, diligence in the particular calling, and fidelity in promises and covenants. Thirdly, That natural and civil relations are not broken or disabled by religion; they must not only love Onesimus as a Christian, but also as one of them, for he was a citizen of Colosse. There is love should be in men as they are fellow-citizens, and of the same trade or profession, or the like.

Thus of the narration.

Ver. 10. *Aristarchus, my prison-fellow, saluteth you, and Marcus, Barnabas' sister's son, touching whom ye received commandment. If he come unto you, receive him.*

Ver. 11. *And Jesus, which is called Justus, which are of the circumcision. These only are my work-fellows unto the kingdom of God, which have been unto my consolation.*

The salutations follow, and they are either signified or required; signified, ver. 10 to 15; required, ver. 15 to the end.

The salutations signified are from six men, three of them Jews, Aristarchus, Marcus, and Jesus, ver. 10, 11, and three Gentiles, Epaphras, Lucas, Demas, ver. 12-14.

Aristarchus is the first; concerning whom here is set down, with his name, both his estate, 'prison-fellow,' and his salutation. This Aristarchus was a Jew of Macedonia, converted by Paul, who out of the dearness of his respect would never leave him, but accompanied him in his adversities; for he was taken with him in the tumult at Ephesus, Acts xix. 29, 30, and here he is his prison-fellow in Rome. Crosses abide all that will live godly; if he will have grace with Paul, he may perhaps lie in prison with him too. But here we see that adversity doth not lessen that affection that is found either to God or to God's people; they that cannot endure the smiting of the tongue would little endure the iron fetters.

Marcus is the second. This is he about whom the contention was between Paul and Barnabas, Acts xiii., because he had forsaken them and the labour of preaching with them. Now he is commended by his alliance to Barnabas. Certainly the kindred of worthy men are to be regarded even for their sakes, much more their posterity. It is a great fault that when men have spent themselves in the labour and service of the church, their posterity should be neglected, and exposed to want and misery. And is it a credit to be Barnabas' sister's son? What is it then to be the child of God by regeneration?

Concerning whom you have received commandment. Some think that Marcus brought them to the decrees of the council at Jerusalem, and these read it, 'of whom ye received,' &c. Some say the meaning hereof is not revealed, and therefore they will not inquire. Some think, that upon his forsaking of the apostle, the churches had notice not to receive him if he came unto them, and that he had written to them himself. Some think the latter words 'whom receive' are an explication, and so they shew what was commanded, viz., to receive him.

Now for the observations we may note: first, That scandalous persons are not to be received. Secondly, That the greatness of the offences of men are not to be measured by carnal reason, but by the consideration of the person, manner, place, time, &c. A lesser offence aggravated by circumstances may give cause of private separation from voluntary company. Thirdly, That an ingenuous nature is much affected with the distaste of discreet Christians. Fourthly, That repenting sinners are to be received, if unto God's mercy, then much more unto our houses and companies. It is an ill quality to be hard to be reconciled. In general it is our duty and God's commandment that we should receive one another, Rom. xv. 7. Thus ministers must receive their people, Luke ix. 11, when they are with them, to speak to them of the kingdom of God, Acts xxi. 26; and the people must receive their ministers also, and the people must receive one another, even the meanest Christians as well as the greatest, the little ones that believe in Christ, Mat. xviii. 5, all the disciples of Christ are to be received, Mat. x. 40, 41.

Now because this point of receiving one another is exceeding needful, and there may be much mistaking about it, I think good therefore to give out of several scriptures rules how we are to carry ourselves in this business of receiving one another.

1. That we entertain with all heedfulness, so Acts ix. in Paul's case, and Acts xviii. 27, in Apollos' case. This condemns the carnal hospitality in the world, which promiscuously admits any of any profession, where the basest and vilest sort of people are soonest chosen for the table and company; yea, many of the better sort are to be blamed, such as are over credulous, many times to their own singular disgrace, and hurt of the church.

2. That when we are assured of the faithfulness of any, we receive them with all Christian respect, freely and liberally, Rom. xv. 17, bearing with their infirmities, Rom. xv. 1, yea, if need be, pardoning their offences, Philem. 12, 17.

3. That in society with weak Christians, we take heed of entangling them with questions and controversies, Rom. xiv. 1, as the manner of some is.

4. That great respect be had of our callings.

5. That the employment be chiefly about holy things. Receive them in the fellowship of the gospel, not for recreation or idle discourse; either labour to strengthen them, Acts xviii. 26, or to be furthered in obedience by them, 2 Cor. vii. 15.

6. That great respect be had of frugality, Luke x. 8. Thus of ver. 10.

Ver. 11. *And Jesus, which is called Justus, which are of the circumcision, &c.*

The third person that doth salute is described by his proper name, 'Jesus,' and his surname, 'Justus.'

Quest. May the name of 'Jesus' be given to any man?

Ans. Before it was appropriated to the Son of God, it was both lawful and usual to give it to men, as appears by Joshua's name, which is the same, and the son of Sirac. But now it is not expedient any way; and therefore the Jesuits may change their names, like Jebusites as they are.

The name 'Justus' was not given him by the Jews, but by the Romans, as the varying of the language showeth; and in all probability given in praise of his faithfulness and true dealing with all men.

Quest. What may we do to win the reputation of just persons?

Ans. 1. Be peaceable and make peace, and do all things without murmuring or reasonings, Mat. v. 8, Phil. ii. 15.

2. Be watchful unto chastity, and the honesty of the seventh commandment, 1 Pet. ii. 11, 12.

3. Let your conversation be without fear, 1 Pet. iii. 2.

4. Be not vain in apparel, 1 Pet. iii. 3.

5. Get a meek and quiet spirit, 1 Pet. iv. 3, 4.

6. In yielding apology, be constant, and unmoveable with all cheerfulness, will to give answer with all meekness, and reverence, and good conscience, 1 Pet. iii. 15, 16.

7. Show all uprightness in thy calling; and this uprightness hath three things: 1. Diligence; 2. All true and faithful dealing in words and promises; 3. A conversation without covetousness.

Finally, To live inoffensively is a strong inducement, even to the worst men, many times to draw from them a good testimony even of God's children.

Thus of their names.

In the second place they are described: 1. By their country, they were of the circumcision, that is Jews; 2. By their praises, and thus they are commended, either for what they were to the church in general, they were labourers, fellow-workers, or for what they were to Paul, they were to his consolation.

Which are of the circumcision. This is added perhaps to note, that even those men, though they were Jews, did subscribe to the apostle's doctrine concerning the abolishing of Jewish ceremonies.

But by this periphrasis the Jews were noted, not so much because God did once hereby distinguish and separate them from the world as by a partition wall, but because of pertinacy in refusing, though they were Christians, to lay down circumcision. This obstinacy of the Jews should teach us resolution for the truth, and to be more constant in all good courses than they obstinate in evil.

In the praise of their pains, I note: 1. Their paucity or fewness, 'these only;' 2. Their labour, 'work-fellows;' 3. The subject about which they labour, 'the kingdom of God.'

These only. Here observe: 1. That when God hath any work to do, there are found few faithful men to do it. 2. That a people that hath had the means and been convinced, if they turn not speedily, prove of many others the most obdurate and hard-hearted; thus almost the whole nation of the Jews resisted Christ. 3. Persecution drives many hearers into apostasy; this was not the case of the Jews in Rome only, but would be our case if the times altered.

Quest. What hearers amongst us are like to fall away if the times should change?

Ans. 1. Such as hear without affection; 2. Such as have only a temporary faith; 3. Such as now forbear society with God's servants in the fellowship of the gospel: for if now they shame their presence, how far would they stand off in perilous time? 4. If these three only of all the Jews were faithful labourers in Rome, where was Peter if he had been at Rome? Either Paul much wrongs him, not to mention him, and his eminent praises, or else the gaining of a bishopric made him give over his work.

Work-fellows. Here consider: 1. Their labour, 'work;' 2. Their honour, 'fellows.' For the first, observe: 1. That God's kingdom on earth is erected by man's hands, as the outward instruments, an honour done to man which is denied to the angels; 2. God's kingdom needs much labour and help. Ministers must work, they may not be loiterers; yea, they must work hard, for cursed is he that doth God's work negligently; yea, they must work in their own persons, not by substitutes. Magistrates also must help forward this work by protecting the ministry and good men, by compelling such as are by the highways to come into God's house, and by reforming abuses which hinder God's grace and kingdom amongst men. Private persons must help by instruction, admonition, consolation, &c.

Fellows. Here note: 1. The honour of these labourers, they are all one, fellows, though differing in gifts, 1 Cor. iii. 8, 9; 2. Their unity, some are workers, but not co-workers, for they preach not Christ purely; 3. Humility in the apostle, imitable in all, though never so much excelling in place or gift.

Uses of all. 1. For instruction: First, pray to the Lord of the harvest to send forth more labourers; though clergymen are very corrupt, and few of them faithful, yet it is better our mouths be filled with prayers than with reproaches.

Secondly, Ministers must study to approve themselves workmen that need not be ashamed, 2 Tim. ii. 15.

Thirdly, The people must take heed they hinder not God's work by disobedience, 1 Cor. xvi. 16.

Lastly, Must ministers in their callings labour? surely then must every man work in his calling also, else just with God if poverty attend sloth; yea, women must work, and not destroy their houses by pride and idleness; and all, both men and women, must not talk of it, as many do, but set to it, Prov. xiv. 23, nor begin only, but persevere, Prov. xviii. 9; but some are so settled upon their lees in this point, that they are wiser in their own conceit than seven men that can give a reason.

2. Secondly, For consolation to all God's workmen, especially ministers; though they have not so great gifts as others, yet if they shew all good faithfulness in discharge of their places, they are fellows even to apostles; though all that wrought at the tabernacle had not Bezaleel's skill, yet all were co-workers; yea, God's workmen differ from all the workmen in the world; for, 1. God himself will work with them, so

will no prince though the work be never so princely; 2. Though their work be not finished, yet they shall receive their wages, 'Though Israel be not gathered, yet their judgment is with the Lord, and their work with their God,' Isa. xlix. 4, 5.

Unto the kingdom of God. There is a threefold kingdom of God : first, Of nature, Ps. ciii. 19; secondly, Of grace, Mat. iii. 2; thirdly, Of glory, John iii. 3.

The kingdom of grace is here meant. Here I observe: first, The privileges of this kingdom; secondly, The properties or signs of the subjects; thirdly, The uses.

For the first, the excellent condition of such as by true conversion are admitted into the kingdom of grace may be three ways considered ; for they are happy: first, In their King; secondly, In their laws; thirdly, In the personal prerogatives of the kingdom.

1. They are happy in their King, for he is nobly born, the Son of the Most High. 2. He comes rightly by the crown, Ps. ii. 7. 3. He is of eminent sovereignty ; he hath a name written on his garments and thigh, the King of kings and Lord of lords, Rev. xix. 16 ; Prince of the kings of the earth, Rev. i. 5. 4. He is a Prince of admirable qualities, Wonderful, Counsellor, the mighty God, an everlasting Father, Prince of Peace, one that keeps the government upon his own shoulders, Isa. ix. 6. 5. Lastly, He is immortal, 1 Tim. i. 17. In the earth, if a prince were never so good, yet in this the subjects are unhappy that they shall lose him, but Zion's King will never die.

2. They are happy in their laws, for they are not only clearly digested in God's sacred volume, but they are every way most perfect to make men wise to salvation, and absolute to every good work, such as need no repeal nor addition, a perfect rule to all ages, and so are no laws of man under heaven, 2 Tim. iii. 3, 15, 16, 17.

3. They are happy in the personal prerogatives of the kingdom ; for first, Here is certain safety and quiet habitation for all the King's subjects, Isa. xxxiii. 20, 21, Jer. xxiii. 5, 6. Secondly, To all the subjects it is given to know the mysteries of this kingdom, Mat. xiii. 11. Thirdly, In this kingdom poor men may get advancement as easily and as soon as rich, James ii. 6. Fourthly, If any of the subjects fall into desperate crosses that they be without all means, yet they are prisoners of hope, and shall be saved and delivered by the blood of the covenant, Zech. ix. 9, 11. Fifthly, The King doth quiet himself in the love of every subject, and doth rejoice over them with joy. It is a great benefit to live under a good king, though the subject be not known unto him ; but a great favour that the king should take notice of the subject by name ; but exceeding great comfort it is if the king love some subject with a special love : thus doth Christ to all his subjects, which no king can do, because his heart is finite. Sixthly, Here all subjects are sons, Rom. ix. 25, 26. Seventhly, They are all kings, Rev. i. 5, 6, v. 10, Rom. v. 17. Eighthly, Here if any two of the subjects do agree on earth upon anything, whatsoever they desire their heavenly Father will grant it, Mat. xviii. 19, 20. Lastly, The properties of the kingdom shew the felicity of the subjects of this kingdom.

First, Is in power, not in word, 1 Cor. iv. 20 ; secondly, Is not of this world, but as far more excellent, as it differs in nature from the kingdoms of the world, John viii. 36 ; thirdly, It is without end, Luke i. 33, Heb. xii. 28.

Thus of the privileges.

The second thing is the properties of the subjects, or the signs by which they may be known ; and they are six.

First, They are a poor and penitent people, Mat. v. 3, iii. 2. Secondly, They do gladly and constantly subject themselves to be ruled by the powerful preaching of the gospel, and esteem the comforts thereof above all treasures, Mat. xiii. 44, 45, hence called the gospel of the kingdom. Thirdly, They are a patient people, and do willingly forgive each other his brother's trespasses, Mat. xviii. 33, 35, Rev. i. 9. Ordinarily men cannot more darken their evidence than by their unruly passions unbridled. The King of Zion is meek, Mat. xxi. 5, and so are the subjects. Fourthly, They may be easily known by their easy access to their King in their daily troubles ; you may see them betimes every morning at the court gates, Gal. iv. 7, Ps. v. 2, 3 ; where he gives his Son, he gives the spirit of his Son into their hearts, &c. Fifthly, They fear their King and his goodness ; they are more affected with fear upon the sense of his mercy than upon the sight of his judgments, Hosea iii. 5. Sixthly, They make conscience of the least commandments, fear as well to swear by lesser oaths in common talk as perjury in courts of justice; they make conscience of drinkings as well as drunkenness, of filthy speaking as well as whoredom, Mat. v. 19, xiii. 33; they are new creatures, they have not a new leg or an arm only, they labour to abound in grace and duties, 2 Pet. i. 11.

The uses follow.

First, For instruction. If the estate of Christians converted by the powerful preaching of the gospel under the regiment of Christ be so excellent an estate, and so happy and king-like condition, it should teach: first, All that are not yet converted to settle their hearts about this point; and that they may get into the kingdom of God, they must get an holy estimation of the happiness of that estate. A kingdom should move them much. Satan knew if anything would prevail with Christ it must be the glory of kingdoms. Behold here God offers thee a kingdom. Secondly, Pray daily and earnestly that God's kingdom may come upon thee, Mat. vi. Thirdly, Practise what thou prayest, and by practice seek the kingdom of God first, Mat. vi. 33; and to this end observe four rules:

First, Remove what might hinder; that is, by repentance cast off thy sins; no unclean thing must enter here, and it is plain it is required, Mat. iii. 2. Secondly, Wait upon the preaching of the gospel, for it is the gospel of the kingdom, and the keys of heaven; only take heed thou neither betray it by security, nor choke it by care, Mat. xiii. Thirdly, Remember to seek it with all zeal and earnestness, for the kingdom of heaven suffers violence, and the violent take it by force, Mat. xi. 12. Fourthly, Take heed thou give not over when thou come near to the kingdom of God, Mark xii. 34, for the children of the kingdom may be cast out.

2. Take heed of despising poor Christians, for God hath chosen them to make them heirs of the kingdom; they must not be accounted of according to their outward estate in the world.

3. Those that have attained this excellent estate must be exhorted to three things.

First, By godly conversation to walk worthy of the kingdom of God, 1 Thes. ii. 12, 1 Pet. ii. 9. Secondly, To rejoice in their King, and speak of the praises of the great renown of the sacred kingdom that thus cometh in the name of the Lord, Ps. cxlv. 10, 11, cxlix. 2, Mat. xi. 10; for many prophets and great kings have desired to see such days, and have not seen them in that clearness we now see them. Thirdly, Willingly to suffer for righteousness, 2 Thes. i. 5.

Lastly, Ministers should here be informed and provoked by all means possible, in season and out of season, to exhort, persuade, beseech men, and turn themselves into all forms to prevail, for it is about a kingdom they labour.

Thus for instruction.

2. It serves for reproof, first, of such as can be so easily content either to want or lose the means; the kingdom of God is taken from them, Mat. xxi. 43. Secondly, Of the waywardness of cavilling hearers that can never be set down, but are still objecting against this word of doctrine or the estate of Christians: these are condemned, Mat. xi. 16, &c. Thirdly, It is a great terror to rich men in special, who are threatened with impossibility to enter into this kingdom, if they do not above all other men look to themselves, Mat. x. 23, 24. Fourthly, Of the discontentments of God's servants under crosses. Is there no King in Zion? or is it no privilege that the first dominion is come unto them? Micah iv. 9. Fifthly, It especially reproves those wicked persons that profess by their works they will not have Christ to reign over them by his word, Luke xix. 14, 27, Zech. xiv. 17; woe is unto them, and woe to such as shut up the kingdom of God before men, Mat. xxiii. 13.

3. For comfort to all God's servants. Did so great kings and prophets desire to see these things we see? What is it to enjoy such a kingdom? Was it a great offer in Herod to offer half his kingdom? What is it in God to give a whole kingdom, better than any kingdom on earth? Yea, this comfort is the greater, in that such Christians, whose grace is but like the grain of mustard-seed, may be possessed of this kingdom.

Which have been to my consolation.

Doct. The labours of God's servants are a great comfort unto good men, it is a comfort to see God's work prosper, and besides joy in the Holy Ghost is wrought in their hearts by the power of the word preached.

Quest. What should be the reason why many that come constantly to hear God's servants, yet get not consolation, or not the comfort they desire?

Ans. The lets of comfort are either: first, In men; or, secondly, In God.

In men, they are either of frailty, without any great sin, or such as arise of sin.

The lets of frailty are specially two: first, Bodily distemper, by sickness or melancholy, but this may be tried thus, if they be dead-hearted in all other things, as well as hearing and prayer, &c. Secondly, Waywardness in the distress of conscience, when the soul refuseth comfort, Ps. lxxviii. 3.

The lets of comfort that arise of sin may be considered two ways: first, As they are in the worser sort of men; secondly, As they are also in the better sort. In the worser sort these are the lets: first, Impenitency, Jer. viii. 6-8. Secondly, Perverseness, Jer. vi. 10. Thirdly, Vile affections, such as are: 1. Worldly grief or fretting; 2. Worldly cares, these are thorns; 3. Rage and passion, Rom. xv. 4; 4. Lust, 2 Tim. iii. 6; 5. Envy, 1 Pet. ii. 12. Fourthly, A spirit of slumber, Rom. xi. 7, 8, &c. Fifthly, Contrariety or contradiction in opinions, Phil. ii. 1, 2.

In the better sort: 1. Want of preparation; ploughing must go before sowing, Mat. xvii.; of attention, Isa. lv. 3, 4; of estimation of comfort received, Job xv. 11; of godly sorrow, Isa. lxi., lxii.

Secondly, Prevailing of other joys.

Thirdly, An over high expectation.

Fourthly, Presumptuous sins.

Fifthly, Spiritual satiety and fulness, when they seem to have grace enough, and want nothing too, like the Laodiceans, Rev. iii.

Thus in men.

Secondly, God doth restrain consolation, sometimes for reasons secret to himself, sometimes for reasons revealed, but not to us, as:

First, To teach us to know that comfort is his gift, and to draw us to look above the means. Secondly, To teach us to live by faith and not by sense. Thirdly, To scourge unthankfulness. Fourthly, To compel us to the use of other his ordinances, too much neglected.

Thus of the lets.

To pass from this point, we may here observe: 1. An imitable praise in the apostle; he envies not the labours of his brethren; he is so far from it, that he rejoiceth in it. 2. We may see that the wisest and greatest men have need to be comforted of meaner men. 3. Here is a reproof of such workmen as by their labour grieve God's people, and are as thorns and goads in their sides, but comfort them they do not.

Thus of the salutations of the Jews.

The salutations of the three Gentiles follow. The first is Epaphras, who (besides the report of his salutation) is described: 1. By his office, the 'servant of Christ;' 2. By his relation to them, 'who is one of you;' 3. By his love to them, shewed by striving in prayer for them; 4. By his zeal, not only for them, but for the two neighbour churches, ver. 13.

This Epaphras was the city's preacher among the Colossians; he is kept back at Rome for a time, that so Tychicus might confirm the doctrine before taught by Epaphras.

Quest. But why is the apostle so long in speaking of him, being so short in the mention of the rest?

Ans. It is the apostle's discretion to honour him before his own people.

A servant of Christ. He was a servant of Christ: 1. As a man, and so by the necessity of creation, he must serve Christ whether he would or not. 2. As a Christian man, and so he serves him willingly and in religious works; 3. As a preacher of the gospel, and so he serves Christ in a special function in the church.

Doct. 1. Ministers are Christ's servants, whence follows two things: first, They must do his works; secondly, They must not be servants of men.

Doct. 2. The estate of the ministers of God is an estate of serving, not of reigning; they are not lords over God's heritage, nor must they think to be like the princes of the nations.

Doct. 3. It is a great honour to be Christ's servant, for all his servants are freemen, and their wages is everlasting, and therefore we should love to be his servants, neither should it ever seem evil unto us to do his work. Besides, it is a great comfort to poor Christians, though they cannot be kings and apostles, yet they may be Christ's servants, which kings and apostles have accounted their greatest honour. Thirdly, Men must take heed of despising or abusing ministers, seeing they are Christ's servants; yea, it is not safe to abuse any Christian for that very reason. Lastly, Seeing it is so great a dignity to serve Christ, both ministers and people must be careful to perform Christ's service, with observation of what Christ requires for the manner or rules of his service.

Ministers must not seek their own things, Phil. ii. 21; they must not be given to wine, nor to filthy lucre, nor fighters, nor covetous, nor profane in their families, not young scholars, not scandalous, 1 Tim. iii. 3-7, 2 Tim. ii. 24; they must faithfully care for all the matters of the church, Phil. ii. 20, they must serve with all modesty and tears, Acts xx. 19.

Christians in their service of Christ must remember to lay aside all immoderate cares for the profits and pleasures of this world; ye cannot serve Christ and mammon; 2. That Christ will not be served but in newness of spirit. The old heart can do Christ no work Christ will accept, Rom. vii. 6.

Quest. But who are Christ's servants?

Ans. If you speak of ministers, it is answered negatively, Gal. i. 10. He that preacheth man's doctrine, or goeth about to please men, he is not the servant of Christ. If you ask of Christians in general, it is answered, Rom. vi. 16. His servants ye are to whom ye obey. If ye conscionably endeavour to obey the word of Christ, you are the servants of Christ, otherwise ye serve sin unto death.

For conclusion, let us so settle our hearts to serve Christ, that we remember to do it: 1. Constantly, at all times; 2. Sincerely, by doing all his works, both public and private.

Which is one of you. *Doct.* There is a special love due to fellow-citizens. This I have noted before; but I add, that the love of citizens must shun five things, as great rocks to make the shipwreck of true affection upon: 1. Opposition or quarrel, and suits in matter of estate. 2. Envy at the prosperity or trade of others. 3. Faction or banding into sides in matters of government. 4. Schism in matter of religion; but it is to be noted, that it is profane and fleshly men that have not the Spirit of God, that cannot abide others, because they run not with them into the same excess of riot, for God's servants would fain live at peace, Judges xviii. 19. 5. A rejoicing together in evil. The love that leads men from their calling to go from tavern to tavern, or from sport to sport, is not true citizen-like love; it is base and unwarrantable.

The third thing in the description is his love to his people, shewed by his praying for them. In his prayer note:

1. The action, that he doth pray; 2. The subject persons for whom—'for you;' 3. The circumstance —he prays 'absent;' 4. The variety of his prayers —'prayers;' 5. The fervency of his prayers— 'striveth;' 6. The constancy of his prayers— 'always;' 7. The matter he prays for: (1.) Their perseverance—'that ye may stand;' (2.) Their perfection amplified, by the measure—'full,' and by the extent of the subject—'in all the will of God.'

Prayer. *Doct.* Prayer is the usual remedy and refuge for God's children in their griefs and desires; a remedy, I say, for all times, persons, and places. As for griefs and fears, it is of force and available: 1. Against the troubles and cares of this world, Phil. iv. 6; 2. Against the stings of secret temptations and prevailing sins, 2 Cor. xii. 9, Mat. ix.; 3. Against the shame of evil works past, both the blushing and gnawing of the conscience inwardly, and outwardly the reproach of name, Zeph. iii. 11; 4. Against sickness, James v. 15; 5. Against ill tongues, Ps. cxix. 4; 6. Against the fear of apostasy, 2 Tim. ii. 19. And these are the most usual things that need to trouble any child of God. And as for desires, it is a plain proposition that God is rich to all that call upon him, Rom. x. 12. This shews the felicity of every child of God, to whom God hath given the Spirit of his Son into his heart as a spirit of prayer; for we see he cannot be miserable that can pray. And it should teach us that if we would be counted God's people, to shew that we trust God, by pouring out our hearts before him in all places and at all times, Ps. lxii. 8, 1 Tim. ii. 8.

For you. *Doct.* 1. Ministers must pray for their

people as well as preach to them. And as this may humble ministers under the sense of the neglect hereof, so it should teach the people to requite their labour in the Lord, by praying for them again; but especially they should take heed they send not their teachers with hearts full of grief to complain of them.

Doct. 2. Prayer for others is a principal sign of our love to them. Hereby ministers may try whether they love their people, and parents whether they love their children, &c.

Doct. 3. In that Epaphras prayeth for them absent, he is therein a pattern of a true pastor; no distance of place can make him forget the love of his people.

Prayers. There be divers kinds of prayers; for they are varied: first, By the place; for there is public prayer and there is private prayer, either with our families or alone by ourselves. Secondly, By the manner; and that either for form or affection. For form; there are not only ordinary set prayers, but ejaculations, short requests or desires, cast out upon sudden opportunities, and accepted by God, though the words be few or abrupt; for affection in prayer there is prayer unto which is required the usual devotion of the heart, and there is supplication which is with special instance and importunity, Phil. iv. 7. Thirdly, By the instrument; there is the prayer of the mouth, and the prayer of the heart. Fourthly, By the matter; for there is deprecations for turning away of judgment, and confessions with acknowledgment of sin, and petition in matter of request, and thanksgiving for benefits received.

Striveth. But why must we strive in prayer? Because of the greatness of our own wants and necessities, and because it is a great loss to lose our prayers.

Quest. But what doth striving import?

Ans. 1. It imports earnestness, as it is opposed to coldness, when we draw near to God with our lips, but our hearts are far from him; or spiritual fainting in prayer, Luke xviii. 1. 2. Tenderness of affection, both sorrowing and rejoicing in prayer, according to our occasions and the matter of prayer. 3. A resolution to take no denial. 4. Difficulty; for fighting imports opposition.

Quest. But what must we fight against in prayer?

Ans. 1. Carnal counsel; 2. Distractions by the lusts of the flesh or cares of the world; 3. The objects of our own flesh; 4. Our own unskilfulness to pray: strive to learn to pray better; 5. Hardness of heart; 6. Sleepiness of our body; 7. The temptations of Satan; 8. We must strive against God himself, as Jacob did by wrestling to get the blessing.

Use. For reproof of such as never complain of any impediments in prayer, nor care how they speed. Their condition is as far from happiness, as their practice is from duty. And they are to be blamed that complain of their lets and discomforts in prayer, but yet they strive not. But we should learn to harness ourselves, and conscionably strive against all that may hinder us; and to this end set ourselves in God's presence, and beseech God to heal our infirmities, and help us against all the lets of prayer, and stir up in our hearts the promises made to prayer, observing fit times, and watching to all opportunities, to be importunate when any door is opened.

Lastly, Would one be fervent in spirit? They must then look to four things: first, They must serve the Lord, for a profane person can never be fervent; secondly, They must labour to rejoice their souls with the hope of a better life, for such comfortable meditations inflame the spirit; thirdly, We must get patience under worldly crosses and tribulations, else the cares and vexations of the world will choke all true fervency; fourthly, We must continue in prayer, for use and experience breeds fervency.

Always. We must be constant in prayer, 1 Thes. v. 16, Luke xxi. 36. To pray always is to keep a constant order in the daily performance of this duty, and besides to pray upon all occasions and opportunities. The profit comes by this constancy in prayer appears by the proofs to be: 1. Much joy, 1 Thes. v. 16; 2. They that pray continually shall escape the last terrible things, and be able to stand in the day of Christ, Luke xxi. 36.

Here we may see the difference between a godly mind and a carnal heart. The godly mind is always praying, but the carnal heart is seldom without a sense of tediousness, with a desire to be rid of the burden of it.

The reason why God's children be so willingly employed in much and often prayer, is partly because God commands them to pray always, partly because they find unutterable benefit and refreshing in prayer, and partly they daily get hereby what they desire, Mark xi. 24.

If any take unto them the words of those wretched Jews, Mal. iii. 16, and say, what profit is it to keep God's commandments, or to walk humbly? and that they could never find any good by it, I can soon answer, that in their prayers and obedience there was no profit, for indeed they did not walk humbly, nor in the power of godliness did they keep God's commandments.

Object. But have not the best of them all their sins, distractions, and wants, as well as others? How, then, can they be so bold and frequent in prayer?

Sol. The children of God have privileges, others have not; for their wants are covered by Christ's intercession, and their suits are followed in heaven by Christ's advocation, 1 John ii. 1, and framed in earth by the Spirit, Rom. viii. 26.

Object. But how can they find matter for so much prayer?

Sol. If men had by the law gathered the catalogue of their sins, and learned to see and fear the judgments sin might bring; if they had observed the daily straits of a mortal condition; if they had considered the almost infinite occasions of prayer for themselves and others, they would not thus object.

Object. But there are some that do pray, and that always, too, against their corruptions, and yet cannot speed, nor get strength against them.

Sol. If they have constantly prayed, which yet I doubt, then the reason is either they watch not in practice to cut off the occasions of evil, Luke xi. 36, or they strive not with importunity to prevail with God, Luke xviii., or else they cannot be truly affected towards God's grace in others; for if envy at the graces and estimation of others reign in thee, it is just with God to deny to give thee that grace thou enviest in others.

To conclude, if any man hitherto careless of this duty, be now desirous to be instructed how to pray as he ought, with words, affection, and success, let such a man put on a mind to observe the rules following:—

1. Thou must forgive all thine enemies, and resolve to live without malice, Mat. vi.

2. Thou must constantly hear God's word, else thou canst never pray, but God will abhor thee and thy prayers, Prov. xxviii. 10.

3. Thou must get and show a merciful heart to man, if thou wouldst prevail to obtain mercy with God, Prov. xxi. 13, Mat. v. 7.

4. Thou must carry thyself orderly and quietly in the family, 1 Pet. iii. 7.

5. Take heed of hypocrisy in praying to be seen of men, Mat. vi.

Object. But I want words.

Sol. Pray God to give thee words, and mind thine own way, by considering thy sin and wants by the law.

Object. But I want the affections of prayer.

Sol. Search whether there be not some vile affections, lusts, and passions unmortified, Ps. lxvi. 18; 1 Tim. ii. 8, and pray God to give thee the spirit of compassion, Zech. xi. 12. Yet in all this take heed of security, rest not in beginning. God will take that at the first which he will not still be content with. Learn to pray better.

Thus of the sixth thing.

The last is the matter he prays for.

That ye may stand. Concerning perseverance here are four things to be observed:

Doct. 1. That in the visible church there may be such as will not stand, and this is true both in true members, and in seeming members. The true members may fall either by infirmity; and so the righteous falleth seven times and riseth again, or by presumption falling to the practice of gross evils, out of which they cannot recover but with extreme sorrow. The only seeming members not only may, but certainly will fall, and that most an end, finally, without recovery. So Demas, Judas, Joash, and many more.

This should teach us not to think it strange if we see apostasy in men that have rooms in the church, and have acknowledged the truth according to godliness.

Doct. 2. That it is a fearful thing to fall away; a

worse condition likely a man cannot choose for himself, 2 Pet. ii. 20, 21. For Satan will re-enter, and gain a stronger possession than ever he had; yea, their dispositions unto evil may seven times more be inflamed than ever before. Seven devils worse than the former may enter. It were better to be ground under a millstone than thus to live in apostasy, Mat. xxi. 44. Such persons are abolished from Christ, Gal. v. 4. They are in the power of Satan, 2 Tim. i. 18. Their latter end is worse than their beginning. It had been better for them never to have known the way of righteousness, than having known it to depart from the holy commandment given unto them. They are as hateful to God as dogs and swine, 2 Pet. ii. 20-22, yea, they may so order the matter, that they may fall into such a condition as there will remain no more sacrifice for sin.

Quest. But what should be the causes of their apostasy?

Ans. The causes are either without them, or in themselves. Without them are ill counsel, as in the case of Joash, and the effectual working of Satan, not only to glut himself in the blood of their souls, but thereby to work scandal in the weak and scorn in the wicked.

Within themselves, the causes are, in some, unbelief, Rom. xi. 20; in some, pride and the vanity of our own conceits, 1 Tim. vi. 21; in some, covetousness and ambition, so in Judas and Demas; in some, the very levity and inconstancy of their natures; in some, the concupiscence of the lusts of the flesh, 2 Tim. iii.; in some, certain opinions wilfully received, as justification by the law, Gal. v. 4, or that the resurrection is past, 2 Tim. ii. 16-18, or the like; but the general cause is the want of practice of that we hear, Mat. vii. And therefore 'let him that standeth take heed lest he fall,' or 'by any means be turned away from the love of the truth,' 2 Pet. iii. 18, 2 Cor. x. 11, and the rather considering that many that are fallen had great knowledge, Heb. vi. 4, and great joy in hearing the word, Mat. xiii., and great affections to the ministry, for so had the Galatians to Paul, Gal. iv., and besides they were such as in reformation did forsake the filthiness of the profaneness of the world, 2 Pet. i. 20, and had a taste of the heavenly gift, and were partakers of the Holy Ghost, and tasted of the powers of the life to come, Heb. vi. 4, 5.

Object. But some one may say, they that are fallen find no such misery in their estate.

Ans. Thou knowest not what they find. They are for the most part cast into a 'spirit of slumber.'

Object. But they fall not from religion; for they are protestants still, and not papists.

Ans. There is a total apostasy, and an apostasy in part. They fall from the sincerity of religion. Demas did not turn gentile, or the Galatians; nay, the pharisees that committed the sin against the Holy Ghost, did not openly renounce religion. And therefore let men take heed of falling from 'the simplicity that is in Christ Jesus,' 2 Cor. xi. 13.

And thus of the second doctrine.

Doct. 3. Perseverance may be obtained; a man may stand and hold out to the end, Rom. v. 1-3; 'God is able to establish us,' 1 Cor. xv. 1. And the word of God is God's power, not only to regeneration, but to salvation, Rom. xiv. 4. 'The weapons of our warfare are mighty,' 2 Cor. x. 4, and great power is made known in weakness, 2 Cor. xii. 10. Only believe, and use the means.

Doct. 4. Much prayer is a great means to obtain perseverance, and will prevail. Though this be not the only means, yet it is an effectual means.

Perfect. A Christian man may be said to be perfect divers ways:

1. In the cause or fountain of holiness; so good gifts are said to be perfect, James i. 17, viz., as they are from God.

2. In respect of consecration or calling; so the word that some translate to make perfect, is translated by others to consecrate, Heb. i. 10, v. 9, which importeth that Christ may be said to be perfect, because he was separated, or dedicated, or called to perfection, or hath a perfect calling.

3. In respect of acceptation, not in respect of operation, the Lord accounting our confession of imperfection for perfection.

4. In respect of parts, though not in respect of degrees. He is perfect in that he hath holiness in every part, though not in such measure. Thus to be perfect is to be 'sanctified throughout.'

5. Comparatively, not positively. Comparatively,

I say, either with carnal men, or ordinary hearers, or infants in grace. A Christian that makes conscience of all his ways, and can love his enemies, is perfect in comparison of carnal men, Mat. v. 48, that follow the swing of their own corruptions and affections; and so he is too in respect of ordinary hearers, that seek not the power of godliness. And as for infants in grace, it is perfection to be of ripe age, or strong in the grace or knowledge of Jesus Christ, 1 Cor. xiv. 20, Eph. iv. 12, Hosea v. 14. And so the doctrine that is to be propounded is called the doctrine of perfection, Heb. vi. 1.

6. In respect of truth, though not in respect of absoluteness. Thus he is perfect because he desires and endeavours after perfection, though in act he attain it not. Thus uprightness is the perfection of a Christian after calling.

7. In respect of men or common estimation; and so he is perfect that is unrebukable.

8. In respect of the end; and so he may be said to be perfect three ways—

1. In intention; because he sets perfection as a mark to shoot at, Phil. iii.

2. In respect of duration; because he holds out to the end.

3. In respect of accomplishment; because he finisheth what he undertaketh in godliness or mortification; he doth it not by halves, or in some parts of it; for so to perfect is translated to 'finish,' Acts xx. 24, John iv. 34, xvii. 4.

Here, then, we see what we must do to be perfect men: we must confess conscionably our imperfection; we must live in uprightness, and not in any gross or presumptuous sin; we must finish what we undertake in godliness, and we must strive after perfection; we must love our enemies, and rule our tongues, James iii. 1, i. 5, and let patience have her perfect work: he that doth this is a perfect man.

But a man shall never attain unto this unless he labour for much knowledge, 1 Cor. xiv. 20, and to that end exercise himself in the word of righteousness, Heb. v. 14; and besides, a man must withdraw himself from the world, and devote himself to sincerity; and especially a man must get a great deal of love; for that is the bond of all perfectness, Col. iii. 14.

Full. The faithful are said to be full, both in respect of the number of faithful persons added to the church, and in respect of the plentiful performance of the rich promises of God, 2 Thes. i. 11, and in respect of holding out till their course be fulfilled, Rom. xi. 25; but I take it to be meant of fulness in graces and duties; in both fulness is required. In duties fulness is taken for abundance, and sometimes for the fulfilling of some particular office or charge; both are required, Acts ix. 36, Phil. i. 11, Acts xii. 14, 26. In graces there is a fulness of grace and knowledge, and of zeal, Acts vi. 3, 5, 8, and of joy, John iii. 29, xv. 11. The fulness of faith is the confidence and undaunted assurance of it; the fulness of knowledge is the largeness of understanding and discretion; the fulness of zeal is the power of words and affections; the fulness of joy is the truth and contentment of it.

Hence we may discern the state of the soul of a Christian: it is like a vessel under the conduit-pipe of God's ordinances, filling more and more by the influence of Christ, till it come to be brim-full.

Hence we may see cause to be greatly humbled because our works are not full before God.

Now if any shall think this doctrine of fulness to be a doctrine of discouragement, he may note these things for removal of that objection:

First, That it is a kingdom men labour about, and therefore should not think much if much be required of them; secondly, We may fill spiritually, though we do not discern it; thirdly, God requires not fulness at first, but by degrees; fourthly, That the Lord hath in many scriptures promised to help us against all temptations and impediments, whether arising from our own weakness, or from without us.

In all the will of God. Cajetan, a papist, makes a stop at 'all,' and reads it, 'in everything by the will of God,' and delivers the sense thus: That ye may be consummate in respect of yourselves, and full in respect of others, in every spiritual thing, by the will of God, that is, not by your own merits—note that—but by the grace of God's will.

But I think it should be read as ordinarily it is read; and so I observe that we should take counsel for the informing of our faith, and reforming and perfecting of our lives, at the will of God.

Which serves for great reproof of the course of the most men, who are advised and guided either by carnal reason, or by the lusts and wills of their carnal friends, or the lusts and temptations of Satan himself, 1 Pet. iv. 2, John viii. 44, or the inclination of their own flesh. How are worlds of men swayed by these, or some of these, almost in all matters of religion! If reformation, and the practice of the sincerity of the gospel, may not get the consent of their own carnal reason, or of such and such friends, &c., then it must never be gone about. But contrariwise, we should learn to stick to God's will in all things, yea, we should pray earnestly that we might never be beaten from this anchor-hold, but that in all estates—in prosperity and adversity, in life and death—we might constantly exalt the glory of God's will, to yield it for ever our acknowledgment of sovereignty over us, Ps. xl. 8-10.

Secondly, Note here that we must respect all God's will; and thus we are tied to respect all the will of God, both in respect of knowledge and in respect of practice; for we should labour to be made 'rich in all things, in all kind of utterance, and in all knowledge,' 1 Cor. i. 5; we should be 'expert in the word of righteousness,' accustoming ourselves continually to exercise our wits about discerning of good or evil out of the word, Heb. v. 14; in practice we must have respect to every commandment of God, and, as David did, we must labour to do all God's will, and not be like Saul or Herod.

This may serve, first, for confutation of the papists, that will not allow the will of God to be the only rule, though they grant it to be a perfect rule. But let us detest that subtle distinction, and, in the simplicity that is in Christ Jesus, acknowledge that there is a will of God for every opinion and work of every man of God, sufficient to make him perfect in all knowledge and every good work, 2 Tim. iii. 16.

Again, if this doctrine were soundly urged through every commandment, it would ransack the hearts of carnal men, and then manifestly let them see the vanity of their false and wild presumption of civility, and God's liking of them and their honest meanings. It is true they dare not say with their tongues, there is no God; but is there not such talk in their hearts? or could they not wish there were no God? Ps. xiv. 1. They worship not sun, moon, nor stars; but is there in them that warmth of love to the true God, that they can love him with all their hearts and all their souls? Deut. vi. 5. Where is that lively knowledge of God? John xvii. 3; where is that trembling fear of God? Hab. iii. 16; where is that glorying in God? Jer. ix. 24; where is that cleaving unto God? Acts xi. 23. Do these men every day commit their ways and their works unto God? Ps. xxxvii. 5, Prov. xvi. 3. These men use to wonder at heretics; but what forms of God do they conceive in their heads every day! They will not blaspheme God to his face, it is true; but will they not murmur from day to day at the work of his hands? 1 Cor. x. 10. They place no divinity in the signs of heaven; but will they not fear them neither? yet this is condemned as well as the other, Jer. x. 2. It is true popish images are gone out of their sight in the churches; but are the pictures of the Trinity gone out of their houses? They think, indeed, it is too bad never to come to church, or to give God no worship; but do they make conscience of cold service of God, or lukewarmness, and continued hypocrisy? Rev. iii. 15. For may it not be truly said of them that their hearts almost never come to church? Isa. xxix. 13. Sure their souls will be indicted in the day of Christ, and convicted too, for obstinate recusants. Witchcraft, conjuring, and charming is naught, they say; but is going to witches and conjurers and charmers naught too in their opinion? Lev. xx. 6. To forswear a man's self, they hold it somewhat vile if it may be discerned; but what conscience make they of swearing in their common talk, especially by petty oaths, and that which is not good? Mat. v. 34-37. They dare not curse God, but they dare curse the creatures of God by the name or justice of God; they dare not talk directly against God, but they dare use God's titles without reverence, Deut. xxviii. 58. They say they know all comes from God's blessing; but do they daily seek the sanctification of their callings and the creatures by the word and prayer? 1 Tim. iv. 4. We all say the Sabbath must be sanctified; but who makes it his delight? We condemn labour on the Sabbath; but where are those Nehemiahs that will restrain this monstrous abuse in the city of hiring labourers on the Sabbath? Though for many Sabbaths, one after another, they travel hither many hundreds of all sorts from all parts round about, and fill the streets almost with tumults on the Lord's-day, from the morning till near the evening, yet none seeks the reformation of this matchless abuse; or if any would restrain it, how are they opposed? The Lord give repentance to those that have sinned this way, and lay not the toleration of this damned abuse to their charge! Men say at length, it is naught to keep open shops or ride to fairs on the Sabbath-day; but who repents of the idle and fruitless spending of the Sabbath? We do somewhat in public duties; but who cares for the private duties in the family on the Sabbath? Men will not openly rail on magistrates; but how licentious are men's tongues in private? or when do men affectionately pray for their superiors? Where is a well-ordered family to be found? Say that men forbear blood, fighting, do they forbear anger, envy, frowardness, bitter words? They avoid whoredom; but do they shun filthy speaking and lust? Some men shun drunkenness; but do they shun drinkings? 1 Pet. iv. 3. Open stealth is abhorred, but secret fraud and deceit is common, 1 Thes. iv. 6, Deut. xxv. 13. Covetousness is condemned; but in worldliness men are drowned and see it not. Gaming for pounds and hundreds is easily censured, but for crowns and shillings it is no offence. Men make some conscience of false witness in courts, but at home they make no conscience of evil speaking, or suspicions, or censures. It may be men would be loath to be found guilty of raising slanders, but yet men love lies, Rev. xxii., if anybody else will invent them; and they will go about with tales and spread them, Lev. xix. 16; they will discover secrets, Prov. xi. 13; they will slander by scoffing or jesting, Eph. v. 4; they will report part of men's words, but not all, or not in their sense, Mat. xxvi. 61, John ii. 19; and evil thoughts and worlds of contemplative wickedness these men never care for.

Object. But some may say, What need all this ado? it is preciseness to be so curious.

Ans. It is true it is preciseness, and we are commanded to walk precisely, for so the word is, Eph. v. 15. And besides there is that necessity of it, that unless our righteousness exceed the righteousness of the scribes and pharisees, who yet lead a civil life, we cannot enter into the kingdom of heaven, Mat. v. 20.

Object. But we see the most men, and those too men of great place and learning, do not favour such strictness.

Ans. What then? Such is the calling of a Christian that not many mighty, not many wise, nor many noble, &c., will be drawn to deny themselves that they may be saved. But yet we must enter in at that strait gate few find, 1 Cor. ii. 27, Mat. vii.

Object. But there is none can do as you require.

Ans. In many things we sin all, but yet God's children do endeavour after the holiness required, confessing their failings, and no sin hath dominion over them; but now other men allow themselves in these evils, and think all is well, and have no desire or endeavour to shew their respect to all God's commandments, but venture all to God's mercy, yea, they will not forego such sins as they can leave if they list, they will continue in sins that neither bring them pleasure nor profit.

Object. But, might some one of the better sort say, What! are we bound to respect all God's wills, and to be perfect and full, and to stand so too? Who is able to bear it? Is it not a heavy yoke?

Ans. It is true that all this is required, and hereby we may see whither sin hath brought us, and what impotency is now in us. It is true also that a mortal condition is a hard condition. Our Saviour meant something when he said, 'Strive to enter in at the strait gate.' Yet a Christian needs not faint, for it is all good work, and he is to obey no worse a will than God's will, and for no worse an end than his own good, and with no worse company than all the saints.

Object. But the multitude of my former sins troubles me, that I cannot with that comfort address myself to undertake this strict course.

Ans. This is thy comfort, that in Christ there is a propitiation for all thy sins past; and now that God calls for this obedience, he will accept thee as righteous by forgiving thee all former accounts, Rom. iii. 25.

Object. But if all were forgiven me, yet I cannot do all that God requires of me in his law.

Ans. Thou art 'not under the law, but under grace,' Rom. vi. 14, thou art freed from the rigour of the law; so that thou extend thy desire and endeavour to all the will of God, thy perfection is but uprightness.

Object. But in my best services there is much evil.

Ans. Christ makes request for thee, and by the virtue of his intercession the evil of thy good works is hid and covered.

Object. But I am so weak, I cannot find strength almost to do any work of God, much less all, and to hold out too.

Ans. As weak as thou have subjected themselves to all God's wills, of which some now sleep in the Lord, who from small beginnings grew to great ability in God's service. What may not grace, like a grain of mustard seed, grow to in short time? Mat. xiii.; besides, God's ordinances are mighty through God to fulfil our obedience. 2 Cor. x. 4, 6, and God will shew his power in thy weakness, 2 Cor. xii. 9, yea, it is his covenant not only to require all his will, but to give us his Spirit to cause us to do them, Ezek. xxxvi. 27.

Object. But if I were set in never so good a case, and had for the present never so good success, yet I fear falling away.

Ans. God 'will keep the feet of his saints,' 1 Sam. ii. 9.

Object. But I have tried a great while, and I have great helps, and yet I find not any such graces or fulness, or any such likelihood to stand.

Ans. 1. It is one thing what is, and another thing what thou feelest. 2. Consider whether thou hast not desired to do all God's will, and endeavoured it as thou knewest it, and that with desire to do all perfectly; certainly the will, study, care, desire is accepted with God. 3. Consider whether God hath not let thee see all this while that thou art accepted as full and perfect. What sin hast thou begged pardon for, and not obtained it? what duty or grace is it that thou hast prayed for constantly, and God hath utterly denied to answer thee? If God have accepted thee, why doest thou charge thyself falsely?

Object. But I know not all God's wills, much less can I do them.

Ans. It shall be to thee according to what thou hast, and not according to what thou hast not; increase in knowledge, that thou mayest increase in grace. What shall I say? Consider but the recompense of reward, God will reward every work, and should we not then do all his wills? Though the task be hard, and labour great, yet the pay and gain is exceeding great; if we had so many ways to thrive in our estates we would refuse no labour. Oh why should we not seek the gain of doing every will of God?

Thus of the twelfth verse.

Ver. 13. *For I bear him record, that he hath a great zeal for you, and them that are in Laodicea, and them in Hierapolis.*

Ver. 14. *Luke, the beloved physician, and Demas, greet you.*

In the 13th verse the zeal of Epaphras, which is the fourth thing, is described: first, By the testimony of Paul, 'I bear him record;' secondly, By the quantity of it, 'a great zeal;' thirdly, By the person for whom, 'for you,' &c.

The apostle useth all these words to set out his zeal, because he was desirous to have him in great respect with his hearers, for he knew if he were once contemned or suspected, his doctrine would be unfruitful, and his hearers made a prey to false teachers. Besides, perhaps he found the people inclining to grow to have enough of him, or to suspect him, or to lessen their regard of him.

I bear him record. Note:—

1. That the witness of one apostle is a sufficient testimony and infallible, which should encourage us to study their writings, seeing we are sure to find nothing but truth there.

2. That the best testimony is not our own record of ourselves; 'Let thy neighbour, not thine own mouth, praise thee,' Prov. xxix.

3. Godly ministers should be ready and forward to preserve the fame of their brethren, and in particular willing to give record for them; but if we would have record from others, we must not be idle, or ignorant, or corrupt, or scandalous. Oh, the misery of these times! How are insufficient or wicked ministers written for to the patron, to the bishop, to the congregation, concerning whom there can be no sufficient testimony in the day of Christ! And happy were it if no churchmen had their hands in such records. The Lord pardon and purge the sins of the sons of Levi!

Zeal. *Doct.* Zeal is needful in a minister; now, his zeal is twofold, either for God, or for God's people. A minister should shew his zeal for his people: 1. By praying for them; 2. By painful preaching to them, in season and out of season; 3. By protecting them against the reproaches and scorns of the world, striving by doctrine not only to comfort them, but to wipe away the aspersions cast upon them; 4. By earnest rebukes and admonitions; he must cry aloud and not spare, not suffering them to sin; 5. By suffering either with them or for them.

The use is to excite zeal in ministers, and to awake them out of that coldness or deadness, especially in teaching. It is a wonderful scourge to the people, and a dishonour to the glorious doctrine of God, where the teacher is without life or spirit in the enforcing of his doctrine.

And is zeal good for a minister? then sure it is good for the people too; indeed, it is of exceeding praise in all sorts of men, of what degree soever. Neither will it be amiss here a little to consider more seriously of zeal, seeing there is much need of it in the world, and there is much mistaking about it.

Now if men will be rightly ordered in their zeal, let them look to these things:

1. Let it not be a pretended zeal, as in Jonah; 2. Nor a superstitious zeal, as in Paul, Gal. i. 14; 3. Nor a passionate zeal, only for fit, as in John at his first entrance; 4. Nor a malicious zeal, as in persecutors, that think they do God good service in vexing men wrongfully, Acts vii. 9, Gal. iv. 17; 5. Nor a wrong-intended zeal, such as is the zeal of meritmongers, Rom. x. 2; 6. Nor a contentious zeal, such as theirs that make needless rents in the church, Rom. xiii. 13, 1 Cor. iii. 3; 7. Nor a secure zeal, that is a zeal not raised by godly sorrow, 1 Cor. vii. 10, or that is carried without care or fear of falling away; 8. Nor an idle zeal, that is all words without works,—the word is rendered labour sometimes, and it is certain true zeal is spent about good works, Titus ii. 14; 9. Nor an over-curious zeal, shewed either by sticking too much to the letter of scripture, Acts xxi. 20, 21, or by prying into or harsh censuring of the lesser faults of others, Mat. vii.; 10. Or a bitter zeal, James iii. 13, 14, that spends itself in railing and fiery reproaches,—railers seldom stand long; 11. Or an ignorant, bold zeal, such as was in the Jews, Rom. x. 2; or lastly, a self-conceited zeal, when men trust too much to themselves and their own judgments.

True zeal hath in it six things:

1. The affections of worship and spiritual compassion; it will not rest in the bare work done, either of piety to God or spiritual mercy to men; it cannot be cold or lukewarm in praying, hearing, preaching, admonishing, &c.

2. An ardent love to such as fear God, shewed by desire, mourning, and fervency of mind towards them, 2 Cor. vii. 7.

3. An utter hatred of the wickedness and profaneness of the world, with a willingness to shew and maintain, according to a man's calling, a spiritual opposition against it.

4. An affectionate desire after God's house and the purity of it, thus the zeal of God's house should eat us up.

5. A great wrestling within a man against the corruptions of his own nature, expressed by indignation, sorrow, confession, strong cries to God, and revenge upon the flesh.

6. The coveting of all spiritual things as the best things in the world.

Lastly, Observe that he saith, much zeal or great zeal, which sheweth that men ought to thrive in zeal as well as in other graces, howsoever the world judge of it, only let men look to themselves according to the former rules, that they deceive not themselves nor the world.

For you and for them of Laodicea and Hierapolis. I will not trouble the reader with the topography of these towns; it is out of question they were near bordering cities. Only observe here three things:

1. That the care of faithful teachers, and their desire to do good, extends to other churches; also hence they are compared fitly to stars, that give light not only to the orb in which they are, but to places further off; and this good ministers may do by prayer, example of faithfulness and diligence, or by counsel or writing, or confirmation of doctrine, by preaching as there is occasion. And this shews the worth of painful and sincere teachers; they are a great benefit to the whole country where they live, and therefore they should be protected and encouraged by all them that would be accounted lovers of their country.

2. That ministers owe a special love and care to the neighbour churches, for as nearness of habitation increaseth the strength of civil bonds, so should it much more in spiritual.

3. That the care of other churches should not cause men to neglect the flock that depends upon them, it is not sufficient that men preach somewhere. God calls for an account of their stewardship in their own charge, they must tend their own herds; he were a strange husbandman that would plough his neighbour's field and let his own lie untilled; it is vile corruption to be intent when we labour for others, and remiss when we labour for our own people.

Luke, the beloved physician. There is some ado amongst interpreters who this Luke should be, but I incline to them that think it was Luke the evangelist, but whosoever it was, three things may be here observed:

1. That the church of God hath always consisted of men of divers callings; so as no lawful calling is excluded, nor yet any only taken.

2. That physic hath been of ancient honour and use in the church; we see it here in the apostle's time, and it was long before also, for there were physicians in Joseph's time, Gen. l. 2.

Four sorts of men may be reproved concerning physic or physicians:

1. Such as totally neglect them though they have need to use them; yet our Saviour Christ saith, 'the sick need a physician;' 2. Such as are wayward and will not be cured, that is, such as through impatiency will not be ordered by this means in the manner they should be; 3. Such as put their whole trust in physic, as Asa did, neglecting to seek unto God for help; yea, it is to be noted in Asa, that his disease being but ordinary, yet to neglect the Lord in it was a great sin, for though God hath allowed physic as a help, yet it was never his meaning to rob himself of his own glory; 4. Such as will out of pride and niceness be tampering with their bodies in physic when there is no need, contrary to that of our Saviour Christ, 'The whole need not the physician.'

Now inasmuch as many times it is manifest physic doth no good to the diseased, we are to understand three things: 1. That this may be the fault of careless and ignorant physicians; 2. That as we grow monsters in the world by sinning, overpassing the deeds of the wicked, so the Lord sometimes by bringing in strong and new diseases doth overpass the skill of the physicians; 3. God for sins or trial may restrain the blessing upon the means, which else would be available.

The third thing I note is, that the Holy Ghost gives this praise to a godly physician, importing that a physician should be a man sound in religion, and zealous for the truth, and known and beloved in the church; for as it is certain godly and religious physicians may do much good in the dangers of their patients, so miserable experience shews that popish and superstitious physicians do exceeding much hurt, by working upon those opportunities to seduce and pervert men.

And Demas. This is that Demas that afterward forsook Paul, and embraced this present world, from the consideration of whose estate we may observe three things:

First, That the vices of men, by the profession of the truth, may be restrained when they are not cured. This man's love of the world was in him when he was at the best, but it was curbed and held down; and so it is with many hypocrites, and therefore men should be warned and look to themselves, that they be not deceived by taking the restraint of the outward practice of some evil for the true mortification of them.

Secondly, It is many times a great hand of God upon unsound-hearted men, that at their best they are seen into and not greatly esteemed. It seems it was so with this man, for, if we mark it, the apostle not only reckons him in the last place, but he names him also without any manner of praise, as if he would import that he durst not commend him to the churches. We should here learn what to do towards such from the example of the apostle.

Now if any would know more fully what is to be done, and how they should carry themselves towards such as they justly doubt and fear not to be right, though they make profession, there are three rules to be observed:

1. Pity them, pray for them, and admonish them.

2. Commit not thyself unto them, but be well

advised before thou converse inwardly with them. It is true that the practice of this rule is strangely censured when those kind of people perceive themselves not to be regarded so much as they would be; for usually, if in discretion men prove before they trust, they are taxed of pride and haughtiness; yet considering the vile hypocrisy that is in many, it is better to be so censured without cause than to be beguiled by men that make their religion but a cloak to their own ends.

3. The third rule is, that while they stand and fall not into open sin, thou mayest not traduce them, but conceal thy dislikes till God lay them open, unless greater danger might ensue by the concealment, for the Lord may make him sound and give him repentance. Paul doth not dispraise Demas here, as he doth not commend him.

Thirdly, We may in this man note the property of many hypocrites, they will not be discountenanced, they are usually impudent. This man thrusts himself into the apostle's company, and will be commended to the churches; he will have a place, though it be the last place.

Ver. 15. *Salute the brethren which are in Laodicea, and Nymphas, and the church which is in his house.*

Hitherto of salutations signified; now the salutations required follow, and these are particular, ver. 15, 16, 17, general, ver. 18.

The particulars concern either Laodiceans, ver. 15, 16, or the Colossian preacher, ver. 17, who is not only saluted, but exhorted or rebuked by intimation.

In the salutation of the Laodiceans, observe two things: first, The persons who are to be saluted, ver. 15; secondly, A special direction for the open reading of two epistles, ver. 16.

The persons are the brethren in general, and Nymphas in special, and the household of Nymphas.

Salute the brethren which are at Laodicea. 1. Christian courtesy ought to have in it a holy remembrance of absent friends.

2. It is not vanity or weakness, but may stand with singular gifts and graces of mind, to be industrious and large-hearted in the many remembrances of all sorts of Christians.

3. It is profitable that men of great gifts and place should preserve their memory with others, though it be but in these lighter compliments of salutation; for many times it may inflame much affection to godliness in such to whom they send their salutations.

4. God hath his choice amongst men, for here he takes notice of the brethren in Laodicea only. God doth not drive in whole towns of men into the field of his grace at once; for as it was then in turning men from gentilism, so it is now in turning men from profaneness, the gospel doth not work upon all promiscuously.

And Nymphas. This Nymphas was not a woman, as Ambrose, and Dionysius, and Catharinus, and the gloss would have it, for it is αὐτοῦ in the end of the verse, 'his' house, not 'her' house.

This Nymphas, as it seems, was some eminent Christian, whom Paul would specially honour before the congregation, and so it shews that a special respect should be had of such as did excel in gifts amongst such as profess the sincerity of the gospel.

And the church that is in his house. By the church he means those in the household that fear God, whether they were women, or children, or servants.

Now here, first, I consider of these persons, and then of the title the apostle gives them in calling them a church.

In that the apostle thus with honour remembers the household of Nymphas, it shews his singular uprightness, in that he can respect grace in whomsoever he finds it; he loves a good servant as well as a good master, and can commend good order in a household as well as in a congregation. This should teach us not to have the grace of Christ in respect of persons; and hereby also we may try our love to God's children, by examining ourselves whether we can love such as can neither profit nor pleasure nor grace us in the world. And this may be a great encouragement to the young and meaner sort, in that they may perceive from hence, that if they get true grace they shall be respected both of God and good men.

Now in that the apostle calls this household a church, we may note, that a religious and well-ordered family is, as it were, a little church. Here in one family is prescribed what all families should be. This family is called a church, because his people were godly, and the word of God was read there, and prayers made to God, and psalms sung, and the younger sort were catechised and instructed.

Now, do we learn from hence that our houses are churches? Then these things will follow:

1. That God's worship and piety must be set up in them. How can they be churches of God, if God be not served in them?

2. All must be done there in order, and quietness, and silence, for so it is or should be in the church.

3. Evil persons that are incorrigible must not dwell there, but must be cast out, Ps. ci.

4. The husband or master of the family must dwell there as a man of knowledge, and wives, children, and servants must obey as the church doth Christ.

Again, are our families churches? Why then religious families are in a happy case, for then God himself will dwell there; so as a stranger coming to such places may say, as Jacob did of Bethel, surely God is in this place.

Lastly, should our families be churches? Oh, then, woe unto the world of profane households! Should a church be without sacrifice? and can their families escape God's wrath, seeing there is neither prayer nor piety in them, but instead of God's service, there is cursing, and swearing, and lying, and chiding, and filching, and whoring, and railing, and fighting, and what not? The most families are very cages of unclean spirits, where not God or good men, but very devils, dwell, they are very styes of uncleanness and unholiness.

Thus of the fifteenth verse.

Ver. 16. *And when the epistle is read amongst you, cause it to be read also in the church of the Laodiceans, and that you likewise read the epistle from Laodicea.*

These words contain a direction for reading: 1. Of his epistle, and that both privately and publicly; 2. Of an epistle from Laodicea.

In the general we may observe, that the scripture may be read; it is men's duty to do it; it is a flat precept, search the scriptures, John v. 39. And this may evidently reprove the profane neglect of the most herein in this great light. Many are so drowned in carelessness that they have not yet so much as a Bible in their houses, and others, though for their credit sake they have gotten them Bibles, yet they read them not.

This epistle. In that this epistle may not be neglected, but must be read, it shews that whatsoever is revealed to the church to be a part of the word of God, it must be read. So soon as this epistle is written, it must be read of all Christians, which shews that every part of God's word is to be read.

Now for the persons that must read the scriptures, it is here set down indefinitely 'of you,' meaning of all sorts of people, which is in other parts of the word of God distinctly expressed, For, 1 Tim. iv. 13, 15, ministers must read the scriptures, and Deut. i. 17, 19, it is required also of kings, and magistrates also—none are too good or too great to be employed herein; young men must study in the word, Ps. cxix. 10, so must women also, Acts xvii. 12. Priscilla was ripe in the knowledge of the scriptures, able to instruct others, Acts xviii. 27. What should I say? Every good man must read the scriptures, Ps. i. 2.

The use may be to stir us up to do it, and to do it constantly, for the same word of God that requires it to be done shews it should be done frequently. We must read all the days of our life, Deut. xvii. 19, and that daily, Acts xvii. 11, day and night, Ps. i. 2; they read four times a day, Neh. ix. 4.

And the rather should we be excited to this daily reading of the word, considering the profit comes thereby. It would exceedingly comfort us, Rom. xv. 4; it would be a lantern to our feet, and a light unto our paths, Ps. cxix. The word is the sword of the Spirit, Eph. vi.; and how can we resist tentations with, 'It is written,' if we read not what is written? And without reading we can never be expert in the word of righteousness; thereby we are made acquainted with the mysteries of the kingdom, and come to understand all the counsel of God; it will teach us the fear of the Lord, and keep that our hearts be not lifted up, Deut. xvii. 19, 20.

Quest. But what should be the reason that many get no more good by reading the word, and cannot find any great profit in their reading?

I *answer* diversely: 1. Some men are poisoned with the inclinations of atheism and security; they

3 F

come to the word to observe it, not to let the word observe them.

2. Men seek not a blessing by prayer, whereas it is certain the flesh will not of itself savour the things of the Spirit.

3. Men bring not a humble and meek spirit, whereas unto the fruitful meditation of the word, a heart quiet and patient, and a mind free from pride and passion is requisite, Ps. xxv. 9.

4. Men lay not down their cares and lusts, they have marred their taste before they come, they do not empty their heads, and separate themselves to seek the wisdom of the word. Care or lust will choke the word.

5. Men read not all God's word, nor do they read constantly; they will not wait daily at the gates of wisdom. To read seldom, or by starts and here and there, will do little good.

6. One great cause of not profiting is the not seeking of the law at the priest's mouth, that is, want of conference and propounding of doubts.

7. In many, unprofitableness is the scourge of unthankfulness for the good they have found in reading.

8. In reading men do not mind their own way, for if men did propose unto themselves what sin of their own they might find rebuked, and what directions might be collected out of that they read for their lives, or did note how the word did offer comfort when they need it, they could not but find many excellent experiences of God's providence and power in the word; they could not live in any sin, but either reading or hearing would discover it; nor could they go long without some word of comfort when they needed it; yea, they might observe how God in the word they read did counsel them too when they were in distress; therefore let him that readeth mark and read for himself.

Lastly, The cause is, in the most, that their hearts are not turned to God, and so the veil is not taken away, 2 Cor. iii. 16.

Cause to be read. Observe here:—

1. That it is not enough to read ourselves, but we must cause others to read, by exhorting, encouraging, commanding, &c.; especially parents and ministers should see to it, so should magistrates also.

2. From the coherence note, that we must cause others to read when we have read ourselves; it is vile hypocrisy for a minister or parent to urge their children or servants to read the scriptures, when they neglect reading themselves.

In the church. Here we have a plain proof for reading of the scriptures publicly in the church; we see it was anciently both required and practised. Add for the further confirmation hereof these places: Deut. xxxi. 11, 12, Neh. viii., Luke iv., Acts xiii. And this may assure us: 1. That public reading is no invention or ordinance of man; 2. That the people of God have found in all ages great need of this help. And therefore they are miserably transported with humour that so vilify or neglect this ordinance of God, and it may be just with God that thou shouldst not profit by reading at home, when thou carest not for reading in the church. Thus of the reading of the Epistle to the Colossians.

Epistle from Laodicea. Here is a great ado among interpreters to find out what epistle this was.

1. Theophylact thinks it was the first Epistle to Timothy, which was written from Laodicea, another town of that name, not this Laodicea before mentioned.

2. Some think Paul did write an epistle to the Laodiceans, which was apocrypha; and so Dionysius tells of a third Epistle to the Corinthians. Jacobus Stapulensis caused such an epistle to be printed, but Catharinus could easily avouch that it was a bastard and counterfeit.

3. Some think the Laodiceans wrote to the apostle, and propounded their doubts, unto which the apostle hath answered in this epistle; and therefore required that his answer might be compared with their doubts; this is the most public opinion.

But in the general it shews us thus much, that we must read other good books as well as scriptures.

Thus of the sixteenth verse.

Ver. 17. *And say to Archippus, Take heed to the ministry which thou hast received in the Lord, that thou fulfil it.*

These words concern the Colossian preacher, who is not only saluted, but exhorted.

This Archippus, as it seems, was their pastor,

joined with Epaphras, who was now at Rome with Paul. It is likely he was grown negligent in teaching, and careless and idle.

Many times it comes to pass, that men that sometimes were painful in their ministry, do afterwards grow slack and negligent.

1. Sometimes from very discouragements from their people, either because they profit not, or because they weary their teachers with indignities and wrongs. Thus the very prophets have been sometimes so tired that they could have been almost willing never to speak more in the name of the Lord.

2. Sometimes this comes from the corruption of their own natures, they grow soon weary of God's work; or else having taken more work to do than they are sufficient for, they grow to neglect all; or else they are drawn away with the love of the world; or else forbear of purpose to preach often lest they should be thought to be too precise; or else to win applause, they set out at first with such a strife to seem eloquent and learned that they quickly spend their store, and then rather than they will be observed to want, they will give over preaching.

3. Sometimes God himself, for the wickedness of their lives, casts a barrenness upon their hearts, and blasteth their gifts.

In this exhortation four things may be noted:

1. Who he is that exhorteth, 'say to Archippus.'
2. The matter charged upon him, 'see to thy ministry.'
3. The reason by which it is urged, 'thou hast received it of the Lord.'
4. An explication of the matter charged by the extent of it, 'to fulfil.'

Say to Archippus. Here I observe seven things:

1. The sinner must be told of his sin, Lev. xix. 17.
2. Such as offend publicly, must be told of it publicly.
3. Ministers as well as others may be rebuked, though some clergymen are so sore and so proud that they may not be touched; and many times it is a just judgment of God that no man should rebuke them that their sores might not be medicined, but, like unsavoury salt, they should be cast out of God. No man's learning or greatness of place can so protect them, but that they may be told of their faults. It is too commonly known they can sin as well as others, why, then, should they not be rebuked as well as others?

Doth Archippus need to be told? The Lord be merciful to the land and church! There be many Archippuses in the Church of England had need to be wakened with a loud trumpet of rebuke, and to be told of their faults, even of their ignorance, silence, sloth, pride, covetousness, simony, dissoluteness, ambition, contempt of their brethren, and soul-murder of many kinds.

4. The people may put their teachers in mind of their faults; as they ought to encourage them in well-doing, so may they admonish them for what is evil. Therefore ministers should strive so to live and so to teach as their people should not have cause to find fault.

5. Ministers must be told of their faults by their people, with great reverence and heedfulness and wisdom, according to that direction, 'Rebuke not an elder, but exhort him as a father;' here they must 'say to Archippus,' not directly reprove him.

6. They must say it to him, not say it of him. Ministers ought not to be traduced behind their backs.

7. He doth not threaten him if he do not, which implies, he hoped their exhortation would speed. Certainly it is a great praise to profit by admonition.

Take heed to thy ministry. This 'take heed' hath in it three things:

1. Consideration, a weighing and meditation of the greatness of the function, of the dignity of it, and the duty also, with the accounts he must make to God, and his high calling and the great price of souls, &c.

2. It notes divers of the worthy qualities of a minister, as care, attendance, watchfulness, aptness to teach and divide the word aright, discretion, to give every one his portion, diligence, gentleness, in not marring the doctrine with passion, patience to endure the work and labour of his ministry, &c.

3. It notes caution, and so ministers must take heed both of what is within them and what is with-

out them; they must take heed of their own divinations; they must take heed of sloth and idleness; they must take heed of the objections of their own flesh, and the tentations of the devil; without them they must take heed of the new errors that will daily rise; they must take heed of the sins of the people, with all the methods of Satan in devising, committing, or defending of sin; they must take heed of men's fancies; and for persons they must take heed of hypocrites and open adversaries, domestical vipers, and foreign foes, false brethren, and professed idolaters.

The use may be for great reproof of our sleeping watchmen and blind guides, that take no heed to their ministries. Oh, the woes that will fall upon them! who can recount the miseries that the blood of souls will bring upon them!

Which thou hast received in the Lord. A minister is said to receive his ministry in the Lord in divers respects: first, Because it is God's free grace that he is chosen to be a minister, Rom. i. 1; secondly, Because he is inwardly called and qualified by God; thirdly, Because he received his outward authority, though from men, yet by direction and warrant of God's word; fourthly, Because he receives it for the Lord, that is, to God's glory, and the furtherance of his kingdom over the mystical body of Christ.

The use is threefold: first, The people should therefore learn to seek their ministers of God; secondly, Ministers should hence learn, neither to be proud nor idle; not proud, for they received their ministry of God—it was his gift, not their deserts; not idle, for they are to do God's works; thirdly, Ministers may hence gather their own safety notwithstanding the oppositions of the world, that God that called them will perfect them.

To fulfil it. Ministers are said to fulfil their ministries two ways: 1. By constancy, holding out in it to the end; to fulfil it is to go on, and not look back when they are at plough; 2. By faithful performance of it, with a due respect of all the charge they have received of God: thus to fulfil it is to shew the people all the counsel of God; it is to rebuke all sorts of sins and sinners; it is faithfully to do every kind of work that belongs to their ministry, whether public or private.

Ver. 18. *The salutation by the hand of me Paul. Remember my bonds. Grace be with you. Amen.*

There are three things in this verse, a sign, a request, a vow or wish.

The salutation by the hand of me Paul. To write with his own hand he calls 'the token in every epistle,' 2 Thes. iii. 17. Here two things may be noted:

1. The great care that anciently hath been to provide that none but the true writings of the apostles should be received of the church; it should cause us so much the more gladly to receive and read these apostolical writings.

2. It implies that even in the times of the apostles, Satan raised up wicked men who endeavoured to counterfeit books and writings, and to father them upon the apostles themselves, or other eminent and worthy men; this continued successively as a most devilish practice in divers ages after.

Remember my bonds. The observations are: 1. God's children have been in bonds.

2. It is profitable to remember the troubles and afflictions of God's children, and to meditate of them: for 1. It may serve to confirm us when we find like hatred from the world; 2. It is an alarm to preparation, and the harnessing of ourselves against the fight of affliction; when one part of the host of God is smitten, should not the rest prepare for the fight? 3. It will soften our hearts to mercy, both spiritual and corporal; and, 4. It may learn us wisdom and circumspection.

Quest. How should they shew it that they did remember his bonds?

Ans. 1. By praying for him to God; 2. By shewing like patience under their crosses; 3. By constant profession of the doctrine he suffered for; 4. By a care of holy life, that they might strive to be such, as he need not be ashamed to suffer for them; 5. By supplying their wants.

3. As any have been more gracious, so they have been more straitened and oppressed by the wicked.

4. The actions of great men are not always just; a worthy apostle may be unworthily imprisoned.

5. The people should be much affected with the troubles of their teachers; and therefore they are far wide, that instead thereof trouble their teachers.

Grace be with you. By grace he means, both the

love of God and the gifts of Christ ; as he began so he ends, with vows and wishes of grace, which shews :

1. That in God we have wonderful reason continually to exalt the praise of his free grace and love.

2. That in man there is no greater happiness than to be possessed of the love of God and true grace ; it is the richest portion and fairest inheritance on earth.

When he saith 'be with you,' it is as if he said three things : 1. Be sure you have it, be not deceived, nor satisfied till ye be infallibly certain ye have attained true grace and God's love ; 2. Be sure you lose it not—never be without it ; it matters not though ye lose some credit or wealth or friends, &c., so you keep grace still with you ; 3. Be sure you use it, and increase it ; employ it upon all occasions, be continually in the exercise of it.

Thus of the whole epistle.

There followeth a postscript or underwriting in these words :

Written from Rome, and sent by Tychicus and Onesimus.

There is a difference about the reading ; some copies have not *Tychicus* and *Onesimus;* in some Latin copies read, *Misso ab Epheso.* But the Greek copies generally agree that it was from Rome.

But it is no great matter for the certainty of the reading, for the reader must be admonished, that the postscripts are not part of the canonical scripture, but were added by the scribes that wrote out the epistles. If any desire to be more particularly informed herein, he may peruse a learned tractate of this argument published by Master Rudolph Cudworth upon the subscription of the epistle to the Galatians.

ΤΩ, ΔΥΝΑΜΕΝΩ, ΥΠΕΡ ΠΑΝΤΑ ΠΟΙΗΣΑΙ ΕΚ ΠΕΡΙΣΣΟΥ 'ΩΝ 'ΑΙΤΟΥΜΕΘΑ 'Η ΝΟΟΥΜΕΝ, ΚΑΤΑ ΤΗΝ ΔΥΝΑΜΙΝ ΤΗΝ ΕΝΕΡΓΟΥΜΕΝΗΝ 'ΕΝ 'ΗΜΙΝ, 'ΑΥΤΩ; 'Η ΔΟΞΑ 'ΕΝ ΤΗ, 'ΕΚΚΛΗΣΙΑ, 'ΕΝ ΧΡΙΣΤΩ, 'ΙΗΣΟΥ 'ΕΙΣ ΠΑΣΑΣ ΤΑΣ ΓΕΝΕΑΣ ΤΟΥ 'ΑΙΩΝΟΣ ΤΩΝ 'ΑΙΩΝΩΝ. ΑΜΗΝ.

THE END.

PRINTED BY BALLANTYNE AND COMPANY, EDINBURGH.

www.ingramcontent.com/pod-product-compliance
Lightning Source LLC
Chambersburg PA
CBHW030554300426
44111CB00009B/972